Humanism, Culture, and Language in the Near East

Georg Krotkoff

Humanism, Culture, and Language in the Near East

Studies in Honor of Georg Krotkoff

Edited by

Asma Afsaruddin

and

A. H. Mathias Zahniser

Winona Lake, Indiana
EISENBRAUNS
1997

The publication of this volume was made possible by generous donations from:

- The Department of Near Eastern Studies, the Johns Hopkins University
- The Middle East Students Association, the Johns Hopkins University
- Mr. Erik Harrell
- Dr. Wells Harrington
- Ms. Maleka Khatun
- Ms. Diane Krasner
- Mr. Firas Raad
- Dr. and Mrs. A. H. Mathias Zahniser

Printed in the United States of America.

Library of Congress Cataloging-in-Publication Data

Humanism, culture, and language in the Near East : studies in honor of Georg Krotkoff / edited by Asma Afsaruddin and A. H. Mathias Zahniser
p. cm.
Includes bibliographical references.
ISBN 1-57506-020-5 (cloth : alk. paper)
1. Arabic philology. 2. Aramaic language. I. Afsaruddin, Asma, 1958– . II. Zahniser, A. H. Mathias, 1938– . III. Krotkoff, Georg.
PJ6024.K78H48 1997
492.7—dc21 96-51074
CIP

The paper used in this publication meets the minimum requirements of the American National Standard for Information Sciences—Permanence of Paper for Printed Library Materials, ANSI Z39.48–1984.⊗™

Contents

Preface viii
Acknowledgments x
Publications xi
Abbreviations xxii

Introduction: Georg Krotkoff as Scholar and Teacher 1

PART 1
Humanism, Culture, and Literature

George Makdisi • Philadelphia
Inquiry into the Origins of Humanism 15
Michael G. Carter • New York
Humanism and the Language Sciences in Medieval Islam 27
Julie Scott Meisami • Oxford
Cosmic Numbers: The Symbolic Design of Niẓāmī's *Haft Paykar* 39
Fedwa Malti-Douglas • Bloomington, Indiana
Playing with the Sacred: Religious Intertext in *Adab* Discourse 51
Werner Ende • Freiburg, Germany
From Revolt to Resignation: The Life of Shaykh Muḥsin Sharāra 61
A. H. Mathias Zahniser • Wilmore, Kentucky
Sūra as Guidance and Exhortation: The Composition of *Sūrat al-Nisāʾ* 71
Barbara Freyer Stowasser • Washington, D.C.
The *Ḥijāb*: How a Curtain Became an Institution and a Cultural Symbol 87
Roger Allen • Philadelphia
The Development of Fictional Genres: The Novel and Short Story in Arabic 105
Issa J. Boullata • Montreal
An Arabic Poem in an Israeli Controversy: Maḥmūd Darwīsh's "Passing Words" 119
Asma Afsaruddin • South Bend, Indiana
Bi-lʿArabī al-faṣīḥ: An Egyptian Play Looks at Contemporary Arab Society 129

Part 2
Arabic

Carolyn Killean • Chicago
Learning Arabic: A Lifetime Commitment 145
Karin C. Ryding • Washington, D.C.
The Alchemy of Sound: Medieval Arabic Phonosymbolism 155
Karl Stowasser • College Park, Maryland
Al-Khalīl's Legacy 165
Wolfhart Heinrichs • Cambridge, Massachusetts
The Etymology of *Muqarnas*: Some Observations 175
Manfred Woidich • Amsterdam
Egyptian Arabic and Dialect Contact in Historical Perspective 185
Benjamin Hary • Atlanta
On Later and Modern Egyptian Judeo-Arabic 199
Hans-Rudolph Singer • Germersheim
Ein arabischer Text aus Constantine (Algerien) 225

Part 3
Aramaic

Anton Schall • Heidelberg
Zur griechischen Nebenüberlieferung im Syrischen 237
John A. C. Greppin • Cleveland
Syriac Loanwords in Classical Armenian 247
Robert D. Hoberman • Stonybrook, New York
The Modern Chaldean Pronunciation of Classical Syriac 253
Gary A. Rendsburg • Ithaca, New York
Double Polysemy in Proverbs 31:19 267
Otto Jastrow • Heidelberg
Zum neuaramäischen Dialekt von Hassane 275
Michael L. Chyet • Berkeley
A Preliminary List of Aramaic Loanwords in Kurdish 283
Yona Sabar • Los Angeles
The Story of Balaam and His She-Ass in Four Neo-Aramaic
Dialects: A Comparative Study of the Translations 301
Edward Y. Odisho • Chicago
A Comparative Study of Pet Names in English and Assyrian 319

Part 4
Afroasiatic

Carleton T. Hodge • Bloomington, Indiana
The Trickle-Down Approach 337
Herrmann Jungraithmayr • Frankfurt am Main
Ablaut im Verbalsystem osttschadischer Sprachen 345
Werner Vycichl • Geneva
Akkadian *lišān-u-m,* Arabic *lisān-u-n*: Which Is the Older Form? 355

Part 5
Ancient Egyptian, Ottoman Turkish, and Other Linguistic Matters

Yoël L. Arbeitman • Princeton
You Gotta Have Heart 363
Peter T. Daniels • Chicago
The Protean Arabic Abjad.................................. 369
Alan S. Kaye • Fullerton, California
A Matter of Inconsistency: Variations of Arabic
Loanwords in English 385
Claudia Römer • Vienna
The Language and Prose Style of Bostān's *Süleymānnāme* 401
Hans Goedicke • Baltimore
Language and Script in Ancient Egypt 419

Contributors 429
Index of Authors 433

Preface

On a warm spring evening in the backyard of Georg Krotkoff's cozy residence in Baltimore, the plan to launch a volume of essays in his honor was conceived. The occasion was a dinner party that was held to commemorate Georg's retirement from the Department of Near Eastern Studies at the Johns Hopkins University after a distinguished thirty-year record of service. Among the invitees were the three future editors of the volume in the making: Asma Afsaruddin, Georg's last graduate student at Johns Hopkins; Karl Stowasser, a dear friend and colleague, who then taught in the Department of History at the University of Maryland, College Park; and Mathias Zahniser, Georg's former student, who had gone on to a successful teaching career. The three of us agreed with great excitement to undertake this project. We forged ahead, even though Diane Krasner, Georg's wife, whose assistance we enlisted, warned us ominously that Georg would not be warmly predisposed to the idea. For those of us who know our honoree well, it was a truism that he was of "the old school," which meant, among other things, that he did not subscribe to shameless self-promotion, nor did he go out of his way to seek the accolades of his peers. The project was thus conceived in secrecy and remained a secret for several months. In an unfortunate development, Karl in the course of the next few years would contract a serious illness and be forced to withdraw from the editorship. (It is our sad duty to report here that Karl succumbed to his illness on Feb. 13, 1997, just a few months before final publication of the volume.) As the two remaining conspirators, we however continued full throttle ahead.

The response from Georg's colleagues and friends who had been invited to jump on board was overwhelming. We were greatly encouraged by the outpouring of support we received from the future contributors to this volume. As the table of contents shows, their scholarly contributions reflect Georg's own eclectic and broad-ranging interests in philology, comparative linguistics, literature, history, and religion, both as distinct and as interpermeable disciplines. A word about the various transliteration and transcription methods used by our various authors seems apposite here: because of the many languages represented and the various scholarly conventions our contributors are accustomed to, we have on the whole honored their own systems and have not attempted to impose a global consistency on them.

Before the first year was up, we decided to summon all of our courage and let the cat out of the bag, bracing ourselves for possible disapproval on Georg's part. To our relief, Diane's dire prediction never came true. Georg was both touched and flattered by our initiative and heartened by the robust enthusiasm displayed by his colleagues for participating in the project. The rest, as they say, is history.

This volume, as all involved in its evolution know, has been seven years in the making. We are grateful in particular to the contributors, who have borne with us graciously for what must have seemed an unconscionably long time. It was a rare opportunity for us to work closely with so many distinguished scholars in such a worthy endeavor. On behalf of this special community of people, we dedicate this modest tangible token of our affection and esteem to Georg Krotkoff, teacher and mentor to some, friend and colleague to us all.

May you continue to prosper and keep on enriching our lives!

زادك الله تعالى مجدا من فضله ومنه!

Asma Afsaruddin
South Bend, Indiana

Mathias Zahniser
Wilmore, Kentucky

Acknowledgments

We would like to thank Ken Boyd, Executive Director of Information Technology at Asbury Theological Seminary, and his staff for assistance in obtaining materials and carrying out tasks necessary for the editing of this volume. We are indebted to Jane Dreyer of the Department of Near Eastern Studies at Johns Hopkins University and to Pat Richmond of the E. Stanley Jones School at Asbury Theological Seminary for their help in duplication, mailing, and record-keeping.

We should mention the help that we have received from the Department of Near Eastern Studies at Johns Hopkins University and the E. Stanley Jones School at Asbury Theological Seminary in defraying the costs of the volume. Jerry Cooper, who at the time the project was conceived was chair of the Department of Near Eastern Studies at Johns Hopkins University, and who promised us financial support, significantly encouraged the carrying out of the project.

We should also thank David Bundy of Christian Theological Seminary in Indianapolis and, especially, Diane Krasner for valuable advice and encouragement along the way. Steve Vinson and Ann Zahniser, our spouses, offered invaluable support and advice. Ann helped immensely with the tedious job of proofreading.

Jim Eisenbraun and his staff, especially Beverly Fields, have gone beyond the call of duty in bringing this book to fruition.

Had it not been for a serious illness, Karl Stowasser, a contributor to the volume, would have served with us as an editor. His involvement would have lightened the load; notwithstanding, he encouraged us with the inspiration of his wit and support.

Publications by Georg Krotkoff

1950

1. *Taschenbuch der russischen Grammatik.* Vienna: Globus. Reprinted 1954, 1956.

1954

2. *Lehrbuch der deutschen Sprache mit arabischer Anleitung.* Cairo. Reprinted 1955; Baghdad, 1957.
3. "Review of *The Arab City of Gedi*, by J. S. Kirkman." *Egyptian Gazette.* July 9.

1955

4. "Review of *A History of the Sudan*, by A. J. Arkell." *Egyptian Gazette.* July 15.
5. "Review of *Foundations in the Dust*, by Seton Lloyd." *Egyptian Gazette.* July 15.

1956

6. "Zur Abwehr des bösen Blicks in Ägypten." Pp. 217–20 in *Studia Orientalia*, Volume 1. Cairo: Centre des Études Orientales de la Custodie Franciscaine de la Terre Sainte.
7. "Austrian Diplomat Became One of Pioneers of Oriental Studies in Europe." *The Iraq Times.* November 26. The same in Arabic: "Al-Dhikrā

al-Miʾawīya li-Wafāt al-Mustashriq al-Nimsāwī Hammer-Purgstall." *Al-Zaman*. November 23. [Brief communication]

1957

8. "The *Kitāb laḥn al-ʿawāmm* by Abu Bakr az-Zubaydi: Description of a Lexicographical Manuscript." *Bulletin of the College of Arts and Sciences* 2: 1–14. [Baghdad]

1958

9. "An Unknown Work of Yaḥyā at-Tibrīzī." *Bulletin of the College of Arts and Sciences* 3: 211–25. [Baghdad (Arabic)]
10. "Die arabischen Akademien und die Sprachreform." *Österreichische Hochschulzeitung*. May 1.

1959

11. "Review of *Arabsko-russkiy slovar'*, by Ch. K. Baranov." *Zeitschrift der deutschen morgenländischen Gesellschaft* 109: 212.
12. "Review of *Das einzige Wörterbuch der deutschen und arabischen Sprache*, by Riad Gayed." *Zeitschrift der deutschen morgenländischen Gesellschaft* 109: 212–13.
13. "Review of the *Military Dictionary* of the Egyptian Army." *Zeitschrift der deutschen morgenländischen Gesellschaft* 109: 213–14.

1960

14. "Beduinenrecht und gesatztes Recht." *Wiener Zeitschrift für die Kunde des Morgenlandes* 56: 99–108.
15. "'Die Sommerreise,' von Mahmud Taimur." Translated from the original Arabic by Georg Krotkoff. Pp. 593–99 in *Die Reise zum wonnigen Fisch: Die besten Humoresken der zeitgenössischen Weltliteratur.* Edited by R. Hoffmann and W. A. Oerley. Vienna: Paul Neff.
16. "Review of *Supplement zum arabischen Wörterbuch*, by Hans Wehr." *Wiener Zeitschrift für die Kunde des Morgenlandes* 56: 319–20.
17. "Review of *Klyuch arifmetiki* and *Traktat ob okruzhnosti*, by Jemshid Ghiyath al-Din al-Kashi." *Wiener Zeitschrift für die Kunde des Morgenlandes* 56: 321.

1961

18. "Ali Hussein al-Wardi: Die Persönlichkeit des Irakers." *Bustan* 2/1: 7–11. [Vienna]
19. "Review of *Grundriß und System der altarabischen Metren*, by Gotthold Weil." *Wiener Zeitschrift für die Kunde des Morgenlandes* 57: 228–30.
20. "Review of *Wörterbuch der klassischen arabischen Sprache*, Part 1. In cooperation with A. Spitaler. Edited by J. Kraemer and H. Gätje." *Der Islam* 36/3: 286–88.

21. "Beobachtungen zum Neu-Ostaramäischen." *Zeitschrift der deutschen morgenländischen Gesellschaft* 111: 393–95.

1962

22. "Review of *Le minaret de Djam*, by André Maricq and Gaston Wiet." *Wiener Zeitschrift für die Kunde des Morgenlandes* 58: 250–51.
23. "Review of *Die Brunnen der Wüste*, by Wilfred Thesiger." *Wiener Zeitschrift für die Kunde des Morgenlandes* 58: 252.
24. "Review of *A New Method of Spelling and Writing in the Arabic Language*, by Abdul Majid Taji Farouki." *Wiener Zeitschrift für die Kunde des Morgenlandes* 58: 253.
25. "Review of *Introduction à l'histoire de l'Orient Musulman*, by Jean Sauvaget." *Wiener Zeitschrift für die Kunde des Morgenlandes* 58: 253–56.
26. "Review of *Wörterbuch der klassischen arabischen Sprache*, Part 2." *Der Islam* 38/1–2: 205–6. [See item #20 above]
27. "Bagdader Studien, I: Das Weberhandwerk in Bagdad." *Zeitschrift der deutschen morgenländischen Gesellschaft* 112: 319–24 + 4 illustrations.

1963

28. "A Possible Arabic Ingredient in the History of Spanish *Usted*." *Romance Philology* 17: 328–32.
29. "'Auf den Hund kommen': Etymology and Ideology." *Modern Language Notes* 78: 532–35.
30. "Review of *Ma^{c}dān*, by Sigrid Westphal-Hellbusch and Heinz Westphal." *Zeitschrift der deutschen morgenländischen Gesellschaft* 113: 666–68.

1964

31. "Bagdader Studien, II: Ein Einakter im Bagdader Dialekt." *Zeitschrift der deutschen morgenländischen Gesellschaft* 114: 66–90.
32. "Nochmals: Mağhūra, mahmūsa." *Wiener Zeitschrift für die Kunde des Morgenlandes* 59–60: 147–53.
33. "Arabic *^{c}lm* 'to know'." *Journal of the American Oriental Society* 84: 170. [Brief communication]
34. "Some Philological Remarks on a Linguistic Publication." *Journal of the American Oriental Society* 84: 263. [Brief communication]
35. "The Emperor's New Art." *Goucher Weekly*, Baltimore. December 4. [Brief communication]
36. "Review of *Traité de philologie arabe*, Volume 1, by Henri Fleisch." *Wiener Zeitschrift für die Kunde des Morgenlandes* 59–60: 239–42.
37. "Review of *Die Geheimnisse der Wortkunst*, by Abdalqahir al-Curcani." *Wiener Zeitschrift für die Kunde des Morgenlandes* 59–60: 243.
38. "Review of *Arabic Lexicography*, by John A. Haywood." *Wiener Zeitschrift für die Kunde des Morgenlandes* 59–60: 243–45.

39. "Review of *A New Arabic Grammar of the Written Language*, by J. A. Haywood and H. M. Nahmad." *Wiener Zeitschrift für die Kunde des Morgenlandes* 59–60: 245–47.
40. "Review of *Untersuchungen zur Sternnomenklatur der Araber*, by Paul Kunitzsch." *Wiener Zeitschrift für die Kunde des Morgenlandes* 59–60: 247.
41. "Review of *Syriac and Arabic Documents regarding Legislation Relative to Syrian Asceticism*, by Arthur Vööbus." *Wiener Zeitschrift für die Kunde des Morgenlandes* 59–60: 248–50.
42. "Review of *Sammlung Eduard Glaser II*, by Maria Höfner and J. M. Solá Solé." *Wiener Zeitschrift für die Kunde des Morgenlandes* 59–60: 250–51.
43. "Review of *Die arabische Rangstreitdichtung und ihre Einordnung in die allgemeine Literaturgeschichte,* by Ewald Wagner." *Wiener Zeitschrift für die Kunde des Morgenlandes* 59–60: 251–53.
44. "Review of *Contributions to Arabic Metrology II*, by George Miles." *Wiener Zeitschrift für die Kunde des Morgenlandes* 59–60: 253.
45. "Review of *Le Dictionnaire des autorités de Abd al-Muʾmin ad-Dimyati*, by Georges Vajda." *Wiener Zeitschrift für die Kunde des Morgenlandes* 59–60: 253–54.

1965

46. "Review of *Wörterbuch der klassischen arabischen Sprache*, Parts 3 and 4." *Der Islam* 41: 284–86. [See item #20 above]
47. "Review of *Catalogue of the Mingana Collection of Manuscripts*, Volume 4, by Derek Hopwood." *Zeitschrift der deutschen morgenländischen Gesellschaft* 115: 366.
48. "Review of *Mufākahat al-khillān fī ḥawādith al-zamān*, by Shamsaddin Muhammad ibn Tulun." *Zeitschrift der deutschen morgenländischen Gesellschaft* 115: 367.
49. "Review of *The Jat of Pakistan*, by Sigrid Westphal-Hellbusch and Heinz Westphal." *Zeitschrift der deutschen morgenländischen Gesellschaft* 115: 417–18.

1967

50. "Review of *Wörterbuch der klassischen arabischen Sprache*, Parts 5 and 6." *Der Islam* 43/1–2: 284–86. [See item #20 above]
51. "Review of *Spoken Arabic of Baghdad*, by R. J. McCarthy and Faraj Raffouli." *Der Islam* 43/1–2: 207–8.
52. "Review of 'The Evidence of Language,' by W. F. Albright and T. O. Lambdin." *Journal of the American Research Center in Egypt* 6: 167.
53. "Review of *Egypt and the Fertile Crescent 1516–1922*, by P. M. Holt." *Journal of the American Research Center in Egypt* 6: 182.

54. "Review of *The Practical Visions of Ya^{c}qub Sanu^{c}*, by Irene L. Gendzier." *Journal of the American Research Center in Egypt* 6: 182.
55. "Review of *The Arabic Triliteral Verb*, by Afif A. Bulos." *Journal of the American Oriental Society* 87: 315.
56. "Review of *Deutsch-arabisches Wörterbuch*, by Günther Krahl." *Wiener Zeitschrift für die Kunde des Morgenlandes* 61: 201.
57. "Review of *Arabic Inscriptions* and *Arabic Papyri from Hirbet el-Mird*, by Adolf Grohmann." *Wiener Zeitschrift für die Kunde des Morgenlandes* 61: 202.
58. "Review of *Key to a New Arabic Grammar*, by J. A. Haywood and H. M. Nahmad." *Wiener Zeitschrift für die Kunde des Morgenlandes* 61: 203.
59. "Review of *Sabaean Inscriptions from Mahram Bilqis*, by Albert Jamme." *Wiener Zeitschrift für die Kunde des Morgenlandes* 61: 203.
60. "Review of *La Berbérie orientale sous les Zirides*, by Hady Roger Idris." *Wiener Zeitschrift für die Kunde des Morgenlandes* 61: 204.
61. "Review of *Grundzüge der Grammatik des arabischen Dialekts von Bagdad*, by Nizar Malaika." *Wiener Zeitschrift für die Kunde des Morgenlandes* 61: 204–6.

1968

62. "Kazimen: Ein schiitischer Wallfahrtsort." *Bustan* 9: 59–62. [Vienna]
63. "Review of *Syrisch-arabische Grammatik*, by Heinz Grotzfeld." *Der Islam* 44: 296–97.
64. "Review of *Spoken Arabic of Baghdad*, Part 2: Anthology of Texts, by R. J. McCarthy and Faraj Raffouli." *Der Islam* 44: 298.
65. "Review of *The World of Islam*, by Ernst Grube." *Journal of the American Research Center in Egypt* 7: 143.

1969

66. "*Laḥm* 'Fleisch' und *leḥem* 'Brot'." *Wiener Zeitschrift für die Kunde des Morgenlandes* 62: 76–82.
67. "Review of *Arabische Texte im Dialekt von Hama mit Einleitung und Glossar*, by Bernhard Lewin." *Journal of the American Oriental Society* 89: 834.
68. "Review of *The Jewish Neo-Aramaic Dialect of Persian Azerbaijan*, by Irene Garbell." In *Wiener Zeitschrift für die Kunde des Morgenlandes* 62: 346–48.
69. "Review of *Handbook of Classical and Modern Mandaic*, by Rudolf Macuch." *Wiener Zeitschrift für die Kunde des Morgenlandes* 62: 348–50.
70. "Review of *Taha Husein*, by Istituto Universitario Orientale." *Wiener Zeitschrift für die Kunde des Morgenlandes* 62: 350–51.

71. "Review of *The Emergence and Linguistic Background of Judaeo-Arabic*, by Joshua Blau." *Wiener Zeitschrift für die Kunde des Morgenlandes* 62: 351–52.
72. "Review of *Damaszenisch-arabische Texte*, by Ariel Bloch and Heinz Grotzfeld"; *Laut- und Formenlehre des Damaszenisch-Arabischen*, by Heinz Grotzfeld"; and *Die Hypotaxe im Damaszenisch-Arabischen*, by Ariel Bloch." *Wiener Zeitschrift für die Kunde des Morgenlandes* 62: 353–54.
73. "Review of *Egyptian Guilds in Modern Times*, by Gabriel Baer." *Wiener Zeitschrift für die Kunde des Morgenlandes* 62: 355.
74. "Review of *Der arabische Dialekt von Bishmizzin*, by Michel Jiha." *Wiener Zeitschrift für die Kunde des Morgenlandes* 62: 355–56.
75. "Review of *Le parler arabe du Caire*, by Nada Tomiche." *Wiener Zeitschrift für die Kunde des Morgenlandes* 62: 356.
76. "Review of *Untersuchungen zur Ragazpoesie*, by Manfred Ullmann." *Wiener Zeitschrift für die Kunde des Morgenlandes* 62: 357–58.

1970

77. "Review of *A Mediterranean Society*, Volume I, by S. D. Goitein." *Journal of the American Research Center in Egypt* 8: 182.

1972

78. "Bagdader Studien, III: Miszellen von Bagdader Märkten; IV: Metallgefäße; V: Kopfbedeckungen; VI: Vom Baugewerbe; VII: Ein toponymisches Kuriosum; VIII: Zu Weissbach, ZS 4." *Zeitschrift der deutschen morgenländischen Gesellschaft* 122: 93–101.
79. "Die Erzieher sägen am eigenen Ast." *Die Presse*, Tribüne der Leser. Vienna: September 2, 1972, 18. [Brief communication]
80. "Review of *Kloster und Mausoleum des Farag ibn Barquq in Kairo*, by S. L. Mostafa." *Journal of the American Research Center in Egypt* 9 (1971–72): 157.
81. "Review of *ᶜIsa ibn Zurᶜa: Philosophe arabe et apologiste chrétien*, by Cyrille Haddad." *Journal of the American Research Center in Egypt* 9 (1971–72): 158.
82. "Review of *Archives du couvent Saint-Sauveur*, by Rachid Haddad." *Journal of the American Research Center in Egypt* 9 (1971–72): 157.
83. "Review of *Manuscrits du couvent de Belmont*, by Rachid Haddad and Faèz Freijate." *Journal of the American Research Center in Egypt* 9 (1971–72): 157.
84. "Review of *Kulturhistorische Studien zur Genese pseudo-islamischer Sektengebilde in Vorderasien*, by Klaus Müller." *Wiener Zeitschrift für die Kunde des Morgenlandes* 63–64: 334–36.

85. "Review of *Les bibliothèques arabes publiques et semi-publiques . . . au Moyen Age*, by Youssef Eche." *Wiener Zeitschrift für die Kunde des Morgenlandes* 63–64: 336–37.
86. "Review of *Medicinalia Arabica*, by Albert Dietrich." *Wiener Zeitschrift für die Kunde des Morgenlandes* 63–64: 337–38.
87. "Review of *Der Orient in der Forschung* (Otto Spies Festschrift), Edited by Wilhelm Hoenerbach." *Wiener Zeitschrift für die Kunde des Morgenlandes* 63–64: 338–39.

1973

88. "Review of *Bell's Introduction to the Qur*ʾ*an*, by W. Montgomery Watt." *Journal of the American Oriental Society* 93: 363.

1974

89. "The Arabic Line in the *Cancionero de Baena*." *Hispanic Review* 42: 427–29.
90. "Rejoinder to 'Kritik einer ungerechtfertigten Kritik.'" *Wiener Zeitschrift für die Kunde des Morgenlandes* 65–66: 282–83.
91. "Review of *Bulletin d'études orientales*, Volume 22, by the Institut Français de Damas." *Wiener Zeitschrift für die Kunde des Morgenlandes* 65–66: 366–67.
92. "Review of *Dhat al-Himma*, by Udo Steinbach." *Wiener Zeitschrift für die Kunde des Morgenlandes* 65–66: 367–70.
93. "Review of *Le parler arabe de Cherchell*, by Jacques Grand'Henry." *Wiener Zeitschrift für die Kunde des Morgenlandes* 65–66: 370.
94. "Review of *Der historische Gehalt der Aiyam al-Arab*, by Egbert Meyer." *Wiener Zeitschrift für die Kunde des Morgenlandes* 65–66: 371.
95. "Review of *Damas, Bagdad: Capitales et terres des Caliphes*, by J.-Ghislain de Maussion de Favières." *Wiener Zeitschrift für die Kunde des Morgenlandes* 65–66: 371–2.

1976

96. *Langenscheidts Taschenwörterbuch der arabischen und deutschen Sprache*, Part 1: *Arabisch-Deutsch*. Berlin: Langenscheidt.
97. "Review of *Miskawayh: Traité d'éthique*, by Mohammed Arkoun." *Wiener Zeitschrift für die Kunde des Morgenlandes* 68: 239–40.
98. "Review of *Arabic Poetry: Theory and Development*, Edited by G. E. von Grunebaum." *Wiener Zeitschrift für die Kunde des Morgenlandes* 68: 240–41.
99. "Review of *Recherches de Kurdologie*, by Mohammad Mokri." *Wiener Zeitschrift für die Kunde des Morgenlandes* 68: 258.

1977

100. "Review of *Die Natur- und Geheimwissenschaften im Islam*, by Manfred Ullmann." *Journal of the American Oriental Society* 97: 338.
101. "Review of *Hochsprache und Dialekt im Arabischen*, by Werner Diem." *Der Islam* 54/1: 163.
102. "Review of *Wörterbuch der klassischen arabischen Sprache*, Volume 2/ Part 1." *Der Islam* 54/1: 164. [See item #20 above]

1978

103. "Review of *The Classical Heritage in Islam*, by Franz Rosenthal." *American Journal of Philology* 99/2: 272.
104. "Review of *Greek Wisdom Literature in Arabic Translation*, by Dimitri Gutas." *American Journal of Philology* 99/2: 273.
105. "Review of *Wörterbuch der klassischen arabischen Sprache*, Volume 2/ Parts 2–4." *Der Islam* 55/1: 112–13. [See item #20 above]

1979

106. Population Information Center. *Twenty-Two Dimensions of the Population Problem.* Population Reports J–11. Baltimore: Johns Hopkins University Press. Translated by Georg Krotkoff from the original English into Arabic.
107. "Review of *Le livre des sept vizirs*, by Zahiri de Samarkand; *Le livre du Dedans*, by Djalaluddin Rumi; *Odes mystiques*, by Djalaluddin Rumi." *Wiener Zeitschrift für die Kunde des Morgenlandes* 71: 240–42.
108. "Review of *La grande assemblée des Fidèles de Verité au tribunal sur le mont Zagros*, by Mohammad Mokri." *Wiener Zeitschrift für die Kunde des Morgenlandes* 71: 248–50.

1981

109. "Review of *Arabic Grammar: A First Workbook*, by G. M. Wickens." *Journal of the American Association of Teachers of Arabic* (= *Al-Arabiyya*) 14: 92–95.

1982

110. *A Neo-Aramaic Dialect of Kurdistan: Texts, Grammar, and Vocabulary.* American Oriental Series 64. New Haven: American Oriental Society. 172 pp.
111. "Review of *Islam and Development*, Edited by J. L. Esposito." *Journal of Church and State*, April: 383–85.
112. "Review of *A Dictionary of Modern Written Arabic*, by Hans Wehr." 4th Edition. *Der Islam* 59/1: 157.

113. "Review of *Poetische Namengebung*, by Hendrik Birus." *Wiener Zeitschrift für die Kunde des Morgenlandes* 74: 309–10.

1983

114. "ABJAD." Pp. 221–22 in *Encyclopaedia Iranica*, Volume 1. Edited by E. Yarshater. London, Routledge & Kegan Paul.

1984

115. "Colour and Number in the Haft Paikar." Pp. 97–118 in *Logos Islamicos: Studia Islamica in Honorem Georgii Michaelis Wickens*. Edited by R. M. Savory and D. A. Agius. Toronto: Pontifical Institute of Mediaeval Studies.
116. "Review of *Arabisch-deutsches Wörterbuch*, Parts 1–4, by Götz Schregle." *Der Islam* 61/1: 107–8.

1985

117. "Studies in Neo-Aramaic Lexicology." Pp. 123–34 in *Biblical and Related Studies Presented to Samuel Iwry*. Edited by A. Kort and S. Morschauser. Winona Lake, Indiana: Eisenbrauns.

1986

118. "Review of *The Finite Passive Voice in Modern Arabic Dialects*, by Jan Retsö." *Der Islam* 63/2: 362.

1987

119. "Hammer-Purgstall, Hajji Baba, and the Moriers." *International Journal of Middle Eastern Studies* 19: 103–8.
120. "The Arabic Language and Script." Pp. 58–60 in *The Rise of Islam*. Silver Burdett Picture Histories. Morristown, New Jersey: Silver Burdett.

1988

121. "Arabic Wordprocessing: *AlKaatib*." *Journal of the American Association of Teachers of Arabic* 21: 131–35.
122. "Review of *Grundriß der arabischen Philologie*, Edited by Wolfdietrich Fischer." *Journal of the American Association of Teachers of Arabic* 21: 137–40.

1989

123. "Majhūra/Mahmūsa Revisited." *Journal of the American Association of Teachers of Arabic* 22: 217–18. [Brief communication]

124. "Review of *Die semantische Entwicklung arabischer Wörter im Persischen*, by Asya Asbaghi." *Journal of the American Association of Teachers of Arabic* 22: 181–83.
125. "Review of *The Book of Genesis in Neo-Aramaic in the Dialect of the Jewish Community of Zakho*, by Yona Sabar." *Jewish Quarterly Review* 79: 388.

1990

126. "An Annotated Bibliography of Neo-Aramaic." Pp. 3–26 in *Studies in Neo-Aramaic*. Edited by W. Heinrichs. Harvard Semitic Studies 36. Atlanta: Scholars Press.
127. "Review of *The Sound System of Modern Assyrian*, by Edward Y. Odisho." *Zeitschrift der deutschen morgenländischen Gesellschaft* 140: 157.

1991

128. "Remarks on the Iraqi-Arabic Lexicon: Problems and Characteristics." Pp. 886–89 in *Semitic Studies in Honor of Wolf Leslau on the Occasion of his Eighty-Fifth Birthday*, Volume 1. Edited by Alan S. Kaye. Wiesbaden: Harrassowitz.
129. "Review of *The Syntax and Semantics of Verb Morphology in Modern Aramaic: A Jewish Dialect of Iraqi Kurdistan*, by Robert D. Hoberman." *Journal of the American Oriental Society* 111/1: 138.

1993

130. *Langenscheidts Taschenwörterbuch der arabischen und deutschen Sprache*, Volume 2: *Deutsch-Arabisch*. Berlin: Langenscheidt.
131. "Hammer-Purgstalls Schrift 'Das Kamel'." *Wiener Zeitschrift für die Kunde des Morgenlandes* 82 [1992]: 261–68.
132. "Review of *Der neuaramäische Dialekt von Hertevin (Provinz Siirt)*, by Otto Jastrow." *Journal of the American Oriental Society* 113/3: 505.
133. "Brief Review of *Der arabische Dialekt der Juden von ᶜAqra und Arbîl*, by Otto Jastrow." *Zeitschrift der deutschen morgenländischen Gesellschaft* 143/1: 228.

1994

134. "Aus der Werkstatt eines irakischen Volksdichters." Pp. 558–66 in *Festschrift Ewald Wager zum 65. Geburtstag*, Volume 2. Edited by Wolfhart Heinrichs and Gregor Schoeller. *Studien zur arabischen Dichtung*. Beirut Texte und Studien 54. Beirut and Stuttgart: Franz Steiner.
135. "Wilhelm Czermak and Spatiality in Language." Pp. 125–33 in *Essays in Egyptology in Honor of Hans Goedicke*. Edited by Betsy M. Bryan and David Lorton. San Antonio, Texas: Van Siclen.

136. "Der ägyptische Ursprung von slawisch *bes* 'Dämon.'" *Zwischen den beiden Ewigkeiten: Festschrift Gertrud Thausing*. Edited by Manfred Bietak, Johanna Holaubek, Hans Mukarovsky, and Helmut Satzinger. Vienna: Institute for Egyptology.

1995

137. "Review of *Das Neuwestaramäische, III: Volkskundliche Texte aus Ma*^{c}*lûla*, by Werner Arnold." *Journal of the American Oriental Society* 115: 176.
138. "Remembering Umberto Rizzitano (1913–1980)." A Review Article of *Studi arabo islamici in memoria di Umberto Rizzitano*, Edited by Gianni di Stefano. *Die Welt des Islams* 35/1: 126–30.

1996

139. "Review of *Christian Arabic of Baghdad*, by Farida Abu-Haidar." *Journal of the American Oriental Society* 116: 602–3.
140. "A Response to Marina Tolmacheva's 'The Medieval Arabic Geographers and the Beginnings of Modern Orientalism.'" *International Journal of Middle East Studies* 28: 461.

Abbreviations

General

f.	feminine
JPS	Jewish Publication Society Version of the Bible
m.	masculine
MT	Masoretic Text
pl.	plural
sg.	singular
VE	siglum for "Il Vocabulario di Ebla." *Testi Lessicali Bilingui della Biblioteca L. 2769, Parte I.* Materiali Epigrafici di Ebla 4. Edited by G. Pettinato et al.

Reference Works

ÄA	*Ägyptologische Abhandlungen*
AbrN	*Abr-Nahrain*
AJSL	*American Journal of Semitic Languages and Literature*
AnOr	Analecta Orientalia
AOS	American Oriental Series
ArOr	*Archiv Orientální*
ASORMS	American Schools of Oriental Research Monograph Series
BASOR	*Bulletin of the American Schools of Oriental Research*
BHS	*Biblia Hebraica Stuttgartensia*
Bib	*Biblica*
BIFAO	*Bulletin de l'institut français d'archéologie orientale*
BKAT	Biblischer Kommentar: Altes Testament
BSO(A)S	*Bulletin of the School of Oriental (and African) Studies*
CBQ	*Catholic Biblical Quarterly*
EI[1]	*Encyclopaedia of Islam.* Leiden, 1913–36
EI[2]	*Encyclopaedia of Islam.* New edition. Leiden, 1960–
EncJud	*Encyclopaedia Judaica*
GLECS	*Comptes Rendus du Groupe Linguistique d'Études Chamito-Sémitiques*
HALAT	W. Baumgartner et al., *Hebräisches und aramäisches Lexikon zum Alten Testament*

HAR	*Hebrew Annual Review*
IDBSup	Supplementary volume to *Interpreter's Dictionary of the Bible*
IJMES	*International Journal of Middle East Studies*
IOS	*Israel Oriental Studies*
JA	*Journal asiatique*
JAATA	*Journal of the American Association of Teachers of Arabic (= al-ʿArabiyya)*
JAOS	*Journal of the American Oriental Society*
JARCE	*Journal of the American Research Center in Egypt*
JBL	*Journal of Biblical Literature*
JEA	*Journal of Egyptian Archaeology*
JNES	*Journal of Near Eastern Studies*
JPS	*Tenakh: The Holy Scriptures.* Philadelphia: Jewish Publication Society, 1985.
JSS	*Journal of Semitic Studies*
JQR	*Jewish Quarterly Review*
LÄ	*Lexikon der Ägyptologie.* Edited by W. Helck and W. Westendorf. 7 vols. Wiesbaden: Harrassowitz, 1975–92
MAD	Materials for the Assyrian Dictionary
MEE	Materiali epigrafici di Ebla
MLS	*Modern Language Series*
Or	*Orientalia*
REI	*Revue des Études Islamiques*
RIS	*Rasāʾil Ikhwān al-Ṣafāʾ*
RMM	*Regensburger mikrofiche Materialen*
SEI	*Shorter Encyclopaedia of Islam*
TDAY	*Türk Dili Araştırmaları Yıllığı*
UAJb	*Ural-Altaïsche Jahrbücher*
UT	C. H. Gordon, *Ugaritic Textbook.* Rome: Pontifical Biblical Institute, 1965
VE	*Vocabolario di Ebla* (in MEE 4)
VOHD	*Verzeichnis der orientalischen Handschriften in Deutschland*
VOHD Sup	Supplement to *Verzeichnis der orientalischen Handschriften in Deutschland*
VT	*Vetus Testamentum*
WZKM	*Wiener Zeitschrift für die Kunde des Morgenlandes*
ZA	*Zeitschrift für Assyriologie und vorderasiatische Archäologie*
ZAL	*Zeitschrift für arabische Linguistik*
ZDMG	*Zeitschrift der Deutschen Morgenländischen Gesellschaft*
ZGAW	*Zeitschrift für Geschichte der arabisch-islamischen Wissenschaften*

Georg Krotkoff as Scholar and Teacher

Asma Afsaruddin and
A. H. Mathias Zahniser

As Ralph Tingey and Matt Zahniser, the two students who represented Dr. Krotkoff's whole seminar in Arabic texts, entered his office for their Tuesday seminar, they were startled by an invitation to go with him to Columbus, where Ohio State University would soon host the ninth annual Conference on Islam and the Medieval West. "It doesn't make any sense," he said, "to carry on as usual here when so much is going on at Ohio State. Let's go to Columbus."

And to Columbus they went at his expense in Zahniser's tan Dodge Dart—Krotkoff's Volkswagen beetle being too small for the three of them and their luggage. Krotkoff had a very practical end in view for the trip: jobs for his students and contact with others in their field. But this was also innovative education with a vengeance; it not only provided his students with an opportunity to hear some valuable lectures, to witness scholarly interchange, and to meet many of the scholars whose work they had studied; it gave them a chance to see their teacher at work as an international linguist who knew languages and could converse in any being used that week in Columbus—English, French, German, and Russian. Traveling, eating, and living at close quarters afforded them an unanticipated intimacy with him.

As this experience make clear, Georg Krotkoff was a teacher and learner who was not bound to a pedagogy familiar to us for the transmission of knowledge and method. In retrospect, it is possible to discern that his methods and values as a teacher and learner were significantly shaped by his childhood.

Childhood: Enthusiasm for Language

Georg Krotkoff was born in Vienna on May 21, 1925, to Russian immigrant parents. In time, his father, Boris Krotkoff, became lecturer of Russian literature, first at the Higher Institute for Commerce, and later at both the higher institute and the University of Vienna.

Before he secured a position at the university, the elder Krotkoff gave Russian lessons to individual students in his home. The bilingual Georg was permitted to observe these lessons. In at least one instance, when his father was delayed, Georg took the waiting student through his drills. The linguist and teacher was five years old.

Georg's fascination with language started with scripts. At the age of ten he copied any alphabet he could get a hold of into a little black commonplace book that his aunt had given him. Noting the seriousness and care with which the child studied and recorded his scripts, his father obtained for him a secondhand copy of Karl Faulmann's ponderous volume *Geschichte der Schrift.*[1] Georg did not, however, abandon the copybook procedure. Rather, he obtained a larger copybook, which he filled with careful notes and charts from Faulmann and some supplementary material. In fact, he continued to copy words, paradigms, and other details from languages into copybooks. Later, he would encourage his students to make dictionaries for the languages they studied. "Even if you don't use them much, the effort is part of learning," he advised.

The elder Krotkoff was a master teacher. An earlier career as an actor helped him become the teacher of a whole generation of Austrians who learned Russian. His unique methods would be used by his son throughout his career as a language teacher. These procedures and principles are worth mentioning.

First of all, only the language being learned would be used; a simple vocabulary and grammar being built up through question and answer, focusing upon objects at hand: "This is a pencil"; "That is a book"; "The pencil is on the book," etc. Later on, a transition would be made to the usual classroom language,

1. K. Faulmann, *Illustrirte Geschichte der Schrift* (Vienna: Hartleben, 1880).

the language already known to the learners, to facilitate explanations about the structure and the meaning of the various features of the language being learned. But even after the known language was in use, at the beginning of each lesson some time would be given to using only the new language.

Early in the course of study, a simple poem or other short text would be memorized. This served two purposes: the obvious purpose was to give students a small corpus of examples upon which the instructor could draw for explanation of the grammar and the morphology of the language; the more subtle purpose was to emphasize a fundamental principle of Krotkoff language learning: the text always comes first.

After the war, while he was a doctoral candidate, Krotkoff taught Arabic in an adult education program. He had twenty students, including an Austrian employee at the Egyptian embassy. He used his father's method, which involved memorizing a simple children's poem in the language. An official at the Egyptian Embassy, Mr. Maraghi, needed a driver's license. Krotkoff's Austrian student, Mr. Howenstein, helped Maraghi by serving as his interpreter for the oral examination. The official of the traffic division would ask Maraghi a question in German through Howenstein; the latter would then quote a section from the poem, the only Arabic he knew, to Maraghi. The embassy official could then say in Arabic whatever he pleased, for Howenstein would simply substitute the correct answer in German.

His father's purchase of Faulmann's *Geschichte der Schrift* illustrates another axiom of Georg Krotkoff's pedagogy: facilitate fascination and encourage learning. He facilitated and encouraged any interest evidenced in his students. Long after graduating, his students still receive an occasional clipping or reference on topics in which they have shown an interest.

Trubetskoy and Jansky: The Lure of Linguistics

The elder Krotkoff facilitated his son's fascination with Prince Nicolay Trubetskoy, the great linguist. The Prince, a commanding figure in the Russian immigrant community, in the Russian refugee church, and at the university, was of course known socially to the Krotkoff family. Since the elder Krotkoff was teaching Russian and was interested in language, he sat in on some of the Prince's lectures.

In his speech of acceptance into the Viennese Academy of Science at the age of 39, the Prince described himself as "mentally deranged"; the subject of his mania—language. The imprint of this passion stayed with Georg Krotkoff, who made the Prince's mania his own and still associates himself with the Prague School.

In the year Trubetskoy died at age 49, the elder Krotkoff was appointed lecturer in Russian at the University of Vienna. If the model for the linguistic career of Georg Krotkoff was his father, and a major inspiration Prince Trubetskoy, his practical mentor was Herbert Jansky at the *Konsularakadamie* or school for diplomats in Vienna. Put in other terms, Georg Krotkoff was both a product of the Russian immigrant community in Vienna between the world wars, and the product of that great city itself, described by Blake Ehrlich and Ronald John Hill as "an invigorating distillation of human energy and imagination."[2]

Among the many wise decisions of her forty-year reign (1740–80) was Empress Maria Theresa's establishing of the *Orientalische Akademie* in Austria's capital city. After World War I, the Akademie was made into the school for diplomats, including diplomats from other nations. The elder Krotkoff, himself, had taught at this school before his appointment to the Higher Institute; and Georg, later, during his days as a doctoral candidate at the university, would teach in the *Lehranstalt für orientalische Sprachen*, the evening extension for the general public of the *Konsularakadamie*. And it was the Turcologist Herbert Jansky, that tireless teacher of Near Eastern languages and Modern Greek at the *Lehranstalt*,[3] who would contribute so much to Georg Krotkoff, the Arabist. It was Jansky who suggested that the young Georg start with Arabic as the basis for the study of Persian and Turkish. So at the age of thirteen Georg began his life as an Arabist. By the time he was out of his teens, Krotkoff had also taken Persian and Turkish from Jansky, whose practical orientation to language study would also influence Krotkoff's teaching.

"Inventing the Language Lab"

During these formative years, another city and another set of teachers were an influence, behind the scenes, honing the expertise of the young Krotkoff. He was at this point, as he later termed it "inventing the language lab." The city was London and the "language lab" was the Arabic broadcasts of the BBC. From his early days as Jansky's student, his real teachers were the readers of the news and other speakers in the British Broadcasting Company's Arabic division. Georg would listen to the various readers and identify words that he did not know. He would then look them up in his dictionary and be ready to add to them at the time of the next broadcast. Especially in news reports, there was enough continuity in vocabulary that each "lab session" built upon the other,

2. "Vienna," *The New Encyclopædia Britannica* (1990 ed.) 493.

3. Dr. Claudia Römer, a contributor to this volume (see pp. 401–18 below) was also a student of Jansky in the late 1960s.

increasing his working vocabulary, familiarizing him with the structure of the language, and tuning his malleable young ear to its distinctive sounds. Two years into his university studies he would spend the summer at an international harvest camp in rural England to establish his use of the English language. A visit to London provided an opportunity to visit the offices of his language lab and to thank its director, Neville Barbour, and his staff for their help.

Before the end of the Second World War, Georg had sat for the exam to register his qualification to be a military interpreter (*Sprachmittler*) in Arabic. This he hoped would qualify him for military service using Arabic, lest his knowledge of Russian send him to the Russian front. Passing the exam did keep him away from the front and in a reserve unit for some six months. In the end, however, when his knowledge of Russian was discovered, he was placed in a signal battalion on the eastern front which by then had moved to Poland. As it turned out, the war lasted only a few more weeks, and in June of 1945, he was able to return to Vienna and enter the university to study his life's passion—languages.

The University of Vienna and Wilhelm Czermak

As a preparation against the danger of bombing, the volumes in the university library had been cached in other buildings outside the danger zone. Incoming students were immediately put to work collecting the library and restoring it to its proper place—that is, if they were very fortunate. The tougher jobs involved cleaning up the rubble from no less than sixteen bombs that had struck the university complex. Krotkoff would later remember that "these were happy occasions giving us a sense of accomplishment in a life otherwise characterized by deprivations and shortages at every level of existence."[4]

At the University of Vienna, Krotkoff was especially influenced by Wilhelm Czermak, an Egyptologist and African linguist, who also taught Arabic after the untimely death of Arabist Hans Kofler. Like Krotkoff himself, Czermak was exposed to Arabic at an early age, in his case in its Egyptian dialectal variety. Czermak spoke several languages with the fluency of a near-native

4. Krotkoff, "Wilhelm Czermak and Spatiality in Language," *Essays in Egyptology in Honor of Hans Goedicke* (ed. Betsy M. Bryan and David Lorton; San Antonio, Tex: Van Siclen, 1994) 125–33. In this fascinating article (pp. 129–33), Krotkoff includes an English summary of Czermak's obscure but seminal article, itself "buried in a Festschrift" ("Die Lokalvorstellung und ihre Bedeutung für den grammatischen Aufbau afrikanischer Sprachen," in *Festschrift Meinhof: Sprachwissenschaftliche und andere Studien* [Hamburg, 1927] 204–22).

speaker, including Egyptian Arabic, Nubian, and Somali. Georg would describe Czermak's acquaintance with African languages as "thorough."[5] He was also an accomplished lecturer who handled the German language with rhetorical skill. Philosophically oriented, he saw the world whole, making room for language both as the rhythmic expression of primal human experiences of pain and joy and as the vehicle for the spatial ordering of the human spirit. Krotkoff was attracted to this man of such visible excellence, and Czermak liked him because of his unusual skill with Arabic. Georg took many courses from his mentor and chose African languages as his minor, registering for Arabic, Ethiopic, Fulani, Somali, Swahili, and Tashilhait under Czermak. Krotkoff was clearly one of those "addicts who would not miss a Czermak lecture as long as they could afford the time."[6] He also subscribed to Czermak's concern for all the dimensions of a language in all the aspects of its culture.

Hans Gottschalk, the Arabist who was newly appointed during Krotkoff's student days, had only a limited influence on him. More important was the Arabic that he learned in the process of teaching German to Arab medical students in Vienna. But Gottschalk, as supervisor, and Herbert Duda, as second reader, teamed up to guide Krotkoff's dissertation on a collection of optical questions by the Mālikī jurist, al-Qarāfī. In his analysis, he worked from a manuscript that the well-known physician and expert on Arab medicine, Max Meyerhof, had commissioned. Krotkoff completed his dissertation and received his doctorate in Arabic philology from the University of Vienna in October of 1950.

Cairo and Baghdad: Apprenticeship and Fieldwork

Eager to become acquainted with the Islamic world, the young scholar took the first opportunity that presented itself. In the summer of 1951, he went along with a geographical expedition to the High Atlas in Morocco as a photographer and interpreter. Before that, he had written a letter to Ṭāhā Ḥusayn, then minister of education in Egypt, offering his services as a lecturer in German at the newly founded Ibrāhīm Pasha University, which after the Revolution was renamed ᶜAyn Shams University. To his great delight and surprise, he received a positive response, notifying him of his appointment as lecturer of German in the department of Egyptian archaeology, under the chairmanship of Dr. Aḥmad Badawī.

5. Krotkoff, "Czermak and Spatiality," 126.
6. Ibid., 127.

The Cairo experience was an apprenticeship in Arabic-speaking society and culture. The young Viennese scholar met orientalists, including W. Montgomery Watt and Umberto Rizzitano, the latter becoming a real mentor for Krotkoff, introducing him to many important people and events in Egypt. His was the privilege of meeting and engaging in scholarly interaction with Egyptian scholars and literary craftsmen such as Ṭāhā Ḥusayn; Tawfīq al-Ḥakīm, director of the Dār al-Kutub in Cairo; and Maḥmūd Taymūr, that towering literary figure, one of whose short stories Krotkoff translated into German.[7] He picked up no little Egyptological lore in the process, as he accompanied the students on their excursions to many archaeological sites up and down the Nile.

If his four years in Egypt represented apprenticeship, his four years in Baghdad marked the beginning of significant fieldwork and publication as a scholar in his own right. Traveling back and forth from Egypt to Vienna by ship during the summers, Krotkoff met up with Desmond Stewart, the classically trained author and novelist, then teaching in Baghdad. Stewart invited him to visit him in Baghdad at Christmas time to see if he would like to continue his teaching fieldwork there, where the university needed a German lecturer. The chemistry was evidently right, because Krotkoff moved to Baghdad and taught at the University under Dean of Arts and Sciences, ᶜAbd al-ᶜAzīz ad-Dūrī. Before he left Baghdad, Krotkoff had collected the material he would use for the substance of his major contribution to Modern Aramaic grammar,[8] for his Baghdad studies,[9] and a number of other individual studies, including one published only recently.[10] Fourteen of his articles and books would either be published during his tenure at the University of Baghdad or be based on research carried out during that tenure.

7. Mahmud Taimur, "Die Sommerreise," in *Die Reise zum wonnigen Fisch: Die besten Humoresken der zeitgenösischen Weltliteratur* (Vienna: Paul Neff, 1960) 593–99.

8. Krotkoff, "Beobachtungen zum Neu-Ostaramäischen," *ZDMG* 111 (1962) 393–95; *A Neo-Aramaic Dialect of Kurdistan: Texts, Grammar, and Vocabulary* (AOS 64; New Haven: American Oriental Society, 1982); "Studies in Neo-Aramaic Lexicology," in *Biblical and Related Studies Presented to Samuel Iwry* (ed. A. Kort and S. Morschauser; Winona Lake, Ind.: Eisenbrauns, 1985) 123–34; and "An Annotated Bibliography of Neo-Aramaic," in *Studies in Neo-Aramaic* (ed. Wolfhart Heinrichs; HSS 36; Atlanta: Scholars Press, 1990) 3–26.

9. Krotkoff, "Bagdader Studien, I: Das Weberhandwerk in Bagdad," *ZDMG* 112 (1963) 319–24; "Bagdader Studien, II: Ein Einakter im Bagdader Dialekt," *ZDMG* 114 (1964) 66–90; "Bagdader Studien, III: Miszellen von Bagdader Märkten; IV: Metallgefäße; V: Kopfbedeckungen; VI: Vom Baugewerbe; VII: Ein toponymisches Kuriosum; and VIII: Zu Weissbach, ZS 4," *ZDMG* 122 (1972) 93–101.

10. Krotkoff, "Aus der Werkstatt eines irakischen Volksdichters," *Festschrift Ewald Wagner zum 65. Geburtstag*, band 2: *Studien zur arabischen Dichtung* (ed. Wolfhart Heinrichs und Gregor Schoeler; Beiruter Texte und Studien 54; Beirut: In Kommission bei Steiner Verlag Stuttgart, 1994) 558–66.

In Baghdad he became aware of an Aramaic-speaking minority. While Arabic philology was clearly the major focus of his scholarly interest, his fascination with language in general and with Near Eastern languages in particular made research in Modern Aramaic attractive. In addition, the community of Aramaic speakers merited attention, and the literature about Modern Aramaic was scarce. Thus, need and opportunity came together and yielded the fieldwork that would become *A Neo-Aramaic Dialect of Kurdistan: Texts, Grammar, and Vocabulary*, published in 1982, and dedicated to that precarious Aramaic-speaking community whose discourse it analyzed and preserved.[11] Having resigned from his post in 1959 due to political unrest, Krotkoff returned to Vienna, seeking academic employment. On the heels of his return he received an invitation to the Johns Hopkins University, where he would teach until his retirement in 1990. Ironically, the Baghdad connection had been crucial in his selection for the invitation.

A Hopkins Career

Wilfred Lambert, then the chair of the Oriental Seminar at Hopkins, had heard about Krotkoff from Edith Penrose, wife of Ernest Penrose, Professor of Geography, then in retirement. The Penroses had been in Baghdad one year while Professor Penrose was a visiting professor of geology in the College of Arts and Sciences at the University of Baghdad and had become aquainted with Krotkoff. Mrs. Penrose, a political scientist interested in the Arab world and attempting to learn Arabic, thought that Hopkins should have a specialist in Arabic like Krotkoff. Thus, when Professor Lambert later brought up the question of hiring an Arabist, she suggested Krotkoff. Lambert's letter of invitation, however, arrived in Baghdad just after Krotkoff had returned to Vienna; it never reached him. Lambert persisted and sent another letter to the Institute in Vienna. This letter connected, and in the fall of 1960, Krotkoff began his life's work at the Johns Hopkins University. He taught there for thirty years. His teaching was characterized by a commitment to text and context, and his research was motivated by problem-solving.

11. Krotkoff, *Dialect of Kurdistan*, iii. Under the dedication, which is set prominently in capital letters, Krotkoff pasted a color photograph of Shabo, his informant, and his family. He also inserted an update on the village of Aradhin in copies of the work that he distributed. In reviewing Otto Jastrow's *Der neuaramäische Dialekt von Hertevin* (1988), Krotkoff took some of his limited space to draw readers' attention "to the existential plight of human beings in whom we are too easily inclined to see nothing but speakers of a language under study and potential informants." He commended Jastrow for his own obvious concern for the people of Hertevin (*JAOS* 113/3 [1993] 505).

Commitment to Text and Context

The Krotkoff that we knew was fascinated with languages in their literary and cultural contexts. He was committed to seeing that his students found for themselves the meaning of the language under investigation and examined meaning in relation to the living situation of the speaker or author of the text. He was impatient with facile emendations to texts and with translations that were preposterous in the light of the probable life situation of the text and its author. He demurred when a translator or interpreter of a text who obviously did not understand the passage under discussion would not admit it. He himself had no false humility about his strengths and made no attempt to disguise or deny his limitations.

A Pedagogy of Process and Example

Both Krotkoff's skills and his struggles with a text were in full view for his students. We approached a text together in the seminar atmosphere of his office with his most important resources at hand, many of them carefully locked in a metal cabinet. When a problem arose, we went straight to these resources for a solution. His interpretive materials included his own files, usually made up of discarded library cards he had frugally amassed for this purpose. When an interesting philological phenomenon arose in a text, out came the file, and a slip of paper was added to it. This would be the grist for such things as his *Taschenwörterbuch der arabischen und deutschen Sprache*,[12] or some other future article, brief communication, or review. Rather than appearing the omniscient expert, he played the role of the collegial example.

He allowed his students to argue at whatever length necessary for their interpretation of a text, patiently countering their argument step by step with his own, almost always—as it turned out—superior interpretation. In the end the student was taken again through the steps of analysis and was granted the luxury of recovering the sense of closure about the more accurate meaning of the passage that had originally led him or her to such certainty about the less accurate meaning. Only teachers who really know what they are doing can afford such lavish vulnerability. But the result is students who are able to work on their own.

Seminars focused on texts. No other organization of the curriculum was obvious besides the texts we were to study in a given semester. Yet anything could be brought to the text for its understanding. Even though Krotkoff possessed a

12. Krotkoff, *Langenscheidts Taschenwörterbuch der arabischen und deutschen Sprache, 1. Teil: Arabisch-Deutsch* (Berlin: Langenscheidt, 1976); *2. Teil: Deutsch-Arabisch* (Berlin: Langenscheidt, 1993).

virtually inexhaustible supply of experiences of interest to us, he was reticent about sharing them and did so only in relation to the point at hand. Experience was hermeneutic, not diversionary. Yet he had no sense of the passage of time. We often stayed three or four hours in these seminars, which were scheduled for an hour and a half. On rare days he would dismiss the class early with the comment, "We have learned enough for today."

Krotkoff's field experience was motivated by the same conviction that drove his pedagogy. "You want to get acquainted with and understand everything involved in the life of the culture," was the simple, direct way he stated it. His convictions that the living context of the language is its culture, that the text is the literary context of written discourse, and that these two contexts have to be known and respected as wholes show up in the two selections in this Festschrift by his students: one an analysis of a modern Egyptian play, the other a structural contribution to the interpretation of a Qurʾānic sūra.

For Krotkoff, language is the focal point of analysis, since language covers all aspects of life. Most of his publications are the product of this conviction. For this reason many of his contributions look like anthropology. His articles on weaving are full of detail with illustrations and pictures. He also wrote on folk poetry, basing his analysis upon data obtained from a skilled and knowledgeable informant. Though these studies of poetry may seem more obviously linguistic, his other cultural studies also represent ingredients in the mastery of Iraqi Arabic in particular and of language in general. In order to understand the language associated with a craft, the researcher must grasp the craft; in order to understand the language of popular songs, one must have a handle on the whole ethos of popular music. As Krotkoff put it, "You have to have somebody explain it to you, because it is not self-explanatory."

This is true not only of dialectal and modern studies. In the study of medieval and ancient texts, Krotkoff tried in his classes and seminars to get the text to "talk to" the student. He sought to show the plausibility of what was described in the discourse. He urged his students to imagine the characters in the text and to imagine its author, to listen to the characters making their statements, to see the author writing the statements. Sense was to be made out of them within their setting and environment. In essence, understanding the message of the text demands the same effort and sensitivity whether the focus of analysis is a medieval manuscript or a piece of folk poetry.

"Things that Bother"

If the word *context* typifies the major dimension of Krotkoff's scholarship and teaching, the word *bother* typifies another dimension of his life's work. In

1988, he presented an informal talk to the Department of Near Eastern Studies at Hopkins entitled, "Things That Bother." Although the springboard for the appeal was the bother of student evaluations, the speech was really about the motivation for his research and writing. If something "bothered" him, he investigated it until he "resolved the bother." The focus of this talk was etymology, so his examples were taken from that field. He revealed what lay behind his study of the Spanish pronoun *usted* 'you'.[13] It bothered him that no Spanish philologist had derived this pronoun, used in polite address, from the Arabic *ustāḏ*, a derivation that seemed to him much simpler and more direct than deriving it from the combination *vuestra merced* 'your mercy', through attrition. This "bother" led to a foray into Spanish philology and resulted in the article mentioned in n. 13.

Being bothered by what he called pseudosociological etymologies led to other investigations, one of which he published in *Wiener Zeitschrift für die Kunde des Morgenlandes* in 1969.[14] It bothered him that scholars had attributed the fact that *leḥem* in Hebrew means 'bread' and its cognate in Arabic means 'meat' to the agricultural basis of the former and the nomadic society of the latter. After all, just as there were settled Arabs, there had also been nomadic Hebrews. His struggle led him to the wider meaning of the common root in Semitic languages as 'that which sticks together', a notion from which both 'meat' and 'bread' can be derived. The diversity of his published materials is explainable at least in part by this tendency to be bothered. His seminal article "Color and Number in the *Heft Paikar*"[15] was a result of being bothered by the fact that none of the scholars who had analyzed that epic had seen the compositional function of color and number. He took a sabbatical to improve his Persian in pursuit of a resolution to this bother.

Professor and Professional

Georg Krotkoff served a term as chair of the Department of Near Eastern Studies at Hopkins and was active in a number of professional societies. He served one term as president (1982) of the American Association of Teachers of Arabic and two terms (1968–70 and 1978–80) on the executive board. He has been active in the Middle East Studies Association since 1969, serving as a member of the program committee for its annual meeting for 1987. He was the

13. Krotkoff, "A Possible Arabic Ingredient in the History of Spanish *usted*," *Romance Philology* 17 (1963) 328–32.

14. Krotkoff, "*Laḥm* 'Fleisch' und *leḥem* 'Brot'," *WZKM* 62 (1969) 76–82.

15. Published in *Logos Islamicos: Studia Islamica in Honorem Georgii Michaelis Wickens* (ed. R. M. Savory and D. A. Agius; Toronto: Pontifical Institute of Mediaeval Studies, 1984) 97–118.

convener of the North American Conference on Afroasiatic Linguistics when it met in Baltimore in 1983, and has been active in that organization. He has held memberships in the American Oriental Society since 1960, the American Research Center in Egypt from 1966 to 1981, serving as advisory editor for its journal for most of that time, and the Middle East Institute, from 1970 until his retirement.

This Festschrift is testimony to the many friends he made in his professional life and to both the integrity with which he pursued his own work and the kindness with which he facilitated the work of his colleagues.

Part 1

Humanism, Culture, and Literature

Inquiry into the Origins of Humanism

George Makdisi

In a previous study on scholasticism, I wrote that its basic institutions originated in classical Islam. In a more recent study,[1] I have come to the conclusion that classical Islam appears to have provided the model for Italian Renaissance humanism. In this article, we will observe the rise of these two movements and follow their full development. Classical Islam affords us knowledge not only of *what* happened, but also *why*.

There is a continuing controversy regarding the concept of the renaissance, as well as that of humanism. I have nothing to say here about the concept of the renaissance, and the only humanism that will be dealt with is that which has been described as a cycle of studies, called the *studia humanitatis*, including grammar, poetry, rhetoric (as applied to letter-writing and speech-writing), history, and moral philosophy (mainly moral tracts). Further, since

Author's note: An abbreviated version of this paper was given at a conference sponsored by the Rockefeller Foundation in Bellagio, Italy, in 1989.

1. Makdisi, *The Rise of Humanism in Classical Islam and the Christian West* (Edinburgh: University of Edinburgh Press, 1990).

there is in classical Islam a connection between scholasticism and humanism, there will be some mention of scholasticism. Although scholarly studies on these two movements as they existed in the Christian West are highly developed and have yielded a mine of information and knowledge, there is still need, in the Christian West, for an adequate answer to the question *why*.

The Origins of the Movements and The Origin of the University

One place to begin in examining the *what* and *why* questions is with the phenomenon of the university. Our universities go back to medieval Europe; this is as far as we have been able to trace them. In a relatively recent work on medieval universities, A. B. Cobban makes the following statement:

> collectively the distinguishing features of the medieval university seem to have been nowhere reproduced in previous institutional form; and there does not appear to be any organic continuity between the universities which evolved towards the end of the twelfth century and Greek, Graeco-Roman, Byzantine, or Arabic schools.[2]

The author was justified in including the "Arabic schools" in his statement because their true nature was not generally known. Islamic higher learning is still in the process of being studied.

A more recent author writing on the origins of the university says,

> there is one myth that still hinders our understanding of the university's origins and development: the idea that the university was born naturally, or even inevitably, out of the diversification of the utilitarian and professional demands made upon education in the later Middle Ages and that it was shaped by the struggle of scholars to gain freedom and autonomy from external, and especially, from ecclesiastical domination and control.[3]

This author argues that "the university originated, not out of acquiescence to the demands for more specialized and practical learning, but out of resistance to these pressures."

We are thus still as uninformed regarding the origins of the university as we were with the fundamental *Medieval Universities* of Hastings Rashdall.[4] There

2. A. B. Cobban, *The Medieval Universities: Their Development and Organization* (London: Methuen, 1975) 21–22.

3. Stephen C. Ferruolo, *The Origins of the University: The Schools of Paris and Their Critics, 1100–1215* (Stanford, Calif.: Stanford University Press, 1985) 2–3.

4. H. Rashdall, *The Universities of Europe in the Middle Ages* (ed. F. M. Powicke and A. B. Emden; 3 vols.; Oxford: Oxford University Press, 1936).

are also other matters that have no previous institutional form, and their appearance on the scene still calls for adequate explanation: for instance, a fixed curriculum excluding certain fields of knowledge, a scholastic method leading to the *license to teach*, and the true nature of this doctorate.

It is not easy to accept the thesis of the influence of classical Islam on the Christian West, one of the reasons being that our scholarship in Islamic studies is at least a century behind that of the Christian West. Islamic studies suffer from underdevelopment and from the attempt to apply the methods of the social sciences to them before the manuscript sources have been edited in sufficient quantity and preliminary studies have sufficiently prepared the ground for such studies. The general image conveyed by the manuals on classical Islam makes it difficult to imagine that its civilization could have had anything to do with Western civilization in the areas of scholasticism or humanism. Under the circumstances, to consider that classical Islamic civilization could be at the origins of these two intellectual movements seems somehow to weaken the strength of Western European ties, both real and imagined, with classical antiquity.

Let us first deal with the names applied to these two movements, for they both rose and developed without being identified as "scholasticism" and "humanism." In classical Islam, they never had such names, and any reference to them in Modern Arabic would be in a translation or transliteration of a European language. In the Christian West, it was not until long after their development and decline that these two movements received their names. Therefore, any comparison of the two sets of movements in both civilizations would have to be done by considering the personnel involved, their professional activities, and their literary compositions.

The sequence of the appearance of both movements in classical Islam differs from what the sequence is believed to have been in the Christian West. Humanism was the first to develop in classical Islam, followed more than a century later by scholasticism. The dawn of humanism may be placed in the latter part of Islam's first century (seventh A.D.) and its products recorded as of the second. The beginning of scholasticism may be placed in the latter part of the third century (ninth A.D.), its products being recorded in the fourth. In the fourth/tenth century, scholasticism began to exert some influence on the development of humanism, and by the twelfth century, humanism had exerted some of its own on scholasticism. It was thus over a number of centuries that these two movements had their rise and development in classical Islam, the reasons for which are clearly traceable in its intellectual and religious history.

In the Christian West, scholasticism is said to date from the twelfth century, its dawn beginning with the *Sic et Non* (1122) of Abelard (d. 1142). The dawn of humanism is said to have been around the year 1280. In this scheme regarding the sequence of the two movements in the Christian West, we would have the reverse of their sequence in classical Islam. However, there is reason to believe that the reception of these two movements in the Christian West occurred at about the same time, in the second half of the eleventh century and that they proceeded to develop at two different paces. Scholasticism had experienced its full development and was on the decline when humanism, first proceeding partially, began to develop at a more rapid pace. What is known as Renaissance humanism began with the *ars dictaminis* restricted mainly to letter-writing and did not flourish as the fuller cycle of studies until the fourteenth. In this scheme of the history of the Christian West, it has been possible to know *what* happened regarding these two movements, but we have yet to have an adequate answer to the question *why*.

Summary of the Development of Scholasticism and Humanism in Classical Islam and the Christian West

I have dealt in detail with the scholastic movement in *The Rise of Colleges* (Edinburgh, 1981) and in *The Rise of Humanism* (Edinburgh, 1989), where special reference is made to scholasticism. Here I will confine myself to a brief listing of a few details, mainly in order to show the similarities between the two cultures. This will cover the *what* of humanism. I shall then remark on the *why* of both humanism and scholasticism, in an attempt to show that their essential elements, which constitute the model for two movements in the Christian West, are products of the exigencies of Islamic religious history.

The major fields of humanism, known by the term *studia humanitatis*, come under the Classical Arabic term, *adab*, and may be referred to as the *studia adabiya*:

- grammar (*naḥw*) and lexicography (*lugha*)
- poetry (*shi*ᶜ*r*)
- oratory (*khaṭāba*), especially applied to
  letter-writing (*tarassul*), whether
  official (*sulṭānīyāt*) or
  private (*ikhwānīyāt*), and
- speechmaking (*khiṭāb*, *wa*ᶜ*ẓ*)
- history (*ta*ʾ*rīkh*, *akhbār*)
- moral philosophy (ᶜ*ilm al-akhlāq*)

Philology: Grammar and Lexicography. In addition to grammars and lexicons, books were composed on how to avoid *laḥn*, barbarisms, and solecisms, in order to preserve the purity of the classical language.

Poetry. Poetry pervaded all intellectual products of humanism. Indeed it pervaded all of the divisions of knowledge in the classical Islamic organization of learning, so much so, that one categorization of poetry was according to the various humanistic professions and specializations: (1) the poetry of the intellectuals, grammarians, and so on; and (2) the grammar, law, theology, philosophy, and so on of poetry. Not all of this poetry, needless to say, was even then considered by the critics to be good poetry; nor were those who composed the poetry under such an impression. Writing poetry was something of a humanist pastime. There were also, of course, many great poets. Their poetry was categorized as "the poetry of poets."

Rhetoric. Rhetoric included the two branches of applied rhetoric: (1) epistolography, official, and private letter-writing; and (2) oratory, including religious preaching and sermon-writing, the academic sermon, and public speeches.

History. History included the diaries, annalistic histories, annalistic-biographical histories, biographies, autobiographies, memoirs, chronicles, and *akhbār*-history, including the historical novel.

Moral philosophy. Although works in the field of moral philosophy were written (for example, Avicenna's *Kitāb al-barr wa-ʾl-ithm* 'The Book of Piety and Sin'), the majority are moral tracts.

There were two categories of humanists: amateurs, such as jurists, physicians, philosophers, theologians, astronomers, astrologers, mathematicians; and professionals, such as chancellors, secretaries (of all ranks, from the secretary of state down to the simple clerk), tutors, boon companions. Notaries belonged to both categories: as lawyers they were amateur humanists, and as composers of formal documents they were professional humanists. The literary products of both cultures include treatises, formularies of notaries and epistolographers, commentaries, books on rules to be observed in certain professions, collections of speeches, and the like. *All the essential elements of humanism, as this movement has come to be known, are to be found in both cultures.*

Eloquence and the Dignity of Man

What is most typical of humanism and most essential is the concept of eloquence, the integrating element in humanism. Another concept of fundamental importance is the dignity of man. In chapter twenty of his great Qurʾānic commentary, entitled *Mafātīḥ al-ghayb* ('The Keys to That Which Has Been Concealed'), Fakhr al-Dīn al-Rāzī discusses speech (*nuṭq*) as a perfection of momentous importance and cites two verses from Sūrat al-Ḥijr (15:2–4), which refer to God:

> He created man, He taught him eloquence
> (*khalaqa ʾl-insāna ʿallamahu ʾl-bayāna*)

Al-Rāzī points out that in these two verses God did not use the adjunctive particle 'and'. He did not say, "He created man and taught him eloquence." Had he done so, He would have introduced a contrasting element. In the absence of 'and', the verse 'He taught him eloquence', comes as proof that 'He created man'. Al-Razi then goes on to say:

> It is as though God performs the act of creating man only when He has taught him *bayān* ("eloquence"). This goes back to the well-known dictum that the essence of man is that he is a rational animal. The second point is that intelligent men are in agreement as to the great importance of language. The poet Zuhayr put it this way: "A man's tongue is half of him; the other half, his mind . . ." (*lisān al-fatā niṣfun wa-niṣfun fuʾāduh . . .*).[5]

Indeed, the Qurʾān is clear regarding man's exceptional worth: the word *bayān* ('eloquence'), applied only to God and to man as taught by God, is not an attribute of any other creature, not even of the angels. Thus, in the Qurʾān man appears superior to the angels through the knowledge and dignity that God bestowed upon him and the faculty of clear, articulate, eloquent speech. Speech is the mark of man, and the degrees of clarity and eloquence in his speech determine his position on the scale of excellence in this most essential of human attributes. The following advice is that of al-Maʾmūn's prime minister to his sons:

> Learn how to speak well, for man's superiority over all other beings is through speech; and the more skillful you are in speaking, the more worthy you are of humanity.

This emphasis on eloquence, typical of the Arabians of old, is rooted in the Sacred, with the advent of Islam. For Muslims, the authenticity of the Qurʾān as God's own words rests on the miracle of its inimitable eloquence. Al-Razi's commentary cited above had the effect of indicating that *bayān* is not mere speech. Indeed, mere speech, according to the Qurʾān, was given to all things: "God has given us speech, *(He) who gave speech to all things*." But whereas God gave mere speech to all things, making the very skins of the damned to witness against them, He gave *eloquent* speech, *bayān*, to man alone. It was man alone who was challenged to produce a chapter of the same class as the chapters in the Qurʾān. By imitating the language of the Qurʾān, Muslim intellectuals strove to achieve eloquence in speech and in writing. Some tried consciously and deliberately to equal, and even to outclass, the eloquence of the Qurʾān. The humanist of classical Islam was imbued with the notions of

5. Al-Rāzī, *Mafātīḥ al-ghayb* (32 vols. in 16; Cairo: Dār iḥyāʾ turāth al-ʿarabī, 1980–89) 6.43–44.

eloquence and the dignity of man, from his tender years, through his memorization and recitation of the Qurᵓan.

Regarding man's dignity, it was Pico della Mirandola (d. 1481) who made a famous speech. At the very beginning of his *Oration on the Dignity of Man*, he cited the Arabs:

> I have read, reverend Fathers, in the works of the Arabs, that when Abdala the Saracen was asked what he regarded as most to be wondered at on the world's stage, so to speak, he answered that there was nothing to be seen more wonderful than man.
>
> *Legi, patres colendissimi, in Arabum monumentis interrogatum Abdalam Sarracenum, quid in hac quasi mundana scaena admirandum maxime spectaretur, nihil spectari homine admirabilius respondisse.*[6]

We also have these lines on the dignity of man from a tenth-century Muslim jurist, secretary, and poet-humanist, Abū ᵓl-Fatḥ al-Busṭī (d. 363/973–74) [my translation]:

> O Slave of the body! How you toil to serve it!
> Where there's nothing but loss, you seek to profit.
> Turn to the mind, which you need to perfect:
> You are man, not by the body, but by the intellect.
>
> *Yā khādima ᵓl-jismi! Kam tashqā bi-khidmatihi!*
> *Li-taṭluba ᵓr-ribḥa mimmā fīhi khuṣrānu.*
> *Aqbil ᶜalā ᵓn-nafsi, wa-ᵓstakmil faḍāᵓilahā:*
> *Fa-anta bi-ᵓn-nafsi, lā bi-ᵓl-jismi, insānu.*[7]

Underlying Motives of the Movements: Humanism

The first fact of Islam is the Qurᵓān. As already pointed out, it declares itself to be the word of God and its authenticity to rest on the matchless eloquence of its language, Classical Arabic. The risk of losing this language, felt by Muslims who mixed with the conquered peoples, gave impetus to philological studies pursued by urbanized Arabs who spent a number of research years in the

6. Giovanni Pico della Mirandola (d. 1481), "*Oratio de dignitate hominis*, Oration on the Dignity of Man," in *The Portable Renaaissance Reader* (ed. James B. Ross; New York: Viking, 1953) 476; Florence A. Gragg, *Latin Writings of the Italian Humanists* (New York: Scribner's, 1927) 213.

7. Ibn al-Jawzī, *al-Muntaẓam fī tārīkh al-mulūk wa-ᵓl-umam* (vols. 5–10; ed. Krenkow; Hyderabad: Dāᵓirat al-maᶜārif, 1357–59/1938–40) 7.73 (lines 17–18) (read: *tashqā* instead of *tashfī*).

Arabian peninsula. This was a massive effort to collect and record the language of the Arabians and what they still remembered of the pre-Islamic prose and poetry of the ancients. The reason for this effort was to preserve and practice using the classical language in order to continue to understand the sacred Scripture. In the latter part of the nineteenth century, Charles James Lyall, translator of *Ancient Arabian Poetry*, called these early philologists "eminent humanists."[8] At the beginning of the twentieth, he was seconded by Reynold A. Nicholson, author of the *Literary History of the Arabs*, who called them "the great Humanists," agreeing that "they have been well named by Sir Charles Lyall."[9]

This concern for the classical language of the Qurʾān and the scholarly activity that it brought into existence resulted in a humanistic movement called *adab*, consisting of a number of philological and literary fields, varying in number from four to fourteen. The first fields to develop were the philological sciences of grammar and lexicography. In the introduction to his *Prolegomena to Grammar*, the second/eighth-century Khalaf al-Aḥmar (d. 180/796) says that

> he who reads it [his grammar], memorizes it, and engages in disputations on it, will know all those principles of grammar which will reform his tongue with respect to a book he writes, or a poem he declaims, or a speech or letter he composes.[10]

In this statement by an early grammarian, four of the subjects of humanistic studies are listed: grammar, poetry, speeches, and letters. Such was the philological beginning of humanism in classical Islam and the motivation behind it.

Underlying Motives of the Movements: Scholasticism

Scholasticism came into being after the Inquisition (*miḥna*) set afoot by the Rationalists against the Traditionalists under al-Maʾmūn and carried on by three of his successors. Fifteen years later, in the middle of the ninth century, the Inquisition collapsed to the detriment of its protagonists and in favor of its victims, the Traditionalists. To ward off a recurrence of the struggle and to consolidate their gains in perpetuity, the Traditionalists brought into existence

8. Charles James Lyall, *Translations of Ancient Arabian Poetry* (London: Williams & Norgate, 1930 [1st ed., 1877]) xxxix n. 2.

9. R. A. Nicholson, *A Literary History of the Arabs* (Cambridge: Cambridge University Press, 1953 [1st ed., 1907]) 32.

10. Khalaf al-Aḥmar, *Muqaddima fi'n-naḥw, Prolegomena on Grammar* (ed. ʿIzz al-Dīn al-Tānūkhī; Damascus: Dār iḥyāʾ al-turāth al-qadīm, 1381/1961) 34.

certain innovations. They created professional legal guilds, professionalized their legal studies, and created the professional *license to teach and to profess legal opinions*. These guilds were created, among other things, to exclude philosophical theology from the colleges, all of which were based on the charitable trust, completely within the control of the juridical theologians. The positive function of the colleges was to produce the juridical theologians in whom resided the "authority to teach," the jurisdictional authority to define orthodoxy in classical Islam: that is, the *magisterium*.

Although they excluded the philosophical theologians from participating in the *magisterium*, the Traditionalists did not put a stop to philosophical theology; they simply banned it from the curriculum, excluding it from the program leading to the doctorate. In doing so, it relegated philosophical theology and philosophy itself to the role of defending Islam against its enemies; it relegated those fields to an apologetic function. Thus the designation of philosophical theology, *kalām*, as the "scholastic" theology of Islam, is a glaring example of our misunderstanding of the school movement in Islamic religious history. It had no place in the "schools."

Such, briefly, were the beginnings of scholasticism and humanism and the underlying motives that brought them into existence. These two movements, which developed over a period of centuries in classical Islam, appear in the Christian West without an adequately explained background. The doctorate of classical Islam and the process that led to it had an impact not only on the development of higher education in the medieval university but also emerged in Christianity as an intrusive element in the Church's authority to teach, the *magisterium*. The Church had no need for a second *magisterium*, utterly foreign to its hierarchical organization, a *magisterium* that was to compete with Christianity's original authority to teach.

Channels of Communication

The West is known to have received and translated works of Arab physicians and philosophers. These intellectuals wrote not only works on medicine and philosophy but also, as amateur humanists, works in various fields of the humanistic studies. Western intellectuals would have come across these humanistic works of philosophers and physicians in the process of searching for the works they sought on philosophy and medicine. Arabs were in contact with the West not only in Spain but also in Sicily and Italy. Their schools, in which humanistic subjects were taught, were established in great number, in Sicily as well as in Spain. The tenth-century geographer and traveler Ibn Ḥawqal (d. 367/977) states that Palermo had 300 such schools. Arab merchants were active in commerce and trade in many parts of Italy, and books were an item of commerce. Some books on humanism were translated, such as the *Disciplina clericalis*, the *Secretum secretorum*, and the *Liber philosophorum moralium antiquorum*, while others are known to have been read, as we can see from the statement of Pico della Mirandola. It may be noted in passing that the *Disciplina clericalis* belongs to a genre of Arabic humanistic literature, is a literal translation of the Arabic, and its contents belong to fields of *adab* humanism.

It appears that there were two moments in the reception of humanism in the Christian West: the first, in the translation movement of Monte Cassino in the eleventh century; the second, in the twelfth and thirteenth centuries in the period of Roger II and Frederick II in the two Sicilies, and in the translation movement in Toledo, Spain. The books of the Arab philosopher-physicians that were sought for translation in Monte Cassino and Toledo could account for the reception of humanistic writings by these amateur humanists. As for the second moment, it is well known that in the chanceries of Frederick II, the secretaries, backbone of the professional humanities, representing the three great medieval civilizations, regularly wrote their documents in Arabic, Greek, and Latin, as colleagues in the same government administration.

It seems to me that there would have been some reluctance on the part of a Christian to admit using materials from a Muslim author in the field of religion or its related fields involving Classical Arabic. There are two exceptions: the complaint of Alvaro and the statement of Pico. The former's complaint shows that the Christian youth imitated and emulated the Arabs in emphasizing Classical Arabic to the neglect of medieval Latin. Pico's statement also tells us that Arabic books were read, not just translated. Moreover, if the fact that we have three books in the field of humanism that were translated into Latin is evidence that they may have come down to us in translation because their authors were not known to have been Arabs.

There is another reason why we cannot expect much by way of direct evidence. It was in the very nature of humanistic literature not to cite one's sources for ideas. Borrowing ideas from others without citing the sources was the custom in both humanistic cultures; it could even be said to be a principle of their methodology. The creativity of the author was not always considered to be in the idea itself but in the form it was given. Even as late as the seventeenth century, when Corneille had to admit that he borrowed his Le Cid from Guillen de Castro's *Las mocedades del Cid*, he pleaded that he had improved on the original. Much of the Arabic literature of commentary on poetry is involved with the commentator's ability to trace the poetic ideas to previous poets, the purpose being to give the reader a basis on which to judge whether the poet's rendition was an improvement on that of his predecessor(s).

It is important to keep in mind that what is essential to humanism is eloquence; that is to say, form, elegant form. It is not so much what a humanist says that distinguishes him as a humanist, but rather how he says it. His language is classical, the vernacular being considered incapable of eloquence as lofty as the classical. The *Thousand and One Nights* that had so much influence on European literature, was never considered to be a part of the literature of *adab*, since it was written in the vernacular with a thin coating of syntax. Nor was the *Divine Comedy* of Dante considered a part of humanistic literature, because of its vernacular form.

This is how I see the development of humanism in Italy: the impetus for humanism was given by the Arabs who also supplied the model. The substance was sought in classical antiquity: in the case of humanism, from Cicero. The case of scholasticism is similar. The Arabs furnished the model; the substance was sought in classical antiquity from Aristotle, first as received from the Arabs, then directly from Aristotle's works. Further study will be needed to determine exactly what substance was derived from *adab* humanism.

The historian studying a period long before his own has little chance of finding direct evidence; he has to be satisfied with indirect, circumstantial evidence. History, especially medieval history, is based for the most part on such evidence. All that the historian can claim is that the explanation he offers is more reasonable than the alternatives and if so, should stand until better evidence or a more reasonable explanation is offered. Kristeller uses such evidence when linking the humanists of the Italian Renaissance to the *dictatores* of the earlier Middle Ages. Sam Dresden does the same when linking French humanism with the humanism of the Italian Renaissance. The link between the two sets of movements in classical Islam and the Christian West is based on the same methodological treatment. Rather than setting higher standards of evidence when classical Islam is involved, we would be better served to see whether the case for the formative influence of Islam on the West makes sense and whether it is the best available explanation for the phenomena involved in the two sets of movements. If such is the case, it should be allowed to stand until more evidence is available or until a better explanation is offered.

Kristeller has rightly argued that the humanists of the Italian Renaissance had certain interests and ideals that set them apart from intellectuals of the Middle Ages. After describing the cycle of the *studia humanitatis* circumscribing the intellectual range of Renaissance humanism as found expressed "in the professional activities and literary compositions of the humanists," he goes on to say that "the result of these activities represents *a peculiar and unique combination of intellectual interests* . . . ."[11] There was no way for Kristeller to know that this combination of intellectual interests was already unique to the humanists of classical Islam, not only because he does not read Classical Arabic, but also because studies in the field of Islam are not as advanced as those in the Christian West, especially as regards scholasticism and humanism. The problem is further aggravated by the lack of sufficient and adequate comparative studies on Islam and the West.

If Western humanism had its rise in Italy and not in France, it is because of that distinctive relation of Italy to classical Islam that was brought out clearly by Jacob Burckhardt.[12] It is this relationship that gives meaning to the distinction that is made between the humanism of the Italian Renaissance and the humanism of the Renaissance of the twelfth century. If it is now possible to link the humanism of the Italian Renaissance to that of classical Islam, in its ideals, its professional activities and its literary compositions, it is because of the fundamental work of Paul Oskar Kristeller.

11. P. O. Kristeller, *Eight Philosophers of the Italian Renaissance* (Stanford: Stanford University Press, 1964) 156–57, emphasis mine.

12. J. Burckhardt, *Die Kultur der Renaissance in Italien: Ein Versuch* (3d ed.; ed. L. Geiger; 2 vols.; Leipzig, 1877); trans. of 2d ed.: G. C. Middlemore, *The Civilization of the Renaissance in Italy: An Essay* (New York: The Modern Library, 1954).

Humanism and the Language Sciences in Medieval Islam

Michael G. Carter

Although at first sight the terms humanism and Islam might seem incompatible, there is good evidence that they are not. The highly developed urbanism of Islam, its elaborate bureaucracy, wealthy courts and associated patronage, and a universal respect for learning all combined to provide a fertile environment for the emergence of a kind of humanism analogous to that which arose in the West. The supreme importance of Arabic on the religious, cultural, administrative, and commercial levels made it inevitable that whatever kind of humanism appeared, it would have to give a special place to language. The topic is therefore particularly apposite for this volume dedicated to a colleague known for his special interest in language.

Author's note: This essay is based on a paper of the same title delivered at the Sixth International Penn-Paris Colloquium on Humanism, Bellagio, Italy, November 27–December 2, 1989.

The secondary literature has in fact already identified four distinct kinds of Islamic humanism, namely philosophical, literary, religious, and legal humanism, to which this paper proposes to add a fifth, labeled for convenience intellectual humanism. These five varieties of humanism will now be reviewed, with a brief discussion of their relationship to the language sciences. The names of one or two representative authors and typical works of grammar or philology will be mentioned to illustrate the literary output associated with each category, beginning with the one most deeply influenced by the same Greek philosophical ideals that were the foundation of European humanism.

1. Philosophical Humanism

Philosophical humanism is the name given by Arkoun and Kraemer[1] to the humanism of the Islamic philosophers and their circle, mainly in the tenth and eleventh centuries. It is characterized by total commitment to the Greek model from which it is derived, although for obvious reasons the entire Greek mythology disappears and Allāh replaces the impersonal First Cause of the Greek cosmos (helped by the neo-Platonist filter through which the Arabs became acquainted with Greek thought). In keeping with its Greek inspiration, this type of humanism is fundamentally secular—"man is a problem for man," said al-Tawḥīdī (d. 1023)[2]—which partly accounts for the general hostility of orthodox Islam to the philosophers.

In philosophical humanism, the philosopher sees himself as a courtier, statesman, and adviser of kings. A concept of education is cultivated that is virtually identical with the *paideia* of the Greeks (though not with that of the *adab* model in type three below), where philosophy, rather than the established religion, occupies the highest place as the ultimate guide to perfect conduct, both of the state and of the individual. From this perspective, language is regarded by the philosophers as a mirror of rational thought, a verbalization of the logical process, essentially abstract and internal, in contrast with the

1. Cf. M. Arkoun, *L'humanisme arabe au IVe/IXe siècle, Miskawayh, philosophe et historien* (Paris, 1982) 357; J. L. Kraemer, *Humanism in the Renaissance of Islam, the Cultural Revival during the Buyid Age* (Leiden, 1986), and see the same author's earlier article "Humanism in the Renaissance of Islam: A Preliminary Study," *JAOS* 104 (1984) 135–64. In both works, Kraemer assumes that philosophical humanism is the only form of humanism in Islam.

2. Arkoun, "L'humanisme arabe d'après le *Kitāb al-Hawāmil wa-'l-Šawāmil*," *Studia Islamica* 14 (1961) 79, reprinted in *Essais sur la pensée islamique* (Paris, 1984) 112; and cf. idem, *L'humanisme arabe,* 357; all based on Miskawayh's *Kitāb al-hawāmil wa-'l-shawāmil* (ed. A. Amīn and A. Ṣaqr; Cairo, 1951) 180. Cf. A. Azmeh (*Arabic Thought and Islamic Societies* [London, 1986] 63), who cites the idea of man as a microcosm from al-Tawḥīdī's *al-Imtāᶜ wa-'l-muᵓānasa* (ed. A. Amīn and A. al-Zayn; 2 vols; Cairo, 1939–44) 1.147.

grammarians' (and lawyers') view of language as a set of social acts more physical and external in nature, as in type five, legal humanism.

The most conspicuous example of the purely philosophical approach to language is provided by al-Fārābī (d. ca. 950), for whom Arabic is simply an instance of the universal category of language and not, as orthodox Islam maintained, the privileged and unique receptacle of absolute truth. Al-Fārābī, on the contrary, believes that the truth is accessible to all those who are properly competent in logic, regardless of their language. And although he acknowledges the place of language sciences in the curriculum, they are merely elements in a universal system of knowledge with no special link to religion.[3]

2. Intellectual Humanism

Intellectual humanism is an ad hoc label for an attitude that deserves to be considered a possible type of humanism, though the claim is here being made for the first time.[4] The term *intellectual* is chosen to set this form of humanism apart from type one, philosophical humanism, and the rest, for reasons which should soon become apparent.

While relying heavily on the logic of the Greeks, intellectual humanism differs from the philosophical kind in its complete immersion in the ideas and values of Islam and its dedication to the task of demonstrating that Islam is a rational religion fully compliant with the laws of logic. Unlike philosophers, who were often branded unbelievers, the members of this second group tended to be found guilty of the lesser charge of heterodoxy. They are collectively known as the Muᶜtazilites, a name that by popular etymology signals their ideological detachment from the Islamic community. Their activities span the eighth to eleventh centuries, the time it took Islam to achieve its ultimate doctrinal perfection, much of this thanks to the tenacious Muᶜtazilite insistence on identifying, debating, and sometimes even resolving dogmatic issues with relentless dialectic.

3. Well summarized by G. Bohas, J.-P. Guillaume, and D. E. Kouloughli, *The Arabic Linguistic Tradition* (London, 1990) 8–9. Detailed treatments of the conflict between the philosophers and the grammarians are in A. Elamrani-Jamal, *Logique aristotélicienne et grammaire arabe (étude et documents)* (Paris, 1983) and G. Endreß, "Grammatik und Logik, arabische Philologie und griechische Philosophie im Widerstreit," in *Sprachphilosophie in Antike und Mittelalter* (ed. B. Mojsisch; Bochumer Studien zur Philosophie 3; Amsterdam, n.d.) 163–299.

4. Arkoun hints at it ("L'humanisme arabe," 98 = *Essais,* 93), discussing the possible influence of Muᶜtazilism on al-Tawḥīdī. But I prefer to consider al-Tawḥīdī not a philosopher (which would put him among the philosophical humanists) or an *adīb* (he was a social misfit in fact), but the intellectual kinsman of Ibn Jinnī; see below, p. 30.

Language for these people is no longer the image of a universal mental activity: they are concerned instead with only one language, Arabic, for them the unique bearer of revelation and the medium of a specific, Islamic truth. In keeping with their conviction that man himself is rational, they regard Arabic as the reasonable activity of the reasonable Muslim, that is, while it does not have the rigor of pure logic, it is as consistent, harmonious, and systematic as any human activity can be.

Two representatives of this Muᶜtazilite position may be mentioned. Al-Rummānī (d. 930) is outstanding for the freedom with which he uses logical techniques in analyzing Arabic without shrinking from the theological consequences.[5] The other figure is Ibn Jinnī (d. 1002), an extraordinarily original thinker whose ideas were simply too adventurous to find ready acceptance among the orthodox, not because they were particularly dangerous, but because the current of orthodoxy was by this time in full flow and had no need of such notions. Apart from hostility on the fringe of fundamentalist Islam (particularly the Ḥanbalī Ibn Maḍāʾ al-Qurṭubī, d. 1196), Ibn Jinnī was not so much refuted as merely ignored. We return to him below.

3. Literary Humanism

The literary variety of humanism has long been recognized as probably closest to the humanism of Europe, with which it has several features in common. In Arkoun's phrase, it is the product of an "aristocracy of the mind,"[6] a combination of cultural and social ideals that were acquired through a more or less formal education and exercised in the refined environment of the court, the intelligentsia, and the religious dignitaries. This acquired culture is usually referred to as *adab*, which in the sense of 'upbringing' is obviously closely related to the Greek *paideia*. *Adab*, however, denotes not only the process of training but also its result, namely literature and polite social intercourse. Indeed, it is particularly striking that the several meanings of the term *adab* 'correct behavior, discipline, literature, education' correlate directly with the various denotations of the medieval Latin *mores*, namely, *disciplina*, *litterae*, and *paideia* respectively. The eclecticism of *adab* is perhaps a quality that distinguishes it from European humanism: insofar as the Arabs were open to Greek, Syriac, Persian, and Indian sources, their *adab* has a much broader base than the *litterae (humaniores)* of Europe, which drew only on classical antiq-

5. See M. G. Carter, "Linguistic Science and Orthodoxy in Conflict: The Case of al-Rummānī," *ZGAW* 1 (1984) 212–32.

6. Arkoun, *L'humanisme arabe*, 357.

uity (and also, ironically, on Arabic). The *Mujtanā* of Ibn Durayd (d. 933) is a convenient illustration of the Arab taste, containing as it does material not only from within the Arab tradition, but also Greek and Persian wisdom, and even sayings attributed to Jesus. The two greatest representatives of early Arab *adab*, Ibn al-Muqaffa^{c} and al-Jāḥiẓ, are both too well-known to be discussed in detail here.[7]

In the context of *adab*, language was a means of social interaction, a mode of communication completely different in purpose from the previous two categories. It is part of a person's external appearance, both the form and the content being learned in the same way that appropriate dress and behavior for the court were learned. Everything that the term *manners* implies can be assumed to underlie the combination of correct demeanor, comportment, and diction encompassed by the word *adab*. There is here a noteworthy resemblance between the qualifications expected of the Islamic *kātib* and the secretary of Western Europe, whose humanist milieu likewise comprised the court, statecraft, and diplomacy.[8]

In this regard, both Islam and the Latin West are in clear agreement on the primacy of language studies as the key to all other branches of knowledge: compare "morphology is the mother of all the sciences and grammar their father" from the early fourteenth-century grammarian Ibn Mas^{c}ūd[9] with John of Salisbury's "grammar is the cradle of all philosophy."[10] This principle was eventually institutionalized in the *madrasa*, the school of higher learning (which may be a forerunner of the European university),[11] together with the whole edifice of scholasticism that determined the curriculum, methods of study, and granting of degrees at these establishments. Naturally this led to a huge output

7. C. Pellat (*The Life and Works of Jāḥiẓ: Translations of Selected Texts* [trans. from the French by D. M. Hawke; Berkeley, 1969] offers an illuminating access to the mind of Islam's greatest litterateur. On Ibn al-Muqaffa^{c}, see F. Gabrieli, "Adab," EI^2; S. Y. Labib, "Ibn al-Muḳaffa^{c}," EI^2; and C. Brockelmann, "Kalīla wa-Dimna," EI^2. It is interesting to note that a translation of *Kalīla wa Dimna* recently appeared under the title *Le pouvoir et les intellectuels, ou les aventures de Kalīla et Dimna* by R. R. Khawam (Paris, 1985).

8. A whole genre of works evolved under such titles as *Adab al-kātib*, *Adab al-nadīm*, *Adab al-qāḍī*, etc.; see Gabrieli, "Adab."

9. The opening words of Ibn Mas^{c}ūd's *Marāḥ al-arwāḥ* (many editions; see C. Brockelmann, *Geschichte der arabischen Litteratur* [5 vols.; Leiden, 1949] 2.21).

10. John of Salisbury, *The Metalogicon of John of Salisbury: A Twelfth-Century Defense of the Verbal and Logical Arts of the Trivium (*trans. D. D. McGarry; Berkeley, 1962) 37. At various places in J. Koch, (ed.), *Artes Liberales: Von der antiken Bildung zur Wissenschaft des Mittelalters* (Leiden, 1959), the fundamental importance of grammar is stressed; for example, p. 70: grammar is the "guardian of history" (St. Augustine).

11. See G. Makdisi, *The Rise of Colleges: Institutions of Learning in Islam and the West* (Edinburgh, 1981), esp. chap. 4.

of textbooks, dictionaries, manuals of style, treatises on poetics, and so forth, and we are reminded of Erasmus's comment that there are now "almost as many grammars as grammarians,"[12] which was also certainly true for Islam from the eleventh century onwards! Pedagogical grammars of a purely scholastic nature (that is, arranged in an arbitrarily schematic manner that has little to do with the structure of the language itself and designed expressly for use in the *madrasa*) were produced in abundance: the *Muqaddima* of Ibn Bābashādh (d. 1077) and the *Mufaṣṣal* of al-Zamakhsharī (d. 1134) may be taken as typical of scores of grammars that present language as a part of *adab*, which is to say, as a recognized component of an all-inclusive pedagogical system.

4. Religious Humanism

Arkoun uses religious humanism as a term for a kind of humanism that was distinct from philosophical and literary humanism and remained entirely within the religious framework, in "confident submission and reference to God."[13] While it accepted a minimum of influence from Greek (as much as was necessary to sustain the scholastic system and to organize orthodox beliefs), religious humanism was perhaps best understood as a serene contentment with the non-transcendental aspects of Islamic life alongside an unreserved acquiescence to all the conditions of the faith, thus integrating a humane and satisfying earthly existence with the hope of eternal salvation. It may be left for others to decide whether this Islamic religious humanism had anything in common with the biblical humanism that emerged in Europe in the time of Erasmus and sought to recover the linguistic reality of the scriptures with the help of the vastly increased knowledge of the original Greek and Hebrew versions.

Language for the religious humanist is the medium in which the facts of Islam, and by the same token its authority, are perpetuated.[14] It is therefore necessary to preserve language from change, whether it be human language, which must remain stable to protect its contents from changing with it, or divine lan-

12. Erasmus, *The Praise of Folly* (trans. Clarence H. Miller; New Haven, 1979) 81.

13. Arkoun, *L'humanisme arabe*, 356.

14. Latin served Christianity in the same capacity: St. Augustine is reported to have said that "rightly ordered speech is a consequence of the Incarnation" (M. L. Colish, *The Mirror of Language: A Study in the Medieval Theory of Knowledge* [New Haven, 1968] 33). There is remarkable agreement between Arkoun's characterization of Islam as "logocentric" (M. Arkoun, "Logocentrisme et vérité religieuse dans la pensée islamique," *Studia Islamica* 35 [1972] 5–51, reprinted in *Essais*, 185–231) and B. Stock's notion of the medieval "textual community" (*The Implications of Literacy, Written Language and Models of Interpretation in the Eleventh and Twelfth Centuries* [Princeton, 1983], esp. chaps. 2 and 4).

guage, that is, the Qurʾān, which raised Arabic to a level beyond human power to imitate and cannot by its nature ever change. Unlike the Bible, the Qurʾān does not offer a model of literary style for writers: although the Qurʾān is frequently *quoted* in prose and verse works, it has hardly ever been imitated.[15]

For this reason, it is not strictly philology that concerns the religious humanist in Islam, but rather the huge corpus of text generated by the Qurʾān and the commentary literature it inspired, including the extra-Qurʾānic record of Muḥammad's every word and deed and the ancillary historical and biographical resources. In collecting and transmitting this enormous quantity of data, there was a need not so much for logic and critical analysis as for simple power and accuracy of memory combined with a method (principally the *ijāza* system) for controlling and disseminating the material. Islam supported various professions to fulfill this task, from tutors for juveniles, teaching small children to memorize the Qurʾān and basic grammar, to encyclopedic memorizers of the collected sayings and actions of the Prophet. Exegetes, biographers, and historians may also be counted among those whose careers depended on texts, to which perhaps ought to be added the writers and preachers of sermons.

5. Legalistic Humanism

The final species of humanism, legalistic humanism, has been somewhat neglected in the secondary literature. The idea that the Islamic legal system had in itself the capacity to produce an indigenous humanism was suggested by Kunitzsch in 1976.[16] That there was a form of legal humanism in medieval Europe is also known, though there can hardly be any historical connection between the two.[17]

Law in any culture has an intrinsic dependence on language, all the more so in a religion as logocentric as Islam, so that it is no exaggeration to claim,

15. J. van Ess ("Some Fragments of the Muʿāraḍat al-Qurʾān Attributed to Ibn al-Muqaffaʿ," in *Studia Arabica et Islamica: Festschrift for Iḥsān ʿAbbās on His 60th Birthday* (ed. Wadād al-Qadi; [Beirut, 1961]), refers on p. 152 to the discovery of a few fragments as "something new, almost a sensation" but goes on to argue that even if genuine (which they might well be), they are not attempts to create a rival Qurʾānic text but simply a demonstration that it might be possible to do so (p. 161). Cf. also A. F. L. Beeston et al., (eds.), *The Cambridge History of Arabic Literature* (2 vols.; Cambridge, 1983): vol. 1, *Arabic Literature to the End of the Umayyad Period*, 212 and 260–64.

16. P. Kunitzsch, "Zur Problematik und Interpretation der arabischen Übersetzungen antiker Texte," *Oriens* 25 (1976) 116–32, esp. 132, where the footnotes indicate his debt to Plessner and ultimately to Bergsträßer for this insight.

17. It was the theme of a paper by E. Peters at the Bellagio Colloquium (see author's note above) entitled "The Sacred Muses and the Twelve Tables: Jurists and Humanism in the Later Middle Ages," but it is not known where, or even whether, this paper has appeared.

as Makdisi has done, that law is "the climax and kernel of Islamic learning."[18] Islam allows the student and executor of the law an intimate and comprehensive insight into the entire range of the believer's actions on both the spiritual and the temporal planes: the Sharīᶜa, which is by no means as insensitive to the complexities of man's nature as is sometimes thought, in fact obliges the enforcers of the law to scrutinize the behavior of their fellow Muslims so closely that some kind of humanist perception is inevitable.

From the legalistic standpoint, language is a form of behavior, and grammar is the means of controlling it; hence it was recognized as a general obligation (*farḍ kifāya*) that certain members of society in the "textual community" of Islam must have a mastery of Classical Arabic. Legal reasoning is impossible without recourse to linguistic factors, and forensic argument and pleading likewise require appropriate language skills, as many legal textbooks acknowledge. One grammarian, Ibn al-Anbārī (d. 1181) even wrote a treatise demonstrating that the systems of Arabic grammar and Islamic law were fundamentally identical.[19] Language, as seen by the legal profession, is no longer the abstract process of pure thought as the philosophers saw it. Instead, it is a set of actions conducted in the open and subject to the same criteria as all the other actions constituting the recommended behavior of the Muslim. The very term for grammar, *naḥw* 'way', reveals that correct speech is a subset of the *Sunna*, the ideal "Way" to behave, for in this context *naḥw* and *Sunna* are synonyms.[20]

Arabic grammar still retains this legalistic character. The first systematic grammarian, Sībawayhi (d. late eighth century), was first trained in law and transferred the legal methodology to his analysis of language with such effect that his method has so far not been totally superseded. Many grammarians were also active as judges or jurists and occasionally took the trouble to stress the interdependence of law and grammar, for example, Ibn Fāris (d. 1004/5),[21] as well as Ibn al-Anbārī, already mentioned.

It is now time to return to Ibn Jinnī, who was assigned to humanism type two above. He displays such a curiosity about the personal aspects of language

18. G. Makdisi, "Institutionalized Learning as a Self-Image of Islam," in *Islam's Understanding of Itself* (ed. R. G. Hovannisian and S. Vryonis; 8th Giorgio Levi Della Vida Biennial Conference; Malibu, Calif., 1983) 73–85, esp. 74.

19. Ibn al-Anbārī, *Lumaᶜ al-adilla* (ed. A. Amer Stockholm: 1963). See also U. Haarmann, "Religiöses Recht und Grammatik im klassischen Islam," in *XVIII. Deutscher Orientalistentag 1972* (ed. W. Voigt; ZDMG Sup. 2 Wiesbaden, 1974) 149–69.

20. Cf. M. G. Carter, "Les origines de la grammaire arabe," *REI* 40 (1972), esp. 81–82.

21. Ibn Fāris (*Al-Ṣāḥibī fī fiqh al-lugha* [ed. M. Chouémi; Beirut, 1964] 64–66) laments the jurists' ignorance of Arabic grammar and stresses the dependence of Islam on correct language. Cf. M. G. Carter, "Language Control as People Control in Medieval Islam: The Aims of the Grammarians in their Cultural Context," *al-Abḥāth* 31 (1983) 65–84.

that it is impossible to deny him a place in this paper. The following extracts from his views on language are not intended to be exhaustive but only to provide some impressionistic justification for adding a category of "intellectual humanism" to the other four.

Like most scholars, Ibn Jinnī pursued his career through the patronage of courts (in his case Aleppo, Baghdad, and Shiraz) where learning was enthusiastically promoted. Rulers liked to surround themselves with literary and cultural figures, and it is very significant that the courts Ibn Jinnī attended, particularly those of the famous Sayf al-Dawla (reigned 944–967) in Aleppo and of the Buwayhids in Baghdad, were hosts to the most influential philosophers, such as al-Fārābī, who died just before Ibn Jinnī himself came to Aleppo, and poets, such as al-Mutanabbī, who was a personal friend of Ibn Jinnī's. We may gain some idea of the academic environment simply by noting the readership to whom Ibn Jinnī addressed his most important book: "theologians, jurists, philosophers, grammarians, secretaries and others,"[22] a group that, if we count Ibn Jinnī among the "others," fits comfortably into the five types of humanism outlined above! From the range of his own writings, it is clear that Ibn Jinnī was at home in all the disciplines implied by this list.

Theologically he was squarely in the Muᶜtazilite camp, that is, he held to the belief that Islamic dogma was entirely compatible with human reason. This is not the place to describe his Muᶜtazilite views in detail: his works are larded with their terminology and, more to the point, their conclusions (for example, God has no knowledge of particulars, religious language is not to be taken literally, man does not "acquire" actions already created for him by God, thus becoming responsible for them by such 'acquisition' *kasb*, and so on). One single phrase of Ibn Jinnī is enough to confirm his Muᶜtazilite allegiance: when discussing certain syntactically ambiguous constructions, he describes them as having an 'intermediate status' (*manzila bayn al-manzilatayn*), using an expression peculiar to the Muᶜtazilites and originally referring to the intermediate status of the grave sinner hovering between the prospect of eternal damnation and forgiveness. Ibn Jinnī's application of this theological principle to a point of grammar is not only typical of his intellectual fearlessness but also reminds us that issues of language were always likely to be issues of theology in Arabic.

His fascination for language is all-consuming, and he is one of the few to take seriously the questions of the origins of language and whether linguistic causality is closer to logical or legal principles in its operation. The former problem is of course an echo of the debate in *Cratylus* with the terms changed

22. Ibn Jinnī, *Khaṣāʾiṣ al-ᶜarabiyya* (3 vols; ed. M. A. al-Najjār; Cairo, 1952–56) 1.67.

to suit the theological demands of Islam. Thus, the opposition of *physis* and *thesis* is replaced by divine inspiration (*ilhām*) and human convention (*waḍ*ᶜ, a direct lexical equivalent of *thesis*). Ibn Jinnī is, to be sure, somewhat ambivalent in his answer, but seems in the end to favor the position that whatever its origins (probably a mixture of both), language is now a wholly conventional phenomenon, a notion that accords well with the Muᶜtazilite concern to maximize man's own choice of and responsibility for his actions.[23] On the nature of linguistic causality he is more explicit, and understandably so. Linguistic causes, he says, are closer in nature to those of dogmatic theology (*kalām*), meaning that they are at bottom rational and follow an underlying *ḥikma* ('wisdom', both human and divine!), unlike religious prescriptions, which are a priori facts for which no rational cause can be assigned. For example, with regard to the five daily prayers, there is no reason other than a religious one why the number should be five.[24]

Where Ibn Jinnī unmistakably reveals a humanist outlook is in his insatiable interest in all the shortcuts, idiosyncrasies, rationalizations, imprecisions, and ambiguities in human speech arising from the vagaries of man's nature. He delights in whimsical formulations, "what becomes less when you add something to it?"[25] and he notes with obvious amusement that when the pronoun suffix *-ka* loses its personal reference and becomes a mere demonstrative, as in *dhālika* 'that', the meanest subject can address it to a king without fear of losing his head![26] He boldly theorizes as to why certain combinations of sounds are not used, tries to persuade the reader that all words containing the same root consonants in whatever order share a common meaning (his so-called *al-ishtiqāq al-kabīr*, the 'major derivation', contrasting with the 'minor derivation', *al-ishtiqāq al-ṣaghīr*, of words formed from a single root), and converts the Aristotelian theory of substance and accident into a general linguistic rule to account for a wide range of structural and semantic features of Arabic.[27] He describes a man who is reluctant to talk to people when he cannot see them, crit-

23. See H. Loucel, "L'origine du langage d'après les grammairiens arabes," *Arabica* 10 (1963) 188–208 and 253–81; and *Arabica* 11 (1964) 57–72 and 151–87 (Ibn Jinnī is in vol. 10, pp. 275–76).

24. See Ibn Jinnī *Khaṣāʾiṣ*, 1.48 ff., summarized in A. Mehiri, *Les thèories grammaticales d'Ibn Jinnī* (Tunis, 1973) 141–42.

25. The answer is an independent sentence when subordinated by the conjunction *anna* 'that' (*Khaṣāʾiṣ, 2.272*).

26. *Khaṣāʾiṣ*, 2.188. Compare the accusation against Cardinal Wolsey of giving himself precedence over Henry VIII in the (grammatically correct) "ego et rex meus" (Shakespeare, *Henry VIII* 3.2.314).

27. Cf. M. G. Carter, "Ibn Jinnī's Axiom: 'The Adventitious Determines the Rule'," in *Semitic Studies in Honor of Wolf Leslau* (ed. A. S. Kaye; 2 vols.; Wiesbaden, 1991) 1.199–208.

icizes the Bedouin and scholars alike for ignorance of their own language, invites us to speculate on the pronunciation of words consisting entirely of glottal stops, and proposes that Arabic grammar is a useful brain exercise not unlike mental arithmetic, throwing out a challenge to solve such conundrums as "if 5 times 7 is 40, what is 3 times 8?"[28]

In short, this is more than a pedantic, theoretical preoccupation: it is an apparent obsession with the human dimension of language far beyond the needs of scientific description or pedagogy.[29] If curiosity and concern for the individual are diagnostic for humanism, Ibn Jinnī must certainly qualify as a humanist. While he is probably unique in the breadth of his enthusiasm, he must have enjoyed the intellectual stimulation and the encouragement of a circle who appreciated his experiments even if they did not unreservedly accept them. He therefore stands as a representative of a class of thinkers, neither identical with the philosophers on the one hand nor the literary humanists on the other, and on these grounds it seems reasonable to consider "intellectual humanism" as an independent variety of humanism in Islam.

Since four types of humanism have already been explicitly identified in the secondary literature, it might seem rather hairsplitting to add a fifth, and the reader is left to judge whether the attempt is justified. There is certainly some flexibility in the scheme. For example, lexicography could be placed in type three (literary), four (religious), or five (legal) humanism, according to whether this particular science is conceived of as an aid to literature, a device for preserving the vocabulary, or a repository of the technical terms of Islamic law and society. Likewise, one might question whether a Muᶜtazilite can also be an *adīb* or vice versa, though it is hoped that the above excursus on Ibn Jinnī will have shown that Muᶜtazilites and *udabāᵓ* are only partly overlapping categories of two essentially different kinds of people. And lest it should appear that the whole of Arabic literature is somehow included in one or another humanist category, let it be remarked that all mystical writing is absent, as well as fantastical works such as the *1001 Nights* (but not *Kalīla wa-Dimna*), a great deal of poetry, most devotional literature (prayers, prayer tables, pilgrimage guides, creeds, lives of saints), magic, pure science, medicine,[30] astronomy, and the

28. The answer is $27\frac{3}{7}$; *Khaṣāᵓiṣ*, 3.329; the operation would have been second nature to a *farāᵓiḍ* specialist, a professional inheritance divider. In the same work (2.478–88), Ibn Jinnī claims that morphology drills are good training for the mind, even when they produce impossible words!

29. Bohas et al. (*Arabic Linguistic Tradition*, 11–12 and 27–28) gives a condensed account of Ibn Jinnī that supplements the above information.

30. Since many philosophers earned their living as doctors and medical training certainly encompassed the full range of the medieval "liberal arts," perhaps this profession could be added

other exact sciences. Geography, however, probably does have a claim to be regarded as humanist to some degree.[31]

For what it is worth, at least two other forms of humanism have been detected: Watt's pre-Islamic "tribal humanism"[32] and Dale's "steppe humanism,"[33] though neither has any relevance to the present topic! The purpose of this paper has merely been to demonstrate that the Islamic religion and the Arabic language could and did form a relationship not unlike that between medieval Christianity and the classical languages of Europe, where Latin in particular fulfilled the same kind of dual role as Arabic, at once a vehicle of divine revelation and the medium of a cosmopolitan secular culture in which real humanism emerged and flourished.

---

to type one, philosophical humanism (cf. M. Dols and A. S. Gamal, *Medieval Islamic Medicine* [Berkeley, 1984] 24ff.). We would then have to consider Ibn Sīnā's writings on articulatory phonetics as part of the scope of this paper.

31. Al-Masᶜūdī, who was mainly a historian and geographer, has rightly been claimed as a humanist by A. Shboul, *Al-Masᶜūdī and His World: A Muslim Humanist and His Interest in Non-Muslims* (London, 1979), esp. p. xxvi.

32. W. M. Watt, *Muhammed at Mecca* (Oxford, 1953) 24, using "humanism" in its modern sense of non-religious, secular culture à la Bertrand Russell. A couple of years later, Gabrieli refers, presumably independently, to the "humanism" of the pre-Islamic period, albeit with some scepticism; see "Literary Tendencies," in *Unity and Variety in Muslim Civilization* (ed. G. E. von Grunebaum; Chicago, 1955) 91.

33. S. F. Dale, "Steppe Humanism: The Autobiography of Zahir al-Din Muhammad Babur (1483–1530)," *IJMES* 22 (1990), 37–58, esp. 42 and 49–50. S. D. Goitein has turned the picture completely round by proposing that the study of Islam by *Western* scholars is a humanist—and humanizing—discipline ("The Humanistic Aspects of Oriental Studies," *Jerusalem Studies in Arabic and Islam* 9 [1987] 1–12), which makes a very appropriate conclusion to this paper!

Cosmic Numbers: The Symbolic Design of Niẓāmī's *Haft Paykar*

Julie Scott Meisami

In an important essay, Georg Krotkoff has dealt with many significant aspects of the complex network of astrological, number, and color symbolism that informs Niẓāmī's *Haft Paykar.*[1] There is little I can add to his masterful analysis, which focuses primarily on the symbolism within the seven tales that constitute the poem's central core. My purpose here will be to concentrate on the importance of number and its symbolic associations to the overarching design of Niẓāmī's vast ethical romance.

The *Haft Paykar* presents a complex web of interwoven journeys. Its overall framework is the journey of its protagonist, the Sassanian king Bahrām

1. Georg Krotkoff, "Colour and Number in the *Haft Paykar*," in *Logos Islamikos: Studia Islamica in honorem Georgii Michaelis Wickens* (ed. R. M. Savory and D. A. Agius; Toronto: Pontifical Institute of Medieval Studies, 1984) 97–118.

Gūr, from birth to death, from exile to rightful kingship, paralleled by his inward, ethical, and spiritual journey from ignorance to wisdom, from kingship by will to kingship by law, from human birth to spiritual apotheosis.[2] Bahrām's own journeys are further paralleled by those of the protagonists of the seven tales, journeys both outward and inward that culminate in loss or gain, both material and spiritual; they are further anticipated by the description in the prologue of the Prophet's *Mi^{c}rāj*, in which he passes from earth through the heavens to attain the Beatific Vision.[3] All these journeys take place in various dimensions of space and time—historical, fictional, magical, spiritual; all, moreover, stand in some relation to that ultimate journey which provides the poem's central, if unspoken, metaphor: the soul's journey through this world, from its divine origin to its return.

I have discussed elsewhere the various interlocking patterns that characterize the structure of the *Haft Paykar*: the linear pattern of the biographical-historical narrative; the alternation between the extended "kingship" segments that make up the bulk of that narrative, and the four "adventure" episodes that chart Bahrām's ethical and spiritual progress; the alternation in the seven tales between the moral faculties of the soul, concupiscence and irascibility; and the encompassing circle (or overarching spiral) of Bahrām's spiritual biography.[4] Here I will deal chiefly with the philosophical and ethical associations of the numerical patterns that organize the poem: its overall tripartite division into narrative–tales–narrative; the quadripartite adventure episodes; and the summation of these key numbers, three and four, in the seven tales.

In his lengthy exordium, following the praise of discourse (the one created thing that can attain immortality), Niẓāmī announces:

> He who his own self truly knows
> triumphant over this life goes.
> Who knows not his design must die;
> but who can read it, lives for aye (7:9–10).[5]

Knowledge of the self and knowledge of the design (*naqsh*) that determines man's place in creation and his relation to his Creator are the goal of the soul's

2. On the concepts of kingship by will and by law, see my *Medieval Persian Court Poetry* (Princeton: Princeton University Press, 1987) 205–6 and passim.

3. For a detailed discussion of these and other journeys untreated here, see my "Theme of the Journey in Niẓāmī's *Haft Paykar*," *Edebiyât* n.s. 4/2 (1993) 155–71.

4. See Meisami, *Medieval Court Poetry*, 205–24, 299–304; idem, "Fitnah or Āzādah? Niẓāmī's Ethical Poetic," *Edebiyât* n.s. 1/2 (1989) 51–54; idem, "Theme of the Journey."

5. All references are to H. Ritter and J. Rypka (eds.), *Heft Peiker: Ein romantisches Epos* (Prague: Orientálni Ustáv, 1934); translations are my own (see my translation: Nizami Ganjavi, *Haft Paykar: A Medieval Persian Romance* [Oxford: Oxford University Press/The World's Classics, 1995]).

journey through this world, as of Bahrām's journey through the poem. *Man ᶜarafa nafsahu fa-qad ᶜarafa rabbahu* 'He who knows himself knows his Lord': self-knowledge leads to the understanding of higher truths, of Truth writ large, and right reading is essential to this process.[6] As Bahrām learns the nature of his own design through discourse—and specifically the structured discourse of the seven tales—so the discourse of the poem itself reveals to the audience the nature of the cosmic design, to which the principle of number is central.

In so doing, it relies on other discourses that invoke the sacred symbolism of number to define both the quest itself and its goal. The Ikhwān al-Ṣafāᵓ, whose writings Niẓāmī must have known, identified three stages of self-knowledge: the observation of the body and its characteristics, the observation of the soul and its qualities and faculties, and finally, the observation of the two in concert.[7] The similarity with the *Haft Paykar*'s tripartite structure is striking: the first portion of the poem is dominated by physical action, in the form of hunting, warfare, feasting, and so on; the second is constituted by the tales, reflection on which helps Bahrām to progress towards wisdom; while in the third and final portion, Bahrām's actions (for example, his trial of the evil vizier) are informed by reflection on the principles he has learned, that is, he has become able to exercise both faculties in combination.

The four linked adventure episodes, each of which represents a significant stage in Bahrām's spiritual progress, also evoke the discourse of the Ikhwān al-Ṣafāᵓ. The Ikhwān associate the four degrees of human perfection with four classes of humanity: craftsmen, religious and learned men and political chiefs, kings and sultans, and prophets and sages.[8] In the four adventure episodes (which in this context appear as four initiatory rituals), Bahrām's progress in some way reflects his mastery of each category: of craftsman (through his skill in hunting); of political chief, as he achieves world rule; of ideal ruler, combining temporal with spiritual kingship (in harmony with the Law); and of sage or prophet, as he disappears into the cave.[9]

6. On the importance of self-knowledge, see, for example, *Rasāᵓil Ikhwān al-Ṣafāᵓ* (4 vols.; Beirut: Dār Bayrūt/Dār ṣādir, 1957; hereafter *RIS*) 2.378–79; Miskawayh, *Tahdhīb al-akhlāq, The Refinement of Character* (ed. Constantine K. Zurayk; Beirut: American University of Beirut, 1967) 1.

7. *RIS*, 2.379; compare Naṣīr al-Dīn Ṭūsī on the perfection of the theoretical (speculative) and practical faculties, *The Nasirean Ethics* (trans. G. M. Wickens; London: Allen & Unwin, 1964) 51–53. It is possible to see the Ikhwān's tripartite "philosophic liturgy," consisting of "personal oratory," a "cosmic text," and a "philosophical hymn," reflected in the narrative, the first "personal" element exemplified by Bahrām's achievement of temporal rule, the third by his final dedication to justice, and the "cosmic text" as consisting of the seven tales, linked with the seven planetary spheres. (On the Ikhwān's liturgy, see Seyyed Hossein Nasr, *An Introduction to Islamic Cosmological Doctrines* [Boulder, Colo.: Shambhala, 1978] 35).

8. Nasr, *Introduction*, 31–32; see *RIS* 4.119–23.

9. That there are some anomalies in this identification testifies to the complexity of Niẓāmī's thought. Bahrām's skill as craftsman/hunter is definitively established in the first adventure episode

The Ikhwān's classification was expanded by Naṣīr al-Dīn Ṭūsī, whose *Akhlāq-i Nāṣirī* often reads like a gloss on the *Haft Paykar.*[10] Naṣīr al-Dīn divided men into "ranks of perfection or deficiency . . . determined according to will and reason." According to the degree of their perfection of these faculties, men are able to rise to "the highest of the ascending degrees of the human species," that is, the third stage, of persons who "by revelation and inspiration, receive knowledge of truths and laws from those brought close to divine majesty." They are then able to proceed to the fourth, "And so to the limit, where is the abode of Unity, and there the circle of existence meets, like a curved line beginning from a point and returning to the same point."[11]

I shall return to the significance of this statement, as well as to the further implications of these tripartite and quadripartite divisions, below. The interaction of patterns based on three and on four reflects a more general pattern of alternation that informs the poem as a whole: in the narrative, in the alternation between "kingship" segments (containing one or more episodes) and "adventure" episodes, and in the tales by a further three/four pattern of alternation between tales whose action is motivated by the concupiscent faculty (I, III, V, and VII) and those whose action is motivated by the irascible (II, IV, and VI). The concupiscent faculty (*shahwa, ārzū*) impels humans towards the things in which they find both pleasure and gain (food, drink, sexual activity) and thus ensures the survival and prosperity of the species; it is represented in the *Haft Paykar* by the motifs of temptation and the desire for gain. The irascible faculty (*khashm*) motivates the search for name and renown, resistance to oppression, revenge for wrongs; it is represented by anger, aversion, and steadfastness.[12]

(§14), in which he kills a dragon and finds a treasure. The second, that of Fitna (§25), by casting doubt on his inherent virtue by showing him still tied to the world of action and capable of injustice, inaugurates his spiritual progress. Here (as in the contiguous kingship segments) he is merely political chief, with the limitations that implies. It is the lesson taught by the shepherd in the third (§41) that enables his transformation to ideal ruler; while his apotheosis in the fourth (§52) allies him with sage and prophet by granting him the reward reserved for such figures: the Beatific Vision, vouchsafed to the Prophet Muḥammad in the *Miᶜrāj* (§3). Bahrām's spiritual ascent thus parallels that of the Prophet, who similarly passed through the seven planets (as Bahrām does, symbolically, in the tales). See further Meisami, "Theme of the Journey."

10. While there is no evidence that Naṣīr al-Dīn Ṭūsī was familiar with the *Haft Paykar*, the parallels between his thought and that of Niẓāmī are striking. This is due neither to influence nor yet to coincidence; both writers encapsulate and sum up various tendencies of philosophical, ethical, and esoteric discourse that reached a culmination in the late twelfth century (although Naṣīr al-Dīn is slightly later, he is firmly rooted in this tradition) and that are based in such common and diverse sources as the writings of the Ikhwān al-Ṣafāᵓ and of Miskawayh. (The *Akhlāq-i Nāṣirī* was, indeed, first conceived as a translation of Miskawayh; cf. Ṭūsī, *Nasirean Ethics*, 25–26).

11. Ibid., 46.

12. Cf. Miskawayh, *Tahdhīb*, 15–16; Ṭūsī, *Nasirean Ethics*, 43.

These faculties can motivate for either good or evil; what is important is that equilibrium is established between them, a necessity reflected by the pattern of alternation as the balance swings from one to the other. As to how such equilibrium may be achieved, Naṣīr al-Dīn Ṭūsī writes:

> The student of virtue must first examine the state of the faculty of appetite, and then that of the faculty of irascibility, ascertaining whether either is naturally disposed in accord with the law of equilibrium or divergent therefrom. If it is in accord with the law of equilibrium, he must strive to preserve that equilibrium and to make habitual the procession therefrom of that which is fair relative to the faculty; if it be divergent from equilibrium, he must take steps first to restore it to equilibrium, and then to acquire the habit in question. When he is acquitted of the correction of these two faculties, he must occupy himself with perfecting the speculative faculty, observing (due) classification therein.

Once these faculties are corrected,

> he should show zeal in preserving the articles of justice . . . . If he observes this minute point also, he has become a human being in very fact, and the title of wisdom and the mark of virtue are his.[13]

The tales exemplify divergences from equilibrium; through contemplating them, Bahrām is enabled to perfect his speculative faculty, so that he can later interpret the lesson of the shepherd and bring about moral equilibrium in his own person and justice in his kingdom.

The tales thus make possible Bahrām's spiritual progress from ignorance to wisdom, from political chief to ideal ruler, inaugurated in the Fitna episode and achieved in that of the shepherd, framed by his embodiment of craftsman/hunter and prophet/sage. This progress itself recalls another classification found in the writings of the Ikhwān al-Ṣafāʾ: that of the sixth type of motion, defined as "translation, or local movement (*naqla*)—passage in space and time from one point to another," which may be physical (*jismānī*) or spiritual (*rūḥānī*). This type of movement is further divided into straight (*mustaqīma*), circular (*mustadīra*), or a combination of the two (*murakkaba minhumā*).[14] The two parts of the biographical narrative represent physical and spiritual movement respectively; while the biographical movement is linear (*mustaqīma*), the spiritual progress is circular (*mustadīra*), and the poem as a whole is a "combined" (*murakkaba*) arrangement.[15]

13. Ṭūsī, *Nasirean Ethics*, 111–12.

14. See Nasr, *Introduction*, 66; *RIS*, 2.13–16.

15. Niẓāmī refers to the *Haft Paykar* as a *tarkīb*; on some of the possible connotations of this term, see Meisami, *Court Poetry*, 202 n. 30. *Tarkīb* has obvious associations, not only with "combined" movement but with the combination of four elements/humors that constitutes the body and with the combination of body and soul, matter and spirit.

In a passage quoted above, Naṣīr al-Dīn Ṭūsī observed that those who have perfected the human faculties of will and reason and have risen to the third and highest degree of humanity are able to proceed to the fourth: "And so to the limit, where is the abode of Unity, and there the circle of existence meets, like a curved line beginning from a point and returning to the same point." The chiastic arrangement of the four adventure episodes completes the circle, as well as the spiritual journey that is inaugurated when Bahrām slays the dragon in the cave and that culminates in his final disappearance as he consigns his own "kingly treasure" to the cave. This journey thus constitutes just such a departure and return. The curved line of this journey reaches the third degree as Bahrām, wedded to Justice, becomes the perfect king, and the fourth when his apotheosis confirms him as Perfect Man: "In the perfect man, who has realized his Divine Origin, the process [of ascent towards the Creator] has come to an end."[16]

Of the Perfect Man, Naṣīr al-Dīn Ṭūsī writes:

> When Man reaches this degree, so that he becomes aware of the ranks of generables universally, then are realized in him, in one way or another, the infinite particulars subsumed under the universals; and when practice becomes his familiar, so that his operations and acts are realized in accordance with acceptable faculties and habits, he becomes a world unto himself, comparable to his macrocosm, and merits to be called a "microcosm." Thus he becomes Almighty God's vice-gerent among His creatures, entering among His particular Saints, and standing as a Complete and Absolute Man. . . . At length, between him and his Master no veil intervenes, but he receives the ennoblement of proximity to the Divine Presence.[17]

Bahrām's achievement of this degree is symbolized in the fourth adventure episode by his disappearance into the cave to become one with the *yār-i ghār*, the Companion of the Cave.[18] As the Prophet, at the end of his celestial *Miʿrāj*,

16. Nasr, *Introduction*, 73; see also J. T. P. de Bruijn, *Of Piety and Poetry: The Interaction of Religion and Literature in the Life and Works of Ḥakīm Sanāʾī of Ghazna* (Leiden: Brill, 1983) 216–18; and R. Arnaldez, "al-insān al-kāmil," *EI*². The concept of the ruler as Perfect Man is a logical extension both of the connection between kingship and imamate (the ruler as the Regent of God) and of the concept of man as microcosm (the king embodying the highest level of mankind) and is adumbrated perhaps most fully in al-Farābī's ideal of the philosopher-king.

17. Ṭūsī, *Nasirean Ethics*, 52.

18. For a discussion of the significance of this event see Meisami, *Court Poetry*, 223–24, 233–35; idem, "Fitnah or Āzādah?" 62, 72 n. 60; idem, "Theme of the Journey." Bahrām's disappearance into the cave links him with such figures as the Sunnite *imām mahdī*, the Shiite *imām ghāʾib*, and the Zoroastrian Saoshyant, the savior who will combine the functions of king and priest and bring about the renewal of the world, prefigured by the ancient Iranian god Varhran (= Bahrām). Niẓāmī's eclecticism incorporates various currents of esoteric thought by underlining their common elements,

was granted the Beatific Vision, so at the end of his journey through this world the king returns to his divine origin. Just so the human soul, at the end of its earthly journey full of trials (*fitan*, sg. *fitna*), through which it learns the nature of its own design forgotten at its birth, will rejoin its Creator.

The unifying structure of the circle encompasses and gives meaning to the other patterns in the poem. Before considering its ultimate significance, however, we may look briefly at some of the other cosmic implications of the numbers three and four, whose sum, of course, is seven. In the Pythagorean number symbolism adopted by neo-Platonic esotericism both East and West, three and four are both numbers of the cosmos, three representing the soul and four, matter.[19] The tripartite division of the universe (the material world, the astral world, and the world of universals), applied earlier to poetic structure by Sanāʾī in his *Sayr al-ʿibād ilā l-maʿād* (an important model for Niẓāmī), symbolizes the three levels the human soul may occupy.[20] Three, the number of the soul, signifies its vegetative, animal, and rational dimensions; it is also the number of the "three kingdoms" of creation, mineral, plant, and animal, and of the three astral agents of the Universal Soul: the signs of the Zodiac, the spheres, and the planets.[21]

Four is of course the number by which the categories of nature are subdivided: the four elements, the four humors, the four seasons. (We might also note that the Ikhwān al-Ṣafāʾ described their sources as consisting of four "books": "the mathematical and scientific works written before them; the Scriptures; the archetypes, or Platonic 'ideas,' of the forms [the Book] of Nature; and the angelic, or . . . intellectual intuition," that is, the sum total of knowledge of the created universe.[22] Also recall the comparable importance of the *quadrivium*—arithmetic, geometry, astronomy, and music—to medieval learning.[23]) The total

suggesting a topical connection with the efforts of the Caliph al-Nāṣir (1181–1223) to reorganize and strengthen the position of *futuwwa* groups, important bearers of esoteric knowledge (see Fr. Taeschner, "futuwwa," *EI*²; al–Nāṣir later came to an accommodation with the Ismaʿīlis, which may have been in the wind by the late twelfth century when the *Haft Paykar* was composed).

19. See S. G. Heninger, Jr., *Touches of Sweet Harmony: Pythagorean Cosmology and Renaissance Poetics* (San Marino, Calif.: The Huntington Library, 1974) 152–78 and passim.

20. See de Bruijn, *Of Piety and Poetry*, 205. Although in the *Sayr al-ʿibād* Sanāʾī depicts the soul's progress towards perfection, his goal, as de Bruijn points out, is not eschatology but panegyric: "The depiction of the process of moral purification does not end in looking towards an eschatological fulfillment; it stops at the top of the scale of human perfections in the contemplation of a specimen of the fullest development among the living contemporaries of the poet" (ibid., 213).

21. See Nasr, *Introduction*, 61.

22. Ibid., 39–40; *RIS*, 4.106. On further tetrads and their correspondences, see *RIS*, 1.229–32.

23. See Russell A. Peck, "Number as Cosmic Language," in *Essays in the Numerical Criticism of Medieval Literature* (ed. Caroline D. Eckhardt; Lewisburg, Penn.: Bucknell University Press, 1980) 21–22; Nasr, *Introduction*, 48–50.

of these numbers, seven, the first perfect number, is also the number of man, the microcosm, as it is a number of totality.[24]

The four elements and humors (in other words, the bases of all creation), when maintained in equilibrium, are symbolized by the image of a square within a circle. It is this cosmic symbol that lies at the heart of the *Haft Paykar*'s design, for the progression of the four adventure episodes transforms the straight line of Bahrām's physical journey (now a square, symbolizing its material aspect) into a circle of perfection representing his spiritual journey, which is not merely from ignorance to wisdom, but from *mabdaʾ* to *maʿād*. The transformation of line to circle, symbol of unity, harmony, and wholeness, evokes further the figure of the spiral, said to have "symbolized the 'helicoidal movement', which . . . descends from God to the soul of man and then returns heavenward to its Maker."[25] The Prophet's *Miʿrāj*, the prototype for Bahrām's spiritual journey, involved an ascent and a return; Bahrām's own journey both completes the circle (the meeting of beginning and end, *mabdaʾ* and *maʿād*) and is informed by the upward motion associated with his acquisition of self-knowledge.

In his exordium, Niẓāmī calls attention to the design of the *Haft Paykar*, returning again to the motif of right reading.

> This written temple I've adorned,
> with seven brides, like Magian Zand,
> So that, should the sky-brides decide
> to turn their gaze upon *my* brides,
> through like affairs and ornaments,
> each of them aid to mine might lend.
> For when the seven lines converge,
> one point at center shall emerge.
> The painter, ten designs in hand,
> of one main thread yet grasps the end.
> If that thread from the line should stray,
> the others would be set awry.
> Though one trace not this thread aright,
> rightness remains, nor quits our sight.
> I follow this thread, painter–wise;
> on that main thread I've fixed my gaze (4:33–40).

24. Peck, "Number," 18–19.

25. A. Papadopoulo, *Islam and Muslim Art* (trans. R. E. Wolff; New York: Abrams, 1979) 102; on the importance of the spiral as a compositional principle in Islamic art (especially in painting), see ibid., 96–102. Georg Krotkoff suggests another structure pattern based on the astrological Grand Trine (3 + 3 + 3), the symbol of perfection, rather than the 3 + 3 + 1 sequence of the seven tales, which he has identified ("Colour and Number," 109–10, and see the chart between pp. 108–9). This would create a spatial pattern of three triangles, combining into a pyramid. While this suggestion is intriguing, it does not account for the overall structure of the poem, as it does not take into consideration the material in the first part of the narrative, prior to the tales.

By comparing the design (*naqsh*) of his poem to the "Magian Zand," the Zoroastrian scripture (more properly, to the Middle Persian translation of the Avesta), he affirms its sacral dimensions.[26] The reference to "lines and points" (7:36) has been read as an allusion to geomancy (*raml*), in which an arrangement of lines produces the "point of prosperity" (*nuqṭa-i saᶜādat*);[27] but the passage as a whole appears to allude to procedures for generating patterns in architecture and painting.[28] More importantly, it suggests that the true meaning of the poem—like that of the divine plan itself—can be achieved only by a right reading that attends to the principle of number, the embodiment of truth. The Ikhwān al-Ṣafāᵓ discuss 'intellectual geometry' (*al-handasa al-ᶜaqliyya*) as the means of passing from material to spiritual understanding;[29] while in his *Ḥadīqat al-ḥaqīqa*, Sanāᵓī likened "the ability to behold the divine manifestation . . . to the intellectual way of perception of a geometrician":

> You only see with your imagination and your senses,
> When you have not learned about lines, planes and points.[30]

26. The Zand was understood by Muslim writers as a commentary on the Avesta and an example of *taᵓwīl*, allegorical exegesis; cf. al-Masᶜūdī, *Murūj al-dhahab wa-maᶜādin al-jawhar* (ed. and trans. C. Pellat; 7 vols.; Beirut: Université Libanaise, 1971–79) 1.549. It was presumably decorated with astronomical figures. A variant of line 33 has *naqsh* 'design' for *dayr*. The image of a temple adorned with figures is not uncommon in Islamic writings, since contact with Sabian and (in Persia) Buddhist sacral art gave rise to many of the motifs and commonplaces of the poetic tradition. Cf. H. Corbin, "Sabian Temple and Ismailism," in *Temple and Contemplation* (ed. H. Corbin; trans. by Philip Sherrard; London: KPI, 1986) 132–82; A. S. Melikian-Chirvani, "L'Evocation littéraire du Bouddhisme dans l'Iran musulman," in *Le Monde Iranien et l'Islam*, vol. 2: *Sciences et cultures* (Geneva: Droz, 1974) 1–72.

27. This refers to the astrological version of *raml* rather than to the traditional method of divination using lines and points drawn in sand; cf. E. Savage-Smith and M. B. Smith, *Islamic Geomancy and a Thirteenth-Century Divinatory Device* (Malibu, Calif.: Undena, 1980) 1–10; see also Heninger, *Touches of Sweet Harmony*, 240–43, on geomancy and number symbolism.

28. The poet refers to himself as a *naqshband* and a *rassām*, terms that can designate a painter or an architect, skills combined in the two architects in the *Haft Paykar*, Simnār, the builder of Khavarnaq, and his apprentice Shīda, who constructs the seven domes. Little is known about Islamic architectural techniques, which appear to have been secrets closely guarded within the guilds of artisans (cf. Papadopoulo, *Muslim Art*, 100–101). If, as has been suggested, Niẓāmī was indeed associated with the Akhīs, who may have included such craftsmen among their numbers, he might well have been initiated into such secrets. Cf. Jan Rypka, *History of Iranian Literature* (Dordrecht: Reidel, 1968) 210; idem, "Poets and Prose Writers of the Late Saljuq and Mongol Periods," in *Cambridge History of Iran*, vol. 5: *The Saljuq and Mongol Periods* (ed. J. A. Boyle; Cambridge: Cambridge University Press, 1968), 579; see also Fr. Taeschner, "Akhī," *EI*², and idem, "Futuwwa," *EI*². The Anatolian Akhīs revered the caliph al-Nāṣir as their original patron.

29. See *RIS*, 1.101–13; on the spiritual importance of geometric patterns in Islamic art, see David Wade, *Pattern in Islamic Art* (Woodstock, N.Y.: Overlook Press, 1976) 7–13.

30. De Bruijn, *Of Piety and Poetry*, 216; see M. T. Mudarris Raẓavī (ed.), *Ḥadīqat al-ḥaqīqa* (Tehran, 1339/1951) 69.

In Pythagorean arithmology, lines and points, though present and eternal in the cosmic design, are conceivable only as abstractions, since the senses can perceive reality only as space and volume, represented by the first "real" numbers, three and four.[31]

The passage quoted above introduces yet another symbolic number, seventeen, the sum of the "seven lines and ten designs." According to Jābir ibn Ḥayyān, seventeen was the key to the understanding of nature.[32] Seventeen is the sum of the sequence 1:3:5:8; for the Pythagoreans, it was associated with the harmonic proportion 9:8. Fifty-one, the product of 3 x 17, was important for the Shiᶜites and is the number of the *Rasāᵓil* of the Ikhwān al-Ṣafāᵓ. The culmination of the *Haft Paykar*, Bahrām's marriage to Justice and his apotheosis, occurs in sections 51 and 52, making the Fitna episode and its continuation (25–26), in which Bahrām is set on his spiritual quest, the poem's numerological midpoint.[33]

Niẓāmī's linkage of his poem to such cosmic principles of number relates its ordering design to that of the created universe, as well as to the ordering design of man himself. Even if one fails to read this design correctly, "rightness remains, nor quits our sight." Niẓāmī's words recall those of Augustine, who, centuries earlier, "had explained that if a man comprehends number it is not changed; yet if he fails to grasp it, its truth 'does not disappear; rather, it remains true and permanent, while man's failure to grasp it is commensurate with the extent of his error.'"[34] The poet's construction (his *tarkīb*) parallels the design of the cosmos itself and affirms their kinship; in so doing, it places the poet in a position analogous to that of the Creator.

The *Haft Paykar* is thus a literary microcosm based on the principles of divine geometry; the structural patterns chosen by the poet imply knowledge of the geometric skills necessary for perception of the divine order itself. Like astronomy, the purpose of whose study "is to prepare pure souls and make them

31. Peck, "Number," 24.

32. Nasr, *Introduction*, 38 n. 61.

33. See further Meisami, *Court Poetry*, 213–21; idem, "Fitnah or Āzādah?" 57–59. Fitna, who is the first of Bahrām's spiritual guides, is praised for her musical skills; on the association of music with natural order and with ethics, see Heninger, *Touches of Sweet Harmony*, 103. On the symbolic significance of seventeen (particularly for Shiᶜite thought), see Irène Mélikoff, "Nombres symboliques dans la littérature épico-religieuse des turcs d'Anatolie," *JA* 250 (1962) 435–45. The actual midpoint of the *Haft Paykar* is the fourth tale; on the significance of this tale, see Krotkoff, "Colour and Number," 106–7.

34. Peck, "Number," 17; Peck comments, "The 'artist,' as writers such as Augustine . . . so often insist in their discussions of the creative process, is a structurer. He is also an imitator of the idea held firm and well shaped in his mind. Though he may work with mutable images, the one idea remains true and discernible through the numbers of his varied structures. In the discovery of that idea is the observer's delight" (ibid., 32–33).

desirous of celestial ascent,"[35] geometry leads man to an understanding of the divine wisdom; it is scarcely coincidence that these are the two sciences to which Bahrām devoted himself during his early education. Like the created universe itself, the *Haft Paykar* is a work of art through which knowledge of the creator may be achieved. The unicity of nature, subsumed in its geometric structure and symbolized by the unifying circle, points to the Unicity of God, the source and return of all, the transcendental center lying at the heart of its unending pattern. "He who knows himself, knows his Lord."[36]

35. *RIS*, 1.91; quoted by Nasr, *Introduction*, 78.

36. Space prohibits a discussion of the relations of these structural patterns with notions of time, briefly suggested in connection with the concept of motion. Time may be linear (chronological and biographical time), cyclical (astronomical and historical time, characterized by recurrence and expressed in liturgy and in typology), and eternal; the three were often represented as three concentric circles (see Peck, "Number," 34–44). Time, bound up with notions of space and of motion, is intimately connected with the figure of the circle (ibid., 39–40). The structure of the *Haft Paykar* presents an overall view of time as cyclical; that "ancient instrument of Iranian symbol . . . uniting the primordial beginnings with the eschatological end" (A. Bausani, "Muhammad or Darius? The Elements and Basis of Iranian Culture," in *Islam and Cultural Change in the Middle Ages* [ed. Speros Vryonis, Jr.; Wiesbaden: Harrassowitz, 1975] 48), which incorporates and overrides linear time. This recalls al-Bīrūnī's cosmological system, in which "the traditional idea of cycles implies a qualitative notion of time in such a way that an analogy exists between two points in the unfolding of time. This conception can be symbolized by a helix whose turns have analogies with each other without ever repeating one another" (Nasr, *Introduction*, 119 n. 6). On the contrast between cyclical and linear time and their complementary relationship, see also Heninger, *Touches of Sweet Harmony*, 220–27.

Playing with the Sacred: Religious Intertext in *Adab* Discourse

Fedwa Malti-Douglas

Four-letter words seem to have a fascination for the West, and the Arabic word *adab* is no exception. Appealing and elusive at the same time, this innocuous term has caused more ink to be spilled than perhaps any other word in the history of Arabic literary criticism. Since I have done so elsewhere, I will not review this discussion here.[1] Suffice it to say that *adab* can be understood as a spirit,

Author's note: An earlier version of this study was delivered at the colloquium on "Medieval and Renaissance Humanism," at the Rockefeller Foundation Bellagio Study and Conference Center, Bellagio, Italy, November 28, 1989.

1. For an analysis of the discussions of *adab*, see my *Structures of Avarice: The Bukhalāʾ in Medieval Arabic Literature* (Leiden: Brill, 1985) 7–16. The recent work by George Makdisi, *The Rise of Humanism in Classical Islam and the Christian West with Special Reference to Scholasticism* (Edinburgh: Edinburgh University Press, 1990), effectively defines *adab* as a collection of separate subjects, that are then equated with Western humanism, understood as a collection of similar subjects.

but more concretely as a discourse (itself based on characteristic ways of manipulating texts of certain kinds) that could be said to express this ideal. *Adab* literature is an intertextually rich anecdotal and narrative literature designed to be at once didactic and entertaining. A mixed form that combines prose and poetry, the *adab* work includes Qurᵓānic verses, *ḥadīth*s, poetic selections, and anecdotes. One of the key issues in an examination of *adab* as cultural focus has been its relationship to the Islamic religious tradition. Despite the attention to this problematic in discussions of the meaning of *adab*, the matter has not been subjected to a systematic investigation based on the texts themselves.[2] It is clear that any understanding of *adab* as a worldly counterpart to the otherworldly focus of the religious sciences (a dichotomy that is highly questionable in the Islamic context anyway) needs, at the least, to be carefully nuanced, if for no other reason than the systematic and consistent presence in prototypical *adab* works of religious materials, like the aforementioned *ḥadīth* and Qurᵓānic citations. In the overwhelming majority of cases, these religious materials are presented in a manner consistent with the way they would be used in religious works, for example, *ḥadīth* works, works of moral theology, and so forth.[3] Religious materials play other roles in *adab* texts, however. They are sometimes assimilated into the *adab* texts in ways that apparently subordinate them to the *adab* spirit. From a world of authority, they enter a world of play.

A close examination of the religious intertext in a representative group of *adab* anecdotes will allow us to examine this distinctive use of sacred materials. The authors of these anecdotes are some of the greatest names in Arabic prose and are certainly representative of the major strands of Arabic *adab* literature: al-Jāḥiẓ (d. 255/869), Ibn Qutayba (d. 276/889), al-Thaᶜālibī (d. 429/1038), al-Khaṭīb al-Baghdādī (d. 463/1071), and Ibn al-Jawzī (d. 597/1200). The dynamics of the *adab* discourse has a certain consistency, as we shall see throughout the analysis.

Western critics have called ample attention to the need for a reexamination and a rereading of the Western cultural and literary corpus. The provocative

2. For a discussion and references, see my *Structures*, 9. See also, Mohammed Arkoun, *Essais sur la pensée islamique* (Paris: Maisonneuve et Larouse, 1973) 210–16; cf. Makdisi, *Rise of Humanism*, 113–15. On *adab* anecdotal literature, see also, Yūsuf Sadān, *al-Adab al-ᶜarabī al-hāzil wa-nawādir al-thuqalāᵓ* (Tel Aviv: Maṭbaᶜat al-sarūjī, 1983); Ulrich Marzolph, *Der Weise Narr Buhlūl* (Wiesbaden: Franz Steiner, 1983).

3. See, for example, Ibn al-Jawzī, *Akhbār al-ḥamqā wa-l-mughaffalīn* (Beirut: al-Maktab al-tijārī li-l-ṭibāᶜa wa-l-nashr wa-l-tawzīᶜ, n.d.) 21; Ibn ᶜAbd Rabbihi, *al-ᶜIqd al-farīd* (ed. Aḥmad Amīn, Aḥmad al-Zayn, and Ibrāhīm al-Abyārī; Cairo: Maṭbaᶜat lajnat al-taᵓlīf wa-l-tarjama wa-l-nashr, 1965) 1.232, 235; al-Rāghib al-Aṣbahānī, *Muḥāḍarāt al-udabāᵓ wa-muḥāwarāt al-shuᶜarāᵓ wa-l-bulaghāᵓ* (Beirut: Manshūrāt dār maktabat al-ḥayāt, n.d.) 1.121, 142, 403.

Rewriting the Renaissance is only one such effort.[4] Critics have also investigated the literary properties of religious texts, as has been done, for example, by Northrop Frye in his masterful *Great Code*.[5] This essay differs. Rather than subjecting the Islamic holy texts, such as the Qurʾān or the *ḥadīth*, to critical investigation (as Mohammed Arkoun does in his *Lectures du Coran*, for example),[6] I propose to analyze the permutations of religious material in *adab* works: how is the religious intertext used or misused? How does this help us to understand *adab* discourse?

The controversial eleventh-century religious traditionist al-Khaṭīb al-Baghdādī authored works ranging from *ḥadīth* criticism to history and *adab*.[7] His anecdotal corpus includes a delightful work on uninvited guests (*ṭufaylīs*), in which the following appears.[8] Al-Ḥasan ibn al-Sabbāḥ al-Nisāʾī relates that he went to Jaʿfar ibn Muḥammad, who asked him his opinion of sweets. The guest replied that he did not pass judgment on something absent, upon which the host called for an etched bowl in which was an almond pastry. Following a description of the pastry, the guest uttered a verse from the second *sūra* of the Qurʾān, "Your God is one God,"[9] upon which the host presented him with one piece of pastry. The guest then followed with another verse of the Qurʾān that exploits the number two and received a second piece of pastry. The narrative continued in this way, with the guest bringing forth a verse from the holy book containing the appropriate number, at which point he was given yet another piece of pastry. At the number twelve, followed by the twelfth piece of pastry, the guest jumped to the number twenty, at which the host threw the bowl at him, telling him to eat and addressing him with an insult. The guest merely replied that had the host not thrown the bowl, he would have said (again quoting the Qurʾān): "Then We sent him unto a hundred thousand, or more."[10]

4. Nancy J. Vickers, Margaret W. Ferguson, and Maureen Quilligan (eds). *Rewriting the Renaissance: The Discourses of Sexual Difference in Early Modern Europe* (Chicago: The University of Chicago Press, 1986).

5. Northrop Frye, *The Great Code: The Bible and Literature* (New York: Harcourt Brace Jovanovitch, 1982).

6. Mohammed Arkoun, *Lectures du Coran* (Paris: Maisonneuve et Larose, 1982).

7. For a biographical assessment of al-Khaṭīb and the controversy surrounding him, see my "Controversy and Its Effects in the Biographical Tradition of al-Khaṭīb al-Baghdādī," *Studia Islamica* 46 (1977) 115–31.

8. Al-Khaṭīb al-Baghdādī, *al-Taṭfīl wa-ḥikāyāt al-ṭufayliyyīn wa-akhbāruhum wa-nawādir kalāmihim wa-ashʿāruhum* (ed. Kāzim al-Muẓaffar; Najaf: al-Maktaba al-ḥaydariyya, 1966), and for the anecdote, pp. 53–54. On this work, see my "Structure and Organization in a Monographic *Adab* Work: *al-Taṭfīl* of al-Khaṭīb al-Baghdādī," *JNES* 40 (1981) 227–45.

9. Sūrat al-Baqara, 2:163; A. J. Arberry (trans.), *The Koran Interpreted* (2 vols.; New York: Macmillan, 1974) 1.48.

10. Sūrat al-Ṣāffāt, 37:147; Arberry, *The Koran Interpreted*, 2.155.

This would seem a relatively straightforward anecdote. The *ṭufaylī* will stop at nothing to achieve his goal, including the exploitation of the Holy Book. His reply to the host's insult at the end of the anecdote illustrated this well: if necessary, he would have recited numbers into the thousands. And without a doubt, the tactic worked: each Qurʾānic verse brought forth pieces of pastry. This is obviously not the original signification of the verses in their Qurʾānic context. The *ṭufaylī* was redirecting the religious text to fulfill his physical (and psychological) desires for the food. He could not have done better than to begin on his gluttonous path with the assertion of the unity of God, present in the verse.[11]

Other dimensions add to the complexity of the narrative and help redefine the presence of the religious intertext. An underlying orality permeates the narrative: something emanating from the mouth (the verse from the Qurʾān) brings forth something that enters the mouth (the piece of pastry). That this orality is not a random component can be seen if one examines the guest's initial description of the pastry, which appears before the recitation of the first verse leading to the host's offer of the pastry. The guest has not yet partaken of the delicacy, but nevertheless describes elements of it that can only be assessed after he has sampled it. The description of the external physical appearance is followed by the sounds the piece of pastry makes as first it is pulled out (a squeaking like that of Sindī sandals)[12] and then put into the mouth (a sizzling like that of iron being taken out of the furnace). Both of these images create interesting but certainly unsavory bisociations: the first with sandals and the second with iron.

The religious text is here used to produce food. In another Khaṭībian anecdote, this one drawn from his book on misers, the dynamics are reversed. If, as its name suggests, the *Kitāb al-taṭfīl* is about uninvited guests (and by extension about guests who abuse their rights), the *bukhalāʾ* or miser literature tends to concentrate on the problem of hospitality and, therefore, to a considerable degree on hosts who may be niggardly with their guests. We are on opposite sides in the tug-of-war between host and guest. A Bedouin came to visit a man, who happened to have a platter of figs in front of him. Seeing the visitor, he covered the platter with his garment. This did not go unremarked upon by the newcomer, who then sat in front of the man. The latter asked the guest if he knew something from the Qurʾān well, to which the latter replied "Yes." Told to recite, he proceeded with the following: "By the olive and the

11. For the interpretation of this verse, see, for example, al-Bayḍāwī, *Tafsīr al-Bayḍāwī* (Beirut: Dār al-kutub al-ʿilmiyya, 1988) 1.97.

12. On this type of sandal, see al-Jāḥiẓ, *Kitāb al-tarbīʿ wal-tadwīr* (ed. Charles Pellat; Damascus: Institut Français de Damas, 1955) 84–85.

Mount Sinai."[13] The man then asked where the fig was, to which the guest replied, "Under your garment."[14]

This anecdote only makes sense if one knows that the protagonist has changed the Qurʾānic text. Recited properly, the verses should be: "By the fig and the olive and the Mount Sinai."[15] The textual play does not work, however, the guest not receiving any figs for his trouble. The circumstances of the fruit hidden under the man's robe would certainly suggest a sexual implication, and figs have been associated with male organs in other traditions.[16] But in Arabic, the term *tīna* (the noun of unity as opposed to *tīn*, the collective, in the Qurʾānic verse) signifies the behind or anus, which does not fit the anecdote.[17]

In another example, a *ṭufaylī* was asked about his knowledge of the Qurʾān. Replying that he was one of the most learned people in it, he was then requested to interpret a part of the following verse: "Enquire of the city wherein we were."[18] He replied that it referred to the people of the city, adducing as proof that when one says that one ate the table of so and so, he means he ate what was on it.[19]

This *ṭufaylī* is at once learned, as he himself claimed, and creative. His explanation of the Qurʾānic verse from the *Sūrat Yūsuf* concords with its traditional interpretations, hence showing his knowledge of *tafsīr* (Qurʾānic exegesis).[20] His creativity, spurred clearly by his one-track mind (centered as it is on food), lies in his analogical reasoning. One synecdoche has been replaced by another; and in the process, the holy text is placed in an associative relationship with the *ṭufaylī*'s object of desire. There is clearly nothing in the Qurʾānic text itself that calls up this bisociation, and the relationship between the divine original and its anecdotal context remains external, artificial. Hence, the Qurʾānic text is in no sense redefined; there has been no real semantic interference between intertext and context.

In effect, this has been the case with all the anecdotes thus far discussed. The first with numbers is a perfect example. The use of the Qurʾānic citations

13. Sūrat al-Tīn, 95:1–2; Arberry, *The Koran Interpreted*, 2.343.

14. Al-Khaṭīb al-Baghdādī, *al-Bukhalāʾ* (ed. Aḥmad Maṭlūb, Khadīja al-Ḥadīthī, and Aḥmad al-Qaysī; Baghdad: Maṭbaʿat al-ʿānī, 1964) 75–76. On this book, see my *Structures*.

15. Sūrat al-Tīn, 95:1–2; Arberry, *The Koran Interpreted*, 2.343.

16. I am grateful to Speros Vryonis and the participants in the colloquium on "Medieval and Renaissance Humanism" for this information.

17. See, for example, al-Zabīdī, *Tāj al-ʿarūs* (Beirut: Dār ṣādir, n.d.) 9.154.

18. Sūrat Yūsuf, 12:82; Arberry, *The Koran Interpreted*, 1.263.

19. Al-Khatīb, *al-Taṭfīl*, 56.

20. See, for example, al-Bayḍāwī, *Tafsīr*, 1.493; Jalāl al-Dīn al-Maḥallī and Jalāl al-Dīn al-Suyūṭī, *Tafsīr al-Qurʾān al-karīm*, printed on the margins of *al-Qurʾān* (2 vols.; Cairo: Muṣṭafā al-Bābī al-Ḥalabī, 1966), 1.274.

is anecdotal. There is a genuine semantic identity in the case of the occulted fig, but this relationship remains superficial and has no influence on the semantic field of the Qurʾānic verse. (It should also be noted that the alimentary interpretation of the fig and the olive is doubled with a geographic one in the exegetical tradition.)[21] This does not mean that the games played here remain exclusively rhetorical. The Qurʾān retains its status as normative text (to say the least), and its use in this context opens up questions about the relationship between its inherent textual truth and its exploitation (in both senses of the term) in situations of varied and occasionally dubious morality. The bisociation with food, so natural in the context of *ṭufaylī* and *bukhalāʾ* literature, does nevertheless expand the horizons of the holy texts into another domain, suggesting implicit redefinition.

The interpretation of a religious text, however, can be perverted. Al-Jāḥiẓ, the acknowledged master of medieval Arabic prose, provides us with a good example. In his defense of avarice included in al-Jāḥiẓ's famous *Kitāb al-bukhalāʾ*, Ibn al-Tawʾam reinterprets a *ḥadīth* of the Prophet in which the latter advises someone to hold on to his money, turning it into a justification for not spending and effectively, therefore, for avarice (*bukhl*).[22] The argument is clever (and not without echoes in al-Jāḥiẓ's *Bukhalāʾ*), but it is fundamentally dishonest because it confuses the virtue of economy with the vice of avarice. In the process, it has altered the meaning of the sacred text (here a *ḥadīth*). However, it is the semantic similarity between sacred text and context that permits this transformation. As we shall see, other anecdotes exploit varying levels of semantic similarity to effect different kinds of reinterpretation.

This ingenious technique is also evident in the case of the *ṭufaylī* who was asked if he were not ashamed of his behavior. What is wrong with it, he replied, since even the Israelites practiced it, for they said (again citing the Qurʾān): "O God, our Lord, send down upon us a Table out of heaven, that shall be for us a festival"?[23]

Here, the brief interpretation is presented first in the justification of the asocial behavior. The Qurʾānic verse is both evidence and clarification of the interpretation, adding, of course, the weight of the divine word. This clever protagonist is, however, not as honest (or as learned?) as some others of his type, for the speaker in the Qurʾānic verse is actually Jesus and not the col-

21. See, for example, al-Bayḍāwī, *Tafsīr*, 2.607.

22. Al-Jāḥiẓ, *al-Bukhalāʾ*, (ed. Ṭāhā al-Ḥājirī; Cairo: Dār al-maʿārif, 1971) 186. On these missives, for and against miserliness, see my *Structures*, 51–52. This text is textually attributed to Ibn al-Tawʾam, but there is no reason why it could not have been written by al-Jāḥiẓ himself. See ibid., chap. 3.

23. Sūrat al-Māʾida, 5:114; Arberry, *The Koran Interpreted*, 1.146; Al-Khaṭīb, *al-Taṭfīl*, 34.

lectivity of Israelites. A sort of mangling of the Qurʾānic text is effected. The shift alters the implications of the verse since Jesus, not here asking for himself, could in no sense be acting as a *ṭufaylī*; and even without this change, the *ṭufaylī's* interpretation constitutes a moral hijacking of the Qurʾānic intent.

The area of bisociation need not be limited to food. The Ḥanbalī theologian and polyhistor Ibn al-Jawzī, in the chapter on *ṭufaylī*s in his *Akhbār al-adhkiyāʾ* ("Stories of the Clever and Witty"), relates an anecdote about the prototypical uninvited guest, Bunān. The latter came to a banquet and the door was locked before he could enter. So he rented a ladder and placed it on the man's wall, looking out on the man's family and daughters. The man said to him: "O you, do you not fear God? You have seen my family and daughters." Bunān replied: "O *shaykh*, [and here the Qurʾānic citation begins] 'Thou knowest we have no right to thy daughters, and thou well knowest what we desire.'"[24] The man laughed and told Bunān to come down and eat.[25]

In this concise narrative, it is as though we had come full circle. The Qurʾānic verse alludes to the people of Lot, whose homosexual inclinations are part of what causes their downfall. But Bunān is not interested in the sexual; his appetites lie elsewhere. He borrows this Qurʾānic allusion and redirects it to his own desires. Clearly, the anecdote revolves around a tension between sexual and alimentary desires. And this is manifest from its very beginning. The closing of the door, the climbing of the ladder, Bunān's scopic activity—these all form part of the sexual discourse in the anecdote. Pulling at this is the alimentary component: the banquet, implying food. When the host confronted the prospective *ṭufaylī* with the sexual (the scopic), Bunān replied with a verse about sexuality but shifted it to a nonsexual use.

The manipulation of sexuality and the religious intertext is a fairly consistent element in the anecdotes about women in the *adab* corpus. Relatively atypical is the case of the woman who passed by a group of men from the Banū Numayr, who persisted in staring at her. She admonished them with both a verse from the Qurʾān directed against looking ("Say to the believers, that they cast down their eyes")[26] and with a line of poetry of similar import. The men were ashamed and bowed down their heads.[27] The female speaker in this anecdote uses the verse from the holy book in the exact way it was intended: as an admonition against looking. Her goal is achieved: the men lower their

24. Sūrat Hūd, 11:79; Arberry, *The Koran Interpreted*, 1.248.

25. Ibn al-Jawzī, *Akhbār al-adhkiyāʾ* (ed. Muḥammad Mursī al-Khawlī; Cairo: Maṭābiᶜ al-ahrām al-tijāriyya, 1970) 189.

26. Sūrat al-Nūr, 24:30; Arberry, *The Koran Interpreted*, 2.49.

27. Ibn Qutayba, *ᶜUyūn al-akhbār* (4 vols. in 2; Cairo: Dār al-kutub, 1963) 4.85.

eyes. But the religious intertext does more. It reverses the power of the sexual situation, which begins with the male scopic in a superior position. The male gaze has been deflected by the religious text.[28]

More typical is an anecdote relating that when a man who wished to buy a slave girl asked her price, she replied: "And none knows the hosts of thy Lord but He."[29] Her refusal to answer a prospective buyer was effected through the holy book. She silenced the male voice by using a verse whose content in no way denoted sexuality and was essentially irrelevant.

Two women, one a virgin and one not, were shown to a buyer and he favored the virgin. The nonvirgin then asked him why he preferred the virgin, given that there was only one day between them. The virgin then replied: "And surely a day with thy Lord is as a thousand years of your counting."[30] The man liked both women and bought them both.[31] Here, the virgin responded to her colleague's question, which the latter had addressed to the male buyer. Through the use of the verse, she created a bisociation between the religious and the sexual—and one that played up to the sexual power of the man. The Lord in the Qurʾānic verse became the lord and master of the house. His sexual possession of the woman is compared with the deity's domination of the universe. Patriarchal religion, one might say, has been reduced to patriarchy. The response does more, however. The verse from *Sūrat al-Ḥajj* is embedded in a section on the punishments inflicted by the deity. This context of punishment serves to reinforce the negative implications of the loss of virginity.

This kind of dialogue mediated through a religious intertext is even more prominent in a story found in the *Laṭāʾif al-luṭf* by al-Thaʿālibī, one of the most indefatigable scholars of his time. The vizier al-Faḍl ibn Yaḥyā explained to the ʿAbbāsid caliph Hārūn al-Rashīd that he was consorting with two of his slave girls, one Meccan and one Medinan. The Medinan aroused him and proceeded to the sexual act, at which point the Meccan slave girl overpowered her. The Medinan replied that she had more right to this, adducing the *ḥadīth*, according to which the Prophet said: "He who revives a dead land, it belongs to him."[32] But the other responded with another *ḥadīth*: "The quarry belongs

28. For the dynamics of this problematic in *adab* chapters on women, see my *Woman's Body, Woman's Word: Gender and Discourse in Arabo-Islamic Writing* (Princeton: Princeton University Press, 1991) 29–53.

29. Ibn al-Jawzī, *Adhkiyāʾ*, 238. The verse is Sūrat al-Muddaththir, 74:31; Arberry, *The Koran Interpreted*, 2.311.

30. Sūrat al-Ḥajj, 22:47; Arberry, *The Koran Interpreted*, 2.33.

31. Ibn al-Jawzī, *Adhkiyāʾ*, 236.

32. This *ḥadīth* is a reasonably popular one, as evidenced by A. J. Wensinck, *Concordance et indices de la tradition musulmane* (8 vols; Leiden: Brill, 1936–88) 1.539. See, for example, Mālik ibn Anas, *Kitāb al-muwaṭṭaʾ* (ed. Fārūq Saʿd; Beirut: Dār al-āfāq al-jadīda, 1983) 637–38.

not to the one who arouses it but to the one who hunts it."[33] The caliph laughed and the two slave girls were given to him.[34] A change of registers is effected here through the use of the nonsexual *ḥadīth* in a clearly sexual context. The interchange between the women is restricted to the two religious texts. Through this exploitation, the female speakers succeed in turning the male into a sexual being, if not into a merely sexual object. But it is precisely their verbal skills, their ability to manipulate the religious discourse, that makes them desirable females, themselves objects of desire, as they are the property first of one male and then of another.

These anecdotes, thus, vary in the degree to which they reinterpret or redefine the religious text. Of course, this reinterpretation is in no sense absolute. The orthodox or received interpretations of these verses or *ḥadīths* are never really eliminated. In fact, the authoritative nature of the *ḥadīth* or Qurʾānic citations is key to their use in the power plays of the anecdotes. The religious texts are assimilated into the systems of *adab* anecdotes: the struggles over food and sex, the clever stratagems, the displays of wit. They show us that *adab* must be understood not (or at least not exclusively) on the basis of the nature of the materials included in it, still less their origin, but in terms of the specific ways in which these materials are presented, exploited, or manipulated.

33. I have not been able to locate this *ḥadīth* in the standard compilations.

34. Al-Thaʿālibī, *Laṭāʾif al-luṭf* (ed. ʿUmar al-Asʿad; Beirut: Dār al-masīra, 1980) 99–100.

From Revolt to Resignation: The Life of Shaykh Muḥsin Sharāra

Werner Ende

One of the most prominent features of the Middle Eastern educational system in the nineteenth and twentieth centuries was the founding of numerous institutions of higher learning. The founders included governments (for example, those of the Ottoman Empire), Christian missionary societies and orders, as well as Muslim educational associations and foundations. Almost all of these new colleges and universities were based on European or American models as far as their internal organization and the shaping of their curricula were concerned. The tradition of the Islamic *madrasa* played no role in them at all, or if it did, only a limited and marginal one. The founders of the new schools proceeded on the assumption that the *madrasa* was outdated and that it could not be reformed.[1]

1. For a general survey of this development, see articles "Ma^{c}ārif" and "Madrasa" in *EI*^{2} 5.902–21 and 1123–54, respectively.

The relatively broad success of these new places of learning, evident above all in the careers in public service of many of their graduates, acted as a decisive impetus for the development of ideas to reform—and for actual attempts at reforming—traditional and sometimes highly renowned institutions. One outstanding example is the Azhar in Cairo. Its history after about the year 1865 can in part be regarded as a constant—though laborious and sometimes unsuccessful—process of reform. One of its aims is still to secure its graduates a place in Egyptian society and the Islamic world under conditions of increasing competition from more modern, "secularly" oriented universities.[2]

Admittedly, there are, or were, centuries-old and well-known centers of Islamic learning that underwent no significant change in curriculum or teaching activity. Some of them lost their importance or disappeared during the course of the nineteenth and twentieth centuries; others were swallowed up by reformed or newly established institutions that were happy to be able to make use of the one-time fame of the *madāris*.

One example of a university, or rather a complex of *madāris*, at which there was no fundamental change until the 1970s, is Najaf. In this respect, and with regard to their history as well as to their political and social functions, Shīᶜī Najaf and Sunnī Azhar can hardly be compared meaningfully. This is obvious already from the different situations in which they found themselves at the beginning of the nineteenth century. While al-Azhar was drawn into the conflict between the populace of Cairo and the French occupants, the people of Najaf had to fear the attacks of Wahhabi Bedouin, that is, anti-Shīᶜī zealots who actually succeeded in conquering and plundering Kerbela in 1802.

We may well ask whether the idea of reforming instruction in Najaf was actually considered in the nineteenth century and if it was, as of what year and by whom. It cannot be ruled out that it was, but there is no clear evidence available to me that such considerations ever took place.

More or less concrete indications of a certain awareness of crisis among leading theologians at Najaf are noticeable during the early years of the twentieth century. They center on Muḥammad Kāẓim al-Khurāsānī (d. 1911), an Iranian *mujtahid* who was known as "Ākhūnd" to his students and friends. In a petition addressed to the Persian Shah, Muḥammad ᶜAlī, in 1907, he advocated, among other things, the promotion of the *modern* sciences. He is credited with having founded both traditional religious as well as modern schools.[3]

2. *EI*² 1.813–21, esp. 817ff.; also Wolf-Dieter Lemke, *Maḥmūd Shaltūt (1893–1963) und die Reform der Azhar* (Frankfurt, 1980); A. Chris Eccel, *Egypt, Islam and Social Change: Al-Azhar in Conflict and Accommodation* (Berlin, 1984).

3. See "Ākhūnd" in *Encyclopaedia Iranica* (ed. E. Yarshater; London, 1985) 1.732–35. In addition to the literature mentioned there, see ᶜAbd al-Raḥīm Muḥammad ᶜAlī, *al-Muṣliḥ al-mujāhid*

Among his students were several who were responsible for spreading modernist ideas and who stressed the necessity of an open confrontation with the modern sciences. One of them was Hibat al-Dīn al-Ḥusaynī al-Shahrastānī, who in 1910/11 published a book called *al-Hayʾa wa-l-islām*.[4] Writing in the style of the Egyptian modernists of the times, he tries to prove the compatibility of the knowledge gained from modern astronomy—which he probably knew from journals like the *Muqtaṭaf* published in Cairo—with certain sayings in the Qurʾān, the prophetic *ḥadīth* and the *ḥadīth* of the Twelver Shīʿī imams. The journal *al-ʿIlm*, which was edited by al-Shahrastānī,[5] was published under the patronage of Khurāsānī and was the most important voice for his reform ideas and those of his circle. In 1906, when ʿAlī Bāzārgān, a young Baghdadi, called for the founding of a school in which Shīʿīs in particular would be taught modern sciences and Western languages, he came under heavy attack. But he was supported by Muḥammad Saʿīd al-Ḥabbūbī, a *mujtahid* (also known as a poet), who was a member of Khurāsānī's circle. The school is said to have been founded in 1908 and to have taken up teaching activity in 1909.[6]

It can be assumed that in Shīʿī modernist circles, consideration was given not only to the founding of new schools of general education such as those just mentioned, but to the consequences for the traditional *madāris* of Najaf as well. An article written under the pseudonym "ʿIrāqī" on the texts and instructional methods used by the Shīʿīs, particularly with reference to Najaf, appeared in 1911 in the journal *Lughat al-ʿarab*, which was edited in Baghdad by Father Anastase-Marie al-Kirmilī. In 1913, al-Kirmilī published a French version signed by "Un Mésopotamien" in the *Revue du monde musulman*.[7] Neither the original nor the French version contains any outspoken criticism of the teaching methods in Najaf, but the latter does end with a weighty sentence that had either been omitted in the Arabic or was added in the French version: "Tel est, en résumé, le programme des études. J'espère qu'il sera modifié tôt ou

al-Shaykh Muḥammad Kāẓim al-Khurāsānī (Najaf, 1972); on schools, etc., pp. 135–46. Further ʿAbd al-Ḥusayn Majīd Kafāʾī, *Margī dar nūr* (Tehran [?], 1359 h/sh).

4. Reprints and translations of this book are mentioned by Kūrkīs ʿAwwād, *Muʿjam al-muʾallifīn al-ʿirāqīyīn* (Baghdad, 1969) 3.440ff.

5. On al-Shahrastānī's life and activities, see, for example, Āghā Buzurg al-Ṭihrānī, *Ṭabaqāt aʿlām al-shīʿa* (11 vols.; Najaf, 1954ff.) 1/4 (1968) 1413–18; and Jaʿfar al-Khalīlī, *Hākadhā ʿaraftuhum* (Baghdad, 1968) 2.193–212.

6. Wamīḍ Jamāl ʿUmar Naẓmī, *al-Judhūr al-siyāsīya wa-l-fikrīya wa-l-ijtimāʿīya li-l-ḥaraka al-qawmīya al-ʿarabīya al-istiqlālīya fī l-ʿIrāq* (2d ed.; Baghdad, 1985) 123; concerning Ḥabbūbī, see al-Ṭihrānī, *Ṭabaqāt*, 1/2.814–23.

7. A.-M. al-Kirmilī, "Kutub al-qirāʾa wa-ṭarīqat al-tadrīs ʿind al-shīʿa fī l-ʿIrāq," *Lughat al-ʿarab* 2 (1911) 439–44; "Le programme des études chez les chiites et principalement chez ceux de Nedjef," *RMM* 23 (1913) 268–79.

tard, pour marcher avec les progrès du siècle. Que ce jour arrive au plus vite!"[8] (The question of the authorship of the article signed "^{c}Irāqī" and the circumstances under which it was published in *Lughat al-^{c}arab* and *RMM* lie outside the purview of the present article).

The reform movement in Najaf appears to have gone through a certain period of crisis following the death of al-Khurāsānī at the end of 1911 and the defeat of the forces of the constitutional movement in Iran. The succeeding years, up to the end of the First World War—indeed, up to the establishment of the kingdom of Iraq under British mandate in 1921—were not favorable to the discussion of reform ideas among the Shī^{c}īs. After 1921, developments were strongly influenced by the efforts of Sāṭi^{c} al-Ḥuṣrī; as Director General of Education, he tried to establish an Arab nationalist, secular educational system. His memoirs, in which he also discusses the conflicts between himself and ministers of education of Shī^{c}ī origin—among them Hibat al-Dīn al-Shahrastānī—reveal a general aversion to the Shī^{c}ī clergy and a lack of understanding for the concerns of Shī^{c}ī modernists.[9]

The so-called Nuṣūlī affair of 1927, prompted by a book on the Umayyads by a Sunnī teacher from Lebanon who was working in Baghdad, turned the tensions created by al-Ḥuṣrī's educational policy into a crisis.[10] Under the influence of this crisis, the majority of the Twelver Shī^{c}īs in Iraq formed a defensive front, and it would have seemed most likely that the resulting atmosphere would not be conducive to the expression of internal, Shī^{c}ī criticism or self-criticism. However, what we find is that the most radical and detailed criticism of the teaching methods and the cultural climate in Najaf ever written by a Shī^{c}ī appeared in 1928, that is, just a year after the Nuṣūlī affair. (It seems that since then there has never again been such a vehement attack by a Shī^{c}ī theologian.) The article bore the title "Bayn al-fawḍā wa-l-ta^{c}līm al-ṣaḥīḥ." Its first part was published in the journal *al-^{c}Irfān* in Sidon (Lebanon) in September 1928.[11] The author was Muḥsin Sharāra, who described himself as a Shī^{c}ī from the Jabal ^{c}Āmil in southern Lebanon but who was living in Najaf.

8. Ibid., 279.

9. S. al-Ḥuṣrī, *Mudhakkirātī fī l-^{c}Irāq* (2 vols.; Beirut, 1967–69).

10. Werner Ende, *Arabische Nation und islamische Geschichte* (Beirut and Wiesbaden, 1977) 132–45; Hanna Batatu, *The Old Social Classes and the Revolutionary Movements of Iraq* (Princeton, N.J., 1978) 398–99.

11. M. Sharāra, "Bayn al-fawḍā wa-l-ta^{c}līm al-ṣaḥīḥ," *al-^{c}Irfān* 16 (1928) 201–7. Concerning the second installment, see p. 67 (n. 19) below. On *al-^{c}Irfān* and its importance for modern Shī^{c}ī thought, especially in Lebanon, see Tarif Khalidi, "Shaykh Ahmad ^{c}Arif al-Zayn and *Al-^{c}Irfan*," in *Intellectual Life in the Arab East, 1890–1939* (ed. Marwan R. Buheiry; Beirut, 1981) 110–24.

Shortly after it appeared, the article became known in Najaf, where it received a great deal of attention. It begins with a few comments on the ethnic background of the students and teachers at the educational institutions in Najaf and with remarks on the number of buildings devoted to education and their architectural style. This is followed by an affectionate and proud description of Najaf, dedicated by the poet and subsequent politician ᶜAlī al-Sharqī, a contemporary of Sharāra's, to his hometown.[12]

Sharāra's criticism sets in quite unexpectedly: the summers in Najaf are marked by an extremely dry heat; the houses there are built in an unhealthy fashion. This is especially true of the basement apartments beneath the houses (*sarādīb*), which are filled with standing and ill-smelling air. The city's entire supply of drinking water, which reaches Najaf over very salty terrain, is full of impurities and the urine of animals. This represents a constant danger to the students' health, and many a scholar (*fāḍil*) has fallen victim to these conditions and died, thus being torn away much too early from the Islamic community. Sharāra then writes: "The present situation of Najaf is therefore not at all suited to the presence of a university (*madrasa jāmiᶜa)* where a large number of foreigners from distant regions gather." In addition, the author says, there is an economic consideration: Prices in Najaf are in general too high, particularly those of vegetables during the summer months. In light of these conditions, the great reform theologian Mīrzā Ḥasan Shīrāzī had already considered transferring all teaching activities (*ḥaraka ᶜilmīya*) to a more favorable location, and he took the first step himself by moving from Najaf to Sāmarrā, which is better situated and has pure air and sweet, clean water. After Shīrāzī's death, however, the *madrasa* he established in Sāmarrā was closed.[13]

The person referred to is the Shīᶜī scholar of Iranian origin who issued the famous *fetwa* that played such an important role in the so-called tobacco protest in Iran in 1891–1892. For reasons more complex than those given here by Sharāra, he had moved to Sāmarrā with his pupils and followers in 1875. He died in 1895 in Sāmarrā but was buried in Najaf.[14]

Sharāra's negative opinion of the fundamental suitability of Najaf as the location for a center of Islamic learning, based on climatic, geographical, and economic reasons, would have sufficed to turn the people of Najaf against him. Their very existence depended to a considerable degree on Najaf's role as a center of Shīᶜī scholarly tradition. And although Sharāra does not express himself

12. On al-Sharqī, a Shīᶜī dissident who may have had some influence on Sharāra, see ᶜAbd al-Ḥusayn Mahdī ᶜAwwād, *al-Shaykh ᶜAlī al-Sharqī: Ḥayātuhu wa-adabuhu* (Baghdad, 1981).

13. Sharāra "Bayn al-fawḍā," 202.

14. Al-Ṭihrānī, *Ṭabaqāt*, 1/1 (1954) 436–41; Nikki R. Keddie, *Religion and Rebellion in Iran: The Iranian Tobacco Protest of 1891–1892* (London, 1966); for Shīrāzī's role, see index, 162.

anywhere in his article in a way that could be understood as an attack on the sanctity of Najaf or its importance as a place of pilgrimage, his ill-disguised proposal that consideration should again be given to transferring teaching activity to a more favorable location would have involved a considerable loss as far as the functions and prestige of Najaf were concerned.[15]

But Sharāra goes even further: there is, he continues, scarcely any intellectual life in Najaf, and this applies to both theology and literature. As far as theologians are concerned, if it were not for the well-known *mujtahids* Mīrzā Ḥusayn Nāʾīnī, Sayyid Abū l-Ḥasan Iṣfahānī, Shaykh Muḥammad Ḥusayn Kāshif al-Ghiṭāʾ, and Shaykh Āghā Ḍiyāʾ al-ʿIrāqī (all of them his teachers!),[16] as well as a few others of equal standing, the entire faculty would have disbanded long since and everyone (teachers and students) would have gone home. In what follows, Sharāra speaks more directly about the reasons for this situation.

As far as literary life is concerned, he argues that there are indeed some teachers and writers who have emphasized the necessity for reform in their works, and here he names the theologian already mentioned—Kāshif al-Ghiṭāʾ—as well as (Hibat al-Dīn) al-Shahrastānī, (Muḥammad Saʿīd) al-Ḥabbūbī, (ʿAlī) al-Sharqī, (Muḥammad Riḍā?) al-Shabībī, and "the (two?) Jawāhirīs"; but they represent only a minority, and most of the scholars in Najaf remain silent.[17]

After lamenting the widespread lack of intellectual activity in Najaf, the lethargy of the educated, the fear of reform (for example, in the form of a confrontation with modern science), Sharāra, in another section of his article, turns to the conditions under which students and teachers live in Najaf: every (modern) university both near and far operates according to fixed statutes and rules that establish the rank of professors and students in accordance with their educational level. In Najaf, however, there are—in addition to some outstanding scholars (not the least those from Jabal ʿĀmil)—a large number of turban-bearers who cause harm to the *umma* and the reputation of the *sharīʿa* through their lack of knowledge and their inactivity. So much so, he writes, that students from Najaf travel to other places in Iraq for instruction. The declining

15. It should be noted that already in 1910 a student of al-Khurāsānī's, Shaykh Asadullāh Māmaqānī, in a book published in Istanbul, is said to have proposed "that the Shiite centers of learning be moved from the Ottoman Iraq to one of Iran's holy cities . . . and the Shiite educational system be thoroughly reformed on the model of ʿAbduh's reform of al-Azhar in Egypt" (Said Amir Arjomand, "Ideological Revolution in Shiʿism," in *Authority and Political Culture in Shiʿism* [ed. Said Amir Arjomand; Albany, N.Y., 1988] 183).

16. Muḥsin al-Amīn, *Aʿyān al-shīʿa* (56 vols.; Beirut, 1958) 43.180–81.

17. For general information about the persons mentioned here, see, for example, Pierre-Jean Luizard, *La formation de l'Irak contemporain: Le rôle des oulémas chiites à la fin de la domination ottomane et au moment de la création de l'Etat* (Paris, 1991); and Yitzhak Nakash, *The Shiʿis of Iraq* (Princeton, N.J., 1994).

reputation of the *ᶜulamāʾ* has even led to a decrease in the size of the yield from endowed property directed towards the Shīᶜī holy places. There is in fact no such institution, as is the case elsewhere, that registers income and expenditures, distributes to each what is rightfully his, accepts those who are suited and turns away the unsuited, and sends out missionaries to the whole world after the conclusion of their studies. Where, Sharāra asks, is the reformer who is willing to place his own reputation at the service of the public good, who does not fear for his name—where is such a man in this center of learning where proposing an organized system of financial administration is regarded by many of the *ᶜulamāʾ* as contrary to the *sharīᶜa*?

Sharāra then lists the Islamic sciences and the subordinate disciplines that have to be studied in order to attain the standing of *mujtahid*. They include grammar, *tafsīr*, *ᶜilm al-rijāl*, and *ᶜilm al-ḥadīth*. And actually, he writes, a knowledge of the sciences of astronomy, medicine, geography, geometry, Islamic history, and other fields must be included—all subjects to which Islamic scholars of earlier generations devoted their attention and through mastery of which they became the teachers of other nations as well. In this context, Sharāra does not fail to refer to the *direct application* of those sciences in the fulfillment of a Muslim's duties, for example, in determining the direction of the *qibla* or the duty to fast. In addition to these sciences, the subjects of philosophy and *kalām* are extremely important at present, not least in the evaluation and proper uses of modern sciences, such as sociology, psychology, comparative history of religions, and foreign languages.

Sharāra adds: If we ask what is *really* taught in Najaf,[18] we find only the following subjects: *naḥw* and *ṣarf*, *ᶜilm al-manṭiq*, *balāgha*, *uṣūl al-fiqh*, and *ᶜilm al-fiqh*. In the next issue of the *ᶜIrfān* Sharāra discusses the method by which these subjects are taught.[19]

Sharāra then refers to the achievements of Shīᶜī scholars of the past in these areas: Bahāʾ al-Dīn al-ᶜĀmilī, al-ᶜAllāma al-Ḥillī, Sayyid [Muḥammad] Mahdī Baḥr al-ᶜUlūm, al-Shahīd al-Awwal, and al-Shahīd al-Thānī. The work

18. For a good survey of the curriculum and the methods of teaching, see Peter Heine, "Traditionelle Formen und Institutionen schiitischer Erziehung in der Gegenwart am Beispiel der Stadt Nadjaf/Iraq," *Zeitschrift für Missionswissenschaft und Religionswissenschaft* 74/3 (1990) 204–18, and the literature mentioned there; see also Seyyed Hossein Nasr, "The Traditional Texts Used in the Persian Madrasahs," *Traditional Islam in the Modern World* (London, 1987) 165–82, and Sabrina Mervin, "La quête du savoir à Naǧaf. Les études religieuses chez les chiᶜites imâmites de la fin du XIXᵉ siècle à 1969," *Studia Islamica* 81 (1995) 165–85.

19. "Bayn al-fawḍā wa-l-taᶜlīm al-saḥīḥ," 331–37. It should be noted here that Shaykh Muḥsin had published, in August 1928, an article in *al-ᶜIrfān* (pp. 95–100) concerning the necessity of reforms in general and at al-Azhar in particular (98ff., an article taken over from the journal *Al-Muqtaṭaf*). Obviously he did this in preparation for his attack on the system prevailing in Najaf.

of the last two, *al-Rawḍa*, still forms the basis of *fiqh* studies. (Sharāra is referring here to *al-Rawḍa al-bahīya,* a commentary by al-Shahīd al-Thānī [Zayn al-ᶜĀbidīn al-ᶜĀmilī] on the *Lumᶜa dimashqīya* by the first Shahīd, Muḥammad ibn Makkī.) In Sharāra's day, however, when the *fuqahāʾ* get to the chapter on the *qibla* in their teachings, they skip over some of the pages because they do not want to have to deal with questions of astronomy, about which they understand nothing. Similarly, there are some problems of arithmetic in questions of inheritance law that are ignored by them for lack of knowledge. The excuse given is that, in cases of need, one could turn to a merchant (God willing that one could be found at the right moment), who could carry out the computation on behalf of the *faqīh*.

Present-day scholars, Sharāra continues, would not pass the test in any of the sciences that were once cultivated by Muslims; in fact, they seek pretexts for avoiding them, raise pointless objections, or counter with the argument that true scholarship has nothing to do with these disciplines, although they are highly regarded by some contemporaries. He does not deny, says Sharāra as he concludes his argument, that in some of the *zāwiyas* in Najaf there are individuals who understand a great deal about these sciences. They received their knowledge from scholars of the preceding generation; but few of them are passing on this knowledge, and they have few students. This is the case because the disciplines have a 'modern' (*ᶜaṣrīya*) tinge and, therefore, appear to be sinful to more than just a few people in Najaf. Such a mistaken judgment, Sharāra says in the end, should arouse the indignation of all free-thinking men.

Muḥsin Sharāra's article contains many points that had already been expressed by Muslim modernists, such as Sayyid Aḥmad Khān, Muḥammad ᶜAbduh, and others, several decades earlier. But Sharāra was a young theologian at the *beginning* of his career, and besides, he raised his voice *from within* a center of traditional Islamic learning, namely Najaf. There, his critical comments and suggestions for reform, influenced in part by earlier Sunnī and Shīᶜī modernists and in effect not very original, were a provocation. Threats on his life forced him into hiding for some time.[20]

The nature of the situation in which Sharāra found himself resulted, at least in part, from his biography. Muḥsin Sharāra was born in Ṣafar 1319 (May–June, 1901) in Bint Jbayl in the Jabal ᶜĀmil in southern Lebanon and died there in 1946.[21] When his critical article on Najaf appeared, he was 27

20. Muḥammad Jawād Mughnīya, *al-Islām maᶜ al-ḥayāh* (2d ed.; Beirut, 1961) 288.

21. The most important Arabic sources available to me are the following: Jaᶜfar al-Khalīlī, *Hākadhā ᶜaraftuhum* (Baghdad, 1963) 1.121–28; al-Amīn, *Aᶜyān al-shīᶜa*, 43.179–86; Muḥammad Jawād Mughnīya, "al-Shaykh Muḥsin Sharāra," *al-ᶜIrfān* 33 (1947) 82–86; and idem, *al-Islām maᶜ al-ḥayāh*, 288–89; ᶜAlī al-Khāqānī, *Shuᶜarāʾ al-gharīy* (Najaf, 1955) 7.279–94.

years old. He was a member of an important family of scholars that had resided in Bint Jbayl for a long time,[22] and he had been sent to Najaf in 1919. There he gave early evidence of his literary talent and his interest in areas of knowledge such as mathematics and philosophy that received little attention at the *madāris* in Najaf. In addition, he sought contact with Lebanese and Syrian teachers who were employed at a state-run secondary school in Najaf. He took private instruction in English from them, a fact that was criticized by some of his fellow students and his teachers.[23]

In poems that he published in Iraqi newspapers and journals as well as in the Lebanese *ᶜIrfān*, Sharāra spoke out about cultural and social problems and ridiculed the backwardness, passivity, and false piety of many *ᶜulamāᵓ*.

Shortly after the publication of his attack on teaching in Najaf, he made himself unpopular with the people of the city once again: Sharāra took an active part in the inner-Shīᶜī controversy over the permissibility of self-flagellation and passion plays during Muḥarram. The debate had been initiated during the early twenties by the polemical writings of Sayyid Muḥsin al-Amīn. It reached its culmination at the end of 1928 and the beginning of 1929. Sharāra was one of a small group in Najaf who openly supported Muḥsin al-Amīn's call for the suppression of these practices.[24] He and others of like mind were reviled as "Umayyads" by the far more numerous defenders of self-flagellation and the passion plays, who called themselves 'the partisans of ᶜAlī' (*ᶜalawīyūn*). Muḥsin Sharāra once again had to fear for his life and went into hiding. It would appear, however, that in both of these critical situations, some of his teachers and a few other influential people in Najaf extended him their protection, perhaps in consideration of his grandfather's and his father's reputation as prominent Shīᶜī scholars.

With two *ijāzas* that, incidentally, he apparently made little effort to receive, Shaykh Muḥsin returned home in 1936 in order to attend to the needs of the community of his village. It may be that he regarded this as a kind of retreat after it became clear to him that, given what had happened, he had no future among the clergy in Najaf.

For a time, he was successful in gathering about him a large part of the youth of Bint Jbayl and in arousing their enthusiasm for his ideas of a modern,

22. See Muḥammad Hādī al-Amīnī, *Rijāl al-fikr wa-l-adab fī l-Najaf* (Najaf, 1964) 245, and the literature mentioned there.

23. Years later, Sharāra planned a full translation of Dwight M. Donaldson's *The Shiᶜite Religion* (London, 1933); see his article "Kitāb madhhab al-shīᶜa aw al-islām fī Īrān wa-l-ᶜIrāq," *al-ᶜIrfān* 31 (1945) 354–59.

24. Werner Ende, "The Flagellations of Muḥarram and the Shiᶜite ᶜUlamāᵓ," *Der Islam* 55 (1978) 19–36.

socially committed Islam. It was such young people who one day drove out of Bint Jbayl, under a hail of stones, two Shīᶜī scholars from Tyre, who had been among the opponents of Sharāra's modernist activities in Najaf. (One of the two was Sayyid ᶜAbd al-Ḥusayn Sharaf al-Dīn, an uncle of Imām Mūsā Ṣadr).[25] The general atmosphere in Jabal ᶜĀmil, however, which was determined by the dominant Shīᶜī *zuᶜamāᵓ* in consort with conservative *ᶜulamāᵓ*, was not favorable to Shaykh Muḥsin's modernist efforts. During the last years of his life, he was increasingly overcome by a sense of failure. In addition, he contracted tuberculosis, which was eventually the cause of his death in 1946.[26]

With the exception of the excitement he caused in Najaf in 1928–29, Muḥsin Sharāra's life was relatively undramatic. His attempt to cast off the shackles of traditional education is not a complete exception within the world of Shīᶜī centers of learning in the twentieth century. But very few expressed themselves with the same kind of clarity, and of those few, there were only a handful, for example, Sharāra's compatriot Ḥusayn Muruwwa[27] or the Iranian ᶜAlī Dashtī,[28] who were able to free themselves early on from the influence of their families and from the careers as religious scholars that had been marked out for them.

This was not the case with Muḥsin Sharāra. A better understanding of the dilemma of the Shīᶜī modernists up to the present would be well served, I think, by a more detailed study of the biography, writings—still unedited—and social activities of Muḥsin Sharāra, both in Iraq and in southern Lebanon.

25. Khalīlī, *Hākadhā*, 1.127.

26. Ibid., 128.

27. Both Sharāra and Muruwwa were members of a modernist group in Najaf called "*al-shabība al-ᶜāmilīya al-najafīya*." See ᶜAbbās Bayḍūn (ed.), *Ḥusayn Muruwwa: Wulidtu shaykhan wa-amūtu ṭiflan* (Beirut, 1990) 39 (and photograph p. [74]); on Muruwwa, see also Peter Gran, "Islamic Marxism in Comparative History: The Case of Lebanon, Reflections on the Recent Book of Husayn Muruwah," in *The Islamic Impulse* (ed. Barbara Freyer Stowasser; London, 1987) 106–20.

28. F. R. C. Bagley, "Note on the Author," in *Dashti: Twenty Three Years* (trans. Bagley; London, 1985) ix–xiv. For a rather critical assessment of Dashtī's career as a writer, see Bozorg Alavi, *Geschichte und Entwicklung der modernen persischen Literatur* (Berlin, 1964) 222ff.

Sūra as Guidance and Exhortation: The Composition of *Sūrat al-Nisāʾ*

A. H. Mathias Zahniser

My studies under Georg Krotkoff at the Johns Hopkins University focused on Arabic, Persian, and Syriac texts. Every session of Professor Krotkoff's seminars involved creative interaction between mentor, student, and text. Held in his office where his resources for textual analysis were at hand, the seminars provided a setting where he could serve as both teacher and model. Rather than merely checking the results of our textual analysis against his, he enabled us to share in the process by which he obtained his results. The reward for me has been a lifetime of enjoyment in the study of texts. This essay is presented in gratitude to him for the depth of his expertise in both the subject matter and process of his teaching, and for his attitudes toward his students, humane learning, and the interpretation of texts.

Author's note: An abbreviated version of this study was presented at a session of the Qurʾān and Ḥadīṯ at the American Academy of Religion, November, 1994.

In this process-oriented pedagogy, we followed one dictum religiously: suggest an amendment to the text only as a remote possibility—an absolute last resort. We listened long and carefully to any text, seeking inductively to grasp its meaning.[1] This conviction also informed Professor Krotkoff's view that future breakthroughs in the study of the Qur^ᵓān would be literary.

This literary emphasis informs the present study, which rests on two convictions: (1) that the canonical text of the Qurᵓān, whatever its historical development may have been, has an integrity of its own and a commensurate impact on its readers and hearers; and (2) that, since position is hermeneutic,[2] attention to composition and structure can contribute significantly to understanding the meaning of the sūra.[3] These convictions have informed a number of recent Qurᵓānic studies, most of which focus on sūras from the Meccan period of the Prophet Muḥammad's mission.[4] I have chosen to focus on the composition of a sūra from the Medinan period.

Sūrat al-nisāᵓ ('The Sūra of Women') has been chosen for analysis partly because, on the surface, it appears to defy a fully satisfactory accounting of its compositional structure. At best, it might be characterized as "stream-of-

1. Another aspect of Professor Krotkoff's approach was to study a text in its religious context intertextually. For example, we read the Sūra of the Cave, then Arabic and Persian commentaries on it, and finally a modern play based on the People of the Cave.

2. I am grateful to Stanley D. Walters for this useful formulation (*The Book of Reversals: An Essay on the Organization and Purpose of Samuel* [Toronto: Self-published, 1990] p.45). It is not altogether dissimilar to the conviction of the Pakistani Qurᵓānic interpreter Amīn Aḥsan Iṣlāḥī and his teacher Ḥamīd al-Dīn ᶜAbd al-Ḥamīd al-Farahī that Qurᵓānic *naẓm* (thematic and structural coherence) is an exegetical principle; see Mustansir Mir, *Coherence in the Qurᵓān: A Study of Iṣlāḥī's Concept of Naẓm in* Taddabur-i *Qurᵓān* (Indianapolis, Ind.: American Trust Publications, 1986).

3. I do not claim to have discerned the final or complete meaning of the Sūra of Women. That would depend upon far more than I have brought to this analysis. For example, very little attention has been given to the commentaries in this paper. The method followed in my contribution requires the full attention of the analyst to the sūra itself. I, therefore, offer only what such a procedure can offer.

4. For the Meccan period, see Anne A. Ambrose, "Die Analyse von Sura 112," *Der Islam* 63 (1986) 219–47; Pierre Capron de Caprona, *Le Coran aux sources de la parole oraculaire: Structures rhythmique des sourates mecquoises* (Paris: Publicationes Orientalistes de France, 1981); Angelika Neuwirth, "Zur Struktur der *Yusuf*-Sure," in *Studien aus Arabistik und Semitistik: Anton Spitaler zum siebzigsten Geburtstag von seinen Schülern überreicht* (ed. Werner Diem and Stefan Wild; Wiesbaden: Harrassowitz, 1980); idem, *Studien zur Komposition der mekkanischen Suren* (Studien zur Sprache, Geschichte und Kultur des islamischen Orients, n.s. 10; Berlin: de Gruyter, 1981); Michael Sells, "Sound, Spirit, and Gender in Sūrat al-Qadr," *JAOS,* 111 (1991) 239–59; and Irfan Shahid, "The Sūra of the Poets: Another Contribution to Koranic Exegesis," *Journal of Arabic Literature* 14 (1983) 1–21. For the Medinan period, see Mir, *Coherence*, especially pp. 45–63; and my "Word of God and the Apostleship of ᶜIsā: A Narrative Analysis of ᵓĀl ᶜImrān (3):33–62," *JSS,* 37 (1991) 77–112.

consciousness" discourse;[5] at worst, as disjointed and confused.[6] The clear difficulty in discovering the sūra's over-all compositional structure, however, does not necessarily mean that it has been haphazardly composed, or that it has no organizing principle.[7] On the other hand, if an intentional ordering does characterize the sūra, an adequate accounting of its structure may very well reveal that structure to be unprecedented. By means of a relatively close reading of the whole sūra from the lexical level on up, I have attempted to understand its overall structure. Although I have used a number of models for inductive study of texts,[8] I have tried to do so heuristically, striving to allow the sūra to guide me to its own structure.

5. See the discussion of the stream-of-consciousness novel in William F. Thrall, Addison Hibbard, and C. Hugh Holman (eds.), *A Handbook to Literature* (2d ed.; New York: Odyssey, 1960) 471–72.

6. For example, H. A. R. Gibb says that "the present composition of the longer suras" are characterized by "unevenness and . . . rough jointing" (*Mohammedanism* [London: Oxford University Press, 1964] 36). According to . . . Richard Bell, Qurʾānic discourse is "disjointed." He indicates that one rarely finds a "sustained unified composition" of any significant length (*Introduction to the Qurʾān* [Edinburgh: Edinburgh University Press, 1953] 72; see also pp. 85ff.). His assessment, however, does not apply to the "short units" of which, according to him, the longer sūras are composed (p. 72). Moḥammad Khalīfa has collected some of these negative assessments in *The Sublime Qurʾān and Orientalism* (London: Longman, 1983) 20, and Mustansir Mir, who takes a more sober look at the phenomenon, also references Western assertions about the lack of coherence in the Qurʾān (*Coherence*, 2).

7. Recent cross-cultural studies of discourse have emphasized the variety of ways in which discourse can be organized. What looks like disorganization to one culture might be clearly organized by the standards and conventions of another. See, for example, the different partitioning devices treated by Joseph E. Grimes in *The Thread of Discourse* (Janua Linguarum, Series Minor 207; Berlin: Mouton, 1975) 102–7. Such a cultural insight stands behind Mir's report of al-Farahī's insight that "following the standard literary practice of its time, the Qurʾān usually omits what are known as the transitional words and expressions—a Qurʾānic stylistic feature that can be most exasperating to a modern reader, accustomed as he is to styles that make abundant use of such connecting links" (*Coherence*, 41–42).

8. David Bauer, *The Structure of Matthew's Gospel: A Study in Literary Design* (Bible and Literature Series 15; Sheffield: Almond, 1988); John Beekman, John Callow, and Michael Kopesec, *The Semantic Structure of Written Communication* (5th ed.; Dallas: Summer Institute of Linguistics, 1981); Neuwirth, "Zur Struktur"; idem, *Studien*; H. Van Dyke Parunak, "Transitional Techniques in the Bible," *JBL* 102 (1983) 525–48; Robert A. Traina, *Methodical Bible Study* (New York: Bookroom of the Biblical Seminary in New York, 1952); and Stanley D. Walters, "Wood, Sand and Stars: Structure and Theology in Gn 22:119," *Toronto Journal of Theology* 3 (1987) 301–30. The method of Amīn Aḥsan Iṣlāḥī is also thoroughly inductive. His work must also be considered with these other inductive approaches. Since his work is in Urdu, I have not yet been able to study it. Since Mustansir Mir has given us a thorough analysis of his work in English, I have been able to make use of it in this study. In fact, Mir chooses to summarize Iṣlāḥī's analysis of Sūrat al-Nisāʾ as a sample of the Pakistani scholar's treatment of Medinan sūras (*Coherence* 45–63). Unfortunately space does not permit a thorough engagement with Mir's significant book.

While thematic analysis contributed the most to discerning the overall structure, attention to formal features such as verse structure,[9] rhyme pattern,[10] and concatenation[11] were also important for the analysis.[12]

In order to make the discussion more accessible for readers who do not know Arabic, wherever possible I use my own English translation, rather than the Arabic text from which the analysis was made.[13] Where reference to the Arabic text is necessary, an English translation is given in the text or in the notes.

The Women Material

We begin our analysis by identifying a block, a cluster, and a verse dealing with women through attention to theme borders, repeated phrases, and rhyme-pattern change.

The material dealing with women from which the sūra takes its name is confined to three parts of the sūra: a major block that begins it (vv. 1–43),[14] a

9. See Neuwirth, *Studien* 16–19 and 117–73.

10. See ibid., 14–16 and 65–115.

11. Concatenation is a transition device used by a narrator. Narrators may foreshadow an approaching section of their discourse by advancing a thematic element from the next section. They may also include an element from the previous section in the early cola of the section following it (Parunak, "Transitional Techniques in the Bible," 526). Neuwirth discovered that rhyme change in the Meccan sūras plays a significant role in indicating structure. Often the transition from one unit indicated by a given rhyme scheme to another unit indicated by a different rhyme scheme is signaled by concatenation. That is, the rhyme scheme change does not take place immediately at the break between the two units of discourse, but a verse or a few verses before or after it (*Studien*, 113). In *Sūrat al-Nisāᵓ*, thematic concatenation occurs as a transition device. This device may be a substitute for the transitional words, the absence of which al-Farahī contends makes the Qurᵓānic discourse exasperating at times (*Dalāᵓil al-niẓām* [Asamgarh, India: al-Dāᵓira al-hamīdiyya wa-maktabatuhā, 1388/1968] 65–67. See the full quotation from Mir (*Coherence*, 41–42) in n. 7 above.

12. This study is being presented in the reverse order from that in which it was carried out. I started with verses as the basic units of revelation (Neuwirth, *Studien*, p. 117) and worked up thematic units (Neuwirth's *Gesätze* [ibid., 6]) based on verse clusters. Next, I identified larger units of composition based mainly on thematic content and then moved to the larger indicators of structure, such as repeated cola. Counting verses and cola was the last step of all. That is, the analysis was carried out at first without considering symmetry or proportion.

13. I worked from a colometric transliteration of the text of the sūra. Angelika Neuwirth's colometric analysis ("Zur Struktur der *Yusuf*-Sure" and *Studien zur Komposition der mekkanischen Suren*) contributed significantly to the refining of my own structural diagrams (see "The Word of God," 83, 90–92). The structural diagram of *Sūrat al-nisāᵓ* from which I worked can be obtained by writing to me (Asbury Theological Seminary, Wilmore, KY 40390).

14. I am including v. 43 in this block, even though it is a transition verse, the subject matter of which differs from the subject matter of the preceding and succeeding thematic units. The word *an-nisāᵓ* does, however, occur in the verse. Iṣlāḥī also finds vv. 1–43 a major unit of the sūra. He refers to its content as social reform (*Tadabbur-i Qurᵓān,* 8 vols. [vols. 1–2: Lahore: Dār al-ishāᶜāt

cluster of verses that features a brief summary of the earlier block along with a case not treated there (vv. 127–35),[15] and an isolated long verse at its very end (v. 176). These three passages will be referred to in what follows as the Women Block, the Women Cluster, and the Women Verse.[16]

In addition to its thematic continuity with the Women Block, the Women Verse is linked to the block by rhyme-pattern divergence. The final clause (*fāṣila*) of v. 176 has a rhyme pattern (CaCīC)[17] that differs from the main rhyme pattern of the sūra (CaCīCā) and that occurs in six other verses, all but one of which are within the Women Block (vv. 12, 13, 14, 25, 26, and 44). In fact, if three of the five Islamic traditional versification systems are correct, the verse break between vv. 44 and 45 is a mistake, leaving all the divergent verses within the women material.[18] Angelika Neuwirth finds this kind of rhyme change significant as an indicator of the structure of the Meccan sūras.[19]

The divergent rhyme scheme in the Women Verse, being identical to that of the Women Block and found nowhere else in the sūra, serves to strengthen the link between the verse and the block. The only other divergent rhyme pattern in the entire sūra (CaCūCū) occurs in v. 3.[20]

---

al-Islāmiyya, 1387–91/1967–71; vols. 3–4: Lahore: Anjuman-i Khuddām'ulqurʾān, 1393–96/1973–76; vols. 5–8: Lahore: Fārā Foundation, 1398–1400/1977–80] 2.9–10; cited in Mir, *Coherence*, 46–47).

15. Verses 137–43 make up a unit with a chiastic structure, and vv. 127–34 represent a thematic unit. Verses 135–36, each of which begins with an address to those who believe, represent a transition device in that v. 135 is thematically connected with the verses preceding it, and v. 136 with verses following it.

16. The related subjects of orphans and inheritance are also confined to this "women" material. Both of these subsidiary themes occur in vv. 1–43, orphans in vv. 127–35, and inheritance in v. 176.

17. All of these final words end in /n/ or /m/.

18. Anton Spitaler, *Die Verszählung des Koran nach islamischer Überlieferung* (Munich: Bayerischen Akademie, 1935) 35. In fact, the versification traditions treated by Spitaler for Sūrat al-Nisāʾ differ only here and at v. 173, where the Syrian tradition alone makes a verse division at *ʿalīman*, one colon before the verse ending in the other traditions. Gustav Flügel (*Corani textus arabicus* [3d ed.; Leipzig, 1883]) eliminates the verse division between vv. 44 and 45, against the Cairo text, that is, the Kufic tradition, and inserts one in v. 173 with the Syrian tradition. He inserts a verse division on his own in the middle of v. 46 (at *fī l-dīn*) and in the middle of v. 172 (at *muqarrabūn*). The presence of the divergent rhyme, whether at 44 or in 46, could also be attributed to rhyme concatenation (see n. 11 above) and thus contribute to my argument here. I do not understand why Flügel posited *muqarrabūn* as a rhyme ending (*fāṣila*)—technically it rhymes with *muqarrabīn*—but no similar rhyme divergence occurs in sūra 4.

19. Neuwirth, *Studien*, 91ff.

20. I cannot establish any structural significance for this unique rhyme pattern. Verse 47 ends with *mafʿūlā*—a slight divergence from the standard pattern. Verse 47 is closely connected with v. 48, which in turn is identical with v. 116. Since these verses figure prominently in my analysis, I am tempted to see the rhyme divergence as marking the prominence of vv. 47–48.

Furthermore, the Women Cluster and the Women Verse are linked by the fact that they begin with parallel phrases. Verse 127 begins, "And they will ask you for a pronouncement about women. Say: . . ."[21] And v. 176 starts with, "They will ask you for a pronouncement. Say: . . ."[22] No other instances of this phrase occur in the Qurʾān. The phenomenon of repeated phrases has proven an indicator of sūra divisioning in other sūras,[23] and, thus, it is safe to say that the Women Cluster and the Women Verse are linked in a structurally significant way.[24]

Before we can proceed to a discussion of the other obvious thematic block in the sūra, we must deal with the question as to why v. 176 comes at the end, as though it were simply tacked on to the sūra. It is of course possible that the verse was simply placed there because of its connection with similar motifs in the sūra, no attempt being made to integrate it with the Women Block or the Women Cluster. But if this is the case, the sūra must have represented such a compositional unity that the putative redactor felt obliged not to embed the verse in some other place. The most likely answer to the question about the position of v. 176 seems to be that it is meant, along with vv. 127–35, to serve some compositional purpose. Obviously without v. 176, there would be no section five, vv. 127–76, corresponding thematically with section one, vv. 1–43. Before we can lay out the major sections of the sūra, we must deal briefly with its center section.

The Battle Block

The section comprising vv. 71–104 contains all of the references in the sūra to fighting in the way of God. I have therefore referred to it as the Battle Block.[25]

21. *Wa-yastaftūnaka fī n-nisāʾi qul. . . .* The translations of the Qurʾān are mine.

22. *Yastaftūnaka qul. . . .*

23. Neuwirth, *Studien*, 239–41.

24. Iṣlāḥī also considers vv. 127–76 one of the three main sections of sūra 4. Section one, according to his analysis is mentioned in n. 14 above, section two consists of vv. 44–126 and deals with the Islamic community and its opponents, and section three he calls the conclusion to the sūra. The long verse, 176, he considers a supplement to v. 12 in section one (*Tadabbur*, 2.9–10; cited in Mir, *Coherence*, 46–47).

25. *Qitāl* and other words from its root are repeated again and again throughout vv. 71–93. Although vv. 94–104 do not contain any more instances of *qitāl* words, they do continue to involve the subject matter of fighting in the way of God. The participle, *al-mujāhidūn*, occurs three times in v. 95. As far as I can tell from Mir's presentation, Iṣlāḥī does not pick up on the thematic uniqueness of vv. 71–104. Rather he treats its three major subdivisions as parts of his central section (vv. 44–126) (ibid.). For other aspects of Iṣlāḥī's analysis, see nn. 24 and 14.

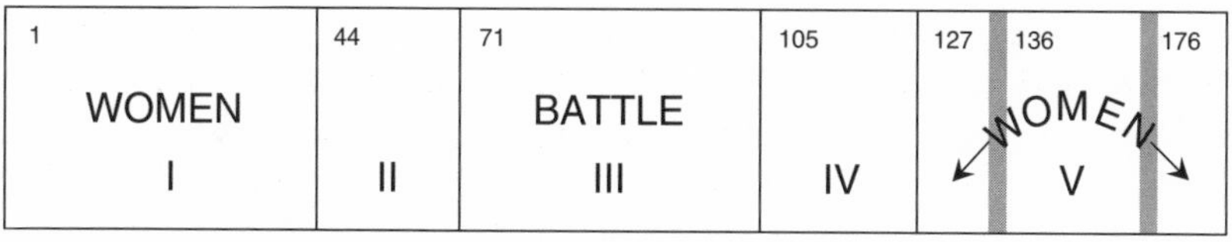

Figure 1. The Five Sections of Sūra 4

Like the Women Block, the Women Cluster, and the Women Verse, its major theme is not found outside its borders.

The Major Divisions of the Sūra

So far we have identified three major thematic sections of material in the sūra, two sections related to the theme from which the sūra takes its name, and a third determined by the theme of fighting in the way of God. The first section, the Women Block, begins the sūra; the second section, bounded by the Women Cluster and the Women Verse, ends the sūra; and the third section, the Battle Block, lies at the center. On the basis of this analysis, then, we can divide the sūra into five main sections (see fig. 1): section I, the Women Block (vv. 1–43); section II, the material between it and the Battle Block (vv. 44–70); section III, the Battle Block (vv. 71–104); section IV, the material between the Battle Block and the last section (vv. 105–26); and section V, the unit beginning with the Women Cluster and ending with the Women Verse (vv. 127–76).

Two questions arising from the analysis, summarized in fig. 1, must be addressed: what are the content and the role of sections two and four, and what is the import of the hollowness of section V? Answers to both questions prove crucial for the interpretation of the sūra; but before we address them directly, we must look at the impact on structure of two related phenomena: formulas of address and repeated cola.

Formulas of Address

Since the five formulas of address that occur in the sūra obviously represent caesuras in the discourse, we must investigate their significance for its overall compositional structure. We shall discuss the first formula, "O you people," which occurs at three strategic places for the composition of the sūra (vv. 1, 170, and 174) after we have dealt with the sūra's overall structure more thoroughly.

While the instances of the second formula, "O you who believe" (vv. 19, 29, 43, 59, 71, 94, 135, 136, and 144), play a role in the structuring of the narrative, they do not help us to discern the overall composition of the sūra. Both the third and the fourth formulas, "O you to whom the book has been given" (v. 47) and "O people of the book" (v. 171), occur only once, the latter in a strategic place, which will be discussed below in connection with the first formula. The occurrences of the fifth formula, addressed to the Prophet, "Have you not observed" (vv. 44, 49, 51, 60, and 77), relate to the sūra's overall structure. All but the last occurrence of this formula come between the Women Block (vv. 1–43) and the Battle Block (vv. 71–104). Since the occurrence of the formula in v. 77 amounts to an instance of the transition device common to Quranic discourse known as concatenation,[26] this formula of address ends up being distinctive of the second section of the sūra (vv. 44–70), a conclusion further supporting the overall structure illustrated in fig. 1. We turn now to a recurrence of cola and verses other than formulas of address, which will further establish that section V (vv. 127–76) is a discrete unit of discourse.

Recurrent Cola

We have already seen that the recurrent colon "they will ask you for a pronouncement" (vv. 127 and 176) serves to link the Women Cluster and the Women Verse. We saw how the formula of address to the Prophet "have you not observed" is peculiar to section II and thus supports the structure of the sūra that I am advancing here. Another set of recurring cola also supports that structure.

A Sovereignty Colon

The sentence "God owns everything in heaven and on earth," with slight variations, recurs six times in the sūra (vv. 126, 131 [2x], 132, 170, and 171).[27] Except for verse 126, which can be considered an instance of concatenation, all these cola fall within the fifth section of the sūra.

The fact that this colon, repeated often in the Qurᵓān, occurs generally in contexts emphasizing the sovereignty of God (e.g., ᵓĀl ᶜImrān [3]:29 and al-Tawba [9]:116, both Medinan sūras) and often in connection with passages denying that God has begotten a son (e.g., al-Baqara [2]:116, a Medinan sūra, and al-Anᶜām [6]:101, a Meccan sūra) will be significant for an interpretation

26. See n. 11 above.

27. A merism meaning "everything belongs to God."

of one aspect of the meaning of the sūra's structure.[28] This aspect of the meaning of the sūra's structure is related to the appearance in sections II and IV of a striking doublet.

A Striking Doublet

Verse 48 in section II reads as follows: "Never will God forgive associating any being with him, although he will forgive whomever he pleases for lesser sins. Whoever, therefore, associates any being with God has committed a great transgression." Verse 116 in section IV differs only in its rhyme colon (*fāṣila*), so that its last sentence reads, "Whoever, therefore, associates any being with God has gone far astray." Since these verses have no counterpart in the other sūras of the Qurʾān, they form a striking set of recurrent cola. Verses 57 and 122 are almost identical as well. While this fact reinforces the argument of this paragraph, it is less telling than the parallel character of vv. 48 and 116 because the parallel cola of these verses occur frequently in the Qurʾān.[29] Angelika Neuwirth concludes in her study of the Meccan sūra of Joseph (12) that an occurrence of identical cola (or even closely parallel cola) in different scenes of a sūra indicates that the respective scenes reference each other.[30] Her conclusion, although about a Meccan sūra, suggests that we should at least pay careful attention to such a prominent set of exactly parallel cola as vv. 48 and 116 in our Medinan sūra. If we can establish a plausible link between the sections of the sūra in which they are located, we would be warranted in considering this doublet an indicator of the comparative or contrastive import of the passages in which the verses are embedded. This link, which I will establish below, reinforces the fivefold structure of *Sūrat al-nisāʾ* illustrated in fig. 1. Thematically, like the recurrent colon "the heavens and the

28. The affirmation "the heavens and the earth belong to God" in its several forms occurs in a sizable number of both Meccan and Medinan Qurʾānic verses. The verses are of several types: some feature God's unqualified transcendence (e.g., al-Baqara [2]:255); some refer to his all-inclusive knowledge and power (e.g., al-Baqara [2]:284); others stress God's unchallengeable transcendence (e.g., ʾĀl ʿImrān [3]:129); some verses with this phrase stress God's invulnerability (e.g., al-Nisāʾ [4]:131); and some stress his sole sufficiency (e.g., al-Baqara [2]:107). It is God's all sufficiency that is frequently connected with the denial that he has begotten a son (al-Baqara [2]:116, al-Nisāʾ [4]:171, al-ʾAnʿām [6]:101, Yūnus [10]:68, al-ʾAnbiyāʾ [21]:26, al-Furqān [25]:2).

29. I did a careful study of this whole section and failed to uncover any significance in the occurrence of both 48/116 and 57/122, unless it serves to reinforce the fact that these sections of the sūra should be read together. I am indebted to Neal Robinson for comments on this passage received in a personal communication, in the spring of 1994.

30. Neuwirth, "Zur Struktur," 144; see also my "Word of God," 97–98.

TABLE 1. The Relative Size of the Panels of Sūra 4

Panels	*Verses*	*Cola*	*Words*
I (1–43)	43	241	1,060
V (127–76)	50	245	999
II (44–70)	37	99	464
IV (105–26)	22	92	350
III (71–104)	34	204	856

earth belong to God" discussed above, these verses relate to the exhortation of the People of the Book not to make exaggerated claims about Christ and to believe in God and his prophet (vv. 170–73). We shall return to this theme below. But here we note that the linking function of these verses reinforces the structural analysis so far advanced. We are now ready to compare the relative sizes of the five sections into which the sūra is divided.

Size and Structure

The structure of the sūra discerned so far by thematic and structural indicators finds support in the relative balance of sections I and V and sections II and IV. Section I (241 cola) is roughly equivalent to section V (245 cola), and sections II (99 cola) and IV (92 cola) correspond closely. Table 1 demonstrates this relative balance in size of the sūra's corresponding sections.

Two structural questions must be answered before a final interpretation of the meaning of the sūra's structure can be offered: first, what is the relationship of sections II and IV signaled by the doublet, vv. 48 and 116? Second, how should the "hollow" nature of section V be understood? The two problems turn out to be related.

The Prominence of the People of the Book

Section II and the "hollow" part of section V (vv. 135–75) both feature the People of the Book prominently (vv. 44–58, 153–62, and 170–75) but not exclusively. Structural signals in both of these sections, however, indicate the prominence of the People of the Book in the intentionality of the sūra. The first signal is the relation between the formula of address "O you people" (vv. 1,

170, and 174) and the tidy structure of the thematic unit (vv. 170–74) for which the formula serves as an inclusio.[31]

"O You People!"

After the opening colon, "In the name of God the compassionate, the merciful," the words "O you people" are the first words of the sūra.[32] The content of its first verse suggests that the sūra addresses the broadest possible audience, since its controlling verbs are parallel imperatives that enjoin reverent fear toward God, supported by propositions that introduce thematically the women material from which the sūra takes its name:[33]

> O you people!
> Fear your Lord who created you from one person,
> and from him created his counterpart,
> extending from the two of them many men—and women;[34]
> fear God about whom you question each other, and the wombs.
> Surely God sees you.

This formula occurs again only at the beginning of vv. 170 and 174, where it functions as an inclusio for the penultimate thematic unit of the sūra (vv. 170–75).[35] Since both the content and the structure of this impressive thematic unit

31. According to H. Van Dyke Parunak ("Oral Typesetting: Some Uses of Biblical Structure," *Bib* 62 [1981] 158–62), the term *inclusio* goes back to David H. Müller (*Die Propheten in ihrer ursprünglichen Form* [Vienna: Alfred Holder, 1896]).

32. According to Fakhr al-Dīn al-Rāzī, the consensus of interpreters is that the formula under discussion addresses all those in general upon whom the regulations of the sūra are incumbent. He supports this with the following points: (1) the definite article with the collective noun (*al-nās*) conveys the idea of completion; (2) the fact that men and women are portrayed as all descendants of Adam indicates that God must intend the formula to be understood as 'all people'; and (3) the charge to revere God is the right of all people in general (*al-Tafsīr al-kabīr* [33 vols.; Cairo: Maṭbaᶜat al-bahīya, 1938] 9:157–58).

33. According to Muḥammad Jamāl al-Qāsimī (*Tafsīr al-Qāsimī: Maḥāsin al-taʾwīl* [ed. Muḥammad Fuʾād ᶜAbd al-Bāqī; 17 vols.; Cairo: ᶜĪsā al-Bābī al-Ḥalabī, 1957] 5.1093), the sūra is called the Sūra of Women because more is revealed about women in it than in any other sūra.

34. The structure of this colon marks 'women' as prominent: *wa-baththa minhumā rijālan wa-l-nisāʾan*.

35. Both members of the inclusio are followed by an announcement of the reliability of the revelation that has come to the people. Parunak identifies two types of inclusios, internal and external. Internal inclusios are integral to the paragraph(s) in which they occur and segment material into discrete units like any chiasm. External inclusios are not integral in this way and serve to mark off material that, like a footnote, is not crucial to the flow of the discourse ("Oral Typesetting," 162). On strictly formal grounds, the inclusio we are discussing (170–74/75) is of the external type, since vv. 170 and 174/75 stand out from verses 171–73 by the fact that they are typical

figure in the analysis of the meaning of the compositional structure of the sūra advanced here, a complete translation follows:

O you people!
The Apostle has come to you with the truth from your Lord.
So believe! It is better for you.
But if you disbelieve,
so what? God owns everything in heaven and on earth.
God is all-knowing and wise (170).
O People of the Book!
Do not go beyond the truth in your religion,
speak correctly about God.
The Messiah, Jesus son of Mary,
is strictly the apostle of God
and God's word, which he delivered to Mary—
and a spirit from him.
So believe in God and in his apostle.
And do not say "Three."
Desist! It is better for you.
God is strictly one God.
He is exalted well beyond having a child.
He owns everything in heaven and on earth;
God needs no deputy (171).
The Messiah will never be too proud to be a servant of God,
nor will God's intimates, the angels.
Those too proud to be God's servants, who are haughty,
he will force to come to him *en masse* (172).
But to those who believe and do good deeds
he will give their full due,
and even more from his bounty.
But those who despise servanthood and exalt self,
those are the ones he will painfully punish;
and for them—other than God—there will be neither
benefactor nor helper (173).
O you people,
a proof has come to you from your Lord,
and we have revealed to you clear light (174).
Those who believe in God and cling to him,
them he shall plunge into his own mercy and grace,
and lead them to himself upon a straight path (175).

Confirmation of Revelation verses that have proven significant for structuring the Meccan sūras (Neuwirth, *Studien*, 250–53).

The prominence of this formula of address at the beginning of the sūra and the fact that its only other occurrences make up the inclusio of its penultimate thematic unit suggests three considerations for determining the interpretation of the Sūra of Women. First, the position of these formulas suggests that the core of the thematic unit which the inclusio includes is important for an interpretation of the sūra as a whole. Second, since the position of these formulas would make such an impressive beginning and end for the whole sūra, the position of the Women Verse as the sūra's final thematic unit must be significant for understanding the message of the sūra as a whole. Both of these considerations are based on the principle, identified at the outset of the essay, that position is hermeneutic. The third consideration is of the same order. The position of vv. 170–73 between the formulas in vv. 170 and 174 gives their theme a certain prominence. The fact that they address the People of the Book[36] who believe in Jesus, warning them against making exaggerated claims for him and against saying that God is three, or that he could have a child, makes this emphasis significant for the interpretation of the sūra as a whole.

Thus, the penultimate thematic unit, embedded in the last section of the sūra, which is formed by the Women Cluster and the Women Verse, contains an elaborate plea to the People of the Book who believe in Jesus. Of course the sūra addresses people other than Christians: the Prophet, believers, Jews, hypocrites, and unbelievers. But the Christians are made prominent among them by this final appeal within an inclusio addressed to the broadest audience of the sūra. This conclusion accords with the connection between the recurrent formula "the heavens and earth belong to God," which occurs only in section V, and the conviction that God would not have begotten a son. This connection is made explicit in v. 171, "He is exalted well beyond having a child. He owns everything in heaven and on earth; God needs no deputy" (171). The connection between sections II and IV, identified by the doublet, vv. 48 and 116, relates to this theme.

A Charge of Idolatry

The second major signal indicating the prominence of the People of the Book in the sūra is the doublet identified above (vv. 48 and 116) connecting sections II and IV. At first glance, these sections appear to have little in common. The focus in section II is on the People of the Book (a theme reintroduced in section V), where the charge is to believe in Muḥammad as God's messenger and in the scripture that has been given to him. Verse 48 appears intrusive in this context.

36. *Yāʾahla l-kitāb* (171). These "scriptuaries" include Jews, Christians, and Sabians.

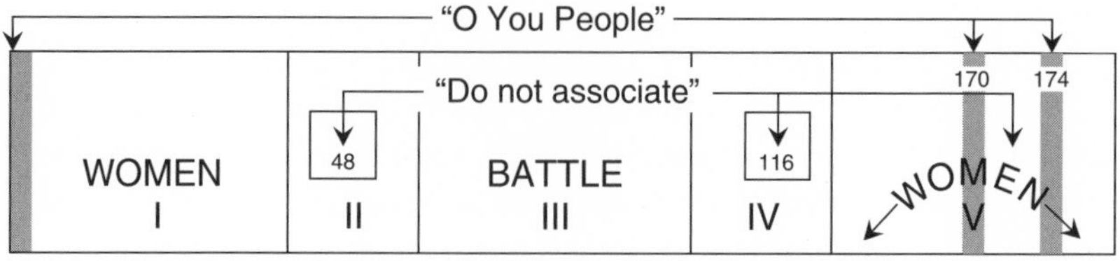

Figure 2. The Composition of Sūra 4

The focus in section IV, however, is on those among the Qurʾān's audience who are from a traditional Arabian religious background. In the immediate context of v. 116, the people addressed are the ones who, having once received the message, split off from the Apostle (v. 115), invoking females or Satan instead of God (v. 117). In this context, the verse seems to fit well.

What relationship between their respective contexts do these identical verses signal? If we interpret the passage in which the verse appears angular in the light of the passage in which it fits well, we become aware of another dimension of the sūra's warning to the People of the Book. They are being warned against the kind of 'association' of which the "pagans" are guilty: "Whoever associates [*yushrik*] any being with God has committed a great transgression" (v. 48). The relationship of sections II and IV, interpreted by means of the doublet, now appears clearer. In the light of that relationship, the doublet represents a foreshadowing of the final and prominent appeal in section V to the People of the Book (vv. 171–73) which we have just quoted and discussed.

Structure and Meaning

Figure 2 offers a more elaborate schematic of *Sūrat al-nisāʾ*. While it necessarily oversimplifies the content of the sūra, it demonstrates the impact of its overall structure. Ignoring for the moment the "hollowness" of section V, we notice that sections I, III, and V deal with guidance for the community of faith in such areas as family relations, marriage, divorce, inheritance, treatment of orphans, and the obligation to fight in the cause of God. The palindromic structure of the sūra endows this aspect of the sūra's guidance with an unchangeable and eternal quality. The focus is on its center, the Battle Block, which stresses the requirement, incumbent upon the community of faith, of fighting in the cause of God and in the cause of the community's weaker members: "And what is with you not fighting in the cause of God, and for helpless men, women, and children who are saying, 'Our Lord, Get us out of this city whose people are oppressors;

and provide your own guardian for us; and provide your own helper for us'?" (v. 75).

But the sūra also exhorts the whole of humanity, including the People of the Book. Christians in particular are exhorted to jettison the accretions that have crept into their faith and to accept only God as God and Muḥammad as his prophet. This function is not only signaled by the doublet connecting sections II and IV, but also by the very movement of the sūra indicated by the People-of-the-Book material embedded in section V and connected with the opening verse of the sūra through the formula of address, "O you people." In contrast with the changeless quality of the sūra as guidance, the sūra as exhortation suggests movement. The linking of sections II, IV, and the prominent penultimate thematic unit of V endows the sūra, as exhortation, with a dynamic quality and a sense of urgency.[37]

In fact, the guidance and the exhortation may be linked by the suggestion that the People of the Book may have asked Muḥammad for at least some of the guidance. The final section of the sūra begins and ends with the formula "they will ask you for guidance" (vv. 127 and 176). Is it not possible that the subject of this asking that brackets the fifth section was the People of the Book who are addressed in its "hollow" interior?

37. Iṣlāḥī also suggests that sūra 4 is both legislation or guidelines and exhortation or summons to Islam (*Tadabbur*, 2.16; cited in Mir, *Coherence*, 55.

The *Ḥijāb*: How a Curtain Became an Institution and a Cultural Symbol

Barbara Freyer Stowasser

Exegetical and Semantic Background

The Classical Arabic dictionary *Lisān al-ᶜarab*[1] relates the noun *ḥijāb* to the verb *ḥajaba* 'to cover, to hide from view, to conceal'. *Ḥijāb* is anything by which something or someone is veiled, hidden, screened off, or separated; *ḥijāb* is anything that intervenes or comes in between. In semantic terms, then, the first meaning of *ḥijāb* as 'barrier' includes both the objective limitation of space (the mark of a border or threshold or of a separation) and also the subjective

1. Ibn Manẓūr (d. 1311/12 A.D.), *Lisān al-ᶜarab* (15 vols.; Beirut: Dār ṣādir, 1955–56) 1.298ff.

perception of that limit (the veiling of an object, that is, how it is removed from view). Second, *ḥijāb* as 'barrier' can be a positive means of "protection" for something potentially vulnerable, exceptional, or holy; or else it can connote a separation from something negative, from a distraction, disturbance, or taboo that might otherwise come between seekers and their spiritual goals. The concept of *ḥijāb*, therefore, involves both the concrete and the metaphorical; it has come to concern both the concrete and the abstract.

In the Qurʾān,[2] the term *ḥijāb* appears seven times. In three instances it has a clearly metaphorical meaning, twice it means a concrete spatial and visual separation, and once, in an eschatological context, its meaning has been interpreted as a mixture of the two. In chronological sequence of revelation,[3] *ḥijāb* first appears in sūra 19:17 (of the middle Meccan period) as the 'curtain' or 'barrier', behind which Mary sought refuge from her people in preparation for the birth of her son, the prophet Jesus. In sūra 38:32 (also middle Meccan), the prophet Solomon is quoted as having loved the goods, *al-khayr* (of this world, that is, beautiful horses, at the expense of remembering his Lord) "until (the sun) hid behind the *ḥijāb*, curtain (of night)." Sūra 17:45 (middle Meccan) speaks of the 'veiled' or 'invisible' screen or barrier (*ḥijāb mastūr*) that God places between the Prophet Muḥammad and those who do not believe in the hereafter. In sūra 41:5 (late Meccan), the unbelievers speak to the Prophet saying: "Our hearts are veiled from that to which you are calling us, and in our ears there is a deafness, and between us and you is a *ḥijāb*, barrier. Act! And we also will act." In sūra 42:51 (late Meccan), the *ḥijāb* appears as the barrier between God and His prophets:

> And it is no human's right that God should speak to him, except by inspiration or from behind a curtain/partition/screen/barrier or that He send a messenger who (then) inspires by His permission what He wishes. He is exalted and wise.

Sūra 7:46 (late Meccan) refers to the eschatological barrier that separates the blessed from the condemned in the hereafter:

> And between them twain (inhabitants of heaven and inhabitants of hell) is a barrier, and on the heights [? *al-Aʿrāf*] are men who recognize all (believers as well as unbelievers) by their sign; and they call to the inhabitants of paradise: Peace be upon you! They (the people destined for hell) do not enter it (paradise), even though they so desire.

2. All Qurʾānic translations in this article are mine.

3. According to the chronological attribution of Qurʾānic passages by Theodor Nöldeke, as schematized in (Richard) *Bell's Introduction to the Qurʾān* (ed. W. M. Watt; 2d ed.; Edinburgh: Edinburgh University Press, 1970) 205–13.

Finally, in sūra 33:53 (Medinan), the *ḥijāb* is a screen, partition, or curtain that spatially separates and segregates the Prophet's wives from nonrelated male visitors to their quarters. The verse reads:

> O believers, do not enter the Prophet's houses except that permission is given you for a meal, without waiting for its time. But when you are invited [or: called], enter, and when you have eaten, disperse, without seeking familiarity for talk. This used to cause the Prophet annoyance, and he is ashamed [or: bashful] of you. But God is not ashamed of what is right. And if you ask them (the women) for a thing, then ask them from behind a *ḥijāb*. That is purer for your hearts and their hearts. And it is not for you to cause annoyance to God's Messenger, nor that you should marry his wives after him. Truly this with God would be enormous.[4]

In some instances, though not in all, later uses of the term *ḥijāb* derive from these Qurʾānic bases.[5] A shared semantic theme of most of the meanings of *ḥijāb* is the concept of 'separation', most commonly in the sense of a (desirable) protection or an (undesirable) obstacle, which is either concrete, metaphorical, or abstract. The dictionary gives examples of *ḥijāb* as a concrete protective device in a number of membranes by that name in the body, such as *al-ḥijāb al-ḥājiz* (or: *ḥijāb al-jawf*) 'diaphragm';[6] *al-ḥijāb al-mustabṭin* 'pleura';[7] and *ḥijāb al-bukuriyya* 'hymen'.[8] A related meaning, even though involving the concrete as well as the abstract, inheres in the *ḥijāb* as "a supra-terrestrial protection, in fact an amulet . . . which renders its wearer invulnerable and ensures success for his enterprises."[9] At the same time, the *ḥijāb* in a metaphorical sense can be an obstacle to union, communion, indeed, comprehension of and participation in the truth. Just as the Qurʾān speaks of the *ḥijāb* as a screen that mystically veils the hearts of the Meccan pagans so that they cannot perceive the truth of Muḥammad's message (sūra 41:5; cf. 17:45), so the mystics

4. This *ḥijāb* verse is followed by a revelation that establishes the classes of individuals "in whom there is no sin [or: harm] for them; their fathers, sons, brothers, brothers' sons, sisters' sons, their women, and their slaves" (33:55), a revelation commonly thought to belong together with the *ḥijāb* verse and to concern the categories of relatives and servants with whom the Prophet's wives were permitted to deal face-to-face rather than from behind a partition.

5. J. Chelhod, "hidjāb," *EI*[2] 3.359.

6. Ibn Manẓūr, *Lisān al-ʿarab*, 1.288.

7. Ibid.

8. Chelhod, "hidjāb," 359. Similar protective function is ascribed to *al-ḥajibān*, "the eyebrows . . . , i.e., the bones above the eyes with their flesh and hair . . . or, just the hair which grows on the bones, because it keeps the sun's rays away from the eye" (Ibn Manẓūr, *Lisān al-ʿarab*, 1.298–99).

9. Chelhod, "hidjāb," 361.

define the *ḥijāb* as that painful barrier between man and God that, rooted in man's sensual or mental passion, conceals the truth and impedes man's progress toward God.[10] In this instance, the *ḥijāb* connotes a painful deprivation, and he who is *maḥjūb* 'separated by the *ḥijāb*' is deprived, excluded from the light of truth and grace, "damned."[11] Lastly, the *ḥijāb* is both the concrete means to segregate an individual or a group of individuals from society at large and also the abstract institution of such segregation. In medieval royal circles, the *ḥijāb* was the curtain behind which the ruler was hidden from the eyes of courtiers and commonors alike. This practice, first documented for the Umayyads and Abbasids, later became part of an elaborate system of court ceremonials of, especially, the Fatimids.[12] While the custom of screening off was unknown among the Prophet and his four rightly-guided successors (*al-khulafāʾ al-rāshidūn*), it was divinely legislated for the female elite of the first Medinan community, the Prophet's wives.

The Revelation of 33:53: The *Ḥijāb* as 'Curtain' or 'Screen' in the Prophet's Household

The majority of Ḥadīth and Tafsīr accounts identify the occasion for revelation of the *ḥijāb* verse as the Prophet's marriage to Zaynab bint Jaḥsh, which occurred in Medina in the fifth year after the *Hijra*. Zaynab was Muḥammad's first cousin on her mother's side. The Prophet had arranged her marriage with Zayd ibn Ḥāritha, a former slave of Muḥammad's first wife Khadīja, whom he had freed and adopted as a son. This marriage, however, was not harmonious, and even though Muḥammad had instructed him to retain her, Zayd decided to divorce Zaynab. Thereafter, the Prophet received the divine command to marry her himself (33:37–38). In spite of this revelation, some members of the community were scandalized because adopted sons were then regarded as the full equals of natural sons, and in their understanding, the adoptive relationship between the Prophet and Zayd rendered his marriage to Zaynab incestuous. The communal debate persevered until two revelations established that "adopted sons are unlike real sons" and that "Muḥammad is not the father of any of your men" (33:4, 40). Ibn Kathīr[13] and others call the revelation of 33:40 "the (di-

10. Ibid.

11. Fatima Mernissi, *The Veil and the Male Elite* (trans. Mary Jo Ekland; Reading, Pa.: Addison-Wesley, 1991) 97. This Moroccan feminist writer extends the negative connotation of the *ḥijāb* as a barrier of deprivation (of the mystics) to the *ḥijāb* as a device to seclude the women of Islam "from the privileges and spiritual grace to which the Muslim has access."

12. Chelhod, "hidjāb," 360–61.

13. Ismaʿīl ibn ʿUmar Ibn Kathīr (d. 1373), *Tafsīr al-Qurʾān al-ʿaẓīm* (4 vols.; Cairo: Dār ʾiḥyāʾ al-kutub al-ʿarabiyya, n.d.) 3.492.

vine) rejection of the hypocrites' suspicion surrounding (the Prophet's) marriage to the wife of Zayd, his protégé and adopted son." This statement is important in that it links the events with a prominent faction of Muḥammad's enemies in Medina, the 'hypocrites' (*munāfiqūn*), who, though in name Muslims, were given to vicious rumor-mongering, harrassment of Muslim women in the streets (especially at night), and other activites intended to disturb and divide the community. Their influence was especially keen during periods of Muslim military and economic difficulties, such as in 5 A.H., when the Meccans besieged Medina. Both the rumors initially surrounding Muḥammad's marriage with Zaynab and also the *ḥijāb* as a protective device for Muḥammad's household, revealed soon thereafter, have been placed in the context of hostile *munāfiqūn* activities during that year.[14]

Most traditions maintain that the *ḥijāb* verse was revealed after some guests had overstayed their welcome at the nuptial celebration in Zaynab's house. On this occasion, the *ḥijāb* "came down" in a double sense: First, it was, literally, a 'curtain' that the Prophet lowered while he was standing on the threshold to Zaynab's chamber (with one foot in the room and the other outside) in order to bar his servant Anas ibn Mālik from entering.[15] Second, the *ḥijāb* also "came down" by way of God's revelation of 33:53, which the Prophet recited to Anas at that time.[16] Other traditions report that the *ḥijāb* was decreed after the Prophet saw some men loitering in the vicinity of Zaynab's house on the morning after the wedding night[17] or after the hand of Muḥammad's wife ᶜĀ᾽isha bint Abī Bakr had accidentally touched the hand of ᶜUmar ibn al-Khaṭṭāb, while they were eating together.[18] A third strand of traditions mentions ᶜUmar ibn al-Khaṭṭāb in the role of "counselor" who urged the Prophet to conceal and segregate his wives because "both the righteous and the wicked enter into your houses."[19] In this context, it may be important to note that, first, ᶜUmar ibn al-Khaṭṭāb appears in the Ḥadīth as spokesman in favor of the segregation,

14. Cf. Mernissi, *The Veil*, 105ff., 170ff.

15. Anas ibn Mālik is the main authority on the traditions that desribe this event.

16. Ibn Saᶜd (d. 845), *Kitāb al-ṭabaqāt al-kabīr* (14 vols. in 9; ed. Carl Brockelmann; Leiden: Brill, 1905–28) 8.74–75, 81–82, and 124–25; Abū Jaᶜfar Muḥammad ibn Jarīr al-Ṭabarī (d. 923), *Jāmiᶜ al-bayān fī tafsīr al-Qur᾽ān* (30 vols. in 12; Beirut: Dār al-maᶜrifa,1972) 22.26; Maḥmūd ibn ᶜUmar al-Zamakhsharī (d. 1144), *Kashshāf ᶜan ḥaqā᾽iq ghawāmiḍ al-tanzīl* (ed. Muṣṭafā Ḥusayn Aḥmad; 4 vols.; Cairo: Maṭbaᶜat al-istiqāma, 1953) 3.437; Ibn Kathīr, *Tafsīr*, 3.503–4; Nabia Abbott, *Aishah: The Beloved of Mohammad* (Chicago: University of Chicago Press, 1962) 20–24; and Mernissi, *The Veil*, 85ff.

17. Ibn Saᶜd, *Kitāb al-ṭabaqāt*, 8.74.

18. Ibid., 8.126; also al-Ṭabarī, *Jāmiᶜ al-bayān*, 22.28; al-Zamakhsharī, *Kashshāf*, 3.439; ᶜAbdallah ibn ᶜUmar al-Bayḍāwī (d. 1286?), *Anwār al-tanzīl fī asrār al-ta᾽wīl* (ed. H. O. Fleischer; 2 vols.; Osnabrück: Biblio, 1968) 2.134; Ibn Kathīr, *Tafsīr*, 3.505.

19. Al-Ṭabarī, *Jāmiᶜ al-bayān*, 22.27–28; al-Zamakhsharī, *Kashshāf*, 3.438–39; al-Bayḍāwī, *Anwār al-tanzīl*, 2.134; Ibn Kathir, *Tafsīr*, 3.503 and 505.

domesticity, and marital obedience of the Prophet's wives. Second, the sources record some spirited opposition on the part of the Prophet's wives to ᶜUmar's "interference"; here it is the aristocratic Umm Salama of the noble Meccan clan of Makhzum who often appears as spokesperson for Muḥammad's harem.[20] Third, for some of the later medieval exegetes, such as al-Bayḍāwī and Ibn Kathīr, ᶜUmar's vigilance "for the good of the Prophet's wives" rates greater consideration as the "occasion of revelation" for 33:53 than do the accounts of the Prophet's annoyance at the guests who lingered in Zaynab's house on the night of the wedding.[21]

Muslim interpreters, past and present, state that the Prophet's wives participated fully in the communal affairs of Medina until the revelation of the *ḥijāb* verse. They ascribe the women's exclusion from public life at that time to several factors. One of them was that the living conditions in Medina were extremely crowded, especially in the area around the mosque, itself the very center of public activity. It was here that the Prophet's wives' quarters were located; indeed, they stood so close to the mosque that the women's rooms were natural extensions of its space. The Ḥadīth gives a vivid picture of throngs of Muslims seeking audience with the Prophet while he sat in the chamber of one of his wives. The *ḥijāb* revelation, then, is seen mainly as the legislation of a means to provide domestic comfort and privacy for the female elite of Islam. This notion, in turn, connotes an element of "privilege." And, indeed, the medieval Ḥadīth informs us that the *ḥijāb* was imposed on the Prophet's wives as a criterion of their elite status.[22] In addition, the *ḥijāb* is also seen as a protective device, especially during the periods of civic tension when the hypocrites were instigating disorder and stirring up intercommunal fears. Thus, according to Muslim interpretation, both the privileges of privacy and also physical protection were accorded Muḥammad's wives by way of seclusion in their home, which, in turn, was achieved through the architectural means of 'a single curtain', *sitr wāḥid*.[23] While the literal Qurᵓānic meaning of the term *ḥijāb* in 33:53 is that of a concrete object ('curtain, partition, or screen'), the term's meaning in the Ḥadīth evolved to connote both the concrete and also the abstract, a domestic fixture to ensure seclusion and also the seclusion itself.

In addition to the *ḥijāb*, an obligation imposed on the believers in their dealings with the Prophet's wives ("[W]hen you ask them for a thing, ask them from behind a curtain"; 33:53), the Qurᵓān also legislates a number of

20. Al-Ṭabarī, *Jāmiᶜ al-bayān*, 22.28; al-Zamakhsharī, *Kashshāf*, 3.438–39; al-Bayḍāwī, *Anwār al-tanzīl*, 2.134.

21. Ibid.; Ibn Kathīr, *Tafsīr*, 3.503.

22. E.g., Ibn Saᶜd, *Ṭabaqāt*, 8.84, 91, 93.

23. Ibid., 8.126.

restrictions for the Prophet's wives directly that both limit their social visibility and also regulate their domestic comportment. The revelations bearing these restrictions form part of a group of verses (33:28–34) thought to have been revealed after a major crisis in the Prophet's household, which involved the Prophet's seclusion from all of his wives for the period of a month.[24] While Nöldeke dates these revelations to the end of 5 A.H.,[25] that is, shortly after the revelation of the *ḥijāb*, Abbott's date is considerably later, between 7 and 9 A.H.[26] In 33:28–29, the Prophet is commanded to ask his wives to choose between "God and his Prophet" and "the world and its adornment (*zīna*)." In 33:30–31, the Qurʾān establishes double punishment for the Prophet's consorts in case of clear immoral behavior and double reward for obedience to God and His Apostle and for the working of acts of righteousness. In 33:32, Muḥammad's wives are then told that they are "not like any (other) women" and are enjoined: "do not surrender in speech [or: be complaisant of speech] so that he in whose heart is a disease should desire but speak with conventional [or: befitting, good] speech (*qawl^{an} maʿrūf^{an}*)." Both 33:33 and 33:34 then impose domesticity, modest behavior, obedience and piety: "And stay in your houses, and do not strut about [or: display your charms] (*wa-lā tabarrajna*) in the manner of the former [or: first, or: foremost] Jāhiliyya (*al-jāhiliyya al-ʾūlā*), and perform the prayer and give the alms, and obey God and His Prophet . . ." (33:33). "And recollect what is rehearsed to you in your houses of God's verses [or: signs, *ʾāyāt*] and of wisdom (*ḥikma*) . . ." (33:34).

In the meantime, and probably soon after the revelation of the *ḥijāb* verse, self-protection of "the Prophet's wives, his daughters, and the women of the believers" had been enjoined in Qurʾān 33:59–60 by way of God's command that Muslim women cover themselves in their 'mantles' or 'cloaks' (*jalābīb*; singular: *jilbāb*) [when abroad] . . . "so that they be known [as free women, not slaves] and not molested [in the streets] by the hypocrites and those in whose hearts is a disease and those who stir up sedition in the City (al-Madīna)."[27] This piece of legislation differed from the *ḥijāb* of 33:53 in two ways: first, it was concerned with individual female appearance when outside of the home, not seclusion within it; and, second, it applied to all Muslim women, not just

24. Ibid., 8.123–24, 129–39; al-Ṭabarī, *Jāmiʿ al-bayān,* 21.99–101; al-Zamakhsharī, *Kashshāf,* 3.422–23; al-Bayḍāwi, *Anwār al-tanzīl,* 2.127; Ibn Kathīr, *Tafsīr*, 3.480–81 and 4.385–90.

25. T. Nöldeke, *Geschichte des Qorans* (Dritter reprographischer Nachdruck der 2. Auflage; 2 vols.; Hildesheim: Olms, 1981 [orig., Leipzig, 1909–38]) 1.207.

26. Abbott, *Aishah*, 51.

27. This Qurʾānic verse clearly indicates both that the veil as head-cover was known in Arabian society and also that its wearing was the mark of women of social stature. Its imposition upon the Prophet's wives, daughters, and "the women of the believers" thus marks them as members of the new elite.

the Prophet's wives. Once again, classical exegesis has here identified ᶜUmar ibn al-Khaṭṭāb as the main spokesman in favor of this clothing law, which he is also said to have "enforced" on several occasions. A subsequent revelation concerning male and female modesty was vouchsafed in sūra 24:30–31, of which 24:30 is directed at Muslim men and 24:31 at Muslim women in general terms. The first verse reads as follows: "Tell the male believers that they restrain their eyes and guard their private parts. This is purer for them. God is well aware of what they do" (24:30). The next verse says:

> And tell the female believers that they restrain their eyes and guard their private parts and not display of their adornment [or: finery, *zīna*] except for what is apparent [or: external], and not display their adornment except to their husbands or their fathers or their husbands' fathers or their sons or their husbands' sons or their brothers or their brothers' sons or their sisters' sons or their women or their slaves or male subordinates who have no natural force (*ᵓirba*) or the children who have no knowledge of women's private parts. And that they not stamp their feet to give knowledge of the adornment which they hide. Turn to God in repentance, O believers; perhaps you will prosper [or: perhaps it may be well with you] (24:31).

With Islam's expansion into areas formerly part of the Byzantine and Sasanian empires, the scripture-legislated social paradigm that had evolved in the early Medinan community came face-to-face with alien social structures and traditions deeply rooted in the conquered populations. "Fusion and assimilation took place in a broad variety of ways, including in the lives of individuals, in administrative and bureaucratic practice, and in the literary, cultural, and intellectual traditions."[28] Among the many cultural traditions assimilated and continued by Islam were the veiling and seclusion of women, at least among the urban upper and middle classes. As they became a part of the Islamic way of life, these traditions of necessity helped to shape the normative interpretations of Qurᵓānic gender laws as formulated by the medieval (urbanized and acculturated) lawyer-theologians. In the latters' consensus-based prescriptive systems, the Prophet's wives were recognized as models for emulation (sources of *sunna*). Thus, while the scholars provided information on the Prophet's wives in terms of, as well as for, an ideal of Muslim female morality, the Qurᵓānic directives addressed to the Prophet's consorts were naturally seen as applicable to all Muslim women.

Semantically and legally, that is, regarding both the terms and also the parameters of its application, Islamic interpretation extended the concept of

28. Leila Ahmed, *Women and Gender in Islam* (New Haven: Yale University Press, 1992) 81.

ḥijāb. In scripturalist method, this was achieved in several ways. First, the *ḥijāb* was associated with two of the Qurʾān's "clothing laws" imposed on all Muslim females: the "mantle" verse, 33:59, and the "modesty" verse, 24:31. On the one hand, the semantic association of domestic segregation (*ḥijāb*) with garments to be worn in public (*jilbāb, khimār*) resulted in the use of the term *ḥijāb* for concealing garments, which women wore outside of their houses. This language use is fully documented in the medieval Ḥadīth. However, unlike female garments such as *jilbāb, liḥāf, milḥafa, ʾizār, dirʿ* (traditional garments for the body), *khimār, niqāb, burquʿ, qināʿ, miqnaʿa* (traditional garments for the head and neck),[29] and also a large number of other articles of clothing, the medieval meaning of *ḥijāb* remained conceptual and generic. In their debates on which parts of the woman's body, if any, are not *ʿawra* (literally, 'genital, pudendum') and may therefore be legally exposed even to nonrelatives, the medieval scholars often contrastively paired woman's *ʿawra* with this generic *ḥijāb*. This permitted the debate to remain conceptual rather than getting bogged down in the specifics of articles of clothing whose meaning, in any case, was prone to change, both geographic/regional and chronological. At present we know very little about the precise stages of the process by which the *ḥijāb* in its multiple meanings was made obligatory for Muslim women at large, except to say that they occurred during the first centuries after the expansion of Islam beyond the borders of Arabia and then mainly in the Islamicized societies still ruled by preexisting (Sasanian and Byzantine) social traditions. With the rise of the Iraq-based Abbasid state in the mid–eighth century of the Western calendar, the lawyer-theologians of Islam grew into a religious establishment entrusted with the formulation of Islamic law and morality, and it was they who interpreted the Qurʾānic rules on women's dress and space in an increasingly absolute and categorical fashion that reflected the real practices and cultural assumptions of their place and age.[30] Classical legal compendia, medieval Ḥadīth collections, and Qurʾānic exegesis on this subject are mainly formulations of the system "as established" and not of its developmental stages, even though differences of opinion on the legal limits of the *ḥijāb* garments survived, included among the doctrinal teachings of the four orthodox schools of law (*madhāhib*).

The Prophet's Medina-born biographer Ibn Isḥāq, an early source (d. 767), makes an interesting remark on the face veil while describing the nasty end of

29. On these items, cf. R. P. A. Dozy, *Dictionnaire détaillé des noms de vêtements chez les Arabes* (Beirut: Librairie du Liban, 1969; photomechanical reproduction of Amsterdam: Jean Muller, 1845), s.v.

30. Cf. Ahmed, *Women and Gender*, 79–101.

Muḥammad's uncle Abū Lahab (an enemy of Islam), who died of "pustules." In fear of the disease, Abū Lahab's sons left his body unburied for three days, then

> threw water at the body from a distance [instead of properly washing it]. . . . They did not bury Abū Lahab, but he was put against a wall and stones were thrown against him from behind the wall until he was covered. It is said that when [Muḥammad's wife] ᶜĀᵓisha passed the place, she used to veil her face.[31]

For the later scholars of Islam, the female face veil would be a hotly debated item; not, however, in the context of individual choice, such as horror of a place, but within the parameters of the *ḥijāb* as legally prescribed female "concealment." In addition to differences between the early law schools, a chronological factor appears also to have had its impact. With the progression of time, *ᶜulamāᵓ* opinion, even within a particular *madhhab*, came to prescribe the female face veil (as part of the woman's *ḥijāb)* in increasingly absolute and categorical terms. Al-Ṭabari (d. 923), a *Shāfiᶜite* who later founded his own short-lived school of law,[32] maintained that a woman's "lawful" dress permitted her to leave hands and face uncovered.[33] By contrast, the popular Qurᵓānic exegete al-Bayḍāwī (d. 1286 or 1291), also of *Shāfiᶜite* affiliation, opined that the Muslim freeborn woman must conceal her whole body, including face and hands, except during prayer and in cases of "necessity," such as medical treatment and the bearing of witness in court.[34] This restrictive position was later heightened and emphasized by, for example, al-Khafajī (d. 1659), author of a *ḥāshiya* ('marginal commentary') on al-Bayḍāwī's Qurᵓānic commentary, who, again on the authority of *al-Shāfiᶜī*, argued in agreement with al-Bayḍāwī that "the whole body of the Muslim woman, including face and hands, is *ᶜawra* ('pudendal') and must, therefore, be concealed."[35] While al-Khafajī continued to allow for women's bare-facedness in cases of prayer, medical emergency, and testimony in court as lawful exceptions from "the established rule," he also presented these cases as more marginally acceptable than did his source, the thirteenth-century exegete al-Bayḍāwī.[36]

31. Ibn Isḥāq, *The Life of Muḥammad* (trans. A. Guillaume; Lahore: Oxford University Press, 1955; 3d impression, 1970) 310–11.

32. Al-Ṭabarī founded his own, short-lived *madhhab* called *Jaᶜfarī*. Al-Ṭabarī opposed Aḥmad ibn Ḥanbal in the capacity of jurist, that is, as an authority on *fiqh*, but recognized him as a traditionist, that is, an authority on Ḥadīth. Consequently, his relations with the supporters of Aḥmad ibn Ḥanbal were strained.

33. Cf. al-Ṭabarī, *Jāmiᶜ al-bayān,* 17.92–98, on the exegesis of Qurᵓān 24:31.

34. Al-Bayḍāwī, *Anwār al-tanzīl,* 2.20, on the exegesis of Qurᵓān 24:31.

35. Aḥmad ibn Muḥammad al-Khafajī, *Ḥāshiyat al-Shihāb al-musammā bi-ᶜināyat al-qāḍī wa-kifāyat al-rāḍī ᶜalā tafsīr al-Bayḍāwī* (8 vols.; Beirut: Dār Ṣādir, 1974) 6.371–73.

36. For greater detail on this medieval exegetic debate, see my "Status of Women in Early Islam," in *Muslim Women* (ed. Freda Hussain; London: Croom Helm, 1984) 25–28.

The provisions of Qurʾān 33:33, God's command to the Prophet's wives to stay in their houses and to avoid *tabarruj*, also acted as additional enforcement, extension, and enrichment of scripturalist arguments in this medieval establishment paradigm of female comportment and domesticity. Classical exegesis gives the meanings of *tabarruj* (33:33) as (1) strutting, or prancing about, (2) flirting, coquettishness, (3) embellishment, the showing off of finery, the flaunting of bodily charms, "as was practiced by women in the period before Abraham's prophethood, when women wore shirts made of pearls, open at the sides, or other garments which did not conceal their persons."[37] Some said that *tabarruj* included "the unfastened head-veil which permits glimpses of the neck and necklace, ears and earrings of its wearer."[38] In general terms, *tabarruj* meant a woman's public display of her physical self, including her unrestricted gait and the wearing of revealing garments that aided in the display of physical features, ornaments, makeup, and the like. Today, the meaning of *tabarruj* includes everything from the elaborate salon-type coiffure to the hairpiece and wig; facial foundation, powder, and blushers; lid color and mascara for the eyes; manicure and enamel for the nails; "revealing" dress of any sort, but also including all Western clothing in generic terms, especially if it is of the *couture* kind or is intended to be fashionable in the Western sense.[39] While the exact definition of what constitutes *tabarruj* has varied over the ages, its condemnation by the custodians of communal morality has always included the Qurʾānic reference that it is un-Islamic, a matter of *jāhiliyya* (33:33), and thus a threat to Islamic society. Applied to all women, *tabarruj* thus came to signify the very antithesis of *ḥijāb* in the extended meaning of a concealing garment worn outside the house.

Second, the Qurʾānic command to Muḥammad's wives to "stay in your houses" (33:33) was likewise applied to Muslim women in general; in tandem with the *ḥijāb* rule in its original meaning—"screen of separation" from strangers in the home (33:53)—it legitimized the domestic segregation of women[40] that became a distinctive feature of life for at least the upper-class urban dwellers among them. According to some oft-quoted traditions, the Prophet himself is said to have likened the merit that men gain by fighting for God's cause (*jihād*) to the merit gained by women who stay quietly in their houses

37. Al-Ṭabarī, *Jāmiʿ al-bayān,* 22.4; al-Zamakhsharī, *Kashshāf,* 3.425; al-Bayḍāwī, *Anwār al-tanzīl,* 2.128; Ibn Kathīr, *Tafsīr*, 3.482–83.

38. Ibid.

39. Niʿmat Ṣidqī, *al-Tabarruj* (Cairo: Dār al-iʿtiṣām, 1975) passim (62 pp). This small treatise is very popular in Islamist circles and is available in a large number of editions.

40. Cf., e.g., al-Ṭabarī, *Jāmiʿ al-bayān,* 22.3–4; al-Zamakhsharī, *Kashshāf,* 3.425; al-Bayḍāwī, *Anwār al-tanzīl,* 2.12.

and thus remove themselves from becoming Satan's tools in societal corruption.[41] The "scripture-based" legality of women's seclusion in the house, and even within the house (subsumed under the concept of *ḥijāb*) thus also signified the legality of the Muslim woman's exclusion from any institutionalized participation in public affairs. Thus the pairing up of specific key Qur^ɔānic concepts, *ḥijāb* and confinement versus *tabarruj*, as antonyms or metonyms and tropes of each other led to mutually enforced semantic extensions of the concepts' original meanings. Women's secluded space, concealing clothing, and unfitness for public activity emerged as three powerful determinants in the medieval Islamic paradigm on women's societal role.

The Place of the *Ḥijāb* in Contemporary Islam

When the nineteenth-century, French-educated, pro-Western Egyptian journalist, lawyer, and politician Qāsim Amīn first spoke about bringing Egyptian society from its state of "backwardness" into a state of "civilization" and modernity, he did so by lashing out against the *ḥijāb*, in its expanded sense, as the true reason for the ignorance, superstition, obesity, anemia, and premature aging of the Muslim woman of his time.[42] As Amīn pitted the objectionable (because "backward") *ḥijāb* against the desirable modernist ideal of a woman's right to an elementary education, supplemented by her ongoing contacts with life outside of the home to provide experience of the "real world" and combat superstition,[43] he understood the *ḥijāb* as an amalgam of institutionalized restrictions on women that consisted of sexual segregation, domestic seclusion, and the face veil. He insisted as much on the woman's right to mobility outside the home as he did on the adaptation of *shar*ᶜ*ī* Islamic garb, which would leave her face and hands uncovered.[44] Domestic seclusion and the face veil for women, then, were primary points in Amīn's attack on "what was wrong with the Egyptian social system" of his time. Thereafter, both of these items came to be the focus of the conservative Islamic defense, in Egypt and elsewhere. This reaction is recorded, for instance, in a monograph on *The Ḥijāb* by the Indian Muslim Abū al-Aᶜlā al-Mawdūdī, whose writings have since inspired conservatives and fundamentalists all over the Islamic world.[45] Al-Mawdūdī's Is-

41. E.g., Ibn Kathīr, *Tafsīr*, 3.482.

42. Qāsim Amīn, *Taḥrīr al-mar*ɔ*a* (1899), in *al-A*ᶜ*māl al-kāmila li-Qāsim* ɔ*Amīn* (ed. Muḥammad ᶜAmāra; 2 vols. in 1; Beirut: al-Muɔassasa al-ᶜarabiyya li al-dirāsāt wal-nashr, 1976) 2.20, 54ff.

43. Ibid., 35–37, 54ff., 68.

44. Ibid., 43ff.

45. Abū al-Aᶜlā al-Mawdūdī published a series of articles, written in Urdu, on women's *purdah* in the *Terjumān al-Qur*ɔ*ān*, which he then edited in book form in 1939. The English translation of this volume was done by al-Ashᶜarī, *Purdah and the Status of Woman in Islam* (Lahore:

lamic formula to avoid the tragic societal consequences of the secularization of culture that had occurred in the West[46] lay in the preventive measures of the established, that is, traditional Islamic social system,[47] of which women's segregation was the main feature. According to al-Mawdūdī, the Qurʾānic injunctions of sūra 33, vv. 33 and 53, even though addressed to the Prophet's wives, were and are binding on all Muslim females.[48] For al-Mawdūdī, the laws of what constitutes Islamic dress (*satr* 'coveredness') fall *within* the social system of the *ḥijāb*; that is, they are but one of its many features.[49] Like his medieval predecessors, al-Mawdūdī infers from the Qurʾānic *jilbāb*, or 'mantle', verse (33:59) that the woman's Islamic dress must include the face veil and also gloves. The question of female concealing garments, including the face veil "except in cases of necessity," stirs him to a passionate defense of their Islamic nature. "Though the veil has not been specified in the Qurʾān, it is Qurʾānic in spirit"; indeed, the Muslim women living in the time of the Holy Prophet were attired in these very garments, which symbolized their commitment to a righteous way of life. According to al-Mawdūdī, the clear and rational laws of Islam stipulate that the modern believing Muslim woman must do likewise, even if this means ridicule by the West and its hypocritical, pseudo-Muslim spokesmen. The latter speak of "progress" and "civilization" while they engage in unprincipled behavior and are beset by bankruptcy of reason and lack of moral courage.[50]

Amīn's call for the bare-faced Muslim woman to be given access to the outside world in order to acquire knowledge of "what is real" and al-Mawdūdī's call to uphold and defend the moral and authentic Islamic tradition of the segregation of women, including the complete veiling of their body and face, both bear a close relationship to the history of European imperialism in the Islamic world. As most recently shown by Leila Ahmed,[51] women's seclusion and veiling in Muslim societies acquired multiple "symbolic" meanings when the Western colonialist establishments, though themselves patriarchal, began to attack these traditions as the primary reason for Muslim "backwardness" and

---

Islamic Publications, 1972). By then, the book had been translated into Arabic; it was first published in Damascus in the early 1960s under the title *al-Ḥijāb*. This book is now widely available in the Arab world, from a variety of publishing houses. The Arabic translation accessible to me is in the form of a Saudi-Arabian publication entitled *al-Ḥijāb* (Jeddah: al-Dār al-saʿūdiyya li al-nashr wa al-tawzīʿ, 1985). All of the quotations in this article are from the 1972 English translation.

46. Al-Mawdūdī, *Ḥijāb*, 39–72.

47. Ibid., 135–216.

48. Ibid., 149ff.

49. Ibid., 183–204.

50. Ibid., 198–203.

51. Ahmed, *Women and Gender*, 144–68.

the obstacle to their progress toward "true civilization," that is, their remaking in the Western mold. Western missionaries and feminists further strengthened this imperialist formula, which resulted in a fusion of Muslim women's issues with Islamic culture as a whole. The formula acquired an inner-Islamic class dimension when indigenous but Westernized, upper-class intellectuals such as Qāsim Amīn criticized traditional, that is, lower-class Muslim society by focusing on women's issues while using the foreigners' language on the inferiority of Muslim traditions and the superiority of the West. The indigenous Islamic response of resistance was as complex as the original challenge. As here exemplified in al-Mawdūdī's passages, it embodied the call to pitch Islamic cultural authenticity (formulated in terms of Islamic morality) against foreign colonialism, neocolonialism, and their pseudo-Muslim Westernized mouthpieces. True to the challenge, however, the focus of the debate remained on women's issues, especially female domestic seclusion and the veil, as symbols of the validity and dignity of Muslim tradition as a whole.[52] While the linkage of women and culture continues as a dominating theme in Muslim religious theory, socio-economic changes have now also left their mark on the precise "meaning" of the *ḥijāb* in its practical, though not its symbolic, terms.

Today's Muslim societies have largely developed beyond the past paradigm of women's seclusion, no matter how fervently Islamic conservatives and fundamentalists would wish it otherwise. On the one hand, upper and upper–middle-class women, formerly the only truly "housebound"/"segregated" ones, now have access to education and thereby to professional careers, which spell the end to their institutionalized domestic seclusion. If given a choice, the women of these classes tend to favor modes of dress different from the traditional. Simultaneously, middle-class women have gained access to education as well, and many of them are now taking on paid jobs outside their homes, motivated sometimes by choice perhaps, but also more frequently by economic necessity. For lower-class women, the situation may not be new, since the women of this class have traditionally had to work both inside and outside their homes. Consequently, the Islamic call for women's *ḥijāb* has changed its tenor. On the one hand, the religious message is now addressed to the Muslim woman herself rather than to her man (formerly "her guardian" in all things); this is because the Muslim woman now listens to the radio, watches television, and, most of all, is now able to *read*. On the other hand, the Islamic call is now also directed at a new constituency, the women of the urban middle and lower middle class, in a quasi-democratized fashion. Inasmuch as its target audience are Muslim women who are often compelled to work, the Islamic call for the *ḥijāb*

52. Ibid., 164.

has also had to shift in semantic content. By socioeconomic necessity, the obligation to observe the *ḥijāb* now often applies more to female "garments" (worn outside the house) than it does to the older paradigmatic feature of women's domestic "seclusion."

Conservative and Modernist Cultural Paradigms

True to the fact that any religious paradigm is persistent by nature, the issue of women's *ḥijāb* as spatial seclusion and as domesticity continues to linger on in the discourse of Muslim conservatism. In the sermons and writings of the popular Egyptian preacher Muḥammad Mutawallī al-Shaᶜrāwī, for instance, "the house" is celebrated as the woman's God-given space. As is predetermined through her God-given physical and mental attributes, the woman's place is in her home. Here she may pursue the noblest of all professions on this earth, which is to raise the next generation. When a woman stays at home, she contributes through her domestic labor far more to the family budget than when she earns a salary outside but has to pay for the support staff who replace her.[53] Other conservative voices point to the disastrous cost of women working outside the home in terms of the damage done to the Islamic family order. A woman who contributes part of the household expenses undermines both her man's divinely appointed obligation to be the family's provider (Qurʾān 4:34) and also his *qiwāma* 'guardianship' over her (Qurʾān 4:34); indeed, a working woman's husband is selling his *qiwāma* for a trifle, since she takes away his manhood in exchange for a mere portion of her salary. By permitting his wife to work, the man loses his dignity, his substance, and his willpower.[54]

Thus, for these interpreters, a woman's best *ḥijāb* is still her home.[55] But "necessity" here represents the extenuating circumstance. Even the spokesmen of conservatism now agree that in emergency situations the Muslim woman may work abroad, provided that she behaves with all modesty and also returns to domestic life as soon as the emergency has been taken care of.[56] However, since it is economic necessity that drives increasing numbers of middle-class

53. Muḥammad Mutawallī al-Shaᶜrāwī, *Qaḍāyā al-marʾa al-muslima* (Cairo: Dār al-Muslim, 1982) 18ff.

54. Muḥammad Kāmil al-Fīqī [Former Dean of the Faculty of Arabic and Islamic Studies, al-Azhar University], *La taẓlamū al-marʾa* (Cairo: Maktabat Wahba, 1985) 59–66.

55. Ibid, 34.

56. Some say that it is the duty of the State and/or of society at large to save the woman's morals and reputation by paying her one-fourth of her salary as a "pension" in order to enable her to return to domestic life. Cf. al-Shaᶜrāwī, *Qaḍāyā al-marʾa*, 18ff.; and al-Fīqī, *Lā taẓlamū al-marʾa*, 57ff.

women (the conservatives' new target group) to work without the prospect of early retirement, this formula is becoming more and more untenable. As a consequence, the semantic focus of the concept of *ḥijāb* has begun to shift; in the contemporary normative Islamic language of Egypt and elsewhere, the *ḥijāb* now denotes more a 'way of dressing' than a 'way of life', a (portable) 'veil' rather than a (fixed) 'domestic screen/seclusion'.

It is indicative of this semantic shift that in conservative primers for the Muslim woman, the material on "the veil" holds center stage.[57] Echoes of past imperialist attacks on this garment, awareness of its having been discarded by members of the Westernized upper class, but mainly the need to salvage at least some aspects of the hallowed *ḥijāb* complex of old now lead conservative writers and preachers to exhort the Muslim woman to "wear the *ḥijāb*" for the sake of God, her own dignity in youth and in old age, and as a protection of her own morality and that of all males whom she encounters in her daily life outside of the home. In partial continuation of traditional premodern usage, then, *ḥijāb* is here used as a generic term for women's clothing. On the basis of Qurʾān 24:31, Egyptian conservatism, for instance, reckons that this *ḥijāb* must cover the woman's hair, neck, throat, and the upper part of her chest; on the basis of the Qurʾānic reference to hidden anklets in sūra 24:31, it must also be a long and loose-fitting gown that reaches to the heels; as established by Prophetic tradition, only the hands and face should remain visible. Other ḥadīths are quoted to prove that the material of the *ḥijāb* should be heavy, not light; that the garment should not be molded to the body and revealing of its contours; that it should not be perfumed or smell of incense; that it should not resemble men's clothing; and that it should not be "showy."[58] As in past tradition, however, its precise cut is not prescribed. Indeed, the conservative preacher al-Shaʿrāwī leaves the shape and "doing-up" of the head cover to the individual wearer, because "you women know more about this than we men do."[59]

In terms of 'garment', the *ḥijāb* has in some Arab Muslim contexts acquired a spectrum of meanings that spans the semantic field from a specific article of clothing to the general concept of modest female attire reflecting religious commitment. In Egypt, for instance, the *ḥijāb* as a specific garment presently denotes the basic head covering ('veil') worn by Islamist women as part of Islamic dress (*zayy ʾislāmī* or *zayy sharʿī*); this *ḥijāb* head covering con-

57. In his booklet *Qaḍāyā al-marʾa al-muslima*, for instance, al-Shaʿrāwī's remarks on the *ḥijāb qua* 'veil' are about four times longer than his treatment of women's rights or women and work and even surpass in length what he has to say about women and the family.

58. Ibid., 43–63.

59. Ibid., 49.

ceals the hair and the neck of the wearer and resembles the head covering of Catholic nuns of the reformed orders, except that for Muslims, the throat is also covered. The Egyptian fashion industry, however, has begun to market new designs of *ḥijāb* head coverings as well, some of which consist of whimsical ornaments, berets, or pillbox hats to be worn with and over the "veil," so that the whole effect resembles the *1001 Nights* more than it does the chaster "wimple." In categorical terms *qua* "modest attire," the *ḥijāb* simultaneously stands for a variety of dress. It can typically mean a bulky, high-necked, long-sleeved, ankle-length robe in a muted color worn with the "wimple." Simultaneously, a long-sleeved blouse and long, tightly belted skirt ensemble with head veil, even if colorful and/or of tailored elegance, also qualifies as *ḥijāb*. In her guide to the symbolic functions of dress in contemporary Egypt, Andrea B. Rugh here differentiates between "fundamentalist" and "pious" styles of dress, indicating that both styles can accommodate grades of (externalized) pious commitment, the highest of which entails full face-veiling and the wearing of gloves.[60] While the *ḥijāb qua* "fundamentalist" dress is now mainly a middle-class phenomenon that serves to distinguish between educated and uneducated classes, the lower-class women in Egypt still wear folk-dress styles that accomplish the same modesty aims but are more related to community norms than to pretensions of piety;[61] consequently, their wearers are also not referred to by the term *muḥajjabāt*.

The urbanized elite of Egypt and elsewhere who now (ideologically) opt against the *ḥijāb* in favor of Western fashions, if interested, may find their Islamic legitimation in modernist exegetic works such as those by the contemporary Egyptian intellectual Muḥammad Aḥmad Khalaf Allāh. He has argued that the Qur^ɔān gives women full political rights as well as the right/obligation to work but does not prescribe a particular "Islamic dress," because both Qurɔān 33:59 and 24:31 were revealed as calls for the reform of public conduct and etiquette in the early Medinan comunity against the then-prevailing customs of pre-Islamic paganism. Addressed as they were to the needs of seventh-century Arabia, these norms were of time-specific, not absolute, validity.[62] Here, as elsewhere, Khalaf Allāh proves his discipleship to the founder of Arab Islamic modernism, the Egyptian theologian Muḥammad ᶜAbduh (d. 1905), who had called for the fresh interpretation and adaptation of the Qurɔān's social laws by each generation of Muslims in light of the practical needs of their own age.

60. Andrea B. Rugh, *Reveal and Conceal: Dress in Contemporary Egypt* (Syracuse: Syracuse University Press, 1986) 149ff.

61. Ibid., 155.

62. Muḥammad Aḥmad Khalaf Allāh, *Dirāsāt fī ɔl-nuẓūm wal-tashrīᶜāt al-islāmiyya* (Cairo: Maktabat al-anglo al-miṣriyya, 1977) 189–99.

In traditionalist Sunni countries like Saudi Arabia, itself the main part of the Arab world that escaped Western colonization, the religious debate on women's issues (including the *ḥijāb* in its multiple meanings) has proceeded within the parameters of the established Sunni *sharīᶜa*, now still formulated by conservative juridic authorities of the Ḥanbalī *madhhab*. While contemporary Shiᶜite Iran is worlds apart from the contemporary Wahhabi-based paradigm of Saudi Arabia, there the *ḥijāb* issue regarding women's clothing laws has also seen enforcement by the state. Most other Muslim countries are not quite as strictly ruled by the *sharīᶜa*. In many, the *ḥijāb* has to some degree become an "option" that entails a spiritual, ideological, and social dimension. When European colonialism first attacked the *ḥijāb* as an obstacle to Muslim "progress" (in the Western mold), the Arab/Middle Eastern conservative establishment, on this issue later joined by fundamentalists, responded by redefining traditional women-related institutions as the core of Islamic "authenticity," while modernism's response, in some measure acculturationist, sought and continues to seek legitimate change on these issues within the parameters of the Islamic scripturalist paradigm. All the while, however, the core meaning of *ḥijāb* in this debate has undergone a semantic shift from women's general societal segregation and invisibility to 'a garment' (a 'portable' veil) that educated and working women from the great part of the middle and lower middle classes now wear as a badge of both morality and cultural authenticity, while performing new tasks in the public sphere.

The Development of Fictional Genres: The Novel and Short Story in Arabic

Roger Allen

For Georg Krotkoff,
with admiration and affection

As translation continues to fulfill its function as a process of "carrying across" textual expressions from one culture to another, it becomes clear that Arabic fiction today is in a position to become not only a participant in, but an active contributor to, the creative development of literary genres within the wider context of world literature. The award of the Nobel Prize to the Egyptian novelist Najīb Maḥfūẓ in 1988 reflects this important function of translated texts and serves perhaps as the most visible token thus far of the increasing awareness on the part of a broader readership of the sheer existence and artistic merits of an

Arabic literary tradition that, in its modern manifestations, has been largely ignored outside the scholarly community that specializes in its productions.[1]

The variety and vigor of this developing fictional tradition have been accompanied by the emergence of an equally lively corpus of critical works that have analyzed the way in which each genre has developed, mostly within the context of a single nation or geographical area within the larger Arab world. However, while we can look back today on the process that has brought fiction to its present stage of development in the Arab world and differentiate the various genres and their critical adjuncts, the situation at the outset of that process is somewhat less clear. Discussion is complicated by two principal factors. The first is too well known to need underlining, namely the generally poor state of our knowledge of that large "black hole" in our understanding of Arabic culture termed the "Period of Decadence" (thirteenth–eighteenth centuries, approximately). In the case of literary production, it seems clear that previous generations of scholars have, at least in the case of elite literature, found themselves almost completely unsympathetic to the esthetic norms of the period. With regard to popular literary expression, they have followed the lead of the indigenous culture itself in not regarding such expression as part of the Arabic literary canon at all. Thus, while a wide awareness in the Western world of the narrative riches of *The 1001 Nights*, for example, is reflected in a vast number of studies, the number in Arabic has, till recently, been extremely small; the same can, in fact, be said for studies that analyze the tales in this famous collection as narratives.

The second complicating factor is the fact that classical Arabic narrative provides no convenient parallels to the fictional genres that now predominate in the contemporary Arab world. There is one classical narrative genre whose continuing popularity throughout the intervening period we have just described clearly did reflect the esthetic norms of the readership for Arabic literature, and this is the *maqāma*. It is thus hardly surprising that one of the first manifestations of neoclassicism in the nineteenth century takes the form of compositions in this genre, from direct imitations at the hands of Nāṣīf al-Yāzijī (1800–1871) in his *Majma^{c} al-baḥrayn*, to the more innovative and complex experiments of Aḥmad Fāris al-Shidyāq (1804–87) in *al-Sāq ^{c}alā al-sāq*. Meanwhile,

1. A brief glimpse at most anthologies and encyclopedias of "world literature" confirms this impression. While volumes such as *The Encyclopedia of World Literature in the 20th Century* (New York: Ungar, 1981–84) have been endeavoring to include the more famous modern Arab authors, a collection such as *Prentice Hall Literature: World Masterpieces* (Englewood Cliffs, N.J.: Prentice-Hall, 1991) includes under the rubric of "Persian and Arabic Literature" extracts from two texts that are not considered as "literature" at all within the Arabic critical tradition itself, the Qur$^{\supset}$ān and *The 1001 Nights*. The whole of modern Arabic literature is represented by a poor translation of one short story of Maḥfūẓ.

many of the tales from *The 1001 Nights*, segments of which had for centuries been performed in public by storytellers at festivals and other societal and familial occasions, found their way into another sphere of public performance, the developing genre of the drama.[2]

Novels and Short Stories

While both the novel and short story give every appearance of fulfilling their generic purposes in the Arab world today, with a tremendous variety of themes and experiments reflecting the various influences on and priorities of littérateurs in the various nations involved, it is interesting to look back and notice that the pattern of development for each genre shows signs of cross-fertilization and even of some confusion between the two. This reflects a similar situation to be found at certain stages in the development of the Western fictional tradition.

I have suggested elsewhere that nomenclature may contribute to the confusion (while other critics would go further and suggest that the very concept of genres is the primary underlying factor).[3] The use of the adjective *short* in the English term *short story* (replicated in the Arabic *qiṣṣa qaṣīra*[4]) has led many critics to be concerned with the issue of length, in some cases even resorting to the counting of words or, as with Poe, estimating reading time. This in turn has led to the development of a notion much resented by short-story writers, namely that the short story is a kind of testing ground for the more arduous, time-consuming, and serious work of novel writing. These feelings are well represented in the following two quotations:

> The short story is often seen as the "little sister" of the novel—and because it is defined in terms of the novel, it is bound to fail in many respects when it comes up for judgment. . . . Because it is short, the material must be fragmentary, subjective, partial. . . .[5]

2. Tales from *The 1001 Nights* have provided themes for plays by Abū Khalīl al-Qabbānī, Tawfīq al-Ḥakīm, Alfred Faraj, and Saᶜdallāh Wannūs—to provide just a short list of examples. Regarding public performances in the nineteenth century, Edward Lane reported that "the great scarcity of copies . . . is, I believe, the reason why recitations of them are no longer heard." See Edward Lane, *Manners and Customs of the Modern Egyptians* (London: Everyman, 1954) 420.

3. See Roger Allen, "Narrative Genres and Nomenclature: A Comparative Study," *Journal of Arabic Literature* 23/3 (November, 1992) 208–214.

4. The term *uqṣūṣa* is preferred by a few critics, precisely because of the issues that I am discussing here. *Qiṣṣa qaṣīra*, however, remains the predominant term. See Ṣabrī Ḥāfiẓ, "Khaṣāᵓiṣ al-uqṣūṣa al-bināᵓiyya wa-jamāliyyātuhā," *Fuṣūl* (July, 1982).

5. Clare Hanson, "'Things out of Words'; Towards a Poetics of Fiction," in *Re-reading the Short Story* (ed. Clare Hanson; New York: St. Martin's, 1989) 23.

> Even though academic critics continue to describe the short story as the poor relation of the novel, neglected at every turn, the short story is, nonetheless, the current contemporary form in fashionable currency.[6]

The question of contemporaneity is one to which I will return below in the Arab world context. However, the extent to which short-story writers believe that theirs is actually the genre that requires the greatest artifice and craftsmanship can be illustrated in the following remark by H. E. Bates:

> because a short story is short it is not therefore easier to write than a novel, ten, twenty, or even thirty times its length—the exact reverse being in fact the truth.[7]

Alberto Moravia supports this assessment:

> a definition of the short story as distinct and autonomous literary *genre*, with its own special rules and laws, may well be impossible, for, among other things, the short story has an even wider sweep than the novel.[8]

In the context of this quotation, one can point to an interesting aspect of the apparently self-conscious craft of the short story: it seems to have led a number of its practitioners to analyze and explain their techniques and the techniques of others in a number of critical studies of the short story genre itself. Besides H. E. Bates, one can cite V. S. Pritchett, Katherine Porter, Hallie Burnett, Sean O'Faolain, and Nadine Gordimer. Shukrī ᶜAyyād, Yaḥyā Ḥaqqī, and Yūsuf al-Shārūnī, all distinguished critics and short-story writers, have shown the same tendencies (and devotion) in the Arab world.

In the Western context then, the short story has continued vigorously to assert its right to separate and equal status as a literary genre. To achieve this, it has carved out its own creative and critical space in a fictional arena already populated by the formidable, popular, and variegated genre of the novel (and its even earlier forebear, the novella). I will suggest below that the process of generic development within the *nahḍa* may have led to interestingly different sequences of development in the Arabic context, but the beginnings of the tradition, with the complexities that I have tried to outline above, presented those who would create works of fiction (and analyze them) with a task of monumental proportions. What terms were to be used to identify these new types of stories? And with what could they be compared or contrasted? Without going into an elaborate discussion of the defining characteristics of each genre, the

6. William O'Rourke, "Morphological Metaphors for the Short Story: Matters of Production, Reproductions, and Consumption," in *Short Story Theory at a Crossroads* (ed. Susan Lohafer and Jo Ellyn Clarey; Baton Rouge: Louisiana State University Press, 1989) 198.

7. H. E. Bates, *The Modern Short Story, 1809–1953* (London: Robert Hale, 1988) 2.

8. Alberto Moravia, "The Short Story and the Novel," in *Short Story Theories* (ed. Charles E. May; [Athens]: Ohio University Press, 1976) 147.

following quotations may suggest the difficulty of the task that confronted the literary communities in the countries of the Arab world as they tried to distinguish examples of the different categories of Western narrative, and, in particular, the novel—Hegel's "burgher's epic," Trilling's "agent of the moral imagination"—from the short story:

> [The short story] is the glancing form that seems to be right for the nervousness and restlessness of modern life . . . . The novel tends to tell us everything whereas the short story tells us only one thing, and that intensively. . . . Above all, more than the novelist who is sustained by his discursive manner, the writer of short stories has to catch our attention at once not only by the novelty of his people and scene but by the distinctiveness of his voice, and to hold us by the ingenuity of his design; for what we ask for is the sense that our now restless lives achieve shape at times and that our emotions have their architecture.[9]

> The short story is much more end-oriented than the novel; that is, . . . the short story is carefully constructed so as to give us a feeling of completion at its conclusion. . . . [T]he plotting functions more neatly to lead to a conclusion that is a true denouement.[10]

These two quotations supply examples of contexts within which the novel and the short story have been analyzed and compared. The criteria can be applied to examples from the contemporary Arabic literary tradition that I outlined in my opening paragraph, but clearly the features that these authors identify are the result of a prolonged process of development involving both creative writing and critical analysis. For those in the Arab world who endeavored to follow these Western generic models, whether as creative writers or critics, the process whereby these genres were introduced, translated, adapted, and imitated produces some interesting variations.

The Development of Modern Arabic Fiction

There is one feature that can be identified immediately as being common to the development of fiction in both the West and the Arab world: the role of developing technology in providing increased publication opportunities and, most particularly, the institution and rapid expansion of a press tradition. While printing in Arabic had been available for some time, advances in printing techniques that became available in the Arab world in the nineteenth century made the publication of books considerably more convenient. This obviously had a direct impact

9. V. S. Pritchett, "Introduction," in *Oxford Book of Short Stories* (ed. V. S. Pritchett; London: Oxford University Press, 1981) xi and xiv.

10. Viktor Shklovsky, quoted in Robert Scholes, *Introduction to Structuralism* (New Haven: Yale University Press, 1974) 85.

on libraries, whether private or public, as with the Egyptian Dār al-Kutub, founded in 1870 under the direction of ᶜAlī Mubārak, himself the author of a work of fiction entitled *ᶜAlam al-dīn* (published in Alexandria between 1881 and 1892).[11] The speed with which newspapers proliferated, particularly after the arrival of a number of Christian émigrés from Syria in the 1870s and 1880s, can be gauged from the documentation provided in Fīlīb dī Tarrāzī's well-known study.[12]

Within the context of a discussion of the emergence of fictional genres, what is clearly of major importance is first, that publication avenues became more available and convenient; second, that, as newspapers became the favored locus for political expression, a more direct link could be forged between political and societal issues and literary expression; and third, that the readership was vastly expanded and, as is emerging from more recent research, included a large number of women readers (who had access, among other things, to journals and magazines published for such a readership).[13] But, in addition to these changes in the social context of fiction, the press was instrumental in another important change, namely in language usage and attitudes to style. As newspapers and journals came to be appreciated as a powerful force for debate and change, many writers began to realize the need to clarify and to simplify the level of discourse that was used to communicate information and opinion to an ever-widening readership. Pioneers such as ᶜAbdallāh Nadīm and Yaᶜqūb Ṣannūᶜ used their publications to offer examples of articles and short narratives that transcribed the colloquial language into a written representation of the liveliness of spoken dialogue. Needless to say, this was a crucial precedent to the appearance of an authentic expression of dialogue in any emerging fictional genres.[14]

Within this press tradition, a large number of literary works were published during the earliest stages of *al-nahḍa*: poems, anecdotes (such as those of ᶜAbdallāh Nadīm), fictional essays (such as the famous examples of al-Manfalūṭī), and serialized novels. Initially, many of the novels to be published were translations—a pattern repeated in other Middle Eastern countries such as Turkey, and the fact that one of the first and most popular selections was Dumas' *The*

11. See J. Brugman, *An Introduction to the History of Modern Arabic Literature in Egypt* (Leiden: Brill, 1984) 65–68.

12. Fīlīb Dī Tarrāzī, *Tarīkh al-ṣiḥāfa al-ᶜarabiyya* (4 vols.; Cairo: al-Maṭbaᶜa al-amīriyya, al-Maṭbaᶜa al-amrīkiyya, 1913–33).

13. See, for example, the introductions to *My Grandmother's Cactus* (trans. Marilyn Booth; London: Quartet Books, 1991); and Margot Badran and Miriam Cooke (eds.), *Opening the Gates* (London: Virago / Bloomington: Indiana University Press, 1990).

14. For discussions of the writings of these two pioneers, see Roger Allen, *A Period of Time* (Reading, England: Garnet, 1992) 23–25; Pierre Cachia, *An Overview of Modern Arabic Literature* (Edinburgh: Edinburgh University Press, 1990) 62–64; Sabry Hafez, *The Genesis of Arabic Narrative Discourse* (London: Saqi, 1993); and Matti Moosa, *The Origins of Modern Arabic Fiction* (Washington, D.C.: Three Continents Press, 1983) 43–66.

Count of Monte Cristo gives us some idea of popular tastes at the time and also points to some of the perceptions of both the generic purpose of the novel and the direction(s) it might take—at least initially. Special journals were established to publish both translated novels and the early efforts at imitation that soon followed.[15] As had been the case many centuries earlier with Ibn al-Muqaffaᶜ (d. 757) and his translations into Arabic, the sheer process of translating Western fiction in this way was another contributor to the process of change in the written language that would make available a clear and malleable vehicle for fictional expression. It is interesting to speculate what may have been the more practical effects of such serialization in the press on perceptions regarding the particular features of fictional genres. From the point of view of plot and structure, for example, we know that Dickens was clearly influenced by the reception of his serialized works in the press and made adjustments of some significance. The same holds true of Muḥammad al-Muwayliḥī (1858–1930) and his *Ḥadīth ᶜĪsā ibn Hishām*.[16] However, considering some of the criteria for *differentiating* the fictional genres that have been identified above with regard to their development within the Western tradition, one can begin to see clear reasons as to why the development of each genre should have taken different paths and at different paces. For example, not only does the publication of a novel in serial form make each segment of a length quite similar to that of a short story, but also when the work in question is as diffuse in structure and plot as some examples of the incipient novel in Arabic, the task of learning "to see the wider and deeper relationships of life on a large scale" and "to understand the unity and inner logic of a whole epoch" (to cite Medvedev/Bakhtin) is rendered especially difficult, if not impossible.[17]

The Short Story

As we turn to considering the way each genre developed, the context of the press and the new readership for fictional writing that it created and fostered provides another parallel:

> The fact of serial publication, and the popularity of serialized novels among the English middle classes inadvertently gave the short story its break.[18]

15. Examples include Salīm al-Bustānī, *al-Huyām fī jinān al-Shām* (1870) and serialized in *al-Jinān*; and Saᶜīd al-Bustānī, *Dhāt al-khiḍr*, published in *al-Ahrām* in the 1880s.

16. See Roger Allen, *A Period of Time*, 35–44.

17. These are features of the novel as presented by P. N. Medvedev and M. M. Bakhtin (*The Formal Method in Literary Scholarship* [Baltimore: John Hopkins University Press, 1978] 134–35).

18. Suzanne Ferguson, "The Rise of the Short Story as a Highbrow, or Prestige Genre," in *Short Story Theory at a Crossroads* (ed. S. Lohafer and J. E. Clarey; Baton Rouge: Louisiana State University Press, 1989) 182.

The narratives that Nadīm and al-Manfalūṭī published in Egyptian newspapers in the late nineteenth century may not contain all the features of the short story as identified by Pritchett above and by many others. We should obviously not be too concerned at this early stage with "ingenuity of design," but there can surely be no denying in their writings the concision of expression that needs to be the stock in trade of anyone writing in the journalistic realm; and their short narratives certainly reflect "the nervousness and restlessness of modern life" as it impacted upon Egyptian society at the time. In the final decades of the nineteenth century when these writers were publishing their stories, there was much discussion and argument concerning the status of women in society, particularly with regard to educational opportunities. This was a cause for which Qāsim Amīn (1865–1908) became famous as an advocate. The very same theme was picked up by both Jubrān Khalīl Jubrān (1883–1931) and Mikhāʾīl Nuᶜayma (1889–1988) in their earliest stories, composed in the first two decades of this century. The trials of "Martā from Bān," snatched from the rural simplicity of her home and placed in the dens of iniquity in the evil city, and of "Wardā al-Hāniyya," who deserts a comfortable home with a husband she hates in order to live with her real love—these stories are told by Jubrān with both passion and sentimentality.[19] Mikhāʾīl Nuᶜayma's early stories show a greater sense of both subtlety and detachment, something that he acquired, no doubt, from his extensive readings in the works of Russian masters of the short story, such as Chekhov and Gogol; their influence is clearly visible in the themes and techniques of stories such as "Sanatuhā al-jadīda" and "Maṣraᶜ Sattūt."[20]

Such early experiments in short fiction as these, matched somewhat later in other parts of the Arab world,[21] laid the thematic and linguistic groundwork for

19. Jubrān Khalīl Jubrān, "Martā al-Bāniyyah," in *ᶜArāʾis al-murūj*, trans. H. N. Nahmad as "Martha," in *Nymphs of the Valley* (New York: Knopf, 1968) 3–9 [abridged]; "Warda al-Hāniyya," in *al-Arwāḥ al-mutamarrida*, trans. H. N. Nahmad as "Warde el-Hani," in *Spirits Rebellious* (New York: Knopf, 1969) 3–28.

20. See Nadeem Naimy, *Mikhail Naimy: An Introduction* (Oriental Series 47; Beirut: American University in Beirut, 1967) 85–105; and C. J. Nijland, *Mīkhāʾīl Nuᶜaymah, Promotor of the Arabic Literary Revival* (Istanbul: Nederlands Historisch-Archaeologisch Instituut, 1975) 18 and 49–63. For the stories, see "Sanatuhā al-jadīda" in *Kān mā kān* (Beirut: Maṭbaᶜat al-ittiḥad, 1937), trans. John Perry, in *A New Year* (Leiden: Brill, 1974) 23–32; and "Maṣraᶜ Sattūt," in *Akābir* (Beirut: Dār Ṣādir, 1956).

21. The situation in Iraq, for example, is described by ᶜAbd al-Ilāh Aḥmad in *Nashʾat al-qiṣṣa wa-taṭawwuruhā fī al-ᶜIrāq 1908–35* (Baghdad: Maṭbaᶜat Shafīq, 1969). For Tunisia, see Muḥammad Ṣalīḥ al-Jābirī, *al-Qiṣṣa al-tūnisiyya: Nashʾatuhā wa-ruwwāduhā* (Tunis, 1975). For Egypt, the list of studies is long; among the most famous are Yaḥyā Ḥaqqī, *Fajr al-qiṣṣa al-miṣriyya* (Cairo: al-Hayʾa al-miṣriyya al-ᶜāmma li-al-kitāb, 1975); ᶜAbbās Khiḍr, *al-Qiṣṣa al-qaṣīra fī Miṣr mundhu nashʾatihā ḥattā sanat 1930* (Cairo: al-Dār al-qawmiyya li-l-ṭibāᶜa wa-al-nashr, 1966); and Sayyid Ḥāmid al-Nassāj, *Taṭawwur fann al-qiṣṣa al-qaṣīra fī Miṣr min sanat 1910 ilā sanat 1933* (Cairo: Dār al-kātib al-ᶜarabī, 1968).

the emergence of a remarkable outpouring of talent in Egypt. The pioneer of the group was, by general consent, Muḥammad Taymūr (1892–1921), who, in spite of his early death, made a major contribution to the development of the short-story genre.[22] He was followed by a group of writers known as *al-Madrasa al-ḥadītha* (The New School)—including such major figures as Maḥmūd Taymūr (younger brother of Muḥammad, 1894–1973), Yaḥyā Ḥaqqī (b. 1905), and Maḥmūd Ṭāhir Lāshīn (1894–1954), who brought the short-story genre in Arabic to a truly remarkable level of technical and artistic sophistication. Space does not allow a full assessment of the achievements of this group; in the context of a discussion of the development of the short-story genre in Arabic, however, I would suggest that the remarkable rapidity with which a genuine maturity was achieved in this genre may be due in no small part not only to the appropriateness of its generic characteristics for the literary expression of the societal needs of the time (with the analysis of the status of women at the head of the list) but also to the fact that the development of the short-story genre itself and, in particular, its Russian and French traditions (from which these Arab pioneers clearly derived so much inspiration) is itself of comparatively recent vintage.

The Novel

It is hardly surprising that the development of the novel, in comparison with the short story, was a more complex and even disjointed process. The ability to project aspects of "life on a large scale," to place realistically drawn characters into authentic environments, and to do so in a style that was palatable to a newly emerging readership—these were skills that needed a lengthy and concentrated period of application and technical development, something that was, and in many cases remains, a luxury that many would-be novelists cannot afford.

Pioneers in modern Arabic prose-writing honed their descriptive skills in a series of works that discuss visits to Europe and its various institutions, from the narratives of Rifāᶜa Rāfiᶜ al-Ṭahṭāwī (*Takhlīṣ al-ibrīz fī talkhīṣ Bārīz*) and ᶜAlī Mubārak (*ᶜAlam al-dīn*) to the *maqāma*-inspired works of Nāṣīf al-Yāzijī, Aḥmad Fāris al-Shidyāq, and Muḥammad al-Muwayliḥī. Incidentally, this theme—of Arabs visiting Europe—was to become a major focus of the Arabic novel in the course of its development. In a succession of works by Tawfīq al-Ḥakīm, Shakīb al-Jābirī, Yaḥyā Ḥaqqī, al-Ṭayyib Ṣāliḥ, and ᶜAbd al-Raḥmān Munīf, one can follow the course of a love-hate relationship between two cultures;

22. Muḥammad Taymūr's contribution is well discussed in the recent study of E. C. M. de Moor (ed.), *Un oiseau en cage: Le discours littéraire de Muḥammad Taymūr (1892–1921)* (Amsterdam: Rodopi, 1991).

while for Ṣāliḥ, Europe is an arena for violent confrontation, for Munīf it serves (as is all too frequently the case in real life) as a place of exile. However, before al-Muwayliḥī sends his narrator, ᶜĪsā ibn Hishām, to Paris to visit the Great Exhibition of 1899 (in the "second journey" [*al-Riḥla al-thāniya*] of *Ḥadīth ᶜĪsā ibn Hishām*), he has already made a crucial contribution to the development of modern Arabic fiction in the first part of his famous book. ᶜĪsā ibn Hishām conducts a pasha from the previous generation on a tour of Cairo in the 1890s. Recognizable Egyptian stereotypes are shown behaving in characteristic ways in settings that, although depicted in rhyming prose of the utmost classical virtuosity, were sufficiently accurate and indeed witty enough to make the work an instantaneous success when it was published in 1907. One crucial feature of novel-writing—the depiction of contemporary society in the often confrontational process of change—had been put into place. However, al-Muwayliḥī's work illustrates for us at the same time a feature of society that was to remain a stumbling block in the development of the novel in Arabic for some time. *Ḥadīth ᶜĪsā ibn Hishām* has extremely few female characters; the only one who emerges from the background and participates in the action in any real sense is a dancer-prostitute. In one of the later chapters that depicts a visit to a theater, al-Muwayliḥī uses one of his "characters" to make it abundantly clear that he finds it utterly inappropriate that women should be seen in public or portrayed in amorous situations in a literary text.[23] The implications of this type of attitude were to affect the choice and portrayal of female characters in Arabic novels for some time to come.

We have just drawn attention to the brilliant style in which al-Muwayliḥī's depiction of the realities and foibles of Egyptian society are drawn. The work was published in serialized form in the al-Muwayliḥī newspaper, *Miṣbāḥ al-sharq*, and was enjoyed by readers from among the intellectual elite. However, such exercises in neoclassicism were clearly not designed to appeal to an expanding popular readership, whatever the subject matter might be. It was part of the literary (and commercial) genius of the Lebanese émigré journalist Jūrjī Zaydān (1861–1914) to appreciate that popular interest in the growing library of adventure novels could be exploited for educational and even nationalist purposes. Using his own magazine, *al-Hilāl* (founded in 1892), he published a whole series of historical novels. The episodes that he selected from Islamic history allowed him to portray in fictional form significant events from the Arabic national heritage. The benefit of historical distance allowed him to make each scenario the framework for a local "human-interest" story, often including

23. See Muḥammad al-Muwayliḥī, *Ḥadīth ᶜĪsā ibn Hishām* (Cairo: al-Dār al-qawmiyya, 1964) 278–79; trans. Roger Allen, in *A Period of Time* (Reading, England: Garnet, 1992) 368–77.

a pair of lovers. But clearly a major feature of these works that may account for their continuing popularity (they remain in print today) is the style in which they are written. In contrast to al-Muwayliḥī, for example, Zaydān set out to write works that could be accessible to a wider audience, using familiar vocabulary and uncomplicated sentence structures. Following Zaydān's example, a number of writers made use of such journals as *al-Riwāya al-shahriyya* (Monthly Novel) to publish historical fiction, including Nīqūlā Ḥaddād (d. 1954), Yaᶜqūb Ṣarrūf (d. 1927), and Faraḥ Anṭūn (d. 1922).

Somewhere in the midst of these divergent trends we must place Muḥammad Ḥusayn Haykal's novel *Zaynab*, published in Egypt in 1913, but apparently written in France at an earlier date (1911?). *Zaynab* has often been termed "the first real Arabic novel" in that, unlike many of the other works that we have described above, it depicts authentic Egyptian characters in an indigenous setting. To a certain extent this may be true, but even when compared with the descriptive detail of al-Muwayliḥī's work of a decade earlier, *Zaynab* comes up short on "authenticity." The countryside of Egypt is depicted with the overwhelming sentiment of a writer in a foreign country, recalling it in its most idealistic and romanticized garb—man at one with his environs. Apart from the epistolary mode used for communication between the hero, Ḥāmid, and his cousin, ᶜAzīza—a favorite device among early writers of love fiction—the behavior of male and female characters in *Zaynab* can hardly be considered authentic; by way of comparison, consider, for example, the remarkable short story written several decades later by Yūsuf Idrīs, "Ḥādithat sharaf," in which he gives a vivid description of the "fishbowl" atmosphere of a similar microcosm.[24] However, there is one area in which Haykal does make a gesture towards realism in *Zaynab*, and that is in the use of the colloquial dialect in the dialogue; even though there is rather little of it, it represents an important step in an area of continuing debate on the language of fiction.

In the light of a historical retrospective such as this, *Zaynab* emerges as a significant stage on the path to the development of the novel in Arabic but one that would clearly benefit from being relieved of the burden of being designated "the first" of any particular subcategory, a role that it does not fulfill with particular success. It is here, I would suggest, that the course of development of the short story becomes relevant. Following the end of the First World War and the 1919 Egyptian Revolution, the 1920s were a period of great expectations, changes, and political upheavals. The period witnessed further advances in the

24. Yūsuf Idrīs, "Ḥadīthat sharaf," *Ḥadīthat sharaf* (Cairo: ᶜĀlam al-kutub, 1971) 94–123, trans. Nadia Farag as "Peace with Honour," in *Arabic Writing Today: The Short Story* (ed. Mahmoud Manzalaoui; Cairo: Dar al-Maaref, 1968) 234–55.

continuing debate on the status of women. An Egyptian Feminist Union was founded in 1923, and there was a significant increase in publications by and for women. All this ferment was reflected in the short stories that were published at the time, including the highly successful first anthologies of short stories by Maḥmūd Taymūr.[25] Male and female characters were portrayed in vignettes culled from real-life situations within the family and in society at large; their tales were told in a language that was both accessible and adaptable. Moreover, in 1926, Ṭāhā Ḥusayn published in serial form an account of his early childhood, which, in its skillful use of fictionalizing devices, showed a keen awareness of narrative techniques.[26]

The Arabic novels that appear in the 1930s reveal a group of authors experimenting with aspects of the craft of writing in a new genre—Ibrāhīm al-Māzinī, Tawfīq al-Ḥakīm, ᶜAbbās Maḥmūd al-ᶜAqqād, Maḥmūd Taymūr, Shakīb al-Jābirī, Dhū al-Nūn Ayyūb, Tawfīq Yūsuf ᶜAwwād—each author brings a concern with particular aspects of the novelistic craft to bear and contributes to the larger project. The very fact that such a montage of distinguished Arab littérateurs should be experimenting with the composition of novels (and with such varying degrees of success) two decades after the initial publication of *Zaynab* is surely further evidence of the need for a more realistic assessment of its qualities and place in the development of this complex fictional genre. During this same decade of the 1930s, a member of a younger generation of writers, Najīb Maḥfūẓ, at first tries his hand at the short story, but then, having translated an English work on Egyptology into Arabic, begins a long career as a novelist with three works set in ancient Egypt. At the same time, he sets himself the task of reading novels from all the major Western traditions and of equipping himself for the process of turning the eye of the novelist in Arabic to a critical analysis of the ills of his own society and people. Maḥfūẓ undertook this assignment in the early 1940s, and the Arabic novel has been in his debt ever since. Reflecting the concerns of an entire generation of readers across the Arab world in the decades following the Second World War, his works have stimulated a whole younger generation of writers, who have been able to use the solid basis that his *oeuvre* provides to explore reality in all the ways that make the novel genre a continuing focus of experiment and debate.

25. The earliest writings of Maḥmūd Taymūr are discussed in detail by Rotraud Wieland, *Das erzählerische Frühwerk Mahmud Taymurs: Beitrag zu einem Archiv der modernen arabischen Literatur* (Beirut: Franz Steiner, 1983).

26. This craft has been analyzed with great perception by Fedwa Malti-Douglas, *Blindness and Autobiography:* al-Ayyam *of Taha Husayn* (Princeton: Princeton University Press, 1988).

Conclusion

Each of the fictional genres that we have been discussing here is fulfilling an important role in the intellectual life of all the nations of the Arab world. While the vagaries of influence and a host of local factors may produce a considerable diversity in both subject matter and literary quality, recent years have seen the appearance of a number of journals (and critics who write for them) that are willing to view Arabic fiction within a more than purely local perspective.

Among general issues that seem to impinge upon fictional writing, the status of the writer within society is clearly one that has a major impact. Censorship is a given in many of the societies in which Arabic fiction is published. Some writers have gone to prison for their opinions, even though expressed through the supposed ironic distance of fiction; others have preferred either silence or exile. Beyond these direct assaults on the fictional endeavor, however, we need to bear in mind the fact that creative writing is still not a career by which one may earn a living in the Arab world. The more fortunate writers may obtain a job in a conducive field, such as journalism and magazine editing (often subjecting themselves even further to the control of the state's cultural apparatus), but for many other writers, even this is not an option. It is thus hardly surprising that the short story is currently the Arab world's most popular literary genre, both because the process of composition is comparatively shorter than the process required for the novel and also because there is a plethora of publications to which to submit short fiction.

Here we note an interesting difference between the situation in the Arab world and the West. A large number of Arab-world authors publish short stories for the first time in various magazines and newspapers and then, at a certain point, gather a group together and publish them. In the Western world, by contrast, the process of publishing short story collections *in book form* is a much more arduous task. We thus return to the question of attitudes to the two genres that was discussed earlier. Except at the hands of the most illustrious practitioners of the short-story craft, the genre in the West tends to be regarded as a somewhat ephemeral phenomenon, appearing in a number of well-known monthly magazines on a regular basis, but then disappearing.[27] By contrast, the time and commitment required to produce a novel become a considerable handicap for the would-be novelist writing in Arabic. The list of those who have written just one such work and then moved on to other genres and spheres is

27. Yūsuf Idrīs, arguably the Arab world's most accomplished writer of short stories to date, made this point to me with a certain amount of glee in our final telephone call before his death in 1991.

a large one. Other writers have persevered, often in the face of considerable personal and societal odds. Better publication opportunities and book distribution, not to mention contacts between scholars and critics in the Middle East and the West, mean that we have a better awareness than ever of the breadth and depth of new fiction-writing across the Arab world.

The different paths taken by these fictional genres in the various parts of the Arabic-speaking world, the ways in which each has influenced the development of the other, and failures and successes of various experiments—these have been explored briefly above in an attempt to reveal the way in which the generic purposes of each found appropriate expression at the different stages of the complex process known as *al-nahḍa*. The vibrant creative and critical tradition that has emerged shows clearly that, from such early experiments—some successful, others not—a lively tradition of fiction has resulted.

An Arabic Poem in an Israeli Controversy: Maḥmūd Darwīsh's "Passing Words"

Issa J. Boullata

Three months after the beginning of the Palestinian *intifāḍa* on December 9, 1987, against the Israeli occupation of the West Bank and the Gaza Strip, Maḥmūd Darwīsh published a poem in the Arabic-language weekly of Paris, *al-Yawm al-Sābi*^{c}, entitled "^{c}Ābirūn fī kalām ^{c}ābir." Unlike many of the Arabic poems on the *intifāḍa* published before and after it, this poem attracted a great deal of attention in Israel and occasioned a heated debate among Israeli intellectuals and politicians.

A short piece in free verse consisting of about 250 words, disposed in about fifty lines of various lengths, and organized in four unequal stanzas, it addresses the Israelis, without naming them, as "you who pass between passing words" and asks them to leave Palestinians alone. The images used by Darwīsh touched a raw nerve among certain Israeli Jews, both on the right and on the left of the political spectrum, because the poem put forth in the language of everyday life a powerful expression of Palestinian identity and attachment to the land. Furthermore, it strongly conveyed the simple aspirations of the Palestinians who, according to the poet, want only to be left alone in their land, to live in it as they like and know how to do, and not to be interfered with. The poem's emotional appeal to Palestinians and others is based on the natural desire of all human beings to be masters in their own country, enjoying all human and civil rights. But the irritation of the Israeli Jews who criticized it was caused by what they considered to be the poet's portrayal of them as a negation of that natural desire, which they recognize in themselves but cannot apparently tolerate in Palestinians. It was also caused by the poet's call on them to withdraw, for the time of withdrawal has come, and Palestinians, as the poet says, have a great deal to do in their country other than to go on suffering and dying at Israeli hands.

The poem was translated into Hebrew soon after its appearance in the Arabic press and was published in *Yediᶜot Aḥronot*, the Israeli daily with the largest circulation, accompanied by an ill-conceived, foggy article that unwarrantedly suspected a criticism by Darwīsh of the direction of the Palestinian movement. A few days later, the Israeli daily with the second largest circulation, the right-wing *Maᶜariv*, offered a new translation on the first page of its March 17, 1988, issue along with a photograph of Maḥmūd Darwīsh and an article with a headline declaring: "Poet Maḥmūd Darwīsh, PLO cultural official, calls on Palestinians to kick out the Jews from the sea to the Jordan." Although the new translation was incorrect in many places, it—accurately—did not contain such a call. On the next day, *Haᵓaretz* published a telephone interview with Darwīsh, conducted the day before by one of its journalists, in which the poet said he was inspired by the *intifāḍa*, that the *Yediᶜot Aḥronot* translation was closer than others to the original, and that his poem called on the Israelis to withdraw from the occupied territories so that the Palestinians could establish in them their own independent national state. He added that neither the poem nor he personally had advocated throwing the Jews into the sea, as was wrongly claimed.

The Israeli daily *Davar* entered the fray with a new Hebrew translation of the poem. Thus the poem in translation, the accompanying articles, and the *Haᵓaretz* interview unleashed a continuous, almost daily, flow of other articles in the Israeli press as well as angry comments in the Israeli Knesset for several weeks, a critical account of which has been given in French by Simone Bitton, an Israeli journalist of Moroccan origin, now living in France.[1] I do not need to recapitulate the Israeli debate here, which seemed to have been fostered by right-wing journalists and politicians and joined in by leftists for internal Israeli political reasons that had little to do with the poem. But it is worth mentioning that the Israeli novelist Amos Kenan, a personal friend of Darwīsh, wrote a very negative response in *Yedi^{c}ot Aḥronot* (March 25, 1988), that Professor Mattityahu Peled (a former general in the Israeli army, later a leader of the peace movement, d. 1995) wrote a criticism of the Hebrew translations and a literary appreciation of what he called "a poem of anger," and that Uri Avneri (editor of the Israeli weekly *Ha^{c}olam Haze* and advocate of dialogue and peace with the Palestinians) wrote an article denouncing what he termed the arrogance of the Israeli left.[2] From Tunis, Maḥmūd Darwīsh himself entered into the debate and wrote an article in the Parisian newspaper *al-Yawm al-Sābi^{c}* to refute the wrong interpretations of his poem.[3]

In point of fact, however, the debate in Israel was not about the poem but about the Palestinians, the PLO, and the *intifāḍa* and about Israeli policy toward them. Earlier on, Israeli society was divided concerning its government's policy in relation to the Occupied Territories. Some Israelis argued that the territories should be relinquished in peace negotiations and others that they should be annexed permanently. The Palestinian *intifāḍa* had begun to change the positions of certain groups in Israel in this regard. The poem of Maḥmūd Darwīsh provided an occasion to bring such change of positions to the surface for public discussion; it was also a hard-liner's pretext to rally the Israelis behind a unified policy and to justify the so-called "iron-fist" policy toward the Occupied Territories. It was in these circumstances that Yitzhak Shamir, Israel's Prime Minister, addressed the Knesset on April 28, 1988, to denounce the poem and to warn Israelis of Palestinian designs. Referring to the *intifāḍa* in his speech, he said:

> It is clear that it is not peace that is being sought by the trouble-makers, by those who lead them, and by those who support them. It is not necessary for one to be a seer to surmise their intentions. For the exact expression of the

1. Simone Bitton, "Le poème et la matraque," in *Palestine, mon pays: L'Affaire du poème*, by Mahmoud Darwich, with the participation of Simone Bitton, Matitiahu Peled, and Ouri Avnéri (Paris: Editions de Minuit, 1988) 11–43.

2. See Matitiahu Peled, "Un poème de la colère," in Darwich, *Palestine, mon pays*, 71–79, original Hebrew in *Ha^{c}olam Haze*, April 6, 1988; and Ouri Avnéri, "L'Arrogance de la gauche israélienne," in Darwich, *Palestine, mon pays*, 83–94, original Hebrew in *Ha^{c}olam Haze*, April 13, 1988.

3. See Mahmoud Darwich, "Notre pays, c'est notre pays," in Darwich, *Palestine, mon pays*, 50–59, original Arabic in *al-Yawm al-Sābi^{c}*, March 28, 1988, written as a letter to Samīḥ al-Qāsim, dated March 22, 1988; and idem, "L'Hystérie du poème," in *Palestine, mon pays*, 60–68, original Arabic in *al-Yawm al-Sābi^{c}*, April 18, 1988.

> objectives sought by the gangs of assassins organized under the cloak of the PLO has just been given by one of their poets, Maḥmūd Darwīsh, so-called Minister of Culture of the PLO, regarding whom one asks by what justification he has given himself a reputation of being a moderate.
>
> I could have read this poem before the parliament, but I do not want to give it the honor of appearing in the archives of the Knesset.
>
> Those who have eyes to see and ears to hear did not need the stupid poem of this doubtful poet who orders us not only to quit the country for good, but even to carry our dead with us. They know in advance the real intentions of our enemies and of those who raise the flag of organizations of assassins in the course of their violent demonstrations. But the inhabitants of Israel, the forces of law and order, the soldiers and policemen who face the demonstrations and the violence have the strength, the patience, the determination, and the endurance necessary to suppress and annihilate the trouble-makers.[4]

Other Knesset members from various political parties rose to denounce the PLO and Darwīsh. And *Yediᶜot Aḥronot* appeared on the next day with a headline saying: "Unity found again in the Knesset, thanks to a Palestinian poem."[5]

An English translation of Darwīsh's poem appeared in the *Jerusalem Post* on May 13, 1988, under the title "Those Who Pass between Fleeting Words."[6] The poem was also rendered into German by Angelika Neuwirth soon afterwards and published with the *Jerusalem Post* English translation.[7] A French translation by Abdellatif Laâbi (ᶜAbd al-Laṭīf al-Laᶜabī) was also soon published in *Palestine, mon pays*,[8] a book that appeared in Paris in June 1988, bringing together a lot of information on the "affair" of the poem in Israel.[9]

In the remaining part of this paper, I will concentrate on the poem itself, analyzing its themes and the constituent elements of its images.[10]

Although the Israelis were not mentioned by name in the poem, they seem to have recognized themselves in it when the poet addressed himself to "those

4. See Darwich, *Palestine, mon pays*, 19–20.

5. For details of the Knesset discussion, see Simone Bitton, "Le poème et la matraque," in Darwich, *Palestine, mon pays*, 20–22.

6. *The Jerusalem Post*, May 13, 1988, p. 6. This translation was later published in Zachary Lockman and Joel Beinin (eds.), *Intifada: The Palestinian Uprising against Israeli Occupation* (A *MERIP* Book) (Toronto: Between the Lines, 1989) 26–27.

7. Angelika Neuwirth, "Die da vorübergehen inmitten vergänglicher Rede," in *Moderne arabische Literatur* (ed. Claudio Lange and Hans Schiler; Berlin: Das arabische Buch, 1988) 59–61.

8. See "Passants parmi des paroles passagères," in Darwich, *Palestine, mon pays*, 47–49. Unlike the other translations, which have four stanzas, this French translation is divided into five stanzas, but the text is the same.

9. For a review of this book in English by Hassan El Nouty, see *IJMES* 22 (1990) 487–89; for a review in Arabic by ᶜAbduh Wazin, see *al-Nāqid* 1 (November, 1988) 59–61.

10. All English quotations from the poem are my translation, unless otherwise stated.

who pass between passing words," which he repeats six times in the course of the poem and which is slightly different from the word in the title, using *ᶜābirūn* 'those who cross or traverse', instead of *mārrūn* 'those who pass'. Darwīsh may be making an allusion to the Hebrews in the title, for the Arabic word *ᶜābir* (plural: *ᶜābirūn*) corresponds to the Aramaic word *ᶜibray* and the Hebrew word *ᶜibrî*, which originally meant 'one from the other side (of the river)' and designated one of the Hebrews, the Semitic tribes who were descendants of Abraham, and now means one whose language is Hebrew (in Arabic: *ᶜibrī*).[11] Be that as it may, it is the whole content of the poem, not the title word *ᶜābirūn*, that drew the attention of the Israelis. In the circumstances of the *intifāḍa*, the passing words are probably the words of the *intifāḍa* and whatever expedient words of instructions for action its leaders announce from day to day until it eventually achieves its ends, when Palestinians can once more turn to the other important work that they have to do in their country and that the *ᶜābirūn*, the interfering Israelis, are now preventing.

"Carry your names, and be gone," the poet tells them. Israelis have been known to change the Arabic names of many Palestinian localities to Hebrew names, beginning with the West Bank, which they call Judea and Samaria. The poet wants the Arab identity of the land to be restored and the Israelis to withdraw, along with their names and the names they gave to Palestinian localities. "Pull out your hours from our time," he adds. The *intifāḍa* started a new time, not only in the sense of a new direction in the history of the struggle for the Palestinian homeland, but also in the real sense of setting the hours of the day in a manner not to correspond to Israeli summer or winter time. Moreover, the poet wants Palestinian time, both as actual hours of the day and as history, to be free from Israeli intervention. "Steal what you will from the blue of the sea and the sand of memory / Take what pictures you will," he admonishes the Israelis, advising them to be on their way out with whatever photographs they like to take of the Mediterranean homeland full of memories. But he tells them that, even so, they will never know or understand "how a stone from our land builds the ceiling of the sky." Here the poet uses the very symbol of the *intifāḍa*, its simple weapon against the occupiers that has attracted international attention and sympathy, namely the stone, to say it builds the ceiling of high heaven for the Palestinians. The poet says the Israelis will never understand

11. In the Bible, Abram is referred to as *ᶜAbrām ha-ᶜibrî* 'Abram the passer-over' or 'Abram the immigrant'. See Gen 14:13. Abram was a descendant of Eber (ᶜĀbar), "the eponymous ancestor of the Hebrews" (Isadore Singer et al. [eds.], *The Jewish Encyclopedia* [12 vols.; New York: Funk and Wagnalls, 1946] 5.30a, s.v. "Eber"). See also Gen 10:22, 25–30; 11:18–26. Abram was later called Abraham. See Gen 17:5. The popular etymology of "Abraham" relates the word to *ab-ruhām* ('father of a multitude [of nations]'); *ruhām* in Arabic is still used to mean 'a large number', but it is not used any more in Hebrew. See also ibid.

this fact, for the stone thrown at the Israeli forces of occupation has restored feelings of self-confidence, dignity, and pride to the unarmed Palestinians who, for a long time, have been repressed by the much stronger Israeli forces equipped with the most modern weaponry.

The poet then details some of the odds: "From you the sword, from us our blood / From you steel and fire, from us our flesh / From you another tank, from us a stone / From you a tear gas bomb, from us rain." Yet he points to the fact that it is the same sky and air that both communities have above and around them, implying they could better live cooperatively and in peace. So he adds, "Take then your share of our blood and be gone / Go to a dancing dinner party, and be gone." The poet expects the Palestinians to pay the price of the *intifāḍa* and the Israelis to rejoice at the price, and he will accept these facts, if only the Israelis will leave the Palestinians alone afterwards. He says, "It is for us to guard the roses of the martyrs / And it is for us to live as we like."

At this point in the poem, the poet begins to elaborate on the differences between the two communities. Still addressing those "who pass between passing words," he now says they do so as "bitter dust." So he directs them saying, "Pass wherever you wish but / Don't pass among us like flying insects." Insects have a tendency to disturb human beings when flying very close to them, and the poet presents the Palestinians as a busy people who do not want to be disturbed by such insects. "For we have work to do in our land," he explains. "We have wheat to grow and to water with the dew of our bodies." Before his interlocutors say that they too have work, he adds, "And we have what does not please you here: / Stones or partridges." Though the function of stones as simple projectiles against the occupiers is understandable, the function of the partridges remains enigmatic. Does the poet merely like the alliterative sound of *ḥajar* ('stones') and *ḥajal* ('partridges')? Does he imply the former can be replaced by the latter by his use of the conjunction 'or' between them, meaning that the stones are as good as partridges when they are "flying" stones, that is, when they are stones thrown at the enemy, a matter that of course does not please the occupiers? In his article on the misinterpretations of his poem, Darwīsh wrote regarding this point that there must indeed be a real rupture between the two cultures living on the same land for translators not to know that "a partridge is a bird of the size of a pigeon and lives in the midst of stones."[12] It seems he merely wants his words to be understood at their basic level of meaning, stones and partridges being symbolic of one aspect of the Palestinian

12. See Darwich, *Palestine, mon pays*, 61. Hebrew translators rendered *ḥajal* as 'chain' (*ḥajl*?) and 'shame' (*khajal*?!), and Professor Peled rightly criticized them, but he suggested another far-fetched meaning, namely 'wedding bed' (*ḥajala*?) in the plural, referring to the demographic problem Israelis fear regarding the high birthrate among the Palestinians, causing as much anxiety to Israelis as the throwing of stones by Palestinian youths. See ibid., 76.

landscape, which the poet believes the Israelis do not appreciate, since their attention lies elsewhere.

The poet then returns to the idea of time, now emphasizing the vast difference in the conception of time between the two communities and how they view the past and the future. Though he believes the Israelis allow the past to influence their lives unduly, the poet does not want to change their way of life, but he does want it not to interfere with the Palestinian way of life and the way Palestinians view time, particularly the future. They have work to do in their land, so he says:

> So take the past, if you wish, to the market of antiquities
> And restore the skeleton, if you wish, to the hoopoe
> On a porcelain plate.
> We have what does not please you: we have the future
> And we have work to do in our land.

The poet is sarcastic when asking the Israelis to take the past to "the market of antiquities." But then he makes a challenging reference to the hoopoe, which conjures up the Jewish legend of the beautiful bird with colored plumage and crest that helped in the building of the Temple.[13] He asks his interlocutors to restore the skeleton to the hoopoe on a porcelain plate, implying that it is an unlikely feat and, if realized, would be a very fragile artifact at best and a useless one in any event.[14] But while the Israelis are busy attempting this restoration of the past, the poet indicates that the Palestinians have work to do in their land and that they have the future ahead of them, matters which do not please the Israelis.

The poet becomes more sarcastic in the next thought, when he again addresses those "passing between passing words" and says, "Pile up your illusions in an abandoned pit, and be gone," referring to the Israeli concerns about the past as mere illusions that should be buried. He adds: "Put the clock back to the legitimacy of the holy calf / Or to the timing of the revolver's music / For we have here what does not please you, so be gone." He reminds the Jews of the golden calf, which the Bible tells us the Israelites set up in the desert to worship unlawfully in the absence of Moses on Mount Sinai, and it is as though the poet is telling the modern Jews that what they are doing in Palestine by

13. The legend says that the hoopoe was entrusted with transporting the *shamir*, the miraculous worm that split the stones for the building of the Temple, the use of iron tools for the purpose having been prohibited (see *EncJud* 8.970b, s.v. "Hoopoe"). The hoopoe (*al-hudhud*) in the Qurʾān and in Arab tradition has a different story. See al-Qurʾān 27:20–28 and EI^2 3.541b–42a, s.v. "Hudhud."

14. Professor Peled says only that "this image is an allusion to the stuffed, inanimate bird" and he does not associate it with the building or the rebuilding of the Temple. See Darwich, *Palestine, mon pays*, 76.

depriving a people of their homeland is a similar illegitimate act in the absence of a higher ethical restraint and that it is only possible by the use of force, ironically referred to as "the revolver's music." Then the poet cites another difference between the two communities and says, "And we have what is lacking in you: a homeland bleeding out a people who bleed out / A homeland worthy of oblivion or memory."[15] He stresses the continuous suffering of the Palestinians, reasoning that the shedding of their blood in the national cause is itself a contributing factor in making the homeland, a homeland that has also given them birth in suffering. This homeland, he says, is worthy of forgetting because of the great suffering associated with it, but likewise it is worthy of being remembered because of the great gift of life it has given its people.

Then the poet begins the last section of his poem,[16] in which he reiterates more insistently the demand that Israelis be gone. "It is time for you to be gone," he says, "and live wherever you like but do not live among us. / It is time for you to be gone." It is as though he is telling them enough is enough, he and his people can take it no more: the occupation must come to an end, the Palestinians are sick and tired of it. Then he adds, "And die wherever you like, but don't die among us / For we have work to do in our land." The poet wants to avoid the death of Israelis among Palestinians, so he advises them to die in another place of their choice, because Palestinians have other things to do than witness the death of Israelis or be associated with it in any way. Then he moves to the climax of his poem, his words rising to a crescendo of short, successive phrases:

Here, we have the past
We have the first cry of life
We have the present, the present, and the future

15. The Arabic *waṭanun yanzifu shaᶜban yanzifu / waṭanan* is rendered differently in the *Jerusalem Post* translation by ignoring the fact that *shaᶜban* and *waṭanan* are both in the accusative case and by changing the syntax of the verses. That translation reads:

And we have what you lack
A bleeding homeland of a bleeding people
A homeland fit for oblivion or memory.

See Lockman and Beinin (eds.), *Intifada*, 27. Similarly, the French translation of al-Laᶜabī missed the significance of the two accusatives and it reads:

Nous avons ce qui n'est pas en vous:
une patrie qui saigne, un peuple qui saigne
une patrie utile à l'oubli et au souvenir.

See Darwich, *Palestine, mon pays*, 49.

16. This section is the fifth stanza in the French translation, but it is part of the fourth in all others.

Here, we have this world and the hereafter
So get out of our [native] soil
Out of our land, out of our sea
Out of our wheat, out of our salt, out of our
wound
Out of everything, and get out
Of the memories of memory
O you who pass among passing words.

The poet sums up here the ultimate reasons for the attachment of the Palestinians to their land: to begin with, there is the fact of Palestinian history ("Here, we have the past"); then there is the fact of being born in Palestine ("We have the first cry of life"); then there is the fact of the actual presence of the Palestinians on their land now and their determination to remain on it in the time to come ("We have the present, the present, and the future"), the poet stressing the present because of its importance in determining the future; and last but not least, there is the fact of the Palestinian way of life and Palestinian spiritual values ("We have this world and the hereafter"). If any justificatory reasons are required of human beings living on their ancestral land, these are sufficient reasons for any people to ask the intruders occupying it by force of arms to get out of it. With this frame of mind, the poet asks the Israeli occupiers to leave the soil, the land, the sea, even the wheat and the salt, indeed everything they occupy; he also asks them to get out of the Palestinian wound they have caused and out of the memories they have created in the Palestinian psyche.

Throughout the poem, the poet structures his themes in opposing realities around the separate entities "you" (Israelis) and "we" (Palestinians).[17] Thus, the poem has "your hours" and "our time," "your sword" and "our blood," "your steel and fire" and "our flesh," "your tank" and "our stone," "your tear gas" and "our rain," "your dancing dinner party" and "our martyrs," "your hoopoe" and "our partridge," "your illusions" and "our bleeding homeland," "your holy calf and revolver" and "our memories and oblivion," "your past" and "our present and future as well as our past." In spite of the fact that the same sky and air are above and around the two communities in the Occupied Territories, their people as the poet has shown them are at opposite ends with regard to their values and lifestyles. The poet feels constrained to ask the occupiers to leave, because this is the only sane solution to a problem that has become intolerable. The Palestinians, as the poet has portrayed them, will never give up the land

17. Criticizing Darwīsh, Amos Kenan says, among other things, "He who is 'we' cannot be 'I,' and he who cannot be 'I' is not a poet." Yet in his response, Kenan uses few "I"s and many "we"s. See Simone Bitton's comment in Darwich, *Palestine, mon pays*, 28–29.

because there are many enduring factors binding them to it. It is "those who pass between passing words," those who have temporarily intruded, who have to withdraw, carry their names with them, and take away their time, their photographs, their hoopoe on a porcelain plate, and leave the Palestinians alone to do their work, to build the ceiling of the sky, to guard the martyrs' roses, to grow their wheat, and to water it with their bodies' dew. The time for withdrawal has come, the poet says, so let the occupiers withdraw and rejoice, let them live and die anywhere else they choose, but the essential thing is that they should be gone, for the Palestinians have work to do in their land and want to live the life they like.

The meaning of the poem could not have been put in simpler words, but the effect of the images is powerful. The poet has successfully evoked symbols of collective identity among Palestinians and rightly used the "we" pronoun to fuse their unified aspirations for liberation and for the good life they have been deprived of and want to regain. The poet has also successfully portrayed his people's perception of the Israeli occupation, its brutal methods and aims, and its obsession with the past to justify a present that is unacceptable to the Palestinians and many others, including certain Jews in Israel and elsewhere. No wonder the poem found itself at the center of so much attention and controversy when the Israelis were having a national debate about their government's policy toward the Palestinians and the Occupied Territories in the context of the *intifāḍa*.

Bi-lᶜArabī al-faṣīḥ: An Egyptian Play Looks at Contemporary Arab Society

Asma Afsaruddin

The play *Bi-lᶜArabī al-faṣīḥ* (*In Plain or Clear Arabic*)[1] by the Egyptian playwright Lenin al-Ramlī recently enjoyed a very successful run at the New Opera House in Cairo. Its enormous popularity attracted the attention of even the *New York Times* and the *Washington Post*, both of which carried a feature article on the play by their Middle East correspondents.[2] This study attempts a close analysis of the play with special attention to (1) its use of language as a political symbol and for defining relations between people perceived to be insiders

Author's Note: An abridged version of this paper was presented at the annual conference of the American Research Center in Cairo held in Baltimore, 1993.

1. In addition to having watched the play on stage, I have also had at my disposal the printed edition of the play (Cairo: al-Markaz al-miṣrī al-ᶜarabī, 1992).

2. See the *New York Times*, January 31, 1992, and the *Washington Post*, March 9, 1992, issues.

and people perceived to be outsiders, (2) its overt political message, and (3) its exploration of the collective Arab psyche. Finally, brief attention is given to the reasons for the popular appeal of the play.

The Use of Language

A notable aspect of the play is that the characters, who are from various Arab countries, speak in their indigenous dialects. By having the principal characters speak in their respective dialects, al-Ramlī seems to be underscoring the fact that despite the perceived (linguistic) unity of Arabs, there are (linguistic) diversities among them that reflect other deep-seated differences. In other words, al-Ramlī has created a microcosm of the Arab world, where its inhabitants appear to speak the same language, but on closer analysis, their variations are discovered and come to symbolize the differences that characterize and ultimately divide them.

How people are depicted as speaking the Arabic language provides important clues to their identity, particularly in their roles as insiders and outsiders in relation to the Arab polity. Those who speak in the formal, standard language, *al-Fuṣḥā* (literally, the 'eloquent language'), either exclusively or most of the time, are depicted as being outsiders and out of step with the common people who form the majority of society. Conversely, those who speak the colloquial dialects are the insiders; they are, therefore, granted a potential role in shaping and changing their political destinies.

The play's announcers are two Egyptians, one man and one woman, who speak in the *Fuṣḥā* most of the time. They are, therefore, insiders who are outsiders, who can only observe and comment on the human drama being enacted before them and are denied any involvement in it or any influence on it. They watch from the sidelines and explicate the meaning of the events; they provide the external parameters within which the events are allowed to unfold, but they cannot be the actors because they do not speak the language of the people.

This is no longer true when the announcers step into the fray and become personally engaged in the drama unfolding before them. This occurs towards the end of the play during the mock debate (see below), when the male announcer, Amīn Fāliḥ, assumes an active role in the debate and resorts to the colloquial language. The female announcer, Ṣādiqa Ṣāliḥ, becomes enraged with his arguments and also steps out from the sidelines to make her opinion known in the colloquial language. In both cases, personal involvement is possible for them only when they resort to the *ᶜāmmiyya*, the 'spoken dialect' of the common people, and cast off their formal personae. When the altercation between the two announcers is over and it is time for them to resume their formal roles, the masks slip back on, and they revert to speaking in the *Fuṣḥā*.

Margaret, the English female companion of Muṣṭafā (who is one of the Arab students in London and a key figure in the play), speaks colloquial Egyptian Arabic easily but with an atrocious pronunciation. She cannot pronounce any of the emphatic or laryngeal sounds, sounds that are distinctive to Arabic and that only indigenous speakers can articulate without difficulty.[3] She is, therefore, immediately branded as an outsider, even though she is sympathetic to the Arab cause and has linked her future inextricably (at least at the beginning) to Muṣṭafā's. Much later, at the beginning of the debate between Western and Arab students, it is clearly apparent that Margaret has severed her relationship with Muṣṭafā and switched sides because she refuses to speak colloquial Arabic anymore and responds only in English, thus severing her most important link to the "other" side.

George, the English bartender, speaks colloquial Levantine Arabic, but like Margaret, makes no distinction between the emphatic and nonemphatic sounds. Although most of George's customers are Arabs and he has learned their language after a fashion, he has no emotional investment in their lives. His relationship with the Arab students is strictly mercantile; he is also not above being bribed to withhold certain vital pieces of information, despite his frequent affirmations of honesty. He is merely a disinterested onlooker and sometimes also serves as a conduit for communications between the Arab students and the English authorities. His lack of emotional contact with the Arab expatriates makes him even more of an outsider than Margaret.

Finally, there is Richard Wisdom (rich irony is intended here in coining this last name), Margaret's father, and learned Orientalist by profession. His knowledge of Classical Arabic is superlative, and this fact is underscored when he is first introduced in the play: "He is Professor Richard Wisdom, the Orientalist who excels in Arabic," declares the announcer. Wisdom himself is aware of the fact that his knowledge of the literary language is better than the average Arab's. When Margaret announces proudly that Muṣṭafā taught her to speak Arabic, he sneers at her, "Of course [he did], which is why you cannot speak Arabic well, like most Arabs!"

Wisdom has ostensibly acquired all the accoutrements for understanding Arabic civilization, starting with its hardest-to-acquire artifact, its 'eloquent

3. One is reminded here that Arabic is referred to as *lughat al-ḍād* ('the language of [the letter] *ḍād*'), because the emphatic consonant *ḍ* is peculiar to Arabic. It is no surprise then that the pronunciation of such emphatic sounds often presents a problem for non-native speakers.

language' the *Fuṣḥā*; yet true insight into the culture he studies eludes him, for he will not accord recognition and legitimate status to the language that people actually speak in common discourse. Richard Wisdom, therefore, is an outsider who can only make superficial contact with the insiders. The playwright symbolizes this when Wisdom refuses Arabic coffee spiced with cinnamon, ginger, hyacinth, carraway, tamarind, and carob, proffered by Ḥikmet, one of the Arab students.[4] When pressed to accept, Wisdom insists on his customary cup of plain tea, like the proper English gentleman that he is. It appears that Wisdom can enter into the Arabic way of life only to a certain extent; his sterile, academic perspective, reflected in the too-perfect, artificial tongue that he speaks, prevents full participation. The diglossia has proved to be not just an insurmountable linguistic hurdle but a cultural barrier as well for even the well-informed outsider.[5]

Language is, furthermore, an important medium for the playwright to expose the motives of his characters. One can sense al-Ramlī's cynicism toward the concept of Arab unity, to which ample homage is paid in word but not in deed by the play's characters. To show how words are being manipulated by the speakers to mask their true sentiments and intent, al-Ramlī has his characters resort to pretentious speech in the *Fuṣḥā*. The equation seems to be that the greater the level of dissimulation, the greater the level of "eloquence." The artificial literary language is evoked whenever the artificial sentiments of the

4. Incidentally, Ḥikmet (here in its Turkicized form from the original Arabic *Ḥikma*) means 'wisdom' in Arabic. It is possible to see this interchange between Wisdom and Ḥikmet as exemplifying the tension inherent between the callow, one-dimensional, and uncomplicated knowledge commonly associated with the West, represented by the plain cup of tea, and the multilayered, unfathomable, and mysterious wisdom traditionally attributed to the East represented by the "exotic" spiced coffee.

5. See Carolyn Killean's article in this *Festschrift* (pp. 145–53), where she points out the importance of learning a language together with the cultural baggage that it carries.

Lest one is led to believe that Richard Wisdom is a one-dimensional, negative portrayal of an Orientalist, it must be pointed out in fairness that he also has positive qualities that are readily acknowledged by the other characters. For example, Ṣādiqa declares him to be neutral and perspicacious in his thinking (*Brūfisīr Ritshard yatamattaᶜu bi-qadr min al-ḥiyād wa-l-taᶜaqqul*). He is picked as the moderator in the debate between the European and Arab teams because he straddles both worlds and is perceived as bridging the two cultures. The Arab students also treat him with some deference on account of his scholarly knowledge regarding their heritage and culture. Wisdom considers this to be his calling-card among the Arab students, for he assures them 'You know that I am sympathetic to most of your causes, and that I value and respect the heritage of the east' (*innanī ᶜuqaddiru turāth al-sharq wa-aḥtarimuh*). He is also portrayed as somewhat of an idealist (*rajul mithālī*), who is given to making statements such as:

> All evil springs from ignorance—and dialogue (*al-ḥiwār*) is an important means of learning the opinion of the other side. In this manner, we will conquer doubt and negative perceptions of each other.

characters are expressed. The following is an example of one of these "eloquent" expressions of unity:

Kullunā hunā ikhwa ashiqqāᵓ	All of us here are blood-brothers
Mujtamiᶜūn fī al-sarrāᵓ	Assembled in joy,
Muttaḥidūn fī al-ḍarrāᵓ	United in pain;
Nuqāwimu inḥilāl al-gharb	We combat the West's dissolution
Bi-ᶜazm wa ibāᵓ	With resolve and lofty disdain.

It is interesting to note that this declaration is expressed in *sajᶜ* ('rhymed prose'). It is well known that *sajᶜ* was associated with soothsaying and divination in pre-Islamic times. The soothsayers of the *Jāhiliyya* used to foretell the future and curse their enemies in rhymed prose. As a result, *sajᶜ* as a literary genre fell out of favor for a while in the Islamic period.[6] The use of *sajᶜ* here conveys the playwright's view that public assertions of this nature are to be regarded as official cant and empty blustering.

One of al-Ramlī's characters in the play actually voices such an opinion. At one point, Amīn, the male announcer, steps up to the microphone and asks the audience, "Will you not agree with me that Arab unity is possible?" The cameraman (who like the director is usually behind the scenes but occasionally intrudes into the play) reacts without thinking, "Whose unity, my friend? Do you believe the words of the newspapers and television . . . ?" Suddenly, realizing the import of his words, the cameraman catches himself and falls silent.

There is, moreover, an obsession of the Arab elite with beautifying external appearances, with keeping images tidy and controlled[7] for which purpose the *Fuṣḥā* is the appropriate medium. This implication is reminiscent of the frequent criticism leveled at Arab litterateurs of the medieval period by modern literary critics. These litterateurs have often been accused of merely engaging in literary pyrotechnics in order to exhibit their knowledge of abstruse words and recondite expressions at the expense of a unified theme and/or profundity of meaning.[8] Al-Ramlī seems to be implying the same criticism—that, while

6. See, for example, Ibn Khaldūn, *al-Muqaddima* (ed. M. Quatremère; Paris: Institut impèriale de France, 1858) 1.181–85, where Ibn Khaldūn refers to this relation between soothsaying and *sajᶜ*.

7. One of the characters, the director of the play, makes it clear that according to directives emanating from the highest echelons of Arab governments, his main objective is spin-control. He states, "The proposals of the meeting of Arab ministers clearly stated at the very outset that all efforts were to be directed at changing the image of the Arab."

8. This kind of criticism has been particularly aimed at composers of *maqāmāt* (which are incidentally in rhymed prose) like al-Hamadhānī and al-Ḥarīrī. For example, R. A. Nicholson (*A Literary History of the Arabs* [London: Unwin, 1907] 329) described al-Hamadhānī's work in this manner:

> Each *maqāma* forms an independent whole, so that the complete series may be regarded as a novel consisting of detached episodes in the hero's life, a medley of prose and verse in which the story is nothing, the style is everything.

"the eloquent language" is an elegantly crafted vehicle of communication, it is not a very effective medium for expressing commonplace truths or everyday sentiments. It obfuscates rather than illuminates. It stifles ideas under a thick veneer of grandeur, defying implementation. In other words, the *Hochsprache* does not pack a wallop as the colloquial dialects do. By stripping ideas of their restrictive, grandiose clothing, one can set them free, so to speak—release them into the domain of the common people so that the moral imperative for translating them into action will be recognized.

The Political Message and Exploration of the Collective Arab Psyche

The following is a summary of the events in the play and an analysis of their political content.

A group of Arab students in London hurry off on the night of *ʿĪd al-fiṭr* to a new nightclub[9] in town to attend a masked ball. While they are thus amusing themselves in this unseemly manner,[10] their friend, a young man called Fāʾiz (who is Palestinian), disappears under mysterious circumstances. His friends are mystified by his disappearance. They assume that he has been kidnaped, most likely by hostile, xenophobic Englishmen, who are often given to harrassing Arabs in the streets of London. Fāʾiz, in fact, had been beaten up by such a group of thugs the day before, and his friends had promised retaliation on his behalf; instead they had elected to paint the town red. The students wait for a call from his kidnappers, who are expected to give them details about the amount of ransom to be paid and so forth. A call does come through from an unidentified group, which claims to be holding Fāʾiz hostage for an unspecified reason. This confirms the worst fears of the Arab students, who are

H. A. R. Gibb expressed a similar view (*Arabic Literature: An Introduction* [2d ed.; Oxford: Oxford University Press, 1963] 101–2). G. E. von Grunebaum (*Medieval Islam: A Study in Cultural Orientation* [2d ed.; Chicago: University of Chicago Press, 1953] 288–89) was of the following opinion:

> The *maqāmāt*, the attenuated offspring of the classical *mimoi*, are perhaps the greatest triumph of the principle of art for art's sake [. . .].

For a modern literary critic's careful and persuasive work in challenging this general assessment, see James T. Monroe, *The Art of Badīʿ az-Zamān al-Hamadhānī as Picaresque Narrative* (Beirut: American University of Beirut, 1983), esp. pp. 87–108.

9. The Arabic uses a stronger word, *maʾkhūr*, meaning 'a den of iniquity' or 'a brothel'.

10. *ʿĪd al-fiṭr*, the festival that marks the end of Ramaḍān, is one of the most sacred days (and nights) of the Islamic calendar. Cavorting at a nightclub on such a night would thus not be considered appropriate behavior.

thrown into disarray and confusion over their next course of action. There is a great deal of talk about being united in the face of this adversity and mounting an attack together against Fā^ɔiz's aggressors. But the talk of unity turns to mutual recriminations when they start quizzing each other about their whereabouts on that fateful night. No one wishes to confess to being engaged in unbridled hedonism while a helpless Fa^ɔiz was being spirited away. Refusal to admit the truth and accept the blame creates deep distrust and dissension among the Arab students. These dissensions create serious chinks in their armor and become apparent even to the "foreigners" (the English), who learn to sneer at what they correctly perceive to be a façade of much-trumpeted unity and brotherhood.[11]

The night Fā^ɔiz disappears, an act of arson takes place in London—an angry mob of people burn down a bookstore. When the Arab students file a police report about Fā^ɔiz's disappearance, the English police inspector before whom they appear and who is openly contemptuous of them, links Fā^ɔiz's disappearance to the arson. He makes the accusation that Fā^ɔiz has burned down the bookstore—for Arabs are known for their disregard for knowledge and are prone to burning books[12]—and then gone underground to escape detection. The police inspector, making this accusation from his position of great power, appears so convincing that the Arab students now feel compelled to defend Fā^ɔiz's honor by justifying his purported act of arson. In other words, if Fā^ɔiz is believed to have committed arson, then there must have been a good reason for the act. The students do not deny the accusation anymore—instead, they claim that the bookstore must have contained books hostile to and defamatory of Arabs. Suddenly, Fā^ɔiz has been thrust into the role of a criminal, and his partisans feel compelled to defend his "crime."

To save Fā^ɔiz, the students must admit their true whereabouts on the night of the former's disappearance and acknowledge their own culpability. They realize the moral imperative for doing so, but no one volunteers to do it.

11. Incidentally, all those who attend the masked ball are robbed at gunpoint. When the robbers offer those in attendance a choice between handing over their possessions or taking their masks off in order to save their lives, they hurriedly hand over their valuables. The physical masks, therefore, are manifestations of the false personae of the play's characters and their hypocrisy.

12. This brings to mind the persistent accusation leveled at ^cAmr ibn al-^cĀṣ and his army, mainly in the West, that they had burned down the library at Alexandria when they conquered Egypt. In reality, the main part of the Alexandrian library was destroyed by fire when Julius Caesar beseiged Alexandria in 47 B.C. The subsidiary library at the Serapeum was ransacked by fanatical Christians in 391 A.D., on the orders of the Byzantine Emperor Theodosius. See, for example, Edward Gibbon, *The History of the Decline and Fall of the Roman Empire* (ed. J. B. Bury; London: Methuen, n.d.) 5.455–54. Regrettably, a few Arab historians fell prey to this canard and related it as historical fact; see, for example, al-Qifṭī, *Ta^ɔrīkh al-ḥukamā^ɔ* (ed. J. Lippert; Leipzig: Dieterich, 1903) 355–56.

Eventually, the Arab students become so involved in protecting their reputations while maintaining a show of (verbal) unity in public, that they consequently forget about Fāʾiz. Finally, things deteriorate to the point that the students turn against Fāʾiz and try to blacken his character. They tell Amal, his suffering fiancée, that he has found a new love and deserted her. Due to this alleged act of treachery, they are absolved from their responsibility to seek his return and are justified in turning their backs on him.

The climactic moment of the play is created by preparations for the debate that is organized by Richard Wisdom between the Arab students and a group of European students to discuss the disappearance of Fāʾiz. In order to groom themselves for the real showdown, the Arab students decide to hold a mock debate among themselves. The debate has trouble getting off the ground, for no Arab student wishes to represent the European viewpoint and have his or her 'Arabness' (*al-ʿurūba*) impugned. Finally, the two announcers step in and assume the role of the European adversaries.

As the mock debate heats up and each side hurls a familiar litany of accusations at the other,[13] Amīn, the male announcer, begins to warm to his position, and a strange transformation occurs. He starts to believe in the certitude of what he says and becomes progressively more hostile to the Arab students. His renegade behavior in turn elicits their hostility and suspicion. His fiancée, Ṣādiqa, the female announcer, breaks off her engagement to him. His hostile compatriots cannot dismiss his accusations as easily as they can when the same charges are made by Europeans who may be motivated by political concerns and innate prejudice. The charges take on a new, horrifying dimension when they come from someone among them. The others recoil in horror and do not know how to handle the situation. Incidentally, the real debate between the Arab and European students never takes place, for the Arab students abort the debate by protesting the arguments of the other side even before they are presented.

The playwright's purpose here seems to be to show that the Arab elite cannot accept honest self-appraisal; self-delusion has become a way of life to the extent that even well-intentioned criticism cannot be recognized for what it is.

13. For brevity's sake, I will give only a few examples. The Western side asks the Arab students why, if they were so critical of the Western legal system, had they come to study law in England? The Arab side responds that the West may have created elaborate laws and constitutions, yet they are the first to trample justice underfoot. The Westerners are accused of being prone to homosexuality, robbery, murder, and rape. The Western team poses the question that if indeed the Arabs had a conscience and nobler characters, why did they let their people die of hunger? Muṣṭafā rebuts by asking why, if Westerners were truly happy and free, did such large numbers of them commit suicide? The arguments continue in the same vein.

He is also attempting to underscore the fact that not all external criticism directed at Arabs is invalid and motivated by malevolence. It is not the provenance of the criticism that is important but its nature. Lenin al-Ramlī judiciously balances the validity and invalidity of the (internal and external) criticisms that are leveled as a matter of course against leaders in the Arab world or against Arabs in general.

It must be obvious by now that the central concern of the play is the Palestinian issue. Fā$^{\supset}$iz is Palestine personified and was snatched away while the Arab elite frolicked in the pleasure dens of Europe. When they realize what has happened, it is too late. Every Arab and anyone familiar with the Arab predicament, watching this play, immediately understands the criticism inherent in the play directed at effete Arab rulers, who, to paraphrase a well-known saying, "plucked at the lute while Palestine burned." The play clearly apportions the greater part of the blame to Arab rulers themselves for the loss of Palestine—to their disingenuousness, their self-absorption, and their internal dissensions.

Al-Ramlī, moreover, underscores the inability of the Arab elite to respond in an effective manner to the crisis that looms before them. This invites the scorn of outsiders, who notice the discrepancy between the highly charged rhetoric of the students and the feebleness of their attempts to do something constructive. The English police inspector before whom the students appear is quick to take notice of this phenomenon. He remarks, "You do not really want him to come back to you. All you wish to do is to preserve his good name."

When none of them claims to know anything about Fā$^{\supset}$iz's whereabouts, the police inspector sarcastically explains to them where he must have gone.

> Indeed, he has ascended to the heavens. The most likely scenario is that he spread his wings and flew off. You may correspond with him at his address in heaven, for someone like that must have been an angel, not a mortal!

Impotence on the part of the Arabs has become transmogrified into a tendency to apotheosize the Palestinian issue—so that it becomes an ideal to glorify in the abstract rather than a crisis to be dealt with realistically and decisively.

Arab impotence is compounded by Western alacrity in blaming the Palestinians themselves for their predicament and in portraying them as criminals. A fortuitous act of arson committed on the same night as Fā$^{\supset}$iz's disappearance becomes the vital clue to resolving the mystery from the Western viewpoint. The accusation is justified because it conforms to a negative stereotype of the Arabs; the Arabs are by tradition book-burners—ergo, the genesis of their problem lies in their own criminal natures. The message in this arbitrary accusation appears to be that the Palestinians deserved to lose their country because they were not morally equipped to hold onto their land by virtue of being Arabs. This careless syllogism allows the case to be neatly resolved in the English police inspector's mind, here a microcosm of Western conscience.

To add insult to injury, the English media have kept up a relentless, negative campaign against the Arabs. For example, the newspaper *Guardian*, which advocates that the Arabs be kept out of Britain, publishes a photograph of an Arab man, clearly in a state of inebriation, kneeling at the feet of a sultry siren.

The negative portrayals are not restricted to one side, however. Because both sides share an ineffable fear of the other, they trade unflattering stereotypes of one another. In the same studio, where the Arab director is supervising the scene that depicts 'the debasedness and the dissolution of the West' (*safāla wa-inḥilāl al-gharb*), the English, in the next room, are producing a film that portrays 'the ignorance and the decadence of the Arabs' (*jahāla wa-inḥiṭāṭ al-ᶜarab*). The latter film starts out with an Arab man with a large paunch, walking down the street with four heavily-veiled women, endowed with massive, swaying derrières, in tow.

One might guess, however, that the West with its powerful media is considerably more successful in getting its message across, effectively neutralizing the Arabic countermessage. The imbalance in the power equation between the West and the Arab world becomes patently obvious in one scene. The Arab students are gathered on stage, and the director, about to give the command to start action, watches helplessly as an English policeman walks calmly onto the stage and stands silently yet menacingly in the back. The powerful symbolism of this action is not lost on the director, who comments sarcastically that the scene, supposed to represent the Arab struggle against the West, becomes rather a testimonial to the West's stranglehold over the Arab world.

To combat these negative stereotypes, the collective Arab response is to whitewash their image as much as possible and present the best possible front to 'the supercilious West' (*al-gharb al-mutaghaṭris*) and to themselves. Unfortunately, this leads to repression of the truth and of dissent in many cases, and to the ugly fact of censorship. When one of the Arab students declares that it was impossible for anyone he knew to abase himself in the manner of the inebriated Arab in the newspaper photograph, another student, ᶜAntar, speaks up. He remarks that in fact he knew the man in the photograph and that he was from the country of. . . . At this point, the director steps in and gives the order for the sound to be killed, and the name of the country is never made known to us.

Anger then becomes directed at ᶜAntar because he dared to break ranks with the others in maintaining a united, unruffled front vis-à-vis the West. Khuzāᶜī, another student, berates ᶜAntar for this act of disloyalty and prays that the latter's own family be disgraced for having chosen to disgrace his extended family—the Arab polity.

The play ends inconclusively; Fāʾiz does not return, and his friends have not plotted a course of action. However, there is "hope" in the play. Amal, Fāʾiz's fiancée, is the gently rebuking conscience of the Arab polity. Only Amal really knows Fāʾiz. While others are quick to believe that Fāʾiz has deserted his fiancée and fallen for Eva,[14] a temptress who dispenses her favors easily, Amal maintains her faith in him and protests his innocence. Her incredulous friends ask her how she can be so certain. Amal replies:

> How does a child know its mother? How does a bird sense an impending earthquake? It knows because truth resides in the heart while falsehood lurks outside.

Amal has the disconcerting habit of showing up unexpectedly and when least wanted. She keeps reminding the others of Fāʾiz when they have conveniently chosen to forget him. It is significant that her name is Amal ('hope')[15]—her

14. Eva represents the State of Israel in the play. She is a beguiling vamp, whose meretricious charms invite the homage of all those around her, including the Arab students. In one instance, Eva is shown departing from the stage, with George, the English bartender, dutifully in tow, carrying the gifts that have been showered on her—a scene that evokes the West's financial support for Israel. To accuse Fāʾiz of having abandoned Amal in favor of Eva, would, therefore, be to accuse him of grave treachery.

15. It is necessary to dwell briefly here on the names of some of the characters in the play, for they are indicative of the roles assigned to them. Fā'iz, the central character of the play, means 'a victor, a triumphant one', reflecting the playwright's belief that his cause is a just one and that he will eventually emerge the victor. Significantly, his *kunya* is Abū l-Faḍl, roughly, 'the father of grace or merit'. Elsewhere, a longer *kunya* is given, Abū l-Faḍl ʿAmmār, evoking the nom de guerre (Abū ʿAmmār) of PLO leader Yāsir ʿArafāt. As mentioned before, the name of Fā'iz's fiancée, Amal, means 'hope' [of a final victory], and Ḥikmet (from the Arabic *ḥikma*) means 'wisdom.'

The Arabness of one of the characters is affirmed by a name greatly revered in Classical Arabic literature—ʿAntar (or ʿAntara [ibn Shaddād al-ʿAbsī]), the legendary stalwart poet-warrior, the paragon of manly chivalry and loyal lover of Abla. In our play, ʿAntar is an idealist who believes that acknowledgement of the truth is desirable at all times, regardless of the consequences. Some of the characters also sport names that are intended to highlight the contrast between the literal meaning of their names and their actual personae. Richard Wisdom's name has already been mentioned, whose last name belies the true depth of his knowledge. There is also a marginal character in the play called Luqmān, who is proudly aware of his Qurʾānic namesake, the Prophet Luqmān, celebrated for his wisdom. Luqmān, at one point in the play, introduces himself as Luqmān ibn Sulaymān al-Mārūnī 'Luqmān, the son of Sulaymān, the Maronite'. The name Sulaymān is obviously a reference to the Prophet Sulaymān (that is, Solomon, the Old Testament monarch), who has become a byword for wisdom. Al-Mārūnī adds a modern, cryptic twist to the name. By coining this name, perhaps the playwright intends to indicate an intense nationalism on Luqmān's part, as ascribed to the Maronites of Lebanon today. In the play, however, Luqmān is anything but wise, for he has been taken in by the deception and artfulness that surround him.

purity of purpose and her unfailing loyalty to Fāʾiz signifies the possibility of finding a solution to the Palestinian crisis.

Popular Appeal of the Play

Bi l-ʿArabī al-faṣīḥ appears to mirror faithfully the perceptions of the Arabs themselves concerning the nature of their problem and their attitudes toward those who govern them—and herein lies the reason for its popular appeal. The verbal commitments to Arab unity, the evoking of this mythical unity as an entity that will crush opposition to it and remedy the Palestinian situation, is recognized for what it is—mere window-dressing, juxtaposed as it is against the apparent disarray and disunity among those who are often the self-appointed leaders of Arab societies. The ambience of the play is recognized by viewers as being reflective of the reality that surrounds them.

Although the play criticizes the Arab elite severely, it does so with an honesty that does not antagonize and with a humor that does not hit below the belt. Al-Ramlī brings the Arab elite into comic relief but does not reduce it to buffoonery; nor does he demonize it. The viewers recognize their political leaders in the play and revel in the artful depiction of their foibles.

The playwright's special gift for verbalizing the unvoiced criticisms and aspirations of his audience is another reason for the success of the play. Al-Ramlī responds directly to the people's inchoate need to speak the truth plainly and to step outside the boundaries of the image created by an artificial, frozen medium. At the very outset of the play, the announcers comment,

> We have discovered that the 'recorded image' (*al-ṣūra al-musajjala*) does not present the complete truth; therefore, we have decided that we will present to you, and for the first time, what occurs behind the scenes (literally 'camera').

The play succeeds because it does precisely what it claims—it takes us behind the formal, official "reality" to give us a glimpse of the unadorned truth.

Conclusion

The playwright's ultimate message seems to be that Arab unity, like the literary *koiné* for which it is a metaphor, is shown to be, on the one hand, an artificial construct, not truly representative of reality, and, on the other hand, to be a much too lofty and idealized objective for mere mortals to aspire to.[16] The truly

16. One should not forget that the best example of *al-Fuṣḥā* is the Qurʾān, Islam's sacred scripture, and the *Fuṣḥā* is, therefore, the medium of the divine revelation. The Qurʾān is held to

eloquent language is proved to be the language of the common people, the *^c^āmmiya*. It is after all the medium in which people can express their true feelings and hopes without equivocation.

---

be inimitable, and no human can duplicate its style or its contents (*i^c^jāz al-Qur^ɔ^ān*). By drawing a parallel between the *Fuṣḥa* and the concept of Arab unity, al-Ramlī seems to be implying that the latter cannot be achieved because it is beyond the reach of flawed mortals.

Part 2

Arabic

Learning Arabic: A Lifetime Commitment

Carolyn Killean

Over and over in my life I am accosted by the question, "Why did you study Arabic?" I admit it is a common reaction whenever I tell people that I teach Arabic (which they usually take to mean aerobics), and when I am questioned about my background, I must admit that I am from WASP stock and grew up in Wisconsin without setting foot in the Middle East until I arrived there with a fresh Ph.D. in Arabic linguistics in hand.

Well, the truth is I was "challenged" into learning Arabic. I chose to enroll in first-year Arabic at the University of Michigan because I was attracted to the romance of the desert and captivated by the lovely lines of the calligraphy. But what kept me going as the romance inevitably wore off with the onslaught of weak verbs, shifty case endings, and broken plurals, all encountered on a vast plain of vocabulary, was the challenge presented to me by my first Arabic teacher, who said: "No one can learn this language."

I was dumbfounded—"No one?" But my undergraduate degree depended on my learning at least some of it! Besides, I knew I was bright and had achieved success in other difficult subjects, so why not this? I decided to prove him wrong. But, over the years, reality has proven him right! Very few native speakers of Arabic can claim really to "know" this many-faceted language. As the Muslims say: *Allāhu ʾaʿlam* 'God alone knows best', and since He is the only native speaker of Classical or literary Arabic, He is the only one who knows it all. What can I, a humble WASP learner, hope to achieve, and why is it so difficult to attain mastery in this task?

In the rest of this essay, I will present a personal perspective on why that original prophecy was right and why we who seek to "learn" Arabic spend a lifetime doing it. There will be some anecdotes from my experience with this lifetime occupation. For you who aspire to acquire Arabic or who are currently caught up in studying it, may this article inspire you to keep going. Unfortunately, as you become more and more involved with this obsession with Arabic, the company gets thinner. Those who can empathize with your frustration and your deification of Hans Wehr will become smaller in number as you develop a secondary code language about Arabic, using terms like jussive, *tamyīz*, *inna*, *kāna*, and others. But keep up the quest. The initiates may be few in number, but their quality is exceptional.

Why Is Arabic So Tough to Learn?

I cannot imagine entering a Russian class and being told that I could not learn the language. But it is classified as only a class 3 language by the Defense Language Institute ranking of difficult-to-learn languages, while Arabic, like Chinese, Japanese, and Korean, is classified as a class 4 language. What is the difference? I can see that the latter three share writing systems that are formidable, but Arabic also shares an alphabetic writing system with Persian (class 3), for example, so it is not just the difficulty of the writing system. For a language to be put in the "hardest for Americans to learn" category by DLI, it must be blessed not only with a writing system opaque to Westerners, but it must be difficult to pronounce, structurally unlike the "normal" Indo-European languages, and blessed with a rich vocabulary rooted in an "exotic" culture.

In a very informative article recently published by the National Foreign Language Center in Washington, D.C., Ronald A. Walton discusses this very issue in a most enlightening way.[1] He first makes the distinction that not all foreign languages are equally "foreign." Some are cognate not only in linguis-

1. Ronald A. Walton, *Expanding the Vision of Foreign Language Education: Enter the Less Commonly Taught Languages* (NFLC Occasional Papers; Washington, D.C.: The National Foreign Language Center, 1992).

tic structure, vocabulary, and alphabet, but also in culture. They are easier to comprehend and to learn because less conceptual "newness" is involved.

Walton classifies other foreign languages as "Truly Foreign Languages" or TFLs. I like this division, for it helps to categorize the wide variety of "non-English communication" that is subsumed under the category "foreign language." This range of languages is far more diverse than we commonly recognize.[2]

The toughness of Arabic, its challenge to non-native speakers, lies especially in the variation and diversity with which it requires them to cope. They must deal both with the large amount of variation tolerated in the pronunciation of the literary language and with the wide variation in structural features possessed by the dialects—urban, rural, and Bedouin in each geographical area. This striking variety makes it difficult for non-native speakers to relate to the "core" of Arabic. Again, Arabic requires special learning effort because it is rooted in several different cultures. Finally, a phenomenon known as diglossia, or dual language competence, is widespread.

Diglossia and the Pronunciation of Literary Arabic

I began my study of Classical Arabic with Lebanese teachers, and during all my Stateside training, I heard texts read aloud in a Lebanese dialect. Naively, I assumed that I understood literary Arabic fairly well. Then, a professor from Cairo came to lecture at Ann Arbor, and I eagerly attended his first lecture. He spoke literary Arabic, but it was almost impossible for me to understand. The stress! I had learned to associate stress with long vowels or closed syllables, and he was mispronouncing word after word, stressing a syllable in which there was no long vowel in "correct" Arabic or skipping the correct syllable and stressing the one after it. The word 'school' came out *mad-ra′-sa,* when I knew it was *mad′-ra-sa.*

Not only that, he mispronounced some consonants. To mention only two, the dental fricatives were sibilants, either *z* or *s* and the affricate *j* had become *g*. I, who "saw" pictures of words in my head, was visualizing really weird spellings and misunderstanding the content of the lecture. Not until I went to Egypt and heard and learned to speak the Egyptian version of "correct" Arabic did I learn to follow the special stress patterns and consonant shifts that characterize Egyptians speaking literary Arabic.

2. The current proposal that American Sign Language is a foreign language and therefore learning it can satisfy the college foreign language requirement is an example of just how diverse these "non-English" languages can be.

In particular, Arabic tolerates variation in the pronunciation of consonants—variation that to a Westerner's ear defies easy relating. We are used to variants of English that shift vowels and occasionally tolerate such pronunciations as "da Bulls" in Chicago-ese, but I find that the variation tolerated by Arab ears exceeds my American expectations. The Egyptian version of *j* mentioned above is only one of the surprises awaiting a person who hears Arabs from different dialectal backgrounds speaking together. The common contrast cited by even the Arabs themselves is the variation in the letter *qāf*. Depending on the geographic and social background of the speaker, pronunciation may vary from *q* to *g* to the glottal stop, ᵓ. These pronunciations affect neighboring vowels in different ways, so that more than just consonant variation must be deciphered.

I particularly have trouble with the assimilation that occurs in Egyptian and Jordanian Arabic—the dialects I know. I hear with my inner eyes. For example, I hear a word and tend to visualize its shape in writing in order to comprehend it. When a colloquial word with the sound *z* is spoken by an Egyptian, I do not know how to spell it. Is it really *z*, or is it *dh* in "correct, formal" Arabic? Could it even be a *ẓ* that I am not hearing as velarized? Or could it be *s* in an environment that voices the sound? The options are too numerous and too confusing for me to process rapidly while listening to spoken Arabic.

The pronunciation of the letter *qāf* is cited in many articles about the dialects, since it is pronounced differently, not only according to geography, but also according to class of society—even depending on the "sophistication" of a given speaker. This variation, coupled with the variation mentioned above for *z* and *dh*, leads to the terrible confusion in the Western transcription of the name of the Libyan leader—Qadhdhafi.[3] Try to explain this phenomenon to outsiders, and you appreciate how familiar you have become with the natural problems of Arabic.

Recognizing Vocabulary Relationships

The second really tough challenge to learners of Arabic is to recognize roots as they "pass through" different word forms. The consonants remain the same and in the same order relative to each other, but they are joined by other consonants, usually *m* or *t*, separated differently by vowels, and often doubled in order to form the words we encounter.

Somehow, native speakers have a "root-seeking" software program in their heads, of which I would like to get a copy. Guessing at unknown vocabulary

3. For more on this topic, see the article by Alan S. Kaye in this Festschrift, pp. 385–99.

is much simpler if you can hone in on the root letters and grasp their general semantic drift and then apply the semantic overlay of the vowel and extra-consonant pattern. This may lead to success in guessing the right semantic field, and then the context in which the word appears finishes the solution of the mystery. Otherwise, relating unknown to known vocabulary can be truly frustrating.

The Enigma of the Arabic Script

Beautiful as it is, the Arabic script is extremely frustrating to read. It is a scaffolding on which the reader must hang the finishing information necessary for comprehension. The pictures are annoyingly ambiguous at times and remarkably good at disguising foreign words, generally proper names, under a cloak of long vowels that are not pronounced with any length in the source language. For example, the word *film* can be spelled acceptably as either *flm* or *fylm*, both options reflecting the same pronunciation. The tendency to use long vowels to picture the *quality* of sound in foreign words rather than its *quantity* makes it a challenge for non-native speakers to recognize words they already know well.

The script also contributes to the variation allowable in reading the skeleton pictures aloud. Since the short vowel signs are not written, the reader fleshes out the word orally and in doing so may read the same picture differently from another speaker. Since readers of Arabic who speak a native dialect can understand large variation in pronunciation of Arabic read aloud, they find it hard to understand how the shift of a reader's dialect can be so difficult for us "foreign learners." Diglossia strikes again.

Variation in Spoken Arabic

For me, the principal difficulty in achieving fluency in colloquial Arabic is the wide variation in the vocabulary and pronunciation of the dialects. Since they are not written, and since I am so "visual," grasping and retaining the vocabulary is more difficult for me. It is easier for me to keep a picture of a word in my head than to learn aurally. Arabic speakers who visualize words as I do must encounter a similar problem understanding *gotta*, *havta*, *gonna*, and various other blends so common in American English speech. When I see a dialect form written—as in some cartoon captions—I cannot read it unless I say it aloud. Although I immediately recognize it as colloquial, I struggle to pronounce it and to relate it to some expression I have already heard.

The lack of spelling rules for these word "pictures" hampers my efforts. I remember learning that the future marker for Egyptian verbs was *ḥa–* pronounced with the strong *ḥ* sound produced in the pharynx. Imagine my surprise when I borrowed a textbook from a teacher of colloquial Arabic at the American University in Cairo. She was a relatively untutored Egyptian lady who could not easily read the colloquial words in the textbook presented in phonetic transcription, so she had rewritten all of the text and drills in Arabic script. In doing this, she had consistently spelled the future prefix with *h–*, the weaker sound picture, so that it came out *ha–*. This variation, obviously acceptable to her, puzzled me: What was right? *Ḥa* or *ha*? I wanted a standard of correctness such as exists for literary Arabic to apply to colloquial written forms as well.

Learning Literary Arabic as a Dead Language

The challenge of learning literary Arabic is compounded by its lack of native speakers. Literary Arabic claims a large number of semi-native speakers, but they often disagree as to the correctness of each other's speech in a way that few speakers of other languages do. Having achieved speaking skills by virtue of schooling and listening to speeches, news, sermons, and the recitation of the Qurʾān and/or the Arabic Bible, they have a very skewed set of intuitions. Asked to discuss international politics, theology, and Arabic grammar, they would be at a loss to do so without using almost exclusively literary vocabulary and a fair amount of literary grammar, although the shift to literary grammar is less predictable. Asked to discuss their childhood, their clothing, and their family life, most Arabs would feel uncomfortable trying to keep the style in the literary mode. Humor and expressions of feeling are automatic prods to shift any literary spoken style into the more familiar and comfortable colloquial. Keeping up with such style-shifting is a real challenge to the learner of Arabic.

Structural Complexities

Much of the grammar of literary Arabic that must be mastered for someone to speak this "dialect" seems irrational at best and trivial at worst. Why do case endings keep shifting around, controlled by the presence of certain particles? The mind boggles at rules that, for example, decree that verbs, when they occur before their subjects, are not sensitive to the number (singular, dual, plural) of that subject. However, when the verb follows the subject, it is sensitive to the variation in number.

Another rule decrees that all nouns in Arabic be one of two genders—masculine or feminine. All agreement of other forms with these nouns must also make this same distinction. Feminine nouns take feminine adjectives, demonstrative pronouns, pronoun referents, and verb forms. However, once you pluralize the noun, this dichotomy is discarded in favor of a semantic one—if the plural noun refers to people—thinking beings—then the concord described above continues to hold. However, all other plural nouns, including animals, are treated in the agreement world as feminine singular nouns. That is, when you speak of "big books," you must say "books big (feminine singular)," but when you speak of "men," you must say "men big (masculine plural)" or "women big (feminine plural)."

You can see that for us English speakers, the idea of always watching out for the "concord police" is a real strain. I tell my students that Arabic is a "concord-happy" language. For example, conjugating verbs for thirteen persons in order to keep meaning and relationships straight seems excessive. There are five ways to say 'you' in literary Arabic, depending upon what gender and how many 'you's you are speaking to. Further, there are two ways to talk about 'they two', depending on the gender of the pair of participants. One summer, when I was a "mature" student in the Arabic immersion program at Middlebury College, we students tried very hard to avoid conversations with two other people in order to avoid the whole system of dual verbs, adjectives, pronouns, and so forth.

Broken plurals are the nemesis of all students of Arabic. It would not be so bad if there were no patterns at all and each plural had to be learned as a separate vocabulary item like its singular counterpart. But where there are patterns, they are inconsistent and frustrating to predict. Why is the plural of 'newspaper' (*jarīda*) *jarāʾid*, while the plural of 'city' (*madīna*) is *mudun*, not *madāʾin*? Why is the plural of 'bank' (*bank*) *bunūk,* while the plural of *ʾanf* 'nose' is *ʾānāf*?

The Role of Cultural "Foreignness" in Learning Arabic

The article by Walton mentioned above makes a very important point about the contribution of the "same culture" to the learning of a new linguistic system. In effect, he argues that learning an Indo-European language is eased by the fact that it is rooted in an Indo-European cultural frame that is not language-dependent. In contrast, languages such as Chinese, Japanese, and Arabic are rooted in a "truly foreign" culture and present the people learning the linguistic code with very new and strange customs, assumptions, and cultural clues.

When I first went to Egypt in the fall of 1966, I was advised not to fly directly to Cairo, but to stop en route to get over the worst of the jet lag before encountering Arabic in the "real" for the first time in my life. I took the advice and spent three days in Greece. The culture shock was tremendous. I was truly out of the common European cultural background and in a Mediterranean world with values that startled me and made me feel truly "foreign."

When I went on to Egypt a few days later, I experienced an even greater shock. By that time, I had studied Arabic for years, but I had never encountered in my linguistic study anything to prepare me for the sights, sounds, and smells of that "earthy" country. I was really "foreign" in that culture, and only months of residence helped me comprehend the subtleties of living successfully. For example, I made a game of the process I called MIP (Most Important Person). In order to be waited on in a store, I had to learn to establish upon entering that I was not only Important, but the MIP in the store. This often meant pushing my way to the front of a crowd at the counter, stepping on toes, calling out to the salesperson to get attention in a loud and commanding tone. Such behavior was warranted because, in this society, waiting on customers in chronological order meant nothing, and I would have waited all day if I had not become what to me was offensively pushy.

It happened that this first visit to Egypt ended with the Six-Day War of 1967 and my evacuation from Alexandria to Greece. I looked forward to seeing Greece again, feeling that this time it would not seem so foreign to me. After all, I had coped with Egyptian mores—Greek ones would be a snap. What a shock! Not only was Greece not so foreign, it felt positively European—almost American. I remember laughing at my earlier equation of Greece with foreign. It was all a matter of relativity. The Egypt experience had rendered Mediterranean culture, in my new estimation, equivalent to general European culture.

Walton in his article goes on to argue that in TFLs, students are particularly slow to develop fluency. Not only is the phonetic and structural code significantly different from English, the cultural support for the language arises from a very different set of values. It becomes quite possible to teach students to be linguistically competent while remaining culturally incompetent—if not downright ignorant. It is a dangerous combination. In 1966, I arrived in Egypt with a background in Arabic that included a Ph.D. dissertation on the deep structure of the noun phrase but was unable to converse in colloquial Arabic. I was also unaware of what the hours of office work were, unaware of the importance of the *wasīṭ*, or broker in many transactions, whether business or social, unaware of the importance of effusive greetings, unaware that I must put interaction with people above every other value, so that using the words "I must get back to work" is unacceptable in Arabic as an excuse for leaving a social gathering.

In other words, learning the sounds, letters, words, and grammar of Arabic is not enough. It is only the beginning. The cultural challenge is the really difficult one, and it is made more difficult by the fact that each Arab country has a different culture, and in each, the genders are also separated in cultural worlds of their own. Even without hearing the shift in sounds, one can tell by clothing, by behavior, and even by physical bearing the difference in Arabs coming from the Gulf, the Sudan, and the North African countries. It is truly a lifetime task to feel ahead of the game with this language and its blend of related but separate cultures.

There is no agreed-upon linguistic capital of the Arab world as there is in countries like China that also have extensive language diglossia. The de facto "king" of the dialects is Egyptian because it is the most widely understood. The exporting of its film and TV productions has schooled Arabs all over the Arab world to the nuances of Cairene and other forms of Egyptian Arabic. Only an Egyptian, however, would ever choose to speak this dialect. Our language is our identity badge, and a Saudi would not want to speak Egyptian unless forced to do so in a desperate situation in which communication was possible in no other language system—not even French or English. Thus the dialects tend to keep the Arab world a mosaic of speakers who all acknowledge the hegemony of one written picture of a special "learned" language—literary Arabic—that links them to a vast treasure of literary masterpieces. And we outsiders struggle to make even a minor inroad into that complex system during a lifetime of study. My teacher was right—no one can learn this language fully—but we do our best.

The Alchemy of Sound: Medieval Arabic Phonosymbolism

Karin C. Ryding

The evolution of elaborate systems of esoteric knowledge based on the sounds of language and their permutations is one of the most fascinating, yet least examined, aspects of the history of the Arabic language. Intimately linked with and enhanced by other Semitic linguistic traditions, the most ancient and fundamental ties between phonological form and meaning lies buried, of course, in the roots of natural language itself. The depth and power of connection between sound and meaning and the implications of the birth of semiotic systems for the human race are not only psychologically dynamic but also conceptually numinous, reinforced by the traditional spiritual potency attributed to *logos*.

Semitic Phonosymbolism

Phonosymbolism deals with sound/image, sound/meaning, and sound/archetype correspondences. Up to the present time, it has represented the intuitive, inferential, and conjectural but increasingly sophisticated study of synaesthesia and semantic values associated with submorphemic entities, also called "phonesthemes."[1]

The Semitic cultural tradition developed complex metaphysical systems of connections between sound and meaning, which were exemplified in mystical Arabic disciplines such as *jafr* 'divination'; *ḥisāb al-jummal* 'gematria'; *ᶜilm al-ḥurūf* 'onomatomancy' or *sīmiyāᵓ* 'white' or 'natural' magic—to name some of the most important—and of course the Hebrew *qabbāla*. These included an extensive array of divinatory approaches to the interpretation of sound/meaning correspondences, such as factor analysis, calculation of permutation, the art of chronograms,[2] gematria or isopsephy, astrological associations, and, through the assignment of natural properties (*khawāṣṣ*) to letters and sounds, talismanic ritual practices.[3]

In addition to the esoteric and mystical systems of sound/meaning correspondence, however, there also exists a recondite tradition within Arabic lexicography of the association of everyday meanings or concepts with the names of the letters of the Arabic alphabet. This is also a form of phonosymbolism where meanings are associated with specific phonemes that normally do not bear morphemic status.

The Root *Ḥ-R-F*

Illustrative of the complexities involved in studying any of these disciplines is the problem of the meaning of the term *ḥarf* (plural, *ḥurūf*) 'letter, phoneme, articulated sound, function word, particle, Qurᵓānic reading', itself.[4] The lexical root has the essential meaning of 'limit' or 'edge', seen by Ibn Jinnī (d. 392/1002) as referring to "the limit where the cutting of the *ṣawt* occurs, its end, its

1. Terrence Kaufman, "Review of Robert A. Blust, *Austronesian Root Theory*," *Language* 66 (1990) 626.

2. See Gernot L. Windfuhr, "Spelling the Mystery of Time," *JAOS* 110 (1990) 401–16 for more explicit analysis, especially of Persian chronograms.

3. The knowledge of these natural qualities (*ᶜilm al-xawāṣṣ*) was based on alchemy. In his book on Jābir ibn Ḥayyān, Paul Kraus discusses "la balance des lettres" at length, giving charts that describe the attribution of the four essential qualities—heat, cold, dryness, and humidity—to the letters of the Arabic alphabet (*Jabir ibn Hayyan: Contribution à l'histoire des idées scientifiques dans l'Islam* [2 vols.; Hildesheim: Olms, 1943–89] 2.224–26). These qualities, calculated in an algorithm incorporating the sequence of letters or sounds composing a name, render a formula that is said to reveal the quantitative structure of that substance.

4. See Jonathan Owens, *Early Arabic Grammatical Theory* (Amsterdam: Benjamins, 1990) 245–48, for an analysis of "*Ḥarf* in Morphology and Syntax."

extremity."[5] The range of usage of the word *ḥarf* as a grammatical term has meant that it refers to at least four things: (1) the written letter shape that represents an Arabic sound, (2) the sound itself, (3) the name of the letter/sound (for example, *alif*), and (4) a particle or function word.

One therefore finds treatises on *maᶜānī l-ḥurūf* that deal with the meanings and functions of particles such as prepositions and conjunctions,[6] as well as works by the same title that deal with the meanings attached to the names of the letters of the alphabet;[7] so that in addition to the attribution of numerical and "natural" qualities to *ḥurūf*, there appears to be a tradition of associating a real world meaning (referent) with the letters themselves, or with the names of the letters. This form of symbolism, or semantic marking, which extends to a phonemic or submorphemic level, is attested both in Hebrew and in Arabic and to some extent reflects a very early stage in the development of these writing systems, where individual signs or sounds were originally equated with concrete objects or elements of the natural environment.[8] In his article on proto-Canaanite origins of the Semitic writing systems, Brian E. Colless writes:

> The Egyptian hieroglyphic script would have served as a model, but only its central core. . . . The earliest known forms of the signs in the Semitic linear alphabet are obviously pictorial. By the acrophonic principle, the initial consonant of the Canaanite word for the thing depicted in each case provides the sound for that pictograph. Moreover, in most or all cases the sign is actually a borrowed Egyptian hieroglyph, it would appear, with its meaning translated into Semitic.[9]

Definitions of phonosymbolic primitives appear in the Arabic lexico-grammatical tradition, as well as in scientific and mystical writings, and

5. Ibn Jinnī, *Sirr al-ṣināᶜa*, p. 1, cited in Henri Fleisch, "ḥarf," *EI*².

6. Alī ibn ᶜĪsā Rummānī (d. 384/994), *Kitāb maᶜānī l-ḥurūf* (ed. ᶜAbd al-Fattāḥ Ismāᶜīl Shiblī; Jidda: Dār al-shurūq, 1981); and Ibn al-Sikkīt, cited in Ramaḍān ᶜAbd al-Tawwāb, *Thalāthat kutub fī l-ḥurūf* [al-Khalīl, Ibn al-Sikkīt, and al-Rāzī] (Cairo: al-Khanjī, 1982).

7. Al-Khalīl ibn Aḥmad, discussed below.

8. For further discussion of this topic, especially as it relates to Indo-European roots, see Yakov Malkiel, "Semantically-Marked Root Phonemes In Diachronic Morphology," in *Perspectives on Linguistics* (ed. W. Lehmann and Y. Malkiel; Amsterdam: Benjamins, 1982).

9. B. E. Colless, "Recent Discoveries Illuminating the Origin of the Alphabet," *AbrN* 26 (1988) 31. A further point of interest lies in the fact that the Arabic alphabet is an exact replication of the consonant phonemes of the language. That is, each letter or discrete sound has a phonemic value, which is not the case in the English alphabet, for example, where a letter such as "c" has no phonemic status, but is simply a spelling convention for the phonemes /s/ and /k/. Moreover, there are in English, for example, a number of phonemes with no single-letter orthographic representation, such as /š/ and /č/ and /θ/, and there are no such omissions from the Arabic orthographic repertoire. This means that the "fit" between the Arabic phonological system and the writing system is extraordinarily precise and is an accurate image or mirror of a powerful generative system.

interrelate in intriguing ways.[10] As a very preliminary contribution to the study of Arabic phonosymbolism, I present here a translation of two versions of a treatise attributed to al-Khalīl ibn Aḥmad (d. 791), who is considered the founding father of Arabic lexicography because of his creation of the first Arabic dictionary, *Kitāb al-ᶜayn*, a founder of Arabic grammatical theory, and the discoverer of the rules of Arabic prosody. The texts I use were edited and published by Ramaḍān ᶜAbd al-Tawwāb.[11]

These texts present 'meanings' (*maᶜānī*) associated with the names of the letters of the Arabic alphabet. Even in al-Khalīl's time, these meanings seem to have been in the category of esoterica. But this was one of al-Khalīl's fortes: foraging for and documenting the rare but genuine lexical items that might be inaccessible to the urban Arabic speaker of the eighth century. He provides plentiful citations of poetry to attest to the existence of these items in the language, but editor ᶜAbd al-Tawwāb comments that, "The [poetic] exemplars are not found in any poet's diwaan. One verse is from 'the book of what is read from its end as it reads from its beginnings'[12]—edited by Georg Krotkoff, in *Majallat kulliyyat al-ādāb wa-l-ᶜulūm* in Baghdad, in 1958."[13]

I have omitted the poetic citations, since although each is attributed, the editor seems to consider most of them spurious, and I include in the translation only the names of the letters and their associated meanings. I have provided a brief and admittedly speculative commentary on some of the definitions.

10. See Kraus, *Jābir*, on Jābir ibn Ḥayyān; ᶜAbd al-Tawwāb, *Thalāthat kutub*, especially al-Rāzī's treatise; Georges Vajda's "Les lettres et les sons de la langue arabe d'après Abū Ḥātim al-Rāzi" (*Arabica* 8 [1961] 113–30) on Abū Ḥātim Aḥmad ibn Hamdān al-Rāzī (d. 322/934) and the connection to the *qabbāla*; and Muḥammad ibn Mukarram ibn Manẓūr's (d. 711/1311) introduction to *Lisān al-ᶜarab* ([13 vols.; ed. Yūsuf Khayyāt; Beirut: Dār lisān al-ᶜarab, 1970] 1.ẓ–ṣ). See also Guy Trevoux, *Lettres, chiffres et dieux* (Monaco: Éditions du Rocher, 1979) for an in-depth speculative analysis of the evolution of phonosymbolism in Semitic alphabets; Thomas Willard, "What is Mystical Language?" (in *Papers in the History of Linguistics: Proceedings of the International Conference on the History of the Language Sciences, III* [ed. Hans Aarslev, Louis G. Kelly, and Hans-Josef Niederehe; Amsterdam: Benjamins, 1987] on mystical language in general; and Solomon Gandz, "The Knot in Hebrew Literature, or from the Knot to the Alphabet," (*Isis* [May, 1930] 189–214), for a discussion of the relationship between knots and the Semitic alphabet. For interconnections between Arabic grammar and the "valeur métaphysique des lettres," see Massignon, *Opera Minora* (2 vols.; Beirut: Dar al-maaref, 1963) 2.600–601.

11. See ᶜAbd al-Tawwāb, *al-Ḥurūf, li-l-Khalīl ibn Aḥmad* (Cairo: Maktabat ᶜayn shams, 1969) and *Thalāthat kutub*. The editor expresses his doubts about the attribution to al-Khalīl, since the title of this treatise is not mentioned in the standard biographies. However, it has apparently been in circulation since at least the twelfth or thirteenth century.

12. I assume that this refers to the phenomenon of palindromes.

13. ᶜAbd al-Tawwāb, *al-Ḥurūf*, 5. I happened across this mention of Professor Krotkoff synchronistically just a few months before being asked to contribute to this Festschrift. I therefore felt that this was an appropriate opportunity to present some preliminary thoughts on the issue of Arabic sound/meaning correspondence.

The Treatises

Al-Khalīl opens his treatise with the following words: "I have collected all the letters with their meanings, which have come from the Arabs, and I have compiled them as it has occurred to me, and I ask of God success in this endeavor."[14]

The Arabic letters are listed as follows:

Alif: a wretched, thin man
Bāʾ: a man who often has sexual intercourse
Tāʾ: a cow that is [always] milked
Thāʾ: the choice part of any thing
Jīm: a strong camel
Ḥāʾ: a stout woman; a woman with a sharp tongue[15]
Khāʾ: the hair on the anus [when it is thick and long]
Dāl: a fat woman
Dhāl: cockscomb
Rāʾ: tiny ticks
Zāʾ: a man who eats a great deal
Sīn: a fat, meaty man
Shīn: a man who often has sexual intercourse
Ṣād: a rooster that wallows in the dirt
Ḍād: the hoopoe [when it raises its head and cries]
Ṭāʾ: an old man who often has sexual intercourse
Ẓāʾ: a woman's breast [when it swings]
ᶜAyn: the camel's hump
Ghayn: a camel reaching water
Fāʾ: sea foam
Qāf: a man who can do without other men
Kāf: a man who settles affairs; a chaste man
Lām: a greening tree
Mīm: wine
Nūn: a fish;[16] inkwell;[17] also the Prophet Jonah
Hāʾ: a [white] mark[18] on the cheek of a gazelle

14. Ibid., 28.

15. The Arabic term is *salīṭa*, which translates both as 'stout' and 'sharp-tongued'.

16. The term used is *ḥūt*, which may also mean 'whale'. *Samaka* 'fish' is also mentioned.

17. The Arabic term is *dawāt*, spelled with *tāʾ marbūṭa*.

18. The Arabic term used is *laṭma*, which translates as 'a blow' (Hans Wehr, *A Dictionary of Modern Written Arabic,* 1979 ed.). ᶜAbd al-Tawwāb states that in one manuscript, it is described as *bayāḍ fī wajh al-ẓabīy* 'whiteness on the face of a gazelle', which I interpret as a white marking.

Wāw: a camel with a [great] hump
Lām alif: thong of a sandal[19]
Yāʾ: direction, aspect[20]

These meanings all refer to basic, real-world items, which is to be expected if they were semantic primitives. Ten refer to human beings with specific qualities; two refer to parts of humans; eight refer to animals; three refer to parts of animals; one may well be onomatopoeic (*ḍād*). The only semiabstract concept is that of 'direction' (*nāḥiya*).

The word *nūn* is known to refer to 'fish' in Arabic and even in the Hebrew alphabet, so this meaning is not unexpected.[21] The letter *jīm*, *gimel* in Hebrew, is traditionally associated with the concept of 'camel' (Arabic *jamal*).[22] In the Hebrew/Aramaic tradition, the name of the letter *mīm* is associated with 'water', so the concept of 'wine' is not too distant semantically. The word *ᶜayn*, however, defined as *sanām al-ibil* 'camel's hump', has a number of more standard meanings, including 'eye', 'spring, source', and 'essence', but these are not mentioned here.

In addition to this treatise, ᶜAbd al-Tawwāb has edited another, entitled *al-Ḥurūf*, by Aḥmad ibn Muḥammad ibn al-Muẓaffar ibn al-Mukhtār al-Rāzī (d. ca. 630/1232). Al-Rāzī's book covers the linguistic, lexical, and qabbalistic/mystical meanings associated with Arabic letters and sounds. Apparently he had access to two different versions of the al-Khalīl *Ḥurūf* manuscript and presents both of them in chapter 7 of this work. One of the manuscripts agrees fairly closely with the one I have just cited, but the other differs considerably. It is as follows:[23]

Alif: the individual ['the one'] of any thing
Bāʾ: one who often has sexual intercourse
Tāʾ: a stout woman; a woman with a sharp tongue

19. There may be a relationship between the orthographic shape of *lām-alif* (as well as the fact that it is a ligature) and the way the thongs of a sandal are tied. This is the only member of the alphabet that is not a phoneme, but a written convention, so its meaning may well refer to its script shape.

20. It is interesting to note that both the Arabic words 'right' (*yamīn*) and 'left' (*yasār*) start with the *yāʾ* sound, especially since *yāʾ* as an initial root consonant is fairly rare. This may relate to the word *yad* 'hand' as well, since in the Hebrew alphabet *yod* has this association. Further, the Ethiopic name for this sound, *yaman*, means 'right hand' (Colless, "Recent Discoveries," 42).

21. See Trevoux, *Lettres*, 210–11; and Louis Massignon, *Essai sur les origines du lexique téchnique de la mystique musulmane* (Paris: Geuthner, 1922) 82, for discussions of its origin.

22. Colless ("Recent Discoveries," 33–35) associates [g/j] with the concepts of "angle" and "boomerang." He also discusses its possible association with the roots for 'assembling' *j-m-ᶜ* and 'camel/beauty/grouping' *j-m-l*.

23. Al-Rāzī, *al-Ḥurūf*, cited in ᶜAbd al-Tawwāb, *Thalāthat kutub*, 143–44.

Thāʾ: something that the she-camel is milked into[24]
Jīm: the canopy of a tent[25]
Ḥāʾ: hermaphrodite; the name of a tribe
Khāʾ: pubic hair
Dāl: dangler of a bucket
Dhāl: ashes
Rāʾ: a plant
Zāy: dry skin
Sīn: rope
Shīn: an apple
Ṣād: brass; a pot made of brass
Ḍād: the noise of a sieve[26]
Ṭāʾ: a flat place
Ẓāʾ: an old man
ʿAyn: gold
Ghayn: thirst; clouds
Fāʾ: thigh flesh
Qāf: neck; nape of the neck
Kāf: deputy, agent
Lām: chemise, coat of mail
Mīm: pleurisy[27]
Nūn: a fish
Wāw: death
Hāʾ: uvula
Lām-alif: thong of a sandal
Yāʾ: report of a noise[28]

Thus the only identical items in the two versions are *bāʾ*, *khāʾ*, *nūn*, and *lām-alif*; the stout or sharp-tongued woman has changed from *ḥāʾ* to *tāʾ*, and the idea of a milk-producing camel (now with a container) has changed from *tāʾ* to *thāʾ*. Some words have a grammatical or phonological relation to their definition. The word *dāl*, for example, in addition to being the name of the [d] sound, is identical with the active participle of the verb *dalā*[29] 'to dangle' and

24. *shayʾ tuḥlab fīhi al-nāqa*
25. *surādiq al-bayt*
26. *ṣawt al-munkhal*
27. *al-birsām*
28. *ḥikāyat al-ṣawt*
29. Of course, the active participle has the form *dāl-in*, with the nunated suffix substituting for the weakness of the *wāw* in the root, but the suffix would not appear in script, nor would it be pronounced in pause form.

related to the word for 'bucket'. The word *ghayn* is phonologically similar to *ghaym* 'clouds'.[30] The concept of 'gold', associated here with *ᶜayn*, could well reflect its meaning of 'essence', since gold was considered the quintessential metal. The letters *ṣād*, *qāf*, and *fāᵓ* are the initial letters of the words used to define them: *ṣufr* 'brass', *qafā* 'nape of the neck', and *fakhdh* 'thigh'. Moreover, the *ḍād* once again reflects a sound, and may be onomatopoeic.

Conclusion

The concept of an alphabet lexicon based on the names of the letters is unusual in that most of the names of letters are not in the typical Semitic triconsonantal root-plus-pattern system. Except for the word *alif* and the phrase *lām-alif*, the names are monosyllabic, for example, *rāᵓ* and *dhāl*. Whereas they may be associated with the concept of phonesthemes, or a sort of proto-morphemic structure, they also bear a relation, in their form and meanings, to the highly functional subset of primitive, non-triliteral Arabic nouns: for example, *umm* 'mother', *ab* 'father', *akh* 'brother', *fū* 'mouth', and *dam* 'blood'. While the meanings of the latter have survived to the present day, however, most of the meanings of the letter/sound names have long since become obsolete and represent a lexical curiosity rather than a living legacy.

It is interesting to note, however, that a very similar phenomenon is connected with the Germanic runic alphabet, or *futhark*. One theory is that the alphabet system of representation of discrete sounds by symbols fused with a prehistoric system of pictorial symbols used for representations of "men and animals, parts of the human body, and various implements such as axes, arrows and ships."[31] As a result of the integration of sound/symbols and meaning/symbols, there was

> a gradual amalgamation of the two distinct streams: the alphabetic script on the one hand, the symbolic content on the other. The fusion was made easier because both systems shared some common ground, not only the formal resemblance of certain signs . . . , but more especially the use of individual signs for purposes of casting lots and divination.[32]

Thus, the interweaving of sound and symbol is a potent psychological and perhaps even archetypal phenomenon that, while carrying mundane meanings,

30. Lane has 'thirst' and 'clouds' attested, both in the *ghym* and *ghyn* roots (Edward William Lane, *Arabic English Lexicon*, [2 vols.; Cambridge: Islamic Texts Society, 1984] 2320 [orig. 1877]).

31. Ralph W. V. Elliot, *Runes: An Introduction* (Manchester: Manchester University Press, 1971) 64.

32. Ibid., 64–65.

can also reach into the spiritual realm. The sound/meaning correlations presented in this paper represent only one limited aspect of the multifaceted study of Arabic phonosymbolism. Whereas the correspondences presented by al-Khalīl and al-Rāzī may reflect an archaic, if mundane, set of semantic primitives, further sound/meaning correspondence systems involving occult, alchemical, and spiritual resonances constitute yet other cosmological dimensions of meaning associated with the Arabic sound system.[33] Taken together, these fields of study yield new and nontrivial data regarding the idea of the nature of semantic complexity, and if, as Wierzbicka states, "the main task of linguistics is to discover, and to describe, how meanings are encoded in languages; to describe it . . . on the level of empirical detail,"[34] then all of these sound/meaning correspondences deserve to be explored and analyzed in order to obtain a genuine grasp of the wide-ranging power of Semitic phonosymbolism.

33. As Windfuhr observes in his discussion of the Islamic poetic tradition, "The manipulation of sounds and signs is as constructive or destructive as is the operation on metal compounds in alchemy, continuing a belief in the correspondence of macrocosm and microcosm and the positive effects of proper operations on them" ("Spelling," 401).

34. Anna Wierzbicka, "Semantic Complexity: Conceptual Primitives and the Principle of Substitutability," *Theoretical Linguistics* 17 (1991) 77.

Al-Khalīl's Legacy

Karl Stowasser†

> I used to visit al-Khalīl ibn Aḥmad, and one day he said to me: "If someone were to put his mind to it and put together the letters *alif*, *b*, *t*, *th* the way I picture it, he could in that manner cover the entire speech of the Arabs and thus have a source book from which nothing at all is missing." When I asked him how that would be, he replied: "He would compose (the book) on the basis of the biliteral, triliteral, quadriliteral and quinquiliteral [root], for the Arabs have no known words with more [consonants] than that." I kept asking him for clarification, and he would give a description while I did not understand what he was describing, and so for days and days I went to see him in that matter. Then he took ill, and I went on the pilgrimage. I was all the time worrying about him, fearing that he might die during his illness so that what he used to explain to me would be for naught. When I returned from the pilgrimage and went to see him, there he was: he had written up all the letters the way they are in the first part of this book. From then on he used to dictate to me what he knew from memory and also things he had doubts about, telling me to ask about them and, if true, to fix them in writing, until I had written the book.

Ibn al-Nadīm, citing the Persian lexicologist Ibn Durustawayh (d. 958), offers this anecdote concerning the genesis of the *Kitāb al-ʿAyn*.[1] The narrator

1. Ibn al-Nadīm, *Fihrist* (Cairo: Raḥmāniyya, 1929) 64–65; also Yāqūt, *Irshād* (London: Luzac, 1923) 6.227.

is al-Layth ibn al-Muẓaffar ibn Naṣr ibn Sayyār, the grandson of the last Umayyad governor of Khorasan and a companion and friend of the only slightly older Khalīl ibn Aḥmad. The man who quoted Layth, the jurisprudent/grammarian Muḥammad ibn Manṣūr,[2] could not possibly have known him personally, since he died in 895, whereas Layth, who served as a secretary of some renown for the Barmakids, passed away shortly before the fall of his illustrious sponsors in 803; a possible link could have been the otherwise unknown Abū Maᶜādh ᶜAbd Allāh ibn ᶜĀᵓidh mentioned in the Preface of the *Kitāb al-ᶜAyn*, but that is pure conjecture. Muḥammad ibn Manṣūr then passed the anecdote on to his contemporary, the distinguished grammarian Abū 'l-Ḥasan ᶜAlī ibn Mahdī al-Kisrāwī,[3] who claims to have received from Muḥammad ibn Manṣūr a transcript of the book copied from Layth's autograph. This is related by Ibn al-Nadīm, who is generally critical and discriminating in the choice of his materials.

There is, one must admit, a certain attractiveness to the story. It cuts through the debate about the authorship of the *Kitāb al-ᶜAyn* with admirable simplicity, confirming what most critics are inclined to believe, namely, that al-Khalīl came up with the idea and the proposed organization, even writing the first part of the book, perhaps the *ᶜayn* part,[4] himself, and then left the bulk of the book to be finished by Layth according to the format and the pattern he had established. Even more important is what the story implies about the degree of linguistic sophistication the Arabs had attained by the end of the Umayyad period. The source book, al-Khalīl proposes, would have to be based on the *root* principle of the Arabic language. A mere century and a half after the Arabs' emergence from their homeland, where they certainly had not engaged in any linguistic speculation—in fact, did not need a 'craft' [*ṣināᶜa*] for their language, as Ibn Khaldūn says, because "it was [then] a habit in their tongues that one generation learned from the other, the way our children nowadays learn our dialects"[5]—their grammarians operated confidently with principles that others of longer grammatical tradition never really understood.

Toward the end of our seventh century, Syrian clerics argued whether it was permissible to share their knowledge with the "sons of the Mohammedans," a question answered with a qualified yes by Jacob of Edessa, the leading spirit

2. See al-Suyūṭī, *Bughyat al-wuᶜāh* (ed. Muḥammad Abū 'l-Faḍl Ibrāhīm; Cairo: al-Ḥalabī, 1384/1964) 1.250 n. 461.

3. See Yāqūt, *Irshād*, 5.27–32; al-Suyūṭī, *Bughya*, 2.208.

4. Abū l-Ṭayyib (ᶜAbd al-Wāḥid ibn ᶜAlī al-Ḥalabī, d. 962) says so in his *Marātib al-naḥwiyyīn*.

5. Ibn Khaldūn, *The Muqaddimah* (ed. and trans. by F. Rosenthal; 3 vols; Princeton: Princeton University Press, 1967) 3.321 (Būlāq ed., *Kitāb al-ᶜIbar*, 1.480).

of the time. Their own scholarly output was then directed mostly toward explaining "difficult words" in Scripture and the patristic literature, and the intricacies of Syriac vocalization. For instance, the Nestorian ᶜAnān Ishōᶜ, who flourished between 650 and 690, wrote a booklet on homographs (*damyāyāthā*),[6] a type of literature still imitated in the ninth century by the Nestorian patriarch (824–28) Ishōᶜ bar Nūn, a friend of Johannes Māsawayh (d. 857), the teacher of the famed Ḥunayn ibn Isḥāq. There is very little in ᶜAnān Ishōᶜ's booklet that could have inspired a "son of the Mohammedans." He obviously has no grasp of the triliteral root (participles are listed under *m*, some verbs in the imperfect under *n* or *t*), has trouble distinguishing adjectives from verbs (e.g., *sghī* and *saggī*), and shows only a rudimentary understanding of the difference between *Peal* and *Pael*. Besides, the Syrian linguists and grammarians labored in the grammatical tradition of the Greek language, with its seven parts of speech, whose norms simply do not conform with those of a Semitic language. What the Syrians did teach the Arabs was the vocalization system, for the names of the vowel signs—*fatḥ* and (Syriac) *pthāḥ* 'opening', *khafḍ* and *khvāṣā* 'lowering', *ḍamm* and *ᶜṣāṣā* 'compression'—can hardly be a coincidence.[7] In fact, it was the Syrians who became the students of the Arabs, not the other way around. The first to understand and to describe the nature and the workings of a Semitic language were clearly the Arabs.

The beginnings of this endeavor are still far from clear. The *Fihrist* mentions quite a number of men who were allegedly pioneers in the field, but many of these are just names and the works attributed to them mere titles, their context unknown or, at best, inferable from an occasional reference in later studies. The glottal stop (*hamz*) appears to have aroused scholarly attention first, probably because of the discrepancy between Qurᵓānic norm and actual usage. ᶜAbd Allāh ibn Abī Isḥāq al-Ziyādī al-Ḥaḍramī (650–735), the teacher of both Abū ᶜAmr Ibn al-ᶜAlāᵓ and ᶜĪsā ibn ᶜUmar al-Thaqafī (hence, indirectly, of al-Khalīl ibn Aḥmad), who is said to have devised the branches of Arabic grammar and to have introduced *qiyās* (reasoning by analogy), is credited with having written the first of the many *kutub al-hamz*. Somewhat later appear studies on verbs (*maṣādir*, for instance, or verbs with identical meaning in Forms IV and I) and

6. It is the oldest extant work of its kind and was edited by Georg Hoffmann (Kiel, 1880). On Syriac grammatical tradition, see Adalbert Merx, "*Historia artis grammaticae apud Syros*," *ZDMG*, 9/2 (1889).

7. The Arabic term *ḥaraka*, on the other hand, is rendered by the later Syrian grammarians in loan translation as *zawᶜāᵓ* 'movement'. It is very likely that it was al-Khalīl ibn Aḥmad who introduced the vowel signs and other diacritical marks into Arabic writing (see G. Bergsträsser and O. Pretzl, *Geschichte des Qorantextes*, vol. 3 of *Geschichte des Qorans* [3 vols. in one; ed. Theodor Nöldeke; (Hildesheim: Olms, 1961] 262); among his works mentioned in the *Fihrist* (p. 65) is a *K. al-naqṭ wa-'l-shakl*.

on particular nouns (used, for example, in singular or plural only, nontransparent dual forms, and so forth). Such studies carry over into lengthy (and, to our taste, irrelevant) grammatical disquisitions throughout the *Kitāb al-ᶜAyn.*

That all of this is closely linked to the study of Qurᵓān and Tradition[8] is shown by the lexicological studies ascribed to that period. The collection of strange and difficult words in the Qurᵓān is attributed by some to the Prophet's cousin ᶜAbd Allāh ibn al-ᶜAbbās (d. 687), but it is very unlikely that he produced a written work. The pioneer in the "Gharīb al-Qurᵓān" literature appears to have been Abū Saᶜīd Abān ibn Taghlib al-Jurayrī (d. 758), a Qurᵓān "reader" with extremist Shiite leanings in Kufa, while the first "Gharīb al-Ḥadīth" work is ascribed to Abū ᶜAdnān ᶜAbd al-Raḥmān ibn ᶜAbd al-Aᶜlā, a contemporary of Yūnus ibn Ḥabīb (d. 798) and the teacher of Abū ᶜUbayda (Maᶜmar ibn al-Muthannā). There are early onomastic collections (*kutub al-ṣifāt*) that the world of the Bedouin and the desert: for instance, a treatise on vermin (*ḥasharāt*) ascribed to Abū Khiyara al-Aᶜrābī;[9] or one on the horse attributed to Abū Mālik ᶜAmr ibn Kirkira, who was a contemporary of Yūnus ibn Ḥabīb and is said to have composed yet another first, a treatise on the nature of man (*khulq al-insān*); al-Aḥmar al-Baṣrī (d. ca. 796) is credited with a "book" on the mountains of the Arabs, and Abū l-Wazīr ᶜUmar ibn Muṭarrif (d. ca. 802) allegedly compiled one on their camp grounds (*manāzil*). For someone ready to tackle "the entire speech of the Arabs" in one coherent book, there must have been an abundance of raw material to work with.

Muslim tradition holds that the principal motive for such grammatical and lexicological activity was the desire, indeed the need, to preserve the purity and correctness of the Arabic language, which was in danger of being turned into a vulgar *koine* by the masses of non-Arab converts to Islam. For "it is the ear that begets the linguistic habits," says Ibn Khaldūn.[10] Leaving aside the early studies on dialectical peculiarities and variants (Yūnus ibn Ḥabīb al-Ḍabbī, for instance, is said to have been a collector of such *lughāt*), the question still remains why a people so proud of their idiom which in their Arabian homeland used to be, in Ibn Khaldūn's words, a natural "habit in their tongues," a people dominant politically, socially, and culturally, would unlearn this treasured language and succumb within a few decades to the solecisms of Aramaeans and Greeks and to the accents and inflections of Persians and Copts. In any event, the Kufan ᶜAlī ibn Ḥamza al-Kisāᵓī (d. 805), tutor of one reigning and two fu-

8. This in itself would rule out the Syrians as possible inspirers of Arab grammatical thought, since grammar to the former was an essential preparation for theological study.

9. Nahshal ibn Zayd (or Yazīd); he was one of the teachers of Abū ᶜAmr ibn al-ᶜAlāᵓ. See Yāqūt, *Irshād*, 7.222; al-Suyūṭī, *Bughya*, 2.317.

10. Ibn Khaldūn, *The Muqaddimah*, 3.321 (*ᶜIbar*, 1.480).

ture caliphs, already felt compelled to write a treatise on the ungrammatical speech of the common people.[11] Was al-Khalīl's "source book" then perhaps an attempt to record the "pure" Arabic language at a time when its "corruption continued on account of the close contact and the intermingling [of the Arabs] with non-Arabs . . . so that many Arabic words were not used in their proper meaning"? Ibn Khaldūn seems to imply this when he discusses the origin of Arabic lexicography.[12]

An analysis of one of the root entries—the root q-r-ᶜ, for instance—in the *Kitāb al-ᶜAyn* should provide a clue. The root is, in format and coverage, no different from the other root entries in the book and is chosen here merely because it is relatively short. It begins with a verbal noun,

> *qaraᶜ*: loss of hair on account of disease,

which is to say, alopecia, pathological baldness. This is followed by the adjectives for someone so afflicted: [m.] *aqraᶜ*, [f.] *qarᶜāᵓ*, [f. pl.] *qurᶜ*, [m. pl.] *qurᶜān*, with a grammatical annotation:

> but *qurᶜ* is [also] permissible, although [the masc. pattern] *FuᶜLān* in the *aFᶜaL* group of attributive adjectives is more correct; and [collective] *naᶜām qurᶜ* [bald ostriches].

The verb is then introduced in a sort of contextual definition:

> One says: "Once she got on in years she became bald—*qariᶜat.*"

Then follows:

> In the proverb: *istannat il-fiṣāl ḥattā l-qarᶜā,* that is, [the camel weanlings] become fat, applied proverbially to someone who exceeds his bounds and claims something he does not have. The remedy for *qaraᶜ* is salt and butter from camel's milk, but when they cannot find salt, they pluck out the fur at the affected parts and splash these with water, then drag (the animal) over salty ground.

No definition is given for *qaraᶜ* (which is a skin disease affecting young camels, characterized by white pustules on the neck and the legs), so that one of the definitions given for the following verb is circular:

> *taqarraᶜa*: (of the animal's skin) to become splotchy with sores caused by *qaraᶜ*.
>
> *qurriᶜa taqrīᶜan*: (of a camel weanling) to be submitted to the treatment [described] when there is no salt available.

11. Al-Kisāᵓī, *Risāla fī laḥn al-ᶜāmma*, ed. C. Brockelmann, *Zeitschrift für Assyriologie*, XIII, 31–46. Doubts have been voiced, though, about al-Kisāᵓī's being the author of the treatise, which, some believe, was written by a student of Abū Zayd al-Anṣārī (d. 830).

12. Ibn Khaldūn, *The Muqaddimah*, 3.325–26 (*ᶜIbar*, 1.481).

The latter is illustrated with a hemistich by the pre-Islamic poet Aws ibn Ḥajar (d. ca. 620), after which follows a lexicological comment on the Form II verb *qarraᶜ*:

> The latter is based on [the functional sense of] *salb* ['deprivation'; cf. Wright 1:36 A] because it removes (the animal's) *qaraᶜ* by means of that (dragging), just as one says: *qadhdhaytu l-ᶜayna*, meaning, I removed the foreign body (*qadhan*) from the eye, or *qarradtu l-baᶜīra* I removed the ticks (*qurd*) from the camel.

Then comes an unrelated noun entry:

> *qarᶜ*: the fruit of an acaulescent plant (*yaqṭīn*); unit noun *qarᶜa*.

Next follow several verbs:

> *aqraᶜa*: (of people) to draw lots, as also *taqāraᶜū baynahum*; the noun is *qurᶜa*;
>
> *qāraᶜtuhū fa-qaraᶜtuhū*: I gambled with him and beat him [that is] the lot fell to me before him;
>
> *aqraᶜtu bayna 'l-qawm*: I had the men draw lots (*yaqtariᶜū*) for something, as also *qāraᶜtu baynahum*

and a noun entry *qarīᶜ*, whose definition is utterly ambiguous:

> So-and-so is the *qarīᶜ*, pl. *quraᶜāᵓ*, of such-and-such, meaning, *yuqāriᶜuhū*,

which, in this context, would have to mean 'he casts lots, or gambles, with him' but could also, and more likely, mean 'he battles him with the sword',[13] in which case the entry is out of place. This is followed by a second *qarīᶜ* with reference to camels:

> *qarīᶜ*: stallion; it is so called because it mounts (*yaqraᶜu*) the mare, that is, covers her; pl. of paucity *aqriᶜa*,

which is illustrated with a hemistich by al-Farazdaq (d. 728) and another by Dhū 'l-Rumma (d. 735). Two denominal verb forms are then given:

> *istaqraᶜanī jamalī* [he asked me for the loan of my male camel] and I lent it to him (*aqraᶜtuhū iyyāhu*), meaning, I gave it [to him] to mate with his mares.

Another unrelated noun entry follows:

> *qurᶜa*: a faint mark on the middle of the nose of a camel or sheep.

13. Compare with, for example, Ibn Sīda's "Muḥkam," which has, immediately after *qirāᶜ* and *muqāraᶜa*: "*qarīᶜuka*: he who fights you in battle; also, he is the '*qarīᶜ* or *qirrīᶜ* of the cavalry squadron,' meaning, its leader, and the one who engages in single combat on its behalf."

The last sense complex opens with alternative verbal nouns of Form III,

> *muqāraᶜa* and *qirāᶜ*: combat with the sword in battle,

illustrated with a hemistich by an unidentified poet. Next, without transition, follows:

> *al-qāriᶜa*: the Resurrection [metaphorically from]

> *qāriᶜa*: a (sudden) calamity; one says: such-and-such felt safe from the *qawāriᶜ* of time, meaning, its calamities (*shadāᵓid*); and the *qawāriᶜ* of the Qurᵓān, such as the Throne Verse [2:255]: he who recites them, it is said, will not be struck by a calamity (*qāriᶜah*).

The basic verb is then introduced obliquely with

> anything you 'strike' or 'hit' or 'knock' = *qaraᶜtahū*

and illustrated with a hemistich by the Hudhalī poet Abū Dhuᵓayb (d. ca. 648). This is followed by

> and [metaphorically of] a drinker who 'knocks his forehead' (*yaqraᶜu jabhatahū*) against the drinking vessel when he drains its content,

illustrated with a hemistich by an unidentified poet that is accompanied by a linguistic comment on an unrelated word in the verse. The entry concludes with two instrument nouns,

> *miqraᶜa* and *miqrāᶜ*: a stick with a thong at one end with which one beats mules and donkeys,

and a verbal noun IV,

> *iqrāᶜ*: the act of donkeys kicking each other with their hooves,

the latter illustrated with a hemistich by the contemporary poet Ruᵓba ibn al-ᶜAjjāj (d. 762).

Quite a bit is obviously omitted here (in Ibn Sīda's "Muḥkam," in contrast, the same root entry runs over four columns), and what is treated is presented in a random and discursive manner with a distinct preference for the unusual and the exquisite. There is no discernible principle that may have determined the organization of the various derivatives within a given root, some root entries beginning with a verb, simple or augmented, others with a noun, or a *maṣdar*, or an adjective or a numeral. Nor is there any clue as to what determined the choice of the opening lemma: the root *ᶜ-r-q*, for instance, starts with *ᶜaraq* ('sweat'), surely not a noun in need of explanation, the root *ᶜ-q-r* with the verbal noun *ᶜaqr* ('wounding'), hardly the first sense that comes to mind in that root, and the root *r-q-ᶜ* with the verb *raqaᶜa* ('to patch'), which indeed determines its semantic range. Homographs (here, *qurʿa*) are dealt with in different places without reference to each other, just as clearly related senses, or subsenses, of a given lexical item are scattered about and presented in no apparent order. Definitions throughout the dictionary are of every variety: synonymous, analytical, synthetic, contextual. Here, as in Sībawayh's grammar, one can easily see the influence of Greek logic.[14] Some entries are quite felicitous, such as

> *taʿḍūḍ*: a variety of black, very sweet dates native of Hajar and its villages
>
> *qaʿfāʾ*: a soft, coarse-leafed spring plant with fire-red flowers, its leaves growing upward and its fruit curving downward,

while others are often ambiguous or circular and offer little enlightenment. Illustrative examples, especially the numerous *shawāhid* drawn from poetry, rarely serve to clarify the given sense of a word, but appear to have been chosen mainly as decorative parade pieces or as a pretext for excursuses into grammar and other extraneous matters.

The point here is not to criticize the *ʿAyn* by applying the criteria of modern-day lexicography. That would be most unfair. It is to find a possible answer to how it came about and what it was intended to be. There is no doubt that the *ʿAyn* is a "source book from which nothing at all is missing," as far as the Arabic roots are concerned. They are all there, secured by the anagrammatic permutations of their elements, even those with no known meaning. It is an ingenious device that points to al-Khalīl as the inventor, regardless of who compiled and completed the work. What happens inside these root entries, however, is quite a different thing. Here the intent is clearly didactic, namely, to present and to elucidate selected *aspects* of a given root, not to cover and to explain every conceivable derivative of it. For that purpose, the choice of the opening lemma is then indeed of little importance, since it serves merely as a "starter" for the lexicological disquisition to follow. Nor is the order in which the chosen material is presented of great consequence. The book, after all, was not designed to be a reference work in the usual sense—a concept alien to Khalīl's time anyway—but was meant to adhere in the presentation of its lexical material, albeit in a novel format, to the traditions established by earlier lexicological studies. Moreover, such lexical material was delivered orally, in a way that facilitates memorization. Hence the sometimes baffling assignment of subentries, for only someone familiar with the Baṣran school's lexicological theories would look for *kaʿk* under the root *k-ʿ-ʿ*, and few would choose the root *ʿ-k-k* for a first stab at finding the word *ʿakankaʿ* ('male ghoul').

14. Consider, for instance, *ẓarf*, which as a technical term used by Sībawayh as well as in grammatical concept conforms exactly with Aristotle's perception of place and time as 'the vessel' (*to angeion*) of a thing.

The critics of al-Khalīl's work were many, and they spoke up almost from the moment, more than half a century later, when al-Layth's autograph emerged from the obscurity of the Ṭāhiriyya library in Nīshāpūr on the Baghdad book market, purchased there, we are told,[15] by al-Layth's fellow Omani Ibn Durayd, then a young man of twenty-five, for fifty dinars. The earliest-known contribution along that line seems to have come from the Baghdadi lexicologist and philologist al-Mufaḍḍal ibn Salama (died ca. 903), a man sponsored by the caliph al-Mutawakkil's Turkish vizier Khāqān; his '*Addenda to the* ᶜAyn' (*Al-Istidrāk ᶜalā 'l-ᶜAyn*) chose the most obvious target. As time went on, the gaps in the coverage were filled, errors debated and corrected, the corpus of subsequent dictionaries became enlarged with ever more thorough treatment of root derivatives. But the format devised by Khalīl, the discursive approach, the didactic presentation, remained the same, as is shown by a disrespectful little *urjūza*, by an anonymous rhymster, that Yāqūt claims to have found[16] on the back of one part of al-Azharī's *Tahdhīb*:

Now, Ibn Durayd, he is an ox,
he's vain and he's a glutton,
And in his ignorance he claims
the "Jamhara" to have written,
Which is, in fact, the "Book of ᶜAyn"
by him but changed and altered.
Or take al-Azharī, the toad,
as dumb almost as Dugha,
Yet in his ignorance he claims
he wrote "Tahdhib al-Lugha,"
Which is, in fact, the "Book of ᶜAyn"
dressed up in different color.
And al-Khārzanjī's wits are dim,
he's stupid and he's muddled,
And in his ignorance he claims
he authored the "Takmila,"
Which is, in fact, the "Book of ᶜAyn,"
and all he did was copy.

At the end of the anagrammatic line stands Ibn Sīda's *al-Muḥkam wa-'l-muḥīṭ al-aᶜẓam fī 'l-lugha,*[17] a "real" dictionary singled out with high praise for its accuracy and reliability by Edward Lane in the preface to his *Lexicon*. By that time, Abū Naṣr Ismāᶜīl ibn Ḥammād al-Jawharī (d. 1003) had already invented a less impractical system for arranging the roots of the Arabic language.

15. Ibn al-Nadīm, *Fihrist,* p. 64.
16. Yāqūt, *Irshād*, 6.224.
17. Edited by Muṣṭafā al-Saqqā and Dr. Ḥusayn Naṣṣār (Cairo: al-Ḥalabī, 1377/1958).

In this new mold, the great monolingual dictionaries took shape—the "Lisān," the "Qāmūs," and the "Tāj," true reference works, normative in approach, exhaustive in the treatment of their entries, and monuments to painstaking scholarship and linguistic sophistication amid a sea of declining educational standards. Ibn Khaldūn is referring to his learned contemporaries when he writes:

> Knowledge of the rules is knowledge of how to use them, but it is not the actual use of them. Therefore, we find that many outstanding grammarians and skilled Arab philologists who have a comprehensive knowledge of those rules make many mistakes and commit many solecisms when they are asked to write one or two lines to a colleague or friend. . . . They cannot put [the words] together and express what they want to say in a way that corresponds to the ways of the Arabic language.[18]

Comprehensive coverage for these lexicographers is no longer an option but a must. There is hardly anything one cannot find in their dictionaries. But it takes time, because the root entries in them are as discursive and unorganized as those in the *Kitāb al-ᶜAyn.* Al-Khalīl would probably be pleased.

18. Ibn Khaldūn, *The Muqaddimah*, 3.355 (*ᶜIbar*, 1.492).

The Etymology of *Muqarnas*: Some Observations

Wolfhart Heinrichs

When the first issue of the journal *Muqarnas* came out in 1983, someone is said to have alerted the editors to the fact that they had misspelled the title: the word *muqarnas* should have been written with a *ṣād* rather than with a *sīn*. Fortunately, those fears were unfounded, because both spellings are attested and acceptable and, whereas in modern Arabic writings there seems to be a tendency to prefer the *ṣād* form,[1] in Western publications it is usually the *sīn* form that prevails.[2] The question arises, of course, how are the variants to be explained and would their existence be helpful in any way to determine the etymology of the term?

1. See, for example, Muḥammad Muḥammad Amīn & Laylā ᶜAlī Ibrāhīm: *al-Muṣṭalaḥāt al-miᶜmāriyya fī l-wathāʾiq al-mamlūkiyya* (Cairo: Dār al-nashr bi-l-Jāmiᶜa al-Amrīkiyya, 1990) 113.

2. See E. Diez, "Muḳarnas," EI^1 *Supplement*; and Doris Behrens-Abouseif, "Muḳarnas," EI^2, s.v.

To answer the first part of the question, it is necessary to adumbrate one of the thornier chapters of Arabic (and Semitic) historical phonology, namely the phonetic realization of the so-called "emphatics." *Ṣād*, as every student of Arabic knows, is the "emphatic" counterpart of the—non-"emphatic"—*sīn*. In Arabic as we know it, "emphasis" (which is hardly more than a meaningless label) is produced by velarization, which means that the primary articulation of the "emphatic" sound is accompanied by a secondary articulation, a constriction in the area of the velum which lends a characteristic "dark" timbre to the sound affected by it. Velarization, in most modern Arabic dialects, is, however, not confined to single sounds but constitutes what some modern linguists call a "suprasegmental phoneme," which is to say that it stretches over a whole word (or morpheme), affecting every single sound in it.[3] Thus, whether we spell *muqarnas* with a *sīn* or a *ṣād* does not make any difference, because in present-day pronunciation the whole word is velarized—*ṃụqạṛṇạṣ*, as it were—and the *sīn* would become a *ṣād* anyway. The *ṣād* form is thus accounted for: it is a reflex of the actual pronunciation of the word. But why should there be a *sīn* form alongside it? This is where the historical dimension comes in.

Comparative Semitics shows us that velarization as the phonetic realization of "emphasis" is most likely an innovation of Arabic, whereas the older Semitic method of distinguishing "emphatics" from their non-emphatic counterparts seems to have been the glottalization of the "emphatics."[4] This is what we still find in the modern Ethiopic and South Arabian languages.[5] Glottalization, unlike velarization, is a phonetic phenomenon affecting only single sounds, never whole words, and there is in fact a strong tendency of not having more than one glottalized sound in a root, which means that certain "emphat-

3. *Velarization* and, to a lesser degree, *pharyngealization* are the most commonly used terms for this phonetic feature, although, as Dolgopolsky (see following note), p. 1 n. 1, has pointed out, they are not quite correct and should be replaced by *uvularization*. In other words, the secondary articulation takes place between the velum and the pharynx. One should, however, allow for some variation among the various dialects, so that "in the area of the velum" seems a safe bet. On velarization as a suprasegmental phoneme, see Konstantin Tsereteli: "On One Suprasegmental Phoneme in Modern Semitic," *JAOS* 102 (1982) 343–46.

4. A strong case for glottalization as the original "emphasis" has been presented by Aharon B. Dolgopolsky: "Emphatic Consonants in Semitic," *IOS* 7 (1977) 1–13. The type of glottalization we are concerned with here produces ejective sounds, which is to say, the secondary articulation is a closure of the glottis, which is released after release of the primary articulation through raising of the larynx.

5. This had long been known for the Ethiopic languages, and it was usually assumed to be a Cushitic substratum influence until Thomas Johnston discovered the same phenomenon in the modern South Arabian languages (Mahri, etc.), for a general account of which see his *Modern South Arabian Languages*, vol. 1 / issue 5 of *Afroasiatic Linguistics* (Malibu, Calif., 1975) 6–7.

ics" are incompatible in one root. Unfortunately, we do not know when the shift from glottalization to velarization took place in Arabic, or Proto-Arabic. But we do know one thing: Arabic orthography reflects the pre-velarization stage, as is evidenced by the many instances in which an etymologically correct non-emphatic is written rather than the "emphatic" counterpart that would be expected as the result of "suprasegmental" velarization.[6] From this linguistic consideration, it would appear that the *sīn* form of *muqarnas* is the more original, more correct form of the word, whereas the *ṣād* form would have come into existence due to the spreading of velarization over the whole word. In this particular case, the starting point of the velarization would appear to be the *rāʾ*, possibly in conjunction with the preceding *qāf*; the /r/ sound has a natural inclination for velarization, as can frequently be observed in modern Arabic dialects.[7]

The fact that there is a *sīn-ṣād* variation in this word, as well as in other derivatives of the root, as we shall see below, means that the written tradition of this word is not very firm and not strong enough to uphold the correct spelling. There are two cases in which this is not uncommon: one is foreign (and mainly non-Semitic) loanwords that obviously do not have a traditional orthography and therefore fluctuate, and the other case is rare roots that are only sparsely or not at all attested in the old authoritative literature.[8] The accepted

6. This does not necessarily mean that Arabic still used glottalized sounds at the beginning of its history as a written language, because Arabic orthography was not simply a mirror of the language at that stage but continued a roughly one-thousand-year-old tradition of Arabic names' being written in Aramaic contexts. See Werner Diem, "Untersuchungen zur frühen Geschichte der arabischen Orthographie, I: Die Schreibung der Vokale," *Or* n.s. 48 (1979) 207–57; "II: Die Schreibung der Konsonanten," *Or* n.s. 49 (1980) 67–106; "III: Endungen und Endschreibungen," *Or* n.s. 50 (1981) 332–83; "IV: Die Schreibung der zusammenhängenden Rede—Zusammenfassung," *Or* n.s. 52 (1983) 357–404.

7. Wolfdietrich Fischer and Otto Jastrow, *Handbuch der arabischen Dialekte* (Wiesbaden: Harrassowitz 1980) 56. Another possibility would be to posit *muqarnaṣ* as the original form and *muqarnas* as a hypercorrect variant of it. There is, however, no evidence for this.

8. Examples of *sīn-ṣād* variation in loanwords would be cases like *sirāṭ/ṣirāṭ* < Lat. *(via) strata* 'road'; *isṭabl/iṣṭabl* < Lat. *stabulum* 'stables'; *qallasa/qallaṣa* 'to beat the tambourines' < Syr. *qalles* 'to cheer, celebrate'; and *usṭuquss/usṭuquṣṣ* < Syr. *esṭuk̲sā*, from Greek *stoicheion* 'element' (presumably via a metaplastic use of *stoichos*; see Hans Daiber, *Aetius Arabus* [Wiesbaden: Steiner, 1980] 18). Without prejudice to a closer investigation of these and similar pairs, it would seem that the *ṣād* forms reflect the actual pronunciation, while the *sīn* variants represent hypercorrect forms in the sense that they take into account certain incompatibilities of the "emphatics" in indigenous roots. As for the other group of words with *ṣād/sīn* variation, which is clearly less well defined, a look at one of the medieval *ibdāl* works may be instructive: Abū l-Ṭayyib al-Lughawī (*K. al-Ibdāl* [ed. ʿIzz al-Dīn al-Tanūkhī; 2 vols.; Damascus: Majmaʿ al-lugha al-ʿarabiyya, 1379/1960–1380/1961] 2.172–96) lists altogether 64 items, of which 8 are clearly or presumably of foreign origin. In 14 of them, the variation occurs in the last radical; this is a position where unpredictable and multiple variation is not uncommon (a fact that has led to the theory of root-determinatives

etymology of *muqarnas* is, in fact, that it is a foreign loanword, that it is somehow derived from the Greek word *korōnís*, which supposedly also yielded the English word *cornice* and its relatives in other Western languages.[9] This derivation is not without its difficulties. Let us first look at the semantic aspect of the *korōnís-muqarnas* correspondence. The Greek word, which is related to the word *korōnē* 'crow' (and other meanings), can be used as an adjective meaning 'crook-beaked', 'curved', and as a noun referring to anything curved or bent, in particular to:

a. a 'wreath or garland',
b. a 'curved line or stroke, a flourish with the pen at the end of a book',
c. a figurative use of (b), namely 'end, completion', and
d. as an architectural term, 'the finishing piece placed on the building, the copestone'.

The last meaning, however, must be considered a rare and unusual word, since it is only given in the dictionary of Hesychius, where it is defined as *tò teleutaîon tês oikodomês epíthema*, literally 'the final thing-put-at-the-top of the building'.[10] Whether this definition would cover a cornice is not quite clear. It must be emphasized, however, that the semantic picture that has emerged so far is based on the *classical* dictionaries. In order to evaluate a lexical borrowing from Greek into Arabic, one should, of course, study the situation in medieval Byzantine Greek. Unfortunately, lexicographical treatment of this stage of the language is far from satisfactory. The old *Greek Lexicon of the Roman and Byzantine Periods*, by Sophocles, is rather incomplete and does not give any architectural meaning for *korōnís*. More helpful is the large dictionary by D. Dimitrakos (Dēmētrákos), which covers all periods of the Greek language.[11] Here we find among the architectural meanings of *korōnís* the definition from Hesychius and then, 'by extension "every projecting girding (*perî-*

of originally biradical roots, recently revived by Christopher Ehret, "The Origin of Third Consonants in Semitic Roots: An Internal Reconstruction [Applied to Arabic]," *Journal of Afroasiatic Languages* 2 [1989] 109–202), and for this reason, these cases should be viewed with caution. The rest appear to be either extremely rare words (such as *ikhranmas/ṣa* 'to fall silent', *tabarbas/ṣa* 'to trot', or *shas/ṣib* 'skinny [sheep]') or secondary *ṣād* spellings that take care of "suprasegmental" velarization (such as *ṣa*^{c}*ūṭ* 'snuff', *waṣakh* 'dirtiness', or *ṣukhn* 'hot').

9. The latest statement of this assumption is by Behrens-Abouseif: "Muḳarnas."

10. Hesychii Alexandrini *Lexicon* (ed. Kurt Latte; Copenhagen: Munksgaard, 1966) 2.516. Since the word is preceded by an asterisk, it is a later interpolation from the Cyrillus Glossary, which is dated by Reitzenstein to the time of Justinian (see *Rheinisches Museum* 43 [1888] 443ff.).

11. D. Dimitrakos, *Méga Lexikòn hólēs tês Hellēnikês Glōssēs* (30 vols.; Athens: Asimakopulos, 1964) 3.4061, s.v. *korōnís*, meaning no. 8.

zōma) or crowning (*stephánōma*) of walls or pieces of furniture"' (my translation), followed by the Italian borrowing *korníza*. Thus, at some point in the history of the Greek language (although the dictionary does not tell us when) the word *korōnís* did have the meaning of *cornice*.

As for the Arabic side of the equation, there is no doubt that, whatever the exact use of the word *muqarnas* and the related verbal noun *qarnasa* in the old sources and in modern definitons may be, it certainly does not mean simply *cornice*. Since the *muqarnas* may sometimes function as "a continuous bracket supporting an overhanging wall,"[12] it is at times also used to support a cornice, and it may thus metonymically have received its name from the element it supports. This is, however, a rather unlikely assumption, because the more characteristic uses of the *muqarnas* are elsewhere. Summing up, we may say that the equation *korōnís-muqarnas* is not totally impossible but leaves a lot to be desired on semantic grounds.

I would add two more considerations that would further weaken the derivation from *korōnís*. One is the formal side of the supposed borrowing: it is rather strange that only inner-Arabic derivatives of the hypothetical borrowing have been attested, the verbal noun *qarnasa* and the passive participle *muqarnas*, whereas no trace has as yet been found of an Arabicization of the word itself, that is, something like **qirnīs, *qurnūs,* or **qurānis*. If we compare other Greek loanwords in the general sphere of architecture, such as *fusayfisāʾ, zukhruf,* or *funduq*,[13] we find that this kind of mere root-borrowing is not followed. The other argument is taken from cultural history: we know, of course, that Greek architects and artists played an important role in early Islamic art and that this had its repercussions on the technical vocabulary of Arabic. However, if the *muqarnas* was developed in northeastern Iran, as Oleg Grabar suggests in various places in his writings, the influence of Greek artists is less likely.[14]

One might mention here in passing that the Syriac dictionaries do not register any transliteration or transformation of the Greek word *korōnís*, but given the heavy theological bias of Syriac literature, this may be just a problem of attestation. Moreover, in view of the live contact of Greek artists with Muslim

12. From the definition of E. Diez, "Muḳarnas."

13. *Fusayfisāʾ* 'mosaic' < Greek *psēphos* 'little stone, pebble' via Syriac *pspsʾ* (pronounced **psēfsā*?); *zukhruf* 'decoration (esp. with paints)' < Greek *zōgraphía* '(the art of) painting'; *funduq* 'hostel' < Greek *pandokheîon* 'hostel, inn'.

14. See, for example, Oleg Grabar, "The Visual Arts, 1050–1350," in *The Saljuq and Mongol Periods*, vol. 5 of *The Cambridge History of Iran* (8 vols.; ed. J.A. Boyle; Cambridge: Cambridge University Press, 1968) 626–658, esp. p. 638; and idem, *The Formation of Islamic Art* (New Haven: Yale University Press, 1973) 181 and 211.

sponsors, there seems to be little need for the—otherwise quite common—transmission of the term via Syriac. However, Syriac does offer one interesting item of vocabulary for our purpose: the word *qurnāsā* meaning 'hammer' and the related verb *qarnes* 'to hammer'.[15] The passive participle of this verb would be *mqarnas*, phonetically a very close approximation of *muqarnas*. However, unless one could prove that the use of the term originated in metalwork and was then transferred to architecture this etymology is unlikely.[16]

It remains to test the indigenous resources for a possible etymology. Turning to the medieval Arabic dictionaries, one should keep in mind that they reflect a specific type of Arabic, the authoritative language of the true Bedouin Arabs of pre-Islamic and early Islamic times. Technical terminology, which originated for the most part in the cultural centers of the Islamic empire, was a priori excluded for the most part. And, indeed, when we consult a dictionary like the very comprehensive *Lisān al-^{c}arab*, we find that the architectural term *muqarnas* is nowhere mentioned.[17] Various words are listed under the *sīn* and the *ṣād* form of the root *q-r-n-s/ṣ*. Some of them are identical in meaning despite the *sīn-ṣād* change. Altogether they present a bewildering jumble of meanings with no apparent common denominator. One of these words stands out as a very likely candidate for being the etymon of our *muqarnas*. It is the geographical morphological term *qurnās* (also *qirnās*), which is defined as

15. R. Payne-Smith, *Thesaurus syriacus* (2 vols.; Oxford: Clarendon, 1879) 2.3752; Carl Brockelmann, *Lexicon syriacum* (2d ed.; Halle: Niemeyer, 1928; reprint Hildesheim: Olms, 1966) 698.

16. The medieval Syriac-Arabic lexicographer Bar Bahlūl (ed. R. Duval; 3 vols.; Paris: Imprimerie Nationale, 1901) 2.1755a, provides an interesting detail, the relevance of which is, however, unclear; the entry runs: [Syriac:] *qurnāsā ba-ṣ(ḥāḥā) arzaptā z^{c}ōrtā*; [Arabic:] *miṭraqa, irzabba, āla yunqar bihā l-raḥā l-marwazī, qurnās*; [Syriac:] *ak̲lōnā d̲-qaynāyē*; [Arabic:] *miṭraqat al-ḥaddādīn* '[Syriac:] *qurnāsā* in one codex: a small hammer; [Arabic:] a hammer, a mallet, an instrument with which the Marv-type quern is grooved, a *qurnās* (borrowed from the Syriac?); [Syriac:] a small hammer of the blacksmiths; [Arabic:] ditto'. Depending on the patterns used in grooving millstones (of which I know nothing), there is a slight chance that *mqarnas* in the sense of 'grooved (like a millstone)' is the etymon we are searching for.

17. Ibn Manẓūr, *Lisān al-^{c}arab* (15 vols.; Beirut: Dār Ṣādir-Dār Bayrūt, 1374/1955–1375/1956) 6.173 (*q-r-n-s*); 7.73 (*q-r-n-ṣ*). An architectural meaning, but with a somewhat mysterious explanation, is adduced by al-Ṣaghānī: *al-Takmila wa-l-dhayl wa-l-ṣila li-Kitāb Tāj al-lugha wa-ṣiḥāḥ al-^{c}arabiyya* (ed. Muḥammad Abū l-Faḍl Ibrāhīm; 6 vols.; Cairo: Maṭba^{c}at dār al-kutub, 1973) 3.407: *saqf muqarnas: ^{c}umila ^{c}alā hay$^{\supset}$at al-sullam* 'a *muqarnas* ceiling: made in the shape of a ladder'. Could this refer to the (inverted) stair-like structure of a double, triple, etc. *muqarnas*? Murtaḍā al-Zabīdī points out that the word *saqf*, as al-Ṣaghānī correctly has it, appears distorted to *sayf* in all copies of al-Fīrūzābādī's *Qāmūs* (on which the *Tāj* is conceived as a commentary) (*Tāj al-^{c}arūs* [ed. Maḥmūd Muḥammad al-Ṭanāḥī; Kuwait: Wizārat al-i^{c}lām, 1396/1976] 16.370a). If he is right, this ghost word has proved to be astoundingly resilient, because it has made it even into the Persian lexicographical tradition. Its mere existence would justify the assumption that *muqarnas* as applied to *saqf* was not a household word.

shabīh al-anf yataqaddam fī l-jabal 'something like a nose projecting in a mountain'.[18] The similarity between this *qurnās* and our *muqarnas* is easy to see, and it will become even clearer and more convincing when we study the testimonial verse adduced by the lexicographers. They are two lines from an elegy by the pre-Islamic poet Mālik b. Khālid al-Khunāᶜī[19] from the tribe of Hudhayl, in which the poet, to console the addressee, evokes the image of the ibex, which, although it can reach the most inaccessible spots, cannot escape destiny:

Ta-llāhi yabqā ᶜalā l-ayyāmi dhū ḥiyadin
bi-mushmakhirrin bihī l-ẓayyānu wa-l-āsu
fī raᵓsi shāhiqatin unbūbuhā khaṣirun
dūna l-samāᵓi lahū fī l-jawwi qurnāsu

By God! Not even one with knotty horns will withstand Time
[although being] on a towering [pinnacle], on which there is clematis and myrtle,
on top of a high-rising [mountain peak]—the gorge [leading up] to it is ice-cold
and has between it and the sky a mountain-jut (*qurnās*) in midair.[20]

The image of the overhanging cliff is presented quite vividly in these lines. If we accept the suggested etymology, the verb *qarnasa* would mean something

18. This word is already attested in the first Arabic dictionary; see al-Khalīl b. Aḥmad, *K. al-ᶜAyn* (ed. Mahdī al-Makhzūmī and Ibrāhīm al-Sāmarrāᵓī; [Baghdad]: Dār al-rashīd, 1982), part 5, p. 252. (The wording in *Lisān al-ᶜarab* ultimately goes back to this source, with the variant *min* for *fī*). Other early references to premodern dictionaries: al-Fārābī al-Lughawī: *Dīwān al-adab* (ed. Aḥmad Mukhtār ᶜUmar; 4 vols.; Cairo: al-Hayᵓa al-ᶜāmma, 1974–75) 2.62 [no explanation]; al-Jawharī, *Tāj al-lugha wa-ṣiḥāḥ al-ᶜarabiyya*, (ed. Aḥmad ᶜAbd al-Ghafūr ᶜAṭṭār; 6 vols.; Beirut: Dār al-ᶜilm li-l-malāyīn, 1399/1979) 3.963 (same as *K. al-ᶜAyn* plus *shāhid*); Ibn Durayd, *al-Jamhara fī l-lugha*, (ed. Ramzī Baᶜlabakkī; 3 vols.; Beirut: Dār al-ᶜilm li-l-malāyīn, 1987) 2.1151 (*qurnās al-jabal aᶜlāhu* 'the qurnās of a mountain is its topmost part'); al-Azharī, *Tahdhīb al-lugha* (15 vols.; Cairo: al-Dār al-miṣriyya li-l-taᵓlīf wa-l-tarjama, 1966) 9.395 (on the authority of Abū ᶜUbayd: *al-qurnās shibh al-anf fī l-jabal*; on the authority of Thaᶜlab *ᶜan* Ibn al-Aᶜrābī: *al-qirnās bi-kasr al-qāf anf al-jabal*).

19. On him, see Fuat Sezgin: *Geschichte des arabischen Schrifttums* (9 vols. to date; Leiden: Brill, 1967–84) 2.252. His father's name is also given as Khuwaylid.

20. In the edition of the tribal *dīwān* of the Hudhayl (al-Sukkarī, *Sharḥ Ashᶜār al-Hudhaliyyīn* [ed. Aḥmad ᶜAbd al-Sattār Farrāj; 2 vols.; Cairo : Dār al-ᶜurūba, n.d.] 1.439–40), the first hemistich appears as:

yā Mayya lan yuᶜjiza l-ayyāma dhū khadamin

O Mayya, (even an ibex) with (white) anklets will not thwart Fate (lit. the Days).

In the translation of *ẓayyān* and *ās*, I follow Bernhard Lewin, *A Vocabulary of the Huḏailian Poems* (Gothenburg: Kungl. Vetenskaps- och Vitterhets-Samhället, 1978), s.vv. Al-Sukkarī, however, explains *ās* as *nuqaṭ min al-ᶜasal* 'drops of honey'. The word *qurnās* is defined as *anf yakhruj min al-jabal muḥaddad* 'a jut emerging from the mountain, sharp-edged' and, on the authority of Abū ᶜAmr (al-Shaybānī), as *ṣakhra ṭawīla muḥaddadat al-raᵓs* 'a tall rock with a sharply pointed top'.

like 'to furnish a structure with projecting overhanging elements', and the passive participle *muqarnas* would, thus, originally have meant '[a structure] furnished with projecting overhanging elements'. This is, by the way, not the first time that *muqarnas* is connected with *qurnās*. In the Persian lexicographical tradition, the architectural meaning of *muqarnas* is well documented. In the *Farhang-i Ānandarāj*,[21] the *qurnās* etymology is expressed this way:

> *ᶜimārat-ī ki ān-rā bi ṣūrat-i qurnās sākhta bāshand wa qurnās bīnī-yi kūh*
>
> [*Muqarnas* is] a structure which they used to make in the form of the *qurnās*, the latter being the nose of the mountain.

Unfortunately, it is not exactly clear how the author understood this definition, because he goes on to say that 'the meaning of *muqarnas* is tall structure and high building' (*murād az muqarnas ᶜimārat-i buland wa binā-yi ᶜālī*). This is excruciatingly vague. In this context, it should be mentioned that in the Persian tradition the architectural term *muqarnas* often seems to have had a much broader meaning, covering any kind of cupola, especially one with paintings.[22] For the time being, it seems safe to assume that this is a secondary semantic extension of the term.

If *qurnās* is indeed the etymon of *muqarnas*, the spelling with *sīn* would be the original and etymologically correct one.[23] This is also borne out by

21. As quoted in ᶜAlī Akbar Dihkhudā, *Lughatnāma* (Tehran: Dānishgāh-i Tihrān, n.d.], s.v. *muqarnas,* vol. *mīm* / part 2, p. 924b–c, col. b, lines 13–15.

22. Cf. ibid., lines 17–19:

> *binā-yi buland-i mudawwar wa īwān-i ārāsta wa muzayyan shuda bā ṣūrathā wa-nuqūsh ki bar ān bā nardubānpāya wa rāh-i zīna rawand*
>
> a round tall building and an iwan (here: gallery?), decorated and embellished with figures and paintings, on to which one goes by means of a flight of stairs and by way of ladders.

(The relative clause looks very much like a misunderstanding of the stair-like arrangement of the *muqarnas* that is probably mentioned in al-Ṣaghānī's definition [see n. 17 above] and that recurs more clearly in the Persian lexicographical tradition.) See also the many poetic quotations adduced in the *Lughatnāma* in which the term *muqarnas* is used metaphorically for the sky or the spheres.

23. The word *qurnās* itself is derived by Y. M. Nawabi from an unattested Iranian **gar-nās* 'mountain nose', which is also supposed to have yielded the Persian *qarnīz* meaning 'a horizontal projection running round the wall of a room immediately below the ceiling and over the floor'. See Y. M. Nawabi, *Cornice* (Twenty-Seventh International Congress of Orientalists: Papers Presented by the Iranian Delegation, Canberra, 6–12 January, 1971), a mimeographed brochure of 8 pages. *Qarnīz* is not mentioned in the dictionaries available to me, including the *Lughatnāma*. Of the constituent elements of **garnās*, *gar* 'mountain' is mentioned in D. N. MacKenzie, *A Concise Pahlavi Dictionary* (London: Oxford University Press, 1971), s.v., but *nās* is not and should be **nāha*—anyway in Iranian (many thanks to Oktor Skjærvø for pointing this out to me). Nawabi's proposal should, thus, be discarded. It seems unnecessary, in any case, to posit a non-Arabic origin of the word.

al-Ṣaghānī's *saqf muqarnas* and by the entire Persian tradition. The spelling with *ṣād* would indicate that the etymology was at some point forgotten, thereby allowing the actual pronunciation to influence the spelling. Seeing that the word mostly escaped the attention of the lexicographers and probably belonged to the technical vocabulary of craftsmen (architects, masons, plasterers, carpenters), this does not come as a surprise.[24]

Although the plausibility of the proposed etymology cannot be denied, it does have certain weaknesses, which may be listed as follows:

1. The word *qurnās* is not very well attested. At present, only one attestation is known in a pre-Islamic poem. However, the text in which it occurs has been closely examined by a number of ancient philologists and thus deserves some credence.

2. The semantic relationship between *qurnās* and *muqarnas* is obvious only if the meaning 'mountain-nose' or the like is definitely established for *qurnās*. Some of the *interpretamenta* are less specific, as we have seen, and could refer to a vertical 'pinnacle', and Lewin does indeed render the word 'mountain peak, crag'.[25] It should be noted, however, that the majority of exegetes adhere to the 'nose' idea and that this idea makes better "visual" sense in the context of the line in which *qurnās* occurs.

3. The word *qurnās* has not itself become an architectural term, say, for the geometrical unit whose repetition makes up the *muqarnas*.[26] However, the use of *qurnās* would require a bold metaphorical transfer from a natural phenomenon to an artificial object, whereas the passive participle of the verb *qarnasa,* in the posited sense of creating *qurnās*es, would immediately imply a man-made product.

It would thus appear that the *qurnās* etymology has a number of advantages. Its competitors are derivations (a) from the Greek *korōnís*, about which enough has been said above; (b) from the Syriac *mqarnas* in the sense either of 'hammered' or of 'grooved'—in both cases the aspect of comparison that would allow the transfer from 'hammered' or 'grooved' object to our *muqarnas*

24. In the parallel case of the verb *qarnasa* in *qarnasa l-dīk idhā farra min dīk ākhar* 'the cock does *qarnasa*, when it flees from another cock', Ibn Durayd says, *wa-lā yuqāl "qarnaṣa" kamā taqūluhū l-ᶜāmma* 'one should not say *qarnaṣa* as the common people do' (*al-Jamhara*, 1151).

25. Lewin, *A Vocabulary, sub radice q-r-n-s*.

26. The term for this seems to be *bayt wāḥid*; see Jamshīd al-Kāshī, *Miftāḥ al-ḥisāb* (ed. Nādir al-Nābulusī; Damascus: Wizārat al-taᶜlīm al-ᶜālī, 1397/1977) 381, line 7.

is far from evident; and (c) another derivation from Arabic and possibly Persian, which is too far-fetched to warrant more than a footnote.[27]

Although I have a preference for the *qurnās* etymology, I cannot claim to have moved the solution of the question far beyond a *non liquet*. But it seems to me that it is worthwhile to present the possibilities in order to sharpen the awareness of future researchers as to what to look out for. The scholar we honor in these pages has always shown a keen interest in questions of etymology and has himself enriched us with many etymological contributions in a number of languages. I hope therefore that he will look on my above attempts with a benevolent eye. I submit them to him as a token of my deep esteem.

27. It is a strange coincidence that *muqarnas/ṣ* is also a technical term in falconry, where it refers to a molting or freshly molted young falcon or hawk. With a fair amount of imagination, one may detect a similarity between the breast plumage of a hawk, with its black-and-white designs, and the overall visual impression of the *muqarnas*. If this is more than a coincidence, it seems likely that the borrowing was from the natural to the artificial. In the case of *muqarnas/ṣ* 'freshly molted', the *ṣād* form may be the original one, since the term may be related to the Persian *kurīch* (with variants) 'molting of birds'—the correspondence *ṣād/chīm* in Arabic borrowings from Persian is quite regular. But a number of linguistic difficulties remain to be sorted out, if this line of research were to be taken seriously.

Egyptian Arabic and Dialect Contact in Historical Perspective

Manfred Woidich

When cruising on an Amsterdam canal, a tourist guide was asked by a German tourist for the date of construction of a certain building. Apparently the guide was well prepared to give his commentary in German, but he was not used to answering spontaneous questions, because he replied: “Im 17. Öwe.” In this answer he produced a new word—*Öwe* in place of *Jahrhundert*—unknown so far in Modern German. Of course, this is a case of hyperadaptation to a target language that is another variety within the same language family, in this case to German. It is a simple conversion of the Dutch word *eeuw* to a supposed German correspondent *Öwe*, with the help of a rule formed by analogy to the existing pair Dutch *leeuw* : German *Löwe*. Thus *eeuw* became *Öwe*.

Author's note: An earlier, shorter version of this article was read at North American Conference on Afro-asiatic Linguistics 20 at Harvard University, April, 1992.

For the linguist, this is a nice example of what happens when two closely related languages or dialects of a language come into contact, or let us rather say, when speakers of such varieties are exposed to each other's variety. Since many words and phrases are mutually intelligible, speakers detect the regular correspondences and make more-or-less correct guesses about the conversion rules that govern these correspondences. According to the situation, this contact may result in an attempt to accommodate to the other linguistic variety or, on the other hand, in the speakers' emphasizing their own linguistic features in order to reinforce the identity of their own group. As can be seen from this Dutch-German example,[1] false analogies and heavy overgeneralizations are the natural result of these accommodations to another variety.

Dialect Contact in Egypt

As a matter of course, we find similar examples of conversion rules, or adaptive rules as they are sometimes called,[2] within the field of Arabic dialects. From the evidence adduced below from Egyptian Arabic, we can see how conversion rules are applied in order to accommodate to a target dialect or in order to incorporate something into the native dialect.

(a) In the oasis of Baḥariyya, the glottal stop of the standard variety corresponds to /g/, that is to say, Cairo *ʾalb* is *galb* in Baḥariyya. Correspondingly, the word *hayʾa* 'company', used for the mining company some 40 km away, was pronounced *hayga* by an informant.[3] Another example is *mithayyigli* 'it seems to me' for standard *mithayyaʾli*, which occurs in an Upper Egyptian text.[4]

(b) In the areas of Fayyūm and Bani Swēf, the diphthongs /aw/ and /ay/ are preserved, unlike in Standard Egyptian, the dialect of Cairo. Speakers "know" that Cairo /ō/ corresponds to /aw/ at home. Thus, all words taken over from Standard Egyptian are given an /aw/, even loanwords that historically never con-

1. To be sure, I am not proposing that Dutch is a dialect of German; the only issue here is that the linguistic varieties are so close to each other that these correspondences can easily be detected and conversion rules can be perceived.

2. See Wolfgang U. Wurzel, "Dialektvariation und Grammatik," in *Dialectology and Sociolinguistics* (Essays in Honor of Karl-Hampus Dahlstedt; ed. Claes-Christian Elert et al.; Umeå, 1977; idem, "Adaptionsregeln und heterogene Sprachsysteme," in *PHONOLOGICA 1976* (ed. Wolfgang U. Dressler und Oskar E. Pfeiffer; Akten der dritten Internationalen Phonologie-Tagung, Wien, 1.–4. September 1976; Innsbruck, 1977); and idem, "Grammatik und Nationalsprache," in *Kontexte der Grammatiktheorie* (ed. W. Motsch; Studia Grammatica 17; Berlin, 1978).

3. This must be somewhat startling for a Cairene to hear, because in Cairo *hāyig/hayga* is a "four-letter word" meaning 'randy, horny'.

4. See P. Behnstedt and M. Woidich, *Die ägyptisch-arabischen Dialekte* (3 vols.; Wiesbaden, 1988), vol. 3, *Texte*, 2. *Oberägypten*. 3. *Oasen*, p. 242 n. 5. Compare with the widespread *biyithayyagli*; see ibid., vol. 1, *Einleitung und Anmerkungen zu den Karten*, p. 69, chart 9.

tained a diphthong: *ˀawḍa* for *ˀōḍa* 'room', *ṣawbar* for *ṣōbar* 'fertilizer', *talafawn* for *tilifōn* 'telephone', and so on.[5] This /aw/ is treated like etymological /aw/ and reduced to /a/ before two consonants: *ˀaḍt innawm* 'sleeping room'.

(c) Upper Egyptian Arabic has /ǧ/ where the standard variety uses /g/. A regular correspondence /g/ – /ǧ/ exists, with which every speaker of an Egyptian dialect is familiar. Again, words taken from the standard variety and containing /g/ are pronounced with the corresponding sound /ǧ/ not with /g/, notwithstanding the fact that /g/ would be available. So we find *ǧinē* and *saǧāyir* everywhere, the latter even being developed to *sadāyir* in some places by dissimilation of sibilants.

The Dutch-German and the Baḥariyya cases are examples of short-term adaptation arising incidentally because of a sudden need, whereas the Fayyūm and Upper Egyptian examples are long-term adaptations because they are well established. The resulting items are incorporated in this form into the lexicon of the dialect and are included in further developments (*sadāyir*, *ˀaḍt innawm*).

Certainly, as historical linguists, we are more interested in these long-term developments, but we should not neglect the short-term cases that show us how these conversion rules come about.

Dialect Geography: Transitional Areas

Contact between speakers of close varieties not only provokes conversion rules, but other related phenomena develop as well. Consider the "transitional areas" that are to be found in any dialect atlas, including the dialect atlas of Egypt.[6] In these geographical dialect contact areas, new forms often develop that belong to neither dialect.[7]

(a) In the Middle Egyptian province of il-Minya, the equivalents of 'threshing stick' are *zagla* to the south of il-Minya and *dugla* to the north of il-Minya.[8] Exactly on the borderline between these two areas, there is a small area where neither *zagla* nor *dugla* is used, but *zugla*, which exhibits the voiced sibilant /z/ of the south and the /u/ of the north. So, if we had to reconstruct the original form of 'threshing stick' from *zugla* alone, we would presumably go back to something like *zuqla, which, as we know from *dugla* and *zagla*, cannot be the ancestor of *zugla* and has never existed. The word for 'duck' in Fayyūm and

5. See for more detail, Rudolf de Jong, "More Material on Fayyūmī Arabic," *ZAL* 31 (1996) 57–92, in particular, p. 61.

6. See Behnstedt and Woidich, *Die ägyptisch-arabischen Dialekte*, 1.27ff.

7. See Peter Trudgill, *Dialect in Contact* (Oxford, 1986) 63.

8. See map 473 in Behnstedt and Woidich, *Die ägyptisch-arabischen Dialekte* (Wiesbaden, 1985) 2, *Dialektatlas von Ägypten*.

northern Bani Swēf provinces provides a similar example with *baṭṭa* being used in the north, *biḥḥa* in the south and *baḥḥa* in the in-between area.[9]

(b) A slightly more complicated case is to be found in the northwestern corner of the Delta, in Biḥēra Province.[10] There *šazaṛa* is used for 'a tree' where we should expect to find *sağaṛa* or *sagaṛa*, as in the rest of the Delta. *Šazaṛa* is confined to the Biḥēra, which borders on the area of the Awlād ᶜAli Bedouins, who use *šzira* with the dissimilation of the /ž/ to /z/ that is so typical for them.[11] The Fallāḥīn, however, dissimilate the /š/ to /s/, which results in *sağaṛa* or *sagaṛa*. In fact, many Bedouin have settled in il-Biḥēra and left their traces there. *Šazaṛa*, therefore, displays the consonants of the Bedouin dialect and the syllable structure of the Fallāḥīn dialects.

In the preceding two cases, no conversion rule is involved because there are no other correspondences of this kind that could lead to the evolution of such a rule. In the *zagla-dugla* case, probably both *zagla* and *dugla* were once in use in this border area at the same time, so a blending of the two items occurred that finally resulted in the intermediate form *zugla*. Nevertheless, *zugla* is also the result of an interaction of dialects.

A different case is the use of *šazaṛa* instead of the expected *sağaṛa*. Here not only sounds are involved but syllable structure as well. It seems that the Fallāḥīn who accommodated to Bedouin speakers adapted phonologically only, while retaining the syllable structure of the original *sağaṛa*. The interaction of the dialects here resulted in an imperfect adaptation to one of the varieties involved and the development of an interdialect form.

In other cases, individual words may not, at first glance, look like the results of dialect contact or interdialect forms. It is, rather, the whole paradigm that seems to have developed in this way. Let us examine a third case from the Egyptian dialect atlas, which concerns the formation of the passive-reflexive of the first stem. In the center of the Delta, we find three adjacent regions with the following distribution of the allomorphs of the i-perfect of the strong verb (stem I and its t-stem):[12]

west: *misik* → *itmisik* → *yitmisik*[13] east: *misik* → *itmasak* → *yitmisik*
in-between: *misik* → *itmasak* → *yitmasak*

These three paradigms can be accounted for in terms of the number of allomorphs {misik, masak} and the number of distribution rules, which means, on

9. See map 436 in ibid.

10. See map 416 in ibid.

11. For /š/-/z/ as the typical pattern of the distribution of sibilants in the Awlād ᶜAli dialect, see Behnstedt and Woidich, *Ägyptisch-arabischen Dialekte* (Wiesbaden, 1987), vol. 3, *Texte*, 1: *Delta-Dialekte*, p. 246. Compare *mašzid* 'mosque', *šariz* 'saddle', *šazzal* 'to record'.

12. See map 248 in Behnstedt and Woidich, *Die ägyptisch-arabischen Dialekte*, vol. 2.

13. The root {msk} is to be understood here as 'type', not as 'token'.

the one hand, the distribution of {misik, masak} in stem I and the t-stem and, on the other hand, their distribution in the perfect and imperfect of the t-stem. Thus, starting from the east, we find two allomorphs {misik, masak} distributed according to two rules, whereas in the in-between area, there are also two allomorphs, but there is only one rule accounting for their distribution. Finally, in the west, there is only one allomorph {misik} left, and, of course, there is no need for a distribution rule. Traditionally, all this region can be seen as a transitional area (*Stufenlandschaft*) with a step-by-step reduction of the original number of rules and allomorphs starting from the east.[14]

But this view remains only descriptive, and it is highly doubtful whether rule loss and reduction of the number of allomorphs somehow reflect the historical development. In particular, it offers no historical explanation of how the form *yitmasak* came about. Further, it presupposes a certain homogeneous starting area for this form's development. A homogenous starting area certainly did not exist, because we know that the eastern dialects of the Delta, with their older system *misik-itmasak-yitmisik*, are strongly influenced by the dialects of Bedouins who arrived relatively recently in the region[15] and presumably brought this system with them. Starting from these eastern dialects as the basis of a historical development in terms of rule loss and reduction of the number of allomorphs is therefore not justified.[16]

However, if this narrow strip between the east and the west is viewed as a contact area between eastern dialects and western dialects, there is a good reason for a form like *yitmasak* to develop. The reason is that speakers from the west who used *misik-itmisik* adapted to speakers from the east who used *misik-itmasak*. *Itmasak* was taken over from eastern dialects, and *yitmasak* was simply formed according to their native rule that perfect and imperfect are formed with the same allomorph: hence *itmasak* → *yitmasak*. *Yitmasak,* and with it the paradigm of t-stem I, can thus be considered to be an interdialect paradigm that does not occur in the original dialects involved.

Developments like this are not very unusual, since the reverse apparently took place in Burg Miġīzil and in Alexandria. There, the form *iftikir, yiftikir* 'mean, think', which is used by more literate people, exists alongside the original

14. Another possibility would be to view an in-between area as a relic area. However, *yitmasak* is certainly not a relic form but an innovation.

15. See Fahmi Abul-Fadl, *Volkstümliche Texte in arabischen Bauerndialekten der ägyptischen Provinz Šarqiyya mit dialektgeographischen Untersuchungen zur Lautlehre* (Ph.D. dissertation, Westfälische Wilhelms-Universität zu Münster, 1961) 2–3.

16. For a similar argumentation concerning the distribution of stem II and III in the Delta, see Manfred Woidich, "Zur Bildung der Verbalstämme in den ägyptisch-arabischen Dialekten: Der II. und der III. Stamm," in *XXIII. Deutscher Orientalistentag, Ausgewählte Vorträge* (ed. Einard Schuler; Stuttgart, 1989) 207.

iftakaṛ, yiftakaṛ.[17] The perfect form *iftikir* is backformed on the basis of the same rule and its reverse application, starting from the Cairene imperfect form *yiftikir.*

Interdialect Forms

Much attention has been paid to interdialect forms in recent publications. Peter Trudgill,[18] in particular, has shown how crucial a role they play in the development of new dialects.

He defines these "interdialectal forms" as follows: "The term 'interdialect' is intended to refer to situations where contact between two or more dialects leads to the development of forms that occurred in none of the original dialects."[19] In situations where speakers of different dialects meet in face-to-face interactions, not only are elements from one dialect borrowed by the speakers of the other dialect, but furthermore, speakers tend to accommodate to these elements in an imperfect manner. This means that they interpret features of the target dialect in their own way or do not succeed in adapting them totally, or, on the opposite side, they react against the accommodation and overemphasize features of their own dialect—"hyperdialectalization," as Trudgill calls it. If, for instance, one dialect enjoys a certain prestige and the other does not, then speakers of the latter may accommodate linguistically, meaning they may adapt their speech to the prestige dialect. Or, depending on the situation, they may demonstrate loyalty to their own speech community by using linguistic characteristics of their dialect where they are not appropriate.

This can happen as a short-term accommodation only, or as a long-term accommodation, with the creation of a new dialect.[20] The latter process is of course of great interest for the linguist and the dialectologist. The "interdialect forms" or "intermediate forms" that may develop in this case do not go back directly to one dialect or another but are mixed forms that result from hyperadaptation, incomplete adaptation, avoidance strategies, and related phenomena.[21]

The concept of *interdialect forms* was developed in dialect areas such as English, Norwegian, and other well-known languages. The dialectal varieties

17. For this and other examples, see Peter Behnstedt, "Die Dialekte des Burullus-Sees: Burg Miğīzil, ein ägyptischer Fischerdialekt," *GLECS, 18–23* (Paris, 1973–79) 132–33; and Behnstedt and Woidich, *Die ägyptisch-arabischen Dialekte*, 1.80–81.

18. For a general discussion of the historical discussion of interdialect, see Peter Trudgill, "On the Role of Dialect Contact and Interdialect in Linguistic Change," in *Historical Dialectology: Regional and Social* (ed. Jacek Fisiak; Berlin, 1988).

19. See ibid., and Trudgill, *Dialect in Contact* (Oxford, 1986) 62.

20. For details, see ibid., 3 and 11.

21. See ibid., 58.

in contact with each other are adequately described, since long-term investigations with dozens of informants have indeed been carried out, yielding considerable and reliable evidence going back over a century. Long-term developments can thus be followed, and the origin of certain varieties can be traced back because the data and the ancestral dialects are well known.

Interdialect Forms and Egyptian Arabic Dialects

Following long-term development is, unfortunately, not as easy in an area like Egypt. Dialect contact, accommodation, and interdialect forms do of course occur here, as well as in other parts of the world. But it is not as easy to adduce conclusive evidence for these phenomena, mainly because of the lack of exact data and thorough research on this subject, but also because, as Hocke writes regarding dialect differences as compared to distinct languages, "the very fact that linguistic differences are minor makes the detection of dialect borrowings considerably more difficult."[22]

Nevertheless, I have attempted to point out some examples of dialect interaction at the beginning of this paper. These are features that can be observed today. But certainly in the past, speakers from different dialect areas also met, were forced to live with each other, intermarried, and interacted linguistically in one way or another. Hence, when approaching the Egyptian dialects as historical linguists, we should take into account the possibility of the development of new dialects by dialect contact. The problem is that we do not have exact records of the earlier states of the Egyptian dialects, so we can only tentatively look for candidates for dialects that perhaps developed in this way. Since linguistic contact can only be the consequence of the contact of the speakers, we will have to search in places in which we know that such contacts have taken place, whether peacefully or belligerently, by migration or by conquest. There are two main areas that are likely to show elements of dialect contact, that is, of long-term accommodation and the emergence of interdialect forms.[23] First, we must consider the large towns and the effects of urbanization during the 19th century. A "notable movement from country to town"[24] took place, and large numbers of peasants from the countryside and even from

22. Hans Henrich Hocke, *Principles of Historical Linguistics* (Berlin, 1986) 388.

23. A third and slightly different case, not considered here, is the influence of Modern Standard Arabic on Cairo Arabic. This is an ongoing process that in the long run will lead to a new dialect of Arabic, as predicted by Charles Ferguson ("Diglossia," *Word* 15 [1959] 332).

24. Gabriel Baer, *Studies in the Social History of Modern Egypt* (Chicago, 1969) 142. For the growth of the population of Egypt in the 19th century, see the same source, pp. 133–48.

Upper Egypt migrated into Cairo, particularly after 1882.[25] This intermingling of speakers of different dialects must have produced new dialects with interdialect forms. Second, we must consider the areas where Bedouin or other groups settled and intermingled with the Fallāḥīn and gradually became peasants themselves. These areas are primarily the Sharqiyya and Biḥēra Provinces, Upper Egypt, and the Arabic-speaking Oases of the Western Desert.[26]

If we want to trace back how certain features developed, or if, by comparing it with other dialects, we want to reconstruct previous stages of a dialect, we must always take into account the fact that features may not have developed because of an internal evolution of the linguistic system but are triggered by dialect contact and must be seen as interdialect features. In the following section, I will discuss some features of the Bᶜēri dialect[27] spoken on the West Bank of Luxor in Upper Egypt, which, in my opinion, must be regarded as contact-induced, in this case by contact between Fallāḥīn and Bedouin. This view is corroborated by the fact that the effects of this contact are not confined to one subsystem of the dialect but can be found in all parts of the grammar and the lexicon as well.[28]

The Case of Bᶜēri Arabic in Upper Egypt

(a) *Vowel alternations.* Bᶜēri Arabic does not allow sequences of two subsequent /a/s if a third vowel of any kind follows, as a suffix for instance. If it

25. Ibid., 143. Earlier, in 1835, Cairo suffered a severe plague and lost at least one-third of its inhabitants. Massive immigration from the rural areas quickly made up for this loss; see Janet L. Abul Lughod, *Cairo: 1001 Years of the City Victorious* (Princeton, 1971) 83 n. 4. All this must be taken into account in tracing the development of the Cairene dialect.

26. For a discussion of interdialectal phenomena in the Western Oases, see Manfred Woidich, "Die Dialekte der ägyptischen Oasen: Westliches oder östliches Arabisch?" *Zeitschrift für arabische Linguistik* 25 (*Festschrift Wolfdietrich Fischer*; 1993) 340–59.

27. For a sketch and texts of this dialect, see Manfred Woidich, "Ein arabischer Bauerndialekt aus dem südlichen Oberägypten," *ZDMG* 124 (1974) 42–58; and Behnstedt and Woidich, *Die ägyptisch-arabischen Dialekte*, 3.244–46. A text is published in M. Woidich, "Text aus il-Biᶜrāt," in *Handbuch der arabischen Dialekte* (ed. Wolfdietrich Fischer and Otto Jastrow; Wiesbaden, 1980) 235–42.

28. For the importance of this criterion "for establishing external causation in the explanation of linguistic changes," see Sarah Grey Thomason and Terrence Kaufman, *Language Contact, Creolization and Genetic Linguistics* (Berkeley, 1988) 61. Dialect contact may not have consequences solely for the various subsystems of grammar. On the semantic level, the development of the derogatory meaning of *mara* 'woman' in Cairo, for example, might go back to dialect contact, or rather to contact between two communities with closely related dialects. *Mara* is a normal word for 'woman' in the rural dialects and has no negative connotations. Because the townsfolk tend to look down on the peasants, *mara* in Cairo Arabic ceased to be used as a normal word for 'woman' and acquired a derogatory meaning. A similar case is the word *afandi* 'master', with its positive connotations in rural areas and its ridiculing effect in Cairo.

does, /a/ is changed to /i/, or to /u/ in an /u/-coloring environment. This means: *masak* 'he seized' becomes *misikat* 'she seized'; *balaḥ* 'dates' becomes *bilaḥa* 'a date'; *bagaṛ* 'cows' becomes *buguṛa* 'a cow'; *ġanam* 'sheep' becomes *ġinimi* 'my sheep' and *ġinimuk* 'your (f.) sheep'; *watad* 'stake' becomes *wutidēn* 'two stakes'. These alternations can be accounted for by a vowel-alternation rule:

a → i / __K(K)_Kv

The rule does not depend on stress, and there are no exceptions to it.[29] High vowels produced by this rule never undergo the well-known elision rule, which plays the same role here as in Cairo Arabic. This led to the (in my view) not very probable assumption that in B^{c}ēri dialect, "old" forms are preserved that would be the basis of certain vowel alternations in Bedouin dialects.[30] In these Bedouin dialects, intermediate forms such as **misikat*, which definitely look like the existing B^{c}ēri forms, can indeed be reconstructed.

The rule that accounts for the vowel-alternations in many Bedouin dialects is quite similar to the B^{c}ēri rule. Here are some examples:[31]

misak +at	→	**misikat*	→	*msikat*	(Nağdi)	'she seized'	{misikat}
xašab	→	**xišiba*	→	*xšiba*	(Nağdi)	'piece of wood'	{xišiba}
ablaš +at[32]	→	*ablišat*			(Nağdi)	'she involved'	{willidat}

The main difference between the B^{c}ēri rule and the Bedouin rule is not only the rule itself but its relation to the elision rule for /i/ that produces *msikat* from **misikat*. From a descriptive point of view, the vowel-alternation in Bedouin dialects has a feeding relationship to the elision rule. This means that it precedes the elision rule, thus providing contexts for the elision rule to work. B^{c}ēri Arabic also makes use of this elision rule, but there is no such feeding order. The elision there precedes the alternation, which means that the rules are in a non-feeding order. Since in B^{c}ēri there are numerous cases of unelided /i/

29. It does not apply when the *gáhawa* rule (see (b) below) accounts for a sequence with two /a/s. The only real exception is the cardinal numbers *aṛba^{c}a* and *^{c}ašaṛa*, which are pronounced as elsewhere in Upper Egypt. The second syllable may not be affected if the following consonant is a pharyngeal or velar. For a detailed analysis, see Manfred Woidich, "Die 3.sg.f. Perfekt im Dialekt von il-Bi^{c}rāt," in *Festschrift Henri Fleisch* (Mélanges de l'Université Saint-Joseph 48; Beirut, 1973–74) 355–72. Because of this strange phonological rule, B^{c}ēri-speaking peasants are easily recognized as hillbillies by others, in particular by the inhabitants of the East Bank. In order to avoid this, I was told by my informants, B^{c}ēri-speakers do not use these alternated forms in market situations, fearing that they will be cheated.

30. See O. Jastrow, "Die Struktur des Neuarabischen," in *Grundriß der arabischen Philologie*, vol. 1: *Sprachwissenschaft* (ed. Wolfdietrich Fischer; 3 vols.; Wiesbaden, 1982ff.) 1.131ff.

31. These examples come from Bruce Ingham, *North East Arabian Dialects* (London, 1982) 44. Dialects with this feature, among others, are Awlād ^{c}Ali, ^{c}Anaiza, Negev-Bedouin, and Baghdad. The words between braces are the corresponding B^{c}ēri terms.

32. 'Involve the subject in something'.

and /u/ on the surface, the elision rule has more exceptions than applications, which means that it has become totally opaque.

I-elision is certainly historically older than vowel-alternation.[33] Hence, the nonfeeding order of Bᶜēri looks like the historical rule sequence.[34] What happened in Bedouin dialects is that the elision rule was applied to these new opaque cases as well, thus making the surface forms transparent by means of rule reordering.[35] In this way, forms like *msikat* and so on came about. If we assume this historical development, the question arises: why did Bᶜēri not go the same way? All Bedouin dialects that developed vowel-alternations of this kind did so; why not Bᶜēri?

We could stop here and content ourselves with this observation: Bᶜēri did not reorder its rules, it preserved the old and unchanged forms, and it kindly provided us with the historical base forms that allow us to understand how the Bedouin forms arose. But this is not the whole story. It can be argued that this vowel-alternation rule in Bᶜēri developed later via intermediate forms, that is, after establishing the i-elision. An argument in favor of this suggestion is the fact that the Bᶜēri alternation rule shows characteristic differences when compared to the corresponding rules in Bedouin dialects. It affects two syllables, not just one, and it has no exceptions. It gives a strong impression that it is the result of an overgeneralization, as is typical for interdialect forms.

Presumably, these interdialect forms arose when Bedouin settled down and took wives from among the Fallāḥīn living there. Since the Bedouin at that time came as conquerors, the target variety for accommodation was the Bedouin dialect. We know from second-language-learning that syllable structure offers one of the greatest problems in mastering a foreign tongue. When these Fallāḥīn adapted to the Bedouin and tried to pronounce *msikat*, the result must have been something like *misikat*, which displays both the vowel /i/ of the Bedouin variant and the syllable structure of the Fallāḥīn dialect *masakat*.[36] As soon as *misikat* was established alongside *masak*, a rule relating the two allomorphs was formed and applied to the whole paradigm, with the necessary overgeneralizations usual in such cases.

33. If, on the contrary, based on the evidence of the Bedouin dialects, we assume that vowel-alternation is older, we will have to explain why /i/ produced by the alternation rule is not subjected to the elision rule in Bᶜēri.

34. "'Additional' sound changes, invoked to account for apparent irregularities in a particular change, are not always, therefore, to be 'added' after that change. They may precede or follow, and they may bleed or feed it" (Hocke, *Principles*, 44).

35. See ibid., 278: "If sound changes result in enough synchronic alternations to motivate 'productive' corresponding synchronic rules, a reordering of these rules may suggest historically incorrect relative chronologies."

36. See the case of *šazaṛa*, above.

(b) *The gáhawa syndrome.* A similar case is the *gáhawa* syndrome in the same dialect. A cluster consisting of a pharyngeal or a velar fricative and another consonant is separated by /a/ if /a/ precedes:

$$\emptyset \rightarrow a/a\ L\_C$$

Thus we have *gáhawa* 'coffee', *áḥamaṛ* 'red', *maġasūl* 'washed', and so on. This is a typically Bedouin feature, albeit in a slightly different shape here: in Bedouin dialects the inserted /a/ is stressed and the first /a/ is often elided. Not so in B^{c}ēri, because the stress is on the first syllable and no vowel is elided. Again the B^{c}ēri form looks like a reconstructed older form of the Bedouin dialects, and again we must ask why B^{c}ēri did not develop like the Bedouin dialects. The answer is the same as above: speakers of a *gáhwa* dialect accommodated to *ghâwa* and the result was *gáhawa*, because the syllable structure of their dialect did not provide for a word starting with two consonants.

(c) Whereas the two examples above arouse suspicion because there are forms involved that look too old to be genuinely old, in the following case an unexpected distribution of two allomorphs draws our attention. The conjugation of two verbs with a primary *hamza*, *akal* 'he ate' and *axad* 'he took', shows some peculiarities that can be explained by dialect contact: the imperfect has an /i/ in its base form, as in most Bedouin dialects, but the imperative has /u/, as elsewhere in Egypt. So we have the paradigm *yākil—kul*! 'he eats—eat!' And, astonishingly enough, the feminine and the plural forms are stressed on the last syllable, that is, on the corresponding morphemes: *kul—kliy—kluw—klan*. There is, to the best of my knowledge, no way to explain this in a system-immanent manner, and it can best be viewed as further evidence of dialect contact.

(d) There is also evidence from morphology for a strong Bedouin influence on B^{c}ēri. The feminine plural, for instance, is in full use: *malan* 'they filled water', *tamlan* 'you fill water', *bētkan* 'your house', and so on. The possessive suffix of the third-person singular masculine *-a*, the morphemes *-aw* and *-ay* for plural and feminine forms respectively of the verb, and the *ya-*, *ta-*, and *na-* prefixes of the imperfect are typically Bedouin features.

(e) In the lexicon, Bedouin words like *zēn* for 'good' and *šēn* for 'bad' are used instead of the common Egyptian *kuwayyis* and *wiḥiš*; and *gēḍ* 'summer', *naḍar* 'to see', *ḍamyān* 'thirsty' for *šāf, ṣēf, ^{c}aṭšān*, and so on.

Oral history supports these linguistic facts. The B^{c}ēri speakers report that they came to Upper Egypt guided by their leader Ḥasan al-Fazārī and following the *ba^{c}aṛ* 'droppings' of their camels; hence the whole region acquired the name al-Ba^{c}īrāt,[37] and they proudly call themselves *B^{c}ēri afzaṛ*.[38] This means

37. Local pronunciation sounds like *ilBi^{c}ṛāt*, which goes back to al-Ba^{c}īrāt.

38. The Fazāra tribe, a fraction of the Dhubyān and belonging to the Qaysites, is well known in Egyptian and Sudanese history; see H. A. MacMichael, *A History of the Arabs in the Sudan*

that there is external evidence that the B^cēris were originally Bedouin or are mixed with Bedouins, a fact that corroborates the assumption that certain peculiarities of this dialect might be better explained by dialect contact via the development of interdialect forms than in terms of an internal development within the system. This conclusion is further supported by the fact that the Christian village ᶜIzbit il-Basīli, which is situated in the heart of the Bᶜēri region, speaks a different dialect, close to the East Bank dialect,[39] without these Bedouin features. The Basīlis did not mix with Bedouin because of their religion. Needless to say, the Bedouin influx still continues today; and, on the borders of the Nile Valley, in the West in particular, numerous small settlements have recently been established.

Conclusions

There is sufficient evidence that contact phenomena like linguistic accommodation, which lead to conversion rules, transitional areas, and interdialect forms, do exist in Egypt. Indeed, it would be rather surprising and unlikely if there were no traces of them. Certainly, these interdialect forms are not confined to present-day language states, but developed in the past as well,[40] since in many parts of Egypt, Bedouin settled and mixed with local people. From Middle Egypt, people migrated to the oases and put down roots there. Huge cities like Cairo always attracted people from the rural areas. Hence we may conclude that many features found in these dialects are not just consequences of the linguistic systems themselves but go back to dialect contact and variation in a mixed society, which result in accommodation and the development of interdialect forms of various kinds. Unexplainable distributions of sounds,[41] large numbers of unexpected innovations such as sudden and unconditioned variation of allomorphs that may lead to new suppletive paradigms,[42] puzzling simplifications of paradigms and rules due to heavy overgeneralizations, and the "preserva-

(Cambridge, 1922) 144–45 and 293; and E. Kippel, "Études sur le Folklore Bédouin de l'Égypte," *Bull. de la soc. Khéd. de Géographie,* VIIe série, nr. 10 (1911) 557. The Fazāra have been present there throughout the Middle Ages. For an account of Bedouin stems in Upper Egypt in the 14th century, see further Jean-Claude Garcin, *Un centre Musulman de la Haute-Égypte Médiévale: Qūṣ* (Cairo, 1976) 359 ff.

39. According to our classification, this is an OÄ 1 dialect, whereas Bᶜēri is labeled as OÄ 3; see Behnstedt and Woidich, *Die ägytisch-arabischen Dialekte,* 3.154ff.

40. See James Milroy, *Linguistic Variation and Change* (Oxford, 1992) 55.

41. This means the unconditioned variation of two sounds that go back to the same sound etymologically; see Hocke, *Principles*, 388–89. For a case in point, see Woidich, "Die Dialekte."

42. This means a mixture of allomorphs that do not match historically.

tion" of astonishingly "old" forms are the most conspicuous cases and indicate that there may be more at stake than rule loss, rule addition, paradigmatic leveling and so on, and that dialect contact with its consequences has occurred. Interdialect forms do not simply mean borrowing or suppression of the most prominent features, but they may be completely new forms that do not occur in any of the participating dialects. This must be taken into account for the purposes of historical analysis.

On Later and Modern Egyptian Judeo-Arabic

Benjamin Hary

The Periods of Judeo-Arabic

Judeo-Arabic[1] has been spoken and written in various forms by Jews throughout the Arabic-speaking world; its literature is concerned for the most part with Jewish topics and is written by Jewish authors for Jewish readers. The following chart represents the transliteration used by the scribes of the various manuscripts cited in this paper:

TABLE 1.

ض	ص	ش	س	ز	ر	ذ	د	خ	ح	ج	ث	ت	ب	ا
צ̇/ד	צ/ס	ש	ס	ז	ר	ד/ד̇	ד	כ̇/כ	ח	ג̇/ג	ת/ת̇	ת	ב	א
ي	و	ة	ه	ن	م	ل	ك	ق	ف	غ	ع	ظ	ط	
יי/י	וו/ו	ת/ה	ה	נ	מ	ל	כ	ק	פ̇/פ	ג̇/ג	ע	ט̇/צ̇	ט	

1. This paper is an updated version of relevant parts from my *Multiglossia in Judeo-Arabic—With an Edition, Translation, and Grammatical Study of the Cairene Purim Scroll* (Études sur le

The linguistic components of Judeo-Arabic are Classical Arabic, dialectal elements, pseudocorrected features, and standardization of these features. In addition, like other Jewish ethnolects,[2] Judeo-Arabic has several other peculiar features: the use of Hebrew characters, various traditions of orthography, elements of Hebrew and Aramaic vocabulary and grammar, and the language layer of the *šarḥ*—a literal or direct translation of Hebrew sacred texts into Judeo-Arabic. It is crucial to differentiate between the genre of the *šarḥ*, which is the actual literal translation of a Hebrew sacred text into Judeo-Arabic, and the language layer of the *šarḥ*, found in other Judeo-Arabic texts and identified by strong Hebrew influence on the Judeo-Arabic as well as a word-for-word rendering of an imaginary or actual Hebrew version into Judeo-Arabic.

Judeo-Arabic consists of five periods: Pre-Islamic Judeo-Arabic, Early Judeo-Arabic (eighth/ninth to tenth centuries), Classical Judeo-Arabic (tenth to fifteenth centuries), Later Judeo-Arabic (fifteenth to nineteenth centuries), and Modern Judeo-Arabic (twentieth century).[3] This periodization, however,

---

judaïsme médiéval 14; Leiden: Brill, 1992). An earlier version of this paper was read at the twenty-sixth annual meeting of the Middle East Studies Association of North America (MESA), held in Portland, Oregon, in October, 1992. I thank Dilworth Parkinson, who was the discussant at my panel, for his important suggestions and remarks. I also wish to thank Asma Afsaruddin and Matt Zahniser for their careful and meticulous editing. The research on this paper was supported in part by the University Research Committee of Emory University and the Memorial Foundation for Jewish Culture. For Later Egyptian Judeo-Arabic, data are collected from the same documents cited in *Multiglossia: Megillat pūrīm il-miṣriyyīn*; seventeenth-century Egyptian Judeo-Arabic folk tales (Viktor Vladimirovich Lebedev, "Skazka o zolotoi gazele: Obrazočik arabskogo fol'klora XVII veka," [Semitic Languages 2; Moscow: Nauka, 1965] 521–32 [Russian]; and idem, *Pozdnii srednearabskii iazyk* XIII–XVIIIvv [Moscow: Nauka, 1977] [Russian]); *il-Maṣrī wir-Rīfī* (Shlomo Dov Goitein, "Townsman and Fellah: A Geniza Text from the Seventeenth Century," *Asian and African Studies* 8 [1971] 257–61); *Darkhe Noᶜam* (Haim Blanc, "Egyptian Arabic in the Seventeenth Century: Notes on the Judeo-Arabic Passages of *Darxe Noᶜam* (Venice, 1697)," in *Studies in Judaism and Islam Presented to Shelomo Dov Goitein* [ed. S. Morag, I. Ben–Ami and N. Stillman; Jerusalem: Magnes, 1981] 185–202; and idem, "Egyptian Judeo-Arabic: More on the Subject of R. Mordekhai b. Yehuda Ha-Levi's *Sefer Darkhe Noᶜam*," *Sefunot* n.s. 3 [1985] 299–314, xi [Hebrew; English summary]); and a non-Jewish document, *Hazz al-Quḥūf* (Humphrey Davies, "*17th-Century Egyptian Arabic: A Profile of the Colloquial Material in Yūsuf al-Širbīnī's Hazz al-Quḥūf fī šarḥ qaṣīd Abī Šādūf* [Ph.D. dissertation, University of California at Berkeley, 1981]). Data for Modern Judeo-Arabic are gathered from Haggadah-Egypt as well as several manuscripts from the Cairo Collection, especially no. C3 (C stands for the Cairo Collection), which includes a variety of *Haggadot*, *Siddurim*, *Piyyutim*, halakhic works, *šurūḥ*, stories about Moses and Joseph, and prayers from various Jewish festivals. This collection is housed at the Institute of Microfilmed Hebrew Manuscripts in the Jewish National and University Library in Jerusalem. Further data for Modern Egyptian Judeo-Arabic are collected from a *šarḥ* to the book of Esther (MS 1302, located at Ben-Zvi Institute [BZ] in Jerusalem).

2. The word *ethnolect* refers to an independent linguistic entity, which is a language or a variety, has its own history and development, and is used by a distinct ethnic speech community. See also Hary, "Judeo-Arabic in Its Sociolinguistic Setting," *IOS* 15 (1995) 74.

3. In earlier works I divide Judeo-Arabic into four periods only ("The Importance of the Orthography in Judeo-Arabic Texts," *Proceedings of the Tenth World Congress of Jewish Studies*,

should not distract us from the major change that occured in the fifteenth century between the Medieval and the Late periods, which is represented in the following diagram:

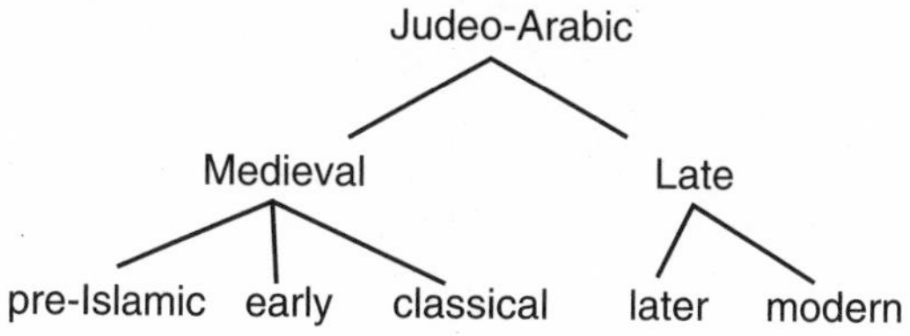

Figure 1.

There is some evidence that the Jews in the Arabian Peninsula had some sort of an Arabic Jewish dialect called *al-Yahūdiyya.*[4] This dialect was probably similar to the dominant Arabic dialect, but it included some Hebrew and Aramaic lexemes, especially in the vocabulary of religious and cultural affairs. Some of these Hebrew and Aramaic words passed into the speech and the writings of the Arabs, thus explaining the Hebrew and Aramaic origins of certain Qurʾānic words. There is no evidence that Pre-Islamic Judeo-Arabic produced any literature, especially if we examine the language of the Jewish poet al-Samawʾal ibn ʿĀdiyāʾ, which did not differ from that of his Arab contemporaries; however, there might have been some writings of *al-Yahūdiyya* in Hebrew characters.[5] Judeo-Arabic elements appear in the writings of every Arabic-speaking Jewish author thereafter. Indeed, after the great conquests of early Islam, the Jews in the newly conquered lands, who had not written or spoken Arabic before, gradually began to incorporate Arabic into their writings and slowly developed their own spoken dialect.

Division D, Vol. 1: *The Hebrew Language, Jewish Languages* [Jerusalem: World Union of Jewish Studies, 1990] 77; "On the Use of *ʾilā* and *li* in Judeo-Arabic Texts," in [*Semitic Studies in Honor of Wolf Leslau on the Occasion of His Eighty-Fifth Birthday, November 14th, 1991* [ed. A. Kaye; 2 vols.; Wiesbaden: Harrassowitz, 1991] 1.595–96); and "The Tradition of Later Egyptian Judeo-Arabic Orthography," *Massorot* 5–6 [1991] 119 [Hebrew; English abstract]). The division here (and in my book, *Multiglossia*, 75–78) is more "refined" and accurate. In previous literature, Vajda divides Judeo-Arabic into two periods, with the fifteenth century as the dividing line (Georges Vajda, "Judaeo-Arabic Literature," EI^2 4.303–7). Stillman discusses two periods, medieval and modern Judeo-Arabic and argues that the latter begins in the late fifteenth century (Norman A. Stillman, *The Language and Culture of the Jews of Sefrou, Morocco: An Ethnolinguistic Study* [Manchester: University of Manchester, 1988] 5). In another article, Stillman defines three "stages": Proto-, Classical, and Modern Judeo-Arabic ("Judeo-Arabic Language," *Dictionary of the Middle Ages*, 1986 ed.).

4. See Gordon Darnell Newby, "Observations about an Early Judaeo-Arabic," *JQR* n.s. 61 (1971) 212–21; idem, *A History of the Jews of Arabia from Ancient Times to Their Eclipse under Islam* (Columbia: University of South Carolina Press, 1988), 21–23; and Moshe Gil, "The Origin of the Jews of Yathrib," *Jerusalem Studies in Arabic and Islam* 4 (1984) 206.

5. Newby, "Observations," 220.

The second period of Judeo-Arabic begins approximately in the eighth (in Egypt) or the ninth century. This is the only period in which a phonetically based orthography is employed, though alongside an Arabicized orthography.[6]

The appearance of Saᶜadyā ibn Yosēf al-Fayyūmī's (882–942 C.E.) translation of the Pentateuch into Judeo-Arabic marks the beginning of the third period of Judeo-Arabic, generally known as that of "Medieval Judeo-Arabic," but more properly called the period of "Classical Judeo-Arabic."[7] Although the written form of this language contains dialectal features as well as pseudo-corrections, it tends to follow the model of Classical Arabic to a certain extent. The works written in this period cover the entire range of literary production: theology, philosophy, biblical exegesis, philology and grammar, law, ritual, and literature, in addition to commercial and private correspondence.[8] Furthermore, the number of such works in this period exceeds the number of Judeo-Arabic works in each of the other periods.

The fourth or "Later Judeo-Arabic" period marks the beginning of the Late period. It starts in the fifteenth and ends in the nineteenth century.[9] During this period, many more dialectal elements penetrated the written language,[10] and the tradition of the *šarḥ* developed. In this period, historical, halakhic, liturgical, and other texts, many of which were aimed at the general public and not only at the elite, were written. Toward the end of this period, and especially during the next period, an extensive folk literature also developed. It was at the beginning of this period that Jewish scholars began to write in Hebrew; by its end, Hebrew was the preferred written language.[11]

6. See Hary, "Adaptations of Hebrew Script," in *The World's Writing Systems* (ed. P. Daniels and W. Bright; New York and Oxford: Oxford University Press, 1996) 727–34, and the references there.

7. I prefer the term *Classical Judeo-Arabic*, not because the language of that period tends to follow the grammar of Classical Arabic, but because most of the classic Judeo-Arabic works were written in this period.

8. Moritz Steinschneider, *Die arabische Literatur der Juden* (Frankfurt a. M.: Kauffmann, 1902); Abraham Solomon Halkin, "Judeo-Arabic Literature," *Encyclopaedia Judaica*, 1971 ed.; Vajda, "Judeo-Arabic"; and Benjamin Hary, "Review of Joshua Blau, *Judaeo-Arabic Literature: Selected Texts* (Jerusalem: Magnes, 1980 [Hebrew])," *Zeitschrift für arabische Linguistik* 11 (1983) 90–91.

9. The shift from Classical to Later Judeo-Arabic was coupled with "the increased social isolation of the Jews of the Arab world at the end of the Middle Ages within restrictive quarters, such as the *mellāḥ* and *ḥārat il-yahūd*" (Stillman, *Language and Culture*, 5). See also Norman A. Stillman, *The Jews of Arab Lands: A History and Source Book* (Philadelphia: Jewish Publication Society of America, 1979) 64–94 and 255–323.

10. Yemen was an exceptional case because the Jewish community there was more isolated. The literary language of the second period continued to be used well into the fifteenth century.

11. Stillman argues that the increased dialectal elements in Later Judeo-Arabic may represent "in part a decline in the general level of education throughout the Islamic world" (*Language and Culture*, 5). While this may be true, one must not forget that Jews in this period began to shy away from Classical Arabic (Hary, *Multiglossia*, 112) and concentrate more on their localized speech.

The literary language of the fifth period, "Modern Judeo-Arabic" of the twentieth century, is characterized by a greater production of *šarḥ* than in Later Judeo-Arabic, as well as a greater production of folk tales and other types of "popular literature."[12] Goitein mentions the large number of Judeo-Arabic books printed in the twentieth century all over the Judeo-Arabic speaking world from India in the east to Morocco in the west. These books contain folk stories as well as entertainment and edification and range from ancient Jewish stories to Arabic romances. Goitein concludes that "a complete survey of that peculiar popular literature would be a useful contribution to the study of folklore in general and to the knowledge of Jewish life in Arab countries in particular."[13] The literary materials from this period are found not only in written form but also in oral form; Goitein discerns four important areas of oral literature: (1) local traditions, where stories are related about the history of a village, for example; (2) folk narratives that vary from one narrator to another in the course of their transmission; (3) poetry; and (4) proverbs.[14] To this, one may add the tradition of the *šarḥ*, which was transmitted orally and not always printed. In sum, literary Modern Judeo-Arabic utilizes, among other things, the special language of the *šarḥ*, which insists on word-for-word translation. The language demonstrates a stronger dialectal influence than that of the preceding period and also exhibits localized elements from the spoken variety.

Multiglossia in Judeo-Arabic

As I have suggested, Arabic multiglossia may be viewed as a continuum with two prototypical varieties standing at either end with complex varieties in between.[15] The left end of the continuum is termed "Variety A" (roughly, the standard variety), the right end, "Variety C" (Colloquial Arabic, or the equivalent of the spoken dialects) and the middle, "Varieties B_n." The two extreme ends, Varieties A and C, are only ideal types; that is, there is no such thing as

12. Alan A. Corré, *A "Diskionary" and Chrestomathy of Modern Literary Judeo-Arabic* (Milwaukee: University of Wisconsin, Milwaukee, Language Resource Center Software, 1989; and Yitzhak Avishur, "The Folk Literature of the Jews of Iraq in Judeo-Arabic," *Peᶜamim* 3 (1979) 83–90 [Hebrew].

13. Shlomo Dov Goitein, *Jews and Arabs: Their Contacts through the Ages*, (3d. ed.; New York: Shocken, 1974) 199.

14. Ibid., 199–204.

15. Hary, *Multiglossia*, 11ff.; and idem, "The Importance of the Language Continuum in Arabic Multiglossia," in *Understanding Arabic* (ed. A. Elgibaali; Cairo: American University in Cairo Press, 1996) 69–90.

"pure" Standard or "pure" Colloquial Arabic.[16] In other words, what is usually perceived as Standard Arabic is the acrolect end of the continuum, and what is usually perceived as Colloquial Arabic is the basilect end of the continuum. Between these ends, one finds the mesolect.[17] This means, in fact, that speakers can employ all the possibilities available on the continuum, subject to certain constraints. They are either closer to the colloquial end, whereby the variety would be considered Colloquial Arabic, or closer to the other end, whereby the variety would be considered Standard Arabic. Speakers may also use intermediate varieties (or the mesolect); in these cases, one sees the result of the speakers' need to move between the standard (acrolect) and the colloquial (basilect) ends of the continuum. The speech used in the middle, "B_n,"[18] can "move" along the continuum. It can be closer to Standard Arabic and exhibit many classical features and fewer colloquial elements, or it can "shift" toward the other end and exhibit more colloquial attributes. It is imperative to remember that this area in the middle is not composed of only one variety or of three varieties as proposed by Badawi;[19] there can be a countless number of lectal varieties on the continuum between the two ideal types. When B_n moves on the continuum to the left, it may eventually be perceived by native speakers as Standard Arabic. On the other hand, when it moves to the right, it is eventually considered Colloquial Arabic. Since we are dealing with the notion of a continuum, there are no boundaries and no commitments to discrete categories. This is illustrated in figure 2.

Note that figure 2 illustrates the situation in both *written* and *spoken* Arabic. Most written materials would be closer to the acrolect end, but most modern (Egyptian) dramatic dialogues, as well as some poetry[20] and dialogues

16. Even in the most "pure" standard text, we may find some colloquial elements. Conversely, standard elements tend to be found even in the most colloquial "texts."

17. On the terms *acrolect*, *mesolect* and *basilect*, which are very useful when discussing the notion of a continuum, see Derek Bickerton, *Dynamics of a Creol System* (New York: Cambridge University Press, 1975). Although these terms are taken from Creole studies, in no way do I intend to embrace a Creole explanation for the history of Arabic dialects, as Versteegh suggests (Kees Versteegh, *Pidginization and Creolization: The Case of Arabic* [Amsterdam and Philadelphia: John Benjamins, 1984]). See Hary, *Multiglossia*, 40–46.

18. The notation "B_n" indicates the almost infinite number of possibilities available to speakers and writers on the continuum. See also Hary, "Sociolinguistic Setting," 77–79.

19. Said Badawi, *Mustawayātu l-ᶜarabiyyati l-muᶜāṣira fī miṣr* (Levels of contemporary Arabic in Egypt) (Cairo: Dāru l-maᶜārif bi-miṣr, 1973). Badawi in fact proposed five varieties altogether, but three in the middle.

20. For example, Nuᶜmān ᶜĀshūr (1918–87), who was one of the most important and prolific playwrights in Egypt, wrote most of his dramatic dialogues in Colloquial Egyptian, and the Egyptian poets Bayram al-Tūnsī (1893–1961) and ᶜAbd al-Raḥmān al-Abnūdī wrote poetry in Colloquial Arabic. Al-Tūnsī also wrote stories in Colloquial Arabic (for example, *As-sayyid wi-mrato fī barīs* "A man and his wife in Paris"). All of these writers enjoy tremendous popularity in Egypt.

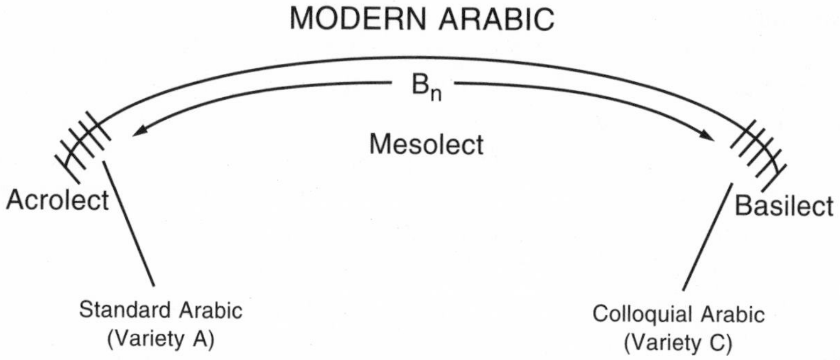

Figure 2.

in prose,[21] can be located closer to the basilect end. The range of oral Arabic, on the other hand, spreads throughout the continuum. In other words, Standard Arabic is primarily written (especially the lects on the far left end of the continuum), whereas Colloquial Arabic is primarily spoken. B_n is usually oral, most often used in the media, but can also be written, for example, in private letters and personal communication. B_n, however, is not usually a vehicle for literary and written expression, with the exception of the above-mentioned examples of some modern Egyptian dramatic dialogues, poetry, and prose. B_n can be (on its left side) an arbitrarily de-classicized form of the fully inflected Standard Arabic used by well-educated native speakers as a pre-planned language employed more often in reading. As B_n moves slightly to the right, it can also be used by well-educated native speakers in more spontaneous discussions of a formal nature. Further to the right, one can find, inter alia, the attempts of semi-literates or illiterates to use Standard Arabic.

An important issue in the complexities of Arabic multiglossia must be raised here: although Standard Arabic is primarily written, written and Standard Arabic are not the same thing. Whereas Standard Arabic is located on the acrolect end of the continuum, written Arabic can be spread far toward the basilect end, as in the examples of modern drama, poetry, and prose that are listed above. It is also useful to adopt the term standard rather than literary for Arabic, since modern Egyptian dramatic dialogues, as well as some samples of poetry and prose, are literary Arabic written in B_n closer to the colloquial end of the continuum and are certainly not composed in Standard Arabic.

Judeo-Arabic, on the other hand, exhibits a different continuum. As is seen in figure 3, the basilect end of the continuum is similar to Modern Arabic,

21. For example, Yūsuf Idrīs (died 1991), one of the most important Egyptian novelists, wrote prose with dialogues in Colloquial Arabic.

where Variety C, or Dialectal Spoken Judeo-Arabic, is located. The rest of the continuum, though, to the left of Variety C, consists of almost countless lects as part of B_n, or Literary Written Judeo-Arabic, the components of which are Classical Arabic, pseudo-corrected features, and standardization of such features. This is in opposition to the use of Modern Arabic, where authors produce most of the literature in Variety A rather than in B_n (with some notable exceptions in prose and dramatic dialogues, poetry, and so on). Variety A, or Standard Arabic, then, is not part of Judeo-Arabic and thus is out of the continuum, but it is in constant contact with the ethnolect and influences its structure and development.

Three additional points should be made about Judeo-Arabic. First, the Jewish authors were unaffected by the ideal of *al-ᶜArabiyya* and therefore allowed colloquial elements to enter their writings.[22] Muslims, on the other hand, were under some pressure to preserve Standard Arabic and to block colloquial elements of the language from entering the written texts. This pressure was due, in part, to the doctrine of the inimitability of the Qurᵓān (*iᶜjāz al-qurᵓān*). The Qurᵓān was viewed as a divine attribute; it was God's speech itself, and therefore Standard Arabic should be protected from "corruption," influenced by the spoken variety. Jews (and Christians) were not under the same pressure, since their sacred texts were not written in Arabic. Consequently, it comes as no surprise that dialectal elements are present in their writings. Second, authors had to take issues of readership competence into account. They wanted to guarantee that they would be intelligible to their readers, many of whom had not mastered Classical Arabic (Variety A). Therefore, they wrote in the Varieties of B_n, with their dialectal components. Finally, some other authors attempted, with varying degrees of success, to elevate their style and write according to the conventions of Classical Arabic (Variety A). As a result, some pseudocorrections arose in their writings.[23]

As can be seen in figure 3, other languages and varieties influenced Judeo-Arabic. Variety A was influential especially in the area of pseudo-corrections. Non–Judeo-Arabic dialects also influenced the ethnolect. They had an impact on Judeo-Arabic dialects as well as on the literary varieties, since many dialectal features are evident in B_n. Hebrew and Aramaic are also important external elements that influence the ethnolect in all linguistic categories, specifically in the lexicon. Their influence is particularly evident in the genre of the *šarḥ* and in its layer.

To conclude, on the one hand, Judeo-Arabic, Standard Arabic, regular Arabic dialects, and Hebrew and Aramaic are all part of the speech community of

22. Versteegh, *Pidginization*, 8.
23. Hary, *Multiglossia*, 62–69.

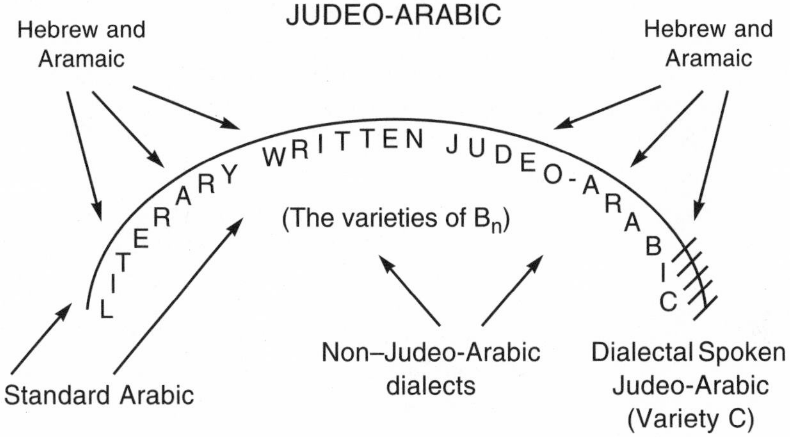

Figure 3.

Jewish society in Arab lands. On the other hand, Standard Arabic, Non–Judeo-Arabic dialects, and Hebrew and Aramaic are not part of Judeo-Arabic multiglossia proper, although they are in close contact with the ethnolect and influence its structure.

The multiglossic situation of Judeo-Arabic changed over the different periods.[24] In Later Judeo-Arabic, B_n ("Literary Written Later Judeo-Arabic") contained a stronger dialectal base than the Judeo-Arabic of previous periods, thus moving the relative position of this variety toward the right end of the continuum. In Modern Judeo-Arabic, the dialectal base of the Varieties of B_n is even stronger than in Later Judeo-Arabic; thus, the relative position of this variety shifts even more toward the colloquial end of the continuum. In this period, many of the literary texts have been transmitted orally and may not have been written; thus B_n should be termed "Literary [Written] Modern Judeo-Arabic."[25] Figure 4 shows the relative position of B_n in different periods of Judeo-Arabic.

This diagram is only a schematic notation of the history of the multiglossia in Judeo-Arabic. The exact place of Literary Written Judeo-Arabic (B_n) is never fixed, even within a specific period, not only because it consists of almost countless lectal possibilities, but also because it may shift on the continuum, depending on the nature of the texts, the writers, and the readers involved. The diagram

24. For analysis of the multiglossic situation in Classical Judeo-Arabic, see Hary, *Multiglossia*, 79–80.

25. These thoughts reflect a slight change from my previous remarks in ibid., 80–81. See also Hary, "Sociolinguistic Setting," 81–82.

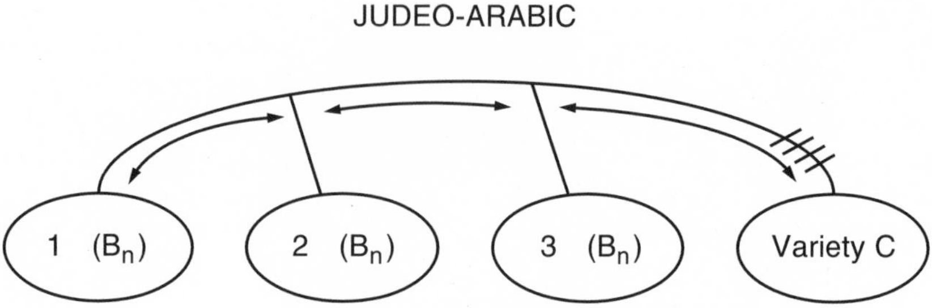

1 = Literary Written Classical Judeo-Arabic
2 = Literary Written Later Judeo-Arabic
3 = Literary [Written] Modern Judeo-Arabic
Variety C = Spoken Dialectal Judeo-Arabic

Figure 4.

attempts to locate, however, the relative positions of average or typical texts of B_n of the different Judeo-Arabic periods; thus, it is clear that the number of dialectal elements in Literary [Written] Modern Judeo-Arabic, for example, is greater than that of Literary Written Later Judeo-Arabic, since the modern variety is located closer to the colloquial end. The same holds true for the relation of Literary Written Later to Classical Judeo-Arabic, in that the dialectal elements in the Later period are more extensive than those of the Classical period.

To conclude, Judeo-Arabic has continually been in a state of multiglossia. It is composed of the varieties of B_n and Variety C, as explained above, divided into five periods, and employed by Jews from Spain in the west to the borders of Iran in the east. There are, of course, geographical dialects, and one can discern localisms in the written language. Although these localisms exist in Early and Classical Judeo-Arabic, they increase significantly in Later and Modern Judeo-Arabic.

Some Linguistic Characteristics of Later and Modern Egyptian Judeo-Arabic

The j̲īm[26]

In a given Later and Modern Judeo-Arabic manuscript, it is customary for the spelling to be rather consistent as part of personal orthographic style (or *schrei-*

26. For a complete treatment of the *jīm*, see Hary, "The *Ǧīm/Gīm* in Colloquial Urban Egyptian Arabic," *IOS* 16 (1996) 153–68.

berschule).[27] On the other hand, there may be consistent differences between some orthographic elements of the various manuscript versions of a text. This, of course, has important consequences. When a manuscript is consistently different from another in the use of a diacritical point, for example, this difference may represent the specific pronunciation of a certain phoneme at the period when the manuscript was copied. Another manuscript, copied at a different period, with the same phoneme marked differently, may represent yet another pronunciation of the same phoneme. A good example of such a phenomenon is the spelling and pronunciation of the phoneme *jīm*.

In mss **R** and **M** of *Megillat pūrīm il-miṣriyyīn*, *jīm* is consistently denoted with ג, whereas in mss **A**, **B**, and **T**, it is usually marked with a dot above the *gīmel* (ג̇), although it is sometimes written without the dot (ג). This may actually reflect a sound shift. In the seventeenth and eighteenth centuries, when **A**, **B**, and **T** were copied, the *jīm* may have been pronounced as an affricate (as reflected in ג̇) and started to show signs of a velar stop (as represented in ג).[28] By the nineteenth and twentieth centuries, however, when **R** and **M** were copied, the pronunciation of the *jīm* had shifted to a velar stop, as is the case today in urban Egyptian dialects.[29] This shift is also seen in Lebedev's published folk passages,[30] and it is confirmed and well documented by Blanc.[31]

The following are several examples from **R** and **M** where Old Arabic *jīm* is consistently denoted as ג (marking the velar stop):

> גמע 'collected' (**R** 1,18; 2,2; 2,4; **M** 7; 9 [× 2]; 22; 28); גלס, גלסו, אגלס, תגלס 'sit, stay' (**R** 1,10; 2,6; 2,10; **M** 5; 26; 35; 36); רגול, ראגל, ראגול 'man' (**R** 1,18; 1,22; 2,4 [× 2]; 2,14 [× 2]; etc.; **M** 9; 39 [× 2]; 49; 53).

In six cases (about five percent) in **R**, however, the *jīm* is spelled with a supralinear dot or an apostrophe following the *gīmel*: וג׳דוהום 'they found them' (**R** 1,26), but also וגדהום 'he found them' (**R** 1,18); רג̇ול 'man' (**R** 2,34), but also רגול (**R** 1,18; 1,22; 2,14 [× 2]; 2,16; etc.); אנג̇מעו, אנג׳מעו 'they joined' (**R** 1,12; 2,6), but also אגתמעו (**R** 2,14; ix); ג׳רא 'happened' (**R** 2,42); צ̇ג׳יה 'noise' (**R** 2,30). This may mean that in 1849, when the manuscript was copied, an affricate for

27. Hary, *Multiglossia*, 97–103.

28. Khan cites other sources indicating the existence of these two pronunciations of the *jīm* at the end of the eighteenth century and the beginning of the nineteenth century; he also discusses the sound shift in progress (Geoffrey Khan, "A Study of the Judaeo-Arabic of Late Genizah Documents and Its Comparison with Classical Judaeo-Arabic," *Sefunot* n.s. 5/20 [1991] 229 [Hebrew]).

29. Peter Behnstedt and Manfred Woidich, *Die ägyptisch-arabischen Dialekte* (2 vols.; Wiesbaden: Reichert, 1985), vol. 2, maps 11 and 12.

30. *Jīm* is marked with and without the dot in the spelling of *xarag* 'he went out': כרג̇; כרג (Lebedev, *Pozdnii*, 76) and כ̇ארג̇א (idem, "Skazka o zolotoi gazele," 528) possibly to represent affricate and stop phonemes respectively.

31. Blanc, "Egytian Arabic in the Seventeenth Century," 189–93.

jīm could still have been heard, although very infrequently. In **M** (copied in 1913), such exceptions do not exist, which indicates that at that time the *jīm* was pronounced only as a velar stop.

On the other hand, the following are several examples from **A**, **B**, and **T**, where Old Arabic *jīm* is usually denoted as ג̇ (affricate) but sometimes as ג (velar stop) to demonstrate the sound shift in progress, which probably took place when these manuscripts were copied:

> ג̇מע (**A** 3a,8; 3a,13; 4a,4; **B** 1b,1; 2b,21; 3a,21), but also גמע 'collected' (**B** 2b,15); ג̇לס, ג̇לסו, תג̇לס (**A** 3b,3; 3b,17; **B** 3a,4; **T** 1b,11), but also תגלס 'sit, stay' (**B** 3a,17); רג̇ל, רג̇ול (**A** 2b,8; 4a,6; 4b,2; 4b,8; etc.; **B** 1b,11; 1b,25; 3b,1; 3b,15; etc.), but also רגל 'man' (**B** 6b,6).

In other instances in **A**, **B**, and **T**, only the ג̇ exists:

> מן ג̇מלת 'among other' (**T** 1a,6); ג̇עלוה 'they appointed him' (**A** 4b,13; **B** 3b,22); תג̇אר, תוג̇אר 'merchants' (**A** 8a,6; **B** 6a,10); ג̇יל 'generation' (**B** 8a,19 [× 2]).

In Modern Egyptian Judeo-Arabic, the pronunciation of Classical Arabic *jīm* has been stabilized as voiced velar stop *g*,[32] as is evident in the manuscripts:

(1) לענד מא גו תלאמיד̇הום *li^{c}ind ma gu talamīẓhum*[33] 'until their disciples came' (C3 2:4);

(2) כאנו ראכעין וסאגדין להמן *kānu rak^{c}īn wi-sagdīn lihaman* 'they bowed down and prostrated to Haman' (BZ 1302 3:2).

The qāf

Qāf is always spelled with a ק in the varieties of B_n of Later and Modern Egyptian Judeo-Arabic, and despite this systematic spelling, the reflex of Classical Arabic *qāf* in sixteenth- and seventeenth-century Cairene dialect was the glottal stop. Grotzfeld has shown that this reflex is attested already at the end of the thirteenth century in Cairo.[34] Furthermore, in Rabat, Fez, Meknes, and Sefrou, Jews also spoke with the glottal stop but wrote with ק,[35] since they were aware that the origin of the glottal stop was the Classical Arabic *qāf*. They also realized that this pronunciation was unique to their communities,

32. Note that even today, affricate *ǧ* is heard quite often in Cairo among religious class speakers.

33. Transcription is used here for the benefit of readers who are not as accustomed to the Hebrew alphabet. It is based on recordings (of an Egyptian Passover *haggadah*) but also on assumptions and speculations and therefore should be considered tentative.

34. Heinz Grotzfeld, "Ein Zeugnis aus dem Jahre 688/1289 für die Aussprache des *qāf* als *hamza* in Kairenischen," *ZDMG* 117 (1967) 87–90.

35. I owe this observation to J. Tedghi, personal communication.

since Jews from other parts of Morocco made fun of this pronunciation. It is surprising, however, that in some texts, such as *Megillat pūrīm il-miṣriyyīn*, the spelling with ק does not have even one exception, since these exceptions do exist in other documents,[36] including several Moroccan texts, where occasionally one can see spelling with א (in cases of "slipping") rather than ק. For example, in the work תוכחת מוסר בלעאראבי by Jacob Dahan (Fez: D. Sharvit and Ḥazzan, 1928), most of the Classical Arabic *qāf*s are denoted with ק. In *maḥberet* 32, however, we find אבלהא 'accept it' spelled with an *ʾālef*:

ida zat si hlika ʾbīḥa	'if a big trouble comes about'	אידא זאת סי הליכא קביחא
ʾbəlha bl-fərḥa	'accept it with joy'	אבלהא בלפרחא
la təskət u-təṭləʾ ṣiḥa	'do not be quiet and therefore yell'	לא תסכת ותטלק סיחא
ḥətta təhbaṭ d-dənya	'until the world turns over'	חתא תבהט (read תהבט) אדנייא

On the other hand, since the Megillah was written by Rabbi Sidilio,[37] a learned man, it is possible that such exceptions do not occur, as is the case in several Moroccan texts that were written by learned חכמים.[38] Furthermore, it is also possible that these authors were using something like the "Saᶜidi Test," that is, they may have asked whether Saᶜidis, as well as speakers in the Delta, pronounced the word in question with g instead of hamza; in other words, if Saᶜidis said *g*, then it must have represented an original *qāf*.

In modern Egyptian Judeo-Arabic, where it is clear that Classical Arabic *qāf* was pronounced as a glottal stop, the scribes have also been very consistent in spelling *qāf* with ק:

(3) מקים מן תראב אל פקיר *muqīm min turāb il-faʾīr* 'raising the poor from the dust' (Haggadah-Egypt 17:2);

36. For example, in *il-Maṣrī wir-Rīfī*, where Goitein fails to read on p. 261, line 21: פי אל 'and he said' ("Townsman and Fellah"). This is the only instance in this manuscript in which the scribe spells Classical Arabic *qāf* with an *ʾālef*.

37. Hary, *Multiglossia*, 125–26.

38. For example: ר׳ ישמ׳ח עובדיה, תשובת השנה [דרשות בערבית־יהודית של צפרו (מרוקו)], פאס, ד. שרביט וחזאן, [אין תאריך]. The son of this author, Rabbi David Ovadiah, delivers a sermon on Israeli radio in Moroccan Judeo-Arabic twice a week. Although in his own dialect he would pronounce the reflex of Classical Arabic *qāf* as a glottal stop, he makes an effort to pronounce it as *q*, since he knows that most non-urban Moroccan Jews use *q*. When his prepared sermon is about the weekly Torah portion, he manages to pronounce each Classical Arabic *qāf* as *q*. On the eve of Holocaust Memorial Day, 1991, however, he "slipped" several times by using the glottal stop because the topic of his sermon, the Holocaust, was not regular. The other two announcers on the Moroccan Judeo-Arabic radio program also employ the glottal stop in their dialect (Fez) but use it on the air as well.

(4) ונטׄר אללה אלה פוקרנה ואלה שקאנה ואלה צׄיקנה *wi-naẓar aḷḷah ila fu*ʾ*rina wi-ila ša*ʾ*āna wi-ila ḍi*ʾ*na* 'and God saw our afflictions, our misery, and our oppression' (C3 9:24);

(5) מוגוד קום ואחד משתֿת ומפֿרֿד בין אל אקואם *mawgūd* ʾ*ōm wāḥid mušattat wi-mufarrad bēn il-a*ʾ*wām* 'there is a certain people scattered and dispersed among the [other] peoples' (BZ 1302 3:8).

The Pattern fuᶜul and Defective Verbs

In Later Judeo-Arabic in general, and in the *Megillah* in particular there is strong evidence for the widespread use of the pattern *fuᶜul*:

> חוצׄור *ḥuḍur* 'he came' (**M** 4; 5; 10) and חוצׄרו 'they came' (**M** 44; 59); חוזנו *ḥuznu* 'they became sad' (**R** 2,24; 2,40; **M** 43); הולכו *hulku* 'they perished' (**M** 61); כֿולצו *xulṣu* 'they saved themselves' (**A** 4b,9; **R** 2,18; **M** 30); כותור *kutur* 'increased' (**R** 1,12);[39] עוצי *ᶜuṣi* 'he rebelled' (**A** 5a,5; 5a,8; 7b,6) and עוציו 'they rebelled' (**A** 5a,6). Two other verbs may belong to this pattern: חוסון *ḥusun* 'it was good' (**A** 5b,6; 6b,3); קותול *ʾutul* (**M** 23)[40] and קותל 'was killed' (**A** 3b,1).[41] In other contemporary texts the *fuᶜul* pattern is also evident. In *il-Maṣrī wir-Rīfī*: חוטור *xuṭur* 'came to mind' (p. 260, §3); in *Darkhe Noᶜam*: סועוב *ṣuᶜub* 'became difficult' (p. 305, lines 17, 18);[42] גורוק *ġuruʾ* 'he drowned' (p. 310, lines 5, 6) and גורקו 'they drowned' (p. 311, line 11); גוטוס *ġuṭus* 'he sank' (p. 310, line 6 [× 2]).

Most of these verbs in modern Cairene can be of the pattern *fiᶜil*, as is seen in table 2.

In modern Cairene, the pattern *fuᶜul* is less common than in Later Egyptian Judeo-Arabic dialect and is restricted to several lexemes, such as *xuluṣ* as a variant of *xiliṣ* 'be finished' and *kutur* as a less common variant of *kitir*.[43] These forms usually occur as the 3d masculine singular of the perfect, all other

39. Probably also כותור in **M** 6. In כֻּתֹר (**T** 1b,15), the vocalization indicates the *fuᶜul* pattern: *kutur* or *kotor*, as an allophonic alternation.

40. See Hary, *Multiglossia*, 279 n. 106, for the possibility that this verb is in the internal passive.

41. The verb טלוע 'he ascended' (**A** 4b,12; **B** 3b,22; **R** 2,18) could also be of the pattern *fuᶜul*, since in modern Cairene, it is of the pattern *fiᶜil*. In many other occurrences in the *Megillah*, however, there is no evidence for this, because the spellings טלע and טלעו are common. Consequently, I prefer to see here an emphatic, back, short *a* (see Khan, "A Study," 226).

42. Note that Davies thought incorrectly that the verb was *siᶜib* 'feel pity for' (if at all, Davies should have referred to *ṣiᶜib* with a *ṣād*) ("17th Century Egyptian Arabic," 107). It is clear, however, from the context in *Darkhe Noᶜam,* that the verb is *ṣuᶜub* 'become difficult' (Blanc, "Egyptian Judaeo-Arabic," 305, 307).

43. More examples can be found in Martin Hinds and El-Said Badawi, *A Dictionary of Egyptian Arabic: Arabic-English* (Beirut: Librarie du Liban, 1986): *ḥimiḍ/ḥumuḍ* 'go bad, sour' (p. 225); *ḍiᶜif/ḍuᶜuf* 'become weak' (p. 522); *ṭiriš/ṭuruš* 'become deaf' (p. 536); *ṭiri/ṭuri* 'become soft' (p. 538); *ṭuhur/ṭihir* 'become ritually pure' (p. 548); etc.

TABLE 2.

Later Judeo-Arabic		*Modern Cairene*
ḥuḍur	'come'	*ḥiḍir*[44]
ḥuzun	'become sad'	*ḥizin*
kutur	'increase'	*kitir/kutur*[45]
huluk	'perish'	*hilik*
xuluṣ	'be finished, save one's self'	*xiliṣ/xuluṣ*[46]
ᶜuṣi	'rebel'	*ᶜiṣi*
ġuruᵓ	'drown'	*ġiriᶜ*
ġuṭus	'sink'	*ġiṭis/ġuṭus*[47]
ṣuᶜub	'become difficult'	*ṣuᶜub/ṣiᶜib*[48]
ᵓutul	'get killed'	missing

forms being *fiᶜil*; thus *xuluṣ* means 'it was finished'; *xulṣu* is not as common as *xilṣu* in the 3d pl. form of the perfect. In the 3d f. sg. form, **xulṣit* is ungrammatical, and only the *fiᶜil* pattern is used (*xilṣit*).

Most of the above-mentioned verbs are intransitive with "low-grade" control and are at times stative. This is similar to the situation in modern Cairene, where the pattern *fiᶜil* is intransitive, as shown in table 3:

TABLE 3.

Transitive		*Intransitive*	
xallaṣ	'finish'	*xiliṣ*	'be finished'
waᵓᵓaf	'stop'	*wiᵓif*	'stop, stand'
naḍḍaf	'clean'	*niḍif*	'become clean'
wallaᶜ	'light'	*wiliᶜ*	'be lit'
taᶜᶜab	'make tired'	*tiᶜib*	'become tired'

This phenomenon is not surprising, since in Semitics, non-*a* is typically a marker of intransitivity or stativity, as demonstrated by the following facts:

44. My informants tell me that the most prevalent use of this verb in modern Cairene is *ḥaḍar*, then *ḥiḍir*, and seldom *ḥuḍur*.

45. See Hinds and Badawi, *A Dictionary*, 735.

46. Ibid., 260.

47. Ibid., 624.

48. Ibid., 503.

(i) In Classical Arabic, the passive forms of the perfect and the imperfect are *fu*^{c}*il* and *yuf*^{c}*al,*[49] respectively.

(ii) Verbs of the pattern *fa*^{c}*ula* are typically stative (the marker of stativity here is the second vowel, *u*):

kabura 'become big'; *ṣaġura* 'become small'

(iii) In Hebrew the passive pattern of *Pu*^{c}*al* and stative verbs such as the following are marked by a non-*a*:

בֹשתי וגם נכלמתי 'I became ashamed' (Jer 31:18); אורו עיניו 'he became delighted' (1 Sam 14:29); מה טובו אוהליך יעקב 'how goodly are thy tents, Jacob' (Num 24:5).

The above analysis indicates that rather than simply viewing the pattern *fu*^{c}*ul* as an older stage of *fi*^{c}*il,*[50] a more complex explanation can be offered, namely, that the contrast between the patterns of Classical Arabic *fu*^{c}*ila* (the internal passive pattern) and *fa*^{c}*ula* was annulled in Later Egyptian Judeo-Arabic, resulting in a single pattern for nontransitive verbs (that is, stative, passive, and so on), with two realizations: *fu*^{c}*ul* and *fi*^{c}*il.* The choice between these two patterns depended on the phonetics of the radicals:

- back radicals (emphatic or guttural) favored *fu*^{c}*ul*;
- nonemphatic radicals, especially defective verbs (where $R_3 = y$) became *fi*^{c}*il.*[51]

In other words, in Later Egyptian Judeo-Arabic, there was a redistribution of the verbal patterns to *fu*^{c}*ul* and *fi*^{c}*il.* Note that even nonstative defective verbs became *fi*^{c}*il* in Later Egyptian Judeo-Arabic as part of the process of generalization. This can be seen in the verb מצ̇י *miḍi* 'passed' (**R** 2,14), which

49. The vowel *a* in *yuf*^{c}*al* does not actually indicate the imperfect passive but, rather, reflects the active vowel *yaf*^{c}*al,* which is not changed in the passive form.

50. Davies believes that the pattern *fu*^{c}*ul* was replaced by the pattern *fi*^{c}*il* long after the seventeenth century, when, he holds, the pattern *fi*^{c}*il* did not yet exist. He supports his hypothesis by claiming that there is "absence of any evidence for it [i.e., the pattern *fi*^{c}*il*] either in the Hebrew-character comparison sources, despite their use of matres. . . ." One would not expect, however, to find conclusive evidence for the pattern *fi*^{c}*il,* since short *i* was not frequently marked in Later Egyptian Judeo-Arabic orthography as short *u* was (Hary, *Multiglossia*, 248–49). Consequently, the use of the matres, as Davies points out, cannot serve as conclusive evidence for the absence of the pattern *fi*^{c}*il,* in Later Egyptian Judeo-Arabic. Moreover, data from the *Megillah* show that the pattern *fi*^{c}*il* indeed occurs in Later Egyptian Judeo-Arabic; thus, an explanation of a more complex nature is required.

51. O'Leary proposes another process: from *fa*^{c}*ul* to *fu*^{c}*ul* through assimilation—for example, *suġur* for *saġur* 'be small' (note that O'Leary suggests that the *s* is not emphatic in Egyptian Arabic); *kusul* for *kasul* 'be lazy' (De Lacy O'Leary, *Colloquial Arabic* [London: Kegan Paul, 1925] 98).

had to be of the pattern *fiʿil* since *ʾalif maqṣūra biṣūrati l-yāʾ* is never denoted by a *yōd* in ms **R**. The verb הדי *hidi* 'became calm' (**A** 3a,5; **R** 1,38) underwent an even more complex change: from a final-*hamza* verb, it became a defective verb (R_3 = ʾ > R_3 = *y*) that changed to the *fiʿil* pattern. These along with other defective verbs in the *Megillah* demonstrate the *fiʿil* pattern also in the 3d f. sg. and 3d pl.: הדיית *hidyit* 'became calm (f. sg.)' (**M** 20; 31); מציו *miḍyu* 'they passed' (**M** 4); גרייו *giryu* 'they chased' (**R** xix); בכיו *bikyu* 'they cried' (**A** 7a,17; **B** 5b,12; **M** 43); בקיו *biʾyu* 'they remained' (**A** 4b,9; **B** 3b,19; **M** 43). The following, then, are the perfect patterns for 3d m. sg.; 3d f. sg.; 3d pl. respectively: *CiCi*; *CiCyit*; *CiCyu.*[52]

The verb עצייו, עציו, עצי *ʿiṣi*, *ʿiṣyu* '(he, they) rebelled' (**B** 1a,2; 4a,9; 5b,17; **R** 1,24; 2,8; 2,22 [× 2]; 2,24; etc.; **M** 33; 34) is even more complex, since it also appears as עוציו, עוצי *ʾuṣi*, *ʾuṣyu* (**A** 5a,5; 5a,6; 5a,8; 7b,6). Consequently, it seems that this verb had two variants: of the pattern *fiʿil,* as expected from a defective verb, and of the pattern *fuʿul,* as influenced by the emphatic radicals. This is similar to current colloquial Egyptian use of *ṭiri/ṭuri* 'become soft'.[53]

At a later point, many of the verbs may have had both variants *fuʿul* and *fiʿil,*[54] and this can be seen in Willmore's listing.[55] He describes late nineteenth-century Egyptian dialect and cites at least thirty verbs that had both variants (note the semantic class of these verbs: stative, intransitive, low-grade control), for example:

> *tuʾul* and *tiʾil*[56] 'be heavy', *ṭuruš* and *ṭiriš* 'become deaf', *ʾudum* and *ʾidim* 'become old', *ḥiḍir* and *ḥuḍur* 'be evident, appear', *ġiliṭ* and *ġuluṭ* 'err', *kisil* and *kusul* 'be lazy', *niʾiṣ* and *nuʾuṣ* 'be lessened',[57] *ḥimid* and *ḥumud* 'become sour'.

52. Note that Davies explicitly cites the absence of *CiCyit* and *CiCyu* from *Hazz al-quḥūf* (Davies, "17th Century Egyptian Arabic," 110) and believes that the occurrence of these patterns in the *Megillah* may indicate a specific Later Egyptian Judeo-Arabic use; however, more conclusive evidence needs to be found to confirm that neither *CiCyit* nor *CiCyu* existed in seventeenth-century Cairene Arabic (as Davies suggests) and that these patterns were exclusively Judeo-Arabic.

53. Hinds and Badawi, *A Dictionary*, 538.

54. Phillott and Powell claim that Form I has three realizations in the Egyptian dialect: *faʿal*, generally transitive; *fiʿil*, usually intransitive; and *fuʿul*, always intransitive or passive (Douglas Craven Phillott and A. Powell, *Manual for Egyptian Arabic* [Cairo: Self-Published, 1926] 122). This, of course, lends support to my analysis.

55. John Selden Willmore, *The Spoken Arabic of Egypt* (London: David Nutt, 1901) 118–20.

56. Willmore gives the example *tuqul* but writes it morphophonemically and mentions on p. 20 that the realization of *q* is very frequently a glottal stop (ibid., 20).

57. Also *nuʾuṣ* 'he missed' (Karl Vollers, *The Modern Egyptian Dialect of Arabic* [trans. F. C. Burkitt; Cambridge: Cambridge University Press, 1895] 33).

Ten verbs are of the *fu*^{c}*ul* pattern only; a few examples are:

> *tuxun* 'get thick', *ḥurun* 'be restive', ^{c}*uṭul* 'be interrupted', *xuruf* 'be impaired'.

Fifty-two verbs, however, are of the *fi*^{c}*il* pattern only; following are some examples:

> *bixil* 'be stingy', *bilid* 'be dull', *birid* 'get cold', *simin* 'get fat', *sikir* 'get drunk', *fiṭiš* 'choke'.

It is safe, then, to assume that toward the end of the nineteenth century, both patterns were still in use. There was, however, a clear tendency to replace *fu*^{c}*ul* with *fi*^{c}*il*, and this tendency continues to the present day.

The šarḥ

As mentioned above, it is important to identify the language layer of the *šarḥ* in Judeo-Arabic documents, though very infrequently the characteristics of the language layer of the *šarḥ* penetrate the spoken dialect. Note that our knowledge about the origin and the language of the *šarḥ* was very limited until several years ago, when scholars of Jewish ethnolects in general and of Judeo-Arabic in particular began to pay special attention to this genre. The *šarḥ* began to develop in the fifteenth century in order to fill essential needs, assuring children basic education and providing the general Jewish public, who did not comprehend Hebrew and/or Aramaic, with proper education.[58] Judeo-Arabic *šurūrḥ* of the Bible replaced Sa^{c}adya Ga$^{\supset}$on's tenth-century translation of the Bible, since his translation, not literal, followed Classical Arabic structure and often changed the structure of the biblical verses in order to adapt them to Arabic style.

The following examples[59] exhibit the language layer of the *šarḥ*, which sometimes violates Arabic structure. In addition, Hebrew words are sometimes

58. Moshe Bar Asher, "The Sharḥ of the Maghreb: Judeo-Arabic Exegesis of the Bible and Other Jewish Literature—Its Nature and Formation," in *Studies in Jewish Languages—Bible Translations and Spoken Dialects* (ed. Moshe Bar-Asher; Jerusalem: Misgav, 1988) 3–34 [Hebrew].

59. There are many more examples: (1) ולם יעט אללה פֿי קלב עסכר אחׄ באשה אן יטרד כֿלפֿהום 'and God did not put the strength into the hearts of the Pasha's soldiers (that would allow them) to pursue (Suleiman's troops)' (**A** 4b,9–11) translates ולא נתן ה׳ בלבם לרדוף אחריהם עוד (**A** 4b, 9–10); (2) וכאן רגֿול פֿריד פֿי אל קלעה ארסלהו אללה מועיני ומוכֿלצי ומונגֿדי מן ידי אל ימין 'There was a single Jewish man in the Citadel whom God had sent as a helper and saver' (**A** 6a,9–12; **B** 4b,19–21; with changes: **R** 2,32; **M** 39) translates איש יחידי היה בפסגת הבירה והאל שלחו עזרי ומושיעי ותומכי ביד ימיני (**A** 6a,9–12; **B** 4b,20–22; **R** 2,31; with changes: **M** 39; see also Esther 2:5); (3) ולא שבעה עינהו; ולם שבעת עינהו/ו 'and his eye (i.e., avarice) was not satisfied' (**B** 1b,2; **R** 1,14; **M** 7) translates ולא שבעה נפשו/עינו (**B** 1b,2; **R** 1,13; **M** 7; see also Jer 50:19). The sentence ורגֿעו כול ואחד מן טריקהי אל וחשה 'and they repented for their evil ways' (**A** 7a, 15–16) is also a literal translation of the Hebrew version, וישובו איש מדרכו הרעה 'and they repented because of their evil deeds' (based on Jonah 3:8). *Raja*^{c}*ū* means 'they returned' in Arabic, whereas in Hebrew, 'return' may also mean 'repent'. The

copied into Arabic to indicate their Hebrew equivalent, although the cognate Arabic terms do not have the same meaning.

(6) ואיצא גמיע אהל אלמדינה *wi-ayḍan gamīᶜ ahl il-madīna* 'and all the people of the country as well' (**A** 5a,14; with changes: **B** 4a,14; **R** 2,24). This is a direct translation of the Hebrew version, וגם כל אנשי המדינה 'and all the people of the province as well'. This is a clear case of Hebrew interference, where the Arabic word order is changed to accommodate the Hebrew וגם. The word ואיצא 'and also' is placed at the beginning of the sentence, before the expression it modifies, rather than after the expression it modifies, as is the case in Standard Arabic. Moreover, the Hebrew word מדינה 'province' is copied into the Arabic version, although in Arabic, *madīna* means 'city' and not 'province'. In the latter case, however, the word may still mean 'city'. That is, the process was reversed: in the Hebrew version of the *Megillah*, the word מדינה 'city' was written as influenced by the Arabic equivalent.

(7) In the sentence ופי כול מדינה ומדינה וכול בלד ובלד *wafi kull madīna wi-madīna wi-kull balad wi-balad* 'and in every province and city' (**A** 5a,2–3), it is clear that the Hebrew word מדינה was copied into the Judeo-Arabic text, while changing its Arabic meaning from 'city' to 'province'; this sentence translates the Hebrew ובכל עיר ועיר ובכל מדינה ומדינה, which is based on Esth 4:3.

(8) ואווגד קבול פי חצרתו *wi-awgad ᵓabūl fi ḥaḍrato* 'and (Ahmad Pasha) found favor in his presence' (**M** 1). This is a literal or direct translation of the Hebrew וימצא חן בעיניו. This translation is a reconciliation of the biblical style and the Arabic, by the Judeo-Arabic author (See Esth 8:5). In this example, the Judeo-Arabic version uses a phrase directly translated from Hebrew, since the expression ואווגד קבול פי חצרתו does not exist in Arabic.

(9) ולם קדרו לייגו עליהום *wi-lam ᵓidru li-yīgu ᶜalēhum* 'and they were not able to overcome them' (**R** 2,14) translates ולא יכלו לבוא עליהם (**R** 2,13). The direct translation is evident in the use of the preposition *li*.

(10) נסכר ללאה פחייאתי נגני לילאהי פמאזאלי *nəskər ḷəḷah fḥyati ngənni l-ilahi f-mazali* 'I will praise God all my life, and sing to my God while I exist'.[60] This sentence, taken from a Maghrebi Siddur, translates the biblical sentence אהללה ה' בחיי אזמרה לאלהי בעודי (Ps 146:2). The need for a word-for-word translation makes the author violate the Arabic structure. In Arabic the phrase *mā zāl* should not take a pronominal suffix or follow a preposition; however, פמאזאלי was interpreted as a noun, and since in Hebrew, בעודי takes a pronominal suffix and follows a preposition, in Judeo-Arabic the same features occurred.

author used the word for 'return' in Arabic to mean 'repent', as a direct translation from Hebrew. Note, however, that *rajaᶜa* can also be associated in Classical Arabic with 'returning to God', as in the sentence *innā li-llāhi wa-innā ilayhi rājiᶜūn* 'to Allah we belong and to Him we shall return' (Qurᵓān 2:157).

60. Joseph Tedghi, "A Moroccan *Maḥzor* in Judeo-Arabic," *Massorot* 8 (1994) 93 [Hebrew].

(11) There may even be a change in gender; for example, מבארך די קאל וכאן דנייא *mbark di ʾāl u-kān d-dənya* 'Blessed be He who said, let the world be'[61] translates the Hebrew ברוך שאמר והיה העולם. The word דנייא is considered masculine (as evident from the masculine verb וכאן), as a reflection of the influence of Hebrew עולם (m.).

Another important feature of the language layer of the *šarḥ*—but not limited just to the layer of the *šarḥ*—is the use of the prepositions *ʾilā* and *li* in Later and Modern Egyptian Judeo-Arabic texts.[62] *ʾIlā* may precede the definite direct object and constitutes a translation of the equivalent Hebrew *ʾet*.[63] In the following Judeo-Arabic examples *ʾilā* indeed translates *ʾet* from the Hebrew version of the text:[64]

(12) ופ̇דו מוסה . . . ושמואל . . . אלה נפ̇סהום *wi-fadu mūsa . . . wi-šmuʾēl . . . ʾilā nafsihum* (Heb. ויפדו משה . . . ושמואל . . . את נפ̇שם) 'and Musa . . . and Shmuel . . . redeemed themselves' (**M** 20);

(13) יפ̇די אלא נפ̇סו *yifdi ʾilā nafso* (Heb. לקנות את עצמו) 'redeem himself' (**R** 1,37–38);

(14) פ̇סמע אלה אלד̇י אנצנע פ̇י אליהוד *fi-simiʿ ʾilā allazi inṣanaʿ fi l-yahūd* (Heb. וישמע את אשר נעשׂה ביהודים) 'and he heard what had been done to the Jews' (**M** 40);

(15) אנא אלד̇י אכ̇ד̇ת אלא רודס *ana allazi axadt ʾilā rūdes* (Heb. לקחתי את רודס אני) 'I am the one who took Rhodes' (**R** 1,15–16);

(16) וכאנו עסכר אל גראכסה באגצ̇ין אלא אל יאוד *wi-kānu ʿaskar il-garāksa bāġḍīn ʾilā l-yahūd* (Heb. ויהיו חיל הגראכסה שונאים את היהודים) 'And the Circassian troops hated the Jews' (**R** 2,25–26);

(17) וחצ̇רו איצ̇ה אלא קורבליס *wi-ḥaḍaru ayḍan ʾilā kurablis* (Heb. ויביאו אותו ואת קרב̇ליס) 'and they brought Kuravlis as well' (**R** 1,31–32);

(18) פ̇למא סמעו אל יאוד אלא אל אמר אל רצ̇י *fi-lamma simʿu l-yahūd ʾilā l-amr il-raḍi* (Heb. ויהי כשמוע היהודים את הדבר הרע הזה) 'and when the Jews heard this evil thing' **R** 39–40);

61. Ibid., 94–95.

62. See Hary, "*ʾilā* and *li* in Judeo-Arabic Texts," for a detailed explanation of this phenomenon.

63. This phenomenon is not new, however. Already Rabbi Yissachar ben Sūsān (sixteenth century) indicated in his introduction to the *šarḥ* of the Pentateuch that he felt that he had to translate Hebrew *ʾet* into Judeo-Arabic (probably because of his need to translate a sacred text word for word), and he chose the Judeo-Arabic morpheme אייא(ת) to serve this purpose. See David Doron, "On the Translation of the Particle *ʾet* in Al-Sharḥ al-Sūsānī Likhamsat Jzāʾ al-Torā," *Arabic and Islamic Studies* 2 (1978) 9–25 [Hebrew]; and Hary, "On the Use of *ʾilā*," 599. On the use of *ʾilā* and *li* in Classical Judeo-Arabic, see Joshua Blau, *A Grammar of Medieval Judeo-Arabic* (2d ed.; Jerusalem: Magnes, 1980) 118–20 and 177–80 [Hebrew], summarized in Hary, "On the Use of *ʾilā*," 597–98.

64. The underlining is mine.

(19) ולמא נטׄרו אליהוד אלה פׄרג אללה *wi-lamma naẓaru l-yahūd ʾilā farag allah* (Heb. ויהי כאשר ראו היהודים את ישועת ה׳) 'and when the Jews saw God's relief' (**M** 57);

(20) אלא אברהם ואלא יצחק ואלא יעקוב *ʾilā ibrahīm wi-ʾilā isḥāq wi-ʾilā yaʿqūb* (Heb. את אברהם את יצחק ואת יעקוב) 'with Abraham, Isaac, and Jacob' (**R** 2,29–30);

(21) לבן פתש ליקלע אלא אל כל *laban fattaš li-yiʾlaʿ ʾilā il-kull* (Heb. ולבן בקש לעקור את הכל) 'and Lavan sought to uproot every thing' (Haggadah-Egypt 9:1);

(22) וכׄדמו אל מצריון אלא בני ישראל באל קאסי *wi-xadamu il-miṣriyūn ʾilā bani israʾīl bil-ʾāsi* (Heb. ויעבדו מצרים את בני ישראל בפרך) 'and the Egyptians subjected the Israelites to hard labor' (ibid., 10:1);

(23) יבארך אלא גומאעת ישראל *yibārik ʾilā gumāʿat isrāʾīl* (Heb. את בית ישראל יברך) 'bless the house of Israel' (ibid., 22:1);

(24) אעטא לנה אלה אל סבת *aʿṭa lana ʾilā s-sabt* (Heb. נתן לנו את השבת) 'He gave us the Shabbat' (C3 17:46);

(25) עלה סבב אלדׄי מררו אל מצארווה אלה חיאת אבהאתנה פׄי מצר *ʿala sabab allazi marraru il-maṣārwa ʾilā ḥayāt ibahatna fi maṣr* (Heb. שום שמררו המצריים את חיי אבותינו במצרים על) 'for the Egyptians embittered the lives of our fathers in Egypt' (ibid., 18:50);

(26) ליעטי לנה אלה אל ארץׄ *li-yiʿṭi lana ʾilā l-arḍ* (Heb. לתת לנו את הארץ) 'to give us the land' (ibid., 19:51);

(27) אלדׄי צנע לאבהאתנה ולנה אלה כל אל עגאיב הדולי *allazi ṣanaʿ li-ibahatna wi-lana ʾilā kull il-ʿagāyeb hadōli* (Heb. שעשה לאבותינו ולנו את כל הנסים האלו) 'who did for our fathers and for us all these miracles' (ibid., 19:52);

(28) אלדׄי פׄכיתנה ופׄכית אלה אבהאתנה מן מצר *allazi fakkitna wi-fakkit ʾilā ibahatna min maṣr* (Heb. אשר גאלנו וגאל את אבותינו ממצרים) 'who redeemed us and our fathers from Egypt' (ibid., 21:55);

(29) ליגיב אלא ושתי אל מלכה *li-yigīb ʾilā fašti il-malika* (Heb. את ושתי המלכה להביא) 'to bring Vashti, the Queen' (BZ 1302 1:17);

(30) דׄכר אלא ושתי ואלא אלזי צנעת *zakar ʾilā fašti wi-ʾilā allazi ṣanaʿit* (Heb. זכר את ושתי ואת אשר עשתה) '. . . remembered Vashti and what she had done' (ibid., 2:1);

(31) לם כׄברת אסתר אלא קומהא *lam xabarit ester ʾilā ʾōmha* (Heb. הגידה אסתר את עמה לא) 'Esther had not informed her people' (ibid., 2:10);

(32) וחב אל מלך אלא אסתר *wi-ḥabb il-malik ʾilā ester* (Heb. ויאהב המלך את אסתר) 'and the king loved Esther' (ibid., 2:17);

(33) כבּר אל מלך אל אזדשירי אלא המן *kabbar il-malik il-azdaširi ʾilā haman* (Heb. גדל המלך אחשורוש את המן) 'King Ahasuerus promoted Haman' (ibid., 3:1).

The use of *ʾilā* as a marker of the definite direct object was so widespread in Later and especially in Modern Judeo-Arabic that sometimes the writer used it even when the marker *ʾet* was missing from the Hebrew version:

(34) פׄי דׄכר להום אללה אלא עהדו *fi-zakar lahum aḷḷa ʾilā ʿahdo* (Heb. ויזכור להם בריתו) 'and God remembered His covenant for them' (**R** 2,29–30);

(35) פֿזכר אלרב אלה עהדו *fi-zakar ir-rabb ʾilā ʿahdo* (Heb. ויזכור להם בריתו) 'and God remembered His covenant' (**M** 38);

(36) וליעמלו אלה יום תמאניה ועשרין מנו יום פורים *wi-li-yiʿmálu ʾilā yōm tamānya wi-ʿišrīn minnu yōm burīm* (Heb. ולעשות יום שמנה ועשרים בו יום פורים) 'and make the twenty-eighth of this month a day of 'Purim' (**M** 58).

This development is important because the spread of the use of *ʾilā* to mark the definite direct object suggests productive use of the preposition to indicate the above-mentioned syntactic function rather than just to represent the mechanism of a literal translation. In other words, in these instances, the language layer of the *šarḥ* undergoes a further development and marks the definite direct object with *ʾilā* as a characteristic of this language layer, regardless of the appearance of that marker in the equivalent Hebrew version.

Sometimes when the Hebrew *ʾet* stands for something other than the definite direct object marker, its meaning is interpreted and translated accordingly:

(37) פֿזכר אלרב אלה עהדו מע אברהם מע יצחק ומע יעקוב *fi-zakar ir-rabb ʾilā ʿahdo maʿa ibrahīm maʿa iṣḥāq wi-maʿa yaʿqūb* (Heb. ויזכור להם בריתו את אברהם את יצחק ואת יעקב) 'and God remembered His covenant with Abraham, Isaac, and Jacob' (**M** 38);

(38) וכֿאפֿו אל קום מן אללה *wi-xāfu il-ʾōm min aḷḷah* (Heb. וייראו העם את ה') 'and the people feared God' (Haggadah-Egypt 13:1);

(39) עלא אלדֿי לם עמלת כאמר אל מלך *ʿala allazi lam ʿamalit ka-amr il-malik* (Heb. על אשר לא עשתה את מאמר המלך) 'forasmuch as she has not done the King's order' (BZ 1302 1:15).

Note also that the Judeo-Arabic text may "interpret" the Hebrew version in other cases as well:

(40) ונטֿר אללה אלא בני ישראל ורחמהם אללה *wi-naẓar aḷḷa ʾilā bani israʾīl wi-raḥimhum alla* (Heb. וירא אלוהים את בני ישראל וידע אלוהים) 'And God looked upon the Israelites and had mercy upon them' (Haggadah-Egypt 10:2). In this sentence, the writer interprets ידע as 'have mercy upon'.[65]

On the other hand, not every Hebrew *ʾet* is rendered by the Judeo-Arabic *ʾilā*:

(41) פֿי למא סמע אל מעי' אברהים דֿאלך אל כלאם *fi-lamma simiʿ il-muʿallim ibrahīm zālik il-kalām* (Heb. וכשמוע אברהם הנז' את הדברים האלה) 'and when Abraham heard these words' (**R** 1,22; with changes: **M** 11);

(42) ליגיבו ושתי אל מלכה *li-yigību fašti il-malika* (Heb. להביא את ושתי המלכה) 'to bring Vashti, the Queen' (BZ 1302 1:11), but in another place, ליגיב אלא ושתי אל מלכה (Heb. להביא את ושתי המלכה) 'to bring Vashti, the Queen' (ibid., 1:17);

65. For further examples of this kind from Judeo-Arabic texts, see Hary, "On the Use of *ʾilā*," sentences 37 (a similar sentence taken from a Baghdadi Passover Haggadah), 50, 55, and 56.

(43) למא צׄרב אל מצריין *lamma ḍarab il-miṣriyīn* (Heb. בנגפו את מצרים) ‘while He struck the Egyptians’ (Haggadah-Egypt 15:2), but in C3 the sentence is expressed with *ʾilā*: פׄי צׄרבו אלה מצר (18:48);

(44) וכׄבזו אל עגׄין *wi-xabazu il-ʿagīn* (Heb. ויאפו את הבצק) ‘and they baked the dough’ (Haggadah-Egypt 16:1), but in C3 the sentence is expressed with *ʾilā*: וכׄבזו אלה אל עגינה (18:49).

When the definite direct object begins a sentence or a phrase, however, it is always preceded by the marker *ʾilā*:

(45) ואלה עלי ביך ואלה גׄאנם אלחמזאווי . . . כׄמׄן אלבאשא *wi-ʾilā ʿali bēk wi-ʾilā ğānim il-ḥamzāwi . . . xamman il-bāša* (ואת עלי ביך ואת גׄאנם אל חמזאווי . . . חשב (Heb. השר ‘and as for Ali Beik, Ghanim al–Hamzawi . . . the Pasha intended’ (**M** 46);

(46) ואלא שקאנא *wi-ʾilā šaʾāna* (Heb. ואת עמלנו) ‘and as for our toil’ (Haggadah-Egypt 11:1);

(47) ואלא ביותנא כׄלץ *wi-ila buyūtna xallaṣ* (Heb. ואת בתינו הציל) ‘and our homes He saved’ (ibid., 15:2);

(48) ואלה צׄיקנה *wi-ʾilā ḍiʾna* (Heb. ואת לחצנו) ‘and as for our oppression’ (C3 11:29);

(49) ואלה מסאכנו קׄפׄרו *wi-ʾilā masakno ʾafaru* (Heb. ואת נוהו השמו) ‘and his dwelling they devastated’ (ibid., 23:13);

(50) ואלא קואנין אל מלך ליתׄהם טאיעין *wi-ʾilā ʾawanīn il-malik lethum ṭayʿīn* (Heb. ואת דתי המלך אינם עשים) ‘and they do not obey the King’s laws’ (BZ 1302 3:8);

(51) ואלא נסכׄת כתאב אל שריעה *wi-ʾilā nusxat kitāb iš-šarīʿa* (Heb. ואת פתשגן כתב הדת) ‘and the copy of the writing of the decree’ (ibid., 4:8).

This may also occur if the Hebrew version features a different word order:

(52) וחרקו אלבלד ואלה נוצׄ דקאדוס חרקוהא *wi-ḥaraʾu il-balad wi-ʾilā nuṣ dʾadūs ḥaraʾūha* (Heb. וישׂרפו את חצי דקאדוס באש) ‘then they set that town and half of Dqadus on fire’ (**M** 55).

Similarly, *ʾet* with pronoun suffixes preceding the verb is rendered in the Judeo-Arabic texts in the same way. In this case the writer is compelled to translate it usually with the inflected *ʾilā* or with the Classical Arabic *ʾiyyā*;[66] he cannot translate the inflected *ʾet* with a pronominal suffix because of the desire to preserve the Hebrew word order:

66. This is similar to Ben Sūsān’s obligatory rendering of אותי with אייאתי if it precedes the phrase or the verb. For example, אייאתי ואייאת רייס אלכׄבאזין (Heb. ויתן . . . אותי ואת שר האופים) ‘and he put . . . me and the chief baker’ (Gen 41:10). On the other hand, if אותי follows the verb, it can be translated as a suffixed pronoun: פיקתלוני (Heb. והרגו אתי) ‘and they killed me’ (Gen 12:12). See Doron, “On the Translation of the Particle *ʾet*,” 16; and Hary, “On the Use of *ʾilā*,” 601 n. 16.

(53) חתא אלנא פך מעהום *ḥata ilna fakk maʿāhum* (Heb. אלא אף אותנו גאל עמהם) 'and even us, He redeemed with them' (Avraham 1865, 31:2);

(54) ואלנא כרג̇ מן תם *wi-ilna xarag min tamm* (Heb. ואותנו הוציא משם) 'and us, He took out of there' (ibid., 31:2);

(55) כמא קאל אל פסוק ואיאנא אכ̇רג מן הנאך *kama ʾāl il-fasūq wa-iyyāna axrag min henāk*[67] (Heb. שנאמר ואותנו הוציא משם) 'as it is written, and us, He freed from there' (Haggadah-Egypt 16:2);

(56) ואייאה צלבו עלא אל כ̇שבה *wa-iyyāh ṣalabu ʿala l-xašaba* (Heb. ואותו תלו על העץ) 'and him they have hanged from the tree' (BZ 1302 8:7).

On the other hand, as a general rule, if the inflected *ʾet* comes after the verb, it is usually *not* translated but rendered as a bound pronominal suffix of the verb:

(57) וייעד̇בוהום ארבע מאית סנה *wi-yiʿazzibūhum arbaʿ miyat sana* (Heb. וענו אותם ארבע מאות שנה) 'and they tortured them for four hundred years' (Haggadah-Egypt 8:2);

(58) ומשיתהו *wi-maššēthu* (Heb. ואולך אותו) 'and I led him' (ibid., 8:1);

(59) ליורת̇ו *li-yuwriso* (Heb. לרשת אותו) 'to inherit it' (ibid., 8:1);

(60) לאג̇ל יג̇יבנא *liʾagl yigībna* (Heb. למען הביא אותנו) 'in order to bring us' (ibid., 16:2).

Furthermore, it is clear that there is a decrease in the use of *ʾilā* in Later and Modern Egyptian Judeo-Arabic texts when indicating direction and, correspondingly, an increase in the use of the preposition *li* for that purpose:

(61) נזל אבראהים . . . לחארת אל יאוד *nizil ibrahīm . . . li–ḥārat il-yahūd* 'Ibrahim went down . . . to the Jewish Quarter' (**A** 6b,12–13; with changes: **M** 41);

(62) וחצ̇רו בהום לחצ̇רת *wi-ḥaḍaru bihum li-ḥaḍret* 'and they brought them to His Highness' (**A** 2b,5; with changes: **R** 1,32; **M** 17);

(63) וטרדו כ̇לף עסכר אל ג̇ראכסה לקליוב *wi-ṭaradu xalf ʿaskar il-ğarāksa li-qalyūb* 'and they chased after the Circassian soldiers to Qalyub' (**A** 9b,7–9; with changes: **B** 7a,7–8; **R** xix; **M** 54);

(64) חוצ̇ור אחמד באשא למצר *ḥuḍur aḥmad bāša li-maṣr* 'Ahmad Pasha came to Egypt' (**M** 4);

(65) ותווג̇ה לבית שמואל *wi-tawaggah li-bēt šmuʾēl* 'and he returned to Samuel's house' (**M** 15);

(66) וארסל אל צולטאן באשה למצר *wi-arsal is-sulṭān bāša li-maṣr* 'and the Sultan sent a Pasha to Cairo' (**R** xxiii);

(67) ונזל למצר *wi–nazal li–maṣr* 'and he went to Egypt' (Haggadah-Egypt 9:1);

67. By reciting *wa-iyyāna* at the Passover table rather than using *wi-* and/or *ʾilā*, the speaker "moved" on the continuum closer to the left end of B_n.

(68) לו כאן אדכ̇לנא לארץ̇ ישראל *law kān adxalna li-arḍ isra*ᵓ*īl* 'had he brought us into the Land of Israel' (ibid., 15:1);

(69) ופ̇י אל צבח הייא תרגע לבית אל נסא *wi-fi ṣ-ṣubḥ hiyya tirga*ᶜ *li-bēt in-nisa* 'and in the morning she returned into the women's house' (BZ 1302 2:14);

(70) אנאכ̇ד̇ת אסתר לל מלך אל אזדשירי *wi-in*ᵓ*axazat ester lil-malik il-azdaširi* 'and Esther was taken unto King Ahasuerus' (ibid., 2:16).

The conclusion is, then, that since ᵓ*ilā* has an additional function that corresponds to Hebrew ᵓ*et*, the writers must have felt that some of its functions (such as direction) could be attributed to *li*, although one must also remember that in the dialect, in general *li* is used to indicate direction.

In Classical Judeo-Arabic there is already evidence that Judeo-Arabic *li* was used to mark the definite direct object;[68] there is, however, no evidence that in this earlier period the Hebrew marker ᵓ*et* had a Judeo-Arabic equivalent. In Later Judeo-Arabic, writers desired to translate word for word from Hebrew to Judeo-Arabic and looked for an equivalent Judeo-Arabic morpheme for Hebrew ᵓ*et*. Yissachar ben Sūsān of the sixteenth century, for instance, used the marker ᵓ*iyyāt*, and later writers started using the preposition ᵓ*ilā*. Writers did not continue to use Classical Judeo-Arabic *li*; they preferred ᵓ*ilā* to indicate the definite direct object, perhaps because *li* is a clitic, while ᵓ*ilā* was written as a separate word, like ᵓ*et*, which is a separate preposition in Hebrew.[69]

This use of ᵓ*ilā* was awkward to Judeo-Arabic writers. They therefore tried to avoid it whenever ᵓ*et* stood for more than a mere definite accusative marker, as has been shown above. We see, then, that as is quoted so often in the literature, the language of the *šarḥ* is characterized as a literal translation from Hebrew into Judeo-Arabic. Sephiha holds that it is characterized by Hebrew צמידות, or 'linking'; that is, every word in Hebrew has a Judeo-Arabic equivalent coupled with similar word order. In the *šurūḥ* themselves, however, many counter examples to this phenomenon are found. I propose that the language of the *šarḥ* exhibits a constant tension between the desire of the writer to translate the Hebrew text word for word and his desire to be understood. He thus needed to interpret the text from time to time by substituting words,

68. Blau, *A Grammar*, 179–80.

69. This idea was suggested to me by Shmuel Bolozky, personal communication. A similar phenomenon exists in Jewish Neo-Aramaic. In a Bible translation into the Jewish dialect of Dehok (Iraqi Kurdistan), the writer translates the Hebrew עונו 'his iniquity' (Lev 5:1) as one word, ᶜ*wndydy*, and *not* as the usual two separate words, ᶜ*āwān dīde*, in order to adhere closely to the Hebrew text and render the Neo-Aramaic exactly as it appears in the Hebrew text. See Yona Sabar, "The Hebrew Bible Vocabulary as Reflected through Traditional Oral Neo-Aramaic Translations," in *Semitic Studies in Honor of Wolf Leslau on the Occasion of His Eighty-Fifth Birthday, November 14th, 1991* (ed. A. Kaye; 2 vols.; Wiesbaden: Harrassowitz, 1991) 2.1388.

paraphrasing, and adding flavor from the local dialect.[70] In fact, the literal translation of the *šarḥ* prompted young students to ask in Morocco:

(71) האחנא שרחנא לעבראן לשרח, ומן ישרח לנא שרח לערבייא דילנא? *ha–ḥna sərḥna l-^{c}bṛan l-s-sərḥ, u-mn isərḥ l-na s-sərḥ l-l-^{c}ṛbiya dill-na* 'here we have translated the Hebrew into the language of the *šarḥ*, but who will translate for us the *šarḥ* into our Arabic?'[71]

The language of the different *šurūḥ* is not constant and may be placed on a continuum. The nature of the language variety may shift on the continuum, depending on the period of its composition, the place, the writers, and the readers. In the language of the *šarḥ* in general, one can distinguish the influence of Sa^{c}adya Ga^{c}on, especially in vocabulary as well as the influence of a local dialect and possibly of a dialect of a Jewish study center.

From the above analysis, it is clear that the desire for word-for-word translation from Hebrew into Jewish ethnolects in general—and Judeo-Arabic in particular—was pressing. It was so pressing that writers of Judeo-Arabic were willing to assign a new function to *$^{\supset}$ilā* in order to preserve the sacred Hebrew text as literally as possible. A similar phenomenon is found in other Jewish ethnolects. Furthermore, it is interesting to note that Judeo-Arabic played an important role in maintaining Jewish identity in the minority communities of the diaspora. The need for word-for-word translation of Hebrew sacred texts into Judeo-Arabic may well reflect a strong desire to maintain contact with Jewish heritage in a non-Jewish environment. In a diaspora where Jews were threatened with assimilation, determined preservation of sacred texts represented one way of preserving Jewish identity against difficult odds.

Summary

In this paper, I place the periods of Later and Modern Egyptian Judeo-Arabic within the general multiglossic history of Judeo-Arabic. As has been so well demonstrated in the last decade, investigation of the marginal is always helpful to our understanding of the center, and, by analyzing several phonological, morphological,and syntactic phenomena found in Later and Modern Egyptian Judeo-Arabic, I hope to have shed some new light on the historical development of Arabic dialects in general and Egyptian Judeo-Arabic in particular.

70. This linguistic tension is analyzed in detail with extensive examples from a nineteenth-century Judeo-Arabic *Haggada* (from the Cairo Collection) in Hary, "The Cairo Collection," Paper presented at the 20th Annual Meeting of the North American Conference on Afroasiatic Linguistics (Cambridge, Mass.: 1992); and in idem, "Sociolinguistic Setting," 82–95.

71. Bar Asher, "The Sharḥ of the Maghreb," 15.

Ein arabischer Text aus Constantine (Algerien)

Hans-Rudolf Singer

Der vorliegende Text wurde—nebst anderen—von einem meiner algerischen Doktoranden vor etwa vier Jahren in Constantine selbst aufgenommen. Sprecherin ist die damals 72 jährige Hausfrau (Lal)la-Ḍawya, die in der Altstadt (*Qaṣba*) geboren, noch immer dort lebt. Nur deren Bewohner bzw. deren Sprache gilt als "echt"; dies wird begreiflich, wenn man bedenkt, daß Constantine, das 1955 ca. 119,000 und 1966 ca. 253,000 Einwohner zählte, nunmehr mehr als eine halbe Million aufweist. Daß die Sprache des Ortes davon nicht unberührt bleiben könnte, ist klar. Bereits 1957 konstatierte Ph. Marçais:

> Il en est parmis elles [den Stadtmundarten], qui ont bien conservé l'usage de l'arabe de la première couche: on le trouve à Tlemcen, Nédroma, Cherchell, Dellys, Djidjelli, Collo. En d'autres, il n'est reconnaissable que chez les vieilles générations et semble voué à une prompte disparition, s'il n'est déjà pas complètement disparu: à Ténès, Miliana, Médéa, Blida, Alger, Bougie, Mila, Philippeville [Skîkda], Constantine. Partout, ces vieilles cités portent la marque printelles ont subies au cours des âges et continuent de subir, celle des ruraux,

celle des bédouins. . . . Dans d'autres, entourées de collectivités bédouins ou bédouines sédentarisées, c'est le langage de ces voisins qu'ont emprunté les citadins: Ténès . . . , Constantine.[1]

Vor allem konstatiert er für Constantine die Realisationen *q* und *g* des Qáf "où les deux sons, pour les mêmes vocables parfois, s'entendent dans les mêmes bouches." Die Interdentale sind wie in Alt-Ténès, Cherchell und Dellys erhalten (so Marçais), aber in C. mit der Einschränkung, daß *ṯ* zu *t* verschoben als [ṭ] realisiert wird. Von Marçais—so weit ich sehe—nicht erwähnt wird, daß C. die Diphthonge erhalten hat; zumeist mit den Realisationen [ẹ^{i}/ọ^{u}], doch kann bei vorangehenden "öffnenden" Konsonanten das erste Element offener gesprochen werden (ę/ạ,ǫ/ạ). Das von Marçais erwähnte "grasseyement du *r* . . . fréquent à Constantine" tritt in diesem Text selten auf.[2] Unsere Mundart (Md.) ist im Hinblick auf die Realisation [ṭ] des /t/ die östlichste der marokkanisch-algerischen Stadt-Mdd., in anderer Hinsicht (Erhaltung der anderen Interdentalen und der Diphthonge, viele morphologische Gemeinsamkeiten) die westlichste Stadt-Md. der alten Ifrîqiya bzw. des Ḥafṣiden-Reiches. Beduinisch ist wohl die Diphthongierung des Auslauts-/ū/ des Plurals beim Verb. Die verwendete Umschrift ist im übrigen mit einigen Vereinfachungen die meiner tunisischen Grammatik.[3]

Der hier vorgelegte Text ist der erste in der Md. dieser Stadt publizierte. Ihm werden—an anderer Stelle—weitere folgen; am Ende der Serie wird ein kleines Glossar beigegeben werden, weshalb hier nur die unbedingt nötigen Bemerkungen zu einigen Vokabeln gegeben werden. Henri Péres erwähnt in seiner Bibliographie[4] folgende Arbeit: "M(aurice) Mercier, Le dialecte arabe de Constantine. Mémoire en vue du Diplôme d'Études Supérieures de Langue et Littérature arabes présenté devant la Faculté des Lettres d'Alger en mai 1910. Inédit." Nachfragen meiner Doktoranden haben ergeben, daß die genannte Arbeit nicht aufzufinden ist und wahrscheinlich bei dem Anschlag der OAS auf die Universitätsbibliothek von Algier im April 1962 vernichtet worden ist.

1. Philippe Marçais, *Initiation à l'Algérie* (Paris, 1957) 215–37, bes. 226.

2. Vgl. dazu meine Bemerkung in *ZDMG* 108 (1958) 109.

3. Außerdem mußte einigen Beschränkungen des für dieses Buch zur Verfügung stehenden Satzes Rechnung getragen werden.

4. Henri Péres, "L'Arabe dialectal algérien et saharien: Bibliographie analytique," *Bibliothèque de l'Institut d'Études Supérieures Islamiques d'Alger* 14 (Alger, 1378/1958) S. 79/Nr. 347.

Text

lᶜęrs

1. laᶜdā́:dᵗ: zzwā́:ž ā́:na ṅgúlləḳ wä:š-idí:ru, ḏǫ́ṛk ˘ṣṣbá:ḥ, laᶜṛǫ́:ṣa ã:hã:[5] ṣṣbâḥ laᶜṛǫ́:ṣa nha:ṛ-ssā́:baᶜ ki:-ṭṣábbẹḥ, yäḫḫé:-ḥná: fi:-dá:ṛ bä:bā́:ha mbā́:tu mᶜá-lğä:ğ,[6] nā́ḫdmu-lğā́-ğ ṭaiⁱbǫ́:h u-lḫúbz, ˘ṣṣbá:ḥ yiṭẹ́:b fə-lkú:ša lbą́qlä:wa ssní: aw-hā́:käð u-mṣą́ffæf b-əlmləbbəs—lmləbbəs haðā́:k li-zā́iyⁱnu bí:h—wu-nḥǫ́ṭṭu haðā́:k lğā́:ğ, kull-ḫúbza b-ṭą́ⁱr-ğä:ğ, ilá: ᶜẹšri:n-ḫúbza ᶜẹšri:n-ṭą́ⁱr, ilá: ṯl̄äṭẹ́ⁱn ṭą́ⁱṛ . . . u-laᶜḏą́:m mšẹršmẹ́ⁱn u-láḥräš f-əzzaᶜfṛá:n mzáᶜfaṛ láḥräš krā́:kəb lḥā́m yiṭẹ́:b mᶜá-lžä:ž wu-lğā́:ğ kā́if-θä:ni[7] ṭa[8]-mən-hú:wa nḥoṭṭṳ́:h f-əzzaᶜfṛá:n, ižẹ́i ṣfą́ṛ ṣfą́ṛ ṣfą́ṛ, ða[9]-bə́kri f-˘Qṣǫnṭẹ́ina; ḏǫ́ṛka[10] ᶜá:du. wä:š-idí:ru rá:ḥu, ḷḷą́:-yuṣṭar ᶜá:du fə́sdu.

2. häðā́:k˘ssḥánaw hā́:k lməlyā́:n-ᵃḥráš gā́:d ma-ᶜándi ma-ngúlləḳ ṣḷá:t-ᵉnbí: nḥoṭṭṳ́:h fəlwṳ́ṣṭ. wu-ssḥā́n nṭā́:ᶜ loᶜḏą́:m ṭā́:ni mənná: wu-lğā́:ğ dā́:yẹr f-əssní: wu-lḫúbz fi-qąṛṭą́ḷḷą, qąṛṭą́ḷḷą gẹdd-mənná lhé:h; ˘lqąṛṭą́ḷḷą häðí:k nṭā́:ᶜ ˢsᶜáf häðí:k, li:-hā́zzu fi:ha lḫúbz—qṛá:ṭaḷ—hị̄:h, guffa wa-hí:ya b-əlᶜẹraᶜ;[11] kí:ma-ṅgú:lu knẹ́ssru kí:ma-lḅá:nyǫᵘ knẹ́sᵗru u-hú:wa sᶜā́f kā́:nu bə́kri idí:ruhum (sic) sᶜā́f; ḏǫ́ṛka ä:m-ᶜá:du idirú:hum ní:lu. ḏǫ́ṛka idirú:hum b-əlgṣą́b iží:u ṣḥá:ḥ. ḥẹ̄ṭtá kúnna ki:-nā́gslǫᵘ lqą́šš nḥoṭṭṳ́:hum ki:-[i]ší:ḥ lqą́šš nḥoṭṭṳ́:h fí:h . . . l-knẹ́strǫᵘ.[12]

3. [Der 7. Tag] hā́:ði ki:-ṭṣą́bbẹḥ ṣṣbá:ḥ lᶜᵃṛǫ́:ṣa, tru:ḥẹ́lha mən-da:ṛ bā́:bä:ha (sic). u-hú:ma häðā́:k lğā́:ğ ki:fā́:š idi:rǫ́:ᵘh? yúnṣbǫᵘ ğā́:ri byą́ḏ u-ṭwā́:gẹn, kí:ma-ṅgú:lu kúll-˘qdí:r u-qą́dru, w-á:ḫaṛ idí:r ğā́:ri u-zā́uğ ṃṃʷą́:ᶜẹn, šṭą́iṭha[13] u-ṭa:ğí:n lḥú:t, waḷḷą́ ṭa:ğí:n lğā́:ğ, gā́:ša-ná:[14] hā́:ði kə́fṭa waḷḷą́ ṭa:ğí:n lğā́:ğ aw-ṛá:yẹḥ mən-ᶜánd bi:ṭ-bā́:bäha. häðā́:k lğā́:ğ yaᶜmlú:h šṭą́iṭha, yiṭfaṛṛágᵏ, wúlli yiṭḫábba yiṭḫábba,

5. Nasalisiert ausgesprochen.

6. /ğ/ wird sowohl als Affrikate wie auch als *ž* ausgesprochen, doch ist zweifellos ersteres die ursprüngliche Realisation der Md.

7. Ein Füllsel: “wie denn gleich, wie heißt es denn gleich.”

8. Man hört sowohl *ḥ˘ṭa* wie *ṭa-* für *ḥẹ́ṭṭa*.

9. Statt *hā́:ða*.

10. *ḏǫ́ṛka* heißt ‘jetzt’, *ḏǫ́ṛk* dagegen ‘sofort, gleich’, z.B. *ḏǫ́ṛk nğí*: ‘ich komme gleich’.

11. “Henkel” an einem Korb, eines Gefäßes; dieser Pl. lautet in Algier *ᶜᵃṛá:wi*.

12. In Tunis (-M) *knā́stru*; vgl. ‘Kanister’.

13. Cf. Beaussier 526 b; in Tunis heißt dieses Gericht *šäkšú:ka*.

14. Verkürzt aus *gä:l-ä:š* ‘sozusagen’.

wúlli:-[i]ḥoṭṭú:h yä:klú:h lġá:ši. yấ:klu la-ᶜá:d lġá:ši bəzzấ:f hấ:m ˘llấ:hi:-bấ:rek häðấ:k [š]ši: yiṛó:ḥ kúll.

4. wu-ssní: ấ:w maḥṭọ́:ṭ fi:-bi:ţ-laᶜṛọ́:ṣa, ţẹḥţ˘ssrí:r, ţấ:kul hí:ya u-ṛạ́:ğelha (sic). hấ:ði ṣṣbá:ḥ u-ṭạnžṛá-nţấ:ᶜ lğấ:ri ṭạ́nžṛa gẹ́dd-hä:k. hấ:ði ṛá:iḥa mən-dá:ṛ bấ:bä:ha.—ğấ:ri b-əddwéidä nţấ:ᶜ ṣṣạbbá:ḥa, ˘ddwéida rrgí:ga. yấ:u ddzi:ri:yéⁱn mä-idi:róu-š ki:ma-ḥnấ:ya, ḥná:-hná: Qṣọnṭéina, idi:rú:h bəzzấ:f.—b-ə́ṣṣaḥḥ-ḥná: ẖwä:ţấ:ţi-läᵓ; ki:-Zohṛa-ẖţí kí:-kull ki̱-Ḫdí:ğa ki-ᶜẤ:iša ki:- . . . [Schwager:] wu-lᶜadấ:ţ a: ẖấ:lţi? hấ:ðu nţú:ma/nţọ́ᵘma hấ:ðu dí:ma yⁱdí:ru kí:ma-yidí:ru hấ:ḳ̥da kí:ma-ṅgú:lu-ḥná:, lấ:zəm hấ:ði nţấ:ᶜ ṣṣbá:ḥ, wussấ:baᶜ . . . [Frau] ᵘṃṃʷá:la! lấ:zəm ḥţá-lli ma-ᶜandú:-ši:-[i]dí:r qádru. lli-ma-ᶜandú:-š ʸidí:r[15] swí:ni:ya gẹdd-hấ:ḳ̥da.

5. wŭ-ssấ:baᶜ wä:š-idí:ru fí:h? ˘ssấ:baᶜ iḥäzzmú:h w-idí:ru ţrí:da, ţrí:d˘t ẹlkẹskấ:s, wu-lğấ:ri; kull-wấ:ḥẹd wä:š-iḥẹ̈́bb, wấ:ḥẹd idí:r tţrí:da ulğấ:ri, wấ:ḥẹd idí:r lmḥấmmạṛ mᶜá:ha u-ṭạ́:ği:n á:ẖọṛ. ð̣óṛk ᶜá:du iḥấzzmu kúnna nnḥấzzmu f-ssấ:baᶜ b-əlmḥấzzma. ki-ţᶜú̱:d ᶜᵃṛọ́:ṣa ma-ţḥazzấm-š. mḥázzma lwí:z waḷḷạ ṣu̱lṭạ́:ni waḷḷạ *simple*. kä:iní:n ḥţa-idi:rú:hum fạð̣ð̣a, kí:ma-nţấ:ᶜ l-Mạṛṛo:k . . . ðhẹ̈́b; kä:n-bấ:ba-äná: igúlli n˘ddéik l-Mạṛṛọ́:k u-nšrí:-lek mḥázzma. dä:irí:nhum ðhẹ̈b θə́mma f-əl-Mạṛṛọ́:k, bi:bấ:n bi:bấ:n hấ:k˘ð ukä:iní:n-ẖṛéⁱn yaᶜm-lú:hum fạ́ð̣ð̣ạ w-i:ᶜú:du b-ṛọ:bí:l θấ:ni mṣạffí:n. hấ:kðä:k iḥäzzmú:-lha nha:ṛ-˘ssấ:baᶜ, u-ð̣óṛk ᶜá:du nha:ṛ-ţelţ-i:yấ:m iḥấzzmu. hé:h gúlt kull-ši-ţbə́ddel!

6. [Schwager] wấ:š kấ:nu bə́kri idí:ru nnsấ:? [Frau] ləmṛá: ţọ̈́ẖdəm ṣṣọ́ᵘf wu-ţẖdə́m lksrá: f-əddá:r, ţọ̈́ẖdəm rrfí:s,[16] ţọ̈́ẖdəm lksrá: u-ţbé:ᵃᶜ, ţdí:rha gᵘṛạiⁱṣá:t[17] hấ:ḳ̥ði, kẹ́sra ki-ššẹ́ḥ̥da ţᶜú:d ţấ:kul fí:ha ma-ţẹ́ḥkəmhấ:-š aᶜla-sẹnní:k nţấ:ᶜ lḥrá:ẹṛ wu-ţbí:ᵃᶜ . . . [Schwager] mú:la-bí:tha mä-igú:lha wấ:lu?[18] . . . [Frau] ma-igú:lha wấ:lu, ṣṣwá:ṛọ̈d zyấ:da! u-f-əddá:ṛ ţə́ṭṛọ̈z u-ţẖáiyẹṭ b-əlmä:ší:na, u-ţə́ṭṛọ̈z b-əţţéll—wä:šenhóᵘwa ţţéll?—˘ţţéll hấ:ḳ̥ða rgí:g—ẖẹ́ⁱṭ! mấ:-uš kí:ma lẖéⁱṭ,

15. Statt *lli-ma-ᶜandú:š* auch *ma-kä:in-lú:-š* möglich.

16. Ein Gebäck; cf. Beaussier 405 a. *késra* ist der sehr dünne Fladen, *ẖmẹ́:ṛa* ein etwas dikkerer (bei uns in türkischen Läden).

17. Sg. *gᵘṛáiⁱṣa* dim.; *gúṛṣa*, pl. *-a:t* ‘kreisförmiger Gegenstand’ (z.b. ~ *ẖubz*, ~ *ġārs* [Dattelpaste], ~ *késra*), auch ‘flache Dose’ z.B. für Schnupftaback. *Šẹ́hda* (mit stimmhaftem *h*!) eigentlich ‘Honigwabe’.

18. In C würde man richtiger *ma-ḥẹţţä:-ši* verwenden; *wấ:lu* weist ins westl. Algerien und nach Marokko.

hú:wa ẖéⁱṭ ki:-lfą́ḍḍa. hú:wa rgúyyig hắ:keð žắ:i, laᶜbắ:ṛak nṯắ:ᶜ laᶜṛǫ́:ṣa, [ẖ]nä bə́kri ndí:ra lᶜabṛǫ́:k u-ḏúṛk yⁱdí:ru lqą́ṣṣą kí:ma hắ:ði, lᶜabṛǫ́:k maṭṛǫ́:ẓ b-ukúll b-əttéll. qą́ṣṣą-rhí:fa kí:ma-idi:rú:hum nnṣą́:ṛa ᶜᵃla-wuğú:[h]hum, rhí:fa, yissə́mma fí:h lḥrí:r—fí:h ṅgóṭ hắkð. ˇnnṣą́:ṛa idi:rú:hum ᶜala-uğú:h-um bą́ṛk, fí:h ngǫ́ṭᵒngǫ́ṭ.—šúġl bṛǫ́:di? —mắ:uš bṛǫ́:di, wä:š-ğắ:bək lə-bṛǫ́:di? hắ:ða ắ:u ki:-lqą́ṣṣą-rhí̱:f, nṯắ:ᶜ laᶜṛǫ́:ṣa ndi:rú:h byą́ḏ b-əṭṭéll, byą́ð u-hú:wa-byą́ð, ḥę́lla, u-b-əlfṭú:l m-əlláuṭ hắ:k Qṣǫnṭą́ina hắ:-si:dí:.

7. ləmṛá: f-əddá:ṛ ṭdí:r ṯlí:ṯli,[19] ṯḥóṭṭ ṭaqᶜę́ⁱda u-ṭə́fṭəl—hắ:i ṭaqᶜę́ⁱda—nᶜámᵐṛu ḏǫ́ṛkha ắ:ðä elwą́qṭ qrí:b-ə-Ṛąm[ḏ]ą́:n[20] ḏǫ́ṛk mən-qbə́l Sí:di Rğə́m (< Rağab) mən-Šaᶜbắ:n. [yẹẖ]ẖí Šaᶜbắ:n húwa llú:wəl? hä-Sí:di Rğə́m, nəbdắ:u mən-Sí:di Rğə́m. nəbdắ:u-lfṯí:l nṭắḥ-tṯlí:ṯli nə́fṭlu u-naᶜğnú:h naᶜğnú:h ndi:rú:-lu ssmə́n; u-nəbdắ:u dắ:k-ˇssä:ᶜ[21] naẖdmú:h kull-yǫ́:ᵘm, kull-yǫ́:ᵘm ṛá:i ṭelgắi ləbyú:ṭ mná:šaṛ. mä-nšrí:u ḥṭắ-ši mǫ-ẓẓqą́:q; u-náᶜmlu tṭréida f-əddá:ṛ, ndí:ru ləmḥámᵐṣa.[22] f-əddá:ṛ ndí:ru lkúsksi f-əddą́:r, ləmzíyyẹṭ, ləmqą́ṛṭfa[23] l-elğę́:ri (sic), rréšṭa, rréšṭa ndí:ruha f-əṣṣayyá:ṛ nqąṭṭᶜụ́:ha ki:-ddwéiⁱda u-näḥkmú:ha f-ˇṣṣayyá:ṛ yắlläh-yắlläh[24] wu-ṭᶜụ́:d hí:ya mhóuᵘda lmą́ġbú:na ki:wắ:š lğắ:ri nṭáḥḥa wä:š iğí:, iğí:-isáẖẖaf. hắ:ði hí:ya ləbnắ:ṭ laᶜwắ:ṭaq f-əddá:ṛ yẹ́ẖdmu. [Schwager] hắ:ða wä:š-kắ:n idí:ru? ma-yẹẖdmú:-š ˇṣṣǫ́:f kí:ma-ṅgú:lu, waḷḷa idí:ru qšắ:šəb,[25] bąṛnú:ṣ,[26] wu-lfrắ:š . . . ?[27] [Frau] ę́:h—yéẖdmu u-yę́ġzlu lǫqyę́:m,[28] ṭélga-lġṛǫ́ṛ[29] hắkð f-əṣṣṭá:ḥ hắ:i-lġǫ́ṛṛa, ulġǫ́ṛṛa mənfǫ́:g wu-ṯẖábbąṭ laqyắ:m lġázla nṭáḥḥa

19. Eine Suppeneinlage; cf. Beaussier 109 b.

20. Hier *Ṛąmmą́:n* artikuliert, gewöhnlich *Ṛąmðą́:n*; Tunis-M *Ṛumðą́:n*.

21. ‘Danach’.

22. Eine Art grober Kuskus; man unterscheidet *nǫ́ᶜma* (auch *bärbú:ša*) den extra-feinen, *ḥmé:ṣ* den feinen, dann *mḥámmṣą* den groben und schließlich den sehr groben *ᶜáiš*, der indes nicht mehr als wahrer Kuskus gilt.

23. Eine Art Nudeln für die Suppe (*ğắ:ri*).

24. ‘Ganz schnell’.

25. Sg. *qąššắ:ba* und *qąššä:bí:ya.* Ersteres hat 3 Bedeutungen: (1) ein knöchellanges Übergewand der Frauen, in Const. nur zu feierlichen Anlässen, aus edlen Stoffen, mit Kapuze; (2) ein Jackett mit Kapuze aus Baumwolle oder Kamelhaar, auch als “saharienne” bezeichnet; (3) für Männer wie 1., aber dunkel, aus Wolle oder Baumwolle, mit Kapuze; (1) und (3) sind für die warme Jahreszeit. Letzteres ist ein knöchellanges Männergewand für die kalte Jahreszeit, aus Wolle oder Kamelhaar, robust; in schwarz, braun oder weiß.

26. Der Burnus ist auch ein Statussymbol.

27. ‘Bettbezug’ auch *ḥá:ik.*

28. *Qyä:m* ist der ‘Kettfaden’ bzw. die ‘Kette’.

29. Cf. Beaussier 701 b.

ţḫáuwud ḥátţa lgá:ᶜ ṣ̣ạ́ṭḥa-llạuṭ,[30] uṭṭạlláḥḥa ðíkssaᶜ.[31] —[Schwager] wǽš-llí: yẹ́ḫdmu búkk[ull]?—

8. [Frau] yéḫdmu lgná:dạṛ,[32] yẹ́ḫdmu lḥnắ:bəl,[33] yẹ́ḫdmu ẓẓṛạ́:bẹi, yẹ́ḫd-mu kull-ḫá:ir. lắ:h kí:ma ð̣óṛka! nnṳ́ṣṣ ắu f-əẓẓqá:q kắ:məl hắ:məl, b-əlkbí:ra b-əṣṣġị̱́:ṛa. wẹḥnắ:-nḫdmu nẹ́ḫdmu šúġlna kúll-ši f-əddá:r.— [Schwager] w-ulmṛá: bə́kri ki-tᶜṳ́:d mzọ́uᵘža máθal kí:ma-ṅgú:lu-ḥnắ:ya ki:-ṭzíyyẹd ləmṛá:, yắ:häntá:ṛa[34] hí:ya ţqṳ́:m b-əlbẹ́:t nţáḥḥa wạ́ḷḷa k[ắ:]šmá:-iží:u nnâ:s iqu:mú:-lha b-əlbẹ́:t nţáḥḥa.—[Frau] hẹ́:h—kắ:ši wắḥda nắ:fsa ţqṳ́:m b-əlbẹ́:ţ, ᶜẹ́ndha ᵐmạ:lí:ha, wí:la ma-ᶜẹndhắ:š ᶜándu hú:wa-ᵐmạ:lí:h,[35] ᶜᵃğú:za ţkú:n f-əddá:ṛ.—[Schwager] gẹddắ:h elyọ́:m hắ:kðắ:k wu-tnọ́:ð̣ ţọ́ḫdəm?—[Frau] hí:ya-u-mskí:na wä:š mṛí:ð̣ạ i:lá: ᶜá:fi ᶜᵃlẹ́:ha ḷḷạ u-msắhhẹl ᶜᵃlẹ́:ha ṛạ́bbi. ṛá:hi ţúqᶜọd sæbᶜ-iyắ:m u-tnọ́:ð̣; ţǽbbᵃᶜ[36]-bạ́ṛk u-tnọ́:ð̣, wí:la ᶜá:ţ[37] mṛí:ð̣ạ mắiš ṣḥí:ḥa túqᶜọd gú:l—ḫṛạ́:in wạḷḷá: ḥẹ́tţa ṛabᶜáⁱn yọ́:m u-mắ:-iməssú:-š.

Übersetzung des Textes

Die Hochzeit

1. Unsere Bräuche? Ja, ich werde dir erzählen, wie damals eine Hochzeit verlief: Die Braut verbrachte die Nacht vor dem Siebten Tag im Vaterhaus, und wir brachten die ganze Nacht mit der Zubereitung der verschiedenen Gerichte zu. Wir bereiteten Hühner vor, das Kochen und das Braten, und am frühen Morgen wird das Brot im Backofen gebacken. Die Baqlâwa wird auf einem Tablett gebracht, und das Ganze wird mit Dragées geschmückt; die Dragées sind nur zur Ausschmückung da. Danach werden die Hühner auf Tabletts serviert; auf jedes Huhn kommt ein Brot, je nachdem, wenn man zwanzig Hühner auf dem Tablett hat, dann kommen zwanzig Brote dazu, wenn man dreißig Hühner hat, dann kommen dreißig Brote dazu.

30. 'Estrich'.

31. 'Dann'.

32. Sg. *gandọ́:ṛa* 'Kleid; Gewand'.

33. Sg. *ḥámbəl* 'Bettdecke' oder 'Wandteppich', sehr bunt; auch *ḥá:ik* (s. Anm. 23) kann 'Bettdecke' bedeuten und zwar eine sehr dicke; sonst bedeutet letzteres Wort in Algerien 'Frauenübergewand', das in Const. *mlắ:ya* genannat wird (heute schwarz, früher weiß, in Tlemsen grau).

34. 'Ob'.

35. 'Eltern'.

36. < *ţsábbaᶜ* 3 sg. f. impf.

37. *Wí:la ᶜá:ţ* < *ᶜá:deţ* 'wenn sie wiederum (krank wird)'.

Dann kommen die Eier an die Reihe, gekochte Eier, und Fleischklößchen. Die Fleischklößchen werden mit einer Safransauce zubereitet, genauso wie die Hühner; sie werden dann in einer Safransauce gekocht; dann werden sie in die Safransauce hineingehalten, und wenn man sie wieder herausnimmt, dann sieht man, wie prachtvoll ihre Farbe geworden ist, ganz und gar gelb!

So war es einst in Constantine. Und heutzutage? Alles vorbei! Alle Leute sind total verdorben. Gott schütze uns.

2. Der Teller ist mit Dragées vollgefüllt bis es nicht mehr geht; diesen Teller stellt man in die Mitte des Tabletts. Das Tablett für die Eier ist genauso voll. Auf einem anderen Tablett haben wir die Hühner angerichtet; das Brot steht in einem großen Brotkorb namens *qaṛṭaḷḷa* bereit. Diese Art von Körben wird aus Palmblättern geflochten. In solchen Körben wird Brot getragen; es handelt sich um einen großen Korb mit Henkeln, ein Behälter, aber eben aus Palmblättern. Früher gab es nur solche aus Palmblättern, heute aber werden sie aus Kunstfasern (Nylon) gemacht oder aus Schilfrohr, sie sind dann sehr solide. Früher hat man sie auch als Wäschekörbe verwendet. Nachdem man gewaschen hatte und die Wäsche trocken war, wurde sie in solche Körbe hineingelegt.

3. [Der Siebte Tag] Dies wird in der Nacht zum Siebten Tag gemacht und zwar im Haus des Brautvaters. Weißt du denn auch, wie die Hühner zubereitet werden?

Zuerst werden eine klare Suppe und verschiedene Ragouts zubereitet; jeder macht, was er sich leisten kann. Man kann z. B. auch eine einfache Suppe und zwei Gerichte zubereiten, etwa eine Ratatouille und ein Geflügelragout oder ein Fischragout. So werden auch z. B. Hackfleischklößchen (*kefta*) oder ein Geflügelragout vom Haus des Brautvaters abgeholt und zum Haus des Bräutigams gebracht.

Aus den Hühnern macht man also eine Art Ratatouille; ein Teil davon wird den Gästen vorgesetzt und der andere Teil wird beiseite gestellt. Ist aber die Zahl der Gäste sehr groß, dann bleibt nichts übrig.

4. Im Brautgemach wird ein volles Tablett unter das [hohe] Bett gestellt, wovon sich [zu gegebener Zeit] die Brautleute bedienen. Am selben Tag holt man auch einen großen Topf voller Suppe mit feinen Nudeln aus dem Haus des Brautvaters.

In Algier verläuft die Sache ganz anders; dort geben sich die Leute nicht so viel Mühe. Allerdings, meine Schwestern, sowohl Zohra, Ḫdîǧa als auch ᶜAiša, alle haben sich sehr angestrengt (obwohl sie in Algier wohnten).

[Schwager] Tante, war es immer so? Ich meine diese Bräuche vom Siebten Tag . . . ich meine, mußte man so verfahren oder . . . ? [Frau] Na klar! Was glaubst du denn? Jeder muß das machen, auch derjenige, der mittellos ist; man macht halt, was man sich leisten kann. Jemand, der mittellos ist, muß sich eben damit begnügen, nur ein kleines Tablett anzubieten.

5. Was wird also am Siebten Tag gemacht? An diesem Tag bekommt die Braut einen Gürtel [wörtl.: sie muß sich gürten]; an diesem Tag werden Dampfnudeln und ein Ragout (*sic*) zubereitet, oder man kocht eben, worauf man Lust hat, der eine macht Dampfnudeln und eine Suppe, der andere macht Braten und Ratatouille. Heute bekommt die Braut ihren Gürtel vor dem Siebten Tag; damals aber hat sie ihn erst am Siebten Tag bekommen, denn als Braut darf man sich eigentlich noch nicht "gürten."

Der Gürtel ist entweder aus Goldmünzen zusammengesetzt oder von der Sultânî-Art oder ein ganz einfacher. Es gibt manche Gürtel, wie die marrokanischen, die aus Silber oder Gold sind. Ich entsinne mich noch, als mein Vater damals zu mir sagte: "Ich nehme dich mit nach Marokko und kaufe dir dort einen Gürtel." Ja, in Marokko findet man solche, die aus Gold und Silber sind, manche sind auch mit Rubinen geschmückt. Also damals durfte die Braut erst am Siebten Tag den erwähnten Gürtel bekommen; heute aber schon am dritten Tag! Ja, ja! Nichts ist heute mehr wie einst!

6. [Schwager] Was haben die Frauen damals so gemacht? [Frau] Die Frau hat damals Strickarbeiten gemacht, zu Hause Brot, und zwar eine Art Fladenbrot, und ein Dattelgebäck gebacken und dies verkauft. Dieses Brot ist ein echtes Meisterwerk, sehr fein, es schmolz wie Honig im Munde! Das hat sie auf dem Markt verkauft.

[Schwager] Ja, hatte denn ihr Mann nichts dagegen? [Frau] Was sollte er dagegen haben? Das war doch ein zusätzliches Einkommen für die Familie! Zu Hause hat sie auch gestickt und mit der Nähmaschine genäht. Für ihre Stickerei hat sie immer einen silbrigen Faden verwendet. [Schwager] Was ist denn das? [Frau] Dieser Faden ist sehr dünn und fein, es ist kein normaler Faden [sondern ein Metalldraht], der wie Silber aussieht.

Damals hat die Braut einen Schleier getragen, der den ganzen Kopf verhüllte; heutzutage aber trägt sie nur eine Art Hutschleier. Der Brautschleier war über und über bestickt. Der "Hutschleier" ist sehr fein, sowas wie die Christinnen tragen, er ist aus einem sehr feinen Stoff, quasi aus Seide und mit vielen Punkten. Die Christinnen tragen nur sowas vor dem Gesicht, mit lauter Punkten [= eine Art Gazestoff]. [Schwager] Ist es eine Art gehäkelter Spitze? [Frau] Wie kommst du darauf? Nein! Er ist wie ein Hutschleier, aber sehr fein. Der Brautschleier ist weiß und bestickt. Er ist wie eine Tunika, am unteren Saum mit Stickereien geschmückt. So war es in Constantine!

7. Die Frau machte auch Tlîtli (eine Suppeneinlage) und zusammen mit anderen rollte sie Kuskus. Wir fangen mit diesen Arbeiten [Füllen der Schüsseln] einen Monat vor dem Fastenmonat Ramaḍân an, und zwar schon vor dem Monat Rağab im Šaᶜbân. Kommt der Šaᶜbân zuerst? Nein, der Rağab. Also fangen wir mit dem Tlîtli an: Wir bereiten den Teig vor, wir geben ein wenig Fett dazu, und dann wird das Ganze geknetet und dann ausgerollt. Es wird an diesen Tagen sehr viel gearbeitet, jeden Tag, ohne Unterbrechung. Die Frauen in ihren Häusern sind sehr beschäftigt; nichts wird auf dem Markt gekauft. Wir machen verschiedene Sorten von Nudeln und Kuskus, wie *trîda* und *l-mqaṛṭfa*, *l-mẓíyyiṭ*, *l-mḥammṣa* und *rešta*. Die *rešta* wird durch ein Sieb gedrückt, dann in kleine Stückchen geschnitten, wie die *Dwîda*-Nudeln, bis sie ganz fein wird, dann eine Sauce dran und du hast ein Gericht, um das du beneidet wirst. Die ledigen Mädchen sind in dieser Zeit voll beschäftigt.

[Schwager] War das alles, was die Frauen damals machten? Haben sie nicht z.B. auch Sachen aus Wolle gewebt, wie z.B. Kleidungsstücke oder Bettwäsche? [Frau] Aber ja! Sie haben Kettfäden gesponnen und auch gewebt. Sie stellen den Webstuhl auf, man kann auf der Terrasse die Löcher sehen [in denen der Griffwebstuhl befestigt wird], die [ġọṛṛa] oben und die Webkette nach unten sich erstreckend, die Wollknäuel [oben angebracht] laufen nach unten bis auf den Boden und sie [die Frau] arbeitet [den zu webenden Stoff] von unten nach oben.

[Schwager] Was haben sie denn noch alles getrieben? [Frau] Sie haben Kleidungsstücke, Bettbezüge, Teppiche, alles Mögliche haben sie gemacht. Nicht wie die heutigen Frauen! Man sieht es doch—die Hälfte von ihnen, ob jung oder alt, treibt sich nur auf der Straße herum. Wir dagegen, wir sind unseren häuslichen Pflichten immer nachgekommen.

[Schwager] Und wie war es denn damals mit den (verheirateten) Frauen, die ein Kind bekamen? Hat sich dann die Frau trotzdem um den Haushalt gekümmert, oder waren Leute da, die ihr geholfen haben? [Frau] Eine Frau kann doch nicht kurz nach der Entbindung ihren Haushalt besorgen; entweder kommen ihre Eltern oder die Eltern ihres Mannes, um ihr zu helfen, oder es wird irgendeine alte Frau zu Hilfe geholt.

[Schwager] Wieviele Tage ungefähr brauchte sie denn, um das Kindbett verlassen zu können? [Frau] Die Arme ist doch krank! Wenn alles gut geht, ist sie nach sieben Tagen wieder obenauf, und wenn sie nicht sehr kräftig ist, dann braucht sie ein paar Tage länger; manche hüten selbst nach vierzig Tagen immer noch das Kindbett.

Part 3

Aramaic

Zur griechischen Nebenüberlieferung im Syrischen

Anton Schall

Die Überlieferung des Griechischen, dieser “anerkannt vollendetsten aller Sprachen,” wie sie noch Theodor Benfey in seiner “Geschichte der Sprachwissenschaft” genannt hat, wird für uns in zweifacher Weise greifbar. Die geschichtliche *Haupt* überlieferung tritt uns unmittelbar in den erhaltenen Originaldenkmälern und in der lebenden Sprache und ihren Mundarten entgegen, mittelbar in den Abschriften und in den Drucken der Originaldenkmäler. Hinter die geschichtliche Hauptüberlieferung führt vereinzelt die geschichtliche *Neben*-überlieferung zurück: “Diese Nebenüberlieferung wird gebildet—ich zitiere aus Schwyzers “Griechischer Grammatik”—einerseits durch Griechisches in fremden Sprachen, andererseits durch Fremdes im Griechischen. Dies Hinüber und Herüber geht in erster Linie den Wortschatz an, betrifft aber mitunter auch die Wortbildung, sogar Formen und Laute, ja Syntax und sprachliches Denken.”

Die Nebenüberlieferung des Griechischen in den orientalischen Sprachen läßt sich in großen Linien etwa folgendermaßen kennzeichnen:

Aus *archaischer* Zeit stammen Verbindungen zu durchweg dürftig bekannten kleinasiatischen Sprachen, Verbindungen, die lange nicht, teilweise überhaupt nicht abrissen. Geringere Beziehungen zu anderen altorientalischen Sprachen schließen sich an, so dem Ägyptischen, vereinzelt dem Libyschen, unter den altsemitischen Sprachen dem Akkadischen und dem Phönizischen, ferner dem Altiranischen und dem Kaukasischen. Außer dem vermutlichen Achäer- und Joniernamen haben diese Sprachen in archaischer Zeit kaum griechische Elemente aufgenommen. Was das Griechische aus ihnen entlehnte, sind neben Namen nur wenige Appellative.

Die Kulturbewegung des *Hellenismus* strahlte besonders nach Osten und Süden aus. Sie schuf neue Beziehungen zu den indischen Sprachen und verstärkte die Beziehungen zum Iranischen. Den Mittler zum Iranischen hin bildete fast durchweg das Aramäische, welches sowohl im Reichsaramäischen wie in den jungaramäischen Dialekten schon mancherlei griechisches Fremdwörtergut übernommen hatte. Die beiden umfangreichen Bände über "Griechische und lateinische Lehnwörter in Talmud, Midrasch und Targum" von Samuel Krauss geben eine Vorstellung, in welchem Ausmaße neben dem Aramäischen auch das nachbiblische Hebräisch sich Griechisches angeeignet hat. Verstärkt wurden durch den Hellenismus auch die Beziehungen zum Ägyptischen und wohl dem Libyschen.

Das *Christentum* knüpfte die Verbindungen des Griechischen zum Syrischen, d.i. dem ostaramäischen Dialekte von Edessa, zum Koptischen, der Literatursprache der christlichen Ägypter, und über letzteres hin zum Altnubischen, der nationalen Sprache der Nubier zwischen dem 8. und 11. Jahrh. Auf welchem Wege die griechischen Streudenkmäler ins Äthiopische, der älteren einheimischen literarischen Sprache Abessiniens gelangt sind, ob direkt oder über das Aramäische oder Koptische, ist noch nicht endgültig geklärt. Bisher fehlt jede umfassendere Vorarbeit. Ebenfalls der Ausbreitung des Christentums verdanken das Armenische und das Georgische den verhältnismäßig umfangreichen Schatz griechischer Fremd- und Lehnwörter, für die wir in beiden Sprachen gründliche Untersuchungen besitzen.

Ins *byzantinische Mittelalter* gehören die Beziehungen des Griechischen zum Osmanisch-Türkischen und auch zum Arabischen, zumindest in der jüngeren Fremdwörterschicht. Die osttürkische Sprache der islamischen Literaturdenkmäler Mittelasiens hat ihre griechischen Lehnwörter jedenfalls durch Vermittlung des Iranischen erhalten.

Welche Wege griechische Wörter zurücklegen konnten, dafür sei nur ein Beispiel angeführt: Das griechische νόμος wurde über soghdisch *nom* ins

Uigurische entlehnt. Wir finden *nom* mit der Bedeutung 'Lehre, Gesetz, Religion' in uigurischen, d.h. alttürkischen Handschriften, deren Fundorte in Chinesisch-Turkestan und in Nordwestchina liegen. Ihre höchste Kulturblüte entfalteten die Uiguren zwischen dem 9. und 12. nachchristlichen Jahrhundert als Bewohner der turkestanischen Oasenstädte.

Die Nebenüberlieferung des Griechischen in den orientalischen Sprachen ist uns in einer geradezu verwirrenden Vielfalt entgegengetreten. Die Beziehungen zum Syrischen seien als Gegenstand eingehenderer Betrachtung gewählt. Während etwa in der Frage des griechischen Elements im Koptischen die Forschung in vollem Fluß ist, sich dort Meinung gegen Meinung erhebt, ist hier nach dem heutigen Stand der Forschung noch fast alles zu tun.

In *geographischer Hinsicht* wurden die Länderbezeichnungen Συρία und Ἀσσυρία jahrhundertelang promiscue verwandt. Erst der Zusammenbruch des assyrischen Reiches und die Bildung neuer Staaten auf seinem ehemaligen Territorium führte allmählich zu einer schärferen Differenzierung der beiden Namen. So setzte sich die Gepflogenheit durch, mit Syrien ein Gebiet zu benennen, das im Norden und Nordwesten von Kappadokien und Kilikien, im Süden von Ägypten und der arabischen Wüste begrenzt wird, im Osten bis zum Euphrat und im Westen bis zur Mittelmeerküste reicht. Der Gesamtname Syria blieb bestehen, auch als das Land zwischen Ptolemäern und Seleukiden geteilt worden war und die Teilgebiete neue offizielle Benennungen erhielten. Nach der Lostrennung der palästinischen und phönikischen Provinzen und der Provincia Arabia blieb dem nördlichen Rest der Name Provincia Suria, die sogenannte reliqua Syria. Ob die griechischen Namen ἡ Συρία und οἱ Σύροι sich von Anfang an mit den ethnographischen und sprachlichen Begriffen Aram und Aramäer deckten, ist nicht sicher auszumachen. Wenn die geographische Bezeichnung ἡ Συρία in weitestem Sinne mit dem aramäischen Sprachgebiet zusammenfällt, kann das nicht wundernehmen. Die Griechen, denen der Name Ἀραμαῖοι erst durch Poseidonios von Apamea bekannt geworden ist, scheinen Assyrer bzw. Syrer und Aramäer meist für dasselbe Volk gehalten zu haben. So wurde "syrisch" schließlich zur Bezeichnung der aramäischen Sprache und Schrift schlechthin.

Historisch bildete Syrien nach der Eroberung Vorderasiens durch Alexander den Großen das Kernland des Seleukidenreiches, vor allem seitdem Seleukos I. Nikator den Reichsmittelpunkt von Seleukeia in Babylonien nach Antiocheia am Orontes verlegt hatte. Er war davon überzeugt, daß hier die Hauptstadt Asiens liegen müsse, wo die makedonische Bevölkerung am stärksten vertreten war. Das Werk der ersten Seleukiden, des Seleukos I. und des Antiochos I., ist von säkularer Bedeutung gewesen. Mit den Ansiedlern aus

Hellas und Makedonien schlug vor allem in den neugegründeten städtischen Zentren, deren Namen oft von alten makedonischen Heimatstädten übernommen wurden—Edessa, Beröa, Chalcis—auch die griechische Kultur feste Wurzeln. Über die wechselvollen Geschicke des Seleukidenreiches zu berichten darf ich mir ersparen. Die unaufhörlichen Prätendentenkämpfe, in die sich auch die Ptolemäer als Herren von Ägypten und die parthische Dynastie der Arsakiden einmischten, zerrütteten jahrzehntelang das unglückliche Land. Schließlich wurde im J. 63 v.Chr. dem Königtum des letzten Seleukiden, Philippus II. Philoromaios durch Pompeius ein Ende gesetzt. Aus dem nordsyrischen Gebiet vom Amanus bis zum Karmel schuf Pompeius die römische Provinz Syria. Einen wirklichen Abschnitt bedeutet für dieses Land erst der Sieg Octavians, seit dessen Alleinherrschaft eine tatsächliche Besserung der Zustände eintrat. Als kaiserliche Provinz mit der Hauptstadt Antiocheia bildete Syrien, ähnlich Gallien im Westen, den Schwerpunkt der zivilen und militärischen Gewalt im Osten. Siebenhundert Jahre sollte Rom, seit der Reichsteilung durch Thodosius im J. 395 Ostrom, im Lande bleiben und ihm eine gewisse äußere Ruhe geben.

Sprachlich-literarisch gesehen gab es auf dem Boden des späteren christlich-syrischen sicher schon früh ein heidnisches Schrifttum im einheimisch-aramäischen Dialekte. Die ältesten syrischen Sprachdenkmäler weisen nämlich beeits eine ziemliche Festigkeit in Schreibung und Sprachform auf. Die Orthographie muß jedenfalls vor dem Schwund von auslautendem langem -ī und -ū festgesetzt worden sein. Dieser Schwund war erst *nach* der Regelung der konsonantischen Orthographie eingetreten, besaß aber schon in der ältesten erhaltenen Literatur Geltung. Das pagane syrische Schriftltum ist bis auf geringe Reste untergegangen. Es soll versucht werden, den Einfluß des Griechischen darzustellen, soweit er in ihnen erkennbar ist. Zum Teil Originaldokumente, sind diese Überreste im allgemeinen nach Ort lund Zeit genauer bestimmbar. Damit sind aber bereits zwei der Gesichtspunkte beachtet, die Franz Rosenthal an der vorhererwähnten Bearbeitung der griechischen und lateinischen Lehnwörter in Talmud, Midrasch und Targum durch Samuel Krauss vermißte, nämlich die zeitliche und örtliche Scheidung des Fremdwörtermaterials. Der dritte Gesichtspunkt Rosenthals, die kulturgeschichtliche Scheidung der Fremdwörter, soll im Rahmen des betreffenden Dokuments berücksichtigt werden. Diesen Weg hat jüngst auch der Koptizist Lefort in seinem Artikel "Gréco-copte" als den wissenschaftlich einzig gangbaren bezeichnet. Jedenfalls werden wir bei diesem Vorgehen ein fundiertes Material erhalten zur Auswertung durch Gräzisten, in Verbindung mit dem Kenner der nachklassischen griechischen Formen auch durch den Semitisten und nicht zuletzt durch den Kulturhistoriker.

Der griechische Einfluß in den Resten des paganen syrischen Schrifttums stellt uns vor ein *Problem*, auf das ein helles Schlaglicht geworfen wird durch die Rubrik, unter der Eduard Schwyzer die Beziehungen des Griechischen zum Syrischen in seiner "Griechischen Grammatik" anführte. Danach wären diese Beziehungen durch die Ausbreitung des Christentums entstanden. Wird dieser Ansatz durch das Texmaterial bestimmt heidnischer oder vorchristlicher Provenienz bestätigt?

Obschon das Material verhältnismäßig gering ist, muß es doch zuerst zum Sprechen gebracht werden. Es kann uns neue Einsichten vermitteln. Texte paganer Herkunft, die später im großkirchlichen Geiste überarbeitet wurden, sind beiseitegelassen worden, so der Aḥīqār-Roman, von dem Bruchstücke bereits in den Elephantinepapyri vorliegen, oder das in den Thomasakten eingeschlossene Lied vom Königssohn und der Perle.

Möglicherweise noch dem 1. Jahrh. n.Chr. gehört der syrische Brief an, den aus römischer Gefangenschaft ein wohl aus Samosata stammender Mārā bar Serapion an seinen nach dem Großvater benannten Sohn Serapion richtete. Diesen Brief hatte schon Heinrich Ewald, einer der Göttinger Sieben, der 1837–48 an der Universität Tübingen lehrte, unmittelbar in die Nähe der jüdischen Katastrophe vom J. 70 n.Chr. hinaufrücken wollen. In unserem Jahrhundert ist Anton Baumstark abweichend von seiner "Geschichte der syrischen Literatur" zu demselben Zeitansatz durchgestoßen und bringt die Deportation des Mārā aus seiner Vaterstadt in Zusammenhang mit dem Vorgehen der Römer gegen Samosata, von dem Josephus im "Jüdischen Krieg" berichtet.

Den Inhalt des Briefes, der in einer Abschrift des 7. Jahrh. erhalten ist, bilden Mahnungen und Warnungen. Mārā bar Serapion hat von dem Lehrer seines in der Ferne weilenden Sohnes erfreuliche Nachrichten über den Fleiß und den Eifer des jungen Mannes erhalten und fühlt sich nun trotz seines Gefangenenelends gedrängt, dem Sohne seine freudige Anerkennung auszusprechen, zugleich ihm in ernsten Worten die Wahrheit ans Herz zu legen, daß nicht Reichtum und Ehre den Menschen glücklich mache, sondern allein die Weisheit. Mārā ist kein Christ, er steht, wie Schulthess gezeigt hat, auf dem Boden der stoischen Popularphilosophie. Doch ist er dem Christentum gegenüber von wohlwollender Gesinnung und erwähnt unter den großen bei der Mitwelt verkannten Männern außer Sokrates und Pythagoras auch den "weisen König der Juden," der von seinem Volke mit Undank belohnt wurde und nunmehr in seinen "neuen Gesetzen" fortlebe.

Bedenkt man die Bildung des Verfassers, der an der hellenistischen Kultur durchaus Anteil hatte, und in seinem ungezwungenen und vertraulichen Privatbriefe keineswegs wissenschaftlicher Termini bedurfte, so darf man vielleicht sagen, daß die im Briefe des Mārā bar Serapion vorkommenden Wörter griechischen Ursprungs im damaligen Syrisch ziemliches Heimatrecht besaßen. Eine Übersetzung des Briefes aus dem Griechischen ist durch die rein syrische Sprache und das angesichts des Inhalts besonders beachtenswerte fast durchweg echt syrische Sprachgut der Schrift völlig ausgeschlossen.

Begriffe aus Philosophie und Ethik sind es vornehmlich, die den Fremwörterbestand der Schrift ausmachen:

ܦܝܠܣܘܦܘܬܐ	'Weltweisheit', mit Hilfe der syrischen Abstraktendung *-ūṯā* aus φιλοσοφία gebildet;
ܢܳܡܳܘܣܳܐ	'Gesetz', umgeformt aus griech. νόμος nach dem syrischen Nominaltyp *qāṭōlā*;
ܐܶܣܟܺܝܡܳܐ	'Haltung' von griech. σχῆμα in der Wendung ܢܛܪ ܐܶܣܟܺܝܡܶܗ 'seinen sittlichen Stand wahren';
ܦܪܘܣ	als status absolutus zu ܦܘܪܣܐ aus griechisch πόρος 'Mittel, Weg' bezeugt schon durch das Auftreten in den verschiedenen Status ein hohes Alter der Entlehnung.
ܐܰܓܽܘܢܳܐ	aus griech. ἀγών steht in der Wendung ܐܰܓܽܘܢܳܐ ܕܚܰܝ̈ܐ 'Lebenskampf';
ܩܪ̈ܝܣܐ	'Unglücksfälle' ist Plural zu ܩܪܝܣܐ, das aus griech. καιρός gebildet wurde. An anderer Stelle weist dagegen der Zusammenhang auf die für dieses Wort gewöhnlich zu erwartende Bedeutung 'Krieg' hin.

Aus dem Gebiete der Politik stammt ܛܘܪܳܢܳܐ 'Tyrann'. Das griech. τύραννος hat bei seiner Übernahme ins Syrische einen Vokalwandel nach dem Muster der syrischen Nominalform *quṭāl* mitgemacht.

In zwei Fällen sind aus griechischen Nomina syrische Verben entwickelt worden: Aus ζεῦγος 'Paar, Gespann' entstand die Paelform ܙܰܘܶܓܢ 'wir verbanden', aus πεῖσαι wurde das Afel ܐܰܦܺܝܣ 'er überredete, überzeugte' gebildet, das an der betreffenden Stelle allerdings fraglich ist.

Ein Beweis der Reinheit der Sprache in diesem Briefe ist es, wenn ein Fachausdruck der stoiischen Philosophie echt syrisch wiedergegeben wird: ܡܰܣܩܳܬܳܐ ܐܶܢܶܝܢ ܓܶܝܪ ܘܡܰܚܬܳܬܳܐ ܐܶܢܶܝܢ ܕܙܰܒܢ̈ܐ 'denn sie, d.h. die Dinge, die du auf der Welt siehst, sind das Auf und Ab der Zeiten'. ܡܰܣܩܳܬܳܐ und ܡܰܚܬܳܬܳܐ finden sich bei Marc Aurel als ἄνω κάτω Bei Seneca, *De tranquillitate animi,* ist zu lesen: "in tanta rerum sursum ac deorsum euntium versatione."

Als ältestes datiertes Sprachdenkmal größeren Umfangs ist in der sogenannten Edessenischen Chronik im vollen Wortlaut ein "Bericht über die Hochwasserkatastrophe" erhalten geblieben, von welcher die Stadt Edessa, das heutige Urfa, im November des J. 201 n.Chr. betroffen wurde. Der Text war noch vor dem Übertritt des Königs Abgar IX. zum Christentum entstanden und ist den Akten des edessenischen Archivs einverleibt worden. Der Bericht, der im Druck einen Umfang von zwei Oktavseiten hat, enthält an griechischen Wörtern aus dem Bereiche des Bauwesens

ܐܣܛܘܐ	'Säulenhalle' von griech. στοά,
ܦܘܪܓܣܐ	'Turm' von griech. πύργος,
ܩܛܪܩܛܐ	'Schleuse' von griech. καταῤῥάκτης,
ܡܘܟܠܐ	'Riegel, Querbalken' von μοχλός
ܠܡܦܐܕܐ	'Fackel' ist vom griech. casus obliquus λαμπάδος oder λαμπάδα her entlehnt worden.
ܐܓܘܪܣܐ	aus griech. ἀγροί steht neben echt syrischem ܦܘܪ̈ܣܐ in der Bedeutung 'Gehöfte', und
ܐܪܟܘܢ	'Archiv', welches dem Bereich der Administration angehört, aus griech. ἀρχεῖον.

Der Bericht über die Hochwasserkatastrophe hat somit nur verhältnismäßig wenige Bezeichnungen materieller Güter dem Griechischen entnommen.

Aus dem Jahr 243 n.Chr. stammt das älteste *nicht auf Stein geschriebene* Originaldokument des edessenischen Syrisch. Es wurde 1933 bei der Ausgrabung der Festung Dura-Europos am mittleren Euphrat nahe bei den Ruinen der Synagoge der Stadt gefunden. Die auf Pergament geschriebene Urkunde wurde in Edessa ausgestellt und handelt vom Verkauf einer Sklavin, den die Gemahlin eines vornehmen edessenischen Bürgers im 6. Jahre des Kaisers Gordian III., also 243 n.Chr., an einen Einwohner von Ḥarrān, dem antiken Carrhae, vollzog. Charakteristisch für das Dokument ist die Zusammensetzung der Eigennamen aus römischen und orientalischen Elementen. Letztere zeigen aramäische, persische und überraschenderweise auch assyrisch-babylonische Bestandteile. Christliche Elemente fehlen.

Um zu einer gerechten Würdigung des griechischen Fremdwörterschatzes zu kommen, der in diesem Text enthalten ist, muß von der in solchen Urkunden üblichen griechischen Phraseologie abgesehen werden. Nicht heranziehen dürfen wir z.B. die griechischen Wörter der Kaisertitulatur, die zur Datierung verwendet wird. Es heißt da: "Im sechsten Jahre des Αὐτοκράτωρ Καῖσαρ Μάρκος Ἀντώνιος Γορδιανὸς Εὐσεβὴς Εὐτυχὴς Σεβαστός, d.i. Imperator Caesar Marcus Antonius Gordianus Pius Felix Augustus. Ähnlich wie in anderen Dura-Texten erfolgt noch eine zusätzliche Datierung nach dem römischen Konsulat, das durch syrisch ܗܦܛܐ aus griech. ὑπατεία bezeichnet wird. Auch die Datierung, die nach den Jahren "der Freiheit der berühmten Antoniniana Edessa, der κολωνία μητροπόλις Aurelia Alexandriana" rechnet, darf nicht für den Fremdwörterbestand berücksichtigt werden. Da hier das Jahr 31 der “Freiheit” gezählt wird, ist zu schließen, daß Edessa seit 213/214 colonia geworden war. Die Bezeichnung “Aurelia Antoniniana” erfolgte zu Ehren des Gründers der κολωνία, des Kaisers Caracalla.

Endlich ist noch angegeben, unter wessen Strategie (στρατηγία) der Verkauf abgeschlossen wurde. Während der στρατηγός, syrisch ܐܣܛܪܛܓܐ auf der Rückseite des Dokuments mit diesem Titel gezeichnet hat, wird anstelle von στρατηγία syrisch ܐܣܛܪܛܓܘܬܐ gebraucht, eine Weiterbildung aus dem vorigen mit der syrischen Abstraktendung *-ūṯā*. Der eine der beiden Strategen ist ähnlich wie der Vertreter Roms ἱππεὺς ῾Ρωμαῖος ‘eques Romanus’. Am Schluß des Dokuments erklärt der ܐܪܟܘܢܐ ܡܢ ܦܘܠܝܣ ܕܬܪܬܥܣܪܐ “der ἄρχων der zwölften φυλή, das Schriftstück im Namen seiner Frau geschrieben zu haben.

Über solche formelhafte Wendungen hinaus bleibt neben den genannten Titulaturen schließlich nur ein Appellativum übrig, das vom Einfluß der herrschenden Ordnungsmacht zeugt, nämlich ܢܡܘܣܐ ‘Gesetz’ von griech. νόμος.

Zur Sachgruppe Schrift- und Buchwesen gehört das schon im Hochwasserbericht erwähnte Wort für ‘Archiv’. Gemeint ist das Archiv von Edessa, in welchem das Original der Urkunde hinterlegt werden sollte. Die Zweitschrift des Dokuments, syr. ܦܪܘܡܝܘܢ aus griech. παρόμοιον, sollte im Besitze des Käufers bleiben.

In das Sachgebiet Handel und Verkehr fällt der Kaufpreis, der für die Sklavin zu entrichten war: 700 δυνάρια, syr. ܕܝܢܪܐ.

Noch bleibt das *epigraphische Material* sicher vorchristlicher Herkunft zu betrachten. Es beginnt mit der Grabinschrift des Ma^{c}nū bei Serrīn, die durch die Datierung 385 der seleukidischen Ära = 73 n.Chr. die älteste datierte syrische Inschrift ist. Von Bedeutung ist neben diesem Epitaph aus der älteren Zeit nur noch die Inschrift auf einer der beiden Säulen, die sich auf der Zitadelle von Urfa-Edessa hoch über der Stadt erheben und in vorchristlicher Zeit den Dioskuren geweiht waren. Die Inschrift stammt vom Erbauer der Säule. Neben diesen beiden bedeutenden vorchristlichen Inschriften gibt es noch eine ganze Anzahl anderer, die meist nicht sehr ergiebig sind und deren Aufzählung zu weit führen würde.

Aus diesem Material gehört zur Sachgruppe Handwerk und Künste die Bezeichnung für ‘Standbild’, ܐܕܪܝܛܐ, das auf den griech. Akkusativ ἀνδριάντα zurückgeht. Die Übernahme im casus obliquus und die Assimilation des *n* an das *ṭ* beweisen, daß das Wort im Dialekte von Edessa heimisch war.

Im Bereich Famile und Gesellschaft begegnet in einer Inschrift wohl noch des 2. Jahrh. n.Chr. aus Sumatar Harabesi etwa 100 km südöstlich Urfa das Wort ܐܦܠܘܬܪܐ ‘Freigelassener’ von griech. ἀπελεύθερος. Es steht in folgendem Zusammenhang:

> Dies ist was gemacht hat Bar Nahar, Sohn des Dinai, Toparch des Arabergaus, zu Ehren des Aurelius Hafsai, des Sohnes des Bar Kalba, des ἀπελεύθεροσ (d.h. Freigelassenen) des Antoninus Caesar, seines Herrn.

In der christlichen syrischen Literatur ist ἀπελεύθερος nicht mehr belegt.

Damit sind die griechischen Elemente in den erhaltenen syrischen Inschriften paganer Herkunft sämtlich aufgeführt. Die überaus knappe Zahl könnte zufällig erscheinen, sie findet aber eine schöne Bestätigung im neuesten epigraphischen Material, das vor zwei Jahren von dem englischen Gelehrten Segal aus dem Raume Sumatar Harabesi veröffentlicht wurde. Zwei der Inschriften sind für das Jahr 164–65 n.Chr. datiert. Weder sie noch die zwölf anderen etwa derselben Zeit angehörenden Epigraphe enthalten trotz teilweise erheblichen Umfangs ein einziges griechisches Wort.

Das gesamte greifbare syrische Textmaterial vorchristlicher Herkunft ist nunmehr in seinen Beziehungen zum Griechischen vorgestellt worden, gleich ob es sich um literarische Texte handelte oder um Originalurkunden auf Stein und Pergament. Auf die strengere Scheidung in Lehnwörter und eigentliche Fremdwörter konnte nicht eingegangen werden, ebensowenig wurde die Frage der Bedeutungs- und Bildungslehnwörter angeschnitten.

Das bisher Erkannte darf trotzdem zur Antwort benutzt werden auf die eingangs gestellte Frage, ob die Beziehungen des Griechischen zum Syrischen, mit anderen Worte, ob die Nebenüberlieferung des Griechischen im Syrischen auf die Ausbreitung des Christentums zurückzuführen sei.

Die Untersuchung ergab, daß diese Beziehungen vor dem Christentum und unabhängig von seiner Ausbreitung bestanden. Der Großteil der übernommenen Wörter betraf Gegenstände der materiellen Kultur. Nur im Briefe des Mārā bar Serapion kamen auch die Bereiche der Philosophie und Ethik zur Geltung. So wird durch die Texte bestätigt, was Theodor Nöldeke in seiner bedeutsamen Besprechung des 5. Bandes der "Römischen Geschichte" Theodor Mommsen entgegengehalten hatte, daß er sich nämlich die Hellenisierung Syriens in sprachlicher Hinsicht zu ausgedehnt vorstellte, daß sie weit mehr in der Übernahme materieller Güter bestanden habe.

Wer nach diesen Darlegungen ein syrisches Wörterbuch zur Hand nimmt und schon bei flüchtigem Durchmustern die Unmenge griechischer Wörter bemerkt, wird mit Recht fragen, wie und wann diese Flut eindrang.

Es ist, wie die parallele Untersuchung der frühesten Texte christlicher Provenienz zeigen würde, die Ausbreitung des Christentums und die mit ihr jäh ansteigende Entwicklung in den Beziehungen der geistigen Kultur, die diese starke Übernahme griechischen Lehn- und Fremdwortgutes verursacht hat.

In ihrer Blütezeit weisen das Syrische und, wie erwähnt, das im 3. Jahrh. n.Chr. zur Literatursprache geadelte Koptische einen hohen griechischen Wortanteil auf, das Koptische eher noch einen höheren als das Syrische. Es steht heute wohl fest, daß der griechische Einfluß in den beiden Sprachen eine wesentlich verschiedene Entwicklung genommen hat. Den Grund für diese verschiedene Entwicklung vermag der Sprachforscher allein nicht mehr anzugeben. Die *Geschichte* zeigt, wie verschieden stark der griechisch-makedonische Bevölkerungsanteil in den beiden führenden hellenistischen Staaten der Ptolemäer und der Seleukiden war, und wird von da aus die Antwort geben können im Sinne des Referats, das Hermann Bengtson auf dem Historikertag Marburg 1951 über die Bedeutung der Eingeborenenbevölkerung in den hellenistischen Oststaaten gehalten hat.

Syriac Loanwords in Classical Armenian

John A. C. Greppin

That there is Syriac vocabulary in Classical Armenian has never been doubted,[1] for since 302 C.E., when the Armenian state embraced Christianity, the Syriac church had competed against the Greek church for Armenia's submission, a triumph that could be achieved only if the Syriac language prevailed in the Armenian liturgy. But the earliest Armenian Christian priests became skilled in both Greek and Syriac, and, having developed their own alphabet, translated religious documents from Syriac and Greek into their newly recorded language. This achievement created the independent Armenian church but, because of the original languages of the translated material, left numerous Greek and Syrian loanwords in Armenian.[2] This cultural closeness brought

1. Never, that is, since people have cared about such questions. Hübschmann, in his *Armenische Grammatik* (1897), 281–321, listed 133 correspondences, though he noted many were doubtful. However, some have suggested that these Syriac loans were actually more ancient, representing Akkadian vocabulary instead. Of this, more will be said later.

2. The Armenian language was set in written form about 405 C.E., in order to have a vehicle into which to translate Christian documents and to have the liturgy in the native language; accordingly

lexical loans that appear in the earliest of Armenian writings, both in literature translated from Syriac into Armenian and in original writing in Armenian. To a great extent, these Syriac loanwords were of religious substance. Examples of this class are Arm. *Ադին* (*Adin*) 'Eden', known in the Armenian versions of Ephrem; but in Gregory of Narek,[3] this existed alongside Arm. *Եդեմ* (*Edem*), from Gk. Ἐδέμ, which is the form that regularly appears in the Armenian Bible. There is other rather specific Syriac vocabulary that largely does not appear outside the Armenian Bible.[4] Here we find such Syriac terms as:

1. *ամտան* (*amtan*) 'cloak', Syr. ܐܡܠܐ (*āmellā*).
2. *զոպայ* (*zopay*) 'hyssop, a holy water sprinkler', Syr. ܙܘܦܐ (*zōpā*).
3. *խմոր* (*xmor*) 'yeast', Syr. ܚܡܝܪܐ (*xəmīrā*).
4. *փրկել* (*pᶜrkel*) 'to redeem, save', Syr. ܦܪܩ (*pəraq*).
5. *քաքար* (*kᶜakᶜar*) 'type of cake', Syr. ܚܚܘܪܬܐ (*xāxurtā*).
6. *թարշիշ* (*tᶜaršiš*) 'precious stone, the tarsus', Syr. ܬܪܫܝܫ (*taršīš*).

These words above are very clearly terms primarily of religious use or words appearing in a sacerdotal text, such as 'hyssop', which probably had no Armenian pre-Christian equivalent. In addition to these narrowly subscribed loans, others—and these are far more common—prevailed not only in religious works but in secular literature as well, much as in the fifth century works of Armenian history. These would include such terms as Arm. *ծնծղայ* (*cncłay*)[5] 'cymbal', Arm. *հեգ* (*heg*)[6] 'syllable, spelling', and Arm. *հաշիւ* (*hašiw*)[7] 'reckoning'. But there were other loans that imply that the exchange of Syriac words was the result of bilingualism, at least on the part of educated Armenian clerics. Note such terms as *թարգմանել* (*tᶜargmanel*)[8] 'to translate' or *տղայ* (*tłay*)[9] 'a youth' and *պողոտայ* (*połotay*)[10] 'street, road'. These have no special theological value and came into Armenian through bilingual speakers as easily as French words enter

---

the Armenians did not need to rely on Greek or Syriac documents and thereby had a church independent of these two early Christian powers.

3. Narekatsi, a writer of the 12th century, was a great one for mining the more curious vocabulary of the earliest Armenian writing and bringing it into his poetry.

4. Armenian does not differ in the substance of its loans of Syriac origin from the substance of its loans from Greek (though these are more numerous). A great bulk of loans from both these languages was of an ecclesiastical nature, taken directly from ecclesiastical or scriptural sources. A good portion, however, were words of general usage, and we will discuss them below.

5. Syr. ܨܨܠܐ (*ṣeṣṣəlā*).

6. Syr. ܗܓܐ (*həgā*).

7. Syr. ܚܫܝܒ (*xešīw*).

8. Syr. ܬܪܓܡܢܐ (*targəmānā*).

9. Syr. ܛܠܝܐ (*ṭalyā*).

10. Syr. ܦܠܛܝܐ (*plāṭīā*).

English. Thus we see that there are various types of Syriac loans in Armenian. First, there are the words that are most restricted to a religious environment, often appearing only in the scriptures; these are followed by religious terms that appear not only in ecclesiastical tractates but in secular sources as well, such as in the fifth-century historians Yeghishé or Lazar of Parp; and finally, there are the Syriac terms that have no special religious value and which appear commonly in Armenian speech and letters, some to this day.

And though Armenian linguistics is a sober and thoughtful discipline, stray philological heresies can develop from time to time. One heretical school was to argue that certain of these Syriac terms were in fact from Akkadian. This ill-founded linguistic conviction enjoyed, especially in Soviet Armenia, no small support.[11] Such correspondences as the ones that follow (among many others) initially found a warm reception:

1a. Arm. խաշ (*xaš*) 'pennroyal', *Mentha pulegium* L. Akk. *ẖašu* 'thyme'.
2a. Arm. ցից (*cʿicʿ*) 'stake, pole', Akk. *ṣiṣṣu* 'id'.
3a. Arm. ագուռ (*aguṙ*) 'brick', Akk. *agurru* 'id'.

Yet, for each of these, a simpler choice presented itself:

1b. Syr. ܚܫܐ (*ḥāšā*) 'thyme'.
2b. Syr. ܨܨܐ (*ṣiṣṣā*) 'nail'.
3b. Syr. ܐܓܘܪܐ (*āgūrā*) 'brick'.

The processes performed here could have been performed for most other of the so-called "Akkadian" words; those that had no Syriac equivalent could be shown to have been derived from Arabic or Persian (presumably via Aramaic or Arabic). Thus, reference to Semitic languages later than Akkadian seems more appropriate.

Syriac loans into Armenian frequently continued on into the Caucasus,[12] and we find numerous examples of Syriac vocabulary not only in Georgian[13]

11. For a survey, with bibliography, see my "'Akkadian' Loan Words in Armenian," *Annual of Armenian Linguistics* 10 (1989) 73–83.

12. Before the intrusion, via Armenian, of biblical vocabulary into Georgian, earlier Armenian words were absorbed. Both these words probably came to Georgian secondarily via Mingrelian; here see Gerhard Deeters, "Armenisch und Südkaukasisch: Ein Beitrag zur Frage der Sprachmischung," *Caucasica* 3 (1926) 37–82, esp. p. 46.

13. They came, in almost all incidents, via Armenian; it is likely that the Georgians consulted the Armenian version of the scriptures as they prepared their translation. For instance, Arm. վաշ (*vaš*) 'excellent, bravo!' is derived by loan from Luvian *wasu* 'good', yet we find this term in Georgian (*vaša*) in the exact same places in the Georgian Bible (e.g., Job 31:29, Ps 34:25) as in the Armenian, and it is most unlikely that the Georgians had contact with the Luvians in the first millennium B.C.E., while Armenians surely did.

but firmly settled in such kindred Kartvelian languages as Laz, Mingrelian, and Svan. In addition, there is passage from Kartvelian to Tsova-Tush,[14] while secondary derivatives spun off from Armenian into Udi and the Daghestani languages. The occasional correspondences found in the northernmost of the northeast Caucasian languages, Ingush, and Chechen, are probably secondary from Tsova-Tush. The original movement from Armenian into Georgian and Udi was no doubt the result of Christian influence.[15] The following are a few examples of the northward dispersion of Syrian loanwords from Armenia into the Caucasus.

1. Syr. ܫܒܬܐ (*šabbaθā*) 'the Sabbath', Grg. *šabati*, Tsova-Tush *šabat*.[16]
2. Syr. ܡܚܛܐ (*maxaṭṭā*) 'awl, large needle', Arm. մախաթ (*maxat*^{c}), Grg. *maxati*, Chechen *maxa*, Tsova-Tush *max*, Udi *maxat*.
3. Syr. ܡܓܠܐ (*maggəlā*) 'sickle', Arm. մանգաղ (*mangał*), Grg. *mangali*.[17] The appearance of the term in Persian as منگال (*mangāl*; cf. Arabic *minjāl*) is probably brought about through Aramaic intercession.
4. Syr. ܟܟܪܐ (*kakkərā*), Arm. քանքար (*k*^{c}*ank*^{c}*ar*), Grg. *kankari* 'talent (weight)'.[18]

There is one final type of Armenian word said to be inherited from Syriac that may, however, like *kakkərā* above, find its origin in the "Mediterranean" realm instead. I have explored this type of word before,[19] giving examples of vocabulary that is widely distributed among the diverse ancient and modern

14. In addition to the Kartvelian family, the Caucasus supports two other distinct language families: the northwest Caucasian family, containing languages such as Abkhaz and Circassian; and the languages of the northeast Caucasus: these include the Lezghian subgroup, which contains Udi, and the Nakh subgroup, which contains Chechen, Ingush, and Tsova-Tush (Bats), as well as the Avar-Andi and the Lak-Dargwa subgroups.

15. Udi, the contemporary term for the ancient Caucasian Albanians, developed Christianity under the influence of the Armenians; indeed, many Udi speakers even took Armenian Christian names. And though the Udi developed an alphabet, they never made much headway on a translation of the Bible. On these matters, see my "Language of the Caucasian Albanians," *Folia Slavica* 5 (1982) 161–180.

16. The Udi equivalent, *šabat*, came to mean 'good, excellent', from 'the good day'.

17. The term is continued in other Caucasian languages: Laz and Mingrelian *magane*, Tsova-Tush *manga*, Udi *manga*; the term is also known in Aghul, another Daghestani language, as *maqqal*, and in Chechen as *mangal*.

18. The term appears also in Egyptian as *krkr*, and it is possible that the word is not original in Semitic, for it is not a productive root.

19. "The Survival of Ancient Anatolian and Mesopotamian Vocabulary until the Present," *JNES* 50 (1991) 203–7; and "Mediterranean Botanical Loanwords in Classical Armenian," in *Proceedings of the Fifth International Conference on Armenian Linguistics* (ed. John A. C. Greppin; Delmar, N.Y.: Caravan Books, 1992) 61–76.

languages of Western Asia and the Caucasus.[20] I would like to add another such term, the word for 'olive, olive tree, and (olive) oil', which in Armenian is ձէթ (*jēt*), and which is widely known in Semitic in the root √*z-y-t*: Syr. ܙܝܬܐ (*zaitā*), Heb. זית (*zayit*), and so on. In Kartvelian the term is known in Georgian *zeti*, Mingrelian *zet*, Svan *zeṭy*; in the northwest Caucasian languages, we find Abkhaz *azet*, Circassian *zeyitin*; in the northeast Caucasian languages, examples appear in Tsova-Tush *zet*, Udi *zeyt*. The term additionally appears in Egyptian *dt*, Copt δοειτ.[21] Clearly this term for the olive is a term functioning well beyond Semitic. Further, in Semitic, the root √*z-y-t* itself is not productive; accordingly, we have no reason to conclude that this term was original in Semitic. It was more likely derived from another language, possibly now lost, spoken in Asia Minor.[22]

20. These include examples such as Arm. առվոտ (*aṙvot*), Arabic رطبة (*riṭbah*) 'alfalfa, the fresh one', Syr. *raṭab* 'be moist', (√*r-ṭ-b*), Grg. *alaverdi* (dialects of Kaxian and Kartlian) 'alfalfa'. Also: Arm. փերփեր (*pᶜerpᶜer*) 'purslane', Arab. فرفح / فر فحين (*farfaḥ* / *farfaḥīn*), Syr. ܦܪܦܚܝܢܐ (*farfaḥīnā*), Grg. *parpina*, Gk. πέπλιον, πεπλίς, 'id'.

21. Here, see also the essay by K. Treimer, "Altarm. *jētᶜ*, *jitᶜeni* 'Öl, Ölbaum'," *Orbis* 5 (1956) 216–21.

22. Erman, *ZDMG* 46, p. 123 (apud Immanuel Löw, *Die Flora der Juden* [Vienna, 1924–34] 2.387), suggests that the Semitic terms are borrowed from Egyptian, "aber die Herkunft des Wortes ist strittig," a suggestion that remains valid to this day.

The Modern Chaldean Pronunciation of Classical Syriac

Robert D. Hoberman

Classical and Vernacular Pronunciation of Syriac

While the traditional pronunciations of Syriac have been described briefly in most grammars of the language, these descriptions are unsatisfactory in that they treat the classical language in isolation from the native languages of the readers. This essay describes how Classical Syriac is pronounced in one modern community, the Chaldeans. The modern Chaldeans are speakers of Aramaic from northern Iraq, members of the Chaldean Catholic Church, which is historically related to the (so-called Nestorian) Church of the East. It is important to examine the traditional pronunciation of Syriac against the background of the speakers' colloquial language for several reasons. In the first place, oral use of Classical Syriac does not exist in isolation; it is one part of the linguistic repertoire of a living contemporary community and, to different extents, of most or all of its members. Consequently, some details of its pronunciation can be understood only in the light of their contemporary speech habits. In the second place, the historical development of the tradition over many centuries went along hand in hand with the historical development of modern vernacular Aramaic, so that they shared many features.

It is sometimes said that there are two "dialects" of Classical Syriac, a western or Jacobite (also Maronite) dialect and an eastern or Nestorian one. The word "dialect" is inappropriate for these varieties, which differ only in rather superficial phonology, in script, and in a few details of morphophonology, but not (insofar as it has been reported in the standard grammars) in morphology, in syntax, or in vocabulary. If these were real dialects that had had separate lives as the vernaculars of separate speech communities, they would differ in all of these respects. In reality, they are two traditions of copying, of annotating with orthographic diacritics, and of pronouncing a body of sacred and otherwise canonical literature. The Classical Syriac language and texts, cultivated by speakers of Aramaic languages, continued to develop and change long after the time when Syriac itself ceased to exist as a vernacular. The pronunciation of the classical language changed, in part, along with the sound changes that the vernacular Aramaic languages underwent. For example, it is no coincidence that the change of [a:] to [o:] is reflected, with some differences of detail, in the vernacular Aramaic languages of Maᶜlūla and Ṭūr ᶜAbdīn (Ṭuroyo) and in the reading of Classical Syriac by Maronites and Syrian Orthodox Jacobites because the Maronite and Syrian Orthodox scholars who cultivated this pronunciation were speakers of vernacular Aramaic dialects that closely resembled the ancestors of modern Maᶜlūla and Ṭuroyo Aramaic. Such vernacular influence became enshrined in the rules for reading that were transmitted in the schools of those denominations.[1] In the relatively infrequent instances in which a speaker of Modern Aramaic follows a Syriac reading tradition with a history separate from that of his vernacular dialect, the divergences are striking. Thus a Syrian Orthodox priest from the village of Barṭille, near Mosul, pronounces the word for 'house' as [bé:θa] in his native Northeastern Neo-Aramaic vernacular, but as [báyto] in Classical Syriac. For the Chaldeans, the case is otherwise. Their vernacular Aramaic language and their Syriac reading tradition are closely allied.

1. That the two varieties of Syriac were not dialects in themselves but reflected influence from vernacular Aramaic languages insofar as they were not artifacts of the separate schools was pointed out by Theodor Nöldeke in the introduction to his Syriac grammar (*Kurzgefasste syrische Grammatik* [2d ed.; Leipzig, 1898]; repr. Darmstadt: Wissenschaftliche Buchgesellschaft, 1966; trans. James A. Crichton, *Compendious Syriac Grammar* [London: Williams and Norgate, 1904] xxxiii), in a comment that was omitted in Crichton's English translation:

> Gewiss wird die Verschiedenheit der Volksdialecte von Alters her auf die Lautform des Syrischen im Munde der Gebildeten verschiedner Gegenden nicht ohne Einfluss gewesen sein. . . .

The tradition of pronunciation that is described here is not merely a reading pronunciation. On the one hand, many Syriac texts are known and recited by memory, such as the Lord's Prayer (part of the corpus we are describing here); on the other hand, many Syriac words are used in speaking modern vernacular Aramaic. The Chaldean pronunciation of Syriac therefore encompasses a range from an ideal normative code for pronouncing written words, which is described by Mingana, to the variable pronunciation of Syriac words borrowed into colloquial Aramaic speech. In this paper I have concentrated on the actual (as opposed to ideal) pronunciation attested in reciting liturgical texts.

The Chaldeans refer to their classical language as "(Classical) Aramaic" or "Chaldean," in Syriac as *ʾārāmāyāʾ* or *kaldāyāʾ*, in Arabic as (*al-lugha*) *al-ʾārāmiyya al-kaldāniyya*. I will use the term *Syriac* for the classical language (justified by Mingana's use of the term Syriaque) and reserve Chaldean for the people and the church.

Sources of Data

This essay is based on evidence from a corpus of transcriptions of actual liturgical and vernacular Syriac/Aramaic discourse and from a textbook presentation of normative Syriac pronunciation.

The Corpus

The first of two liturgical transcriptions is a tape recording made in 1988 by Monsignor Edward J. Bikoma in Chicago of several brief liturgical texts and a passage from the New Testament. This recording is transcribed below in its entirety. All unattributed phonetic transcriptions in this paper are from this source, designated REC. The second liturgical source, designated DLB, consists of transcriptions of Syriac texts into Arabic (with short vowels indicated for most passages) and English-based Latin scripts in Father Michael J. Bazzi's edition of the Divine Liturgy.[2] The pronunciation that this represents can be deduced

Dieser Einfluss der Mundarten auf die Aussprache des Syrischen kann mit jener Trennung [of Syrians in the Roman and Persian empires and of their Monophysite and Nestorian affiliations] nur gewachsen sein. Wenn wir nun so *nestorianische* oder *ostsyrische* Formen auf der einen, *jacobitische* oder *westsyrische* auf der andern Seite haben, so ist darin theilweise ein wirklicher Einfluss dialectischer Spaltung zu erkennen; freilich beruhen aber viele dieser Unterschiede nur auf künstlicher Festsetzung durch die Schulen.

2. Michael J. Bazzi (ed.), *The Divine Liturgy according to the Eastern Chaldean Catholic Rite* (El Cajon, Calif.: St. Peter Chaldean Catholic Church, 1988).

on the basis of one passage, the Lord's Prayer, which we have both in Father Bazzi's Arabic transcription[3] and in Monsignor Bikoma's recording. Likewise, the English transcription can be interpreted on the basis of the texts that are given in both English and Arabic scripts. Two additional sources of the spoken language are the Syriac words that appear in Monsignor Bikoma's colloquial Aramaic speech[4] and in the texts and glossary in Georg Krotkoff's book on a vernacular Aramaic dialect similar to those of Zakho and Tel Kepe, spoken by Chaldeans from the town of Aradhin.[5]

The Description by Mingana

Finally, Alphonse Mingana's *Clef de la langue araméenne ou Grammaire complète et pratique des deux dialectes syriaques occidental et oriental*[6] provides evidence not of actual practice but of an ideal, normative pronunciation. L'abbé Mingana taught Syriac at the Séminaire Syro-Chaldéen in Mosul and may be regarded as (nearly, if not literally) a teacher of the teachers of Fathers Bazzi and Bikoma.

Monsignor Bikoma is from the town of Zakho, Iraq; his vernacular Aramaic is documented in a separate report.[7] Father Bazzi is from Tel Kepe; the dialect of that town has been documented by Sabar.[8]

Transcription Conventions

A work on the relation between sound and script is no place for the kind of classical reconstructed transcription that is usual in grammars and secondary works. In this paper, Syriac letters, sounds, and words are represented in two ways: (1) The actual pronunciation of Syriac, whether taken directly from REC or deduced from DLB, is represented in a broad phonetic transcription in

3. Ibid., 12 and 46.

4. Monsignor Bikoma's vernacular Zakho dialect is described in my report, "Chaldean Aramaic of Zakho," in *Semitica: Serta philologica Constantino Tsereteli dicata* (ed. Riccardo Contini, Fabrizio A. Pennacchietti, and Mauro Tosco; Turin: Silvio Zamorani, 1993) 115–26.

5. Georg Krotkoff, *A Neo-Aramaic Dialect of Kurdistan: Texts, Grammar, and Vocabulary* (AOS 64; New Haven; Conn.: American Oriental Society, 1982).

6. A. Mingana, *Clef de la langue araméenne* (Mosul: Imprimerie des Pères Dominicains, 1905).

7. The transcription in the present paper is slightly more narrowly phonetic than that in my report on the vernacular dialect of Zakho (see n. 4 above). For instance, the vowel that is transcribed here as [ə] is represented there as short *i*.

8. Yona Sabar, "From Tel-Kêpe ('A Pile of Stones') in Iraqi Kurdistan to Providence, Rhode Island: The Story of a Chaldean Immigrant to the United States of America in 1927," *JAOS* 98 (1978) 410–15.

square brackets, using a notation closely following Krotkoff's[9] except that I use [ə] for Krotkoff's [ɨ]; and (2) the letters, vowel diacritics, and other symbols of the eastern Syriac orthography are transliterated mechanically, within angle brackets. The rûkāḵāʾ sign, which marks the letters ⟨bgdkpt⟩ as having their spirantized alternants, is indicated by underlining: ⟨ḇg̱ḏḵp̱ṯ⟩. The vowel symbols are transliterated as follows; note that a circumflex indicates a *mater lectionis*, but neither the circumflex nor the macron always corresponds to a long vowel sound: pṯāḥāʾ: ⟨a⟩; zqāpāʾ: ⟨ā⟩; zlāmāʾ qašyāʾ: ⟨ē⟩; zlāmāʾ pšîqāʾ: ⟨ə⟩; ḥḇaṣāʾ: ⟨î⟩; rwāḥāʾ: ⟨ô⟩; rḇāṣāʾ: ⟨û⟩. Letters marked with mḇaṭlānāʾ, which indicates that they are not to be pronounced, are enclosed in parentheses. Other symbols of the Syriac orthography are disregarded. As there is no symbol in Syriac orthography for consonant gemination, no gemination will be indicated in the transliteration.

Four other symbols are used in phonetic transcription: (1) a dash under a space (_) indicates "linking," where the last sound of one word and the first sound of the next word are in the same syllable, for example, [á:p_əḥná:n] 'also we', syllabified [á: pəḥ ná:n], [bî:_mqá:we] 'abides in me', [u-mma:ṛ_əḷhó:n_i:šó:ʿ] 'and Jesus said to them', or marks the boundary between a word and a following enclitic (such as a pronoun) when they are written separately but pronounced as a single phonological unit; (2) a hyphen (-) marks the grammatical boundary between a proclitic (such as [b] 'in' or [w] 'and') and a following word, or between a word and an enclitic when they are written as a single word, such as [háw-lan] 'give us', [bri:xá:-t] 'blessed are you'; this symbol has no phonetic significance, [d-wa-šmáyya] and [b-áṛʿa] being pronounced [dwašmáyya] and [báṛʿa] respectively; (3) parentheses ( ) are placed around sounds that are not clearly audible; and (4) the comma and the period indicate intonational contours.

The Chaldean Pronunciation of Syriac

Consonants

The Syriac consonants are pronounced as follows, using the order of the Syriac alphabet, with the spirantized variants (with rûkāḵāʾ) immediately following the corresponding basic stops:

(ʾ) b w g ɣ d ð h w z ḥ ṭ y k x l m n s ʿ p p/w ṣ q r š t θ

In most cases, the modern pronunciation of a Syriac consonant is identical to its reflex in Modern vernacular Aramaic. In some cases, this implies that a

9. *A Neo-Aramaic Dialect.*

sound change that took place at some time in the prehistory of the modern vernacular has also affected the reading of Classical Syriac. Thus the reflex in the modern vernacular language of *b̲ is [w],[10] and in Syriac texts ⟨b̲⟩ is read as [w];[11] ⟨p⟩ has lost its spirantized alternant in the vernacular and in pronouncing the classical language.[12] However, the vernacular and classical reflexes are not identical in the following cases: Syriac ⟨g̲⟩ is read as [ɣ],[13] but its reflex in Modern Aramaic is [ᵓ] or zero;[14] ⟨ḥ⟩ is read [ḥ], but its modern reflex is [x];[15] ⟨ᶜ⟩ is read [ᶜ], but its modern reflex is [ᵓ] or zero.[16] Furthermore, for speakers from Zakho, there are an additional two consonants in this category. In the vernacular Aramaic dialect of Zakho, the native language of the primary informant, [θ] and [ð] have become stops,[17] but he pronounces [θ] and [ð] in Syriac and occasionally in Syriac borrowings into the vernacular, such as [za:xú:θa] 'victory', [beθ ḍaṛṛa] 'house [i.e., field] of battle'.

The sounds [ɣ], [ᶜ], and [ḥ] are pronounced in Syriac words borrowed into vernacular Aramaic, even when the words are reshaped to fit the morphology of the modern language, as the following words in Krotkoff's book attest: [páɣra] 'body', [ṭaᶜánwa] 'he endured',[18] [ḥá:ye] 'life',[19] [mzayó:ḥe] 'to extol', [mšabó:ḥe] 'to praise God', [mší:ḥa] 'Christ', [rú:ḥa] 'spirit'.[20] This fact has an interesting implication for the process of historical change. It suggests that these sounds existed continuously in the speech repertoire of the community even as they were changing to [ᵓ], zero, or [x] in the vernacular (and were not merely reintroduced subsequently in borrowings from Arabic). Before the change, the

10. E.g., vernacular Zakho [kim-ya:w-ə́n-na] 'I gave it', [šwúqta] 'abandoned', [twə́rri] 'I broke'.

11. E.g., [háw-lan] 'give us', [ya:héw-na] 'I give', [šwuq] 'leave, forgive', [šwáqqən] 'we have forgiven'.

12. E.g., [á:p] 'even, also', [ḥla:péyn] 'for us'.

13. E.g., [páɣra] 'body', a classicism appearing in Krotkoff (*A Neo-Aaramaic Dialect*, 98, §91) in a context where it is contrasted with its opposite [rú:ḥa] 'spirit'.

14. Ibid., 13, §2.10.5.

15. Syriac [láḥma] 'bread', [ḥna:n] 'we', [ḥað] 'one', [neḥté:θ] 'I have descended'; Tel Kêpe [lúxma] (Sabar, "From Tel-Kêpe," #21 [cited by sentence number]), Zakho [ᵓáxnan], Zakho and Tel Kepe [xa], Zakho [nxá:ta] 'to descend', Tel Kepe [nxə́θli] 'I descended' (ibid., #12).

16. Syriac [ᶜammé:x] 'with you', Tel Kepe [ᵓə́mmid] 'with'; cf. also Syriac [áṛᶜa] 'land', [ša:ᶜat] 'hour of', [ᶜal] 'on', [taᶜlá:n] 'cause us to enter', Tel Kepe [təšᵓa] 'nine' (Sabar, "From Tel-Kêpe," #5), [be-ᵓwāða] 'doing, making' (Sabar, "From Tel-Kêpe," #9).

17. Compare Tel Kepe [θé:lan] 'we came' (Sabar, "From Tel-Kêpe," #17) with Zakho [té:lay] 'they came'; Tel Kepe [ṭḷa:θi] 'thirty' (Sabar, "From Tel-Kêpe," #20) with Zakho [ṭḷá:ti]; Tel Kêpe [bé:θa] (Sabar, "From Tel-Kêpe," #6) with Zakho [béyta].

18. Krotkoff, *A Neo-Aramaic Dialect*, 106, §115.

19. Ibid., 128, "literary for *xa:ye*."

20. Ibid., 8, at the top.

word for 'life' was [ḥá:ye] in both literary and colloquial registers. After the change, it was [xá:ye] in the colloquial language, but remained [ḥá:ye] in contexts that marked it as belonging to the literary register. In a sense it is wrong to call [ḥá:ye] a borrowing; it must have existed continuously in speech in precisely this form. What changed is its stylistic flavor.

The spirantization of ⟨p⟩ is extremely rare in the eastern recension of Syriac, the letter ⟨p⟩ being normally written without any dot above or below, and pronounced [p], regardless of its position within a word. In only a small group of words (a list of 18 is given by Mingana[21]), it is pronounced [w], again identically with ⟨w⟩ and ⟨b̲⟩.[22] Similarly, there are only a few words in modern colloquial northeastern Aramaic in which an Aramaic **p* has a reflex [w] (or [o:] or [u:] derived from [aw] or [əw]/[ew]). It is striking that these correspond to words in Mingana's list:[23] [nawša(:θan)] '(our)selve(s)', ⟨nap̲šāʾ⟩ 'soul'; [ṭḷáwxe] 'lentils' ⟨ṭlāp̲ẖēʾ⟩; [rú:ša] 'shoulder', [rúšta] 'spade, shovel', ⟨rap̲šāʾ⟩ 'shovel'.[24]

Spirantization of the five consonants ⟨*bgdkt*⟩ is pronounced consistently, in the middle and ends of words, for example, [ʾá:xəl], [payréh], [nəθqaddá:š], [ya:héw-na], [ḥayya:wáyn], [šwuq], [šúwḥa] (⟨šûb̲ḥāʾ⟩).[25] However, at the beginning of a word, when the preceding word in the same phrase ends in a vowel—a situation in which the consonant ought to be spirantized[26] and in which the United Bible Societies' Serto New Testament consistently has rûkāk̲āʾ—only the stop variants are pronounced or indicated in the transliterations in DLB (as Mingana points out).[27] Thus, [láḥma_t-sunqá:nan] 'bread of our need', [wlá: taʿlá:n] 'do not cause us to enter', [nə́šre b-ṭu:rá:x] 'he will remain in your mountain'.[28] After a proclitic 'and', 'that', 'in', or 'to', spirantized

21. Mingana, *Clef de la langue araméenne*, p. 3.

22. According to Mingana (ibid.) and Bazzi and Errico (Michael J. Bazzi and Rocco A. Errico, *Classical Aramaic [Assyrian-Chaldean]: Elementary Book I* [Irvine, Calif.: Noohra Foundation, 1989], 35 and 64), it should in such cases be written with a small circle beneath, but the only such word in our primary corpus, ⟨napšātan⟩ [nawša:θá:n] 'our souls' (DLB, 19:3, 21:3 from bottom), is printed twice without such a circle.

23. These words in square brackets are cited in the dialect of Aradhin, from Krotkoff's glossary (*A Neo-Aramaic Dialect*, 117ff.). The transliterations in angle brackets are from Mingana (*Clef de la langue araméenne*, 3). Though Krotkoff indicates that [nawš-] 'self' is literary in Aradhin, it is common colloquial in many other dialects.

24. On the etymology of [rú:ša] and [rúšta], loan-words from Akkadian, see Georg Krotkoff, "Studies in Neo-Aramaic Lexicology," in *Biblical and Related Studies Presented to Samuel Iwry* (ed. Ann Kort and Scott Morschauser; Winona Lake, Ind.: Eisenbrauns, 1985), 126–27.

25. An isolated exception, probably influenced by the vernacular, is [hu:dá:ye] 'Jews' (REC).

26. Mingana, *Clef de la langue araméenne*, 31.

27. Ibid., n. 2.

28. DLB, 15:4 from the bottom, 1 from the bottom.

alternants are usually pronounced: [u-θəšbúḥta], [t-xáršeɤ], [da-wré:h], [d-wa-šmáyya], [o:-šá:ᶜat] (for *[wa-w-šá:ᶜat]), [d-wi:ša] 'of evil',[29] but not in [u-təštú:n] 'and you drink', [w-de:m] 'and my blood'.

As expected, ⟨ᵓ⟩ is silent except at the beginning of a word and intervocalically. Even at the beginning of a word it is sometimes omitted: [u-mma:ṛ_əḷhó:n_i:šó:ᶜ] 'and Jesus said to them'. After one of the orthographically inseparable particles, the [ᵓ] is sometimes pronounced, as in [d-ᵓá:xəl] 'that eats', [u-ᵓə́nna] 'and I', and sometimes omitted, [d-á:xəl], [d-a:máṛ-na] 'that I say', [l-a:lá:ha] 'to God'. Intervocalically, [ᵓ] is pronounced, as in [šari:ra(:)ᵓí:θ] 'truly', [ᵓamme:na:ᵓí:θ] ' forever'.

The conjunction ⟨w-⟩ 'and' is more often a tense, short, syllabic [u] than [w], as in [u-θešbúḥta] 'and praise', [u-láḥma] 'and bread'.

Vowels, Quantity, and Stress

Following are the basic reflexes of the vowels:

⟨a⟩	⟨ā⟩	⟨ē⟩	⟨ə⟩	⟨î⟩	⟨ô⟩	⟨û⟩
[a]	[a:]	[e:]	[ə]	[i:]	[o:]	[u:]

The length of the vowels is intimately dependent on whether the syllable is open or closed and whether it is word-final or nonfinal, and on the location of stress.

In nonfinal syllables, vowels in open syllables are long and vowels in closed syllables are short. Therefore, a vowel letter whose basic reflex is long is pronounced short in a closed syllable. A consonant-letter with no written following vowel closes its syllable, regardless of whether historical or morphophonological evidence shows that a vowel once followed. Thus the first syllable is closed and the vowel (written ⟨ā⟩) is pronounced short in [ᶜalmí:n] '(for)ever' (with a short first vowel in REC and in the Arabic transcription in DLB[30]), [ᵓamrí:n] 'they say', or [qalxó:n] 'your voice'[31] as is the first vowel (written ⟨ē⟩) in [texlú:n] 'you will eat' and [nexlá:n] 'he will eat me'. The vowels ⟨a⟩ and ⟨ə⟩ are always short;[32] hence syllables containing them are always closed. If the following consonant is marked with a vowel, it is geminated, as in [ᵓeykánna] 'as, how', [ḥayya:wéyn] 'our debtors', [paṣṣá:n] 'save us', [ᶜammé:x] 'with you', [nə́šše] 'women', [nə́ḥḥe] 'he will live', [ᵓətté:l] 'I give', [meṭṭo:lá:θ] 'because of me'. This rule also holds in cases where the gemination is nonhistorical, such as [ᵓə́nna]

29. Ibid., 56:2.

30. DLB, 12:2fb and 46:11.

31. DLB, 19:4fb.

32. In Monsignor Bikoma's reading, as in his vernacular Aramaic, short [a] has a noticeably raised, centralized quality that has not been indicated here.

‘I’, [ʾə́xxal] ‘they ate’, [ʾə́mmar] ‘he said’, [ʾaqqi:mí:w] ‘I will raise him’. If, after a consonant that is historically and underlyingly geminate, a vowel is elided by the usual phonological process, no gemination is pronounced: [taʿlá:n] ‘you cause us to enter’, [šadrá:n] ‘he sent me’ (for /taʿʿel+an/, /šaddar+an/). In a few words, gemination after ⟨a⟩ or ⟨ə⟩ is avoided, and the preceding vowel undergoes compensatory lengthening: [ʾá:wun] (written ⟨ʾaḇûn⟩) ‘our father’, [ʾá:wa] (⟨ʾaḇāʾ⟩) ‘father’,[33] [ʾa:wa:haykú:n]] ‘your fathers’, [ʾa:lá:ha] (⟨ʾalāhāʾ⟩) ‘God’, [wa-mwa:rá:x-u] (⟨wambarak̲ (h)û⟩) ‘and blessed is (he)’.[34] (In ⟨mqāwēʾ⟩ [mqa:we] ‘abides’, the lengthening is more ancient and reflected in the orthography.) There is no gemination before or after an epenthetic [ə], as in [ʾax_ə_t-ʾə́xxal] ‘like they ate’, [lə-me:xál] ‘to eat’, and there is no evidence in the corpus for gemination after vowels other than ⟨a⟩ and ⟨ə⟩. Exceptionally, a long vowel appears in a closed nonfinal syllable in [ba-qnu:mxó:n] ‘in yourselves’; ⟨û⟩, however, is not always long, for it is short in [ʾá:wun] ‘our father’, [ṃúṭṭul] ‘because of’.[35] No instances of ⟨î⟩ in a closed nonfinal syllable (such as ⟨brîk̲tāʾ⟩ ‘blessed [fem.]’, ⟨qadîštāʾ⟩ ‘holy [fem.]’ or ⟨md̲î(n)tāʾ⟩ ‘city’) are recorded or transcribed in our corpus.

In a final syllable, the length of the vowel depends on whether or not it is stressed: if stressed, it is long; if unstressed, it is short. Words (of two or more syllables) ending in a vowel have stress on the penultimate syllable, and the final unstressed vowel is generally short (even the tense [i] and [u] in [də-di:lá:x_i] ‘that yours is’ and [wa-mwa:rá:x-u] ‘and blessed is (he)’ are short). Stressed final vowels, found in monosyllables, are long: [lá:] ‘not’, [bí:] ‘in me’.

33. DLB, 49:1.

34. Mingana lists several words in which ⟨r⟩ or ⟨ʿ⟩ preceded by ⟨a⟩ is not geminated (and presumably the vowel is lengthened), implying that in other similar words it is; moreover, in certain verbs, only in the imperative is the consonant doubled (*Clef de la langue araméenne*, 9 and the note there). Cf . Bazzi and Errico (*Classical Aramaic*, 60). In a similar fashion, the Tel Kepe vernacular simplifies geminate [r] and lengthens the preceding vowel compensatorily, as in [mé:ri] ‘I said’, for *[mirri], /mir+li/ (Sabar, “From Tel-Kêpe,” 412 n. 35). The Zakho dialect does not exhibit this: compare [mírri] in Msgr. Bikoma’s Zakho dialect. Even the Tel Kepe dialect retains [rr] in Kurdish loanwords: [šárre] ‘war’ (Sabar, “From Tel-Kêpe,” #15 and n. 44). It cannot be concluded from this that the Chaldean reading tradition is historically linked specifically to vernacular dialects of the Tel Kepe area, since the reduction of geminate [r] is found elsewhere in modern Northeastern Aramaic.

35. REC and DLB, 56:2 transcribed in Arabic letters (without vowel diacritics) as ⟨mṭl⟩. According to Bazzi and Errico (*Classical Aramaic*, 60) and Mingana (*Clef de la langue araméenne*, 11), a consonant is geminated after ⟨û⟩ in a few words, none of which appear in REC. One, ⟨ḥûbāʾ⟩ ‘love’, appears in DLB (56:6), transliterated into Arabic (in a passage without vowel diacritics) as ⟨ḥwbʾ⟩. This undoubtedly stands for [ḥúbba] (cf. Bazzi and Errico, “Ḥubba,” *Classical Aramaic*, p. 60), the Arabic ⟨w⟩ representing the vowel quality without implying length, as it does in ⟨təšbôḥtāʾ⟩ ‘praise’, transliterated ⟨tšbwḥtʾ⟩ (DLB, 56 last line), but pronounced [təsbúḥta] (attested as [w-θəšbúḥta], REC).

Words of two or more syllables ending in a consonant are normatively stressed on the final syllable,[36] but in our recorded corpus, the situation is more complex. We find two cases: final stress with a vowel nearly always pronounced long (. . .V́:C#) and penultimate stress with the final vowel pronounced short (. . .V́C(C)VC#). The former case, final stress and a long vowel, is general when the last vowel is ⟨ î⟩, ⟨ ē⟩, ⟨ ā ⟩, ⟨ ô⟩, ⟨ û ⟩, or a diphthong; examples are [ᵓamrí:n] 'they say', [ᵓətté:l] 'I will give', [neḥté:θ] 'I have descended', [malku:θá:x] 'your kingdom', [ḥayyá:w] 'its life', [ne:xó:l] 'he eats', [texlú:n] 'you (pl.) will eat', [ḥawbéyn] 'our crimes'. If the last vowel is ⟨ə⟩, stress is penultimate, contrary to the normative rule, as in [ᵓá:xəl] 'he eats'. If the final consonant is preceded by ⟨ a ⟩, sometimes stress is on the penult, as in [ṃá:ran] 'our Lord', [l-ᶜá:lam] 'forever', [məškaḥ] 'able'; and sometimes stress is on the final syllables, in which case the vowel is pronounced long: [taᶜlá:n] (REC),[37] [appa:y] 'face of', [bri:xa:t] 'blessed are you' (REC).[38] I have not been able to discover factors that predict which of the two patterns will be found in a particular circumstance. Sometimes the same word is attested both ways: [paɤréh] and [páɤṛe(h)] 'his body', [mə́ṭṭo:l] and [múṭṭul]. One and the same suffix is sometimes stressed and sometimes not: [t-xársеɤ] 'of your belly' and [ᶜammé:x] 'with you'. Sometimes rhythmic considerations seem to influence stress placement, as when [ᵓi:só:ᶜ] 'Jesus' is stressed finally twice at ends of clauses but has penultimate stress in the phrase [ᵓí:so:ᶜ mší:ḥa] 'Jesus Christ', where a clash of two consecutive stresses is avoided. This principle is not followed consistently, however; note [nəθqaddá:š šmá:x] 'hallowed be Your name'.

The question of consistency is crucial, and we cannot answer it on the basis of the corpus we now have. Would the same reader stress the words in the same way every time, and to what extent would two readers' performances be the same? Within our corpus, we can make such a comparison only on a small body of data, the Lord's Prayer, which we have both in the recording by Monsignor Bikoma and in the transcription into Arabic script in Father Bazzi's edition of the Divine Liturgy (the transcription into Roman script does not indicate vowel length or stress). The Arabic transcription shows vowel length, from which the position of stress can be deduced, given the generalizations made in the preceding paragraph. We find a high correlation between the two renditions of the Lord's Prayer in regard to the length of vowels before a final

36. Mingana, *Clef de la langue araméenne*, 33; Bazzi and Errico, *Classical Aramaic*, 63.

37. The word is transcribed ⟨taᶜla:n⟩ in DLB, 46.

38. Bazzi writes it as one word, ⟨brîḵaty⟩ (Michael J. Bazzi [ed.], *The Gospel according to Saint Matthew* [El Cajon, Calif.: St. Peter Chaldean Catholic Church, ca. 1988?] 115). This edition of Matthew's gospel contains copies of a 1950 edition of the Peshiṭta and of George M. Lamsa's English translation, as well as the text of several prayers.

consonant. In both renditions the vowel ⟨a⟩ is long in [ḥná:n] and [ta^{c}lá:n]; short in [háw-lan], [sunqá:nan], and [l-^{c}á:lam]; and vowels other than ⟨a⟩ are long in both renditions in [^{c}almí:n], [$^{\supset}$a:mé:n], [malku:θá:x], [šəwya:ná:x], [d-á:p_ə_ḥná:n], and [paṣṣá:n]. The two renditions differ with regard to ⟨nəṯqadaš⟩, pronounced as [neθqaddá:š] but transcribed into Arabic without a long vowel, and in ⟨$^{\supset}$āp⟩, read as [$^{\supset}$ap̣] but long in the Arabic transcription. In both cases, the Arabic follows the Syriac script, suggesting that the transcription here may represent an ideal pronunciation not realized in practice.

Historically reduced vowels that may have existed in earlier stages of Syriac (stages that preceded the codification of the vowel and other diacritics, at least a millennium ago) are not reflected at all in the modern pronunciation. Thus there is no "shewa mobile" in [šmá:x] 'your name', [^{c}álma] 'world', [máštya] 'drink', [w-man d-nexlá:n] 'and whoever eats me', [šadrá:n] 'sent me', and many similar words.

Conversely, an epenthetic [ə] is inserted before the second-to-last consonant in a sequence of three or more: [d-á:p_əḥná:n] 'that we too', [ta^{c}là:n_əl-nəsyó:na] 'bring us into temptation', [bri:xá:-t_ə_b-nə́šše] 'blessed are you among women', [d-m(n)_ə_šméyya] 'that from heaven', [ḥayyá:w_ə_d-^{c}álma] 'the life of the world', [u-mma:ṛ_əḷhó:n] 'and he said to them', [léyt_əlxó:n] 'you do not have', [$^{\supset}$ax_ə_t-$^{\supset}$ə́xxal] 'like they ate'. None of these is reflected in the English transcription in DLB. On the other hand, the historically epenthetic vowel [ə] in the word ⟨šḇaqn⟩ [šwáqqən], 'we have forgiven' (in the Lord's Prayer), which is indicated (at least optionally) in the Syriac orthography,[39] does receive notice in the transcription: ⟨šwqin⟩ in Arabic script (DLB, 12, 46) and "SHWOQIN" in Latin letters (DLB, 210).

More diphthongs are pronounced than might appear in a classical phonology of Syriac. In accordance with a phonological process of the vernacular Aramaic of Zakho, the written diphthong ⟨ay⟩ is pronounced [ey], except after an emphatic consonant or gutturals ([h] and [ḥ], sometimes [$^{\supset}$], presumably also [^{c}]), in which case it is [ay]: [$^{\supset}$eykánna], [šméyya], [ḥla:péyn], [leyt], [ḥayya:wéyn], [$^{\supset}$áyna], [ḥṭa:háyn], and [ṭaybu:θa].[40] In stressed final position, [á:y] is pronounced, whether written ⟨āy⟩ as in [ṣaḷḷā:y] or ⟨ay⟩ as in [appá:y].

39. This is written with a line above the ⟨q⟩ in Bazzi's *Gospel according to Saint Matthew* (pp. 18 and 115), and Bazzi and Errico (*Classical Aramaic*, 133), but not in DLB (13 and 47). The line functions here as a mhagyānā$^{\supset}$ 'vocalizer', indicating a vowel sound [ə] before a sonorant consonant. Mhagyānā$^{\supset}$ is normally written below the letter, while a line above a letter should be a marhṭānā$^{\supset}$ 'hastener', indicating precisely the absence of an epenthetic vowel (Bazzi and Errico, *Classical Aramaic*, 62; Mingana, *Clef de la langue araméenne*, 34–35).

40. The vernacular of Zakho is unusual among Northeastern Aramaic dialects in preserving historical **ay* and **aw* as diphthongs. Most dialects, including that of Tel Kepe, reduce them to [e:] and [o:].

As is well known, in the eastern recension of Syriac, ⟨aw⟩ is not written but rather ⟨āw⟩ (with morphologically defined exceptions).[41] This is pronounced [á:w] in stressed final position ([$^{\supset}$i:θá:w], [ḥayyá:w], [wá:w] ⟨(h)wāw⟩), and [aw] in nonfinal syllables ([máwtan], [háw-lan], [ḥawbéyn]) (both [aw] and [a:w] with a low central to front vowel). Occasionally, following a phonological process of vernacular Zakho Aramaic, it is pronounced [ow]: [yówma], [yowmá:na]. In accordance with the absence of ⟨aw⟩ in the eastern recension, a pa^{c}əl form with middle-wāw has no gemination: [mqá:we] 'remains', rather than *[mqáwwe].

Because ⟨ḇ⟩ and the rare ⟨p̱⟩ are pronounced as [w], they too may form diphthongs: [ṣəwya:ná:x] ⟨ṣəḇyānāk⟩ 'your will', [nawša:θá:n] ⟨napšāṯan⟩ (DLB, 19:3, 21:3fb) 'our souls', and even [šúwḥa] ⟨šûḇḥā$^{\supset}$⟩ 'praise'.

A word and its enclitic are phonologically a single word with respect to stress and vowel length or shortening, even if not written as such: [$^{\supset}$ənná:_na] 'I am', [nà:ṣe:n_wá:w] 'they were fighting', [šlám_lex] ⟨šlām lēḵy⟩ 'peace to you'. The expression ⟨šqîlā$^{\supset}$ lēh⟩ 'he has received it (fem.)', written as two words, is transcribed in Arabic script as one word, ⟨šqyl$^{\supset}$lyh⟩ (DLB, 23:20, 22, 5), probably to be pronounced [šqi:lá:le(:)h], like the vernacular [šqi:lá:le].

Sample Text

The Lord's Prayer (Matthew 6:9–13)

$^{\supset}$á:wun d-wa-šméyya nəθqaddá:š šmá:x, té:θe malku:θá:x, néhwe šəwya:ná:x, $^{\supset}$eykánna d-wa-šméyya $^{\supset}$ap̣ ḅ-áṛ^{c}a. háw-lan láḥma_t-sunqá:nan yowmá:na. wa-šwúq_lan ḥawbéyn wa-ḥṭa:háyn.[42] $^{\supset}$eykánna d-á:p_əḥná:n šwáqqən (l-)ḥayya:wéyn. u-lá: ta^{c}là:n_əl-nəsyó:na, $^{\supset}$ə́lla paṣṣá:n mən bí:ša:, mə́ṭṭo:l də-di:lá:x_i malkú:θa, ḥáyla w-θəšbúḥta:, l-^{c}á:lam $^{\supset}$almí:n, $^{\supset}$a:mé:n.

The Hail Mary (after Luke 1:28, 42)

šlám_lex máryam. mályaṭ ṭaybú:θa. ṃá:ṛan ^{c}ammé:x. bri:xá:-t_ə_b-nə́šše. wá-mwa:rá:x_u pé:ra_t-xárseɤ_i:só:^{c}. má:ṛt máṛyam. yáldaθ a:lá:ha. ṣaḷḷá:y ḥla:péyn, há:ša, o:-šá:^{c}ad[43]_máwtan, $^{\supset}$a:mé:n.

41. Mingana, *Clef de la langue araméenne*, 9.

42. This combines the wording in Matt 6:12 ⟨ḥawbayn⟩ and Luke 11:4 ⟨ḥṭāhayn⟩.

43. This formula is used here for /wa-w-šá:^{c}aθ/ ⟨waḇša^{c}aṯ⟩ 'and in hour of'.

John 6:51–58[44]

ʾewunga:lí:yun qaddí:ša_d-má:ṛan ʾi:so:ʿ mší:ḥa, ka:ro:zú:θa d-yo:ḥánnan. ʾə́mmaṛ má:ṛan ['The holy gospel of Our Lord Jesus Christ, the Gospel of John. Our Lord said']:

ʾənná:_na láḥma ḥáyya_d-m(n)_ə_šméyya neḥté:θ, w-ən ná:š ne:xó:l mən há:na láḥma, nə́ḥḥə_l-ʿá:lam. u-láḥma:, ʾáynə_d-, d(ə)-ʾə́nna: ʾətté:l, páɣṛ. d(ə)-ʿal ḥay- ʿa:l_appá:y ḥayyá:w_ə_d-ʿálma ya:héw_na. ná:ṣe:n_wá:w, hu:dá:ye, ḥáð ʿam ḥáð u-ʾamrí:n, ʾeykánna mə́škaḥ há:na paɣṛéh nəttel_lán l(ə)-me:xál. u-mma:ṛ_əḷhó:n_i:só:ʿ, ʾa:mé:n ʾa:mé:n d-a:máṛ_na_lxó:n, də-ʾə́n la: texlú:n páɣṛe(h) da-wṛé:(h)_d-ná:ša, u-təštú:n dmé:h, léyt_əlxó:n ḥáyye baqnu:mxó:n. man d-ʾá:xəl dé:n mən p̣áɣṛ (w)-šá:θe mən dé:m, ʾə́θ le:(h) ḥáyye da-l-ʿá:lam u-ʾə́nna ʾaqqi:mí:w b-yówma ḥṛá:ya. p̣áɣṛ gé:r ša:ri:ra:ʾí:θ ʾi:θá:w me:xúlta. w-dé:m ša:ri:ra:ʾí:θ ʾi:θá:w máštya. man d-á:xəl p̣áɣṛ u-šá:θe dé:m, bí:_mqá:we_w-ʾə́nna bé:h, ʾeykánna, t-šadṛá:n ʾá:wa ḥáyya:, u-ʾə́nna: ḥáy_na: ṃúṭṭul á:wa, w-man d-nexlá:n ʾáp hu: nə́ḥḥe: məṭṭo:lá:θ. ha:ná:w láḥma, da-nḥé:(θ) mə(n) šméyya, lá:-wa ʾáx_ə_t-ʾə́xxal ʾa:wa:haykú:n mánna ʾu-mí:θ. man d-á:xəl há:na láḥma, nə́ḥḥe_l-ʿá:lam,

u-šúwḥa l-a:lá:ha ʾamme:na:ʾí:θ. ['and praise to God forever'].

44. A few inadvertent deviations from the printed Syriac text appear here, without comment.

Double Polysemy in Proverbs 31:19

Gary A. Rendsburg

Wordplay of various types is widely recognized by biblical scholars.[1] One of the most unique types is what I call double polysemy, in which two key words in a line of poetry both bear double meaning, with both sets of meanings intended by the author. Thus, for example, in Gen 49:6 and in Job 3:6, the word pairs *tbʾ/ybʾ* and *tḥd/yḥd* mean both 'enter' and 'be united', as well as 'desire' and 'rejoice'.[2]

An excellent example of this device is found in Prov 31:19: ידיה שלחה בכישור וכפיה תמכו פלך *yādehā šillĕḥâ bakkîšôr wĕkappehā tāmĕkû pālek* 'her hands she sends forth to the spindle, her palms take hold of the whorl'. I have translated this passage in the traditional way, recognizing the two words *kîšôr*

1. For basic treatment, see Jack M. Sasson, "Wordplay in the OT," *IDBSup* (Nashville: Abingdon, 1976) 968–70.

2. Gary A. Rendsburg, "Double Polysemy in Genesis 49:6 and Job 3:6," *CBQ* 44 (1982) 48–51.

and *pālek* (nonpausal *pelek*) as technical terms for spinning tools.[3] These are the primary meanings that these words bear in the present passage.

A demur regarding *kîšôr* was raised by W. F. Albright, who claimed that the word does not mean 'spindle', but rather 'skill', from the Canaanite root *kšr*.[4] As support for this view, Albright noted that the early versions understood the term in this manner (Targum *kûšrāʾ*, Peshiṭta *kaššîrûtāʾ*; see also Greek *sympheronta* 'needed things').[5] To be sure, there are lexicographers who have understood Aramaic *kûšrāʾ* (variant *kûnšěrāʾ*) in this passage as 'spindle',[6] but in truth there is no independent confirmation of this meaning beyond the targumic rendering of Prov 31:19.[7] The only other place where *kûšrāʾ* (again with the variant *kûnšěrāʾ*) is used in all of Aramaic literature is in the Targum to Prov 3:8, but here the word refers to a part of the human body ('spine' and 'navel' are the two most common interpretations[8]). In light of these facts, it is understandable that Albright reached the conclusion that *kîšôr* in Prov 31:19 means 'skill'.

In addition, though one cannot be sure, Albright probably found the meaning 'spindle' for *kîšôr* to be problematic due to the lack of an acceptable etymology for the word. But he himself in an earlier treatment discussed two plausible etymologies for *kîšôr* 'spindle', namely Sumerian ki-sur 'spinning place' and Sumerian giš-sur 'spinning instrument'.[9] The former etymology first was proposed by A. Boissier,[10] and he was followed by S. Landersdor-

3. In translating *kîšôr* as 'spindle' and *pelek* as 'whorl', I accept the suggested definitions of Yael Yisraeli, "Melaʾkhah: Malʾakhot ha-Bayit: Ṭevuyyah," *Encyclopaedia Biblica* 4, cols. 998–1003. In the present article I attempt no further exactitude in defining *kîšôr* and *pelek*, and I recognize that cognates of *pelek* (on which see below) often are translated 'spindle' in the standard dictionaries.

4. W. F. Albright, *Yahweh and the Gods of Canaan* (London: School of Oriental and African Studies, 1968) 136 and n. 67.

5. Since the root is properly *kṯr* (cf. Ugaritic), one would expect *ktr* in Aramaic. Accordingly, one will assume Aramaic *kšr* to be a borrowing from Canaanite. Some Targum manuscripts read *kûnšěrāʾ*, with inserted *n*. This, in turn, most likely explains the double *š* in the Syriac form.

6. J. Levy, *Chaldäisches Wörterbuch über die Targumim* (Cologne: Melzer, 1959 [reprint of the 1866 edition]) 374; and M. Jastrow, *A Dictionary of the Targumim, the Talmud Babli and Yerushalmi, and the Midrashic Literature* (2 vols.; London: Luzac, 1903) 1.622.

7. However, see below the discussion concerning *y. Yebamot* 12d in the Jerusalem Talmud.

8. For 'spine' see Levy, *Wörterbuch*, 374. For 'navel' see Jastrow, *Dictionary*, 1.622–23; and G. H. Dalman, *Aramäisch-Neuhebräisches Handwörterbuch zu Targum, Talmud und Midrasch* (Göttingen: Vandenhoeck & Ruprecht, 1938).

9. W. F. Albright, *Die Religion Israels im Lichte der archäologischen Ausgrabungen* (Munich: Reinhardt, 1956) 242, n. 68. I have not found this discussion included in any of Albright's books in English of a similar title, and I assume that Albright later surrendered the idea of *kîšôr* = 'spindle' with a possible Sumerian etymology in favor of *kîšôr* = 'skill'. J. Friedrich ("Zum urartäischen Lexikon," *ArOr* 4 [1932] 69) also noted that *kîšôr* is of foreign origin, but he did not specify the derivation.

10. A. Boissier, "A Sumerian Word in the Bible," *Proceedings of the Society of Biblical Archaeology* 35 (1913) 159–60.

fer.[11] The latter etymology was proposed by F. Cornelius,[12] and it appears (with a question mark) in the dictionary of W. Baumgartner.[13]

Neither of these combinations of vocables occurs in extant Sumerian texts, but they are perfectly in keeping with Sumerian formations. The words ki and giš appear in a variety of Sumerian terms connected with the textile industry,[14] and sur is the common word for 'spin'.[15] Of these two suggestions, I prefer the latter one since giš-sur 'spinning instrument' yields the desired meaning 'spindle' more appropriately than ki-sur 'spinning place'. At the same time, however, I accept the possibility that ki-sur 'spinning place' in time could have come to mean 'spindle'.

In either case, there are no phonological difficulties with these derivations. If ki-sur is posited as the etymology of *kîšôr*, the only issue that requires attention is the use of Hebrew *š* to represent a Sumerian *s*. Note, however, that there are many instances of Semitic (Akkadian) borrowings of Sumerian words with *š* rendering the Sumerian *s*.[16]

If giš-sur is accepted as the etymology of *kîšôr*, two issues require attention. First is the correspondence of Sumerian *g* and Hebrew *k*, but this is typical of Sumerian loanwords in Semitic, for example, Sumerian barag 'chamber' = Akkadian *parakku*; Sumerian é-gal 'temple' = Akkadian *ēkallu*, Ugaritic *hkl*, Hebrew *hêkāl*; Sumerian gu-za 'chair' = Akkadian *kussû*, Ugaritic *ksʾ*, Hebrew *kissēʾ*.[17] There are also particular examples of Sumerian words with giš entering Akkadian as *kiš-*, for example, giš.kin.ti = *kiškattum* 'workers, artisans, forgers'.[18]

The second issue is the sibilant correspondence. Here too there is no difficulty. We cannot be sure exactly how the combination of Sumerian *š* and *s*

11. S. Landersdorfer, *Sumerisches Sprachgut im Alten Testament* (Leipzig: Hinrichs, 1916) 45.

12. F. Cornelius, cited in Albright, *Die Religion Israels*, 242 n. 68.

13. W. Baumgartner, *HALAT* (Leiden: Brill, 1974) 451.

14. See the listings in the index of H. Waetzoldt, *Untersuchungen zur neusumerischen Textilindustrie* (Rome: Istituto per l'Oriente, 1972) 287–88. I am grateful to my colleague David I. Owen for referring me to this very useful volume.

15. B. Hübner and A. Reizammer, *Inim Kiengi II: Sumerisch-Deutsches Glossar* (Marktredwitz: Self-published, 1986) 916; and A. W. Sjöberg, ed., *The Sumerian Dictionary of the University Museum of the University of Pennsylvania* (Philadelphia: University Museum, 1984) 2.28 (see citations listed under *babbar* 'white'), 2.64–65 (see citation listed under *bala* 'spindle').

16. A. Falkenstein, "Lexikalisches Archiv," *ZA* 42 (1934) 153; I. J. Gelb, *Old Akkadian Writing and Grammar* (MAD 2; Chicago: University of Chicago Press, 1961) 35; and most exhaustively, S. J. Lieberman, *The Sumerian Loanwords in Old-Babylonian Akkadian* (Missoula, Mont.: Scholars Press, 1977).

17. For discussion of the phonetics involved, see M.-L. Thomsen, *The Sumerian Language* (Mesopotamia 10; Copenhagen: Akademisk Forlag, 1984) 43.

18. I. J. Gelb, *Glossary of Old Akkadian* (MAD 3; Chicago: University of Chicago Press, 1957) 154; and Lieberman, *The Sumerian Loanwords*, 296.

(as in gìš-sur) was realized, but a Sumerian loanword in Akkadian allows us to see what transpired when the borrowing of a word with these adjoining sibilants took place. I refer to Sumerian garaš$_3$-san 'leek' which is borrowed into Akkadian in a number of forms: *giršanu*, *girišanu*, *geršanu*, and so forth. In all these variations, the Semitic equivalent is written with a single *š* (as in *kîšôr*) and not as a geminated sibilant (either *šš* or *ss*).

In light of the above options, I find it perfectly reasonable to assume that the ancient Hebrew lexicon included a word *kîšôr* 'spindle' of Sumerian origin.[19] This meaning for *kîšôr* certainly has been the favored interpretation in the Jewish exegetical and lexicographical traditions.[20] For example, Rabbi Nathan ben Yehiel of Rome (1035–1110) in the *ʿArukh* defined the rare Hebrew word *ʾimmāh*, which appears in *Mishna Kelim* 11:6, 21:1, as a sewing or weaving tool and then equated it with the Biblical Hebrew word *kîšôr*.[21]

Moreover, there is a passage in the Jerusalem Talmud that needs to be considered, for it may solidify the case for accepting the existence of *kîšôr* 'spindle'. In *y. Yebamot* 12d, a story is related that describes the disguised Rabbi Yohanan ha-Sandlar asking the imprisoned Rabbi Aqiva a legal question using coded language (so that the Roman authorities would not realize that Jewish scholars were engaging in discussions of Jewish law). Rabbi Aqiva, in turn, replied with his own coded language: אית לך כושין אית לך כשר *ʾyt lk kwšyn ʾyt lk kšr* 'Do you have spindles (*kwšyn*)? Do you have *kasher* (is it valid)?'[22]

19. I recognize, of course, that it is a bit speculative to posit a Sumerian etymon for this word, especially when neither of the desired Sumerian forms (gìš-sur or ki-sur) appears in the extant literature. I would point out, however, that our knowledge of Sumerian continues to expand, often from unexpected sources. For example, the textual finds at Ebla in some instances present entirely new Sumerian forms and constructions. In general, see M. Civil, "Bilingualism in Logographically Written Languages: Sumerian in Ebla," in *Il Bilinguismo a Ebla* (ed. L. Cagni; Naples: Istituto Universitario Orientale, 1984) 75–97 (for particular examples where "the Sumerian shows major modifications or is even unattested in standard lists," see p. 88). Moreover, with the finds from Ebla, we need not postulate Akkadian intermediation in the movement of the word for 'spindle' from Sumerian to West Semitic. The process could have been direct and could have occurred as early as the third millennium B.C.E. To be perfectly honest, of course, one can still uphold the presence of *kîšôr* = 'spindle' in Hebrew without recourse to Sumerian. I could state that there is no reason to depart from the traditional interpretation of the word and leave it at that. Thus, for example, O. Plöger, *Sprüche Salomos (Proverbia)* (BKAT; Neukirchen-Vluyn: Neukirchener Verlag, 1984) 372: "*kîšôr* und *pelek* sind Hapaxlegomena und in ihrer Bedeutung unsicher, haben es aber wohl mit der Webtätigkeit zu tun" (though he partially errs in calling both words hapax legomena, since *pelek* also occurs in 2 Sam 3:29). But inasmuch as philologists prefer to discuss the origins of words and their meanings, I believe my discussion of the potential Sumerian etyma is warranted.

20. See the discussion and the sources cited in E. Ben Yehuda, *Millon ha-Lashon ha-ʿIvrit* (Berlin: Langenscheidt, n.d.) 5.2351 n. 2.

21. A. Kohut, *ʿArukh ha-Shalem* (2 vols.; New York: Pardes, 1955) 1.69.

22. I gratefully acknowledge the assistance of Samuel Morell of the State University of New York at Binghamton for the reading and understanding of this talmudic passage. For a recent English

The word *kwšyn* in this passage is known from eastern Aramaic, where the singular *kûšāʾ* means 'reed', but by extension 'spindle'.[23] It is possible, of course, that this word is to be seen in the *kwšyn* of *y. Yebamot* 12d, even though it appears nowhere else in the rather large corpus of western Aramaic material. But as Y. N. Epstein noted, the coded expression of Rabbi Aqiva would be more readily realized if the word were *kwšryn*,[24] that is, an Aramaic cognate to Hebrew *kîšôr*, presumably to be vocalized *kûšārîn*. So, even though no manuscript of the Jerusalem Talmud reads *kwšryn*—all witnesses have *kwšyn*—one is inclined to accept Epstein's emendation of the text from *kwšyn* to *kwšryn*, that is, through simple addition of *r*. This has already been done by M. Sokoloff in his recent dictionary of Jewish Palestinian Aramaic.[25] Accordingly, in this lone passage of the Jerusalem Talmud, if the textual emendation is granted,[26] we gain an independent witness to an Aramaic form *kûšār* (presumed vocalization). This, in turn, solidifies the case for the Hebrew word *kîšôr* 'spindle' (and suggests that the targumic rendering *kûšrāʾ* in Prov 31:19 may mean 'spindle' after all).[27]

---

translation of the pericope, see J. Neusner, *The Talmud of the Land of Israel: Yebamot* (Chicago: University of Chicago Press, 1987) 387.

23. See, e. g., C. Brockelmann, *Lexicon Syriacum* (Edinburgh: T. & T. Clark, 1895) 156. The term continues to the present day in various dialects of Modern Eastern Aramaic; see A. J. Maclean, *Dictionary of the Dialects of Vernacular Syriac* (Oxford: Clarendon, 1901) 129; A. J. Oraham, *Dictionary of the Stabilized and Enriched Assyrian Language and English* (Chicago: Consolidated Press, 1943) 210; and G. Krotkoff, *A Neo-Aramaic Dialect of Kurdistan* (AOS 64; New Haven: American Oriental Society, 1982) 132. My thanks to Robert Hoberman of the State University of New York at Stony Brook for his assistance on this matter. The cognate form *kûš* occurs in post-biblical Hebrew.

24. Y. N. Epstein, *Mavoʾ le-Nusaḥ ha-Mishna* (Jerusalem: Magnes, 1948) 422 n. 1.

25. M. Sokoloff, *A Dictionary of Jewish Palestinian Aramaic of the Byzantine Period* (Ramat-Gan: Bar-Ilan University Press, 1990) 254.

26. The reader familiar with my work in biblical studies will know that I am characteristically reticent to emend the Masoretic Text of the Bible; see, for example, my *Linguistic Evidence for the Northern Origin of Selected Psalms* (Atlanta: Scholars Press, 1990) 16–17. It may seem a bit odd, therefore, for me to accept an emendation of a word in the Talmud. But the history of the textual transmission of the Bible is quite different from that of the Talmud. Furthermore, I invoke this emendation of *kwšyn* to *kwšryn,* not of my own accord but based on the great authority of a giant in the field, Y. N. Epstein, and with the recognition that M. Sokoloff has also accepted it. Presumably, the tradition to read *kwšyn* in *y. Yebamot* 12d arose due to contamination from eastern Aramaic, the dialect of the Babylonian Talmud, and from Hebrew. The word *kûšāʾ/kûš* was more common in texts written in eastern Aramaic and in Hebrew, and Jews traditionally read the Babylonian Talmud and Hebrew sources more frequently than they read the Jerusalem Talmud. Thus, it may have been quite natural to replace the hapax legomenon *kwšryn* in the Jerusalam Talmud with the better-known *kwšyn*. On western Aramaic texts "which due to the copyists are influenced by Eastern Aramaic," see E. Y. Kutscher, *Studies in Galilean Aramaic (*Ramat-Gan: Bar-Ilan University Press, 1976) 7, though I realize that, in the present instance, even the best manuscripts of *y. Yebamot* read *kwšyn*.

27. Is Maᶜlūla Aramaic *xšūra* 'wood, piece of wood' (from the root *kšr*) to be related? From both the artwork and the archaeological remains, especially from Egypt, we learn that spindles

Acceptance of *kîšôr* 'spindle' in the Hebrew lexicon, however, does not require us to oppose Albright's suggestion to interpret *kîšôr* in Prov 31:19 as 'skill', for this meaning is perfectly appropriate in the context of the verse in particular and the poem in general. That is to say, in my view, the poet intended both meanings of the word. It is to be understood simultaneously as both 'spindle' and 'skill'.[28]

If this is true of *kîšôr*, it also should be true of its parallel member *pālek*. The meaning 'whorl' is established from the cognate terms Akkadian *pilakku*, Aramaic *pilkāʾ*, Arabic *falak* (see also Eblaite *pilak*(*k*)*u*, Ugaritic-Phoenician *plk*[29]). But the meaning 'clever' is also inherent in the word, with the cognate evidence forthcoming from the root *flk* 'clever' in Jibbāli (a Modern South Arabian language).[30] Now at first glance it might seem far-fetched to invoke a Jibbāli cognate to substantiate a meaning in Biblical Hebrew. In defense of this methodology, I hasten to add that quite a few words attested in ancient Northwest Semitic have cognates only in Modern South Arabian or in Modern Ethiopian.[31] This phenomenon is due no doubt to "the very close affinity of

---

were made from wood; see Yisraeli, "Melaʾkhah: Malʾakhot ha-Bayit: Ṭevuyyah," col. 1000. If Modern Western Aramaic *xšūra* is related in some way, then one has to posit that the word was borrowed by ancient Aramaic from Sumerian with the meaning 'spindle', but eventually developed into a word for 'wood, piece of wood', presumably because one of the common uses of wood was the manufacture of spindles. The Maᶜlūla Aramaic terms for 'spindle' are *maᶜzla* and *martna* (the latter borrowed from Arabic *mardan*). I thank both Otto Jastrow and Werner Arnold of the University of Heidelberg for kindly supplying me with the lexical data culled from Arnold's fieldwork in Syria (letter from Prof. Jastrow dated January 10, 1992).

28. Additional support for retaining 'spindle' is the use of this item as a symbol of femininity in the ancient Near East. See H. A. Hoffner, "Symbols for Masculinity and Femininity: Their Use in Ancient Near Eastern Sympathetic Magic Rituals," *JBL* 85 (1966) 326–34. I owe this reference also to D. I. Owen.

29. These cognates can be found in the standard dictionaries. The Eblaite term appears as NE-*a-gu* in a bilingual text, for which see G. Pettinato, *Testi lessicali bilingui della biblioteca L. 2769* (MEE 4; Naples: Istituto Universitario Orientale, 1982) 251 (VE 459). This is read as either *bil-a-gu* (Sjöberg, *Dictionary*, 2.65) or *bi-a-gu* (G. Conti, *Il sillabario della quarta fonte della lista lessicale bilingue eblaita* [Miscellanea Eblaitica 3 = Quaderni di Semitistica 17; Florence: Università di Firenze, 1990] 133). In the latter interpretation, the /l/ is not indicated in the writing system, as occurs elsewhere in Eblaite orthography. In either case, the word is clearly *pilak(k)u*. On *plk* in Ugaritic, see the discussion of S. Ribichini and P. Xella, *La terminologia dei tessili nei testi di Ugarit* (Rome: Consiglio Nazionale della Ricerche, 1985) 59–60.

30. T. M. Johnstone, *Jibbāli Lexicon* (Oxford: Oxford University Press, 1981) 57. For a related meaning, see T. M. Johnstone, *Mehri Lexicon* (London: School of Oriental and African Studies, 1987) 93.

31. For examples, see E. Ullendorff, "Ugaritic Marginalia," *Or* 20 (1951) 273–74; W. Leslau, "Observations on Semitic Cognates in Ugaritic," *Or* 37 (1968) 347–66 (in particular nos. 526, 607, 655, 869a, 1215, 1575, 1721, 1985); G. A. Rendsburg, "Modern South Arabian as a Source for Ugaritic Etymologies," *JAOS* 107 (1987) 623–28. See also G. A. Rendsburg, "Hebrew *RḤM* = 'Rain'," *VT* 33 (1983) 357–62 (the main cognate evidence is Modern South Arabian, but there is also support from Arabic dialects).

Semitic tongues, which are no less similar to each other than languages belonging to one branch of Indo-European."[32]

Accordingly, I understand Prov 31:19 as containing a double polysemy. The words *kîšôr* and *pālek* mean 'spindle' and 'whorl' as well as 'skill' and 'cleverness'. The author of Prov 31:10–31 was obviously a master poet who incorporated into his text not only the present instance of artful use of language, but others as well.[33] The following English translation, unfortunately encumbered by the slash marks, illustrates the wordplay:

> Her hands she sends forth to the spindle / with skill,
> her palms take hold of the whorl / with cleverness.[34]

We cannot say how the words for 'skill' and 'cleverness' would have been vocalized, but probably the original text simply read the consonants *kšr* and *plk* (the latter is written thus still in the Masoretic Text), and the reader would garner both meanings from these graphemes.[35]

Our honoree has distinguished himself throughout his career by paying particular attention to the Semitic languages still spoken in the Near East. The present article demonstrates that such research can yield unexpected dividends, for not only do we gain insights into contemporary Semitic speech communities, often we can apply the findings, especially the lexical information culled, to elucidate problems in ancient texts. I offer the present article, which utilizes material from Modern South Arabian in particular,[36] and which also treats a subject of long-standing interest to our honoree,[37] as a token of my esteem for my friend Georg Krotkoff.

Addendum

Several months after this article was submitted to the editors, Al Wolters (Redeemer College) was kind enough to send me the written version of his paper

32. J. Blau, "Hebrew and North West Semitic: Reflections on the Classification of the Semitic Languages," *HAR* 2 (1978) 22.

33. For another example of artistry of a high order, see A. Wolters, "*Ṣôpiyyâ* (Proverbs 31:27) as Hymnic Participle and Play on *Sophia*," *JBL* 104 (1985) 577–87; and the ensuing discussion in my "Bilingual Wordplay in the Bible," *VT* 38 (1988) 354–57.

34. Presumably the preposition *b* in the first stich is a double-duty preposition, thus yielding the second reading 'with cleverness'.

35. The real issue is with *kšr*, which in the MT is written *plene* as *kyšwr*. This orthography, with both *waw* and *yod* as medial vowel letters, most likely would have developed in postexilic times. See the discussion in Z. Zevit, *Matres Lectionis in Ancient Hebrew Epigraphs* (ASORMS 2; Cambridge, Mass.: American Schools of Oriental Research, 1980) 33–36.

36. In addition, I am happy to be able to cite Neo-Aramaic evidence as well, in nn. 23 and 27.

37. See G. Krotkoff, "Das Weberhandwerk in Bagdad," *ZDMG* 112 (1962) 319–24.

entitled "The Meaning of *kîšôr* (Proverbs 31:19)," read at the Annual Meeting of the Society of Biblical Literature, San Francisco, November, 1992.

Wolters's main point is that *kîšôr* means specifically 'doubling spindle', that is, a large type of spindle used especially for doubling already-spun single-ply yarn, and that *pelek* refers to the 'drop spindle', a simpler instrument. In n. 3 above, I stated that I am not interested in the exact definitions of these terms, so to a great extent Wolters's proposal has no direct bearing on the present paper.

Of greater interest for the concerns of the present paper is a tangential point raised by Wolters. He astutely noted that the Sumerian form ki-sur is now attested in the bilingual dictionaries from Ebla.[38] Unfortunately, in all four occurrences of ki-sur, no Eblaite equivalent is given. Of the two possibilities raised above, I stated a preference for giš-sur over ki-sur. With the attestation of the latter now in a Sumerian-Eblaite lexical text, clearly ki-sur claims the position of most likely candidate for the etymology of Hebrew *kîšôr.*

38. See Pettinato, *Testi lessicali bilingui della biblioteca* L. 2769, 213 (VE 141).

Zum neuaramäischen Dialekt von Hassane (Provinz Şırnak)

Otto Jastrow

Mit seinem Buch *A Neo-Aramaic Dialect of Kurdistan* (1982) hat unser verehrter Jubilar den an wenigen Fingern abzuzählenden grundlegenden Beschreibungen einzelner neuaramäischer Dialekte eine wichtige Monographie hinzugefügt. Der Artikel, den ich ihm widmen möchte, ist demgegenüber nur eine erste, noch keineswegs in allen Punkten endgültige Skizze eines neuentdeckten Dialekts aus der türkischen Provinz Şırnak.[1] Hassane (einheimische Namensform *Haṣṣan*,[2] türkischer Verwaltungsname Kösreli) ist ein Dorf im Kreis Silopi, der

1. Vergleiche hierzu meinen Beitrag "Neuentdeckte aramäische Dialekte in der Türkei". In: XXV. Deutscher Orientalistentag in München, 1991. Ausgewählte Vorträge. Hrsg. von Cornelia Wunsch. Stuttgart, 1994: F. Steiner (= ZDMG, Supp. 10) 69–74.

2. Da es sinnvoll ist, für die Dialekte bzw. die Lokalitäten, in denen sie gesprochen werden, eine leicht zitierbare Namensform möglichst ohne Diakritika zu verwenden, da aber der einheimische Name Haṣṣan bei Wegfall der Diakritika leicht mit dem muslimisch-arabischen Namen *Ḥasan*

bis 1990 zur Provinz Mardin gehörte, dann jedoch der neugeschaffenen Provinz Şırnak zugeschlagen wurde. Im türkischen Census von 1965 wird für das Dorf eine Einwohneranzahl von 730 angegeben. Diese Zahl hatte sich, schenkt man den Angaben der ehemaligen Einwohner Vertrauen, bis Mitte der achtziger Jahre etwa verdoppelt, doch dann setzte eine rasche Abwanderungsbewegung ein, und heute ist das Dorf von seinen Bewohnern völlig aufgegeben worden. Grund für diese unfreiwillige Abwanderung war der Krieg zwischen der türkischen Armee und der kurdischen Guerilla, der in dieser Region mit großer Härte tobte, und dem die wenigen Christen, als von beiden Kriegsparteien verachtete Minderheit, schutzlos ausgeliefert waren.

Der Dialekt von Hassane gehört, wie alle östlich des Tigris beheimateten Dialekte, zum Neuostaramäischen im engeren Sinn, unterscheidet sich also grundlegend vom Ṭuroyo. Er unterscheidet sich auch deutlich von dem weiter nördlich gelegenen Dialekt von Hertevin, dem einzigen bislang ausführlich beschriebenen neuostaramäischen Dialekt dieser Region.[3] Die im folgenden vorgestellten Data zu diesem Dialekt stammen aus Tonbandaufnahmen und Befragungen mit Herrn Yosip Kulan aus Bad Oeynhausen. Ich danke ihm und seiner Frau für ihre Gastfreundschaft, ferner danke ich meinem Studenten Šabo Talay, der mich bei seinem Schwager Yosip eingeführt und an unseren Sitzungen teilgenommen hat.

Zur Lautlehre

Die interdentalen Spiranten **ṯ* und **ḏ* sind zu den Verschlußlauten *t* und *d* zurückverschoben worden: *mata* 'Dorf', *matwata* 'Dörfer', *beta* 'Haus', *ida* 'Hand', *idata* 'Hände'.

Anders als in Hertevin haben sowohl altes **ḥ* wie auch altes **ḵ*, d.h. die spirantisierte Variante von altem **k*, den velaren Frikativ *x* ergeben, z.B. *xzele* 'er sah', *kixaze* 'er sieht', *yarxa* 'Monat', *bxele* 'er weinte', *baxta* 'Frau'. Daneben verfügt Hassane jedoch auch über ein Phonem *ḥ*, das teils auf altes **h* zurückgeht, z.B. *betaḥ* 'sein/ihr Haus', teils in Lehnwörtern vorkommt, z.B. *gimaḥke* 'er erzählt' (arab.).

Altes *ʿ hat den Glottalstop ʾ ergeben, der, wie in Hertevin, auch im Wortinneren überwiegend erhalten ist, z.B. *biʾta* 'Ei', *beʾe* 'Eier', *zbiʾta* 'Finger',

(oft *Hassan* geschrieben) verwechselt werden kann, möchte ich vorschlagen, sich in diesem Fall an der kurdischen Namensform zu orientieren und die Schreibweise *Hassane* (zu sprechen als *Hassā́ne*) zu verwenden.

3. Otto Jastrow, *Der neuaramäische Dialekt von Hertevin* (*Provinz Siirt*) (Wiesbaden: Harrassowitz, 1988 [= Semitica Viva 3]).

ṭˀinne ‘er trug’. Auffallend ist *tiˀna* ‘Feige’ mit einem etymologisch nicht begründeten Glottalstop.

Anders als in Hertevin ist *q* stets als uvularer Verschlußlaut erhalten.

Der Dialekt von Hassane verfügt über sechs Langvokale und vier Kurzvokale:

ī ǖ		*ū*		*ĭ ü̆*	*ŭ*
	ē	*ō*		*ă*	
	ā				

Überwiegend stehen die Langvokale in offenen Silben, die Kurzvokale in geschlossenen Silben; in diesem Falle schreiben wir der Einfachheit halber die Vokalzeichen ohne Diakritika, z.B. *mira* ‘gesagt’ (lies: *mīra*), aber *mirra* ‘sie sagte’ (lies: *mĭrra*). Steht dagegen ein Langvokal in geschlossener oder ein Kurzvokal in offener Silbe, schreiben wir Diakritika, z.B. *zabūn armune* ‘Verkaufen von Granatäpfeln’; *kăde* ‘er weiß’, *gĭbe* ‘er will’. Ob das kurze *ü̆* als Phonem oder als Variante von *ŭ* zu werten ist, bedarf noch der Klärung.

Wie Hertevin hat auch Hassane die alten Diphthonge **ay* und **aw* zu *ē* und *ō* monophthongisiert, z.B. *beta* ‘Haus’, *torata* ‘Kühe’; zugleich wurde jedoch altes **ō* zu *ū* und altes **ū* zu *ǖ* weiterverschoben, z.B. *axuna* ‘Bruder’, *armune* ‘Granatäpfel’, *düka* ‘Ort’, *xayüta* ‘Leben’, *tüna* ‘Stroh’ (vgl. Hertevin *aḥona, armone, tuna*).

Pronomina

Die folgende Tabelle zeigt das selbständige Personalpronomen und die Pronominalsuffixe am Nomen:

3. Person:	sg m	*awa*	*betaḥ*
	sg f	*aya*	*betaḥ*
	pl c	*ani*	*beteḥin*
2. Person:	sg m	*ahit*	*betux*
	sg f	*ahit*	*betax*
	pl c	*axnütin*	*betoxin*
1. Person:	sg c	*ana*	*beti*
	pl c	*axni*	*betan ~ beteni*

Das Pronominalsuffix 1 pl c hat eine längere Variante *-eni* (mit Akzentwechsel: *bétan ~ beténi*). Entsprechende Langformen, die mit der Grundform frei wechseln können, finden sich auch beim Verbum, z.B. *xzelan* ~ *xzéleni* 'wir sahen'. Außergewöhnlich ist das Pronominalsuffix *-aḥ* für die 3. Person Singular (ohne Genusunterscheidung).

Zur Verbalflexion

Das Verbum verfügt über drei Grundtempora: Präsens, Präteritum und Perfekt, ferner über einen Imperativ.

Präsens

Das Präsens ist charakterisiert durch die Existenz von fakultativen Langformen in der 2. und 1. Person. Beispiele für die Präsensflexion (ohne Tempuspräfixe) des starken Verbums und des Verbums tert. inf. (*šaqil* 'er nimmt', *xaze* 'er sieht'):

3.	sg m	*šaqil*	*xaze*
	sg f	*šaqla*	*xazya*
	pl c	*šaqli*	*xaza*
2.	sg m	*šaqlit* ~ *šaqletin*	*xazit* ~ *xazetin*
	sg f	*šaqlat* ~ *šaqlatin*	*xazyat* ~ *xazyatin*
	pl c	*šaqlütin*	*xazütin*
1.	sg m	*šaqlin* ~ *šaqlena*	*xazin* ~ *xazena*
	sg f	*šaqlan* ~ *šaqlana*	*xazyan* ~ *xazyana*
	pl c	*šaqlux* ~ *šaqluxni*	*xazux* ~ *xazuxni*

Die Langformen (mit Akzentwechsel: *šáqlan* ~ *šaqlána*) stehen in freier Variation mit den kürzeren Formen; sie treten vor allem bei langsamem und zögerndem Sprechen sowie vor Pausa häufiger auf. Die auffallendste Form des obigen Paradigmas ist die 3. Person pl. c. der Verba tert. inf.: *xaza* 'sie sehen' vs. *xaze* 'er sieht'. Beim Antritt von Objektsuffixen fallen die beiden Formen jedoch in *xaze* zusammen: *xazele* 'er sieht ihn / sie sehen ihn'.

Tempuspräfixe: Die flektierte Form ohne Tempuspräfixe fungiert als Subjunktiv. Das Präsens wird mit dem Präfix *k(i)-* ~ *g(i)-* gebildet: *kišaqil* ~ *kšaqil* 'er nimmt', *gimayit* ~ *gmayit* 'er stirbt'. (Auch wenn der kurze Vokal *i* nicht elidiert ist, richtet sich der anlautende Konsonant des Präfixes nach der Stimmhaftigkeit des folgenden Konsonanten.) Das Futur wird mit *b-* gebildet: *bšaqlena* 'ich (m) werde nehmen'. Das Imperfekt wird durch suffigiertes *-wa* gebildet, wobei das Präsenspräfix in der Regel beibehalten wird: *gidamxinwa* 'ich (m) schlief gerade'.

Präteritum

Es existieren zwei Flexionsreihen, die sich nur in der 3 pl c unterscheiden: (1) Endet die Flexionsbasis auf *l-*, *n-* oder *r-*, lautet das Flexionssuffix 3 pl c *-Ka*, wobei *K* dem auslautenden Konsonanten der Flexionsbasis entspricht. (2) Endet die Flexionsbasis auf einen anderen Konsonanten oder auf Vokal, lautet das Flexionssuffix *-ne*. Beispiele (*šqille* 'er nahm', *mirre* 'er sagte', *dmixle* 'er schlief', *ittüle* 'er setzte sich'):

		(1)		(2)	
3.	sg m	*šqille*	*mirre*	*dmixle*	*ittüle*
	sg f	*šqilla*	*mirra*	*dmixla*	*ittüla*
	pl c	*šqilla*	*mirra*	*dmixne*	*ittüne*
2.	sg m	*šqillux*	*mirrux*	*dmixlux*	*ittülux*
	sg f	*šqillax*	*mirrax*	*dmixlax*	*ittülax*
	pl c	*šqílloxun*	*mírroxun*	*dmíxloxun*	*ittǘloxun*
1.	sg c	*šqilli*	*mirri*	*dmixli*	*ittüli*
	pl c	*šqillan*	*mirran*	*dmixlan*	*ittülan*

Vor Objektssuffixen wird in der 3 pl c *-Ka* durch *-Ke* und *-ne* durch *-le* ersetzt, z.B.:

šqilla + *-le* > *šqíllele* 'sie nahmen ihn'
xzene + *-le* > *xzélele* 'sie sahen ihn'

Im Präteritum fallen mithin bei sämtlichen Verben die 3 pl c und die 3 sg m bei Antritt von Objektssuffixen zusammen.

Das Flexionssuffix 1 pl c hat die fakultative Langform *-leni*, z.B. *šqillan* ~ *šqílleni* 'wir nahmen'.

Perfekt

Das Perfekt wird aus dem Partizip Perfekt entweder mit der vorangestellten selbständigen Kopula oder mit den suffigierten Formen der Kopula gebildet. Beispiele (*hule itya* ~ *ítyele* 'er ist gekommen'):

3.	sg m	*hule itya*	*ítyele*
	sg f	*hula itita*	*itítela*
	pl c	*hune itye*	*ítyene*
2.	sg m	*huwit itya*	*ítyewit*
	sg f	*huwat itita*	*itítewat*
	pl c	*huwütin itye*	*ítyewütin*
1.	sg m	*huwin itya*	*ítyewin*
	sg f	*huwan itita*	*itítewan*
	pl c	*huwux itye*	*ítyewux*

Anders als in Hertevin wird das Perfekt auch von transitiven Verben in aktiver Bedeutung gebildet, z.B. *hule šqila* 'er hat genommen', *hula xzita* 'sie hat gesehen'.

Imperativ

Der Imperativ des Grundstammes lautet beim starken Verbum: sg c *šqul* 'nimm!', pl c *šqülun* 'nehmt!', beim Verbum tert. inf.: sg m *xzi* 'sieh!', sg f *xze* 'sieh!', pl c *xzo* 'seht!'.

Unregelmässige Verben

(a) Verba primae *ʾ zeigen im Subjunktiv und Futur die erwartete Basis mit *a*, z.B. *bamir* ['ba:mir] 'er wird sagen', *bamra* 'sie wird sagen', *bamrin* ~ *bamrena* 'ich (m) werde sagen'. Mit dem Präsenspräfix lauten die Formen dagegen: *kimir* ['ki:mir] 'er sagt', *kimra* ['kimra] 'sie sagt', *kimri* 'sie sagen', *kimrux* 'wir sagen', etc. Der Imperativ lautet: *umir* ['u:mir] 'sage (m/f)!'; *umrün* 'sagt!'. Entsprechend für *ʾxl 'essen': *baxil*, *kixil*, *uxil*, etc. Im Präteritum und Perfekt ist der erste Radikal spurlos geschwunden: *xille* 'er aß', *hule xila* ~ *xílele* 'er hat gegessen'.

(b) Das Verbum *ʾty 'kommen' flektiert im Präsens und Futur wie erwartet als *kite*, *kitya*, *bate*, *batya,* etc., der Imperativ ist jedoch unregelmäßig: *hayyo* 'komm (m/f)!', *hăwun* 'kommt!' Das Präteritum lautet *tele*, das Perfekt (s.o) *hule itya* ~ *ítyele*.

(c) Ganz unregelmäßig ist die Flexion von *zl 'gehen' im Präsens, Futur und Imperativ:

		Präsens	Futur	Imperativ
3.	sg m	*kizil*	*bzale*	
	sg f	*kiza*	*bzala*	
	pl c	*kizi*	*bzane*	
2.	sg m	*kizit ~ kizetin*	*bzalux*	*si!*
	sg f	*kizat ~ kizatin*	*bzalax*	*se!*
	pl c	*kizütin*	*bzáloxun*	*so!*
1.	sg m	*kizin ~ kizena*	*bzali*	
	sg f	*kizan ~ kizana*	*bzali*	
	pl c	*kizux ~ kizuxni*	*bzanne*	

Das Präteritum lautet *zille*, *zilla* etc., das Perfekt *hule zila ~ zílele*, *hula zilta ~ zíltela* etc.

(d) Das Verbum für 'geben', aus **yhb + l-* entstanden, hat wie **ʾzl* 'gehen' nur in der 3 sg m ein auslautendes *-l*, anders als bei 'gehen' ist jedoch der Vokal der ersten Silbe stets kurz, z.B. Präsens *kăwil* 'er gibt', *kăwa* 'sie gibt', *kăwi* 'sie geben', und entsprechend Futur *băwil*, *băwa*, *băwi*. Der Imperativ lautet: sg c *hal*!, pl c *hallo*! Das Präteritum lautet *wille*, das Perfekt *hule wila*.

(e) Ganz unregelmäßig ist **bʾy* 'wollen': Präsens *gĭbe* 'er will', *gĭba* 'sie will', *gĭba* 'sie wollen', Futur *bbaʾe* 'er wird wollen', sg f *bbaʾya*, pl c *bbaʾa*, Imperativ sg m *biʾí*!, sg f *biʾé*!, pl c *biʾó*! Das Präteritum lautet *bʾele*, das Perfekt *hule biʾya*.

A Preliminary List of Aramaic Loanwords in Kurdish

Michael L. Chyet

I am honored to be included in this volume, commemorating Prof. Georg Krotkoff's invaluable contribution to the fields of Neo-Aramaic and colloquial Arabic dialectology. After having read his book *A Neo-Aramaic Dialect of Kurdistan* on the dialect of Aradhin, near Amadia, in Iraqi Kurdistan, I found Prof. Krotkoff's article "Studies in Neo-Aramaic Lexicology" so exciting that I wrote him to tell him so, and our friendship was thus begun. In his aforementioned book, Prof. Krotkoff has a brief section entitled "Iranian influences" (p. 64, 5.1), in which he discusses the influence of Kurdish on Neo-Aramaic. This issue, which is of relevance to the concept of areal features as laid out by Don Stilo

Author's note: Abbreviations used in this essay are spelled out at the end of the essay.

I would also like to take this opportunity to thank my professor Martin Schwartz for his insightful comments and suggestions, which assisted me greatly in the preparation of this paper.

and to the theory of languages in contact, à la Uriel Weinreich, is of great interest and importance.

Aramaic and the Iranian languages have a long history of interaction. During the period of the Achaemenid Empire, although in Persia itself Old Persian was the primary written language, Imperial Aramaic was the spoken lingua franca. This situation is reflected in the Aramaic passages of the Bible (mainly Ezra 4:8–6:18, 7:12–26; Dan 2:4–7:28), which contain several loanwords from Old Persian. In the Middle Persian period (Parthian and Sassanid Empires), Aramaic was the medium of everyday writing, and it provided indigenous scripts for writing Middle Persian, Parthian, Sogdian, and Khwarezmian. Moreover, in Middle Persian there were numerous ideograms (or logograms) in which the Aramaic word was written, while the Persian word was pronounced, much like the case of the abbreviation *lb.* (< Latin *libra*; pronounced *pound*) in English.[1]

In a very fine article by the late Israeli scholar E. Y. Kutscher,[2] the influence of Persian on Classical Aramaic is discussed at length. In the opposite direction, Aramaic words are manifested in Iranian at various stages, including such well-known examples as Middle P *gunbaḏ* and Pahlavi *gmbat* (< Aram *qubeṯā*) and Middle P *šanbaḏ* (< Aram *šabetā/šabatā*).[3] With regard to Iranian languages in the modern period, however, very little research has been done on the relationship between the Aramaic language and Iranian. Because the Jews and Christians of Kurdistan speak dialects of Neo-Aramaic, the interaction between Kurdish, an Iranian language, and Neo-Aramaic (both northeastern Neo-Aramaic, to borrow Robert Hoberman's apt term [henceforth NENA], and Turoyo) is particularly worthy of study. In addition to Krotkoff's aforementioned discussion, two important articles touch on the effect of Kurdish on NENA, I. Garbell's "Impact of Kurdish and Turkish on the Jewish Neo-Aramaic Dialect of Persian Azerbaijan and the Adjoining Regions,"[4] and F. A. Pennacchietti, "Verbo neo-aramaico e verbo neo-iranico."[5] Moreover, Yona Sabar's article "Multilingual Proverbs in the Neo-Aramaic Speech of the Jews

1. See Franz Rosenthal, "Die aramäischen Ideogramme in den mitteliranischen Dialekten," in *Die aramaistische Forschung seit Th. Nöldeke's Veröffentlichungen* (Leiden: Brill, 1964) 72–82.

2. E. Y. Kutscher, "Two 'Passive' Constructions in Aramaic in the Light of Persian," in *Proceedings of the International Conference on Semitic Studies (1965: Jerusalem)* (Jerusalem: Israel Academy of Sciences and Humanities [distributed by Brill], 1969) 132–51.

3. See Paul Horn, 'Neupersische Schriftsprache," in *Grundriss der iranischen Philologie* (Strassburg: Trübner, 1895–1901), vol. 1:2, p. 6. Modern P has *gonbad* (> T *kümbet*) and *šanbe*. See also Weryho, p. 308.

4. I. Garbell, "The Impact of Kurdish," *JAOS* 85 (1965) 159–77.

5. F. A. Pennacchietti, "Verbo neo-aramaico e verbo neo-iranico," in *Tipologie della convergenza linguistica: Atti del Convegno della Società Italiana di Glottologia* (Pisa, 1988) 93–110.

of Zakho, Iraqi Kurdistan,"[6] in which 40 of the 153 proverbs listed are in Kurdish, bears eloquent testimony to the close cultural contact between Neo-Aramaic–speaking Jews and their Kurdish compatriots.

However, hitherto nothing has been written regarding the influence of Aramaic on Kurdish. The present contribution to Krotkoff's Festschrift is a step toward bridging that gap. Whereas the Kurdish loanwords into Neo-Aramaic are too numerous to discuss in the space of a few pages, the number of Aramaic words borrowed into Kurdish seems to be relatively small. Although the list offered here is by no means exhaustive, it should give an idea of the general situation.

I should clarify at the outset that only Aramaic words borrowed directly into Kurdish are discussed here. Arabic and Persian loanwords that are ultimately of Aramaic origin, such as *qurban* (sacrifice, victim) and *zembîl* (basket), are not relevant, since they tell us little about the interaction between Aramaic and Kurdish.

List of Aramaic Loanwords in Kurdish[7]

Besîre, bêsîre *m.* (1) Unripe *or* sour grapes {*syn*: Cûr; Harsim; Şilûr}; (2) sour juice of grapes. {*also*: ⟨bêsîre⟩ (HH)} Also Sor *bersîle* = 'unripe (of fruits)' (K3) < Aram *besar* = 'to begin to boil, be in the first stage of ripening' + participle *besir* (m.) / *besira* (f.) = 'in the early stage of ripening': NENA *bassi:ra* (Krotkoff); cf. Heb *boser* 'unripe fruit'.

Bênder, bêder *f.*, **bêdêr** *m.* (*Amadiya*) Threshing floor (in the Middle East [orig.: 'Orient'] wheat is not beaten but rather crushed with a metal-plated plank that is dragged along by oxen [JJ]). {*also*: [bider] (JJ)} {*syn*: Coxîn} < Akkadian *idru* (vSoden) → Aram *bē(t) + Aram *idrā* / Syr *edrō*; NENA *bidra* (Krotkoff); cf. Arab *baydar*, Iraqi Arab *bēdar.*[8]

6. Y. Sabar, "Multilingual Proverbs," *IJMES* 9 (1978) 215–35.

7. All Kurdish words are Kurmanji (Krm) unless otherwise designated. All Classical Aramaic (Aram) references are from M. Jastrow, ספר מלים: *A Dictionary of the Targumim, the Talmud Babli and Yerushalmi, and the Midrashic Literature* (New York: Judaica, 1971); Syriac (Syr) references are from Payne Smith's *Compendious Syriac Dictionary* (Oxford: Clarendon, 1903); Turoyo references are taken from Hellmut Ritter's *Ṭūrōyo: Die Volkssprache der syrischen Christen des Ṭūr ʿAbdîn*, vol. A: *Texte*, vol. B: *Wörterbuch* (Wiesbaden: Franz Steiner, 1967–79).

8. See Georg Krotkoff, "Studies in Neo-Aramaic Lexicology," in *Biblical and Related Studies Presented to Samuel Iwry* (ed. A. Kort and S. Morschauser; Winona Lake, Ind.: Eisenbrauns, 1985) 130; Siegmund Fraenkel, *Die aramäischen Fremdwörter im Arabischen* (Leiden: Brill, 1886) 136.

(Sor) **Dahoł, daweł** Scarecrow. < Aram *daḥlūlā* = 'scarecrow' (whence Heb *daḥlil*) < √d-ḥ-l = 'to fear'. NENA *daxlūlā* (Oraham: dakh-lue-la); cf. also Early Modern P *dāhōl*,[9] *dāxūl* [*ibi* dākhūl] (Weryho, p. 307).

Dewl, dewil, dewlik, dol, *also* **delûv** *f.* Bucket, pail, e.g.: **Vira dewlçî dewlê hildide** (Ba) Here the bucket carrier picks up the bucket. {*also*: [delou/dōl] (JJ); ⟨dûl⟩ (HH)} {*syn*: E'lb; Sîtil} < Aram *dewal/dawlā* and Syr *dawlō*; NENA *dôlâ* and *dôlchâ* (Maclean); Sor *dołçe* and *dołke*. Cf. Arab *dalw*, Heb *deli*; P *dalv* and *dūl* (Weryho, p. 307), and diminutive *dūlče*, the immediate source of NENA *dôlchâ* and Sor *dołçe*. It is difficult to determine whether the Krm forms come directly from Aram or indirectly via P *dūl*.[10]

Dêr *f.* (1) Church; (2) monastery. Also Sor *dêr* = 'monastery' < Syr *dayrō* = 'dwelling, habitation; monastery'; cf. Arab *dayr* = 'monastery', also of Aram/Syr origin.[11]

Dilop, dilob *f.* Drop (*of a liquid*). {*syn*: Ç'ilk; Niqitk; P'eşk} < Aram *delaf* = 'to drip': NENA *dilpa* = 'leak' (Oraham), *dâlip* = 'to drip, to leak' (Maclean).

(Krm) **Doşav, doşab** *f.* and (Sor) **doşaw** Syrup (esp. of grapes), grape molasses [T *pekmez*, Arm *ṛup*]. Cf. P *dūšāb* = 'syrup made of raisins mixed with butter and cream'; according to JJ, this is derived from Mandaic, although the Classical Aram form is identical: *duvšā* = 'honey, glutinous substance'; NENA *dôshâb* = 'syrup, treacle, from grapes or honey' especially in Salmas (Maclean) and *dyûshâ* (Maclean) / *duyša* (Christian Urmia) = 'honey'; cf. Heb *devaš* = 'honey', Arab *dibs* = 'grape molasses'. The Iranian word for water (P *āb*, Krm *av*, Sor *aw*) may have played a part in the metathesis from the original Aram form. To put it another way, because of the viscous nature of grape molasses, a Kurdish or Persian speaker may perceive **doşav**, etc., as being some sort of water (**av**, etc.). This is similar to what I think happened with **şiveřê** (see below). Although this word is the most common word for grape molasses in Sor and in southern Krm, in Krm other words are in use as well, viz., **aqit** (common also in colloquial Turkish of East Anatolia in the form *akıt* < Arab *ᶜaqīd* = 'thick (of grape molasses)', **dims**,

9. Horn, "Neupersische Schriftsprache." This appears also in Steingass' *Persian-English Dictionary* (London: Routledge & Kegan Paul, 1892) 502, vocalized as *dāhil* or *dāhul*.

10. It is interesting to note that Persian has borrowed both the Aramaic and the Arabic forms, which are cognate to one another.

11. See Fraenkel, *Aramäischen Fremdwörter*, 275.

and **mot/mut. Dims** is derived from Arab *dibs* and is therefore ultimately cognate to **doşav**.

Fehêt, fehît, fihêt *f.* Shame, disgrace, e.g.: **Ev poşmanî şerm e û fihêt e** (JR) This [feeling of] regret is a shame and a disgrace. {*also*: [fehité] (JJ); ⟨fihêt⟩ (HH)} {*syn*: *E't'ib*; *Fedî*; *Sosret*; *Şerm*} < Syr √p-h-y = 'to wander, err': *pahyūtā* = 'error'.

Fetilîn *vi.* **(difetile)** (1) To rip, tear (vi.); to split; (2) to be wrapped up; (3) {*also*: Fitilîn} to come untwisted, come undone; (4) {*syn*: Vegeȓîn; Ziviȓîn} to turn around (vi.), e.g.: **Gava ko usa Stîyêȓa dibêje Memo, Stîyê bi paşva difitile** (Z-3) When Memo says that to Stîyê, she turns right around [and goes back]. < Aram *petal* = 'to twist' and *pattel* = 'to pervert'; NENA *pṯa:la* = 'to throw, discard, twist' (Krotkoff) and *pâtil* = 'to make crooked, twist (Old Syr); 'to turn (vi.), turn the face; to wind a clock' (Maclean); Turoyo *fótəl* = 'to spin (vi.), revolve'; cf. Arab *fatala* = 'to twist together, to twine'. The third meaning listed above, 'to come untwisted', has become confused with the second listed meaning of the following verb:

Filitîn *vi.* **(difilite)** (1) To be rescued, saved, delivered; to get away, escape, e.g.: **Ji bin destê dijmin filitî** (IF) He was delivered from the enemies' hands **Ez ancax ji destê wan filitîm** (B) I just barely escaped from their hands; (2) {*syn*: Fetilîn} to become untied or undone, e.g.: **Qayîş filitî** (B) The strap came undone; (3) ? to pounce on (vt.) (L): **Brayê wî felitî wê xwarinê** (L) His friend (lit. 'brother') pounced on the food [son ami se jeta sur les victuelles]. < Aram *pelaṭ* = 'to discharge, vomit; to escape; to detach, take off' and Syr √p-l-ṭ = 'to escape, slip out or away; to bring forth (young)'; NENA *pḷạ:ṭa* = 'to come out, escape; to become, result' (Krotkoff) and *pâliṭ* = 'to go / come out, leave; to result, ensue, become; to escape; to be heard (of a sound)' (Maclean); Turoyo *fālit* = 'to run'; cf. Arab *falata* = 'to escape, to be set free', with final **t** rather than emphatic **ṭ** in Turoyo and Aramaic. Although the initial f- rather than p- suggests Arabic rather than Aramaic derivation, it should be remembered that whereas NENA has no /f/ excepting in certain loanwords[12]—a feature that it shares with such languages of the Caucasus as Armenian and Georgian—in Turoyo, the /f/ is preserved, as in these verbs √f-t-l (*fótəl*) = 'to spin (vi.), revolve' and √f-l-t (*fālit*) = 'to run'. It is not impossible, however, that

12. E.g., *fha:ma* = 'to understand', Jewish Neo-Aramaic of Zakho and Jizre [Cizre/Cizîr].

both Turoyo and Kurdish have borrowed these words from Arabic, which in turn borrowed them from Aramaic.

(Krm) **Fitîl** *f.* and (Sor) **piłîte** Wick. {Krm *also*: [pilté], [pilta qandili] (JJ)} < Aram *peṯīlā/peṯīltā* and Syr *peṯıltō*; NENA *pṯilta* f. (Krotkoff) and *ptiltâ* f. (Maclean); cf. also P *patīle/fatīle*; Arab *fatīl*; Arm *p'ilt'ay*. The Sor, JJ, and Arm forms feature a metathesis of -tl- to -lt-, which we have seen also in the confusion between **fetilîn** and **filitîn**.

Kezeb, kezev *f.* (1) (also **Kezeba r̄eş** = 'black [kezeb]') Liver {*syn*: Ceger[areş]/Cerg; Pişa reş/Pûş}; (2) (also **Kezeba sipî** = 'white [kezeb]') Lungs {*syn*: Cegeraspî/Cerga sipî; P'işik/Pişa spî; Sîh}; (3) {*syn*: Hinav} Internal organs (K). {*also*: [gezeb] (JJ)} Cf. Aram *kavḏa* and Syr *kavḏō* = 'heaviness; liver [seat of anger and melancholy]': NENA *kôdâ* (Maclean: listed as Old Syr) = 'liver; bowels, entrails; heart'; Arab *kibdah* = 'liver'; Heb *kaved*. It is worth noting that NENA and Kurdish have conducted a mutual swap: NENA *jîgâr* (Maclean) [and the verb *jga:ra* = 'to get angry'] are borrowed from the Indo-Iranian word (P *jegar* and Kurdish *ceger/cerg*), and Kurdish appears to have borrowed **kezeb** from Semitic, most likely from Aram. For this to be the case, two assumptions must be made: (1) -z- for Semitic -d- suggests that this form originally had a voiced interdental fricative in this position [-ḏ-, like the th- in **th**is], which rules out Arabic, while describing the situation in Aramaic; (2) a metathesis occurred, from *-vḏ- > *-ḏv- [and thence > *-ḏev > * -zev; or: thence > *-zv- > * -zev].

K'inoşe, kinûşik *f.* Broom. {*also*: ‹kinoşe› (HH)} {*syn*: Avlêk/Havlêk [from Arm *avel*] (Tunceli/Dersim-Bingöl-Karakoçan dialect); Gêzî; Melk'es [from Arab *miknasah*] (Çinar, south of Diyarbakır); Siqavêl [also from Arm *avel*] (denotes a large broom for sweeping out a stable); Sivnik; Şicing (Kırşehir in Central Anatolia); Şirt (Ergani, north of Diyarbakır)} < NENA *kānüštā* (Maclean); cf. Aram *kenaš* = 'to gather; to sweep' and *kenošaʾah* = 'sweeper'; Syr √k-n-š = 'to gather; to sweep' and *kenōštō* = 'sweepings, rubbish'; cf. also Arab *kannasa* II = 'to sweep' and *miknasah* = 'broom'.

K'irîv, k'irîb *m.* (1) Godfather, the man who holds a male child who is being circumcised (a fictive kinship relationship: East Anatolian Turkish *kirve/kivre*);[13] (2) nickname for various religious minorities: (1) Yezidi;

13. According to Sedat Veyis Örnek, this phenomenon is known in Turkey, south of an imaginary line drawn between Kars and Sivas, and east of one drawn between Sivas and Mersin (roughly

(b) Christian [= Armenian or Assyrian-Nestorian-Chaldean]. {*also*: [qiriw] (JJ); ⟨kirîva⟩ (HH)} < Aram *ḳarev* = 'near, related'; NENA *qarība* = 'relative; godfather, best man' and *qarūta* = 'bridesmaid'. The misleading thing about Kurdish **k'irîv** is the fact that the initial letter is an aspirated **k'-** rather than **q-**: of the Kurdish sources, only JJ gives a form with [q].

Nep'ixîn *vi.* **(dinep'ixe)** (1) To swell up (vi.), be puffed up {*syn*: Werimîn}. This has a corresponding causative **nep'ixandin** *vt.* **(dinep'ixîne)** = To cause to swell, blow, puff up (vt.); (2) to pant, be out of breath. < Aram √n-p-ḥ = 'to be blown up, swell'; cf. Arab *nafaxa* = 'to blow; inflate'.

P'ale *m.* (1) Worker, workman (cf. also, Az T *fähłä* = 'worker'); day-laborer {*syn*: K'arker; Xebatk'ar); (2) harvester, agricultural worker, farmhand. < Aram *pelaḥ* = 'to till, work; to serve, worship' and *pālḥā* = 'worker, servant; worshipper': NENA √p-l-x: *pla:xa* = 'to work' and *pala:xa* (m) = 'worker' (Krotkoff); cf. Arab *falaḥa* = 'to plow, till, cultivate' and *fallāḥ* = 'peasant, farmer, tiller of the land' (perhaps the etymon of the Kurdish word **file[h]** meaning 'Christian; Armenian; Assyrian-Nestorian-Chaldean'?). In light of the fact that Sor has both *fe'le/fa'le/fele* = 'worker' and *fełe/pałe* = 'agricultural worker', perhaps the roots √p-l-ḥ and √p-^{c}-l became confused in Kurdish. This might account for the lack of final -ḥ in **p'ale** and **fełe**.

P'ekandin, peqandin *vt.* **(dip'ekîne, dipeqîne)** [causative] {*also*: paqānd- (JJ-Prym and Socin)/pakánd- (JJ-Garzoni)} (1) To burst, split, crack (vt.); (2) to crush, squash; (3) to cut off, chop off, sever, break off. This must be considered together with the following:

P'ekîn/pekîn *vi.* **(dip[']eke)** {*also*: P'eqîn; [pŭkīn] (JJ)} (1) To come off, break off (vi.), come undone, e.g.: **Gustîlek di destê hakim de bû . . . ji destê wî pekîya** (L) There was a ring on the king's hand . . . it came off his hand; (2) to drop (vi), fall (into) {*syn*: K'etin; Weşîn}; (3) to splash, splatter (*of liquids*) (vi.), e.g.: **Niqitkeke xûna wî dîsa pekîya ort'a Mem û Zînê** (Z-1) A drop of his blood (again) splattered between Mem and Zin; (4) to explode, flash (*of sparks*, etc.), e.g.: **Ew milê Ûsiv digire sîleke usa lê dixe, wekî ji ç'avê wî pirîsk dipekin** (Ba3-3, #25) He grabs Joseph's arm and slaps him so hard that sparks fly out of his

the area of Kurdistan); it is virtually unknown to the west and north of this area (see his *Türk Halkbilimi* [Ankara: Ajans-Türk Matbaası, 1977] 183). The word seems to be unknown in Sorani Kurdish as well.

eyes. < Aram *peqa*^{c} / Syr √p-q-^{c} = 'to burst, break; to escape'; NENA *pâqé/păqî* (Maclean). For the medial -q- of the original Aram, Kurdish has both -k- and -q-. The disappearance of the final ^{c}*ayn* is not uncommon; cf. **civîn** = 'to gather, assemble (vi.)' and **civandin** = 'to gather (vt.), bring together' < Arab √j-m-^{c}; **qetîn** = 'to be split, cracked, torn' and **qetandin** = 'to split, crack, tear' < Arab √q-ṭ-^{c}.

(Southern Krm and Sor) **Qeşe** (m.) Christian clergyman, priest. < Syr *qašō*, contracted form of *qašīšo* = 'elder; ancestor; priest, presbyter'; NENA *qāšā* (Maclean: *qâshâ*) and Turoyo *qāšō*; cf. Arab *qiss/qass, qissīs* [colloquial *qassīs*], colloquial Baghdadi also *kišīš*; P *kašīš*.

Şemitandin *vt.* **(dişemitîne)** [causative] To cause to slip, cause to slide {*also*: Şimitandin; ‹şemiṭandin (dişemiṭîne)› (HH)} and **Şemitîn, şemitîn, şimitîn** *vi.* **(dişemite)** To slip, slide, e.g.: **Beyrim li ser devê çalê şemitî** (L) Beyrim slipped over the mouth of the pit. {*also*: [chemitin] (JJ); ‹şemiṭîn (dişemi(ṭî))› (HH)} < Aram *šemaṭ/šemeṭ* = 'to loosen, detach, break loose, take away; to slip off, glide; to be released, rest, lie fallow' and Syr √š-m-ṭ = 'to draw, unsheath; to pluck, tear out (hair, feathers); to pull off (shoes)'.

Şêt *adj.* Mad, crazy, insane. {*syn*: Dîn; Gêj; Neḧiş} < Aram *šēḏā* = 'devil'. People who are crazy are thought to be possessed by a devil, or a jinn; cf. Arab *majnūn* = 'possessed by jinn'; also P *šeydā* = 'passionate, frenzied' (cf. Weryho, p. 309).

Şitil, şet'el, şetil *f./m.* Sapling, seedling, young tree; young plant, e.g.: **Şitla bîyê** (Z-3) Young willow tree, and by extension a tall, slender and graceful person [cf. Turkish *selvi/servi boylu*]. < Aram *šetal/šetel* [and Heb *šatal*] = 'to plant (trees)'; Syr *šetlō* and NENA *šitla* = 'plant' and *šatalta/štilta* = 'grove of planted trees' (Oraham); cf. also Arab *šatlah* = 'nursery plant'.

Şiver̄ê, şivêle (JB3), **šivîle** (K/A) *f.* Rural road, country road; rough path; path, trail; narrow path through the fields; narrow, non-paved path, e.g.: **R̄okê bazirganekî giran tê şiver̄îya ber bîrêr̄a derbaz dibe** (Ba) One day a large caravan passes by the well on a path (or, country road). {*also*: [chiw-a ri] (JJ); ‹şivarê› (HH)} Cf. Aram *ševīlā* = 'road, path', the modern form *shwîlâ* (= highway) being designated by Maclean as literary or classical. If the form **şiverê** is indeed of Aramaic provenance, the final syllable -lā was identified by Kurds as **r̄ê** (f.), the Kurdish word for 'road' (cf. Persian *rāh*). This identification of the word with Kurdish **r̄ê** would also account for the feminine gender in

Kurdish, whereas the posited original Aramaic word is masculine. Cf. **doşav** for another example of the identification of the final part of a foreign word (in this case -av) with a native word.

Şoşman, şoşban, şoşbîn, şoşpan *m.* "Best man" at a wedding; (at traditional Kurdish weddings) friend of the bridegroom, who during the wedding, together with the groom, throws an apple at the bride (IF). {*also*: [chouch-bin] (JJ)} < Aram *šošvina/šušvina* = 'best man; king's friend, counsellor' (M. Jastrow); Syr *šušvēnō* = 'bridegroom's friend, groomsman; bridesmaid; godparent, sponsor'; NENA *shushebey-na* (Oraham); cf. Assyrian *susabinu* (Del. Assyr. Handw., p. 506); Heb *šošvin* and Arab *išbīn* = 'godfather; best man'.

Şûre, şîhr and **şûhr** (M-Am), **şûr** (M-Ak), **şûrhe** (M-Zx) *f.* (1) {*syn*: Beden; Sûr} Wall, fortification wall, curtain wall of a town, e.g.: **Amêdîê ya li serê girekî, ya ḧisar-kirîye. Domendorêt ẉê şîhrin, hemî şîhrin, di bilindin, bejna do kîlomêtra di bilindin** (M-Am, 718) Amadiye is on the top of a hill and is walled round. All round it there are walls, all walls, high, to a height of two kilometres; **Xulase ker o xudanê kerî her do ji şûra rezî wajî kirin** (SK, 80) In short he tipped both the donkey and its owner over the wall of the (terraced) orchard; (2) wooden fence surrounding a field or a garden (IF). {*also*: [chour/sour] (JJ)} < Aram *šūr(ā)* and Syr *šūrō* = 'city wall, fortification'; cf. Arab *sūr*. According to MacKenzie, "The curtain wall of a town, Rdz. **šūra**, Ak. **šûr**, Am. ***šûhr, sīhr**, Zx. **šûrha** (< Syr. **šūrā**). Elsewhere the Ar. word **sūr** is used" (M, vol. 2, p. 376, n. 718[1]).

T'ixûb, tixub, t'ẍûb *m./f.* (1) Border, limit, boundary, e.g.: **Esker-leşkerê gran, ji t'ẍûbê benî adem derk'etin, ghîştin cîkî usa, wekî r̄eşk-tarî bû, nêzîkî p'er̄ê e'zman bûn** (EH) The great army passed beyond the boundary of human beings, and reached a place which was dark, near the edge (or, "wings") of the sky; **T'ixûba xorta t'uneye** (Dz) There is no limit for young men (= the young think they can do everything) [proverb]; (2) the Tikhub district. {*also*: [tokóbi] (JJ-G); [t'khob] (JJ-Rh); ⟨tuxûb⟩ (HH)} {*syn*: Sînor} < Aram and Heb *teḥum* = 'dominion, area, district, border, limits', originally a surrounded, marked place; cf. Heb *ḥomah* = 'city wall'; Syr *teḥūmō* = 'border, limit; precept, regulation, penalty'; NENA *tikhûb* (Maclean), apparently borrowing the Kurdish form; Sor *tixûb* = 'boundary, frontier'.

Xebat, xevat *f.* (1) Work, labor {*syn*: îş; şuxul; = Sor firman}; (2) struggle; (3) effort, activity (JJ). {*also*: [khebat] (JJ); ⟨xebat⟩ (HH)} Sor *xebat* =

'effort'. This word has a corresponding verb **xebitîn** *vt.* (**dixebite**) = 'to work'.[14] < Syr √ḥ-p-ṭ: *ḥepēṭ* = 'diligent, assiduous, painstaking' and *etḥapaṭ* = 'to take pains, endeavor, be diligent; to work in'; NENA *khpaa-taa* = 'to urge on; to be diligent' (Oraham).

Xuya, xoya, xuyan, xûya, xweya, xweyan, xwîya *adj.* Visible, apparent, obvious, e.g.: **Ya xortê delal, tu zilamekî x̃erîb xwîya ye** (L) (Oh dandy youth, you appear to be a stranger [in these parts]; **-Xuya bûn** = To appear, be seen, e.g.: **Kes xuyan nabe (nake)** (B) There is no one to be seen; **-Xuya kirin** (A): (a) To show, reveal {*syn*: Mewcûd kirin; Nîşan dan; Peyda kirin}; (b) to seem {*also*: [khouia] (JJ); ⟨xuweya⟩ (HH)} {*syn*: Aşkere; Dîhar; K'ifş; Xanê}; and **Xuyan** *vi.* (**-xwên-/-xwey-** [Msr]) (1) To appear, seem: **Tu pir̃ civan dixweyî** (Msr) You look very young; (2) to make one's appearance, show up; to come to light, be discovered, show (vi.), reveal o.s., manifest o.s., be seen. {*also*: Xweyan (dixweye); Xwîngiyan; Xwîngîn (dixwîngê); Xwîyan; Xwuyan; ⟨xuweyan (dixweye)⟩ (HH)} < Aram *ḥawwē/aḥawē* = 'to show; to tell'; NENA *maxwo:ye* (Krotkoff) and Turoyo *máḥwe* = 'to show; to look (vi.), appear'.

Words Whose Aramaic Provenance Is Possible but Not Certain

(Sor) **Kabra** Man, fellow. Cf. Aram *gavrā/gevar* = 'man', NENA *gôrâ* (Maclean). It is doubtful that the Kurdish word is directly derived from the Aramaic. However, the meaning of the latter may have been combined with a similar-sounding word of different but related meaning. There is a Kurdish word for a young ram, **kavir̃** (Krm) = 'male sheep between one and three years old' and **kawur̃** (Sor) = 'lamb three to six months old'. This word is of Indo-European origin and is ultimately cognate with Latin *caper* = 'goat'. In several Middle Eastern languages there seems to be a link between words denoting goats and sheep on the one hand, and those denoting males on the other, e.g., Krm *nêrî* = 'male goat' < *nêr* = 'male animal'; T *oğlak* = 'kid, young goat' < *oğul* = 'son, male child'. The English word *kid*, meaning both 'young goat' and 'child', may also be part of this trend. The word

14. There are several cases of a Semitic root borrowed into Kurdish in the form of a noun in the pattern Fe^{c}al with a corresponding verb in the pattern Fe^{c}ilīn, often with a causative verb in Fe^{c}ilandin. Examples include **zewac** (f.) = 'marriage'—**zewicîn** = 'to get married'—**zewicandin** = 'to marry off (one's children)' (< Arab *zawj*); **nep'ax** (f.) = 'swelling'—**nep'ixîn** = 'to swell up (vi.)'—**nep'ixandin** = 'to swell up (vt.)' (< Aram √n-p-ḥ).

kabra, however, if it is indeed related to *kavir̄/kawur̄*, would pose a problem: whereas both Krm *nêrî* and T *oğlak* are derived from words denoting males, **kabra** would be the source rather than the product of such a derivation. In other words, the direction of transmission is problematic. Perhaps the similarity in form between Aram *gavrā* and Kurdish *kavir̄/kawur̄* combined to create a hybrid in which the shared semantic properties of the two terms (i.e., their denoting males) and their similar phonetic properties yielded: *kabra* = 'man'. Other examples of such hybridization need to be adduced before such a hypothesis can be considered plausible.

(Krm) **Li** and (Sor) **le [lê]** *prep.* At; in, especially in conjunction with the postposition -da, e.g.: (Sor) ***Le aş-eke-da kes niye*** = 'There is nobody in the mill'. In Sor, **le** can also mean 'from' (= Krm **ji**, cognate with P *az*), particularly in conjunction with the postposition *-ewe*, e.g.: (Sor) ***Le mał-î drawsê-m-ewe e-hat-im*** = 'I was coming from my neighbor's house'. Moreover, the simple preposition **di** (Krm)/**de** (Mukri Sor) has been all but replaced in the Sorani dialect of Sulaimania by **le**. Cf. Aram *le-* and Arab *li-*, both of which mean 'to' (indicating motion toward a place) and are written as prefixes to the noun they govern.

Şit'af. This word, which is not well-attested in the dictionaries, occurs several times in a version of the Kurdish romance **Xec û Sîyabend**, at a point where the young man Sîyabend prepares to ride his horse. The relevant passages are as follows:

IS 64. Sîabend dibêje wan xulama: "Hûn her̄in, bêjne aẍayê min, bila rima şit'af, hespê şê bide min, ezê her̄im şer̄e bazirganbaşî. 65. Yanê ez tême kuştinê, yanê ez bazirganbaşî dikujim!"

64. Siabend says to those servants, "You go, tell my agha to give me the [swift?] lance, the bay horse, [and] I will go fight the caravan chief. 65. Either I will be killed, or I will kill the caravan chief!"

IS 90. Sîabend hespê şê—şit'afek dayê, zînê wî bi du tenga li ser piştê şidand, rima şit'af hilda û sîyar bû.

90. Siabend [gave a washing?] to the bay horse, fastened onto his back his saddle with two straps, grabbed the [swift?] lance and mounted.

IS 345. Sîabend rabû, hespê şê k'işand, şit'afek dayê, sîyar bû û rima şit'af hilda.

345. Siabend led out the bay horse, [gave him a washing?], mounted and grabbed the [swift?] lance.

There seem to be two distinct words in this text that have come together as **şit'af**.

(1) **R̄ima şit'af**, which the Soviet scholars Dzhangoev and Tsukerman translate as *kalënoe kop'ë* = 'tempered spear'. I think that **şit'af** is here from Persian *šetāb* = 'haste, rush', and consequently the phrase **r̄ima şit'af** should be translated 'swift spear' (cf. Kurdoev *şetab* (K) = *speška, pospešnost', toroplivost'* = 'haste, rush, hurriedness'). This is the sort of noun + epithet phrase that characterizes the formulaic language of the Homeric epic, Serbo-Croatian epic songs (*junačke pesme*), and such Kurdish romances as *Mem û Zîn* and *Xec û Sîyabend.*

(2) **Şit'af dan**, which A. A. Dzhangoev and I. I. Tsukerman translate as *gladit'* = 'to strike, pat'. A. Jaba and F. Justi [JJ] list the word [chetaoŭ] = 'action de laver un cheval; action de flatter quelqu'un, faire la cour', which is echoed in T. Wahby and C. J. Edmonds (for Sorani) as *shetaw* [= şetaw] *kirdin* = 'to splash water over, wash (animals)'. I suspect that this is from the Aram verb *šəṭef* (cf. Heb *šaṭaf*) = 'to wash, rinse'. Hence, Sîyabend would not be petting the horse, but rather washing him down before riding off on him.

In another text, the form **şt[']ar** occurs twice, in a similar context. This form does not appear in any of the dictionaries. The following are the occurrences of **ştar kirin**:

> *Ewana ser kanîê peya bûn, hespê xwe avdan, ştar kirin, hatin r̄ûniştin, ser û ç'e'vê xwe şûştin* (EH, p. 234).
>
> They dismounted at the spring, watered their horses, [washed them down?], came and sat down, washed their faces [lit. 'head and eyes'].

> *Wana k'incê xwe êxistin û k'etine avê, xwe di avêda t'êr şûştin, dîsa av vexarin, hespê xwe şt'ar kirin* (EH).
>
> They took off their clothes and got into the water, bathed their fill in the water, then drank water, and [washed down?] their horses.

Whatever **şt[']ar kirin** means, it is clear that it denotes an action that requires water. My guess is that **şit'af dan** and **şt[']ar kirin** are two variants of the same word. The consonants -f- and -r- are not regular reflexes of one another, but if the informant for the text in which **şt[']ar kirin** occurs were reaching for a fancy turn of phrase, he could have garbled a word that was not normally part of his active vocabulary. As I mention in my dissertation,[15] until folklorists and linguists start to record the context in which folktales and the like are collected, such comments must remain in the realm of conjecture.

15. *"And a Thornbush Sprang Up between Them": Studies in Mem û Zîn, a Kurdish Romance* (Ph.D. diss., Berkeley: University of California, Berkeley, 1991).

In yet another text, this time from one of the earliest versions of *Mem û Zîn* to have been collected (ca. 1870), paraphrases of the posited meaning of **şit'af/şt[']ar** occur in a similar context:

> [Memo rabû karê xwe kir, hespê xwe îna derê, hespê xwe meĥes û gelveşîn kir. Zînê ser piştê danî, teng û balatengê xwe şidandin . . . şûrê xwe avêt pişta xwe, rumana zerîn bi destê xwe girt û rabû suwar bû] (PS-#31, p. 72).
>
> Mem made preparations, took out his horse and combed him down. He saddled him up, and fastened his saddle-girth . . . fastened his sword to his waist, took his golden lance in his hand and mounted his horse.

> [. . . ew bi xwe rabû hespê xwe îna, li hespê xwe suwar bû, ruma xwe bi destê xwe girt û rabû derket . . . Hespê wî kişand, taze naze meĥes û gelveşîn kir, zîn ser piştê danî. . . . rum bi destê xwe girt, şîr avête pişta xwe . . .] (PS-#31, p. 73).
>
> He himself got up and brought out his horse, mounted his horse, took his lance in his hand and set out. . . . He led out his horse and gently combed him down, put a saddle on his back . . . he took his lance in hand, girded himself with his sword. . . .

In this text, [meĥes û gelveşîn kirin] is a paraphrase for **şit'af dan ~ şt[']ar kirin. Meĥes** (< Arab *miḥassah*) is a curry-comb, a comb made of rows of metallic teeth or serrated ridges, used to curry or dress horses; **gelveşîn** is a rag used for wiping the sweat off a horse. Hence, **meĥes û gelveşîn kirin** = 'to comb and rub down (a horse)', which is comparable to washing a horse down. Note that once again a javelin is mentioned, as with the sentences from IS in which **şit'af** occurs.

Telandin *vt.* **(ditelîne)** [causative] To hide (vt.), conceal {*syn*: Veşartin} and **Telîn** *vi.* **(ditele)** To hide (vi.), conceal o.s., e.g.: **Zînê k'etibû bin qap'ûtê Memê, telîya bû** (Z-1) Zin got under Mem's coat, she hid. Cf. Turoyo t-l-y = 'to be removed'; Aram *telā/telē* = 'to lift up; to suspend, hang; to be hanged' and Syr *telō* = 'to lift up, hang up, suspend; [+ mən] to draw back, take away'. The range of meanings of the original Aramaic and Syriac word include both 'hanging' and 'lifting up'; in Turoyo, the basic meaning is 'removing', which is an extension of the idea of lifting up. The Kurdish meaning, if it is indeed from this root, would require 'removal' to be taken yet a step further, so that 'hiding' is a way of removing oneself. The sample sentence given above, taken from the climax of the story of *Mem û Zîn*, supports this view.

I would like to end with some conclusions based on the preceding word list. Many of the Aramaic borrowings into Kurdish seem to be older than

NENA. The Kurdish word for liver, **kezeb/kezev**, was taken into Kurdish at a time when the Aramaic form was still ***kavḏa** or the like, whereas NENA has **kôda** (-av- > -ô-), which has all but been replaced by the Iranian word *jîgâr*: if the word is not in use in Neo-Aramaic, the Kurds could not have heard it from their Neo-Aramaic–speaking neighbors. A piece of evidence that may prove helpful in dating such borrowings is the presence or absence of the Aramaic emphatic final -a (W Syr -ō) on nouns and adjectives. When it does occur in Kurdish, it seems to take the form of -e, which appears in the list above in the following words: *besîre*, *k'inoşe*, *p'ale* (?), *pil̄îte* (Sor), *qeşe*, *şivêle/şivîle*, *şûr*[*h*]*e*;[16] also possibly in *kabra* (with final -a).

If my suggestion about **doşav** and **şiver̄ê** is correct, there are words in which the final syllable of a foreign word is reinterpreted in Kurdish as a native word, in these instances **av** meaning 'water' and **r̄ê** meaning 'road'. There may be many more examples of this phenomenon that we have yet to identify. Another phenomenon involving the confusion of sounds in borrowed words is the possible conflation of two Semitic roots, √p-l-ḥ and √p-ᶜ-l, in the case of **p'ale** (workman) and related forms.

With regard to phonological correspondences, I would like to make a few observations. The Aramaic *Pe*, which has two realizations in Classical Aramaic, as /p/ and as spirantized /ph/ = /f/, has the same two realizations in Kurdish, although the original Semitic rules do not apply. Whereas in Classical Aramaic initial p is always /p/, and intervocalic and final p is always /f/,[17] NENA has /p/ in all positions, and Turoyo generally has /f/. In Kurdish, initial *Pe* is realized both as /p/, e.g., **p'ale**, **peqandin/p'ekandin**, and as /f/, e.g., **fehêt**, **fetilîn**, **filitîn**. In the case of the word for 'wick', both are in evidence: (Sor) **pil̄îte** and (Krm) **pilte**, as well as (Krm) **fitîl**. Intervocalic *Pe* is realized as /p/ in **nep'ixîn**, which is contrary to the rules of Classical Aramaic but in line with the situation in NENA. Final *Pe* is also realized as /p/ in **dilop**, again with the same relationships vis-à-vis Classical Aramaic and NENA.

Aramaic *Ḥeth* has three realizations in the above list: /h/ in **dahoł**, /∅/ in **p'ale**, and /x/ in **nep'ixîn**, **t'ixûb**, **xebat**, and **xuya**. The most common sound, the latter one, reflects the norm in NENA. Curiously, none of these three phonetic realizations reflects what we think was the original sound in Aramaic (i.e., Arabic /ḥ/). This sound exists in Kurdish and is written as ḧ (h with diaeresis) in Kurdish orthography, although often appearing as h, and occurs in words borrowed from Arabic as well as in many native words, e.g., **ḧirç'** 'bear, ur-

16. This word is particularly interesting because it also occurs within final -e in the following forms: *şîhr*, *şûhr*, and *şûr*. See **şûre** above.

17. Excepting intervocalic geminate p, as in the verbal form *qaṭṭel*.

sus'.[18] In some words borrowed from Arabic, a final /ḥ/ disappears, e.g., **mifte** 'key' (< Arab *miftāḥ*): this may also be the case in our word **p'ale**. Insofar as the /h/ in **dahoł** is concerned, the Early Modern Persian form has the same realization, appearing as D$^{\supset}$HL (rather than *D$^{\supset}$ḤL[19]).

Aramaic *Qof* has two realizations in the list. Both initially and intervocalically, it has the alternative realizations /k/ and /q/. Initially, we have both (a) **k'irîv** and (b) **[qiriw]** and **qeşe**. Intervocalically, both **p'ekandin** and **peqandin** are attested. NENA has /q/ in all these cases.

It is hoped that this line of inquiry may one day be helpful in dating and sorting out the provenance of Aramaic borrowings into Kurdish. Just as W. B. Bishai's article about Coptic lexical influence on Egyptian Arabic[20] was later supplemented and augmented by Peter Behnstedt,[21] let me close by inviting Kurdologists, Aramaists, and other interested scholars to expand our knowledge of the interrelations between these understudied minority languages of the Middle East.

18. According to Otto Jastrow, this sound and the ʿ*ayin* are too well entrenched in Kurdish to have been the result of Arabic influence alone. He suggests that Kurdish borrowed these sounds from Aramaic, the NENA and Mandaic dialects of which subsequently lost them (personal communication).

19. Both H and Ḥ are pronounced /h/ in Modern Persian. The Ḥ appears only in Arabic loanwords.

20. W. B. Bishai, "Coptic Lexical Influence on Egyptian Arabic," *JNES* 23 (1964) 39ff.

21. P. Behnstedt, "Weitere koptische Lehnwörter im Ägyptisch-Arabischen," *Die Welt des Orients* 12 (1981) 81–98.

Abbreviations Used in This Article

A	Musa Anter, *Ferhenga Khurdî-Tirkî = Kürdçe-Türkçe Sözlük* (Istanbul: Yeni Matbaa, 1967) [Mardin, Turkey].
adj.	adjective
Arab	Arabic
Aram	Aramaic
Arm	Armenian
Az T	Azerbaijani Turkish, Azeri
B	Ch. Kh. Bakaev, *Kurdsko-Russkiĭ Slovar'* . . . okolo 14000 slov s prilozheniem grammaticheskogo ocherka kurdskogo iazyka (Moscow: Gosudarstvennoe Uzdatel'stvo Inostrannykh i Natsional'nykh Slovarei, 1957) 618 pp. [USSR].
Ba	Ch. Kh. Bakaev, *IAzyk kurdov SSSR* (= The language of the Kurds of the USSR) (Moscow: Nauka, 1973) 313–[346].

Costaz — Louis Costaz, *Dictionnaire Syriaque-Français* (Syriac-English Dictionary = *Qāmūs Suryānī-ʿArabī*) (Beirut: Imprimerie Catholique, 1963) xxiii, 421 pp.

Del. Assyr. Handw. — Friedrich Delitzsch, *Assyrisches Wörterbuch zur gesamten bisher veröffentlichten Keilschriftliteratur* (Leipzig: Hinrichs, 1887–90), 3 parts.

Dz — Ordikhane Dzhalil and Dzhalile Dzhalil, *Mesele û Met'elokê K'urda bi Zimanê K'urdî û Rûsî* (Kurdskie Poslovitsy i Pogovorki na Kurdskom i Russkom IAzykakh) (Moscow: Glavnaia redaktsiia vostochnoĭ literatury, 1972) 454 pp. [Kurmanji proverbs; also includes Sorani proverbs from Iraq].

E — east

EH — Emin E'vdal, *Heleqetîêd pizmamtîê nav K'urdada* (Erêvan: Neşireta Akadêmîa RSS Ermenîstanêye Ulma, 1965) 213–[237] [A study of kinship relations among the Kurds; contains six folktales as an appendix].

f. — feminine gender (of noun)

Heb — Hebrew

HH — Ḍiyā' al-Dīn al-Khālidī al-Maqdisī, *Al-Hadiyah al-Ḥamīdīyah* (Beirut, 1975) 56, 240 pp. = Mohammad Mokri, *Recherches de Kurdologie: Dictionnaire Kurde-Arabe de Diaʾ Ad-Din Pacha al-Khalidi*: Introduction et notes linguistiques, notice sur la phonétique et la graphie arabo-persane du dialecte kurmandji, Textes et étude religieux, linguistiques et ethnographiques (Langues et civilisation iraniennes 4; Beirut and Paris, 1975) [Muş, Turkey].

IF — D. Izolî, *Ferheng: Kurdî-Tirkî, Türkçe-Kürtçe* (Den Haag: Komeley Xwêndikaranî Kurd le Ewrupa, [1987]) [Turkey].

IS — *Iranskiĭ Sbornik . . . I. I. Zarubina* (Moscow: Izd-stvo Vostochnoĭ Literatury, 1963) 219–48, 249–55.

JB1 — Joyce Blau, *Le Kurde de ʿAmadiya et de Djabal Sindjar: Analyse linguistique, textes folkloriques, glossaires* (Paris: Klincksieck, 1975) [Amadiya (A) and Jabal Sinjar (S), northern Iraq].

JB3 — Joyce Blau, (*Kurdish-French-English dictionary*) *Dictionnaire Kurde-Français-Anglais* (Brussels: Centre pour l'Étude des Problèmes du Monde Musulman Contemporain, 1965) [literary].

JJ — Auguste Jaba and Ferdinand Justi, *Dictionnaire Kurde-Français* (St. Petersburg: Eggers, 1879) [Kurmanji of Hakkari and environs?; JJ-G = citation from: Garzoni, *Grammatica e vocabolario della lingua kurda* (Rome, 1787); JJ=Rh = citation from: Samuel A. Rhea, "Brief Grammar and Vocabulary of the Kurdish Language of the Hakari District," *JAOS* 10 (1872) 118ff.].

JR — Alexandre Jaba, *Recueil de Notices et de Récits Kourdes* (St. Petersburg: Eggers, 1860; repr. Amsterdam: Philo, 1979) 111, 128 pp. [although supposedly collected in Erzurum, the informant's dialect is more southerly, perhaps from the region of Hakkari].

K — K. K. Kurdoev, *Ferhenga Kurdî-Rûsî* (Kurdsko-Russkiĭ Slovar') (Moscow: Gosudarstvennoe izd-vo inostrannykh i natsional'nykh slovareĭ, 1960) [primarily USSR].

K2-Fêrîk "Fêrîk," in *Grammatika Kurdkogo IAzyka (Kurmandzhi): Fonetika, Morfologiiâ* (ed. K. K. Kurdoev; Moscow-Leningrad: Izd-vo Akademii Nauk SSSR, 1957) 328–34 [short story in the standard written Kurmanji of Erevan].

K3 K. K. Kurdoev, *Ferhengî Kurdî-R̄ûsî (Soranî)* (Kurdsko-Russkiĭ Slovar' [Sorani]) (Moscow: Russkiĭ IÂzyk, 1983) 752 pp. [Sorani Kurdish-Russian dictionary].

Krm Kurmanji (northern) Kurdish

Krotkoff Georg Krotkoff, *A Neo-Aramaic Dialect of Kurdistan: Texts, Grammar, and Vocabulary* (New Haven: American Oriental Society, 1982) 172 pp. [Neo-Aramaic dialect of the village of Aradhin, 10 miles west of Amadia, Kurdistan of Iraq].

L Roger Lescot, *Textes Kurdes* (2 vols.; Paris: Geuthner, 1940–42).

m. masculine gender (of noun)

M D. N. MacKenzie, *Kurdish Dialect Studies* (2 vols.; London: Oxford University Press, 1961–62) [Southern Kurmanji forms are from Akre (= Ak), unless otherwise marked: Amadiya (= Am); Sheikhan (= Sh); Zakho (= Zx); Surći tribe (= Sr), Kurdistan of Iraq].

Maclean Arthur John Maclean, *Dictionary of the Dialects of Vernacular Syriac as Spoken by the Eastern Syrians of Kurdistan, North-West Persia and the Plain of Mosul* (Oxford: Clarendon, 1901; repr. Amsterdam: Philo, 1972) 334 pp. [NENA dictionary].

Mal Malmisanij, *Zazaca-Türkçe Sözlük* (Ferhengê Dımılki-Tırki) (Uppsala: Jina Nû, 1987) 431 pp. [Zaza-Turkish dictionary].

M. Jastrow Marcus Jastrow, ספר מלים: *A Dictionary of the Targumim, the Talmud Babli and Yerushalmi, and the Midrashic Literature* (2 vols. in 1; New York: Judaica, 1985).

NENA Northeastern Neo-Aramaic, term suggested by Robert Hoberman to refer to the largest Neo-Aramaic dialect cluster, spoken by the Jews of Kurdistan, and the Assyrians, Nestorians, and Chaldeans.

Oraham Alexander Joseph Oraham, *Oraham's Dictionary of the Stabilized and Enriched Assyrian Language and English* (Chicago: Consolidated Press [Assyrian Press of America], 1943) 576 pp. [NENA dictionary].

o.s. oneself

P Persian

prep. preposition

PS Eugen Prym and Albert Socin, *Kurdische Sammlungen: Erzählungen und Lieder in den Dialekten des Tûr ᶜAbdîn und von Bohtan* (St. Petersburg: Eggers, [1887–]1890) [Tûr ᶜAbdîn (Mardin), Turkey and Zakho, Bohtan (= Behdinan), Iraq] (PS-I = Tûr ᶜAbdîn, Mardin, Turkey; PS-II = Zakho, Bohtan, Iraq).

s.o. someone

Sor Sorani [central] Kurdish

stg. something

syn. synonym

Syr	Syriac
T	Turkish
vi.	intransitive verb
vSoden	W. von Soden, *Akkadisches Handwörterbuch* (Wiesbaden: Harrassowitz, 1959–81).
vt.	transitive verb (with ergative past tense)
W	west
Weryho	Jan W. Weryho, "Syriac Influence on Islamic Iran: The Evidence of Loan-words," *Folia Orientalia* 13 (1971) 300–321.
Z-3	Text no. 3, in Ordikhane Dzhalilov and Dzhalil Dzhalilov, *Zargotina K'urda* (Kurdskiĭ Fol'klor) (2 vols.; Moscow; Nauka, 1978).
Za	Zaza, Dumilî

The Story of Balaam and His She-Ass in Four Neo-Aramaic Dialects:

A Comparative Study of the Translations

Yona Sabar

Either the entire Bible or parts of it have been translated into several Christian and Jewish Neo-Aramaic dialects. However, only a few of these translations have appeared so far in print.[1] For ritual and prayer, the Christian speakers of Neo-Aramaic usually used the Old Syriac translations of the Bible, and the

Author's note: Dedicated to Prof. Krotkoff for his fine contributions to Neo-Aramaic studies in the areas of dialectology and semantics.

Grammatical abbreviations used in this essay are: p.p. (passive participle), pret. (preterite), sg. (singular), pl. (plural), a.p. (active participle), and imperf. (imperfect).

1. For the printed editions, see the bibliography below.

Jews, the Hebrew and the Old Aramaic targums. The Neo-Aramaic translations were used mostly for instruction of children in the traditional schools and were orally transmitted from generation to generation. Only in recent years, most at the initiative of missionaries or scholars of Neo-Aramaic, some of these translations were written down or recorded.

The following story of Balaam and his she-ass is taken from the book of Numbers, which is a part of my project on Jewish Neo-Aramaic Translations of the Pentateuch, which was completed in 1995, in cooperation with the Language Traditions Project of The Hebrew University, Jerusalem, headed by Prof. Shelomo Morag. The story appears in four dialects: (1) the Jewish Neo-Aramaic dialect of Zakho (northern Iraq, near the Turkish border)—based on a tape-recording of the informant, Rabbi Hakham Levi Amram; (2) the Jewish Neo-Aramaic dialect of Dihok [Dohuk on the maps, northern Iraq, southeast of Zakho—eds.]—based on a manuscript (National Library, Jerusalem, #8° 712) by Hakham Elyahu Abraham Mizrahi Dihoki (nicknamed Abu Abdallah); (3) the Jewish Neo-Aramaic dialect of Urmi (northern Iranian Kurdistan)—based on a manuscript by Hakham Yishay (National Library, Jerusalem, #8° 581); and (4) the Christian Neo-Aramaic dialect of Urmi—based on a printed edition (Beirut, 1966) and as recited by Mr. Patros Thoma Begzade, a native of Urmi, living now in Los Angeles.[2]

The Language of the Translations

§1. The translations are generally a word-for-word translation of the Hebrew text, yet there are some interesting deviations from this principle. Even a comparison of just one chapter (Numbers 22) in the four translations shows some typical features of each, as well as some aspects common to all, or to all three Jewish translations versus the Christian one. These differences are, as expected, mostly formal-dialectal, but there are some that are clearly related to contents, that is, interpretations or misunderstandings of Hebrew etymologies and morphology. The Christian version is more "academic" in form (the spelling in Syriac script is mostly etymological but often nonphonetic!)[3] and exact in

2. For more details on the manuscripts and the informants, see the introductions to Yona Sabar 1983, 1988, and 1990.

3. For example, the retention of *ḥ* and ᶜ when they are actually pronounced *x* and ᵓ, respectively: *ḥmrtᵓ* = *xmarta* (v. 23) 'she-ass', *ᶜl* = *ᵓal* (v. 5) 'on'. Yet there are some exceptions, for example, *ṭlᵓ* (v. 28) = *tla* (< *tlāṯā*) 'three'. [Hereafter, a number in parentheses refers to the verse number in the biblical text.]

contents,[4] whereas the Jewish manuscripts are written in a broad phonetic, usually nonetymological, Hebrew script,[5] including an inexact use of vowel letters and diacritical points,[6] and the exactness of translation depends on how knowledgeable the informant is. Hakham Levi Amram (Zakho = Z) is the most learned, followed by Hakham Yishay (Jewish Urmi = JU), and then Hakham Dihoki (Dihok = D), whose manuscript includes marginal "editorial" corrections by two other Hakhamim, one from Nerwa and one from Zakho (appearing in parentheses in our phonetic transliteration as = Dp). For technical and practical reasons, all four versions are copied here in a harmonized (Latin) phonetic transliteration, the Zakho and Christian Urmi (= ChU) being based on the recordings, and the Dihok and Jewish Urmi on the manuscripts, aided by my long experience with reading these manuscripts and general knowledge of these dialects, and for the Jewish Urmi, by a comparison, whenever possible, with the glossary of Garbell.[7]

§2. Some typical dialectal (etymological, phonetic, morphological) differences: *zıqēnīm* (4) 'elders' = Z: *zaqēnīm*, D: *sāwe*, JU + ChU: *xwārdeqne*;

4. See examples in §10 below.

5. E.g., GWRY (D: 9) = *gūre* (< *gub̲rē*), GORY (JU: 9, 20) = *gore* (< *gab̲rē*; but see n. 87 below) 'men'; *kmrtʾ* (D, JU) = *xmarta* (23) 'she-ass'; *ʾrt* = *aret* (JU: 5) (< *ʾarʿā d-*) 'land of'; *ʾalkwn* = *alxon* (JU: 13) 'your land'.

6. D regularly indicates fricative *bgdkpt* by a dot over the letter, but the indication of vowels (quality and length) by vowel points and letters is not accurate (for example, any of *ʾe*, *ʾiy*, *ʾi* may be used to indicate the central vowel *ı*). Another typical feature of D is an addition of either a prosthetic *ʾ* or a vowel to break an initial cluster: *ʾımburxa* (6) 'blessed (p.p.)', *ġızēle* (2) 'he saw'. JU often has *ʿ*, *ḥ*, *ṭ* for, respectively, *ʾ*, *h*, *t* (e.g., *ʿth* = *átta* 'now', *ʾlḥh* = *elha* 'God', *ṭwrʾ* = *tora* 'ox', *bqṭywm/bqtywm* = *baqatyom* 'morning') and only occasionally indicates the difference between plosive and fricative pronunciations of *bg*(*d*)*kp*(*t*). Both D and JU indicate the old proclitic possessive *d-* 'of' routinely as enclitic *-t*. In the ChU printed text it is always proclitic (*d-*), but the informant, Mr. Begzade, often read it as enclitic (joined to the end of the previous word). None of the texts indicates the accent, which, in all Neo-Aramaic dialects, is normally penultimate, except JU, which usually has the accent on the ultimate syllable (the exceptions in JU, that is, penultimate accent, have been marked according to Garbell, for example, *rába*, *bálki*, *átta*). For more details on the orthography and phonology, see the references in n. 2 above.

7. My transliteration of D and JU is primarily based on the manuscripts, and as such, it may not always reflect an "exact" pronunciation. In the case of JU, where emphatic "flat" pronunciation is an important phonetic feature of the dialect, I consulted Garbell 1965 (and Sabar 1975) and have indicated it in my transliteration in bold letters. I did the same for Z and ChU, based on the recordings, but avoided doing so for D, for I have no recording to compare; most likely, "flat" words in D are the same as in Z (but see n. 47 below for some possible differences). Since my main concern in this article is comparative semantics, I have avoided detailed phonological issues, and my transliteration is at times more approximate than exact. Aramaic words are italicized only in the English context. For an etymological glossary for the entire book of Numbers (including the four versions of chap. 22 given here), see Sabar 1993.

nāhār (5) 'river' = Z: *xawōra*, D + JU: *nehra*, ChU: *nāra*; *waydabbırū* (7) 'they spoke' = Z + D: *muḥkēlu*, JU: *tenelu*, ChU: *humzımlun*; *yhwh* (8) 'Lord (Yahweh)' = Z: *ᵓıstaz-ᶜōlām*, D: *y″y* (traditional Hebrew euphemistic abbreviation), JU: *adonay*, ChU: *marya*; *dereḵ* (22) 'road' = Z + D + ChU: *ᵓurxa*, but JU: *werxa*; *bēṯō* (18) 'his house' = Z: *bēse*, D: *bēṯe*, JU: *belev*, ChU: *bētu*; *yāḏī* (29) 'my hand' = Z: *ᵓīzi*, D: *ᵓīḏi*, JU + ChU: *ᵓīdi*; *līnū* (8) 'spend (the night)' = Z: *dmōxun*, D: *bōṯun*, JU: *menzulun*, ChU: *pūšun.*[8]

§3. As a rule, all Jewish versions translate as literally as possible, even at the expense of violating a grammatical agreement; *ḥarbō šılūfā* (31) 'his sword (f.) drawn (f.)' = Z: *sēpa* (m.) *dīde šlıpta* (f.), D: *sēpe* (m.) *ᵓıšlıxta* (f.), JU: *sepev* (f.? see n. 94 below) *šelexta*, but ChU: *sēpu grīša*. This literalness may be carried ad absurdum: *hayyōm hazze* (30) 'today' (lit. the-day the-this) = JU: *édyom ayya* 'today this'.[9]

§4. However, verbal forms (perfect, imperfect) usually are not translated literally but, rather, adjusted to the Neo-Aramaic verbal system, e.g.: *haraġtīḵ* (29) 'I would kill you' (lit. 'I killed you') = Z + D + ChU: *(b)qaṭlınwālax* 'I would kill you', JU: *qaṭlennax* 'I (would) kill you'.[10]

§5. A noun may be translated by a verbal form: *lısāṭān* (22) 'as an adversary' = Z: *lımdažmōne* 'to be hostile', ChU: *līwāya darqul* 'to be against' (but D + JU: *lsaṭan*).[11]

§6. An active participle may be translated by other verbal or nominal forms: *hayyōṣe* (11) 'that came out' (lit., 'coming out') = Z: *ᵓaw mpīqa* (p.p.), D: *ᵓınpıqle* (pret.), JU: *o-palṭana* (nomen agentis), ChU: *plīṭa* (p.p.); *hōlēḵ* (22) 'going' = Z: *bizāla* (gerund), D + JU + ChU: *zılle* (pret.), Dp: *ᵓazāla* (noun 'goer').[12]

§7. A collective (sg.) may be translated by pl.: *bāqār wāṣōn* (40) 'oxen and sheep' = Z: *tōre uᵓırwe*, ChU: *tōrı uᵓırbı*, but D + JU: *tōra wᵓırba.*[13]

8. For additional examples of this type from the first three books of the Pentateuch and comparisons with old and new translations, see the references in n. 2 above (Hebrew) and in Sabar 1991a: 1395–96 (English).

9. Cf. Sabar 1990: 315; 1991: 1387–88.

10. Cf. Sabar 1990: 316–17.

11. *Onqelos* has here *lısāṭān*, but in the next occurrence (32) has *lımisṭan* 'to be hostile'.

12. Cf. Sabar 1990: 316.

13. Cf. ibid., 315.

§8. Slight etymological deviations: *yereq* (4) 'greenery' = JU + ChU: *gella* 'grass', but Z + D: *yırqa*; *ᶜēn hāᵓāreṣ* (5) lit. 'eye of earth' (= view) = ChU: *pātā* 'face'; D + JU: *rang* 'color', but Z: *ᵓēna* 'eye'. Also the root *h-l-k* 'to go' is at times translated by 'to come': *lıḵa* (6) = Z: *ysa*, D: *ᵓıṯa*, JU: *ida*, ChU: *ta*; *halōḵ* (14) = JU: *idaa*, ChU: *lītāya*, but Z + D: *ᵓizāla* 'go'.

§9. A Hebrew root may be translated by a false "cognate": *hiṯᶜallalt* [< *ᶜ-l-l*] (29) 'made a mockery' = Z: *mtōᶜıllax* [< *t-ᶜ-l*], JU: *telax* 'played games', but D: *ᵓıgxıklax* 'laughed', ChU: *musxırrax* 'made a mockery'.[14]

§10. Difficult etymology or morphology may lead to a variety of interpretations, some almost opposing each other: *hahaskēn hiskantī* (30) 'have I been in the habit' = Z: *mo fhāma fhımli* 'did I have the understanding (= was I smart enough)', D: *mıᶜunkırri mıᶜankōre* 'was I stubborn', Dp: *ha ᵓılyāpa lıpli* 'did I learn', JU: *nafaham nafahmola elewada* 'have I been unreasonable?', ChU: *hīč ᵓīt va li ᵓādat* 'Did I have the habit';[15] *yāraṭ haddereḵ* (32) 'the road swerved' (?) = Z: *xlıfla mın ᵓurxa* '(the she-ass) turned away from the road',[16] D: *dwıqli ᵓurxa* 'I (= the angel) blocked the road',[17] JU: *qelebla werxa* 'the road shifted', ChU: *pčilte-la ᵓurxa* 'the road is crooked';[18] *ᵓulay* (33) 'unless' (but normally 'perhaps' = Z + JU: *balkin* 'perhaps', but ChU: *ᵓen lā* + D: *ᵓınkan lā* 'unless'.[19] An interesting case is: *ᵓūlay nūḵal nakke-bō* (6) 'perhaps I-can we-defeat[20] him' = Z + D: *ᶜımṣēna māxēna*, JU: *messen dahen* 'I-can I-defeat', but ChU: *māṣen māxax* 'I-can we-defeat'.[21]

14. Cf. Sabar 1991: 1388–90.

15. Variations in translating obscure Hebrew roots are often based on the traditional targumic translations (mostly *Onqelos*) and commentaries (mostly Rashi), for example, *haskēn hiskantī* (30) = Dp: *ᵓilyāpa lıpli* 'learning I learned' is quite a literal translation of *Onqelos*: *mēlaf ᵓallīfānā* (and supported by Rashi: *kıtargūmō* 'as its (*Onqelos*) translation'); however, all the other Jewish translations: 'was I stubborn', 'was I smart', 'was I unreasonable', seem to be based on guessing from the context or perhaps based on some local tradition; cf. Sabar 1988: 28–30; Sabar 1990: 312–14; Sabar 1991: 1396–98. It is interesting to note that ChU, 'did I have the custom', is similar to *Onqelos*, and is not based on Old Syriac translations, for example, the Peshiṭta, which translates *hahaskēn hiskantī laᶜasōṯ* 'was it my habit to do' by just *ᶜbdt* 'did I'. See following notes.

16. Cf. Rashi.

17. Cf. *Onqelos*; compare with the variants in BHS.

18. Strangely enough, Peshiṭta has *trṣt* 'was straight'.

19. Cf. *Onqelos*, Rashi, BHS: *lwly*; Peshiṭta: *ᵓlw lᵓ*.

20. However, some see *nakke* as an infinitive; see Ibn Ezra, BHS, *Onqelos*: *ᵓkl lᵓgḥᵓ* 'I can fight'.

21. Cf. Rashi: *ᵓanī wıᶜammī* 'I and my people'; BHS: *nwkl* 'we can'; Peshiṭta has all in pl., including the following Heb. verb, *ᵓgršnw* 'I drive him out' = *nwbdywhy* 'we will annihilate him'.

§11. A Hebrew root may be confused with another of similar sound, especially by D: *wayyāġor* (3) 'he feared' [< *g-u-r*, *y-g-r*] = D: *sıkınne* 'he dwelt' [< *g-u-r*], corrected by Dp: *wzıdeᵓle* 'he feared'; *wayyōsef* (15) 'he added' [< *y-s-f*] = D: *wmıjōmıᶜle* 'he gathered' [< *ᵓ-s-f*], corrected by Dp: *wmōzıdle* 'he added'. Also, D may misread a Hebrew word, e.g.: *ᵓereṣ bınē ᶜammō* (5) 'the land of his people' = D: *bane ᶜammōn* 'people of Ammon'.[22]

§12. Minor explicating additions in the translations (especially ChU): *yāmīn usmōl* (26) '(to swerve) right and left' = D: *la yamme wla čappe* 'neither right nor left'; D interpolates in 31: *ha ᵓıxzēlox did xa yōma* . . . 'have you seen any day (that I was stubborn)'; *qısāmīm bıyāḏām* (7) 'divinations in their hand (= power ?)' = ChU: *hāqıd qıṣma bᵓīdē* 'payments for divination in their hand'; *mıšᶜōl* (24) 'lane' = ChU: *ᵓālōla ᵓemqu* 'deep lane'; cf. also ChU 9, 11, 40, and others for all the additions of present and past copula (*īna*, *īle*; *waw*). Moreover, the informant, Mr. Begzade, occasionally misreads or slightly "corrects" the written text, e.g., *lhaw dbārket* (6) is read: *ldāw barkıtte*. All Jewish translations translate Hebrew *nā* (6, 16, etc.) 'please' by *ᵓatta* 'now', following the Old Aramaic translation of *Onqelos*: *kıᶜan* (note: this is done even when preceded by Hebrew *ᶜattā* 'now', e.g., *wıᶜattā lıḵā-nā* (6) 'and now please go' = *Onqelos*: *uḵıᶜan ᵓīṯā ḵıᶜan* 'and now come now'), but ChU has: *parpūlı-wın* 'I beseech'. Similarly, Hebrew *qıṭannā ᵓō gıdōlā* (18) 'small or big (thing)' (f.) = ChU: *sᵓūra yān gūra* (m.), but all Jewish translations have f. form, as in Hebrew. However, *ᵓim raᶜ* (m.) *bıᶜēnēḵā* (34) 'if (it is) bad in your eyes' (= you disapprove) = Z: *ᵓınkan xrūta-la bᵓēnox* (f., as commonly in spoken Neo-Aramaic for the impersonal), ChU: *ᵓın srīte* (f.) *-la bᵓaynux*; but D + JU: *xrīwa* (m.).

§13. The translations tend to harmonize an inconsistent formula: *ᵓeṯ ᵓašer tıḇārēḵ mıḇōrāḵ* (= a.p.) *waᵓašer tāᵓōr yūᵓār* (= imperf.) (6) 'whom you bless is blessed and he whom you curse will be cursed' = D: *ᵓālet ᵓōt ᵓımbarxıtte ᵓımburxa* (= a.p.) *wdid ᵓımṣaᶜrıtte ᵓımṣuᶜra* (= a.p.) 'whom you bless is blessed and he whom you curse is cursed'; cf. JU: *ᵓayıd barxet berixa, waᵓayıd masteret mestira*, ChU: *ldāw barkıtte mburke-le udᵓaw (d)lēṭet-le lıyṭe-le*;[23] but Z: *ᵓōd ᵓāhıt mbarxētın mburxa, ᵓōd ᵓāhıt mṣaᶜrētın kēse mṣaᶜōre* '. . . becomes cursed'.

22. Cf. BHS: *ᶜmwn*; cf. Sabar 1991: 1391–92 (§9).

23. Similarly in *Onqelos* (*mbrk* . . . *lyṭ*) and Peshiṭta (*bryk hw* . . . *lyṭ hw*).

Numbers 22:2–41 in the Jewish Dialect of Zakho

(2) xzēle bālaq bır **ṣıppōr** ʾālıd kulle ʾod ʾuzle yısrāʾel lʾımōri (3) zdeʾle mōʾav mın qāmıd qōm **rāba**, did **rāba** ʾāwa, krehle mōʾav mın qāmıd bnōn **yısrāʾel** (4) mırre mōʾav ʾıl zaqēnīm dmıdyan: ʾatta blahgi jamāʿa ʾāl kullu čārnıkāre dēni, mux lhāgıd tōra ʾāl yırqıd dašta; ubālaq bır **ṣıppōr** ḥakōma ta mōʾav bıd waʿda ʾāya (5) mšōdırre qāṣūde ʾıllıd bılʿam bır pıʿōr ʾıl pātōra,[24] ʾōd ʾıllıd xawōra, ʾarʾıd bnōn qōm dīde, lıṣrāxa ʾılle, limāra: hōna qōm mpıqle mın **mıṣṣır**, hōna mkōsēle ʾāl ʾēnıd[25] ʾarʾa, ʾāwa tīwa mın barqūli (6) ʾatta ysa-ʾatta[26] **mṣāʾır ṭāli** ʾal qōm ʾōha, did qūya ʾawa mınni, balkin **ʾımṣēna** māxēna[27] ʾıbbe, kardınne mın ʾarʾa did yzeʾli, ʾālıd ʾōd ʾāhıt mbarxētın mburxa, ʾōd ʾāhıt **mṣaʿrētın** kēse **mṣaʿōre**[28]

(7) zıllu zaqēnīm dmōʾav, zaqēnīm dmıdyan, xarše bıd ʾīzōhun, sēlu ʾıl bılʿam, muḥkēlu **ṭāle** xabrıd bālaq (8) mırre **ṭalōhun**: dmōxun ʾaxxa ʾızlal, mmadʾırēna[29] ʾalōxun xabra, mux ʾōd maḥke ʾıstax-ʿōlām **ṭāli**; tūlu sardārıd mōʾav ʾımmıd bılʿam

(9) sēle ʾilāha ʾıllıd bılʿam, nırre: mani ʾanya gūre ʾanya ʾımmōx? (10) mırre bılʿam ta ʾilāha: bālaq bır **ṣıppōr** ḥakōmıd mōʾāv mšōdırre ʾılli (11) hōna ʾaw[30] qōm ʾaw mpīqa mın **mıṣṣır**, mkōsēle ʾālıd ʾēnıd ʾarʾa; ʾatta ysa **mṣāʿır ṭāli** ʾāle, balkin ʾāna **ʾımṣēna lınṣāya** ʾıbbe ukardınne (12) mırre ʾilāha ʾıl bılʿam: la ʾāzētın ʾımmōhun, la **mṣaʿrētın** ʾālıd qōm, did mburxa ʾāwa!

(13) qımle bılʿam bıd mbınōke, mırre ʾıl sardārıd bālaq: ysāwun[31] ʾil ʾarʾāsa dōxun, did mʿunkırre ʾıstaz-ʿōlām lıyhāwa dīdi lʾizāla ʾımmōxun (14) qımlu sardārıd mōʾav, sēlu ʾılllıd bālaq, mırru: mʿunkırre bılʿam ʾizāla ʾımmēni

(15) mōzıdle hēš bālaq mšadōre sardāre **ruwwe** ubıš ʿāzīze mın danya (16) sēlu ʾıl bılʿam, mırru **ṭāle**: hatxa nırre bālaq bır **ṣıppōr**: la ʾatta manʾētın mın ʾizāla ʾılli (17) did mʿazzōze mʿazzızınnōx **rāba**, kulle ʾōd ʾamrētın ṭali bōzēna; ysa ʾatta **mṣāʿır ṭāli** ʾāl qōm ʾōha (18) mjōyıble bılʿam mırre ʾıl ʾōdıd bālaq: ʾınkan yāwıl bālaq **mlīs** bēse **nuqra** udehwa, la **ʾımṣēna** lʾwāra ʾāl

24. Erroneously keeping Heb. directional *-a* 'to'.

25. See §8 above.

26. See §12 above.

27. See §10 above.

28. See §13 above.

29. The future prefix *b-* assimilates into *m* with words beginning with *m*; but sometimes it is neutralized as in *maḥkēna* (38) below.

30. Demonstratives such as 'that' function as definite articles.

31. Lit., 'come' (< ʾ-t-y) for Heb. *lıkū* 'go'; see §8. However, this form almost coalesces with *sāwun* 'go' (< ʾ-z-l).

pımmıd ᵓıstaz-ᶜōlām zurta yān **rabsa** (19) ᵓatta tūn ᵓatta bıd ᵓaxxa ham ᵓaxtun ᵓızlal, byāᵓēna mā māzıd ᵓıstaz-ᶜōlām maḥkōye ᵓımmi (20) sēle ᵓilāha ᵓıllıd bılᶜam blēle, mırre **ṭāle**: ᵓınkan lı**ṣrāxa** ᵓıllōx sēlu gūre, qu si ᵓımmōhun, faqqad ᵓālıd xabra ᵓōd maḥkēna **ṭālox**, ᵓāle ᵓōzētın!

(21) qımle bılᶜam bı mbınōke, **mqurṭınne** ᵓāl xmarta dīde, zılle ᵓımmıd sardārıd mōᵓav (22) **jgırra** sāmītıd ᵓilāha, did bizāla ᵓāwa, ḥmılle malᵓax ᵓıstaz-ᶜōlām bıd ᵓurxa lımdāmōne[32] ᵓılle, ᵓāwa rkīwa ᵓıl xmarta dīde utre **ġulamwāsa** dīde ᵓımme

(23) xzēla xmarta ᵓālıd ᵓistaz-ᶜōlām ḥmīla bıd ᵓurxa, sēpa dīde šlıpta[33] bıd ᵓīze, qlībla xmarta mın ᵓurxa, zılla bıd dašta, mxēle bılᵓam ᵓālıd xmarta, lqlāba dīda ᵓılld ᵓurxa (24) ḥmılle malᵓax ᵓıstaz-ᶜōlām bıd kōlānıd karmāne, **ṭān** maxxa **uṭān** maxxa (25) xzēla xmarta ᵓāl malᵓax ᵓıstaz-ᶜōlām, ḥrıšla ᵓıllıd gūda, ḥrıšla ᵓıllıd ᵓaqlıd bılᶜam ᵓıl gūda, mōzıdle lmxāya dīda (26) mōzıdle malᵓax ᵓıstaz-ᶜōlām ᵓwāra, ḥmılle bı dūka ᵓıqta, ᵓōd lēs ᵓurxa lqlāba yamme učappe (27) xzēla xmarta ᵓal malᵓax ᵓıstaz-ᶜōlām, dmıxla xe bılᶜam, **jgırra** sāmītıd bılᶜam, mxēle ᵓāl xmarta bıd ᶜ**aṣṣa** (28) psıxle ᵓıstaz-ᶜōlām ᵓāl pımmıd xmarta, mırra ta bılᶜam: ma ᵓuzli ᵓıllōx, did qam māxıtti ᵓōha **ṭlāha** naqle? (29) mırre bılᶜam ta xmarta: did mtōᶜıllax[34] ᵓıbbi, xwazzī ᵓis[35] sēpa bı ᵓizi, did ᵓatta bqaṭlınwālax! (30) mırra xmarta ᵓıllıd bılᶜam: hala ᵓāna xmarta dīdōx, ᵓōd rkūlōx ᵓılli mın hēštan dīdōx hīl yōma ᵓōha; mo fhāma fhımli[36] lıᵓwāza ᵓıllōx hatxa? mırre: lāᵓ!

(31) glēle ᵓıstaz-ᶜōlām ᵓēnıd bılᶜam, xzēle ᵓāl malᵓax ᵓıstaz-ᶜōlām ḥmīla bıd ᵓurxa, sēpa dīde šlıpta bıd ᵓīze, zıjle kıple ᵓıl paswāse (32) mırre ᵓılle malᵓax ᵓıstaz-ᶜōlām: ᵓıl mā mxēlōx ᵓıl xmarta ᵓōha[37] **ṭlāha** naqle? hōna ᵓāna mpıqli **lsāṭān**, did xlıfla mın ᵓurxa[38] ᵓıl barqūli (33) qam xazyāli xmarta, qlıbla lqāmi ᵓōha **ṭlāha** naqle, balki[39] qlıbla mın qāmi, did ᵓatta ham ᵓālōx b**qaṭ**lınwa, uᵓāla mmaxyınwa (34) mırre bılᶜam ᵓıllıd malᵓax ᵓıstaz-ᶜōlām: **xṭēli**, did la yzeᵓli, did ᵓāhıt ḥmīla lqāmi bıd ᵓurxa; ᵓatta ᵓınkan xrūta-la bᵓēnōx, bdaᵓrēna **ṭāli**[40] (35) mırre malᵓax ᵓıstaz-ᶜōlām ᵓıllıd bılᶜam: si ᵓımmıd gūre, bale ᵓāl xabra ᵓōd maḥkēna **ṭālōx**, ᵓāle maḥkētın! zılle bılᶜām ᵓımmıd sardārıd bālāq

32. See §5 above, but v. 32: *lsāṭān.*
33. See §3 above.
34. See §9 above.
35. Lit. translation of Heb. *yēš*; the correct modal form would be: *hāwēwa* (cf. D here and §4 above).
36. See §10 above.
37. Lit. translation of Heb. *ze*, but for impersonal, one would expect *ᵓēha*, f.; cf. end of §12.
38. See §10 above.
39. See §10 above.
40. Lit. translation of Heb. *lī* 'for me'; one would expect: *ta gyāni* 'for myself' (ethical dative).

(36) šmeʾle bālaq did sēle bılʿam, mpıqle lqamāye dīde, ʾıl bāır dmōʾāv, ʾōd ʾıllıd tıxub ʾarnōn, ʾōd bdūmāyık tıxub (37) mırre bālaq ʾıl bılʿām: hala mšadōre mšōdırri ʾıllōx **lıṣrāxa** ʾıllōx; **ṭamā** la zıllōx ʾılli? mo **trōṣā** la **mṣēna** mʿazzōze dıdōx? (38) mırre bılʿam ʾıl bālaq: hōna sēli ʾıllōx, ʾatta mo **mṣōye**[41] **ʾımṣēna** maḥkōye xa mındi? xabra ʾōd dāre ʾilāha bıd pımmi, ʾāle maḥkēna[42]

(39) zılle bılʿam ʾımmıd bālaq, sēlu lbāžır **ḥūṣōt** (40) **ẓbıḥle** bālaq tōre uʾırwe, mšōdırre ta bılʾam uta dan sardāre ʾōd ʾımme (41) wēle bıd mbınōke, šqılle bālaq ʾāl bılʿam, qam māsıqle ʾıl bāmōt bāʿal, xzēle mın tāma dūmāyık qōm.

Numbers 22:2–41 in the Jewish Dialect of Dihok

(2) wġızēle bālaq ber ṣıppōr ʾālet kulle ʾōt ʾuwıḏle yıṣrāʾel lʾimōri (3) wsıkınne (wzıdeʾle)[43] mōʾav mın qāmet qōm qawi, did rāba ʾāwa (ʾāhu),[44] wkırehle (ʾeqle)[45] mōʾav mın qāmet bınōnet yısrāʾel (4) wmırre mōʾav ʾel sāwet mıḏyan: ʾatta bıdōqi (bılahgi)[46] jamāʿa ʾalet kullu čār kınārēni mux dıwāqet (ʾelhāget) tōra ʾālet yırqa (!) (d)dašta; wbālaq ber ṣıppōr ḥakōma lmōʾav bıwaʿda ʾāwa (ʾahu) (5) wmıšōdırre qāsūde[47] ʾel bılʿam ber bıʿōr ʾel paṭōr ʾawet wīle ʾel nıhret bane ʿammōn(!),[48] lıqrāya ʾāle līmāra: hōna qōm npıqle mın mıṣṣer, hōna mıkōsēle ʾālet ʾēnet (ranget)[49] ʾarʾa wʾāwa ytīwa lıbarqūli (6) wʾatta ʾiṯa ʾatta mıṣāʿer ṭāli ʾālet qōm ʾōha, dīle beš qūya mınne (mınni),[50] balkin ʾımṣēna māxēna[51] ʾılle wkardınne mın ʾarʾa, did yıḏeʾli ʾālet ʾōt ʾımbarxıtte ʾımburxa, wdid ʾımṣaʿrıtte ʾımṣuʿra[52]

(7) wzıllu sāwet mōʾav wsāwet mıḏyan wqısāmīm (wxarše)[53] bʿīḏōhun, wtēlu ʾel bılʿam, wmuḥkēlu ʾılle xabret bālaq (8) wmırre ʾıllōhun: bōṯun

41. An error for *mṣāya* (the infinitive of the basic form).

42. See n. 29 above.

43. See §§1, 11 above.

44. Often D *ʾāwa* 'he, it, m'. is corrected by Dp *ʾāhu* (cf. below, vv. 4, 12, etc.), which seems to be the dialectal form of Nerwa; see §1 above and Sabar 1976: 62 n. 243.

45. D: 'dreaded', Dp: 'felt tight, pressured'.

46. D: 'will seize' (based on context), Dp: 'will devour'.

47. One would expect *qāṣūde* (emphatic *ṣ*), as in Z and JU (< Arabic *q-ṣ-d*). Cf. nn. 63, 80 below.

48. See §11 and n. 22 above.

49. See §8 above.

50. D 'than him' (an error), Dp: 'than me'.

51. See §10 and nn. 20, 21 above.

52. See §13 above.

53. D leaves Heb. word untranslated, usually an indication of not understanding it.

ᵓaxxa ᵓıbēle, wᵓāna madᵓırēna ᵓıllōxun xabra kudax maḥke y″y [= ᵓaḏōnāy, ᵓıstāḏet ᶜōlām][54] ᵓılli; wyıtūlu sardāret mōᵓav ᵓımmet bılᶜam

(9) wṯēle ᵓilāha ᵓel bılᶜam wmırre: mani ᵓanna gūre kıslox (ᵓımmox)?[55] (10) wmırre bılᶜam ᵓel ᵓilāha: bālaq ber ṣıppōr ḥakōmet mōᵓav mıšōdırre ᵓılli (11) hōna qōm ᵓaw ᵓınpıqle mın mıṣṣer wmıkōsēle ᵓālet ᵓēnet ᵓarᵓa; ᵓatta si mıṣāᶜırrēli ᵓılle,[56] balkin ᵓımṣēna lınṣāya ᵓıbbe wkardınne (12) wmırre ᵓilāha ᵓel bılᶜam: la ᵓāzētın ᵓımmōhun, la mıṣaᶜrētın ᵓālet qōm, did ᵓımburxa ᵓāwa (ᵓāhu)

(13) wqımle bılᶜam bet bınōke wmırre ᵓel sardāret bālaq: sāwun ᵓel ᵓarᵓōxun, did la gıᵓājıb y″y lᵓiṯāya (līhāwa) dīdi ᵓımmōxun wlᵓizāla ᵓımmōxun(!)[57] (14) wqımlu sardāret mōᵓav wṯēlu ᵓel bālaq wmırru: mıᶜunkırre bılᶜam lᵓizāla ᵓımmēni

(15) wmıjōmıᶜle (wmōzıdle)[58] bālaq mišadōre sardāre rāba wbeš yaqūre manya (16) wṯēlu ᵓel bılᶜam wmırru ᵓılle: hatxa mırre bālaq ber ṣıppōr: la ᵓatta manᵓēten mın ᵓizāla kısli (17) did mıᶜazzoze mıᶜazzızınnox qawi, wkulle ᵓōt ᵓamrēten ᵓılli bōḏēna, wsi ᵓatta mıṣāᶜer ᵓılli ᵓālet qōm ᵓōha (18) wmıjōwıble bılᶜam wmırre ᵓel ᵓōdet bālaq: ᵓınkan yāwel ᵓılli bālaq mılīṯet bēṯe nuqra wdehwa la ᵓımṣēna lıᵓwāra ᵓālet taneᵓṯet(!)[59] y″y ᵓilāhi lıᵓwāḏa zurta yān rabṯa (19) ᵓatta yıtūlōxun bēha dūka ham ᵓaxtun bılēle (ᵓıḏlal)[60] wıbyāᵓēna ma māzet(!)[61] y″y lımaḥkōye ᵓımmi (20) wṯēle ᵓilāha ᵓel bılᶜam ᵓıblēle wmırre ᵓılle: ᵓınkan lıqrāya ᵓıllox ṯēlu ᵓanya gūre, qolox(!)[62] si ᵓımmōhon(!), wıbas ᵓālet xabra ᵓōt muḥkēli ᵓıllox ᵓılle ᵓōḏēten

(21) wqımle bılᶜam bet bınōke, wmıqurtınne[63] ᵓālet ᵓıxmarte, wzılle ᵓımmet sardāret mōᵓav (22) wjıgırre karbet ᵓilāha did zılle (ᵓazāla)[64] ᵓāwa, wmuḥmılle[65] malᵓax y″y bᵓurxa lsāṭān ᵓılle, wᵓāwa rakāwa[66] ᵓel xımarte,

54. See §2 above.

55. D: 'chez vous', Dp: 'with you'.

56. The object pronoun 'it' is erroneously translated twice.

57. Heb. *lıṯittī lahalōḵ ᶜimmāḵem* 'letting me go with you' is rendered confusedly: 'coming (letting) me with you and going with you'.

58. See §11 above.

59. One would expect *tanēṯet* 'word of', but strangely enough it is spelled here and elsewhere with an *ᵓalep* with *šewa*.

60. D: 'at night' (cf. *Onqelos*: *bılēlyā*), Dp: 'tonight' (Heb. *hallāylā* is ambivalent; cf. JPS: 'overnight').

61. One would expect *māzed* (< Arabic *z-y-d*), but D tends to spell etymological *-d* (including the ubiquitous possessive pronoun *-d*) as *-t*.

62. One would expect *qūlox*; D often has *ḥolem* (o) instead of the expected *šureq* or *qibbuṣ* (u).

63. One would expect **wmıqurṭınne** (emphatic), as in Z here; cf. n. 47 above.

64. One would expect: *wēle bizāla* 'he was going'; see §6 above and n. 66 below.

65. Heb. *wayyityaṣṣēḇ* 'he (the angel) stood' is erroneously translated by D 'He (God) placed (the angel)'.

66. One would expect *rkīwa* (p.p.); see §6 above.

wkutru (wtıre)[67] ġulmāṯe[68] ʾımme (23) wġızēla ʾıxmarta ʾālet malʿax y″y ʾıḥmīla bʾurxa, wsēpe šlīxa bʾıḏe, wqlıbla ʾıxmarta mın ʾurxa, wzılla bet dašta, wmıxēle bılʿam ʾālet xımarta lıqlāba dīda ʾel ʾurxa (24) wḥımılle malʾax y″y bet kōlanket karmāne, ṭan maxxa wṭān maxxa (25) wġızēla ʾıxmarta ʾālet malʾax y″y wpılımla (wḥırišla)[69] ʾālet gūda, wḥızıqla ʾālet ʾaqel bılʿam ʾel gūda, wmōzıdle lımxāya dīda (26) wmōzıdle malʾax y″y ʾıwāra, wʾıḥmılle bıdūka ʾıqta, did lēṯen ʾurxa lıqlāba la yamme wla čappe[70] (27) wġızēla ʾıxmarta ʾālet malʾax y″y wdımıxla xe bılʿam, wjıgırre karbet bılʿam, wmıxēle ʾālet xımarta bet ʿaṣṣa

(28) wpıṯıxle y″y ʾālet pımmet ʾıxmarta, wmırra lbılʿam: ma ʾıwıḏli ʾıllox did ʾıgmāxıtti ʾēha ʾıṯlāha daste (naqle)?[71] (29) wnırre bılʿam lıxmarta: did ʾıgxıklax ʾıbbi; ʾıxwazzī hāwēwa sēpa bʾīḏi, did ʾatta bıqaṯlınwālax![72] (30) wmırra xımarta ʾel bılʿam: hala ʾāna xımartox, ʾōt rıkūlox ʾılli men ʾaw-wel dīdox whīl ʾıdyo (yōma ʾōha),[73] ha ʾıxzēlox did xa yōma mıʿunkırri mıʿankōre (ha ʾılyāpa lıpli)[74] lıʾwāḏa ʾıllox hatxa? wmırre: lā

(31) wgılēle y″y ʾālet ʾēnet bılʿam, wġızēle ʾālet malʿax y″y ḥmīla bʾurxa, wsēpe ʾıšlıxta[75] bʾīḏe, wkıple wzıdıjle lıpaṯwāṯe (32) wmırre ʾılle malʿax y″y: ʾel mā mıxēlox ʾālet ʾıxmartox ʾēha ʾıṯlāha daste? hōna ʾāna ʾenpıqli lıqlāba, did dwıqli ʾurxa lıbarqūli (ʾel dīmen, did ʾıjıblēlox lʾizāla bēha ʾurxa bet la ʾejbōni)[76] (33) wqam-xazyāli xımarta wqılıbla lıqāmi ʾēha ʾıṯlāha daste; ʾınkan la qalbāwa mın qāmi, did ʾatta ʾālox bıqaṯlenwa, wʾāla bımaxyenwa! (34) wmırre bılʿam ʾel malʾax y″y: ʾıxṭēli, did la ḏeʾli, did ʾāhet ʾıḥmīla lıbarakūṯi bʾurxa, wʾatta ʾınkan xrīwa[77] bʾēnox, daʾrēna (madʾer)[78] ʾılli (35) wmırre malʿax y″y ʾel bılʿam: si ʾımmet gūre, wlēkun (wbale)[79] ʾālet xabra did muḥkēli ʾıllox, ʿāle maḥkētēn! wzılle bılʿam ʾımmet sardāret bālaq

(36) wšımeʾle bālaq did ṯēle bılʿam, wnıpıqle lbarakūṯe, ʾel māṯet mōʾav, ʾōt ʾel tıxub ʾarnon, ʾōt bıdıpnet tıxūb (37) wmırre bālaq ʾel bılʿam: hala

67. D: 'and both of them', Dp: 'and two'.

68. One would expect *ġulamwāṯe*.

69. D: 'twisted', Dp: 'pressed'.

70. See §12 above.

71. Heb. *rıġālīm*, lit., 'feet' (= recurrent times) = D: 'hands' (< Kurdish; cf. Bilblical Heb. *yāḏōt*), Dp: 'moves' (< Arabic, both in the sense of 'times').

72. See §4 above.

73. D: 'today', Dp: 'this day'; cf. §3 above.

74. See §10 above.

75. See §3 above.

76. D (confused): 'I went out to turn over, for I occupied the road . . ."; Dp: '(I went out) to (be) hostile, for you wished to follow this route without my wish'; see §10 above.

77. See end of §12 above.

78. D (correctly): 'I will return', Dp (incorrectly): 'take me back'.

79. D: 'lest' (< Arabic), Dp: 'however' (< Kurdish < Arabic).

mıšadōre mıšōdırri ʾıllox, lıqrāya ʾıllox; tamā[80] la tēlox ʾilli? balkin la ʾımṣēna [dōqen] ʾel kāvōd dīdox (ʾetwābi ʾemʿazzızınwālox)?[81] (38) wmırre bılʿam ʾel bālaq: hōna tēli ʾıllox, ʾatta ha mıṣāya ʾımṣēna maḥkōye mındi xabra? ʾōt dāre ʾilāha bet pımmi, ʾāle maḥkēna!

(39) wzılle bılʿam ʾımmet bālaq, wṯēlu qıryaṯ ḥūṣōṯ (40) wḏıbıḥle bālaq tōra wʾırba, wmıšōdırre lbılʿam wılsardāre did ʾımme (41) wēle bet bınōke, wšıqılle bālaq ʾālet bılʿam, sqamāsıqle bāmōṯ bāʿal, wġızēle mın tāma dıpen qōm (xakma mın qōm).[82]

Numbers 22:2–41 in the Jewish Dialect of Urmi[83]

(2) xezele **balaq** ben **ṣippor** el kulle ayid wedle **yisrael** la**emori** (3) zedele **moav** me**qanšar** **qahum** be**had**, gid **rába** o, **ejez**le **moav** me**qanšar** bane **yisrael** (4) merre **moav** el **xewardeqn**et midyan: átta lagxi jamata el kulle **čartarafan** magon lakex tora el gellet dašda; **balaq** ben **ṣippor** šolṭana[84] la**moav** bewaxt ahi (5) šederre **qasude** el **bilʾam**[85] ben **baʾor patora**, ayid el nehra, aret beronawet **qahum**ev, el-qaroe ellev imara: háwna **qahum peleṭ**le me**meṣer**, háwna kesele el ranget ara, wao yetiv mebaranbari (6) waátta ida átta **mesture** elli el **qahum**, gid qewya o menni, bálki **mes**sen dahen alev, **tard**enne min ara, gid yeli el ayıd **barx**et ber**ixa**, waayıd **master**et **mestira**[86]

(7) zellu **xewardeqn**et **moav** wa**xewardeqn**et midyan, xarše beidu, edyelu el bilʾam, tenelu ellev xabret **balaq** (8) merre ellu: menzulun laxxa edlel, madiren alxun xabra, baayıd tane **adonay**[87] elli; yetivlu sardar **moav** gallet **bilʾam** (9) edyele elha el bilʾam, merre: mani gore[88] ayne gallox? (10) merre **bilʾam** el elha: **balaq** ben **ṣippor** **šulṭan**et **moab** šederre elli (11) háwna **qahum** o-**palṭana**[89] me**meṣer** kesela(!) el ranget ara; átta ʾida **mestur** alev,

80. Pronounced emphatic in Z, but D has it with *taw* rather than *ṭet*; cf. nn. 47, 63 above.

81. D: 'I cannot [hold] your honor' (using a Heb. loanword), Dp: 'it was not in my ability to honor you' (using an Arabic root).

82. D: 'the edge of the people', Dp: 'a few of the people'.

83. See nn. 6, 7 above; for more phonetic and phonological details of this dialect, see Garbell 1965: 21–38.

84. Vocalized here with *ḥolem* (= o), but with *šureq* (= u) in v. 10.

85. The Hebrew spelling with *ʿayin* is maintained, but the dialect has no ʿ in its stock of consonants (Garbell 1965: 21–25), and even ʾ (glottal stop) is marginal, only in some medial clusters (ibid., 24).

86. See §13 above.

87. See §2 above.

88. Vocalized with *ḥolem*, but Garbell (1965: 307) has *gure* (as in other dialects; but see n. 5 above).

89. See §6 above.

bálki **messen** el-qerawa iwada ebbev, tardenne (12) merre elha el **bilᵓam**: la si gallu! la **mestur** el **qahum**, gid **berixa** o!

(13) qemle **bılᵓam** bebaqaṭyom,[90] merre ᵓel sardar **balaq**: simun el alxun(!),[91] gid la ebele **adonay** el-hiwali el-izala galxun (14) qemlu sardar **moav**, edyelu el **balaq**, merru: la-ebele **bilᵓam** idaa gallan

(15) mezedle médreš **balaq** šederre sardare **rábe** yaqure meayne (16) edyelu el **bilᵓam**, merru ellev: háxxa merre **balaq** ben **ṣippor**: la átta **menᵓi** meizala elli (17) gid mayqore mayqerennox be**had**, wakulle ayıd mar elli oden; ida átta **mestor** elli el **qahum** ayya (18) mejeble **bilᵓam** merre el nokarawet **balaq**: agar hawel elli **balaq male** belev sehma dehwa, la **messen** el-piyara el xabret **adonay** elhi el-iwada zurta yan **rabta** (19) waátta yetumun átta baayya ham ᵓatxun(!)[92] édlel, waayen ma mazed **adonay** tane galli (20) edyele ᵓelha ᵓel **bilᵓam** lele, merre ellev: agar el-qaroe ellox edyelu gore, qum(!)[93] si gallu, bale el xabra ayıd tanen ellox alev wod!

(21) qemle **bilᵓam** bebaqatyom, **palan** dehele el xemartev, zelle gal sardar **moav** (22) **ṭeperre** nešmet elha gid zelle o, semexle **malᵓax adonay** be**werxa** el **saṭan** ellev, wao **rekiwa** el xemartev, tere nokarev gallev (23) xezela xemarta el **malᵓax adonay** semix be**werxa** wasepev šelexta[94] beidev, qelebla mın **werxa**, zella bedašda; mexele **bilᵓam** el xemarta el-maqlobe **werxa** (24) semexle **malᵓax adonay** be**jadet** karmawe, parjin maayya, waparjin maᵓayya (25) xezele xemarta el **malᵓax adonay**, resla el guda, resla el aglet **bilᵓam** el guda; mezedle el maxoav (26) mezedle **malᵓax adonay** perre, semexle batuka iqa, ayid let **werxa** el-qalobe **saġ sol** (27) xezela xemarta el **malᵓax adonay**, **demexla** xelit **bilᵓam**; **ṭeperre** nešmet **bilᵓam**, mexele el xemarta be**kopola** (28) pelexle **adonay** el pennet xemarta, merra el **bilᵓam**: ma wedli ellox, gid mexelox ᵓali ya **taha** zae (29) merre **bilᵓam** el xemarta: gid **telax**[95] ebbi, tagla it sepa beidi, gid átta **qaṭlennax** (30) merra xemarta el **bilᵓam**: hala ᵓana xemartox ayid **rekeb**lox(!)[96] elli meayolox hal édyom ayya;[97] nafaham nafahamola[98] el-iwada ellox háxxa? mirre: la

90. See n. 6 above.

91. Normally: *ara* with *r*, e.g., *aret* (5).

92. Cf. Garbell 1965: 58; in other dialects usually *axtun.*

93. Garbell (ibid., 291) has only *qu*, as in other dialects; perhaps the retention of *-m* is influenced by Heb.

94. See §3 above; however, Garbell (ibid., 330) has the gender of *sepa* 'sword' as f. for the northern dialects (including Urmi) but m. for the southern ones.

95. See §9 above.

96. The original has a *dageš* in the letter *bet*, indicating *r-k-b*, but Garbell (1965: 291) has: *r-k-w*; cf. *rekiwa* (22) above.

97. See §3 above.

98. See §10 above.

(31) gelele **adonay** el enit **bilʾam**, xezele el **malᶜax adonay** semix be**werxa** usepev šelexta beidev, keple, šudra wedle el **salm**ev (32) merre ellev **malʾax adonay**: el ma mexelox el xemartox ya **taha** zae? háwna ana **peleṭ**li el **saṭan**, gid qelebla **werxa** el baranbari (33) xezelali xemarta, qelebla el **qanšari** ya **taha** zae, bálki[99] qelebla me**qanšari**, gid átta ham ellox **qeṭil**li, waálav mexyeli (34) merre **bilʾam** el **malʾax adonay**: **xeṭ**eli, gid la yeli gid at semixa **qanšari** be**werxa**, wáatta agar xeriwa beenox, daren elli (35) merre **malʾax adonay** el **bilʾam**: si gal gore, bále el xabra ayid tanen ellox, ellev teni! zelle **bilʾam** gal sardaret **balaq**

(36) šemele **balaq** gid edyele **bilʾam**, **peleṭ**le el **qanšar**ev el **ahret moav**, ayid el **haddosad arnon**, ayid ba**axaryid haddosad** (37) merre **balaq** el **bilʾam**: hala šadōre šederri alox el-qaroe ellox; báma la edyelox elli? **terosa** la **messen** mayqerennox? (38) merre **bilʾam** el **balaq**: háwna edyeli ellox, átta **messoe messen** tanoe mendiġ? xabra ayid mattev **adonay** bepenni, alev tanen

(39) zelle **bilʾam** gal **balaq**, edyelu **qiryat** huṣot (40) debale **balaq** tora waerba, šederre el **bilʾam**, el sardare ayid gallev (41) wele bebaqatyom šeqelle **balaq** el **bilʾam**, meseqlele **bamot baʾal**, xezele móka **ʾaxeryet qahum.**

Numbers 22:2–41 in the Christian Dialect of Urmi[100]

(2) uxzīlı bālaq brūnıd **sīpor** lkul dvıdlı ʾısrāyel lʾ**āmūrāye** (3) **uzdīlı** mūʾav mın qam **tāyıppa rāba**, sābab d**rābe**-wa, upıšlı **mūyıqqa** mūʾav mın qam bne ʾısrāʾel (4) umırrı mūʾav lıxwārdıqnıd **madan**: ʾādīya bıt lākıx kınša lkul **xadırwān**an ʾax lākıx tōrā lgıllıd dıšta; ubālaq brūnıd **sīpor** malkıd mūʾav-īwa bo zōna (5) ušūdırrı ʾızgadde lkıs **bılʾam** brūnıd **biʾor lpītor** dīla **ʾal nārıd ʾarʾıd** bne **tāyıppu**, **lıqrāyu** bimāra: hā **tāyıppa plīte**-le mın **mısr(en)**,[101] hā kusīlı lpātıd **ʾarʾa**, uʾāw tīwe-le lbarqūli (6) uʾādīya ta, parpūlı-wın,[102] **lūt** qa dıyyi lāha **tāyıppa**, sābab **dzarbāne**-le mınni, qōma **māsın** māxax-le **utardax**-le mın **ʾarʾa**, sābab dkı **yattın**, ldāw barkıtte (m)burke-le, udʾāw **lētıt**-le **lıyte**-le[103]

99. See §10 above.

100. See §1 and nn. 6, 7 above. For etymology of words in ChU, see Maclean (1972) or Sabar (1993).

101. The segments in parentheses are murmured or not clearly audible.

102. See §12 above.

103. In the original Syriac text: *lhaw dbarxet mburxa* (*y*)*le* [*rukkākā* dot under the *bet*; cf. v. 12; Maclean (1972: 154) has both: *b-r-x* and *b-r-k*] *uhaw dlayṭet līṭa* (*y*)*le*. See §§12, 13 above.

(7) uzıllun xwārdıqnıd mūᵓav uxwārdıqnıd **madan**, uhāqıd qısma[104] bᵓīdē, utīlun lkıs bılᵓam, uhumzımlun **ᵓammu**[105] hemezmānıd bālaq (8) umırrı ᵓıllē: pūšun laxxa blēle ubıt **maddırın** ᵓıllōxun xabra, dāxıd hamzım **marya ᵓammi**; utiwlun **gūrānıd** mūᵓav **ᵓam bılᵓam**

(9) utīlı ᵓalāha lkıs bılᵓam umırrı: manī-na ᵓanni nāše **ᵓammux** (10) (u)mırrı **bılᵓam** lᵓalāha: bālaq brūnıd **sīpor**, malkıd mūᵓav šūdırrı lkısli (11) hā **tāyıppa plīte**-le mın **mısr(en)**, ukūsīlı lpātıd **ᵓarᵓa**; ᵓādīya ta **lūt**-le qa dıyyi, qōma d**māsın**[106] **lıplāša ᵓamme utardınnı** (12) umırrı ᵓalāha l**bılᵓam**: la ᵓāzıt **ᵓammē**, la lētıt l**tāyıppa**, sābab (d)burke-le

(13) uqımlı **bılᵓam** b**sapra** umırrı l**gūrāne** dbālaq: sēmun lᵓ**arᵓōxun**, sābab dmaxpūlı-le **marya** lıšvāqi dᵓāzın **ᵓammōxun** (14) uqımlun **gūrānıd** mūᵓav utīlun lkıs bālaq umırrun: maxpūlı-le **bılᵓam** lītāya **ᵓamman**

(15) (u)mūzıdlı mıdrı bālaq **lšādūrı gūrāne rāba** ubuš myuqrı mın dāni (16) (u)tīlun lkıs **bılᵓam**, umırrun qātu:[107] hatxa bimāre-le bālaq brūnıd **sīpor**: parpūlı-wın, la pēšıt muklīya mın lītāya (l)kısli (17) sābab (d)myāqūrı bıt myaqrınnux **rāba**, ukul (d)ᵓamrıt ᵓılli bıt **ᵓōdın**; uta, parpūlı-wın, **lūt** qa dıyyi ldāha **tāyıppa** (18) (u)jūwıblı **bılᵓam** (u)mırrı lrigāwātıd bālaq: ᵓın yāvıl-li bālaq mılya bētu sīma udāwa, le māsın liwāra lxabrıd marya ᵓalāhi, liwāda **sᵓūra** yān **gūra** (19) uᵓādīya di tūvun laxxa ᵓup ᵓaxtun blēle, **uyatten** mūdi bıt mazyıd **marya** lhamzūme **ᵓammi** (20) utīli ᵓalāha lkıs **bılᵓam** blēle umırrı qātu: ᵓın lı**qrāyux** tīlun ᵓanni nāše, qu sē **ᵓammē**, uᵓaxči lxabra dhamızmın **ᵓammux** ᵓāw **ᵓōdıt**

(21) uqımlı **bılᵓam** (b)**sapra** usūrıglı lxmartu uzıllı **ᵓam gūrānıd** mūᵓav (22) uxımla karbıd ᵓalāha sābab dzıllı ᵓāw, uklīlı mālᵓāxıd **mārya** bᵓurxa līwāya darqul ᵓıllı,[108] uᵓāw rkīwe-wa ᵓal xmartu, utre jwanqu **ᵓammu** (23) uxzīla xmarta lmalāxıd **marya** bıklāya bᵓurxa, usēpe grīša bᵓīde, uqlıbla xmarta mın ᵓurxa, uzılla go xaqla, umxīlı **bılᵓam** lxmarta (l)maqlūba lᵓurxa (24) uklīlı malāxıd **marya** bᵓālōla **ᵓemqu**[109] dkarmāne, šūra māha gība, ušūra mdo[110] gība (25) uxzīla xmarta lmalāxıd **marya**, ubrıkla (t)xot **bılᵓam**, uxımla karbıd **bılᵓam**, **uxlīsala** gyānu lšūra, **uxlısla** lᵓaqlıd **bılᵓam** lšūra, umūzıdlı lımxāyu (26) umūzıdlı malāxıd **marya** liwāra, uklīlı bdukta ᵓiqta, dlıtva ᵓurxa lıqlāba lyammīna ulsımmāla (27) uxzīla xmarta lmalāxıd **marya**, ubrıkla (t)xot **bılᵓam**, uxımla karbıd **bılᵓam**, umxīlı lxmarta b**xutra** (28) uptıxlı

104. In the original: *qeṣma.*
105. Here and in vv. 22, 39, the original text has *ᶜamme*; cf. v. 11.
106. Without *d-* in the original.
107. Here and in v. 20, the original text has *ᵓıllı.*
108. See §5 above.
109. The original text has *mhaw.*
110. See §12 above.

marya lpummıd xmarta umırra l**bılᵓam**: mūdi vittē-van ᵓıllux, dqam māxıtti[111] ᵓāha **tla** gāhe (29) umırrı **bılᵓam** lxmarta: sābab (d)**musxırrax** bıyyi, tuwwa dhāwe-wa sēpa bᵓīdi, dᵓādīya **qatlın**-wa-lax (30) (u)mırra xmarta l**bılᵓam**: hā lē-wan ᵓāna xmartux dırkīwe-wıt ᵓalli mın dwīlox hāl dāha yūma? mıhwāya hīč ᵓıt-vā-li **ᵓādat** livāda ᵓıllux hatxa? umırrı: lā

(31) gūlīlı **marya** lᵓ**aynıd bılᵓam** uxzīlı lmalāxıd **marya** bıklāya bᵓurxa, usēpu grīša bᵓīdu, ukıplı **usġıdlı ᵓal** pātu (32) umırrı ᵓıllı malāxıd **marya**: but mūdi mxēlux lxmartux[112] ᵓāha **tla** gāhe? hā ᵓāna **plıtli** lıhvāya darqul, sābab dı**pčilte**-la ᵓurxux qāmi (33) uqam xazyā-li xmarta uqlıbla mın qāmi ᵓā(ha) **tla** gāhe; ᵓın la hōya-wa qlıbta mın qāmi, mıjjıd ᵓādīya ᵓup ᵓıllux **qtīl**-ın-wa, uldāy[113] xumye-n-va xēta (34) (u)mırrı **bılᵓam** lmalāxıd **marya**: **xtīli**, sābab dla **dīli** dᵓāt bıklāye-(vi)t-va lıtpāqa bıyyi bᵓurxa, uᵓadīya ᵓın srīte-la b**ᵓaynux**, dērın ᵓāna (35) (u)mırrı malāxıd **marya** l**bılᵓam**: sē **ᵓam** danni nāše, uᵓaxči xabrıd hamzemmın **ᵓammux**, ᵓāw hamzemmıt! uzıllı **bılᵓam** mın[114] **gūrānıd** bālaq

(36) ušmīlı bālaq (d)tīlı **bılᵓam**, **uplıtlı** lᵓurxu lmdīta dmūᵓav, dīwa lkıs txub dᵓ**arnun**, dıbmarzıd txūba (37) (u)mırrı bālaq l**bılᵓam**: ha la mšādūri šūdırri lkıslux lı**qrāyux**? qāmōdi la tīlux lkısli? **trūsa** le **māsın**-wa lıvāda **ᵓiqāra** ᵓıllux? (38) (u)mırrı **bılᵓam** lbālaq: ha tīya-vın lkıslux, ᵓadiya **msāya** kı **māsın** lhamzūmı mındi? xabra dmattıv-le ᵓalāha bıpummı, ᵓāw bıt hamzımınne[115]

(39) (u)zıllı **bılᵓam ᵓam** bālaq, (u)tīlun l**quryat xūsut** (40) (u)dwıxlı bālaq tōrı uᵓırbı, ušūdırrı qa **bılᵓam** uqa **gūrāne** dīwa **ᵓammu** (41) (u)vīla (b)**sapra**, ušqıllı bālaq l**bılᵓam**, umūsıqlı ldukānı rāmı d**bāla**, (u)xzīlı mın tāma marzıd **tāyıppa**.

111. The original text has *māxet li.*
112. The original text has just *xmartux* (without *l-*, the object marker).
113. The original text has *ulhay.*
114. The original text has *ᶜam.*
115. The original text has just *hamzımın.*

Bibliography

The following works are found in *Miqraᵓot Gedolot* (a popular rabbinical compendium of commentaries and targums on the Bible, printed many times; for example, New York: Pardes, 1951):

Ibn Ezra's commentary on the book of Numbers
Onqelos (an Old Aramaic targum)
Rashi's commentary

The Peshiṭta used in this essay is *The Old Testament in Syriac according to the Peshiṭta Version* (Leiden: The Peshiṭta Institute, 1991).

The Bible used in this study for the Christian Neo-Aramaic of Urmi was *Syriac Modern Bible* (Beirut: The Bible Societies in the Near East, 1966).

The Elkoosh (Urmi) version used is *The Four Gospels in the Elkoosh Dialect, Urmi* (American Presbyterian Mission, 1873).

Garbell, I.

1965 *The Jewish Neo-Aramaic Dialect of Persian Azerbaijan.* The Hague.

Kittel, R., et al. (eds.)

1977 *Biblia Hebraica Stuttgartensia.* Stuttgart: Deutsche Bibelstiftung.

Maclean, A. J.

1972 *A Dictionary of the Dialects of Vernacular Syriac.* Oxford, 1901. Reprint, Amsterdam.

Sabar, Yona

1975 The Hebrew Elements in the Neo-Aramaic Dialects of Azerbaijan Jews. *Lešonénu* 39: 272–94 [Hebrew].

1976 *Pešaṭ Wayhi Bešallaḥ, A Neo-Aramaic Midrash on Beshallaḥ (Exodus).* Wiesbaden.

1983 *The Book of Genesis in Neo-Aramaic in the Dialect of the Jewish Community of Zakho, Including Selected Texts in Other Neo-Aramaic Dialects and a Glossary.* Jerusalem.

1988 *The Book of Exodus in Neo-Aramaic in the Dialect of the Jewish Community of Zakho, Including Selected Texts in Other Neo-Aramaic Dialects and a Glossary.* Jerusalem.

1990 *The Book of Leviticus in Neo-Aramaic in the Dialect of the Jewish Community of Zakho, Including Selected Texts in Other Neo-Aramaic Dialects and a Glossary.* Jerusalem.

1991 The Hebrew Bible Vocabulary as Reflected through Traditional Oral Neo-Aramaic Translations. Vol. 2, pp. 1385–1401 in *Semitic Studies in Honor of Wolf Leslau*, ed. A. S. Kaye. Wiesbaden.

1993 *The Book of Numbers in Neo-Aramaic in the Dialect of the Jewish Community of Zakho, Including Selected Texts in Other Neo-Aramaic Dialects and a Glossary.* Jerusalem

A Comparative Study of Pet Names in English and Assyrian

Edward Y. Odisho

Introduction

Names are part of the identity of people all over the world; they are also a distinctive feature of their culture. Thomas Fuller, cited by Dunkling, wrote, "A name is a kind of face."[1] Hanks and Hodges see a person's given (first) name as a badge of cultural identity.[2] They further state that the names that people bear are determined in large measure by the culture they belong to.[3] The latter

Author's note: I wish to express my deep gratitude to Dr. Beverly Otto of the Department of Curriculum and Instruction, Northeastern Illinois University, for her comments on this paper.

1. T. Fuller, cited in L. A. Dunkling, *First Names First* (Detroit: Gale Research, 1977) 11.
2. P. Hanks and F. Hodges, *A Dictionary of First Names* (Oxford: Oxford University Press, 1990) vii.
3. Ibid.

statement would have been more realistic, comprehensive, and accurate if language had been added to culture as another factor that determines the nature and type of the names people bear.

In his very impressive study of the Neo-Aramaic dialect of the village of Aradhin, Georg Krotkoff includes a short list of names and nicknames used by the villagers.[4] This short list is so interesting that it inspired me to expand further and investigate the topic of naming among the speakers of Aramaic, with special emphasis on what Krotkoff calls "nicknames." The onomastic materials in this study are based on what is common among Assyrians, as opposed to Chaldeans and Syrians; however, despite this specificity, the materials are generally valid for all the Christian speakers of Aramaic.

My initial intent in this paper was to employ the term *nickname* as a rubric under which more names of the type incorporated in Krotkoff's list would be included. After further readings in the domain of naming, however, I realized that the term is too broad and loose to stand specifically and definitely for the type of names targeted in this study. Franklyn states that everybody knows what a nickname is but few could define it. He further states that even the Oxford English Dictionary has a chink in its armor.[5] He then cites the OED's definition of nicknames as "a name or appellation added to, or substituted for, the proper name of a person, place, etc., usually given in ridicule or pleasantry." Etymologically, a nickname is derived from the Middle English "an ekename," meaning an added name.[6] It can be a diminutive name, such as "Will" for "William." It can also be descriptive, reflecting physical features and character traits, such as "Shorty" and "Honest Abe," respectively.[7] A nickname can also be an "incident" name that arises from a chance remark, a slip of the tongue, or sometimes from a favorite expression.[8] This means that although a nickname is often applied fondly, it may also be derisive.[9]

Of the above three categories of naming that fall under the rubric of nicknames, only the traditional category of diminutive names applies to the type of "nicknames" in Krotkoff's list. That is, the contents of his list do not represent descriptive or accidental nicknames. Consequently, the types of nicknames included in Krotkoff's list would better be labeled as "pet names." Dunkling strongly argues in favor of such a term as a more appropriate one and defines

4. Georg Krotkoff, *A Neo-Aramaic Dialect of Kurdistan* (New Haven, Conn.: American Oriental Society, 1982).

5. Julian Franklyn, *A Dictionary of Nicknames* (New York: British Book Center, 1962) xii.

6. "Nicknames," *Encyclopedia Americana*, 1990 ed.; Franklyn, *Dictionary*, xii.

7. *Encyclopedia Americana*, s.v.

8. Dunkling, *First Names*, 31.

9. *Encyclopedia Americana.*

it as a variant form of the first name that is used in informal circumstances.[10] The term *hypocoristic* has also been used to stand for pet names, but Dunkling hesitates to adopt it because the term hints at baby language as a source for such names.[11] Dunkling's position is readily justifiable because pet names are not the exclusive creation of baby language. Pet-naming seems to be an onomastic device that is more commonly employed by adults and should not be seen as the coinage of baby language. No doubt, baby language is a factor in coining pet names, but it is not the only one.

Pet-naming is more of a linguistic device practiced by adults in a fashion similar to contractions and abbreviations. It is simply a trend in the economical use of language to serve the function of intimacy, informality, and, perhaps, endearment.

Regardless of the somewhat misleading nature of the term *pet name*, due to its other connotation associated with domestic animals, it is adopted here to designate a common sociolinguistic practice of shortening names without necessarily being hypocoristic, descriptive, accidental, humorous, or derisive.

In this study, pet-naming in English and Assyrian is compared in an attempt to find out the patterns of pet-name formation, the rules that dominate those formations, and whether the underlying morphological rules of English and Assyrian have any relevance in this regard.

For the purpose of conducting this study, 200 given names (selected at random) and their pet names are examined, 100 names from each language, equally representing male and female names. The names from each language are meant to represent some of the ones most commonly used.[12] Obviously, the Assyrians, as Christians, have adopted many Anglo-Saxon names through contact with Europeans, especially the British. Those loan-names, however, are not expected to interfere with the objectivity of the overall assessment of facts because most of them have been indigenized (i.e., Assyrianized) in both pronunciation and syllabic structure.

The tables below include first names (names, henceforth) and pet names, followed by a digit indicating the number of the syllables in each item. For English (tables 1 and 2), the names are written with traditional spelling, whereas for Assyrian (tables 3 and 4), they are broadly transcribed in a manner that is generally consistent with the principles of the International Phonetic Association (IPA). Occasionally, the IPA principles are modified to reflect some intricate

10. Dunkling, *First Names*, 80.

11. Ibid., 77.

12. L. R. N. Ashley, *What's in a Name?* (Baltimore: Genealogical Publishing, 1989); L. A. Dunkling, *The Guinness Book of Names* (London: Guinness, 1986).

phonetic characteristics of the Assyrian language, especially in the representation of aspiration and nonaspiration in plosives and affricates.[13] Moreover, since in Assyrian, the palatal plosives, rather than the velar plosives, are dominant, /ɟ/ and /c/ are consistently used where appropriate. In a previous study, I did point out that some investigators tend to transcribe the above pair of plosives as /g/ and /k/, respectively, either because they are not aware of the palatal nature of those two Assyrian plosives or because they prefer the more familiar symbols of /g/ and /k/.[14] In either case, the substitution may be very misleading for anyone who is not familiar with the language.

There may be several variants for the pet names of certain names in both English and Assyrian, but for the sake of neatness and concentration, a minimum number of the variants is cited. This minimum number was decided upon after ascertaining that the omission of the other variants in no way interferes with the accuracy of the results. For a few items in English, it is difficult to agree on the exact number of the syllables involved. Although they are too few to lead to spurious results, both syllable counts are taken into consideration.

In the phonetic transcription of the Assyrian names, certain conventions must be clarified. First, since stress is predominantly penultimate, it is marked only when it is otherwise. Second, the language has many double-plosive clusters or abutting consonants that, if they happen to be aspirated, feature the symbol of aspiration on the second only, even though the first one is also implied (that is, instead of transcribing /$t^h t^h$/, I have spelled /tt^h/). Third, if an item is emphatic but does not contain a traditional emphatic sound, such as /ṣ/ *ṣade* or /ṭ/ *ṭeth*, emphasis is marked either by the use of /ɑ/ instead of /a/ or by placing a dot under another consonant. Fourth, all items in Assyrian are initiated with a consonant; accordingly, in the absence of an initial consonant, a *hamza* (glottal stop) is assumed; thus /awwi/ stands for /ʾawwi/. Fifth, vowels are long when stressed and in an open syllable.

The Data

TABLE 1. English Male Names and Pet Names

Names	*Syllables*	*Pet Names*	*Syllables*
Albert	2	Al	1
Anthony	3	Tony	2
Arthur	2	Art	1

13. For details, see my *Sound System of Modern Assyrian* (Wiesbaden: Harrassowitz, 1988).

14. Edward Odisho, "Phonetic and Phonological Description of the Labio-Palatal and Labio-Velar Approximants in Neo-Aramaic," in *Studies in Neo-Aramaic* (ed. Wolfhart Heinrichs; Atlanta: Scholars Press, 1990) 30.

TABLE 1, *continued.* English Male Names and Pet Names

Names	*Syllables*	*Pet Names*	*Syllables*
Benjamin	3	Ben	1
Charles	1	Chuck	1
Christopher	3	Chris	1
Clayton	2	Clay	1
Clinton	2	Clint	1
Daniel	2/3	Dan	1
David	2	Dave	1
Donald	2	Don	1
Edward	2	Ed	1
Ernest	2	Ernie	2
Eugene	2	Gene	1
Franklin	2	Frank	1
Geoffrey	2	Jeff	1
Gustav	2	Gus	1
Henry	2	Hal	1
Irving	2	Irv	1
James	1	Jim	1
Jerrold	2	Jerry	2
Jonathan	3	John	1
Joseph	2	Joe	1
Kenneth	2	Ken	1
Lawrence	2	Larry	2
Marcus	2	Mark	1
Matthew	2	Matt	1
Maxwell; Maximilian	2; 4	Max	1
Melvin	2	Mel	1
Michael	2	Mike	1
Mitchell	2	Mitch	1
Nicholas	3	Nick	1
Norman	2	Norm	1
Patrick	2	Pat	1
Peter	2	Pete	1
Philip	2	Phil	1
Raphael	3	Ralph	1
Raymond	2	Ray	1
Richard	2	Rich; Dick	1
Robert	2	Rob; Bob	1

TABLE 1, *continued.* English Male Names and Pet Names

Names	*Syllables*	*Pet Names*	*Syllables*
Ronald	2	Ron	1
Samuel	2/3	Sam	1
Sheldon	2	Shel	1
Stanley	2	Stan	1
Steven	2	Steve	1
Timothy	3	Tim	1
Theodore	2/3	Ted	1
Thomas	2	Tom	1
Victor	2	Vic	1
William	2/3	Will; Bill	1

TABLE 2. English Female Names and Pet Names

Names	*Syllables*	*Pet Names*	*Syllables*
Abigail	3	Abby; Gail	2; 1
Alexandra	4	Sandra	2
Amanda	3	Manda; Mandy	2
Argentina	4	Tina	2
Barbara	3	Barb; Barby	1/2
Belinda	3	Linda	2
Beverly	3	Bev	1
Carolyn	3	Carol	2
Catherine	3	Cathy	2
Cassandra	3	Cass; Cassie	1/2
Cecelia	3	Celia	2
Christine/a	2/3	Chris	1
Cleopatra	3/4	Cleo	2
Constance	2	Connie	2
Cynthia	2/3	Cindy	2
Debra/Deborah	2/3	Debbie	2
Delores	3	Lola	2
Dorothy	3	Doll; Dolly	1/2
Edith	2	Edie	2
Edwina	3	Win; Winnie	1/2
Elizabeth	4	Liz; Betsy	1/2
Emily	3	Emmy	2

TABLE 2, *continued.* English Female Names and Pet Names

Names	*Syllables*	*Pet Names*	*Syllables*
Eugenia	3	Genia	2
Faith	1	Faye	1
Florence	2	Flo; Flora	1/2
Geraldine	3	Gerry	2
Gertrude	2	Trudy	2
Gwendolyn	3	Gwen	1
Helena	3	Lena	2
Hildegard	3	Hilda	2
Jacqueline	2/3	Jackie	2
Josephine	3	Josie	2
Margaret	2/3	Meg; Maggie	1/2
Martha	2	Marty	2
Matilda	3	Mattie; Tilda	2
Pamela	3	Pam	1
Penelope	3	Penny	2
Priscilla	3	Cilla; Prissie	2
Prudence	2	Prue; Prudie	2
Rachel	2	Ray	1
Rebecca	3	Becky	2
Roberta	3	Bobby	2
Sabina	3	Bina	2
Susan/na	2/3	Sue	1
Shirley	2	Sherri	2
Theresa	3	Tess; Tracy	1/2
Valerie	3	Val	1
Victoria	3	Vicky	2
Virginia	3	Ginny; Ginger	2
Wilhelmina	4	Wilma	2

TABLE 3. Assyrian Male Names and Pet Names

Names	*Syllables*	*Pet Names*	*Syllables*
ɑmɑnuwwıl	4	ɑmmo/i	2
andriyyus	3	ando/i	2
ap^{h}rım	2	app^{h}o/i	2
at^{h}(θ)niyyıl	3	att^{h}o/u	2

TABLE 3, *continued.* Assyrian Male Names and Pet Names

Names	*Syllables*	*Pet Names*	*Syllables*
awiyya	3	awwi/o/u	2
awšalım	3	awšo/u	2
azız	2	azzo/u	2
barčʰam	2	baččʰo/u	2
bınyamın	3	bınni/o	2
daniyyıl	3	danno/u	2
daryawıš	3	daryo/u	2
dawıd	2	dodo	2
dınxa	2	dıxxo; dıkko	2
ho(u)rmıs	2	ho(u)mme	2
iliyya	3	ıllo/u	2
ınwiyya	3	ınno/u	2
ısxaq	2	ıqqo; ıččo/u	2
jıbrɑyıl	3	jıbbo	2
ɟıwarɟıs	3	ɟaɟɟo/u; gaggu; jajji/o/u	2
ɟoriyyıl	3	ɟawwo/u; ɟiyye	2
lɑzɑr	2	jajo/u	2
mıšayıl	3	miša/u; mıšša	2
mıxayıl	3	mixa/o/u	2
napılyon	3	nappo	2
natʰnıyyıl	3	natʰo/u	2
nikola	3	niqa	2
nımrud	2	nımmo	2
odišo/u	3	dıšše	2
orɑhım	3	oro; ıcce	2
pʰıθyun	2	pʰıtʰ(θ)yo/u	2
pʰilipʰus	3	pʰıllo/u	2
pʰnuwwıl	2	pʰınno	2
pʰolıs	2	pʰola/u	2
puṭrus	2	pıtto	2
sɑnxiru	2	sɑnxo	2
sargon	2	saggo	2
sarɟıs	2	sagga/i	2
šawı(u)l	2	šawwu	2
šımšun	2	šıššo/u	2
šle(i)mun	2	čemo; čımmo	2
šmuwwıl	2	šuwwa; šuma; čuwwe	2

TABLE 3, *continued.* Assyrian Male Names and Pet Names

Names	*Syllables*	*Pet Names*	*Syllables*
ṭɑlyɑ	2	tɑllo/u	2
wɪlyam	2	wɪllo/u	2
xamɪs	2	xamčo	2
xasq(k)iyyɪl	3	xasq(k)u	2
xošaba	3	šaba/e; čaba/o	2
yonan	2	nanno/u; manno/u	2
yosɪp	2	čopa/e	2
yurɑm	2	yurɑ	2
yuxanna(n)	3	canna/o; nanna	2

TABLE 4. Assyrian Female Names and Pet Names

Names	*Syllables*	*Pet Names*	*Syllables*
aglant^{h}ina	4	ajji; ego	2
agnɪs	2	ego; aggo	2
asmar	2	ačče	2
badriyya	3	badre	2
bahija	3	bɪjje	2
bɑt^{h}ɪšwɑ	3	bɑt^{h}u; baɪt^{h}u	2
cɪtrina	3	cɪtte/o	2
dalila	3	dallo	2
ɪstɪr	2	ɪtte	2
f(p^{h})ɑbroniyɑ	4	f(p^{h})ɑbbo	2
gladɪs	2	gado	2
grazɪlda	3	gazzi	2
helane	3	nane	2
ilɪšwɑ	3	ɪššo/u	2
ilizabet	4	zabo; zabet	2
ɪngrɪd	2	ɪnje	2
jak^{h}lɪn	2	jakk^{h}o	2
juliyya	3	juli/o	2
k^{h}leman't^{h}in	3	č^{h}ema	2
layya	2	tayya/o	2
lɪlyan	2	lɪlle	2
ludiyya	3	ludi/o	2
lusiyya	3	sɪyya; luse	2

TABLE 4, *continued.* Assyrian Female Names and Pet Names

Names	*Syllables*	*Pet Names*	*Syllables*
madlen	2	maddi	2
mɑrgret	2	mɑggi/o	2
marɟanitʰa	3	maɟɟo; majje	2
mɑrlɪn	2	mɑnni	2
martʰɑ	2	battʰa	2
mɑryɑm	2	mɑyyi/o	2
melina	2	melo	2
mɪscɪntʰa	3	mɪsku	2
nɑhren	2	nɑhhi/o	2
najiba	3	najjo	2
nɑnɑjɑn	3	nano	2
narɟɪs	2	naɟɟo	2
rabqa	2	čʰaqqo	2
rejina	3	rejo	2
ṣɑbriyya	3	ṣɑbbo	2
sulṭɑne	3	sulṭe	2
šɑmmirɑn	3	šammo	2
šušan	2	šušše	2
tʰo(aw)rɪs	2	tʰoze	2
wardiyya	3	warde/u	2
warjiniya	4	wajjo	2
wɑylet	2	wɑyo	2
wɪkʰtʰoriya	4	wɑkkʰo; ɪkʰtʰu	2
xanzade	3	xazzu	2
xɪzzeme	3	meme	2
yasmine	3	yasme	2
yuliyya	3	yulo	2

Results

Before the results are surveyed, it is necessary to point out that the syllable is used here as a generic yardstick of measurement regardless of the syllable size (that is, regardless of how many segmental elements are involved). Since both English and Assyrian enjoy a wide variety of syllable sizes, the variety evens out any specific differences in syllable sizes.

The mean length of male names in English is 2.16 syllables, whereas for pet names, it is 1.08 syllables, implying that names are reduced to half size (that is, by 50%). The mean length of female names in English is approximately 2.83 syllables, and for pet names, it is 1.75 syllables, a statistic that implies that female pet names are reduced by approximately 38%, which in actual size is identical with the 1.08 syllables to which male names are reduced.

The above figures indicate that, on average, female names are longer than male names by 0.67 of a syllable, which is exactly the same difference between the female and the male pet names (i.e., 2.83 − 2.16 = .67 for female, and 1.75 − 1.08 = .67 for male).

As for Assyrian, the mean length of male names is 2.52 syllables, whereas for pet names, it is an absolute 2.00 syllables, implying that names are reduced by 0.52 of a syllable. The mean length of female names is 2.70 syllables as opposed to an absolute 2.00 syllables for their pet names. These figures indicate that, on average, female names in Assyrian are longer than their male counterparts by 0.18 of a syllable—a differential that is less than for their English counterparts.

The absolute two-syllable mean length for all male pet names in Assyrian implies that the Assyrian pet names are almost twice as long as their English male counterparts. This is further substantiated by the fact that 92% of English male pet names are monosyllabic, against the fact that all Assyrian pet names are disyllabic. Female pet names in Assyrian, however, are longer than their English counterparts by only 0.25 of a syllable.

Turning to another aspect of the comparison, nearly 60% of the English male pet names are of a monosyllabic CVC (Consonant-Vowel-Consonant) pattern. Some less-common syllable patterns are CV, VC, VCC, CCVC, CVCC. For English female pet names, it is difficult to conduct the description in terms of syllable patterns, since approximately 72% of them are disyllabic. A more appropriate description would be in terms of the overall syllabic structure of the pet names. While no syllabic structure predominates, a CV.CV structure tends to be more common.

The syllabic structure of Assyrian pet names is neater and more systematic. The predominant syllabic structure for both male and female pet names is the CVC.CV structure. Approximately 75% of male and 60% of female pet names have this syllabic structure. The abutting consonants (C.C) in the middle are frequently geminated (doubled) consonants, as in /dɪkko/, /danño/, and /pɪtto/; however, nonidentical abutting consonants are also familiar, such as in /daryo/, /sɑnxo/, and /xasku/. The second most popular syllabic structure is CV.CV, as in /dodo/, /soro/, and /šabe/.

Both CVC.CV and CV.CV syllabic structures imply that pet names in Assyrian are consistently initiated with a consonant (a glottal stop being assumed for any item that is initiated without a consonant) and closed with a vowel.

Another process by which the pet names are formed is called here *truncation*, cutting off a section of the name. Although truncation is active in both languages, the manner in which it applies, the extent of its application, and whether it is combined with other processes may vary.

Truncation seems to apply in two different formats. At times, the anterior section of the name is dropped, such as in the English examples of "Eugene" and "Anthony," reduced to "Gene" and "Tony," and in the Assyrian examples of /xošaba/ and /yuxanna/, reduced to /šabe/ and /nanna/, respectively. This format is described as *front truncation*, in opposition to *back truncation*, in which the posterior section of the name is left off. Examples of back truncation in English are "Donald" and "Raymond" reduced to "Don" and "Ray," and in Assyrian /yurɑm/ and /yasmine/ reduced to /yurɑ/ and /yasme/, respectively. Back truncation is undoubtedly more pervasive in English than front truncation.

Truncation is also active in Assyrian. As in English, back truncation is more active than front truncation. In Assyrian, however, truncation does not seem to operate in the same, more-or-less mechanical manner in which it operates in English, that is, cutting off a section of the name. There is clear indication that in Assyrian, truncation tends to be heavily subject to a major constraint, which is labeled here *root identity retention* (RIR). This is realized through the retention of at least two major consonants of the three or four consonants (radicals) of which the root/stem consists. As a further reinforcement of the RIR constraint, one of the consonants is often geminated. In fact, approximately 65% of the Assyrian pet names do have a geminated consonant.

With respect to their segmental (consonants and vowels) sound structure, English pet names hardly undergo any phonetic change. Unlike English, Assyrian evidences several instances of segmental phonetic change that do not have a direct representation in the original names. The /č/ in /čuwwe/ for /šmuwwıl, /ıččo/ for /ısxaq/, or /xamčo/ for /xamıs/; and /č^h/ in /č^{h}aqqo/ for /rabqa/; /k/ in /dıkko/ for /dınxa/; /j/ in /jaju/ for /lɑzɑr/ and /b/ in /batt^{h}a/ for /mart^{h}ɑ/ all represent major phonetic changes. What is interesting, however, is that there may exist some underlying phonetic affinity between the newly emerging sounds and the original radicals. The phonetic affinity may assume the form of manner or place of articulation. For instance, the pairs /m/ and /b/ and /k/ and /x/ in the examples cited above, are related as to place of articulation.

Discussion

As indicated above, the syllable is treated in this study as a generic yardstick (unit) of measurement, regardless of size. This position is adopted because what is targeted is word length, or more accurately, name length. In the light of such a consideration, the English female names are longer than their male counterparts by 0.67 of a syllable—a relatively sizable difference that seems to result from the frequent addition of a female suffix, such as *a*, *ine*, and *ia*, as in "Edwin/Edwina," "Joseph/Josephine," and "Victor/Victoria." With the addition of such suffixes, an additional syllable tends to emerge. Interestingly enough, in our randomly selected names, exactly the same difference is maintained between the female and the male pet names. This latter difference is implicitly related to the original addition of a female suffix to the male names as a distinctive feature. Explicitly, however, nearly 60% of the female pet names end with a suffix /i/ (graphically represented with *y* or *ie*, as in "Abby," "Sandy," "Cathy," "Connie," "Debbie," and "Jackie"). It is mainly due to the absence of such a marker in the male pet names that the overwhelming majority of them are monosyllabic.

The picture in Assyrian seems to be different. Although the female names are also longer than their male counterparts, the difference is minimal and only about 0.2 of a syllable. Since the difference is minimal to this degree, it can be considered accidental and nonessential. In general, though the first names in Assyrian are slightly longer on average than those in English, their reduction is much more restricted. The only reason for this is the two-syllable length constraint imposed on the formation of pet names in Assyrian. It is assumed here that this constraint constitutes the major distinguishing factor in the formation of pet names in the two languages.

Assyrian, being a Semitic language tends to retain strictly the characteristic role of the consonants in the construction of the morphological identity of words. Krotkoff highlights such a relationship by stating that the concept of a consonantal root, so prominent in all Semitic languages, is a corollary of the existence of strict morphological patterning.[15] The consonantal radicals and the sequence in which they are arranged not only signal "the general meaning of a root,"[16] they also signal its formal identity. In other words, consonants carry more weight in signaling the generic semantic and formal identity of lexical items in the Semitic languages, including Assyrian. Certainly, in this study, meaning is not pertinent, but formal identity is. The absolute two-syllable constraint on the formation of pet names in Assyrian implies a strong trend toward the retention of as much of the consonantal root identity as possible; it was this trend that was referred to above as root identity retention (RIR).

A monosyllabic pattern of pet names in Assyrian would be highly incompatible with, and uncharacteristic of, the Semitic languages. Monosyllabic

15. Krotkoff, *Neo-Aramaic*, 19.

16. G. Bergsträsser, *Introduction to the Semitic Languages* (trans. Peter Daniels; Winona Lake, Ind.: Eisenbrauns, 1983) 5.

structures in such languages are rare. Aside from some pronouns and general particles and some disyllabic words, the great majority of bases/roots appears to be trisyllabic.[17] Unlike in Assyrian, in English, an Indo-European language, the concept of the consonantal root/base is less powerful in determining both the semantic and the formal identity of the linguistic items. This characteristic of English is, perhaps, the primary reason behind the greater variety in the syllabic structures of pet names in English and the greater freedom in implementing the truncation process.

The rules of pet-name formation in Assyrian appear to be more powerful. They operate very rigidly and consistently, even with loan-names, regardless of their source. For instance, "Edward," "Napoleon," and "Alfred" strictly adhere to the CVC.CV syllabic structure and become /ɩddo/, /nɑppo/, and /app^{h}(ff)i/, respectively. Besides this strong indigenization tendency, which is an indication of consistency in pet-name formation, uniformity is further portrayed through the absolute validity of the two-syllable structural constraint, the vocalic ending of the items, and their predominant CVC.CV syllabic structure.

The greater segmental phonetic discrepancy between the Assyrian names and pet names may be attributed to the greater influence of baby language (baby talk) in Assyrian than in English. Apparently, such a hypocoristic influence in Assyrian is realized through phonetic changes within the segmental structure of the items concerned, whereas in English, it is frequently realized through suffixation, as in "Jimmy" for "Jim," "Freddie" for "Fred," and "Tommy" for "Tom."

Conclusions and Implications for Future Research

Pet-naming appears to be a very common and pervasive sociolinguistic phenomenon in both English and Assyrian. In fact, preliminary investigation tends to recognize pet-naming as a phenomenon common to most languages and cultures. Perhaps it will turn out to be a universal feature of human culture. However, a final judgment in this respect should depend on further and more exhaustive research.

This limited comparative study reveals some similarities and differences in the manner in which pet-naming functions in English and Assyrian. A major similarity is truncation, which may not be true of other languages. For example, in Arabic, pet names can be generated through internal restructuring without any change or deletion in the consonantal radicals, such as converting

17. L. H. Gray, *Introduction to Semitic Comparative Linguistics* (Amsterdam: Philo, 1971) 34; Bergsträsser, *Introduction*, 6.

/jami:l/, /kari:m/, and /sali:m/ into /jmayyil/, /krayyim/, and /slayyim/, respectively. Arabic can also introduce different pet name variants for the above three names in the form of /jammuli/, /karrumi/, and /sallumi/, respectively. It can also resort to some sort of truncation, as in /ya:s/ from /ya:siin/, but truncation is very uncharacteristic of Arabic. Most likely the rarity of truncation in the formation of pet names in Arabic is attributable to the fact that Arabic names are overwhelmingly derived from verb roots and bear well-defined meanings. This direct association of Arabic names with the meaning and the form of the roots/bases could be the primary reason why pet-naming through truncation is very rare. Such an interpretation is reminiscent of what was hinted at above when RIR constraint was introduced for the formation of pet names in Assyrian, another Semitic language.

The major differences between English and Assyrian reveal themselves in the greater rigidity and consistency in Assyrian. Such a difference is attributed here to the underlying and grossly different morphological rules of word formation in Assyrian, as a Semitic language, and English, as an Indo-European language.

To pass more definitive judgments in this area of study requires additional comparative studies and further investigation. For instance, one needs to account for the greater permissibility of truncation in Arabic loan-names in Kurdish, such as in /muh̲ammad/, /ʾah̲mad/, /maji:d/, and /ʿabdalla/, which become /h̲ama/, /ʾah̲a/, /maja/, and /ʾaba/, respectively. Questions of this nature will, hopefully, be targeted in a forthcoming study.

Part 4

Afroasiatic

The Trickle Down Approach

Carleton T. Hodge

Comparative Semitic has long had a recognized set of phonetic correspondences.[1] At the same time there have been persistent sets of forms that do not fit these correspondences. This has led to a recognition that certain words were related to each other despite differences that were unaccounted for. In his comparative dictionary of Ge^{c}ez (G.), Leslau uses the word *related* to refer to these apparent aberrations.[2] For example, he cites Arabic (Arab.) *^{c}amila* 'to work' as *related*, on some authority, to Ge^{c}ez *^{c}abbala* 'to work'.[3] Such comparisons are usually qualified by the words "with alternation of labials" *aut sim*.

When the wider field of Afroasiatic (AAs) is considered, such comparisons multiply. For example, Egyptian (Eg.) *m* 'in, from' corresponds to both Semitic (Sem.) **b-* 'in' and **m-* 'from'. Another broadly attested set of alternations

1. Cf., e.g., Heinrich Zimmern, *Vergleichende Grammatik der Semitischen Sprachen* (Porta Linguarum Orientalium 17; Berlin: Reuther and Reichard, 1898) 11–12; and Wolf Leslau, *Comparative Dictionary of Ge^{c}ez* (Wiesbaden: Harrassowitz, 1987) xxvii.

2. Ibid., xxii.

3. Ibid., 54.

concerns the glottalized, pharyngealized, or aspirated consonants versus the plain ones. For example, Arab. *batara* 'cut off' vs. *baṭara* 'incise', *habata* 'fall' vs. *habaṭa* 'fall'. It has been proposed that these and related problem correspondences be attributed to the presence or absence of affixes in the protolanguage (whether AAs or Lislakh [LL]). An affix *H* (a cover symbol for affixes adding glottalization, pharyngealization, or aspiration) and an affix *N* (a nasal morpheme) are postulated as having been added to either one, or both of the consonants, of a proto-root or "base." This hypothesis, called "consonant ablaut," has resulted in the establishment of a large number of proto-bases and the assignment to them of AAs (or LL) lexemes (either attested or reconstructed), according to the presence or absence of *H* or *N*. For example, Sem. **b-* 'in' is taken to be from plain proto***b*, while Eg. *m* and Sem.**m-* are from***Nb*.[4] More exactly, these are from a word for 'foot' or 'place' that had shapes***b-C* and***Nb-C*, where *C* is not yet identified.[5]

The explanatory value of this approach has been amply shown elsewhere.[6] We are here concerned with the implications of this hypothesis for the etymological understanding of a single language, Arabic. If *bi-* goes back to ***b-* and the *mi-* of *min* to ***Nb-*, are there not numerous interrelationships of Arabic roots that have not been recognized?

A single base, ***l-b* 'the middle of the body, heart', has been chosen to test this approach. This base is attested in other branches of the phylum, for example, Eg. *(ᵓ-)3-b, (ᵓ-) n-b* 'heart',[7] Cushitic (Cu.) **l-b* 'chest, breast',[8] and it is, of course, widespread in Semitic.[9] ***l-b* plus *H* or *N* gives us nine basic combinations, but only six of these have Arabic reflexes:

	Reconstruction	*Arabic*		*Reconstruction*	*Arabic*		*Reconstruction*	*Arabic*
1.	**l-b	l-b	2.	**l-bH	?	3.	**l-Nb	l-m
4.	**lH-b	r-b	5.	**lH-bH	?	6.	**lh-Nb	r-m
7.	**Nl-b	n-b	8.	**Nb-bH	?	9.	**Nl-Nb	n-m

4. Reconstructions by the author appear with double asterisks.

5. Carleton T. Hodge, "Indo-European and Afroasiatic," in *Sprung from Some Common Source* (ed. Sydney M. Lamb and E. Douglas Mitchell; Stanford: Stanford University Press, 1991) 156.

6. Carleton T. Hodge, "Consonant Ablaut in Lislakh," in *FUCUS: A Semitic/Afrasian Gathering in Remembrance of Albert Ehrman* (ed. Yoël Arbeitman; Current Issues in Linguistic Theory 58; Amsterdam: Benjamins, 1988) 267–76; idem, "Touching the Bases," in *The Fifteenth LACUS Forum 1988* (ed. Ruth M. Brend and David G. Lockwood; Lake Bluff, Ill: LACUS, 1989) 5–21; and idem, "Splitting Homonyms," in *The Sixteenth LACUS Forum 1989* (ed. Michael P. Jordan; Lake Bluff, Ill: LACUS, 1990) 168–76.

7. Revised readings, Hodge, "Indo–European," 158–59.

8. Christopher Ehret, "Proto-Cushitic Reconstruction," *Sprache und Geschichte in Afrika* 8 (1987) 77.

9. Leslau, *Comparative*, 304.

The reflexes of ***bH* in Semitic, if any, are not known, so the middle set of forms (2, 5, 8), though attested elsewhere, is irrelevant here.

The problem is not a simple one. There are other AAs bases with the consonants ***l-b*, and it is not always possible to determine with any certainty to which of these a given Arabic root with *l-b* should be assigned. There is therefore some discussion of alternatives.

Lubb^{un} is defined as 'the heart, kernel, pith, choice part; understanding, intelligence; essence',[10] 'heart, sense, intelligence, discernment, sound judgment'.[11] Any form that we wish to relate to *lubb*^{un} should be semantically compatible with one of the above meanings. Two broad semantic areas may be distinguished: (1) the physical part of the object concerned and (2) mental processes or states (thought, emotion) associated with the physical area. For maximum clarity of presentation, there has been further division within these two. The suggested cognates are listed by subcategory in the order of the consonant ablaut forms of ***l-b* as given above (1, 3, 4, 6, 7, 9).

Since the Arabic roots cited are triconsonantal and we derive them from a biconsonantal base, it follows that the third consonant is an affix. In the reconstructed forms of the various roots, these affixes are given in parentheses and in their appropriate ablaut form. Most suffixes and prefixes are from demonstrative elements, such as *s*, ʾ, *ḥ* (from ***ʾH*), *h*, ʿ (from ***hH*); or prepositional elements, such as *l*, *r* (from ***lH*), *n* (from ***Nl*). The demonstrative elements generally add an actor or indicate that the action has been effected. The affix *l* adds 'pertaining to' *aut sim.*, as one could assume from its prepositional use (Ar. *li-*).[12]

It is neither claimed nor denied that these relationships are evident to speakers of Arabic or have existed historically. Rather, I hold that these Arabic etyma are derived from the same proto-base and were, at the time of the proto-language, recognized as closely related to each other.

The main sources of the forms are Lane and Ullmann.[13] I used later dictionaries[14] where they offered additional forms or meanings. ***l-b* does not occur in its simple form in Arabic but only with affixes. Words are cited in the general order: those with suffixes, those with prefixes. Secondary affixes, such as feminine *t* or verb stem formatives, are not represented in the reconstructions.

10. Edward William Lane (ed.), *Arabic-English Lexicon* (1 vol. in 8 pts.; New York: Ungar, 1956 [1863–1893]), vol. 1, pt. 7, p. 2643.

11. Manfred Ullmann, *Wörterbuch der classischen arabischen Sprache* (Wiesbaden: Harrassowitz, 1973) 2.77.

12. These meanings have been arrived at independently and do not agree with Ehret, "Proto-Cushitic."

13. Lane, *Arabic-English Lexicon;* Ullmann, *Wörterbuch.*

14. J. G. Hava, *Arabic-English Dictionary* (Beirut: Catholic Press, 1915).

The Physical Part of the Object

I divide the words reflecting the physical meanings into two sections: (1) those referring to the body as such, some part of the front central area of the torso, and (2) those referring to that physical part as it relates to other similar parts or to something outside itself.

The Physical Center

1. ***l-b(-C_2)*: *lubb^{un}* 'heart', etc., *lubāb^{un}* 'inside, pith, kernel'. It seems probable that *labba^{tun}* 'the pit above the breast, the upper part of the chest' belongs here. Compare also ***(hH-)l-b(-ˀ)*: *ˁilbāˀ^{un}* 'muscle on the side of the neck'. A possible origin from ***l-b* 'to pierce' is raised by its meaning as the 'place on the throat where an animal is slaughtered'. Most usages of *labba^{tun}* favor the derivation from ***l-b* 'heart'.
   ***l-b(-N_1)*: *labān^{un}* 'breast, middle of the breast (of horse, etc.)'. The meaning of the affix ***-N1,* as the nasal form of ***l-* 'pertaining to', seems clear.
   ***l-b(-x)*: *labaxa* 'to be corpulent', *lubūx^{un}* 'fleshiness of the body'.
   ***(x-)l-b*: *xilb^{un}* 'diaphragm, membrane of the liver'.
   ***(w-)l-b*: *walaba* 'to enter', i.e., to go into the interior of something. ***w* is a known deictic element, occurring in various pronouns.
3. ***l-Nb(-ˀ)*: *talammaˀa* 'to conceal, enclose (*bi-*)'. The derivation of a meaning 'to conceal, hide' from our base is supported by Geˁez *lababa* 'to surround with something, go around the middle'.[15]
   ***(ˀH-)l-Nb*: *ḥalama^{tun}* 'nipple (of breast)'. Cf. *ˀaḥlām^{un}* 'bodies'. The *H* ablaut of *ˀ* is *ḥ*. Both *ˀ* and *ḥ* are known affixes, usually causative or factitive.
   ***(h-)lH-b*: *hurb^{un}* 'fat over stomach and intestines' (Yemeni).
6. ***lH-Nb(-C_2)*: *rimm^{un}* 'marrow', *rimma^{tun}* 'a bone in which is marrow'.
   ***lH-Nb(-C_2-N_1)*: *rummāna^{tun}* 'stomach of ruminant; woman's breast'.

Physical Contact

The next set is often characterized as pertaining to physical confrontation, from which we get mere physical contact.

1. ***l-b(-C_2)*: *labba* 'it faced, was opposed to'. This reflects the position in which one physical *lubb^{un}* is opposite another physical *lubb^{un}* ('stomach to stomach', where English would say 'face to face'). This is generalized

15. Leslau, *Comparative*, 304, q.v.

to its present meaning. *Mulabban*^{un} means 'in the form of a square block', i.e., with a set of binary oppositions of one side to another.[16] *Labab*^{un} refers to a 'chest strap (of horse, etc)', i.e., that which is put on the *lubb*^{un}.

***1-b(-N*$_1$*)*: *labina*^{tun} 'bib, collar'.

3. ***1-Nb(-C*$_2$*)*: *lamma* 'to put together that which is separate', 'to come and stay with a person' (taking *labba* 'to stay [in a place]' as a semantic derivative).

   ***1-Nb(-s)*: *lamasa*. The *lamasnā* of the Qurʾān (72:8) has been a problem and is variously translated. It has been taken from *lamasa* 'touch' and rendered literally as 'we touched the heavens', as well as with extended meanings such as 'we strove after'. Lane correctly identifies the *m-s* of *lamasa* 'touch' with *massa* 'touch',[17] showing that *l-* is a prefix. *Lamasa* 'touch' is, therefore, from ***(1-)Nb-s* and related to *labisa* 'to put on (clothes)' and ***(ʾH-)b-s ḥabasa* 'to put on (gyves *aut sim.*)', hence 'to confine'. It is here proposed to take the Qurʾānic *lamasnā* from ***l-Nb(-s)*, *lamasa* 'to place oneself in opposition to', i.e, 'we breasted the heavens'.

4. ***lH-b(-C*$_2$*)*: *rabba* 'to collect, congregate'.

   ***lH-b(-hH)*: *rabaʿa* 'to be the fourth', *rabbaʿa* 'to make four-square', i.e., with two sets of opposing sides.

   ***lH-b(-s)*: *rabīs* 'courageous'.

   ***(h-)lH-b*: *h-r-b* in *jāʾa muhrib*^{an} 'he came striving or exerting himself in the affair'.[18] This meaning does not appear derivable from *haraba* 'to flee'.

6. ***lH-Nb(-l)*: *ramala* 'he wove (the mat)', i.e., he put one strand against the other.[19]

7. ***(ʾ-)Nl-b*: *ʾannaba* 'to reprehend, reproach'.

9. ***N*$_1$*-Nb(-s)*: *namasa* 'to become a confidant', *namasa* 'to conceal'. Here the base plus affix has specialized in two different ways.

The Case of Milk

In addition to the above, it could be argued that the Arabic words for 'milk' having *l-b* belong here. This is by no means certain, as it also seems reasonable to derive them from a base ***l-b* 'to flow'.[20] As the idea of 'flow' could also derive from 'to milk, suckle', the issue is unresolved. In support of a derivation from ***l-b* 'heart', we find the expression *banātu laban*^{in} 'the intestines

16. Cf. the words for 'four' below.
17. Lane, *Arabic–English Lexicon*, vol. 1, pt. 7, p. 2673.
18. Ibid., vol. 1, pt. 8, p. 2889.
19. Cf. *rabaʿa* 'to make a four-stranded rope'.
20. Cf. *halaba* 'to drench anyone (with dew)', from ***(h-)l-b* .

in which is the milk'.[21] I include the milk forms here without making a final decision on the matter.

1. ***l-b(-ʾ)*: *labaʾa* 'to milk, to draw off biestings, to suckle (for the first time)', *libaʾ^{un}* 'biestings'.
   ***l-b(-Nl)*: *labina* 'to have (a lot of) milk', *labana* 'to give one milk to drink', *laban^{un}* 'milk, sap', *libān^{un}* 'the sucking of milk'. The ***Nl* suffix can again be interpreted as 'pertaining to' (the *lubb^{un}*).
   ***(ʾH-)l-b*: *ḥalaba* 'to milk'.
   ***(hH-)l-b*: *ʿulba^{tun}* 'a milking vessel'.
3. ***(ʾH-)l-Nb*: *ḥalūm^{un}* 'cottage cheese'.[22]
4. ***lH-b(-s)*: *rabasa* 'to fill (a water skin)'.
   ***(sH-)lH-b*: *ṣaraba* 'to make sour milk'.
6. ***(hH-)lH-Nb*: *ʿarama* 'to suck (breast)'. This may be interpreted as 'he effected (ʿ-) the flow (of milk)'.[23]

Mental Processes or States

We come now to the sets of forms reflecting thought, perception, and feeling. I begin with those indicating knowledge or intelligence.

Knowledge and Intellect

1. ***l-b(-C_2)*: *labba* 'to be possessed of intelligence', *labība^{tun}* 'understanding'.
   ***l-b(-x)*: *labbaxa* 'to teach a thing'.[24]
3. ***l-Nb(-C_2)*: *ʾalamma* 'to reach the age of discretion'.
   ***l-Nb(-hH)*: *ʾalmaʿ^{un}* 'sharp-minded'.
   ***(ʾH-)l-Nb*: *ḥalama* 'to attain to puberty'.
   ***(b-)l-Nb*: *balam^{un}* 'stupid'. The prefix *b-* is from the base ***b-C* (negative).[25]
   ***(hH-)l-Nb*: *ʿalima* 'to know'. *ʿAlam^{un}* 'a thing set up for guidance' and *ʿālam^{un}* 'that by which one knows (a thing)' belong here. *ʿAlam^{un}* 'an impression, footstep' and *ʾaʿlama* 'to make a mark on' are from ***l-b* 'to pierce', even though a mark might also be interpreted as something on the basis of which one makes a judgment.

21. Lane, *Arabic-English Lexicon*, vol. 1, part 8, p. 3007.
22. Cf. ***(hH-)l-Nb*: *ʾiʿtalama* 'to flow upon the ground'.
23. Cf. *ʿarm^{un}* 'the dripping that exudes from meat and from fat'.
24. Said to be a loan from Syriac (Ullmann, *Wörterbuch*, 2.107).
25. Hodge, "Indo-European," 156–57.

4. ***(ʾ-)lH-b*: *ʾaruba* 'to be cunning, intelligent'.
   ***(hH-)lH-b*: *ʿarabatun* 'soul, self, mind', *ʾaʿraba* 'to express one's mind clearly (in Arabic)'.
6. ***lH-Nb(-C_2)*: *rummun* 'something intended or meant', *rāmmatun* 'clever girl'.
   ***lH-Nb(-ʾ)*: *ramaʾa* 'to ascertain'.
   ***(ʾ-)lH-Nb*: *ʾiramun* 'a sign set up to show the way'.
   ***(h-)lH-Nb*: *harimun* 'the mind'.
7. ***Nl-b(-ʾ)*: *nabaʾa* 'to inform'.
   ***Nl-b(-h)*: *nabuha* 'to be known', *nabbaha* 'to inform'.
   ***(h-)Nl-b*: *hanabun* 'weakness of understanding'. This is an unusual privative use of *h-*.
9. ***(ʾ-)Nl-Nb*: *ʾalʾanāmu* 'mankind, everything having the breath of life or a soul (*rūḥ*)'.

Perception

3. ***l-Nb(-ʾ)*: *lamaʾa* 'to glance at'.
   ***l-Nb(-ʾH)*: *lamaḥa* 'to glance at'.
   ***(ʾH-)l-Nb*: *ḥalama* 'to dream'.
4. ***lH-b(-ʾ)*: *rabaʾa* 'to watch, consider', *rābaʾa* 'to watch, observe'.

The heart is the seat of emotion as well as of rational thought:

1. ***l-b(-C_1-C_2)*: *lablabun* 'friendly, affectionate'.
3. ***(ʾH-)l-Nb*: *ḥaluma* 'to be forbearing'.
4. ***lH-b(-hH)*: *rabaʿa* 'to be compassionate' (towards: *ʿalā*).
6. ***lH(-ʾH)-Nb*: *raḥima* 'to be compassionate'. This calls for either an infix *-ḥ-* or for metathesis of a prefix or suffix *ḥ*.
7. ***(ʾH-)Nl-b*: *taḥannaba* 'to be compassionate'.

Desire

1. ***l-b(-Nl)*: *lubānatun* 'wish, desire, craving'.
4. ***(ʾ-)lH-b*: *ʾarabun* 'want, need desire'.

The above items appear to belong together from both the point of view of meaning and of form, expanding our concept of relatedness beyond the traditional *l-b-b* root. It is hoped that research on the usage of these and other words both in Arabic and in related languages will further elucidate such relationships. Even this preliminary survey allows us to conclude that many hitherto unrelatable roots have a common origin and can be fitted into a reasonable frame of reference.

Ablaut im Verbalsystem osttschadischer Sprachen

Herrmann Jungraithmayr

0. Ablaut, d.i. der grammatisch relevante Wechsel von Vokalen[1] im Innern eines Morphems—z.B. im Englischen *sing/sang/sung* oder im Arabischen *ḍaraba/ḍuriba* 'er hat geschlagen / er ist geschlagen worden'—ist in afrikanischen Sprachen eine eher seltene morphophonologische Erscheinung. Dementsprechend gibt es nur wenige kleinere Arbeiten—und keine einzige monographische Abhandlung—über diesen typologisch wie genealogisch wichtigen Gegenstand. Im einzigen Beitrag, der ganz Afrika im Titel führt (Klingenheben 1930/1931: 81–198), heißt es: "Einen (. . .) qualitativen Ablaut (. . .) haben wir im Hausa z.B. bei dem Stammvokal des Verbums *mútu* 'sterben', dessen Partizipium *matáčče* lautet" (S.92). Klingenheben definiert 'Ablaut'—in Anlehnung an die Indogermanistik und Semitistik-als Effekt unterschiedlicher Druckstärke: "Ablaut ist (. . .) diejenige Vokalveränderung, die auf den

1. Wir beschränken unsere Betrachtung hier auf den sogenannten qualitativen Ablaut oder Abtönung, d.h. auf den Wechsel von Vokalqualitäten; quantitative Ablautphänomene (Abstufung) werden nur in dem Maße herangezogen, als sie gegebenenfalls in Begleitung von qualitativen auftreten; z.B. im Sokoro *mené* (perfektiv): *mɛ́ɛ̀nà* (imperfektiv) 'füllen'.

Starkton als bewirkende Ursache zurückgeht" (S.84). Der vorliegende Beitrag soll sich aber nicht mit der Frage nach dem Ursprung des Ablauts auseinandersetzen, sondern das Phänomen selbst anhand neuerer Materialien belegen.

Im wesentlichen kommt Ablaut in Afrika nur im Kuschitischen (vgl. Meinhof 1912) und Tschadischen vor, natürlich einmal vom Berberischen und Semitischen (Arabisch und Afrosemitisch), die nicht im engeren Sinne als (schwarz)afrikanisch gelten können, abgesehen.

1. Ablaut im Tschadischen

1.1. In der tschadischen Sprachfamilie, dem am tiefsten nach Afrika hineinragenden Zweig des Hamitosemitischen, dürfte die Zahl der Sprachen, die einen morphologisch differenzierenden Gebrauch von internem Vokalwechsel machen, 15 nicht überschreiten, das sind etwa 10% ihrer Gesamtheit. Innerhalb des Tschadischen wiederum findet sich die stärkste Konzentration ablautführender Sprachen im äußersten Osten, d.h. östlich des Schari-Flusses im südöstlichen Zentraltschad. Im Westen des Verbreitungsgebietes sind Ablaut und ablautähnliche Prozesse (innere Pluralformation durch Einschub eines -a(a)- o.ä.m.) in statistisch erheblicher Weise auf die Ronsprachen (nigerianisches Plateau) und auf das Hausa beschränkt. Im Zentraltschadischen scheint grammatisch relevanter Vokalwechsel keine erwähnenswerte Rolle zu spielen.

1.2. Innerhalb des Ost-Tschadischen im weiteren Sinne unterscheiden wir die Bereiche Südost mit den drei Gruppen 'Kwang-Kera', 'Lai' und 'Sumray' und Nordost mit den vier Gruppen 'Sokoro', 'Dangla-Migama', 'Mokilko', und 'Mubi-Toram'. Ablautphänomene sind in erster Linie im letzteren—nordöstlichen—Bereich zu beobachten; die nachfolgenden Ausführungen konzentrieren sich auf die Sprachen Mokilko, Migama und Mubi. Ich stütze mich dabei auf eigene Materialsammlungen, die ich vor allem in den 70er Jahren bei mehreren von der Deutschen Forschungsgemeinschaft unterstützten Feldaufenthalten im Tschad anlegen konnte und von denen ein Teil publiziert ist (Jungraithmayr 1978, 1990, 1992).

1.3. In den drei Sprachen—Mokilko, Migama und Mubi—verteilt sich das vorherrschende Auftreten des Ablauts folgendermaßen auf die sprachlichen Sektoren Nomen und Verb:

	Nomen	*Verb*
Mokilko	–	+
Migama	+	+
Mubi	+	+

Während im Migama und Mubi Ablautphänomene in beiden Sektoren etwa in gleicher Stärke auftreten, überrascht es, daß das Mokilko im nominalen Sektor weder im Bereich der Pluralbildung noch bei der Genusunterscheidung inneren Vokalwechsel, bis auf ganz wenige Ausnahmen (Reste?),[2] in Anwendung bringt. Beide potentiellen Einsatzbereiche des Ablauts—Genus und Plural—werden im Mokilko vornehmlich durch Suffigierung bzw. Suffixe abgedeckt; z.B. *sìn-tá* f. 'Zahn'; *ʔùló* 'Junge' : *ʔùtó* 'Mädchen'.

2. Ablaut im Verbalsystem des Mokilko

2.1. Dem reichlich komplizierten Verbalsystem des Mokilko liegt eine binäre Opposition der Aspektstämme (AS) Perfektiv: Imperfektiv zugrunde, deren zwei Ablautmuster sich auf sieben temporal-modale Paradigmata verteilen, über denen sich schließlich ein stark differenzierter Überbau von elf Aktionsarten (AA) erhebt. Da die AA vor allem durch modifizierende Elemente, die zwischen Verbalstamm und Subjektspronomen treten, gebildet werden, können wir sie hier beiseite lassen und uns auf die Bildungsprinzipien der AS konzentrieren; auch die Zwischenebene mit den Tempora/Modi (I–VII) braucht uns hier nicht unmittelbar zu interessieren (vgl. Jungraithmayr 1990: 44).

Schema des Mokilko-Verbalsystems

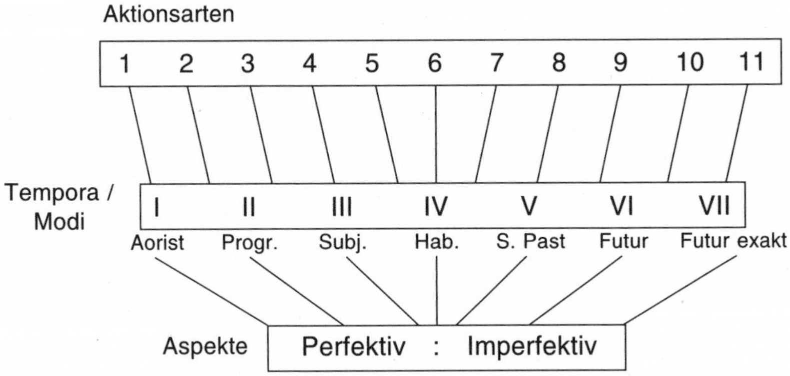

2. Die wenigen Ausnahmen finden sich vor allem im Bereich von Verwandtschafts- und Körperteilnamen: *ʔèèmé* 'Schwiegersohn', Pl. *ʔâmḅí*; *ʔèègó* 'Kopf', Pl. *ʔâwḅí*; vgl. aber auch *ʔûnd-ùmú* 'Baum', Pl. *ʔîndá*, sowie *gédè* m., *gádà* f. 'Hund/Hündin'.

2.2. Auf der Aspektebene bildet der Ablaut des Stammvokals das entscheidende Differential zwischen Perfektiv- und Imperfektivstamm:

	Perfektivstamm	Imperfektivstamm
'zählen'	*gízè*	*kázà*
'werden, wechseln'	*gímè*	*kámà*
'beleidigen'	*gílḍè*	*kálḍà*
'auferstehen'	*bìllé*	*bállìyà*
'ankommen'	*ˀíìnè*	*ˀáànìyá*
'arbeiten'	*nìibé*	*nàabìyá*
'mahlen'	*míssí*	*mássú*
'ziehen'	*ˀílnyè*	*lányà*
'essen' (Hartes)	*ˀíìḍìmá*	*ˀáàḍùmú*
'suchen'	*díˀé*	*déˀú*
'auswählen'	*bíìrè*	*béerìyó*
'jäten'	*gìlzá*	*kòlzé*
'verfolgen'	*gìḍḍá*	*kòḍḍé*
'essen' (Weiches)	*ˀíìmí*	*ˀômḇó*
'saugen'	*ˀùnḍá*	*ˀònḍé*
'lachen'	*gúùbé*	*kóobìyó*
'tanzen'	*ˀìmmìrá*	*ˀòmmìré*
'teilen'	*dìikìḍá*	*dòokìḍé*
'sterben'	*ˀìndá*	*ˀûntó*

2.3. Sieht man von der Vielzahl der Suffixvokale einmal ab, die in diesem System offenbar eine kombinatorische Rolle spielen, so lassen sich folgende Ablautoppositionen beim Stammvokal isolieren:

Perfektiv		Imperfektiv	
i/ii	:	a/aa	= I : A
i/ii	:	o/oo	= I : O
i/ii	:	e/ee	= I : E
u/uu	:	o/oo	= U : O

Das bedeutet, daß den perfektivischen hohen Vokalen I und U die imperfektivischen tief-mittleren Vokale A, O und E gegenüberstehen:

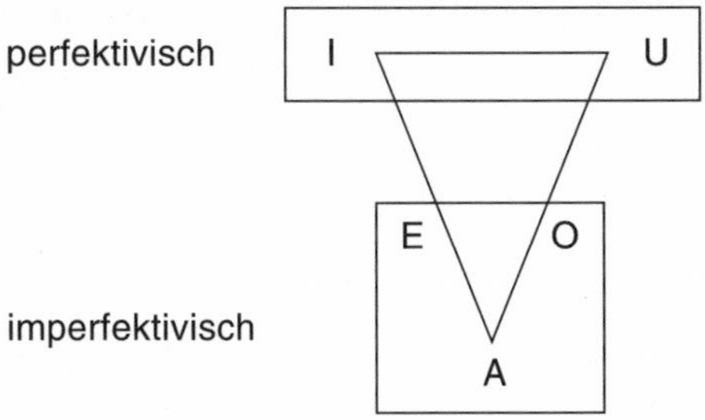

Eine Ausnahme stellt das oben zuletzt zitierte Verb für 'sterben' dar, da hier nicht 'hoch' versus 'tief', sondern 'vorn' (i) versus 'hinten' (u) stehen.

3. Ablaut im Verbalsystem des Migama

3.1. Ähnlich wie im Mokilko liegt auch dem Migama (vgl. Jungraithmayr 1992) eine binäre Opposition vollendete versus unvollendete Handlung bzw. perfektivischer versus imperfektivischer Aspektstamm zugrunde. Die darauf aufbauenden zehn Tempus/Modus-Stämme (TM) setzen sich jeweils aus (1) einem der beiden Stammvokalmuster, (2) einem für den Stamm charakteristischen Suffixvokal sowie (3) einem bestimmten Tonmuster zusammen. Zum Beispiel:

AS		TM	'umdrehen'
Perfektivstamm (pAS):	*pigil-*	→ Perfektstamm:	pìgìlé
Imperfektivstamm (iAS):	*pegell-*	→ Progressivstamm:	*pègèllá*
		→ Rezent-Perf.-St.:	pègèllé

Im Unterschied zum Mokilko sind im Migama für alle Verbalklassen die suffigierten Charaktervokale aller zehn TM-Stämme festgelegt, d.h. der Perfektstamm lautet immer auf *-e*, der Progressivstamm stets auf *-a* aus. Außerdem tritt im iAS bei zwei TM-Stämmen grundsätzlich eine Gemination des letzten (dritten) Konsonanten hinzu, in dieser Form und Funktion eine Einzigartigkeit in den tschadischen Sprachen, die einen natürlich an den Doppelungsstamm im Semitischen erinnert (*iparras*, *qattala*, etc.). Von seiner Valenz (Dauer/Intensität) her gesehen mag dieses Merkmal in Verbindung gesehen werden mit der Entstimmlichung velarer Anlautkonsonanten im Imperfektivstamm des Mokilko (s.o.).

3.2. Die beiden Vokalablautgrundmuster im Migama stehen in fast gleicher Opposition zueinander wie die des Mokilko, d.h. hohen Perfektivvokalen (*i*, *u*) stehen regelmäßig die Mittelvokale *e* bzw. *o* gegenüber; ein pAS mit *a*-, *e*- oder *o*-Vokalisierung verändert dieselbe im iAS nicht, dagegen wird aber eine Folge *a-i* zu *a-a*. Zum Beispiel:

	pAS	iAS
'aufhängen'	*cìkìlé*	*cèkèllá*
'geraderichten'	*míḍìpé*	*méḍéppá*
'nähen'	*ḍyîmmé*	*ḍyémékká*
'sich versammeln'	*gùzìré*	*gòzòrrá*
'blasen'	*gùbùré*	*gòbòrrá*
'etw. Schlechtes tun'	*ḍùwâyyé*	*ḍòwòyyá*
'aussäen'	*lùwé*	*lòwòkká*
'sich aufhängen'	*càkìlé*	*càkàllá*
'hassen'	*ḍàkìté*	*ḍàkàttá*
'ausreißen'	*càlmé (‹*càlìmé)*	*càlàmmá*

Arabische Lehnwörter werden nahtlos in das Migama-Verbalsystem integriert. Zum Beispiel:

'erklären'	*fássìré*	*fàssàrrá*
'sich verspäten'	*ˀákkìré*	*ˀàkkàrrá*
'empfangen'	*láagìyé*	*làagàyyá*

3.3. Im Migama scheint ein harmonisches Gesetz zu herrschen, wonach auch durch Vokal- oder Konsonantenausfall "geschwächte" Perfektivstämme—IIae infirmae und IIae geminatae—, die sich als zweisilbig darstellen—z.B. *tâwwé* 'weiden', *ˀóòmé* 'beißen'—, im Imperfektivstamm wieder als dreiradikalig auftreten müssen. Die Sprache behilft sich dabei mit einem epenthetischen (?) -*k*-, das an dritter bzw. zweiter Position eingefügt wird:

	pAS	iAS
(a) 'weiden, hüten'	*tâwwé*	*táwákká*
'sich waschen'	*ˀàccé*	*ˀàcàkká*
'nehmen'	*ˀíccé*	*ˀécékká*
(b) 'ausgehen'	*ˀòomé*	*ˀòkòmmá*
'beißen'	*ˀóòmé*	*ˀókómmá*
'messen'	*gèemé*	*gèkémmá*

4. Ablaut im Verbalsystem des Mubi

4.1. Für das Mubi (*Mónjúl*), das östlich des Migama bzw. des Abu Telfan-Gebirges gesprochen wird, darf ich u.a. auf meinen Aufsatz "Ablaut und Ton im Verbalsystem des Mubi" (1978) verweisen und mich hier auf einige charakteristische Grundzüge beschränken.

4.2. Das Mubi teilt mit dem Mokilko und Migama das Prinzip der binären Aspektbasis. Zum Beispiel:

	pAS	iAS
'tauschen'	*fílík*	*fíléek*

Was es aber von ihnen unterscheidet, sind folgende Besonderheiten:

(a) es unterscheidet keine weiteren, präponierenden Verbalformgruppen, d.h. weder auf der TM-Ebene noch im Aktionsartenbereich; die beiden Aspektstämme sind also identisch mit den einzigen TM-Stämmen, über die die Sprache—zumindest im präponierenden Bereich—verfügt;

(b) den beiden präponierenden Formengruppen—*à fílík* 'er tauschte' : *à fíléek* 'er tauscht'—stehen zwei entsprechende suffixkonjugierte Paradigmata gegenüber, die ebenfalls eine eigene Ablautstruktur besitzen und deren syntaktische Funktion im Bereich des emphatischen oder Relativsatzes liegt. Zum Beispiel:

	Perfektiv	Imperfektiv
Suffixkonjugation:	*sèerí hárát-ká*	*sèerí híráaḍá-gá*
	'ein Seil flochtest du'	'ein Seil flichtst du'
Präp. Konjugation:	*ká hérít sèerí*	*ká híráat sèerí*
	'du flochtest ein Seil'	'du flichtst ein Seil'

(c) Viele der i- und u-haltigen Verbalstämme bilden einen a-vokalisierten Pluralstamm, so daß sich das Gesamtbild der Ablautmusterverteilung folgendermaßen darstellt:

'tauschen, ändern'	Singularstamm	Pluralstamm
Infinitiv	*fèlègé*	*fàlàgé*
pAS ('Aorist')	*fílík*	*félík*
iAS (Progressiv-Hab.)	*fíléek*	*fíláak*
'zudecken'	*zòd̨ògé*	*zàd̨àgé*
	zùd̨úk	*zèd̨ík*
	zùd̨óok	*zìd̨áak*

Z.B.: *lògòmó fíní dèrèsén* 'ich ließ ein Kamel niederknien'
lògòm sìr dàràsén 'ich ließ zwei Kamele niederknien'.

4.3. Eine große Zahl der Mubi-Verben ist dreiradikalig. Da die finiten Verbalstämme die Struktur KVKVK (pAS) bzw. KVKV:K (iAS) aufweisen— nur der Infinitiv zeigt eine vokalisch auslautende Form—, geht es bei der Frage des Ablauts um das zweivokalige interne Ablautmuster, das folgende Kontraste zeigt:

	Infinitiv	pAS	iAS
(1)	A-A	E-I	I-AA
(2)	E-E	I-I	I-EE
(3)	O-O	U-U	U-OO

Nimmt man die jeweils zweiten Glieder der Vokalpaare als distinktiv an, so geht man wohl nicht fehl in der Annahme, daß bei den Verbtypen (2) und (3) den Ablautveränderungen das gleiche Prinzip zugrunde liegt wie bei (1), nämlich eine Verschiebung des hohen pAS-Vokals (I/U) zu einem mittleren Vokal des iAS, der gleichzeitig auch lang markiert wird (EE, OO). Schematisch läßt sich das folgendermaßen darstellen:

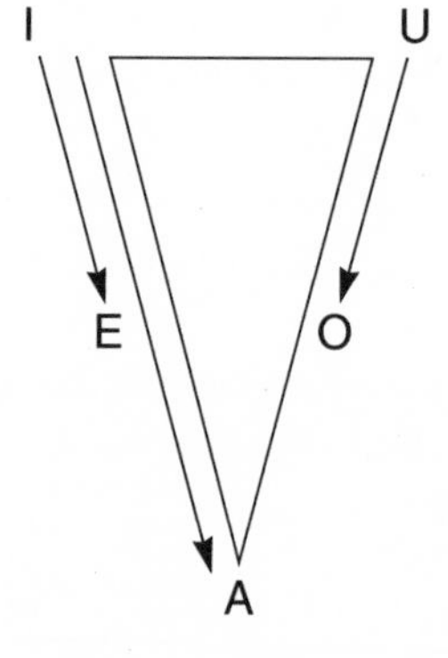

5. Zusammenfassung und Schlußbemerkung

Die Befunde weisen auf eine recht einheitliche Grundausstattung im morphologischen Unterbau der Verbalsysteme der drei osttschadischen Sprachen Mokilko, Migama und Mubi hin, wenn auch die einzelsprachliche Entfaltung und Weiterentwicklung des gemeinsam ererbten Bauplans recht verschiedenartige Wege eingeschlagen haben. Der Grundplan scheint am einfachsten und durchsichtigsten im Mubi—mit der Aspektopposition als der einzigen Operations- und Bildungsebene—erhalten zu sein, während sich das Mokilko—mit seinem immensen Überbau, bestehend aus Dutzenden von 'Tempus-Modi' sowie Aktionsarten—in seiner fast wuchernden Entwicklung am weitesten von der angenommenen Basis entfernt zu haben scheint. Allen drei Sprachen ist aber klar und deutlich die Ablaut-Opposition Hochvokale (I, U) versus Mittel-/Tiefvokale (E, O, A) als Ausdruck einer basissemantischen Opposition Perfektiv (vollendet) versus Imperfektiv (unvollendet) gemeinsam. Damit aber dürften wir im Tschadischen auf hamitosemitisches Urgestein gestoßen sein.[3]

3. Meinen Mitarbeitern Herrn Uwe Seibert, M.A., und Frl. Anne Storch danke ich herzlich für ihre Mithilfe bei der technischen Herrstellung des Manuskripts.

Bibliographie

Jungraithmayr, H.

1978 Ablaut und Ton im Verbalsystem des Mubi. *Afrika und Übersee* 61: 312–20.

1990 *Lexique mokilko*. Berlin.

1992 *Lexique migama*. Berlin.

in Vorbereitung *Lexique mubi*. Berlin.

Klingenheben, A.

1930/1931 Ablaut in Afrika. *Zeitschrift für Eingeborenen-Sprachen* 21: 81–98.

Lukas, J.

1937 *Zentralsudanische Studien*. Hamburg.

Meinhof, C.

1912 *Die Sprachen der Hamiten*. Hamburg.

Akkadian *lišān-u-m*, Arabic *lisān-u-n*: Which Is the Older Form?

Werner Vycichl

Carl Brockelmann, whose aversion to the reconstruction of word forms belonging to a proto-language is well known, denied even the possibility "of reconstructing the common mother of the separate languages with any degree of probability."[1] In spite of this clearly formulated position, he proceeded to reconstruct the Proto-Semitic correspondences of not less than twelve dentals and sibilants.[2]

The examples relevant to the subject of this paper and illustrating the correspondences of Proto-Semitic *ś* in five Semitic languages are the words for 'tooth': Arab. *sinn*, Eth. *senn*, Heb. *šen*, Syr. *šenna*, Assyr. *šinnu*.[3] From this

1. Carl Brockelmann, *Grundriss der vergleichenden Grammatik der semitischen Sprachen* (Berlin, 1908; reprint, Olms, 1961) 1.5.

2. Ibid., 128.

3. See ibid., column XI.

follows that the ancient languages (Akkadian, Hebrew, Aramaic) have *š*, while the younger languages (Arabic, Ethiopic) have *s*. Brockelmann also argues that the shift *š* > *s* occured relatively late in Arabic[4] and that the Akkadian *š* became *s* in late Assyrian, as shown by the biblical renderings of Assyrian names.[5] All this seemingly corroborates a historical development from the Proto-Semitic *š* to *s* in the younger Semitic languages.

Brockelmann came to this somewhat simplistic conclusion because he excluded the Hamitic languages (Egyptian, Berber, Chadic, Cushitic) from his consideration. The latter languages have *s* in the corresponding cognates, just as Arabic and Ethiopic do. The unity of Semito-Hamitic (Afroasiatic) has meanwhile been universally recognized and needs no special justification here.

We do not know when the ancestors of the Hamites penetrated into North and East Africa, but it certainly was long before the third millennium, when Akkadian was first committed to cuneiform script. Some prehistorians think that the first Hamites in North Africa were the authors of the Capsian civilization (eighth millennium B.C.), which corresponds to the mesolithic Natufian in the Near East. The Natufians were ignorant of agriculture, but they collected wild-growing cereals, engaged in hunting, and had only one domestic animal, the dog. For this reason there is no common Hamitic vocabulary for agriculture, animal husbandry, weaving, and ceramics.

Although the Hamitic languages share many easily recognizable structural features, they have only a very limited vocabulary in common. This is undoubtedly due to such factors as phonetic attrition, semantic change, influence of local languages (substratum, adstratum), and innovation. It is for this reason that it is not possible to support the argument with a very large number of examples. As a matter of fact, in this respect all Hamitic languages resemble Mbugu, a language spoken in Tanzania.[6] It combines Bantu grammar with a largely non-Bantu vocabulary. The class prefixes are clearly Bantu: *m-bugu* 'a Mbugu person', pl. *va-bugu*, *ki-mbugu* 'the Mbugu language'; compare Swahili *m-swahili*, *wa-swahili*, *ki-swahili*. Similarly, in the Hamitic languages, as in Egyptian, Berber, Chadic, and Cushitic, the grammatical framework is almost the same as in Semitic: the pronominal elements, the formation of the feminine gender, of the dual (as far as it still exists), of the plural of nouns, and of the conjugation patterns of the verb, but the vocabulary—with only few exceptions—is different. Thus, Egyptian has lost the original word for 'tooth' (a cognate of Arabic *sinn*,

4. Ibid., 129.
5. Ibid., 136.
6. A. N. Tucker and M. A. Bryan "The Mbugu Anomaly," *BSOAS* 37 (1974) 188–207.

Akkadian *šinn-u-m*) and replaced it with *xl* and *njḥ.t*, but the word must have existed in this language since it is preserved in the Berber of the oasis of Siwa[7] (*a-sēn*), in Tuareg (*é-sin*), and on the island of Jerba (pl. *i-sinn-en*). The prefix vowels *a-*, *é-*, and *i-* are remainders of the ancient definite article. This word also shows that the Arabic form with *s* is older than the Akkadian one with *š*.

The following list of words shows that Egyptian (Eg.) almost always has *s* in contrast to the Akkadian *š*.

Personal Pronouns

- Eg. *sw* 'he', *sy* 'she', *sn* 'they'; Akk. *šū, šī, šunu* (m.) and *šina* (f.). It is likely that Egyptian also distinguished the genders in the pl.: **sunu* and **sina*. Contrary to expectations, Arabic replaces the *s* with *h*.[8]

Numerals

- Eg. *srs* 'six'; Arab. *sitt* < **sids* (cf. *sādis* 'sixth'); South Arabian *sdṯ*; Akk. *šiššu*.
- Eg. *sfx* 'seven'; Arab. *sabᶜa*.

Causative Prefix

- Eg. *sa-* (according to Coptic evidence); Classical Arabic has the irregular replacement *ᵓa-* but in the Ḥassānīya Arabic of Mauretania still *sa-*;[9] Akk. *ša-*.

Words with s *in Arabic*

- Eg. *ls* 'tongue' (written *ns*, but pronounced *ls*, as supported by Coptic *las*); Arab. *lisān-u-n*; Akk. *lišān-u-m*.
- Eg. *ḥsb* 'to reckon'; Arab. *ḥasaba*.
- Eg. *wsx* 'to be wide'; Arab. *wasuᶜa*.

7. The examples from Siwa and Jerba are from my own collections.

8. Apparently, such a replacement took place in Chadic Arabic *šam* < **šamh* (Classical *šams*). Personal communication from Mr. Henry Tourneux, CNRS, Paris.

9. Personal communication from David Cohen, Paris.

Words with š in Arabic

- Eg. *šbb.t* 'throat'; Arab. *šibābat* 'throat, reed pipe'.
- Eg. *šmy* 'to go'; Arab. *√mšy* (with metathesis): *mašā, yamšī.*
- Eg. *štm* 'to insult'; Arab. *šatama.*

There are certainly more words with the sibilants *s* and *š* in Egyptian, but the relations are not always visible at first glance. Thus, *snb* 'to be in good health' corresponds to Arabic *salima*, where *l* is transcribed as *n*, just as in the case of *ns* 'tongue', and the final *b* equals *m*. Such cases have been excluded from the examples because the relationships are not immediately obvious.

Also in Berber, Arabic *s* is represented by *s*: *iles* 'tongue' and *isem* 'name' correspond to Arabic *lisān-u-n* and *ism-u-n*.[10] The initial *i* is the old definite article (with metaphony). Such etymologies show in fact that Berber *s* corresponds to both Arabic and Egyptian *s*. Their value, however, is somewhat diminished by the absence of etymologies with *š*, a rather rare sound in Berber. In spite of this, the correspondence between Egyptian *s* and Akkadian *š* is clear. Further afield, the same *s* is evident in Chadic languages, for example, in Mubi (Wadai) *lisi*, pl. *lesas* 'tongue' and *sami* 'name',[11] and in Bidiya (West of Abu Telfan) *līse*, pl. *lisas* 'tongue', *seme*, pl. *semey* 'name'.[12] All of these correspond to Arabic *lisān-u-n* and *ism-u-n*, and not to Akkadian *lišān-u-m* and *šum-u-m*.

Conclusion

In spite of the fact that the three old Semitic languages (Akkadian, Hebrew, and Aramaic) show forms with *š* (Akk. *lišān-u-m*, Heb. *lāšōn*, Aram. *leššān-ā*), while the so-called "young" languages (Arabic and Ethiopian) show *s* (Arab. *lisān-u-n*, Eth. *lësān*), Ethiopian seems to preserve an earlier phonetic realization of this phoneme, since the immigration of the Hamites into Africa took place long before 3000 B.C. (i.e., before Menes, the first king of Egypt, the first dynasty and the beginning of Egyptian history).[13]

This fact is confirmed by the Cushitic languages, for example, by Beja, spoken between the valley of the Nile and the Red Sea, south of Aswan. Here,

10. Emile Destaing, *Dictionnaire berbère-français: Étude sur la tachelḥait marocaine* (Paris, 1938).

11. Johannes Lukas, *Zentralsudanische Studien* (Hamburg, 1937) 155–91.

12. Khalil Aliyo and Herrmann Jungraithmayr, *Lexique Bidiya* (Frankfurt, 1989).

13. Werner Vycichl, "Ménès Thinites: Réalitè ou Fiction?" *Bulletin de la Société d'Égyptologie de Genève* 12, 77–82.

the pronominal endings of the 3d person (m. and f.) are *-s*, pl. *-sna* in the Halanga dialect (other dialects have *-h* or nothing); the causative prefix of the verb is *s-*, *sī-*, or *sō-*, and the word for 'name' is *sim*, pl. *sime*.[14]

Beja has lost all of its Hamitic numerals and adopted a quinary system: 1 *gāl*, 2 *malō-b*, 3 *mehēy*, 4 *fáḍig*, 5 *ēy*. The following numbers are composite: 6 *aságwir*, 7 *asaráma*, 8 *asímhey*, 9 *aššáḍig*, 10 *támin*, and the prefix *as-* or *aš-* seems to go back to a word meaning 'hand' (that is, the 5 fingers).

Since Egyptian and the other Hamitic languages show the same distribution of *s* and *š* as Arabic and Ethiopian, the latter two languages must belong to the oldest stratum of known Semitic languages and be older than Akkadian, Hebrew, and Aramaic. The answer to the initial question must be that *lisān-u-n* is older than *lišān-u-m*.

14. E. M. Roper, *Tu Beḍawie: An Elementary Handbook for the Use of Sudan Government Officials* (Hertford, Herts, England, 1928).

Part 5

Ancient Egyptian, Ottoman Turkish, and Other Linguistic Matters

You Gotta Have Heart

Yoël L. Arbeitman

No analogies are precise; to speak of a "totally precise" analogy is indicative only of a scholar who has taken leave of his senses. For all that, analogies are purposeful. This small paper will be devoted to the support that one Indo-European (IE) item and one Egypto-Semitic (ES) item may be able to offer each other.

I. There are two old and well-known explanations for the isolated Arabic (Arab.) word *qalb* 'heart', isolated in that the Pan-ES lexeme for 'heart' is **lb*(*b*) (for the simultaneous maintenance of this item also in Arabic, see below). Before sketching the two or three well-known theories, we need to ask what a heart is. Its range of meanings is most easily summarized by diagraming them:

Body organ	Seat of emotion	Deanimate[1]
Food for whomever	Item of sacrifice	Prep. phrase

1. I employ *inanimate* for that which by its nature never "had life"; *deanimate* for that which by its nature "had life," but has/had been "rendered lifeless."

1. Paul Haupt declared Assyrian (Ass. = Akkadian) *qablu* 'midst' to be (1) etymologically related to Arabic *qalb* 'heart' and both to be of common origin with Assyrian *qirbu* by a common interchange of liquids; and (2) semantically related to *qablu*, *qirbu*, but also *libbu* as well as *muḫḫu* 'skull' (whose cognates in Hebrew, Arabic, and elsewhere mean 'brain').[2] Prepositional phrases formed with body parts are extremely common in Akkadian, as the next item will also illustrate. But it is necessary first to anticipate and state that Akkadian (Akk.) *qablu* is inanimate,[3] and its meaning 'middle' does not derive from a body organ.

It was thus Haupt's conclusion (a) that the isolated Arab. and Ass. words were interrelated and (b) that this pair was further related to Ass. *qirbu*. He thus arrived at three manifestations of one ES triradical:

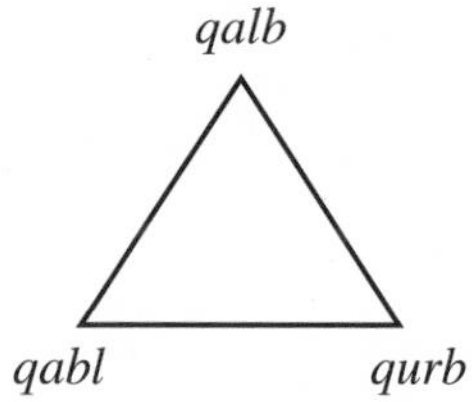

The primary meaning of ES **qrb* is one of body organ, specifically the viscera and the belly (Arab. *qurb*) and the female genitalia[4] with which Arab. *qirba* 'sheath, scabbard, etc.' has to form a semantic pair. The Arab. lexeme has become deanimate as, in a different manner, the Akk. lexeme has. In Egyptian (Eg.) and in Hebrew (Heb.) the prime meaning 'intestine' is still apparent. In Egyptian, Hebrew, Akk., and Ugaritic the noun functions as part of a prepositional phrase. Thus, although the nouns themselves mean respectively 'intestine', 'intestine/middle' (deanimate), and 'female genitalia', in all four languages in a prepositional phrase the meaning of the whole is 'in the midst' or merely a parallel word to 'in'.[5]

In a subsequent article, Haupt offered etymological reasons to detach Ass. *qablu* from the Ass. verb *qabâlu* (and cognates). This verb is barely attested in Akk., only being extant in the I/2 (= Gt) form, the reciprocal participle, m. sg. *muqtablu* 'one who fights with another'. But although Haupt detached "our" noun *qablu* from this verb, the situation is twice as complex, for there is another, homonymous, noun *qablu* II that means 'fight' and is associated with the verb.

2. Paul Haupt, "Critical Notes on Esther," *AJSL* (1908) 134 and 153.

3. See n. 1.

4. See UT, "Glossary," #2269.

5. See ibid.

Totally unconnected with these is "our" *qablu*, I, which means 'middle, middle part, hip, that which is inside' (German *Inneres*: 'heart', 'soul', 'core', and such).

On the other hand, Aram. *qŏḇēl* 'face' (and 'facing'), with its cognates (inclusive of *qablu* II as noted), is connected with this poorly attested Akk. verb.[6]

2. Harri Holma rejected the interchange of liquids inherent in the **qrb* : **qlb* equation. He asserted that Sem. **qrb* is represented in Arab. *qurb* (with a modification of meaning) and that Ass. *qablu* and Arab. *qalb* are identical.[7]

3. The version I first heard came orally from Cyrus Gordon (without any claim to be its author or not to be). This variant states that since Arab. *qalb* has no etymology, and since the **-lb* of the triliteral *qalb* is identical to the **lb*(*b*) pair of Common ES **lb*(*b*), a conflation of this **lb*(*b*) with the *q-* of **q-rb*, another word of generally similar meaning, took place at one point, resulting in **qlb*. Here we have only the attachment of the first consonant of the **qrb* group. This has nothing to do with interchange of liquids or such. This resulted in the relegation of the **lbb* root within Arabic to more specified usages, while *qalb* took over as the main lexeme for 'heart'. Anyone can find a long column of the continued existence of the non-conflated **lbb* in Wehr or Lane.[8]

But we have already come to the conclusion that Arab. *qalb* has a cognate in Akk. *qablu*. If then we are to continue asserting all the hypothetical possibilities along with the Arabic-Akkadian cognation, this conflation process would then have had to occur in Common Semitic, with the resulting new lexeme furthermore undergoing metathesis in Akkadian. I ask those who are wondering why I am pursuing so improbable a course of events to remember that I am concerned with analogy and will bring this to bear.

II. 1. The etymon established for 'heart' in the IE languages is **k̂erd—*[9] for all IE languages, that is, except the Indo-Iranian (IIr.) branch (the umbrella term for the Old Indic and Old Iranic languages). In this latter branch the outcomes necessitate an etymon **ĝherd-*, and there is no trace of **k̂erd-*.

In the two comparative dictionaries of the IE languages that alone are still regnant, those of Alois Walde[10] and Pokorny,[11] this "root" **ĝherd-* is labeled:

6. Paul Haupt, "Some Assyrian Etymologies," *AJSL* 26 (1909) 3.

7. Harri Holma, *Die Namen der Körperteile im Assyrisch-Babylonischen* (Leipzig, 1911) 61.

8. Edward William Lane, *An Arabic-English Lexicon* (8 vols.; London, 1863–93). Hans Wehr, *Arabic-English Dictionary: Dictionary of Modern Written Arabic* (ed. J. M. Cowan; 3d ed.; Ithaca, N.Y., 1976).

9. The IE proto-forms are traditionally given in approximately 4–5 variants. I have selected the one with *e* vowel, so that, having simplified this matter, we may be permitted to give our attention to the problems at hand.

10. Alois Walde, *Vergleichendes Wörterbuch der indogermanischen Sprachen* (Berlin, 1930) 1.424.

11. Julius Pokorny, *Indogermanisches etymologisches Wörterbuch* (Bern, 1959) 580.

"IIr. **žhard-* is merely a rhyme word to *k̂er(e)d-*. . . ."[12] Pokorny's conceptualization is almost identical here. The information concerning several pre–1930 arguments in Walde has—as always—much use and is instructive for later scholars.

2. Walde, under a second, different, lemma, "**ĝherd-* 'heart' (only Indo-Iranian)," notes the earlier attempts in the science of IE comparative linguistics to unite **k̂erd-* and **ĝherd-* etymologically. Although he had dismissed some older proposals s.v. *k̂erd-*, he dismisses others here, whose very dismissal serves the science well.[13] Particularly to be noted is the perspective of Bezzenberger: "the various attempts to unite **ĝherd-* and **k̂erd-* are either phonetic or analogical." Under this latter he notes two such "analogical attempts": (a) **k̂erd* became Indo-Iranian **zherd-* after Old Indic *hr̥ṇī́te* 'is angry' (proposal of Meillet) or (b) an old **ĝherd-* 'gut' (cf. Gr. *khórdē* "gut, string") obtained its meaning from **k̂erd-* 'heart'. He intends here: "The hoary IE word for 'gut' obtained in IIr. a secondary meaning of 'heart', replacing inherited **k̂erd-* in that function."[14] In the notes referred to, Bezzenberger had actually proposed a rather complex set of cross-influences not relevant here.[15]

III. The basic components of the hypothesis on ES **qalb(u)* 'heart' and its relationship to ES **qirb(u)* 'gut' were published nearly 90 years ago. The fundamental building blocks on IE **ĝherd-* 'heart' and its relationship to IE **ĝher-d*[16] 'gut' were published well over a century ago. The two etymological contaminations typologically buttress one another. They also both suggest that the area of this semantic confusion is the specialty of extispicy.

No analogies are perfect, none exact. In the present case, in the proposal for IE, one sort of guttural is substituted for another sort of guttural (**ĝh-* for *k̂-*) in one branch (IIr.). In the analogous proposal that had been made, two semantic items in two branches of ES (Arab. and Akk.) had had a guttural prefixed by contamination ('heart' with 'gut').

IV. For a second time, more than 100 years after scholars struggled with this problem in IE, the very same confusion between these two roots in IE arose. This time the connections made were of a different sort and arose from other bases. So once again the analogy is less than perfect, but it is instructive and not lacking in irony.

12. I have rendered all quotations (all of which happen to be in German) into English.

13. Walde, *Vergleichendes Wörterbuch*, 641.

14. Adalbert Bezzenberger, "Miscellen" and "Etymologien," (both) in *Bezzenbergers Beiträge* 2 (1878) 191.

15. Idem, "Miscellen," 153 and 191.

16. The *-d* here, after the morpheme division, is not part of the root, but rather, a noun formant added to the root.

The oldest attested IE languages are those of Bronze Age Asia Minor, of which Hittite is the best known. It is only quite recently that scholars have made progress in understanding two dialects of one of Hittite's sister languages, Bronze Age (ca. 1500 B.C.E.) Cuneiform Luwian and Iron Age (ca. 750 B.C.E.) Hieroglyphic Luwian. In both dialects, for half a decade, the writing *zart-* was deemed by consensus to (a) mean 'liver'; (b) be cognate with Hittite *karat* 'stomach'; and (c) both to derive from IE **ĝher-d* 'gut'. Within his argument for the meaning 'liver', Poetto pointed out the frequent occurrence within IE of, for example, the root **entero-*, mostly 'innards, entrails', being used in some IE languages for 'liver' (from the more general to the more specific).[17]

Because of the inadequate writing systems of both cuneiform and hieroglyphic for Luwian, the writing *zart-* can equally well represent phonemes deriving from (1a) *k̂ert-*, (1b) *k̂erd-*; (2a) *ĝ/ĝhert-* (2b) *ĝ/ĝherd-*. If they represent (2b), then the writing *zart-* represents a word deriving from *ĝ/ĝher-d* and is possibly pronounced /d^{z}*ard-*/ or /*ǰard*/. If, on the other hand, they represent (1b), then the same writing represents a word deriving from *k̂erd-*, possibly pronounced /t^{s}*ard-*/ or /*čard*/. Philological evidence led Melchert[18] and Morpurgo Davies/Hawkins,[19] both working independently, to be convinced that they were working with "A Luwian Heart" (Morpurgo Davies/Hawkins' title!).

What has been a judgment call regarding the etymology of the IIr. 'heart' "rhyme word" or contamination/conflation with 'gut' in previous examples, is in this case an ambiguity caused by the confluence of two writing systems, also working independently, each impotent to express the phonemes of the language. We have here an analogy of the same two lexemes that were involved in section II; the imperfection in the analogy is that the earlier one never provides any philological difficulty (i.e., in regard to meaning)—providing only a problem for the etymologist; but the later one (almost as fresh as today's newspaper) did indeed provide a philological problem in regard to meaning—the etymologists having early "decided."[20] There is another commonly used form of the name of the Luwian language, and this is with a *v*: Luvian. One cannot

17. See especially Johann Tischler, "Hethitische Etymologie," *Das Etymologische Wörterbuch: Fragen der Konzeption und Gestaltung* (ed. A. Bammesberger; Regensburg, 1983) 283; and Massimo Poetto, "La presumibile parola luvia per 'fegato,'" *Zeitschrift für vergleichende Sprachforschung* 95 (1981) 274ff.

18. H. Craig Melchert, "PIE Velars in Luvian," in *Studies in Memory of Warren Cowgill* (ed. C. Watkins; Berlin and New York, 1987).

19. Anna Morpurgo Davies and J. David Hawkins, "A Luwian Heart," *Studi di storia e di filologia anatolica dedicati Giovanni Pugliese Carratelli* (Eothen I) (Florence, 1988).

20. As in Tischler, "Hethitische Etymologie," 283.

but imagine the alliteration if the conclusions of Morpurgo Davies/Hawkins had led them to title their article *"A Luvian Liver."

V. If the Luwian ambiguity was caused by script inadequacy, the occurrences of the final analogy were brought about by bilingual misprocessing. On March 7, 1981, I was a house guest in an apartment shared by two persons having different degrees of Arabic mastery and linguistic sophistication. These two gentlemen became my accidental informants. Robert Massoud was a second-generation Palestinian-Canadian; Dionisius A. Agius was a Maltese scholar with mastery of several forms of Classical and contemporary Arabic. It chanced that Massoud and I were discussing the presence or lack of presence of the *q* in the respective Arabic */qalb/* and Hebrew */lēb/* words for 'heart'. He had an "if-I-had-to-save-my-life" mastery of colloquial current Palestinian Arabic, the language of his parents. He did not follow my attempts to explain the Hebrew word; so I said, giving the names of the Hebrew graphemes in English, Latin alphabet "l-b" (*el be*). His response was, "But */ˀelbi/* means 'MY heart'. Obviously, in this context, he had processed *qalbi* in its pronunciation current in Palestinian Arabic (and elsewhere) for my intended English letter names. Agius then made a somewhat more successful attempt at putting every word and every letter in its proper place.[21]

VI. To sum up, a century ago, several scholars of the Semitic languages proposed that the isolated Arabic word for 'heart' *qalb* came into being as a conflation of the Pan-Egypto-Semitic (P-ES) word for 'heart' **libbu* with the P-ES word for 'gut' **qVrbu*. About a half-century ago, it was the "common wisdom" among scholars of the Indo-European languages that the word for 'hear', as it appeared in the Indo-Iranian branch of IE, owed its lack of sound law correspondence with the other IE languages, not to chance but to a cause. This cause was that the inherited Pan-IE word for 'heart' **k̂erd* had been conflated with the inherited IE word for 'gut' *$\hat{g}^{h}$*or-d*. The like processes are compared, since they occurred separately within one or two branches of ES and in a single branch of IE.

VII. In conclusion, typological comparison between the events within the Indo-Iranian branch of IE and the same events within two branches of ES, Arabic and Akkadian, strongly suggests that these etymologies are thereby more likely to be valid, made separately, as they were, by different groups of etymologists working in their respective fields.

21. Agius and Massoud suggested on the spot that the conversation be written up. But, like justice, the wheels of scholarship turn very slowly.

The Protean Arabic Abjad

Peter T. Daniels

Script follows religion. It's a truism, but it's true. Christianity carried Roman uncials—in imitation of Greek uncials, in contradistinction to Roman rustic cursive—across Europe (Morison 1972); in the last two centuries or so, Christian missionaries have carried the modern Roman alphabet around the world. Likewise, those who brought Islam to the limits of the known world brought with it literacy in Arabic and a remarkably flexible tool for literacy in scores of other languages: the Arabic script.

Author's note: Prof. Krotkoff has become an annual friend at the meetings of the North American Conference on Afroasiatic Linguistics. The peregrinations throughout the Middle East that he described in his Reminiscences at the 1989 NACAL in New Orleans suggest that this essay is an appropriate contribution with which to honor him. It was presented in part at the 20th NACAL, Cambridge, Massachusetts, 3 April 1992. On that occasion, Prof. Krotkoff brought to my attention the unique feature of Ottoman Turkish orthography noted below. I would also like to thank Charles S. Fineman for his help at the Northwestern University Library, whose peerless Africana Collection provided the scarce materials on African languages cited herein. I thank as well M. O'Connor and David Testen for their valuable comments, and Lloyd Anderson, Jack Cella, and the late Bill McIlwain for technical assistance.

I do not, of course, say Arabic alphabet: in my typology (Daniels 1990), the Arabic script is not an alphabet at all, but a different basic type of script, a consonantary or abjad. A summary of the typology is in order. A script can be a *logosyllabary*, with signs that stand for monosyllabic words of a language and can be used for homophonous syllables. A script can be a *syllabary*, with signs that represent CV syllables (and, in one important case, VC and CVC syllables as well). A script can be an *abjad*[1] and denote only consonants. This covers the Northwest Semitic scripts, basically. A script can be an *alphabet*, where signs individually denote consonant and vowel phonemes. A script can be an *abugida*[2] or neosyllabary, like Ethiopian or Indic, where basic signs denote consonant + *a*, and other vowels are indicated by modifications to the basic shape. Finally, a script can be *featural* (Sampson 1985), where the graphic components of a sign correspond to the phonological features of the sound system. Such scripts include Korean, Gregg shorthand, and Tolkien's Elvish.

The Arabic script is an abjad plus obligatory[3] notation of long vowels. The three additional signs for the three short vowels are easily omissible because the morphological patterning of long vowel insertion plus certain morphophonemic spelling conventions conspire to make the linear skeleton of an Arabic word fairly unambiguous. An interesting exercise for the lexicographer would be to check how many *actual words* are drawn in exactly the same way—I suspect there are not very many. The consonantal shape فعل ⟨fʕl⟩ can have any of the three vowel symbols on the ف, and any of the three vowels or *sukūn* (marking vowellessness) on the ع, giving 12 possible words; but how many of these 12 are found from any particular root? Moreover, the second or third consonants could be provided with *shadda* (which marks gemination of the consonant), allowing 24 or 48 forms total. In practice, however, the only real problems of ambiguity arise with verb forms I and II (*qatala* and *qattala*) and with passives of most verb forms (but a passive predicate will have a different number of arguments from the corresponding active; it is my conviction that the basic purpose of passivization is omission of the subject, rather than, as seems to be generally assumed by syntacticians, promotion of the object).

Islam spread through much of Asia and Africa, and adaptations of the Arabic script are found throughout this vast area. The many adaptations, though, have not been much investigated. I know of one previous study of the application of Arabic script to other languages: C. Mohammed Naim's "Arabic Or-

1. Borrowed from the Arabic word for the numerical order of the Arabic letters.

2. From the Ethiopic word, given to me by Wolf Leslau, for the traditional Hebrew order of Ethiopian consonants, used in liturgy.

3. With a few consistent exceptions deriving from the multidialectal origin of the written text of the Qurʾān, and with some variation in earlier eras of written Arabic.

thography and some Non-Semitic Languages" (1971). This is a survey of nine such Asian languages—Persian, Kurdish, Uyghur (which he calls East Turki), Azerbaijani, Pashto, Sindhi, Urdu, Sulu, and Malay—and is a useful source of data. But some of the treatment and presentation is questionable. For instance, Naim states that these scripts comprise graphemes and vowel diacritics (1971: 114), but, as I have shown elsewhere (Daniels 1991), the term *grapheme* makes little sense and anyway has never been coherently defined. And if one were going to designate units of a script "graphemes," why would the term refer only to the consonant letters and not to the vowels? Moreover, he also refers to the dots that are part of the consonant "graphemes" as "diacritics" (Naim 1971: 119), again with no definition. But the numeral ٢ '2' which is used to mark reduplication of morphemes in Malay and Sulu he says is *not* a grapheme (1971: 136).

Also, Naim is tightly bound to the phonemic analyses he chooses to follow. In the case of Pashto, this means that he must take (1971: 127) four letters as representing *sequences* of phonemes—the affricates that his source, Penzl 1955, analyzes as consonant clusters. Yet M. O'Connor (1983) has understood a script as a "native speaker analysis" of a phonological system; if the native speaker chooses to use the simple letters ج , چ , ځ , and څ, for *j*, *č*, *ɟ*, and *c* respectively,[4] should the linguist not pay attention?

A last difficulty with Naim's article is that he presents the phonemic system of each language in a traditional phonological-space chart in IPA transcription only, then gives the letters added to the Arabic inventory in a randomly ordered list, obscuring the regularities involved in the additions:

> The basic shapes were almost always selected on the basis of phonetic similarity, but no similar attempts were necessarily always made to establish a relationship between the phonetics of the borrowing language and its graphemics. In other words, for example, the graphemes for the palatal consonants in a language do not necessarily show any similarity (Naim 1971: 140).

This is in fact not so.

Let us, then, look at some of Naim's inventory of Arabic-based scripts, and a few that he did not include, in a new way and admire the flexibility (rather than the inadequacy) of this versatile writing system.

First, there is the matter of recording additional consonants. One might suppose that Arabic has rather a large number of consonants, at 28, and these should suffice for most of the world's, or the Muslim world's, languages. But recall that Arabic does not include such common phones as *g* and *p*, and that it

4. Given the uncertainty regarding the phonemic status of these items, it is not possible to notate them in either slant brackets (phonemic) or square brackets (phonetic)!

TABLE 1. Arabic

	P	Θ	T	Ṭ	Č	K	Q	Ḥ	ʾ
P	☐		ت	ط		ك	ق		ء
B	ب		د	ض	ج	☐			
F	ف	ث	س	ص	ش	خ		ح	ه
V	☐	ذ	ز	ظ		غ		ع	
M	م		ن						
W	و		ي ر ل						

Note: In these charts, the left and top axes label the manner and place of articulation respectively.

does include such exotica as the laryngeals and emphatics and interdentals. Of the boxed loci in the phonological chart of Arabic consonant letters (table 1), most languages need the first group (empty boxes), but not the latter set (boxed letters).[5] How are they to cope?

In fact, the Arabic script comes with a nearly built-in solution. As it was developing, many of the letterforms so degenerated that the system of distinguishing dots was introduced. And, to some extent, the dots are used in a phonologically sensible, nearly systematic way—thus ذ /ð/ is a modified د /d/, and ث /θ/ is a differentiated ت /t/, and so on. The Arabic script, to this extent, may be regarded as approaching the featural type. Thus it was reasonable for the mullahs, or whoever "reduced" (to use Pike's [1947] term) the other Muslim languages to writing, to use dots and a few other marks on existing linear bases for denoting new sounds (rather than to create new bases) and to do so in a fairly featural manner. As an example, consider Persian (table 2).[6] Persian needed a letter for /p/; the solution was to change the one dot of ب /b/ for three dots پ. Identically, the one dot of ج / j/ was changed to three for the voiceless

5. The letters of this set, though, are always used in spelling Arabic words, even when their pronunciation has assimilated to the native system, so the character inventory of every Muslim language must include all the Arabic letters, even those that do not occur in native words.

6. Cf. Paper and Jazayery 1955. This and the subsequent tables show only the letters used in spelling native words; for tables of most of the scripts showing their full letter inventories in their traditional orders, see Kaye 1996.

TABLE 2. Persian

	P	T	Č	K	Q	H
P	پ	ت	چ	ك	ق	
B	ب	د	ج	گ		
F	ف	س	ش	خ		ه
V	و	ز	ژ			
M	م	ن				
L		ي ر ل				

/č/ چ. Or, there could be an analogy to an existing pair: palatal ش / š/ puts three dots onto the س /s/ shape; so palatal ژ /ž/ puts three dots onto the ز /z/ shape. There is also the گ /g/ from ك /k/. (A phonetic, though not phonemic, shift is the use of و /w/ for Persian /v/.) Since Persian polities were responsible for much of the spread of Islam into Asia, these additional Persian letters are found in most of the Arabic scripts of the continent.

The Uyghur inventory (table 3) adds ordinary غ /γ/ to Persian (some Persian dialects use this letter themselves as well), and it makes an ⟨ŋ⟩ ڭ from ⟨k⟩ ک plus three dots.[7] Kurdish (table 4)[8] makes ⟨ŋ⟩ with just the digraph ⟨ng⟩ نگ. But Kurdish is interesting because it makes a ⟨v⟩ ڤ from an ⟨f⟩ ف in the same way that it makes a ⟨p⟩ پ from a ⟨b⟩ ب—that is, changing one dot to three dots in this script means switching the value of the voicing feature. Kurdish also adds characters for emphatic /ḷ/ and /ṛ/ by dotting ordinary ⟨l⟩ and ⟨r⟩. A third way of making an ⟨ŋ⟩ is found in Malay (table 5),[9] where it is an ⟨ʕ⟩—or perhaps a ⟨γ⟩—with three dots, ڠ. Perhaps this is coincidental, but it should be noted that /ʕ/ is pronounced [ŋ] in a few dialects of Hebrew (Ornan 1972: 86).

7. Uniquely, the letters used only for Arabic were dropped from the Uyghur script, and the spelling of Arabic and Persian loanwords was assimilated to their pronunciation in Uyghur. Arabic script for Sinkiang Uyghur (controlled by China) was replaced by Roman script in 1959, and Uyghur within Russia is written in a Cyrillic script (Nazhdip 1971: 16–17). In 1984, the Arabic script was reinstated for Uyghur in China (Hahn 1991: 93).

8. Cf. McCarus 1958.

9. Lewis 1958.

TABLE 3. Uyghur

	P	T	Č	K	Q	H			
P	پ	ت	چ	ك	ق		ى	وٰ	ۇ
B	ب	د	ج	گ			ي	ۆ	و
F	ف	س	ش	خ		ھ		ه	ا
V	ۋ	ز	ژ	غ			i	ü	u
M	م	ن		ڭ			e	ö	o
L		ي رل						ä	a

TABLE 4. Kurdish

	P	T	Ṣ	Č	K	Q	Ḥ	ʿ							
P	پ	ت		چ	ك	ق		ء	یبی		ی		ي		وو
B	ب	د		ج	گ					ێ		ه		و	
F	ف	س	ص	ش	خ		ح	ه			ا		ۆ		
V	ڤ	ز		ژ	غ		ع								
M	م	ن			نگ				i		ɨ		ɯ		u
W	و	ي ل	ڵ							e		ə		ʊ	
R		ر	ڔ								ɑ		o		

Malay has, moreover, a palatal nasal ڽ: again, three dots replace the one dot of the ن, but they go *under* the character when it is reduced to a tooth ڽـ, to keep it separate from ث ⟨θ⟩. This is possible because ⟨p⟩ is not made in the Persian way but by placing the three dots on the ⟨f⟩ shape ڤـ. This is also the only case where the shape of the bowl of the independent form is significant, in differentiating between ڽ and ث.

TABLE 5. Malay

	P	T	Č	K	ʾ
P	ڤ	ت	چ	ك	ء
B	ب	د	ج	ڬ	
F	ف	س	ش		ه
Z		ز		غ	
M	م	ن	ڽ	ڠ	
W	و	ي ر ل			

TABLE 6. Pashto

	P	T	Ṭ	C	Č	K	Q	Ḥ	ʾ
P	پ	ت	ټ	څ	چ	ك	ق		ء
B	ب	د	ډ	ځ	ج	ګ			
F	ف	س	ښ		ش	خ		ح	ه
Z		ز	ږ		ژ	غ			
M	م	ن	ڼ						
W	و	ي ر ل	ړ						

Next to be considered are scripts for three languages with full additional series of phones. Pashto (table 6)[10] adds retroflexes. The rule is to add a little circle below, if possible; there is no way to hang it on the teeth of the ⟨s⟩ or the near vertical of the ⟨z⟩ (though it is used on the ⟨r⟩: perhaps it was unesthetic to have a dot and a circle adjacent). It is possible that ⟨z̨⟩ is double dotted to match the ⟨ş⟩.

Urdu (table 7) marks the aspirated series with an initial-⟨h⟩ shape following the basic letter;[11] it marks the retroflexes with a ⟨ṭ⟩ above. Naim is somewhat

10. Cf. MacKenzie 1992.

11. The two alternative medial shapes of Arabic ⟨h⟩ are differentiated consistently. The "two-eyed" shape ھ is used only for marking the feature of aspiration; the independent phoneme

TABLE 7. Urdu

	P	T	Ṭ	Č	K	Q	H
P	پ	ت	ٹ	چ	ك	ق	
PH	پھ	تھ	ٹھ	چھ	کھ		
B	ب	د	ڈ	ج	گ		
BH	بھ	دھ	ڈھ	جھ	گھ		
F	ف	س		ش	خ		ھ = ﮩ
V	و	ز		ژ	غ		
M	م	ن					
L		ي ر ل	ڑ				
ṚH			ڑھ				

distressed (1971: 133) that the script marks an aspirated retroflex [$ʈ^h$], which is in complementary distribution with the unaspirated; but this can simply remind us that a script need not be phonemic to satisfy its users.

So far, we have seen an Arabic-based quasi-featural script developed rather systematically for several languages. But the system seems to falter with Sindhi (table 8).[12] It begins with the basic Persian inventory. First, it adds the retroflexes—and I do not see a pattern. Then, it forms aspirates by adding two dots, up to a total of four, or replacing with two dots, for ⟨$ʈ^h$⟩. Or maybe, then it makes implosives by adding two dots. But note the nasal row of the chart, where the retroflex has a ⟨ṭ⟩ hat and the palatal has two dots. But then the linear bases that have too many dots get ⟨h⟩s for aspiration. There simply seems to be no pattern—let it be a challenge to the reader.

The Asian scripts reveal Persian influence in that they almost all use the Persian forms of ⟨p⟩, ⟨č⟩, ⟨ž⟩, and ⟨g⟩. Turning to the limited information avail-

/h/ is written medially with the double-pointed shape ﮭ, and initially in handwriting with a tooth with a curved stroke below ﮨ (which stroke may also be used medially). In final position, aspiration and independent /h/ are marked by the two-eyed shape ﮪ and the round shape ﮧ respectively (Bright and Khan 1958). This is obscured in Naim's account, which shows the initial ﮪ form as used in medial and final position (1971: 132). This point was clarified for me by Alan S. Kaye.

12. Cf. Yegorova 1971.

TABLE 8. Sindhi

	P	T	Ṭ	Č	K	H
P	پ	ت	ٽ	چ	ڪ	
PH	ڦ	ٿ	ٺ	ڇ	ک	
B	ب	د	ڊ	ج	گ	
BH	ڀ	ڌ	ڍ	جھ	گھ	
ɓ	ٻ		ڏ	ڄ	ڳ	
F	ف	س		ش	خ	ه
V	و	ز			غ	
M	م	ن	ڻ	ڃ	ڱ	
L		ي رل	ڙ			
ṚH			ڙھ			

able for Arabic-based scripts of Africa, we find that Swahili (table 9),[13] the lingua franca of what was once German East Africa, used a Persian-style ⟨p⟩ and ⟨č⟩, a Malay-style ⟨ŋ⟩, and a Kurdish-style ⟨v⟩. It seems safe to say that at least the latter two represent independent creations. (Swahili is now written with the Roman alphabet.) No standard orthography emerged for Hausa or Fulani in British West Africa (tables 10–11),[14] but "some scribes" added letters to the Arabic inventory, and certain characters had pronunciations different from those in Arabic: both had /č/ but expressed it with ث and ش respectively; both used ط, in Hausa for /ts/, in Fulani for /ɗ/ (from the glottalized series of each language). Moreover, the alphabetic order was not that of Arabic, but was the Hebrew-like *abjad* order. Both languages are now written with an augmented Roman alphabet.

In both African and Asian scripts, interesting things happen in the vowels as well, but in most cases I have no information on orthography and no texts to consult. Naim mentions no vowel points for some of the scripts; some just use

13. Cf. Velten 1901.
14. Cf. Taylor 1929.

TABLE 9. Swahili

	P	T	Č	K	H
P	پ	ت	چ	ك	
B	ب	د	ج		
F	ف	س	ش		ه
V	ڤ	ز		غ	
M	م	ن		ڠ	
W	و	ي رل			

TABLE 10. Hausa

	P	T	Č	K	Q	ʿ
P		ت	ث	ك	ف	ع
B	ب	د		غ		
ƭ		ط				
ɓ	ب	ڟ		ك		
F	ڢ	س	ش			ه
V	و ,ب	ز				
M	م	ن				
W	و	ي رل				

the Arabic *fatḥa* /a/, *kasra* /i/, and *ḍamma* /u/; Hausa added a dot beneath the letter for /e/ and used these four vowel points obligatorily; but Pashto and especially Kurdish now apparently include linear vowels. Pashto adds ې for /e/ and final ى for /əy/, indicating "most vowels other than *a ə*" (MacKenzie 1992: 167).

TABLE 11. Fulani

	P	T	Y	Č	K	Q	ʾ
P	ڢ	ت		ش	ك	ڧ	ع
B	ب	د		ج	غ		
ND		ذٜ	ۑ	ڃ	ڠ		
ɗ		ط	ۑ				
F	ف	س					ه
V	و						
M	م	ن					
L		رل	ي				

Kurdish, though, now has a full alphabet: there are nine vowel letters (table 4).[15] The 1984 script reform of Uyghur introduced a full system of vowel notation (table 3), and ⟨w⟩ is now ۋ.

Ottoman Turkish, which uses the Persian inventory plus the optional ڭ for /ɲ/ (table 12),[16] has a system probably unique in the Muslim world for indicating vowels. Turkish has the well-known vowel cube and vowel harmony, so that a root can contain only "hard" (i.e., back) vowels /u o a ı/ or "soft" (i.e., front) vowels /ü ö e i/; it does not have phonemic vowel length. It uses ا, و, and ى to indicate vowel quality; but in addition, it incorporates into the orthographic system for native Turkish words some of the letters elsewhere used only for spelling Arabic loanwords: ص, ط, غ, and ق. These four are used (albeit not fully consistently, apparently) in alternation with س, ت, گ, and ك respectively. The former indicate a following hard vowel, the latter a following soft vowel (in the case of غ/گ and ق/ك, preceding vowel quality as well).[17] This is

15. McCarus 1958: 6f.

16. Cf. Müller 1889. Wahrmund (1869: 23) refers to the frequent omission of the three dots, while Jehlitschka (1895: 12) even denies their use by the Turks, saying that they are limited to European prints.

17. It was surprisingly difficult to find documentation of this phenomenon after it was pointed out by Georg Krotkoff, who referred me to Wahrmund and to Jehlitschka. Wahrmund's quaint

TABLE 12. Ottoman Turkish

	P	T	Č	K	H
P	پ	ت, ط	چ	ك, ق	
B	ب	د	ج	گ, غ	
F	ف	س, ص	ش	خ	ه
V	و	ز			
M	م	ن	ڭ		
L		ل ر ي			

a sensible extension of Arabic practice: in Arabic, the back phonemes /ṣ ṭ γ q/ represented by the first group of letters color allophones of adjacent vowels, but in Turkish there are fewer consonantal phonemes and more vowel phonemes. So the burden of indicating the extra features of vowels is shifted to the surplus of consonant symbols—both sets represent simply /s t g k/. (Curiously, the pair ض/ز = Turkish /z/ was not incorporated into the system.)[18]

These approaches of being obligatorily more explicit about vowels may be contrasted with the solutions in some related scripts that started out as abjad + *matres lectionis*. In Mandaic (Daniels 1996), somewhat as in Greek, various of the consonants were lost, including /ʔ/ and /ʕ/, and their letters and ⟨w⟩, ⟨y⟩, and ⟨h⟩ are now exclusively vowel letters (but vowel quality is not fully specified). Moreover, in Mandaic the vowel letters are visually distinct, being generally smaller than the consonants—a property obscured when Man-

formulation (1869: 11) bears quoting here: "Die schweren Vokale verbinden sich lieber mit den harten Konsonanten [q gh ^{c} ẓ ṭ ḍ ṣ x ḥ], die leichten Vokale lieber mit den weichen Konsonanten [h k s z t]." I have only found two sources for Ottoman orthography published subsequent to Atatürk's spelling reform of 1928–29 (in which a Roman alphabet replaced the Arabic-based script). Gleichen and Reynolds (1944: 69–71) do not mention this. Taeschner (1963: 252–54) notes only the alternation of signs for velar stops.

18. Exactly the same solution of the problem of fitting a script to a quite different phonology was reached in Southeast Asia. The scripts of Thai, Burmese, Khmer, and so on descend from an ancient script of India that provided for the profusion of consonantal places and manners of articulation of Indian languages (cf. Sindhi, table 8). The Southeast Asian languages, however, have quite simple inventories of consonants but variously need to mark tone, vowel quality, or register, and do so using the excess of consonant signs (e.g., Haas 1956, Huffman 1970, Jones and Khin 1953).

daic texts are presented in Hebrew transliteration (only Mark Lidzbarski has published Mandaic documents in Mandaic type).

And in Yiddish, some of the points have fused with the consonants, giving an /a/ letter אַ and an /o/ letter אָ, while the other vowels are fully specified by single or double consonants (Katz 1987: §1.2).

There are also languages outside the Muslim world that might benefit from an adaptation of Arabic script. One is the Mayan language Chuj, as briefly characterized by Ilah Fleming (1991). In this language, the morphophonemics are such that certain vowels in a word do not change, while others may appear or not, or may vary in quality. Linguists have had difficulty in formulating a (Roman-based) orthography for Chuj because of this—is it better to notate all the different shapes of a root, requiring the memorization of many spellings for a single word? or is it better to notate an underlying form of a root, with the reader required to remember when to omit or alter some of the letters? It seems clear that a superior solution would be like the script of Arabic, notating the fixed vowels obligatorily (like the long vowels of Arabic) and using added vowel points—obligatorily or not, as seems appropriate—for the mutable vowels. The shapes of the characters, of course, need not resemble those of Arabic, but the principle of the two strata of signs, linear and supra- or sublinear, seems essential for preserving the basic shape of the root, the recognition of which is essential for fluent reading.

Three different approaches to alphabetizing the Arabic abjad—adding, reusing, and modifying letters—have been described here, and they all work. The Arabic abjad becomes a featural script, and at the same time it becomes an alphabet. Once again, this shows that script is not, like language, constrained by mind; it is a human creation that can be altered at will; emic-and-etic terminology does not apply. And the Arabic script is very flexible—if only the Muslim missionaries had gotten to Indochina before the Indian ones!

Bibliography

Bright, William, and Khan, Saeed A.

1958 *The Urdu Writing System.* Washington, D.C.: American Council of Learned Societies. Repr. 1976, Ithaca, N.Y.: Spoken Language Services.

Daniels, Peter T.

1990 Fundamentals of Grammatology. *Journal of the American Oriental Society* 110: 727–31.

1991 Is a Structural Grammatology Possible? *18th LACUS Forum*: 528–37.

1996 Mandaic. Pp. 511–13 in *The World's Writing Systems*, ed. Peter T. Daniels and William Bright. New York: Oxford University Press.

Fleming, Ilah

1991 Evidences of K. L. Pike's Influence in the Stratified Communication Model. Paper presented at 18th LACUS Forum, Ann Arbor.

Gleichen, Edward, and Reynolds, John H.

1944 *Alphabets of Foreign Languages*. 2d ed. London: Permanent Committee on Geographical Names for British Official Use.

Haas, Mary R.

1956 *The Thai System of Writing*. Washington, D.C.: American Council of Learned Societies. Repr. 1980, Ithaca, N.Y.: Spoken Language Services.

Hahn, Reinhard F.

1991 *Spoken Uyghur*. Seattle: University of Washington Press.

Huffman, Franklin E.

1970 *Cambodian System of Writing and Beginning Reader*. New Haven: Yale University. Repr. 1987, Ithaca, N.Y.: Cornell University Southeast Asia Program.

Jehlitschka, Henry

1895 *Türkische Konversations-Grammatik*. Heidelberg: Groos.

Jones, R. B., Jr., and U Khin

1953 *The Burmese Writing System*. Washington, D.C.: American Council of Learned Societies.

Katz, Dovid

1987 *Grammar of the Yiddish Language*. London: Duckworth.

Kaye, Alan S.

1996 Adaptations of Arabic Script. Pp. 743–62 in *The World's Writing Systems*, ed. Peter T. Daniels and William Bright. New York: Oxford University Press.

Lewis, M. B.

1958 *A Handbook of Malay Script*. London: Macmillan.

MacKenzie, D. N.

1992 Pashto. Pp. 165–70 in vol. 3 of *International Encyclopedia of Linguistics*.

McCarus, Ernest N.

1958 *A Kurdish Grammar: Descriptive Analysis of the Kurdish of Sulaimaniya, Iraq*. New York: American Council of Learned Societies.

Morison, Stanley

1972 *Politics and Script: Aspects of Authority and Freedom in the Development of Graeco-Latin Script from the Sixth Century B.C. to the Twentieth Century A.D.*, ed. Nicolas Barker. Oxford: Clarendon.

Müller, August

1889 *Türkische Grammatik.* Porta linguarum orientalium 11. Berlin: Reuther.

Naim, C. Mohammed

1971 Arabic Orthography and some Non-Semitic Languages. Pp. 113–44 in *Islam and Its Cultural Divergence: Studies in Honor of Gustave E. von Grunebaum*, ed. Girdhari L. Tikku. Urbana: University of Illinois Press.

Nazhdip, E. N.

1971 *Modern Uigur*, trans. D. M. Segal. Moscow: NAUKA.

O'Connor, M.

1983 Writing Systems, Native Speaker Analyses, and the Earliest Stages of Northwest Semitic Epigraphy. Pp. 439–65 in *The Word of the Lord Shall Go Forth: Essays in Honor of David Noel Freedman in Celebration of His Sixtieth Birthday*, ed. Carol L. Meyers and M. O'Connor. Winona Lake, Ind.: Eisenbrauns.

Ornan, Uzzi

1972 Hebrew Grammar. Cols. 77–175 in vol. 16 of *Encyclopaedia Judaica.*

Paper, Herbert H., and Jazayery, Mohammed Ali

1955 *The Writing System of Modern Persian.* Washington, D.C.: American Council of Learned Societies. Repr. 1976, Ithaca, N.Y.: Spoken Language Services.

Penzl, Herbert

1955 *A Grammar of Pashto.* Washington, D.C.: American Council of Learned Societies.

Pike, Kenneth L.

1947 *Phonemics: A Technique for Reducing Languages to Writing.* Ann Arbor: University of Michigan Press.

Sampson, Geoffrey

1985 *Writing Systems.* London: Hutchinson.

Taeschner, Franz

1963 Die osmanische Literatur. Pp. 250–335 in *Turkologie.* Handbuch der Orientalistik 1/5/1. Leiden: Brill.

Taylor, F. W.
1929 *Fulani-Hausa Readings in the Native Scripts*. Taylor's Fulani-Hausa Series 5. Oxford: Clarendon.

Velten, C.
1901 *Praktische Anleitung zur Erlernung der Schrift der Suaheli*. Göttingen: Vandenhoeck & Ruprecht.

Wahrmund, A.
1869 *Praktische Grammatik der osmanisch-türkischen Sprache*. Giessen: Ricker.

Yegorova, R. P.
1971 *The Sindhi Language*, trans. E. H. Tsipan. Moscow: NAUKA.

A Matter of Inconsistency: Variation of Arabic Loanwords in English

Alan S. Kaye

This essay grew out of my curiosity at Garland Cannon's mention of the variant *Allaho akbar* for the far more usual *Allahu akbar* 'God is (very) great', literally, "God is more/most great'. This Arabic phrase is well known in the West as being part of the call to prayer in the countries of the Muslim world, whether Arabic is a spoken language in that country or not.[1] The form *akbar* is really *ᵓakbaru* in Classical Arabic, grammatically speaking, an elative (a fancy and technical

Author's note: I wish to express my gratitude to Garland Cannon, Peter T. Daniels, M. O'Connor, and especially Georg Krotkoff, all of whom have insightfully commented on a preliminary version of this paper. Their fine editorial assistance has particularly enhanced the clarity of my ideas and has saved me from more than one stylistic infelicity. John Algeo, the late A. F. L. Beeston, John Hayes, Wolf Leslau, and Ismail Poonawala have also contributed valuable suggestions to this work, for which I offer my sincere thanks. The usual disclaimers apply, however. An earlier version of this article appeared in *English Today* 8/2 (1992) 32–41.

1. Garland Cannon writes that *Allah akbar* "needs a medial vowel *-u-* or *-o-*" in his "Review of *Loanwords Dictionary*, by Laurence Urdang and Frank R. Abate," in *American Speech* 64

cover term corresponding to the comparative and superlative of English); the *-u* is apocopated or dropped by the Classical Arabic phonological rules of "pause." This is thus known to Semitists and Arabists as a pausal form or a pausal pronunciation. One may compare the Arabic creed *lā ʾilāha ʾillā ḷḷāh* 'there is no god except Allah' (also translated 'there is no god but God'). The final word in this expression shows the contextual and pausal adjustments of *ʾAḷḷāhu* (loss of initial and final vowel).

Since the Middle East and the Arab world (and much of the rest of the Muslim world as well) are so very conspicuous in the daily news since the Iraqi invasion of Kuwait on August 2, 1990, the many variations in English print that one encounters for some high-frequency Arabic loanwords, particularly names, further prompt a study of such variations. Indeed, during this entire period, it is difficult to locate any newspaper or current events magazine published in English anywhere in which there are not Arabic loanwords, frequently more than a few. Most readers are aware of the inconsistencies in the spelling of some of these Arabic loanwords, chiefly names of Arab leaders, but are unaware of the reasons for these confusing, and at times, illogical inconsistencies. Many readers, I submit, have been puzzled or even irritated by the varying orthographies. One complication is that many of these loanwords may have come into English through the intermediary of another language, often Persian or Turkish. Nonetheless, it is important to ask why there is such variation in English. I hope to answer this and related questions, at least in part, by considering a number of frequently occurring names, whose variations have long been a problem for scholars (especially librarians and those who use libraries),[2]

(1990) 269. The vowel ending *-u* is (from the Arabic point of view) the marker of the nominative case. Thus his remark should be amended to read *-u* or *-o* (they are suffixes—not infixes!) The cited variant with *-o* occurs in Mark Channing, *King Cobra* (Philadelphia: Lippincott, 1934) 18. A book titled, *Allah O Akbar: A Journey through Militant Islam*, (London: Phaidon, 1994) has been written by Abbas. Since Abbas is an Iranian, the *o* turns up via a Farsi pronunciation. The version *Allah akbar*, listed in the Urdang and Abate dictionary, does occur, however, so the dictionary's citation form is authentic. A recent occurrence of it was in *Time*, March 11, 1991, 38. In a story about Kuwait, Bruce W. Nelan wrote: "Crowds along the way danced and chanted, '*Allah akbar*!', 'U.S.A! and U.S.A.!', and 'Thank you, thank you!' Thousands swarmed onto the streets, embracing and kissing the arriving soldiers." This transcription mentioned directly above is an accurate transcription of the Arabic, since in the context of applauding and rejoicing, the final *-u* of *Allahu* (*akbar*) is dropped. The expression is spelled "Allah Achbar!" in Washington Irving's nineteenth-century English classic, *The Life of Mahomet* (London: J. M. Dent, repr. 1944) 175. The semantic and pragmatic circumstances are similar to those of the *Time* story. It should be pointed out, however, that the final *-u* or *-o* on the first word *Allah* in the call to prayer is obligatory and can never be omitted, since to do so would destroy the cadence and rhythm of the call. The phrase can also be used in other contexts.

2. John Hayes (personal communication) illustrates the pitiful state of confusion in our libraries. There is an Iraqi Assyriologist by the name of Akram al-Zeebari. Among many other publications,

journalists, and the reading public alike. A detailed discussion of several concrete examples will be instructive in numerous ways and enable the reader to understand the intricacies of the problem of varying spellings.

It is appropriate to begin with the name of the Koran, the holy book for Muslims.[3] Few readers who are not professional Orientalists may know that the following spellings for *Koran* also occur in various English publications of one type or another as alternatives: Kuran, Ḳuran, Kor'an (often with a *spiritus lenis* ᵓ for ', or a curled apostrophe, which need not concern us here), Ḳor'an, Ḳur'an, Ḳor'ān, Kor'ān, Qur'ān, Qoran, Qorān, and Qor'ān (and probably others, too, since there are many permutations possible, filling a continuum of

---

he edited the first volume of the series Texts in the Iraqi Museum (1964). On the English title page of this book, his name appears as Akram al-Zeebari. A major university library listed this book under Al-Zeebari as well as under a more classical form of the same name with the diphthong *ay* for the Iraqi Arabic monophthong *ee*. The *ee* is more likely a mistransliteration of the letter *yā*ᵓ of the unvoweled text as *ī*, rather than an attempt at representing a colloquial pronunciation of the name, which in no case is pronounced al-Zībarī. In any case, the university librarians had two separate author entries for what they thought were two separate books, resulting in one Akram Al-Zeebari and another Akram Al-Zaybari, both of whom edited the aforementioned volume, which just happened coincidentally to be published the same year with the same title and so on. These entries were not cross-referenced, and the librarians had not the foggiest idea that both of these listings referred to the same individual, until a student pointed this out to them. Needless to say, they were completely dumbfounded.

3. Even the spelling *Muslim* has not wholly superseded the previous spelling of *Moslem*, which itself superseded Musulman (a variant from Persian), a form that appears in some desk dictionaries, as well as Muslem. It is difficult to offer a definitive conclusion whether all of these are variations or are just synonyms. Sir William Jones's eighteenth-century English usually employs *Musliman* and *Muselman*, as well, two now archaic variants (cited in Garland Cannon, *The Life and Mind of Oriental Jones, The Father of Modern Linguistics* [Cambridge: Cambridge University Press, 1990] 258 and 286).

The term *Mohammedan*, although used synonymously, is considered to be an offensive or pejorative term by most Muslims and in other circles as well, since it places a human being in the central position in their religion, a position that only Allah may occupy. In other words, Muslims object that the term exaggerates the role of the Prophet: Christians worship Christ, but Muslims do not worship Muhammad. Some Muslims find the spelling *Moslem* offensive as well, for various reasons, chief among which is that it smacks of Orientalism, as depicted by Edward W. Said in his *Orientalism* (New York: Pantheon Books, 1978).

John Algeo (personal communication) notes that none of the English dictionaries he consulted suggest a derogatory meaning for the term *Mohammedan*. I agree with him when he also observes: "I suspect most English speakers are completely unaware of any preference Moslems may have, and regard Mohammedan as just as good (or bad, as the case may be) a term as *Moslem*." In 1782, Sir William Jones published a translation from Arabic entitled *The Mahomedan Law of Succession to the Property of Intestates*. Washington Irving used Mahometan in his *Life of Mahomet* (1849). For the name of the religion per se, Islam, he used the strange-looking (at least by today's standards) *Islamism* (*Life of Mahomet*, 60, 105, and passim). There are many other bizarre Arabic transcriptions in Irving's classic, such as *Cadijah*, the Prophet's wife, normally *Khadijah*; however, the "Irvingisms" more properly belong to another study. It is somewhat surprising that no one, to my knowledge, has yet researched this.

spelling options). (*Q* and *Ḳ* are both intended to represent the back or uvular counterpart of undotted *k*.) One can also find the vowel *a* written with a circumflex (rather than with a macron, *â* versus *ā*) to indicate the Arabic long *a* vowel; with a colon (or dot), indicating the vocalic length (*a*: or *a*·) in the manner of the IPA (International Phonetic Association); or perhaps with a geminated *a*, as in, for example, Qur'aan. Although I cannot recall seeing the latter form, it is a possible rendering and may occur in one genre or other. The long vowel *ā* even shows up as three *a*s in Pakistani English *namaaaz* 'prayer' < Persian *namāz*.[4] These minor discrepancies in the various orthographic conventions mentioned above are of lesser importance for our discussion here, since it is not our purpose to uncover every single possible rendition of the word *Koran*. The *Encyclopaedia of Islam,*[5] as well as the *Shorter Encyclopaedia of Islam,*[6] have *Ḳurʾān*; the form used there, with the Arabic definite article, Al-Ḳurʾān, is the form that is authentic Classical Arabic. (Kuwait in Arabic also always has Al-, like Al-ʿIrāq, Al-ʾUrdunn 'Jordan', and Al-Sūdān.)

A second excellent example of orthographic loanword variation in English, and no doubt in many other languages not written in an Arabic-based script, can be seen in the most popular personal name of all time, Mohammed, cited here in probably its most common English rendition. Its popularity rests in large part on the fact that approximately one out of every five persons in the world is a Muslim[7] and that Islam is the fastest-growing religion in the United States and other countries as well. The following spellings are but a few of the many variations of this name occurring in English: Muhammed, Muhammad, Mahomed, Mahomet (the last made famous by Washington Irving, 1783–1859, who became interested in Islam through his travels in Spain, particularly in Andalusia [Arabic: Al-Andalus]), Mohamed, Mohamad, Muhammad, Moḥammad, and Mohammad.[8] (I do not discuss nicknames for his name, such as Moe, a fascinating study all by itself.)

The Arabic name with perhaps the greatest amount of variation today, at least in the American press, is that of the head of the state of Libya, Muammar or Moammar Khadafy. I shall not be concerned here with the variation in his first name (< Arabic: Muʿammar), which is considerable. His last name has ap-

4. Tariq Rahman, "The Use of Words in Pakistani English," *English Today* 26 (1991) 33.

5. A. T. Welch, "al-Ḳurʾān," *EI*² 5.400–429.

6. F. Buhl, "al-Ḳurʾān," in *Shorter Encyclopaedia of Islam* (ed. H. A. R. Gibb and J. H. Kramers; Leiden: Brill, 1961) 273–86.

7. P. Hanks and F. Hodges (*A Dictionary of First Names* [Oxford: Oxford University Press, 1990] 376) report that one out of seven people in the world is a Muslim.

8. This listing is not alphabetically motivated but, rather, organized to help the reader focus in on some basic contrasts, such as geminated versus nongeminated forms. One could also add Mukhammed, as in the name of a lecturer at Ashkhabad Polytechnic in Turkmenistan, Durdymurad

peared in the press in at least the following forms: Khaddafi, Khadafy, Qaddafi, Gaddafi, Ghaddafi, Ghadhafi, Kaddafi, Qadhafi, Gadhafi, and Kadafi.[9] Although English speakers are hardly compelled to follow one determination only, one

---

Khodzha-mukhammed. This is a transliteration of the Russian spelling of the name Muhammad. See Moscow *News*, Weekly No. 2, January 13–20, 1991, 4. Compare with other Russian names, such as Alimukhamedov and Magomedov, both derivatives of the name of the Prophet. As a wonderful parallel to the variation on Mohammed's name, Schimmel's example of the variation on the name Qāsim is noteworthy: Qassem, Gassem, Gacem, Kaçim, Casem, Kasim, and Ghasim (Annemarie Schimmel, *Islamic Names* [Edinburgh: Edinburgh University Press, 1989] x).

I do not think that Mahound (in Salman Rushdie's *Satanic Verses*) can be considered a variation of the name of the Prophet, yet the allusion to it is surely there. The name Mahound goes back to medieval times. Originally, the name Mahound was a deliberate distortion of the name of the Prophet and was used by Christian opponents of Islam during the Crusades. It was even understood as being the name of the devil himself. According to Georg Krotkoff (personal communication), Mahound is not a variant of Mohammed; rather, the name was intentionally twisted to be negatively associated with "hound" and all its negative connotations, particularly in the context of Islamic culture.

I am not sure how the Moroccan Berber name Mohand fits into the discussion; it seems too far removed from the name of the Prophet, however, to be considered a variant. [*Editor's note*: It seems clear to us that Mohand represents a partial assimilation of the *m* to the *d* after the elision of the vowel; Berbers in general tend to discard vowels.] In Arabic, the name Muḥammad has as variants: Miḥammad (also given as a variant in English by Hanks and Hodges, *A Dictionary of First Names*, 376), Maḥammad, and Muḥ, whereas in Turkish, it has been replaced by Mehmed or Mehmet (where the full form has been reserved for the Prophet). The previous two forms, Mehmed/t, should be regarded not as variants of Mohammed but, rather, as distinct forms. Exactly the same conclusion can be drawn from a consideration of Māmō in West African and Mēmō or Mīm in Kurdish (see Schimmel, *Islamic Names*, 30).

Only a comprehensive study of all genres and styles of English prose can determine the most common spellings for Mohammed or Muhammad, in all likelihood the two most common renditions. The least common variants currently and diachronically are probably Mahomed and Mahomet; yet I have also encountered Mohommed and Mehammed (see Sven Rubenson, [ed.], *Correspondence and Treaties 1800–1854*, vol. 1 of *Acta Ethiopica* [ed. Getatchew Haile and John Hunwick; Evanston, Ill.: Northwestern University Press / Addis Ababa: Addis Ababa University Press, 1982] 3, 98). One impression I have is that the more scholarly the publication, the greater the *tendency* to express gemination and diacritics, a situation that is probably true for all Arabic loanwords. The most common spelling is not the same thing as the "standard" (scholarly) spelling, and examining this in full detail will certainly require a discussion of popular versus formal American spelling, contrasted with British spellings and the English of other countries (for example, India or Australia). This is a huge task, to say the least, and far beyond the scope of the present paper.

9. I omit possible occurrences with the Arabic definite article, *al-*, which is, in fact, part of his name in Arabic; cf. al-Sadat ~ el-Sadat ~ es-Sadat ~ as-Sadat for Sadat, the late President of Egypt. The name Khadafy (any spelling of it) is not listed in P. Hanks and F. Hodges, *A Dictionary of Surnames* (Oxford: Oxford University Press, 1988). The reader should be aware of the fact that the *l* of the article assimilates to certain consonants in Arabic; yet due to transliteration practices, it is often still written. Thus *al-salām* 'the peace' is pronounced *as-salām* in all Arabic dialects (languages). The spelling with *al-* is morphographemic, whereas, in contrast, the spelling with *s* is phonemic; thus the country *al-Sūdān* is pronounced *as-Sūdān*.

might ask which of these alternatives for Khadafy is the most accurate phonetic rendition of the original Arabic? There is no clear-cut answer to this question, in part because there are a variety of languages today labeled Arabic (the parallel to the Chinese situation readily comes to mind, in which, for example, Cantonese and Mandarin are best regarded as two separate languages). This conglomeration of so-called Arabic dialects, related to the continuum of diglossia that has Classical Arabic at one extreme and the colloquials at the other, is similar to the situation of the Romance languages. It is safe to say, however, that in the Modern Standard Arabic of most Arabs, this name is pronounced (Al-)Qadhdhāfī, where *q* is the voiceless uvular plosive, *dh* is the voiced interdental fricative (which is actually geminated in Arabic), and *ā* is, more or less, the /æ/ in *cat* but longer, although this last phonetic realization also depends on many dialectological factors. The final -ī, which is mostly shortened in speech, is similar to the final vowel of English *to be*. Much of this is discussed by David Lamb in his well-known book *The Arabs: Journeys beyond the Mirage*; he too errs, however, when he proclaims: "To set the record straight, an accurate transliteration would be Qathafi, with the *th* pronounced as in *the*."[10] He has ignored the facts of gemination, unfortunately; yet he is right to state that it "is a Bedouin tribal name meaning 'one who throws'."[11]

The other English spellings for Khadafy result from technicalities of Arabic dialectology and matters of English phoneme-grapheme correspondences. The spelling Qaddafi preserves the standard or classical q and is cognizant of the Arabic gemination; the spelling with *g* is related to the fact that this is how the *q* is pronounced in colloquial Libyan Arabic; some Arabic dialects pronounce the *q* as a *k*, hence the spelling with *k*, although this fact may have nothing to do with the orthographic representation *k*. The use of *kh* is an internal English matter, since this digraph is pronounced (as a dorso-velar aspirated stop) exactly the same as *k* (compare the name Khan); its use may be intended to call attention to the fact that the name is Arabic (that is, foreign), although *kh* is often used to signal the Arabic autochthonous, voiceless uvular fricative as in Khodja, the name of the Shiᶜite Ismaᶜili community in the Indian subcontinent (followers of the Agha Khan), or in the Arabic name Khalid or Khaled. Similarly, the spellings with *gh* call specific attention to the fact that it is a foreign name, but more importantly, on the basis of a visual analogy to the variation of Persian toponyms (the Iranian city Qum or Ghom), since the Arabic letter Qāf is pronounced equal to the letter Ghayn in Persian. I owe the observation on Qum to Georg Krotkoff, who also notes in reference to the name

10. D. Lamb, *The Arabs: Journeys beyond the Mirage* (New York: Vintage Books, 1987) 12.
11. Ibid., n. 5.

Ghaddafi: "It cannot be explained as the name read by a Persian, because then it would come out as Ghazzafi."[12]

Commenting now on the *d* versus its geminated counterpart, in some transcription systems, a *d* with a line under it represents an interdental fricative. The omission of the line can be accounted for by technicalities of (typesetting) equipment of one sort or another, which could be part of the reason for the spelling with a double d. More probable, however, is the fact that the interdental has become a dental in the speech of most Arabs. It is unclear, however, to what degree a colloquial pronunciation can be used to explain the incorporation of foreign names by the mass media.

A fourth well-known Arabic name in English is Omar (compare the Egyptian actor Omar Sharif, the Persian poet-astronomer Omar Khayyam, and the American General Omar Bradley). The following variations are possible: Umar, ᶜUmar, ᶜOmar, and perhaps also ᶜUmaru, and ᶜOmaru.[13] Involved here are both Arabic phonology and the influence or interference modifications of other languages, such as Persian; Persian is an Indo-European language heavily indebted to Arabic, from which it has borrowed (as have Turkish, Urdu, Pashto, Swahili, Hausa, and others) much vocabulary since the spread of Islam. In Arabic, the name begins with a voiced pharyngeal fricative, IPA [ʕ], often indicated by the standard Orientalist transcriptional convention that utilizes the Greek *spiritus asper*, ᶜ. In Persian, in initial position, this consonant has become a glottal stop, IPA [ʔ] = Orientalist [ᵓ], or zero, since Persian does not have any pharyngeals. The spelling *ᵓUmar* or the like is probably very rare (I cannot recall seeing it). The realization of the phoneme *u* as an *o* may be the result of an Arabic phonological process, namely the influence of the preceding pharyngeal, or of Persian interference, since this name has been borrowed into English from at least these two languages as the ultimate sources. There is even the possibility that both the aforementioned reasons have worked together to produce the English spelling Omar with the *o*.

In Arabic phonology, there is an allophonic rule lowering the vowel /u/ around pharyngeals, so that /ᶜumar/ sounds very much like [ᶜomar]. In Iranian Persian, Arabic /u/ corresponds to /o/, so that all Arabic words with /u/ are phonetically realized in Persian with /o/. Arabic expressions such as *ᵓalḥamdu lillā(h)* 'Praise be to God' are usually pronounced *alhamdo lellā(h)* by Persian speakers. (I do not wish to discuss the situation with Persian dialects, Afghani

12. Personal communication.

13. I am disregarding the variants ᶜAmr and ᶜAmir listed by Hanks and Hodges (*Dictionary of First Names,* 361 and 383); I also cannot discuss the etymon of Hebrew ᵓŌmār at this point, actually an Edomite name in Gen 36:11.

Persian (Dari), or Persian-Arabic bilinguals at this point, nor am I commenting now on matters of register and stylistic variation.)

The final *-u* in ^{c}Umaru or ^{c}Omaru, if found, would represent a very classical Arabic pronunciation since in Classical Arabic (and elevated Modern Standard Arabic as well), the ending *-u* marks the nominative case for diptotes.[14] This vowel is omitted in Arabic pausal pronunciation, yet is present in a contextual situation, in which case it is then not final. Strangely enough, I am not familiar with an orthographic form Omaru or Umaru or the like in American English; yet there are, for example, Hausa proper names such as Umaru, Aliyu, Muhammadu, Yakubu, and Yusufu, used in the West African varieties of English. The transcription ^{c}Umaru or ^{c}Omaru would be an authentic rendition of the Classical Arabic diptote, whereas the African name Umaru has the final vowel *u* for another reason. One should keep in mind that the second caliph in early Islamic history, to cite but one example, was ^{c}Umaru bnu l-Khaṭṭāb; this name can have many possible renditions in English (see p. 391 and n. 14 for further details).

Now we can return to the variant English spelling *Allaho akbar* cited earlier. This probably reflects a Persian or Persianizing (Persianophile) source, in which the Arabic nominative *-u* is realized as *-o*. Paralleling this, we note other Arabic proper nouns borrowed into English: Hezbollah[15] 'the Party of God' (with Persianized *e* and *o*) versus Hizbullah, the more authentic Arabic form (with *i* and *u*); analogically, Moslem (with Persianized *o* and *e*) versus Arabic Muslim (with *u* and *i*, respectively); and Ayatollah (with *o*) versus Arabic Aya-

14. Most Arabic nouns are triptotes; that is to say, they take all three case endings (nominative, genitive, and accusative). The diptote declension involves only two endings: a nominative and an oblique, meaning genitive plus accusative. Many Arabic names happen to be diptotic, for example, *makkatu* 'Mecca'.

Some African languages that have borrowed Arabic names have *-u* (other vowels, too) for other reasons, most likely due to the phonotactic rules of the borrowing languages, for example, preference for open syllables. Thus we encounter African names such as Yakubu (< Arabic Ya^{c}qūb), Audu and Abdu (both from Arabic ^{c}Abd), Mamadou (< Arabic Muḥammad), Amadou (< Arabic Aḥmad), and so on. Swahili, for example, has the names Hasani (< Arabic Ḥasan), Daudi (< Arabic Dā$^{\supset}$'ū'd), Omari (< Arabic ^{c}Umar), Adamu (< Arabic $^{\supset}$Ādam). Also compare Swahili *mwalimu* 'teacher' < Arabic *mu^{c}allim*. All the Arabic etyma have been cited in pausal forms, since names were always borrowed in pausal forms. All the aforementioned African names can and do occur in the various African varieties of English.

15. One should note that Hizbollah, also occurring in various magazines and newspapers as Hizbalah, can be transliterated *Hizb Allāh* as well (see Bernard Lewis, *The Political Language of Islam* [Chicago: University of Chicago Press, 1988] 123 n. 25). Paralleling Arabic /u/ = Persian /o/, we have, Arabic /i/ = Persian /e/, so Arabic *kitāb* 'book' = Persian *ketāb*, and so on. This aforementioned situation is fairly predictable as opposed to the unpredictability of a name like Yūsuf, which shows up in Singapore English, for example, as Yusof. The *o* can be explained by progressive dissimilation to the preceding *u*.

tullah (with *u*).[16] As in many other Arabic words, there is a variety of possible orthographic traditions utilizing different conventions, such as French *ou* for Arabic *ū*, or English *oo* for the same long *ū* vowel of Arabic and other languages such as Urdu; for example, Mahmoud or Mahmood for Arabic Maḥmūd, which would often result in an English Mahmud or perhaps Mahmuud. Similarly, compare Ibraheem for Ibrahim and the like (= Arabic ʾibrāhīm[u]) or Hindustan, Hindoostan, and [H]indostan.[17] Of course, many Arabic words, including proper names, have come into English through a variety of sources other than direct transfer from Arabic, and the entire story is a very complex one, far too intricate to summarize in these remarks.

Garland Cannon commented as follows on the form *Allaho akbar*:

> I frequently heard the *mullah* (*imam*, if you wish)[18] during my two years in Kuwait in the early 1980's, from two different minarets, in lengthening the Allah in his traditional call to prayer, use something very close to an /o/ rather than /u/. This raises interesting questions about pronunciation in the borrowing. That is, English is not borrowing a classical form that is in the Koran and many other places, but is borrowing a dynamic living form which may well have vocalically changed, especially in something so widely used. During my year in Kuala Lumpur in 1987, the Malay-speaking *imam* always used *Allaho akbar*, though those *imams* would hardly be the source of the loanword item.[19]

I offer the following explanation of this /o/ variant. There were many Iranians, Pakistanis, Indians, and others in Kuwait during the 1980s. I personally met many during a short stay in November and December, 1989. It seems rather likely that the *muezzins* Cannon heard from the two different minarets were subject to the influence (that is, substratum or adstratum) of their native languages, probably Persian.[20] One should keep in mind that many Pakistanis and Indians

16. The Ayatollah's title is rarely given the Arabic spelling Ayatullah Khomeini (see, however, *Time*, January 21, 1991, 43). This is reminiscent of the spelling *Kuran* with *u* versus *Koran* with *o*. The Arabicized orthography seems to me to be reflective of a greater formality belonging to acrolectic English versus the other variants belonging to mesolectic English. Some cases of *o* for short *u* are the result of Francophone ambience (also è for short *i*), according to A. F. L. Beeston (personal communication). He writes (8 June 1992): "For Francophones, short *u* and short *i* are much closer to French *o* and *è* than to o*u*, *i*: hence *Monès* for *Mu'nis*. Spellings like Mohammed have come to us from the French." It seems to me that this reason has combined with Persian influence, with both serving as reinforcements for one another. The use of /i/ and /u/ in Persian has also to do with the phonetic tradition of Farsi in India.

17. On Hindustan, see Cannon, *The Life and Mind of Oriental Jones, 57.*

18. *Muezzin* is technically correct here.

19. Personal communication.

20. The shift to *o* also occurs in Dari or Afghani Persian, and there were some Afghanis in Kuwait, as well. Compare Persian *dūst* 'friend' > Hindi-Urdu *dōst*.

know some Persian, at least as a respected, literary vehicle, following a tradition that dates back to the time of the Muslim establishment of the Mogul Empire in India, and some of them know Persian well. The Malay version with *-o* is possibly the result of a Malay superstratum influence. Garland Cannon has also suggested that this might be accounted for by the non-Hindu (substratal) Tamil speakers "who are settled there, even though there are annual, highly competitive contests to see who can recite the call to prayer most authentically."[21]

Some of the variations in Arabic words I found in the current American press reflect many different linguistic and cultural traditions. Sometimes the newspapers and magazines are internally consistent; sometimes not. The *Los Angeles Times* has Khalid ibn Sultan; *USA Today* and *The Washington Post* have Khalid bin Sultan (both *ibn* and *bin* 'son' reflect different types of Arabic dialects with the latter pronunciation being typical of the North African Arab countries). *USA Today* has Shiite Moslem, *The Orange County Register* and the *Los Angeles Times* have Shiite Muslim. *Time* has Shiʾite, but *Newsweek, The New Republic,* and *The New York Times* have Shiite. *The New Republic* uses both Qaddafi and al-Qaddafi. *USA Today* uses Emir Jaber Ahmed Sabah; *The Orange County Register* has Sheikh Jaber Alahmad al-Sabah (as does the Associated Press) and Alahmed al-Sabah, while *Newsweek* has Sheikh Jabir al-Ahmad al-Sabah (the last form of the name represents the most accurate Arabic phonetic transcription or transliteration, although *Sheikh* has been Anglicized).[22] Reuters has for the Kuwaiti Interior Minister Sheikh Ahmed Hamoud al-Jaber al-Sabah. Here one can notice variations such as between Ahmad (directly above) and Ahmed. Of course, it would be asking too much of the uninitiated to distinguish between the article *al-* and the noun *ʾāl* 'clan'.

21. Personal communication.

22. Tentatively, there is some reason to conclude that a spelling with /i/, as in Jabir, is more Arabicized (Arabophile) in its orientation, while a spelling with /e/ is more Iranicized (Iranophile), namely, Jaber. Compare Moslem and Muslim, in a historical context (see further n. 8). However, as we have mentioned, it seems as though this explanation is far from consistent. Garland Cannon adds: "Even the old word *sheikh* has at least 29 variations, 25 of which are now historically superseded; but *sheikh*, *sheykh*, *shaikh*, and *shaykh* continue to be common" (personal communication).

The spelling *Jabbar* (also occurring in the *Los Angeles Times*, May 15, 1991) is erroneous and is impossible to explain phonologically (just a plain old mistake!). Since Arabic *al-Jabbār* 'the Omnipotent' is one of Allah's epithets, it should not be confused with *Jabir* or *Jaber*. However, Peter T. Daniels has quite ingeniously suggested that this error could be explained by analogy to the former Los Angeles Lakers' basketball superstar, Kareem Abdul-Jabbar (personal communication). It seems possible that a reporter associated *Jabbar* with *Jabir* or *Jaber*, due to similar phonetic makeup (after all, these forms are derivatives of the same root). This makes good sense, especially since the *Jabbar*-form was published in the *Los Angeles Times*.

We have seen that spelling can reveal their Persian or Arabic immediate source. The Shi^{c}ite leader, Hojatolislam[23] Mohammed Bakr al-Hakim, has three *o*s in his title and name, and so we can rightly predict his Iranian identity (similar to the *o* in Ruhollah,[24] Khomeini's "middle" name, counting his title as his first name; compare this with the name of the Kuwaiti Crown Prince Sheikh Saad[25] Abdullah al-Sabah with *u*, pinpointing an Arabic profile or background). To make matters worse, however, there are many exceptions and/or seemingly inexplicable inconsistencies. One might be led to think that Hafez (Al- or al-) Assad (the president of Syria) is Persian by the spelling of his first name with *e*; a more "proper" (that is, usual or standard) Arabic transliteration would be Hafiz. There are numerous apparent, seemingly anomalous, exceptions to the rules given, which are merely tendencies, not laws. These generalizations can be supported by statistical research; yet it is important to note that one often encounters a historically motivated, largely etymological, transcription in which the Arabic system prevails, as in, for example, Hafiz for Hafez, the famous Persian poet. Such is indeed the transcription seen in the form Háfiz, which reflects this type of system or tradition used in books by major publishers such as Cambridge University Press.[26] Phonetically, it is *e* and not *i*.[27] But there are even some inconsistencies to report in the Arabic-type of

23. The spelling with /i/ in the first name is indicative of an Arab background (ethnically or culturally), though there are exceptions such as the case here. One would expect a spelling *Hojatoleslam* with an *e* if it were consistent with the principles stated in n. 15. Peter T. Daniels has noted that *-islam*, spelled with an *i*, is so familiar, that to change it would be to destroy this very familiarity (personal communication). This is precisely the reason why so many authors who write in English write Arabic loanwords that have become accepted English words without any diacritics, such as "ulema," "mufti," or "mollah" (also "mullah" and "moollah"): see, for example, Bernard Lewis, *Political Language*, 123 n. 22. If the first of these were written ^{c}*ulamā*$^{\supset}$, its graphemic recognition in English would be obscured beyond most people's comprehension. Lewis adopts, in all other cases, the system of the *Encyclopaedia of Islam* for the transliteration of Arabic and Persian (with two exceptions) and uses modern Turkish orthography for both Modern and Ottoman Turkish.

24. I have not seen the Arabicized transcription *Ruhullah* with *u* in the second syllable, yet I would not be greatly surprised to learn of its occurrence in some genre or other. I feel, however, that it would be extremely rare.

25. This is *sa*^{c}*d* in Arabic, with the second *a* representing the Arabic voiced pharyngeal fricative. The gemination of *a* often betrays the presence of this consonant, as seen also in the capital of Yemen, Sanaa (Arabic: *ṣan*^{c}*a* or classically, *ṣan*^{c}*ā*$^{\supset}$).

26. See Cannon's recent study of Sir William Jones (*Life and Mind*). Compare *Sháhnáma* (p. 396) to the Iranologist's or Persianist's *Shāhnāmé*, or the writing of the Persian *ezāfé* or genitive marker *-i* for *-e* (for example, *Farhang-i-Jahángíri* [ibid.]), and so on. Once again, Persian Pronunciation in India is important here.

27. Pakistani English has both *-i* and *-e* (see Rahman, "Use of Words," 34).

etymological transcription. In Cannon's book, consider Laylà va Majnún[28] and Yúsuf va Zulaykhá[29] in which Persian *va* 'and' is noteworthy (corresponding to Arabic *wa* 'and'). In contrast to the *e* versus *i* discrepancy mentioned above, the transcription with *v* is phonetically accurate, since Persian does not have /w/ and Arabic does not have /v/. It would be much more phonetically accurate, from the point of view of Iranian Persian, to write Zolaykhá for Zulaykhá, since the *o* reflects the actual pronunciation. See n. 15 above for further details.

The middle name of Iran's president is Hashemi[30] with *e* for Arabic *i*, yet an Iraqi envoy to France during the Persian Gulf War was Abdel Razzak al-Hashimi.[31] Some spellings are unquestionably anomalous (or erroneous), such as *The Economist*'s (February 23, 1991) usage of Ali Akhbar[32] Velayati for Akbar, yet what starts out as an error[33] may soon become accepted, standard, or at least, an alternative spelling. Shifting to cross-linguistic thoughts for a moment, I find it interesting to note, not unsurprisingly, that in the *Asahi Shimbun* (newspaper) of Tokyo, there is also some variation in Japanese: Saddam is Sadamu (compare Spanish Sadam), Mohammad is Mohameddo, but Baghdad is either Bagudaddo or Bagudado.[34]

I began this paper with a comment on Cannon's review of *Loanwords Dictionary*, and it is only coincidental that I will end it with a discussion of Cannon's *Life and Mind of Oriental Jones*, but we can see many of the principles mentioned in the first work illustrated in the latter work (not surprisingly, since it deals with Oriental studies). Cannon's *Life and Mind* and the editorial policies of Cambridge University Press, which published the book, must be seen as

28. Cannon, *Life and Mind*, 397.

29. Ibid., 33, 46, 248, and 291.

30. Also spelled *Hashimi*, but this, I believe, is much rarer. The Iranian president is also cited as Hashemi Rafsanjani.

31. Still, my first explanation here would be a Persianized tradition vs. a straight Arabic or Arabicized (Arabophile) one. The spelling *al-Hashimi* would tend to indicate an Arab, whereas the spelling *Hashemi* would, in all probability, indicate an Iranian.

32. This is, in all likelihood, merely an English orthographic variation designating a dorso-velar stop which marks "foreignness," paralleling the spelling of Khadafy, also with a *kh*. In other words, it is an orthographic signal of foreignness parallel to /ž/ as a phonological signal of foreignness (John Algeo, personal communication). Peter T. Daniels has called attention to Dwight Bolinger's famous notion that this type of phenomenon may best be characterized as a "visible morpheme" (personal communication).

33. "Error" may be the wrong word to use here. *Kh* in English can and does represent a dorso-velar stop; the only question remaining is why the author chose to use it instead of a *k*. He could have been influenced by the often-cited Egyptian journal *Akhbār al-yawm*, which in its correct pronunciation is not similar at all due mainly to the long, stressed second *a*.

34. I hope to investigate the Japanese situation in detail in a future study including Japanese English-language newspapers and magazines.

excellent representations of the formal press, probably half-way between the devices used in the Orientalist-oriented *International Journal of Middle East Studies* (also published by Cambridge University Press and one of the few journals with explicitly different systems for Arabic, Persian, and Ottoman Turkish printed on the inside cover of every issue) and the popular press. Also typical of this formal press are such works as Nicholson's *Literary History of the Arabs*,[35] in which *Muslim* is both *Moslem* and *Muhammadan*, *Soqotri* (the name of a modern South Arabian language) is *Socotrí*, but *Mamlūk* is *Mameluke*.[36] Another example is *A Literary History of Persia*, by Browne,[37] with *z* in the first edition corresponding to *dh* in the latter. Arberry[38] followed in the same tradition as Browne,[39] except that one notes some conspicuous variations that might be confusing to the reader, such as *ḳaṣīda* and *qaṣīda* 'ode'.[40] Cannon uses both the Persianized Nader Shah with *e*[41] and, more often, an Arabicized version of the name of this eighteenth-century Persian king,[42] Nadir. The Persian poet Ferdōsī (ca. 950–1020?), author of the *Shāhnāmé*, is spelled in Arabicized fashion, Firdausi; similarly, the Persian poet Hāfez (c. 1325–80/90) is spelled by Cannon as both Hafiz and Háfiz.[43] Firdausi is also commonly spelled as Firdawsi. The Arabic pre-Islamic poetry known as the *Muᶜallaqāt* is transcribed by Cannon as such but with an accent mark for the long *ā*, yet he also spells it *Moallakát*.[44] Here one can notice that for the *u*- vowel plus the voiced pharyngeal fricative, the Arabic letter *ᶜain*, the vowel has been lowered to an *o*; further, the *q* is *k* (probably through a hypothetical, bypass stage with an intermediary *ḳ*).

The problem of Oriental loanword variation in English orthography is, to be sure, an old one. Even the father of modern linguistics, Sir William Jones,

35. R. A. Nicholson, *A Literary History of the Arabs* (Cambridge: Cambridge University Press, 1962; 1st ed., T. Fisher Unwin, 1907).

36. For Moslem, see pp. ix, xvi, and passim; for Muhammedan, see xvii, xx, and passim; for *Socotrí*, see xvii, xx, and passim; and for *Mameluke*, see p. xxix.

37. E. G. Browne, *A Literary History of Persia* (4 vols.; Cambridge: Cambridge University Press, 1928; vol. 1, originally 1902; vol. 2, originally 1906).

38. A. J. Arberry, *Classical Persian Literature* (London: George Allen and Unwin, 1958).

39. Browne, *A Literary History*, 9.

40. Ibid., 9.

41. Cannon, *Life and Mind*, 40.

42. Ibid., 14, 17, and 404.

43. Ibid., 49 and 36, respectively. Cannon informs me in a personal communication that the latter is, as a matter of fact, a typographical error.

44. Ibid., 17, 263, 403, and passim (*Muᶜallaqat*); ibid., 188 (*Moallakát*). Peter T. Daniels (personal communication) comments that a vowel with an accent mark (V́, e.g., á) is the (early?) Indologist's length marking. Thus, Cannon's form is probably an intentionally archaizing transcription taken from Sir William Jones.

grappled with it.[45] Jones worked with the idea of the phoneme in his transcriptions. According to Cannon,

> his primitive phonemic transcription is a pioneering attempt to approximate the original sounds. This was the first formal essay on transliteration and held the germ of ideas eventually culminating in the International Phonetic Alphabet.[46]

Jones nevertheless used variants in his correspondence and made a point of this to a friend in discussing the variations in spelling the Sanskrit and Hindi word for 'learned person; scholar', the word rendered *pandit*, *pendit*, and *pundit*.[47] The first and last of these variants are still contesting two centuries later. Jones's "effort to standardize Oriental spelling, based on the principle of accurately representing the original sounds within a perspective of general phonetics, started scholars on the road toward the International Phonetic Alphabet";[48] Jones used the values represented by the consonants of English but the vowels of Italian, "a principle adopted by the Royal Geographic Society in 1836."[49] It is indeed ironic that, in these times of supposed phonological breakthroughs and expert transliterations and transcriptions, such variations, if not even worse, are still with us in the highly influential popular press. Jones was fully aware of the problem and offered a solution to it in his "Dissertation on the Orthography of Asiatick Words in Roman Letters" (1786), which came to be called the Jonesian system.

Skipping from Sir William Jones to T. E. Lawrence, we come to our own century. Georg Krotkoff[50] has reminded me (as only he can) that Arabic orthographic loanword variation was a severe problem in the tumultuous, war-ridden times of East versus West, popularized by Lawrence of Arabia—times not unlike those of our own Persian Gulf War. The publisher's note pertaining to the publication of Lawrence's *Revolt in the Desert* says it all:

45. Garland Cannon in a personal communication reminds me that there is a phenomenal amount of variation with other high-frequency non-onomastic items. The English word *mosque* via French (< Arabic *masjid*, which was, in turn, borrowed from Epigraphic South Arabic) has *masjid* as a synonym. These 2 Arabic loanwords are phonemically and graphemically too far apart to be considered synchronic variants (compare, in some ways, with English *skirt* and *shirt*). Cannon informs me that *masjid* has a variant in English *musjid* (through Indian Islam?), along with 24 other superseded variations. Some other *Kulturwörter* mentioned by Cannon are: *minaret*, *munshi*, *jihad*, and so on. These are all discussed in Garland Cannon, and Alan S. Kaye, collaborator, *The Arabic Contributions to the English Language: An Historical Dictionary* (Wiesbaden: Harrassowitz, 1994).

46. Cannon, *Life and Mind*, 249.

47. Ibid.

48. Ibid., 250.

49. Ibid., 379 n. 20.

50. Personal communication.

It seems necessary to explain that the spelling of Arabic names throughout this book varies according to the whim of the author.

The publisher's proofreader objected strongly to the apparent inconsistencies which he found, and a long and entertaining correspondence ensued between author and publisher. The author's attitude can best be judged from the following extracts which show questions and answers.

Q. I attach a list of queries raised by F. who is reading the proofs. He finds these very clean, but full of inconsistencies in the spelling of proper names, a point which reviewers often take up. Will you annotate it in the margin, so that I can get the proofs straightened?

A. Annotated: not very helpfully perhaps. Arabic names won't go into English, exactly, for their consonants are not the same as ours, and their vowels, like ours, vary from district to district. There are some "scientific systems" of transliteration, helpful to people who know enough Arabic not to need helping, but a wash-out for the world. I spell my names anyhow, to show what rot the systems are.

Q. Jeddah and Jidda used impartially throughout. Intentional?

A. Rather![51]

I could conceive of a learned body of linguists in Oxford, Cambridge, or some other city, who would be responsible for publishing a list of words and names from Arabic currently used in English. This list could be made available, and its use could be mandated (with various penalties for nonconformity). This would be an excellent solution to the problem of the varying spelling conventions causing the inconsistencies and lack of uniformity, but I am fully aware that this is neither practical nor feasible in today's English-speaking world. I reluctantly conclude, therefore, by agreeing with Schimmel: "[A]nyone who has looked in the index volume of the *Revue du Monde Musulman* will agree that the possibilities of rendering Islamic names seem to be unlimited!"[52]

51. T. E. Lawrence, *Revolt in the Desert* (Garden City, N.Y.: Garden City Publishing, 1927) xv.
52. Schimmel, *Islamic Names*, 77.

The Language and Prose Style of Bostān's *Süleymānnāme*

Claudia Römer

The *Süleymānnāme*, originally ascribed to someone whose name supposedly was Ferdī, was identified long ago as a work of the Kazasker of Anatolia and then of Rumeli, Muṣṭafā ibn Meḥmed Bostān(zāde) Tīrevī (1498–1569).[1] Since this chronicle is the only historical work among Bostān's writings,[2] it seems natural that up to now only historians should have shown interest in it. In an earlier article, I have dealt with the poems entitled *li-müᵓellifihī* 'by its

1. On Ferdī, see J. Thury, *Török Történetírók* (Budapest: Magyar Tudományos Akadémia, 1894) 2.39–111; J. Karabacek, *Geschichte Suleimans des Grossen, verfasst und eigenhändig geschrieben von seinem Sohne Muṣṭafā* (Zur Orientalischen Altertumskunde 7, Sitzungsberichte der Wiener Akademie, phil.-hist. Kl., 185. Band, 1. Abh.; Vienna, 1917); on the identification of Bostān, see Hüseyin G. Yurdaydın, "Bostân'ın Süleymânnâmesi (Ferdîᵓye atfedilen eser)," *Belleten* 19/74 (1955) 137–202.

2. For the list of his other (mainly religious) works, see ibid., 191.

author' that are inserted into the prose text at various places,[3] so the prose of Bostān's *Süleymānnāme* remains to be studied.

Out of the seven known manuscripts of the *Süleymānnāme*,[4] the one that is best suited to linguistic studies is the Österreichische Nationalbibliothek H.O.42a (Flügel II, no. 99 manuscript 8), which is vocalized throughout—from the first to the last folio. Moreover, it covers the longest period of all manuscripts, namely, from 1521 to 1540. Its major part (up through fol. 331r/3) comprises events up to 1539 and was copied in 1540; its latter part (fols. 331r/4–364r) was copied sometime after 1547. The copyist was Prince Muṣṭafā.[5] From now on I shall neither deal with the other extant manuscripts nor dwell on the contents of the chronicle, since they are well known.[6]

Arabic and Persian Elements

Yurdaydın has mentioned Bostān's style and language in a very cursory manner. He thinks that after having rewritten the first part of the *Süleymānnāme* (the earliest evidence of which is MS Ayasofya 3317), Bostān still uses many Turkish words, although his prose from then on corresponds well to the taste of his time.[7] It is certainly true that in the *Süleymānnāme* there occur quite a number of genuine Turkish words and phrases, for example, *ırğad*[8] 'worker' 71v/1; *ırğadlıq* 'work' 40r/7; *yégrek* 'better' 157r/7; *ḳaçan ki* 'when' 4v/13; *ḳaçmağa yüz dutıcaḳ* 'when he started to flee' 14r/7, *yarındası* 'next day' 21r/5, 22v/9; *bir uzaḳ azmaḳ ve bir ıraḳ bataḳ var idi* 'there was a big flooding and a great swamp' 121r/9–10; *niçe gün ulaşdurı* 'several days running' 355v/11; *ṭopṭolu* 'full to the brim' 116r/11; *Ṭoḳatdan añaru* 'from Ṭoḳat onward' 143r/1; and so forth. Nevertheless, when reading the work as a whole, I could not but feel a strong foreign, that is, Arabic and Persian, influence. To prove this, I have counted words (nouns [i.e., substantives, adjectives, and adverbs] on the one hand and verbs on the other, leaving out all other kinds of words like interjections, pronouns, and so on) as follows: the first noun or verb of every page

3. C. Römer, "Bostān historiographe ottoman en tant que poète," *Anatolia moderna* 3 (1992) 237–46.

4. Yurdaydın ("Bostân'ın") only knew six manuscripts, but recently another one has been found, namely, HS.or.oct.1142, Staatsbibliothek Marburg, *VOHD* 13, Nr. 138, pp. 112–13; cf. Römer, "Bostān historiographe," 237 n. 5.

5. See Yurdaydın, "Bostân'ın," 167.

6. See ibid., 182–85.

7. Ibid., 193–94.

8. The transliteration system used here conforms to that of the *International Journal of Middle East Studies* (*IJMES*); *é* denotes the closed *e*.

TABLE 1. Initial Words of Each Page of the *Süleymānnāme* by Language of Origin

	Noun		*Verb*		*Total*	
A	349	64.27%	91	49.46%	440	60.52%
P	110	20.26%	8	4.35%	118	16.23%
T	56	10.31%	79	42.93%	135	18.57%
M	24	4.42%	6	3.26%	30	4.13%
E	4	0.74%	—	—	4	0.55%
Total	543	100.00%	184	100.00%	727	100.00%

(that is, the recto and verso of each folio) has been counted according to its origin (Arabic: A; Persian: P; Turkish: T; mixed: M; or European: E). A mixed noun would, for example, be *se^cādet-penāh* 'refuge of felicity', whereas an Arabic verb would be *ḳatl étmek* 'to kill'. The total amount of words thus gained is 727, the text consisting of 364 folios, beginning with fol. 1v. Table 1 shows the result of this procedure.[9]

As expected, the amount of Turkish vocabulary is higher among the verbs, but it seems to be extremely low among the nouns.[10] Similar data from the sixteenth century can be found in the *Sūrnāme-i hümāyūn*, whose MS Topkapı Sarayı Arşivi no. 1344 is illuminated splendidly and so far has mainly been considered a valuable source for art historians. Its text, however, has been neglected until recently. Let us look at the statistical evidence from this text, based upon the manuscript of the Österreichische Nationalbibliothek H.O.70 (Flügel II, p. 239, no. 1019):[11] Arabic 38.23%, Persian 26.56%, Turkish 35.19%; in the very elaborate introduction, which covers the first ten folios, the ratio is Arabic 52.13%, Persian 25.66%, Turkish 22.19%.[12] Although the style of the *Sūrnāme-i hümāyūn* is on the whole much more complicated and more abundant with *sec^c* than the style of the *Süleymānnāme* (for details, see below), its vocabulary shows a greater inclination toward Turkish words. This is especially

9. It was impossible, however, to obtain a strictly aleatoric sample, because chapter headings and poems as well as words other than nouns and verbs had to be left out, so that in some cases it was not exactly the first word of a folio that was counted.

10. See my article, "Der Einfluß der Übersetzungen aus dem Persischen auf die Entwicklung des Osmanischen im 14. und 15. Jahrhundert," *WZKM* 73 (1981) 96, and the table on p. 101.

11. The manuscript has been edited and commented upon by Gisela M. Procházka-Eisl, *Die Wiener Handschrift des Sūrnāme-i hümāyūn* (Istanbul: Isis, 1995).

12. Ibid., 63.

TABLE 2. Initial and Final Words of Each Page of Kemālpaşazāde by Language of Origin

	Noun		*Verb*		*Total*	
A	83	65.35%	22	30.99%	105	53.03%
P	27	21.26%	5	7.04%	32	16.16%
T	15	11.81%	43	60.56%	58	29.29%
M	2	1.57%	1	1.41%	3	1.52%
E	—	—	—	—	—	—
Total	127	99.99%	71	100.00%	198	100.00%

true of passages that describe the production of goods offered by the various guilds during the feast.[13]

An objection could be raised, however, that an Ottoman chronicle and a *sūrnāme* belong to quite different categories of literature and, therefore, cannot be compared in regard to language.[14] This is why I have tried the same method of counting words on Kemālpaşazāde. I have used Defters 8 and 9 of his chronicle, which have been edited by Ahmet Uğur.[15] Here, the first and last nouns or verbs of each printed page of the transcription were counted. The results are presented in table 2.

We see that there are even more Turkish words in Kemālpaşazāde than in Bostān but fewer than the average of the *Sūrnāme-i hümāyūn.* The amount of Arabic vocabulary of the *Selīmnāme* is approximately the same as in the introduction of the *Sūrnāme-i hümāyūn.*

Yurdaydın has mentioned fol. 311r as an example of the great amount of Turkish words found in the *Süleymānnāme.*[16] In order to check this, I have counted all the nouns and verbs of fol. 311r (see table 3).

Table 3 shows that the total number of Turkish words on this page is a little higher than the average, whereas the number of Persian verbs is rather high. This is mainly due to the verbs *lenger al-* 'to raise anchor' and *lenger ṣal-* 'to weigh anchor', which occur frequently, the subject of this page being the progress of the Ottoman fleet from one port to the other. The number of Turk-

13. Cf. ibid. 63–64. It is generally accepted that Ottoman prose works combine intricate and simple passages according to the context to be expressed; cf., e.g., B. Flemming, "Bemerkungen zur türkischen Prosa vor der Tanzimat-Zeit," *Der Islam* 50 (1973) 165–66; and P. Kappert, *Geschichte Sultan Süleymān Ḳānūnīs von 1520 bis 1557 . . .* (VOHD sup. vol. 21; Wiesbaden: Steiner, 1981) 39.

14. On the other hand, the *Süleymānnāme* does contain two short *sūrnāme*-like passages (fols. 164r–174r, 316v–331r).

15. *The Rule of Sultan Selīm I in the Light of the Selīmnāme Literature* (Islamkundliche Untersuchungen 109; Berlin: K. Schwarz, 1985).

16. Yurdaydın, "Bostân'ın," 193 n. 147.

TABLE 3. All Words of Folio 311r of the *Süleymānnāme* by Language of Origin

	Noun		*Verb*		*Total*	
A	20	51.28%	9	40.9%	29	47.54%
P	7	17.95%	8	36.36%	15	24.59%
T	9	23.08%	5	22.72%	14	22.95%
M	—	—	—	—	—	—
E	3	7.69%	—	—	3	4.92%
Total	39	100.00%	22	99.98%	61	100.00%

ish words, however, is clearly above the average. This is due to the words *gün* 'day' and *ṣulan-* 'to sail', which occur several times on this page. It seems that whenever Bostān describes concrete actions, he uses shorter sentences with more Turkish words than in the elaborate *sec*^{c} passages on battles, fortresses, feasts, and so forth.[17]

In any case, the Arabic and Persian elements play a predominant part in Bostān's prose (for examples, as well as for Persian syntactical elements, see below). Moreover, the Turkish character of any given text cannot be judged from the mere occurrence of some words of Turkish origin, but the frequency of their occurrence must be checked and contrasted to the foreign vocabulary.

The Degree of Antiquity

The fact that Manuscript ÖNB 42a is vocalized throughout, as has been mentioned before, enables us in an ideal way to find out how modern or how conservative Bostān's—or rather Prince Muṣṭafā's, the copyist's—language is. Ever since Professor Doerfer's study on the vowels in Old Ottoman non-first syllables appeared, we have been provided with an excellent tool to determine the degree of antiquity of a given text.[18] I shall now apply Doerfer's method, as explained in his book.[19]

Doerfer has established a total of 34 relevant items (suffixes and a group of words) to be analyzed, some of which do not of course occur in all texts.

17. See n. 13 above.

18. Gerhard Doerfer, *Zum Vokalismus nichterster Silben in altosmanischen Originaltexten* (Akademie der Wissenschaften und der Literatur, Mainz. Veröffentlichungen der orientalischen Kommission 37; Stuttgart: Steiner, 1985).

19. Recently, Doerfer suggested a slight modification, but it reached me too late to be fully taken into account here and does not in fact change the main conclusions ("Zur Auswertung des Vokalismus nichterster Silben von Xāliṣīs Ẓafer-nāme," *WZKM* 82 [Gedenkband A. C. Schaendlinger: 1992] 97–107).

Except for two instances, the *Süleymānnāme* contains no direct speech, so that there is no evidence of first- and second-person verbal forms or of imperatives (except -AlUm, twice).

The passive, reflexive, and cooperative suffixes are divided into two groups, namely, -Il-/-Ul-, -In-/-Un-, -Iş-/-Uş-, in open and closed syllables, respectively (for example, *olınub/olunub* versus *olındı/olundı*). The same applies to verbs like *oḳı-/oḳu-* and *unıt-/unut-*. The conservativeness or modernity of each item is evaluated by points: 5 for ancient forms without exception, one for modern forms throughout. The suffix -IncI/-UncI, however, can attain only 4 points at the utmost; the total number of items in the *Süleymānnāme*, therefore, is 25.8 instead of 26. If we add up all of the points and divide the sum by the number of items, we obtain the *Altertümlichkeitskoeffizient* (the coefficient of antiquity, abbreviated AK) of the *Süleymānnāme.*[20]

I have gone through the whole prose text of the *Süleymānnāme*, including the headings of chapters, as well as the Turkish poems called *li-müᵓellifihī*; at this point I only omitted poems with the titles *shiᶜr* or *miṣrāᶜ*. Since they are by a different author, they could possibly have interfered with the analysis of Bostān's language.

Table 4 (see p. 407) shows the number of points given to each item and the AK of the *Süleymānnāme.*

If we place these results alongside Doerfer's comparative table for the 30 works he analyzed,[21] we discover that the *Süleymānnāme* belongs in the first column between no. 25 *Şāhnāme* 1511 and no. 26 Pīr 1559, in regard to its date of composition. The second column arranges the 30 works according to the dates of their copies. Our manuscript, however, was copied in two parts, so that we would either have to place it between no. 21, Şeykhī 1523 (1472/3), and no. 22, Şeyyād (1546), or between no. 23, Khiżr (1547), and no. 24, Mevlid (1560). In the third column, which gives the list of works according to their AK, the *Süleymānnāme* would come in between no. 27, Dede (sixteenth century), and no. 28, Ḳānūn (end of the fifteenth century).[22] The last column, therefore, would have −2 and −6 or −4, indicating the distances of the locations through the

20. For further explanations on the method, see Doerfer, *Zum Vokalismus*, 78–81.

21. Doerfer, *Zum Vokalismus*, 87.

22. The abbreviations refer to the following editions (the copies used are not always the oldest ones extant, but the ones preserved best, sometimes vocalized; see Doerfer, *Zum Vokalismus*, 11–16): *Şāhnāme*: A. Zajączkowski, *Turecka wersja Šāhnāma z Egiptu mameluckiego* (Warsaw: Państwowe Wydawnictwo Naukowe, 1965); *Pīr*: E. Rossi, *Parafrasi turca del De Senectute . . . (1559)* (Rendiconti della Reale Academia Nazionale di Lincei: Classe di Scienze morali, storiche e filologiche, Serie sesta 17; Rome: Tipografia della Accademia, 1936) 680–756; *Şeykhī*: A. Zajączkowski, *Poemat iranski Ḫusrev-u-Šīrīn* (Warsaw: Państwowe Wydawnictwo Naukowe, 1963); *Şeyyād*: D. Dilçin, *Yusuf ve Zeliha* (Istanbul: Klisecilik ve Matbaacılık T.A.S., 1946); *Khiżr*: Z. Önler, *Celalüddin Hızır (Haci Paşa): Müntahab-i Şifa* (Ph.D. diss., Elâziğ, 1981); *Mevlid*: A. Ateş, *Süleymān*

TABLE 4. The *Altertümlichkeitskoeffizient* (AK) of the *Süleymānnāme*

Item	*Syllables*	*Points*
1	-Il-/-Ul-open	4
2	-Il-/-Ul-closed	2
3	-In-/-Un-open	2
4	-In-/-Un-closed	2
5	-Iş-/-Uş-open	1
6	-Iş-/-Uş-closed	1
7	oḳı-/oḳu-open	3
8	-IncA/-UncA	4
9	-IcAK/-UcAK	5
10	-AlUm-/AlIm	5
11	-mIş	5
12	-dUK/-dIK	4
13	-dUr-/-dIr-	4
14	-Ur-/-Ir-	4
15	-GUr-/-GIr-	2
16	-dUr/-dIr	5
17	-Ur/-Ir	4
18	-IncI/-UncI	2
19	-Uñ/-Iñ (gen.)	3
20	-(s)I/-(s)U	2
21	-sUz/-sIz	5
22	-lU/-lI after non-labial vowels	5
23	-lUK/-lIK after labial vowels	2
24	bulıt, degül, . . .	2
25	-U/-I	1
26	-Ub/-Ib[23]	0
Total		80
AK: 80 : 25.8 = 3.101		

Çelebi: Vesiletü n-necat, Mevlid (Ankara: Türk Tarih Kurumu Basımevi, 1954); *Dede*: E. Rossi, *Il "Kitab-i Dede Korkut"* (Vatican City: Biblioteca Apostolica Vaticana, 1952); F. Babinger, *Sultanische Urkunden zur Geschichte der osmanischen Wirtschaft und Staatsverwaltung am Ausgang der Herrschaft Mehmeds II., des Eroberers* (Munich: Oldenbourg, 1956).

23. The only modification that I adopted from Doerfer's article was the following: if -Ub never occurs in its longer form -UbAn/-IbAn or in its old form -Ib, even after labial vowels, it is counted as an item but receives no points (0) (see Doerfer, "Zur Auswertung," 102). There is still no sign of the later evolution toward the modern form -Ib^{4}/-Ip^{4}, which means that we can follow Doerfer's pattern of -Ub's being the most modern form for the periods covered by his study.

TABLE 5. Opposition of I versus U with Suffixes -l-, -n-, and -ş- for Open and Closed Syllables of the *Süleymānnāme*

-l-				-n-				-ş-			
Open		*Closed*		*Open*		*Closed*		*Open*		*Closed*	
I	U	I	U	I	U	I	U	I	U	I	U
62	12	3	18	84	469	32	161	—	5	—	4

AK from the dates of composition and copy respectively. This tells whether the text is older (positive numbers) or younger (negative numbers) than one would expect from its date of composition or from its date of copy. The whole line would read: 25a 21a/23a 27a −2/−6(−4).

At first sight, the discrepancy between the AK and the numbers of the second column seems high, but we must not forget that titles 21–24 in this column of Doerfer's table are sixteenth-century copies of much older works and that the table contains a relatively small number of texts originally dating from the sixteenth century (the list starting with Sultan Veled and going down to the eighteenth century). The conclusion therefore seems to be that the degree of antiquity of the *Süleymānnāme* shown by the vowel signs of non-first syllables corresponds well both to the date of composition and the date of copy.

Let us look at a few details: Professor Doerfer has found out that the suffixes -Il-, -In-, and -Iş- first changed into -Ul-, -Un-, and -Uş- after labials when they occurred in closed syllables, and later became -Ul-, -Un-, -Uş- in open syllables. The suffix that was most subject to this change was -Il-.[24] For the *Süleymānnāme*, we can calculate the opposition of I versus U with these three suffixes, as follows (see table 5).

Table 6 shows the relative ratio of I to U (I:U), using the numbers of table 5. The corresponding numbers from Doerfer's analysis are given in brackets; however, they refer to all of Doerfer's 30 works.[25]

Table 7 sums up the data for open and closed syllables in the *Süleymānnāme* in the form of the ratio I:U. It also presents the corresponding numbers from Doerfer's analysis in parentheses.[26]

My numbers differ in many respects from those of Doerfer.[27] (1) I have considered one work only, whereas the relative numbers in Doerfer's list refer to an average of all the 30 works he analyzes. (2) The statistics have perhaps

24. Doerfer, *Zum Vokalismus*, 29.
25. Ibid.
26. Ibid.
27. Ibid.

TABLE 6. The Relative Ratio of I to U in the *Süleymānnāme*, Including a Comparison with Doerfer's Analysis

-l-		-n-		-ş-	
Open	*Closed*	*Open*	*Closed*	*Open*	*Closed*
1:0.193	1:6	1:5.583	1:5.031	0:5	0:4
(1:0.344)	(1:3.107)	(1:0.283)	(1:1.705)	(1:0.104)	(1:0.583)

TABLE 7. Summary of the Data for Open and Closed Syllables in the *Süleymānnāme*, with Comparative Data from Doerfer

Suffixes	*I/U*	*Ratio*	*Doerfer*
-l-	65:30	1:0.462	(1:1.336)
-n-	116:630	1:5.43	(1:0.823)
-ş-	0:9	0:9	(1:0.298)

become a little unbalanced because of the overwhelming frequency of phraseological verbs formed with *olın-/olun-*. (3) On the whole, the AK of the *Süleymānnāme* is rather low. Probably this is partly due to the fact that we are confronted with the latest stage of these three suffixes; that is, -U- is stronger in all positions except one—when -Il- occurs in an open syllable.[28]

An old feature, however, is the reduction of an intermediate vowel (*görinür* > *görnür*).[29] Although I could not find any reduction with this suffix, I found several instances of *olınıcaḳ* > *olıncaḳ* (for example, 52v/9).

The genitive suffix is -Uñ in all of Doerfer's texts except the one from the eighteenth century. Bostān, however, uses -Iñ seven times, mostly in the word *memālikiñ* (for example, 183r/11 and 229r/7), but also in *nehr-i Nīliñ* (84v/6), *Bālī Begiñ* (31r/12).

According to Doerfer,[30] the accusative was the first case ending in which -I changed to -U with the third person of the possessive. In the *Süleymānnāme*, however, we find all the accusatives ending in -InI (if not -In), whereas there are already other case endings (except the nominative) with -U, for example, *ucuna* (170r/8), *oğluna* (206v/6), *ḳullu ḳulunca* (186v/9), *tedārükünde* (145v/1), and *yoluna* (196r/8).

28. Doerfer even suggests that in order to determine a rough AK of any given text, it would be sufficient to investigate these three suffixes (Doerfer, "Zur Auswertung," sub 3.3).

29. Doerfer, *Zum Vokalismus*, 65.

30. Ibid., 49ff., 91, 101.

If the vocalization of a text was influenced by the less conservative spoken language of the author's or the copyist's times, it will betray evidence of an uncertainty in the way the vowel signs were used. There are frequent misspellings in which both possible signs, old and new, are put over or under a word.[31] The *Süleymānnāme* shows many such instances, for example, *eksü/i/k* (50r/1, 59v/3), *degü/i/l* (79v/2, 89r/6), *olı/u/nub* (9r/8, 14v/12, 17v/2, 19r/6), *yüri/ü/yüş* (36r/14), *yüri/ü/yüb* (107v/14), *indü/i/rüb* (34v/9), and *eyledü/i/kde* (148v/5).[32]

The words *ṭoğru, ṭolu* 'hail' and *köprü* originally had final U; the U was changed to I in western Anatolia.[33] Although most of the other features are of a purely diachronic nature, this fact in itself would allow us to classify the *Süleymānnāme* as being of western Anatolian origin. This fits Bostān's biography[34] perfectly, as well as that of the copyist, Prince Muṣṭafā.

Four different stages of the development of vowels in non-first syllables can be distinguished, but some texts belong to intermediate stages because they contain both ancient and modern elements.[35] The *Süleymānnāme* could, on the whole, range between Doerfer's stages 2 and 3.

In works that contain prose as well as poetry, the language of the poetic parts is usually more conservative than that of the prose. This can be seen especially in the case of the passive suffix.[36] Bostān's own poems are of course bound to be on the same linguistic level as his prose. I am not in a position to check this, however, because of the relatively small number of poems called *li-müᵓellifihī* (36).[37] The forms relevant for this purpose occur far too rarely to be significant.

Poems quoted in a prose text which are not by the same author must be older than the text itself. But unless it is a very well-known poem—unfortunately, authors very rarely mention their sources—we cannot determine its age.

In this reason, I tried Professor Doerfer's method on poems with the headings *shiᶜr* or *miṣrāᶜ*. Unfortunately, the majority of poems—all very short ones—are written in Persian, some of them in Arabic, and those composed in Turkish do not provide us with enough material. Apart from the archaic form *olıcağaz* (72v/5), there are no particularly ancient features. As regards the vowels

31. Ibid., 68.

32. For the statistics discussed earlier, I have, of course, counted all such cases as being modern.

33. Doerfer, *Zum Vokalismus*, 58ff.

34. See Yurdaydın, "Bostân'ın," 189–91.

35. Doerfer, *Zum Vokalismus*, 91–92.

36. Ibid., 27.

37. On these, see n. 3 above.

in non-first syllables, I have found old and new forms, just as I did in other contexts throughout the work. It seems that there is one modern aorist in -Ir, *dürişir* (140r/9), but the vocalization is not quite clear. In any case, the sample of vowels in non-first syllables is far too small to allow any conclusions.

The Indifference Stage of Labial Harmony

On the basis of the vowels of non-first syllables occurring in the *Süleymānnāme*, we can classify it as belonging to the second of Johanson's three stages of labial harmony, namely the indifference stage.[38] This is the stage where we can observe (a) an obvious inclination toward using labial and nonlabial forms indiscriminately and (b) variants of vowels that tend toward a neutral position of the lips.[39] The aforementioned double vowel signs like *degü/i/l* could perhaps be interpreted not only as reflecting an uncertainty about the vowel to use but also as a reflex of this development.

Bostān's Style

Let us now look more closely at some striking features of Bostān's style. Yurdaydın has already mentioned briefly that Bostān uses similar phrases when describing similar events.[40] In order to illustrate this I shall quote a passage from each of the two *sūrnāme* pieces. One of the competitions to be won during both feasts of circumcision was to climb to the top of a high pillar.[41]

> 170r/7ff.
> *ʿarṣa-i çeşnigāhda bir yağlu ve müstedīr ʿamūd naṣb olınmış-idiki farḳına rīsimān-i şuʿāʿ-i baṣar ve evc-i semāya mümāss olan ucuna kemend-i naẓar yétişmezdi ol gün baʿż-i cüst u cābük kimesneler zūr-i bāzū ve ḳuvvet-i enāmil ile mezbur ʿamūda ṣuʿūd édüb içlerinden biri ser-i ʿamūda yétişüb ol sebeb-ile ʿināyet-i ʿalīye-i pādişāhiye maẓhar olub ve māl u menāl vérilüb ol devlet-i (!) ensābına yétişdi*

38. Lars Johanson, "Die westoghusische Labialharmonie," *Orientalia Suecana* 27–28 (1978–79) 63–107.

39. See also idem, "Zum Suffixvokalismus in zwei mittelosmanischen Transkriptionstexten," *WZKM* 76 (1986) 165; idem, "The Indifference Stage of Turkish Suffix Vocalism," *TDAY Belleten* (1978–79) 151–56.

40. Yurdaydın, "Bostân'ın," 193.

41. A similar contest is described in the *Sūrnāme-i hümāyūn*, MS ÖNB H.O. 70, fol. 9r–10r, 69r; cf. Procházka-Eisl, *Die Wiener Handschrift*, transliteration.

321r/10 sqq.
ve ᶜarṣa-i çeşnigāhda bir müstedīr ve yağlu ᶜamūd naṣb olundıki fevḳine rīsumān-i şuᶜāᶜ-i baṣar ve evc-i semāya mümāss olan ucına kemend-i naẓar yétişmezdi ol gün baᶜż-i cüst u çāpük kimesneler rūz-i bāzūr (!) ve ḳuvvet-i enāmil ile mezbūr ᶜamūda ṣuᶜūd édüb içlerinden bir niçesi ser-i ᶜamūda yétişüb ol sebeb-ile ᶜināyet-i ᶜalīye-i pādişāhīye maẓhar düşüb ser-firāz u bī-niyāz oldılar

On the field of the feast they had erected an oiled round pillar, whose upper end could not be reached by the thread of the rays of the look and whose top, which touched the summit of heaven, could not be reached by the bow of the glance. That day several select (?) and swift persons climbed onto the aforementioned pillar by the strength of the(ir) arms and the force of the(ir) fingertips. One of them (Some of them) got to the top of the pillar and therefore the lofty imperial grace was bestowed upon him (them), he was (they were) given goods and chattels and attained the (status of) a fellow of the state (?) (and they got high ranks and became content).

We have to confine ourselves to this one example, but there are many more such instances, for example, a show of jugglers during the circumcision (168r/13ff., 322r/5ff.); the causes of the fall of Cānberdi Ğazzālī 11r/11–13), İbrāhīm Paşa (244r/4ff.), and Aḥmed Paşa (84v/13ff.) are described by the same words with very few changes.

Bostān has a repertoire—not necessarily all invented by himself but common to the *inşā* style[42]—of short phrases, partly containing *secᶜ* elements, from which he chooses according to the situation, for example:[43]

- *ḳażā-yi mübrem ve seyl-i ᶜaremrem gibi* 'like a decree of Providence and a torrent of an army'[44] (86v/9, 121r/7, 143r/12, 159r/8, 342v/9, . . .)
- *shevket-i ᶜuẓmā ve ḥaşmet-i kübrā ile* 'with great pomp and big display' (115r/3, 128r/1, 156v/9, 159v/3–4, 171r/10, 241v/2, 345v/12, . . .)
- *ṭabl u ᶜalem khadem u ḥaşem birle* 'with drums and flags, with servants and retinue' (181v/6–7, 198r/3–4, 206r/9, 283r/11, 259v/8, 261v/6, 328r/1–2, . . .)
- *farṭ-i şevket ve ferr-i übehhet ile* 'with abundant pomp and beaming magnificence' (285r/2, . . .)

42. A. Tietze, "Muṣṭafā ᶜĀlī's Prose Style," *Archivum Ottomanicum* 5 (1973) 297–319.

43. Because of limited space, I can neither quote all these phrases nor all the instances in which they occur.

44. It should actually be *seyl-i ᶜarem*, meaning the 'flood that destroyed the city of Seba' (see Redhouse, s.v. *seyl*).

- *rūy-i ḳarārın cihet-i firāra dönderüb* 'they turned their face of stability into the direction of flight' (297r/12–13, . . .)
- *tünd-bād-i devlete süvār olub* 'he (i.e., Süleymān) mounted the swiftly running (horse) of the state (or, "of felicity")' (257v/11, 271r/4, 284v/13, . . .)
- *vadī^{c}āt-i ḥayātı mutaḳażī-yi ecel-i mev^{c}ūda teslīm édüb* 'he entrusted the deposit of life to the importunate appointed term of death' (44v/7–8, 177r/6, 198v/4, 204v/3–4, 251r/6, . . .)
- *şihāb-şitāb ulaḳlar* 'messengers fast as clouds' (192r/7–8, 206r/5, 215r/11, 239v/6, . . .)
- *cengī er ve güzīde leşker* 'warriors and select troops' (310v/6–7, . . .) or *güzīde er ve yarar leşker* 'select men and brave troops' (342r/13, . . .)
- *bāmı şāma ve ṣabāḥı revāḥa ulaşdurdılar* 'they made the morning reach the evening' (161v/3, . . .); the same can be expressed by a different wording, for example, 217r/11, or even in the form of a chiasm: *ṣabāḥı revāḥa ve revāḥı ṣabāḥa ulaşdurmışlardı* 'they made the morning reach the evening and they made the evening reach the morning' (253v/10).
- *sūr-i mevfūrü s-sürūr* 'the feast of manifold happiness' (167r/7, 11; 169r/6, 170v/8, 172r/13, 315v/6, 11–12, . . .)[45]
- *ğirīv-i ṣūrnā ve nefīr ve ṣedāy-i naḳḳāra ve kūs-i rūyīn tāsça-i ^{c}illiyīn u sipihr-i berīni pür-ṭanīn ḳılmışdı* 'the noise of the trumpet and the horn, the voices of the drum and the bronze kettledrum had filled the cup of paradise with buzzing' (167r/8–9, 319v/1–3).

As we have seen, Bostān makes abundant use of short *sec^{c}* phrases as well as longer periods adorned with *sec^{c}*. Of this phenomenon, too well known to be further discussed here,[46] I shall give but two less-common examples. One combines a Qur$^{\supset}$ānic verse with Ottoman *sec^{c}*:

242r/10–12
çün kelām-i i^{c}cāz-i (!) mahṣūṣ inna llāha yuḥibbu llaḏīna yuḳātilūna fī sabīlihī ṣaffan ka-annahum bunyānun marṣūṣun feḥvāsı mūcebince ḥażret-i ṣāḥib-ḳirān. . . .

45. This seems to be a common expression; see Procházka-Eisl, *Die Wiener Handschrift*, passim.
46. See, e.g., A. Tietze, "Muṣṭafā."

> When, according to the inimitable word, "Verily Allah loveth those who fight in His way drawn up in ranks, like a building well-compacted" (61:4), His majesty the lord of the happy conjunction. . . .

The other example to be mentioned here is a purely Turkish imitation of *sec*^{c} quoted earlier: 121r/9–10 *bir uzaḳ azmaḳ ve bir ıraḳ bataḳ var idi* 'there was a big flooding and a great swamp'.

When Bostān introduces the coming of spring or the sunrise, he often uses elaborate but quite usual comparisons, the vocabulary of which suits the context. But he often goes on to explain what he actually means by an extra sentence and/or verse. I have counted more than twenty instances of this throughout the *Süleymānnāme*, for example:

> 61v/6ff.
> *yarındası gün vaḳtī ki fülk-i şafaḳ-sirā*^{c} *u felaḳ-şirā*^{c} *a*^{c}*nī āfitāb-i* ^{c}*ālem-tāb* ^{c}*amūd-i fecirden lenger alub baḥr-i akhżar-i sipihre ṣalub mehābetinden encüm zevraḳları gürīzān ve zemīn u zemān ferr-i vürūdından müteʾelliḳ ve direkhşān olmış-idi a*^{c}*nī bih şi*^{c}*r dar ān dūz (recte: davr) kīn turk(-i) sulṭān-şukūh* zi daryā-yi çīn khayme bar-zad ba-kūh ḥażret-i ṣāḥib-ḳirān-i gerdūn-ğulām a*^{c}*yān ve erkān ve khuddām-i encüm-iḥtişāmı ile bād-seyr ve ṣaḥāb-peyker gemilere binüb.*
>
> On the next day when the ship that sails swiftly in the dawn and twilight, I mean[47] the sun that shines upon the world, had raised anchor from the pillar of dawn and left for the green sea of the firmament, and when the boats of the stars had fled awe-stricken and earth and time had become sparkling and flashing through the glow of his arrival, I mean by this—poem: at this moment when this Turk of sultanic majesty* (coming) from the Chinese sea erected his tent on the mountain[48]—His majesty, the lord of the happy conjunction, who is served by the (whole) world, and his notables, ministers and servants, who are numerous as the stars, went aboard cloud-like ships swift as the wind.

A shortened but otherwise nearly identical version of this description is to be found on 296v/3–4, but the poem inserted there is quite different.

Twelve other characteristic features of Bostān's prose can be identified:

1. He uses *gün günden* 'from one day to the other' frequently (59r/9, 73v/10, 84r/10, 95v/11, 138v/6, 180v/3, 206r/1 . . .).

47. At the end of such passages Bostān also often uses the phrase *bu teşbībden murād budur ki* 'the purpose of this comparison is the following', for example, 84r/3, 139v/1–2, 164r/13, 179r/9, 200r/12.

48. The meter here is *mutaḳārib* v--/v--/v--/v-.

2. The construction . . . *ṣadedinde ol-* occurs about twice as often as *ḳasd ét-* 'to plan' (57v/1, 60r/10, 60v/2, 64r/8, 90v/8, 120r/8, 140r/12, . . .).

3. One finds *muḥāfaẓat* instead of *muḥāfaẓa* 'to keep' (138v/5, 155r/6, 254r/13, . . .).

4. Although the genitive of *ṣu* is quite regular in the *Süleymānnāme*, there are two instances of *ṣunuñ* (85r/10, 356r/3).

5. Normally the form *yıldu*z is used, but *ıldu*z also shows up (109r/12).

6. Verbal composition does occur, although it does not play an important part as a stylistic device, for example, *ḳovagiden* 'who chases' (126v/9), *arayu gitdi* 'he went to search for' (262v/5), *ta*ᶜ*āḳub eyleyügelüb* 'he kept following' (285r/11–12), *dökilüḳalub* 'it was spilt' (290r/11).

7. *Dates.* Bostān has several ways of rendering dates. There is, of course, the normal construction, for example, *sene-i mezbūre Ramażānınuñ ikinci güni ki düşenbe günidür* 'on the second day of Ramaḍān of the aforementioned year, which was a Monday' (151r/7). But about twice as often there is no possessive suffix with *gün*, for example, *sene-i s̱elās̱īn ve-tis*ᶜ*ami*ᵓ*e Ẕī l-ḥiccesinüñ ikinci gün* 'on the second day of Dhū l-ḥijja of the year 930' (92r/3).[49] In these cases one could understand the genitive as an attribute of *gün.*[50] A rather unusual way to express a date, however, is the following: *māh-i mezbūruñ yigirmi üçüncisi gün* 'the twenty-third day of the aforementioned month' (159v/3). This may, of course, be an error, but there still remain many instances of other not-very-common constructions, namely, *muḥārebeden üçünci gün ṣoñra* 'the third day after the battle' (134r/10), *ikinci günden ṣoñra*, literally, 'after the second day' but simply meaning 'two days later' (259r/4, 347v/7, 350r/13, . . .).

8. As will have become evident from the longer quotations, there is no clear strategy as to how complex phrases formed of two synonyms are connected to one another, by *u* or *ve* (e.g., *fülk-i şafaḳ-sirā*ᶜ *u felaḳ-şirā*ᶜ versus *a*ᶜ*yān ve erkān*; see above).

49. For more examples from other texts, see Prokosch, *Studien zur Grammatik des Osmanisch-Türkischen unter besonderer Berücksichtigung des Vulgärosmanisch-Türkischen* (Studien zur Sprache, Geschichte und Kultur der Türkvölker 2; Freiburg and Berlin: Schwarz, 1980) 37ff.

50. Cf. my *Osmanische Festungsbesatzungen in Ungarn zur Zeit Murads III, dargestellt an Hand von Petitionen zur Stellenvergabe* (Vienna, 1995) 82–84; for similar constructions, see Andreas Tietze, "Der freistehende Genitiv im Türkei-Türkischen," *UAJb* 30 (1958) 187–88.

9. There is no regularity for using the Izafet-sign with names, for example, *dārü l-mülk-i maḥrūse-i Istanbula* (135r/12, 145r/12, . . .) versus *dārü l-mülk maḥrūse-i Ḳosṭanṭinīye* (163r/5, 166r/1, . . .); and *Venedīk melāᶜīn* 'the cursed Venetians' (309v/6) versus *Ḳızılbaş-i melāᶜīn* 'the cursed Ḳızılbaş' (301v/3).

10. Often Bostān combines two verbs by using *-ub ve*, but he also leaves out the conjunction in other instances, for example, *ḳonub göçüb* (127v/7) versus *ḳonub ve göçüb* (156v/7). In the colloquial language, the use of *ve* after the gerund in *-ub* indicates that *-ub* is treated almost as a finite verb.[51]

11. *Phraseological verbs.* Besides the normal phraseological verbs with *ét-*, *eyle-*, *ol-*, *olun-*, and so forth, Bostān uses the verb *ṣal-* in a variety of cases, especially when referring to the sultan or the sun.

- *sāye-i vuṣūl ṣal-* 'to throw the shadow of arrival on. . . .' (e.g., 213v/10, 220r/3–4)
- *pertev-i vuṣūl ṣal-* 'to throw the light of arrival on . . .' (e.g., 212r/6, 228v/2)
  pertev-i nüzūl ṣal- 'to throw the light of settling down on . . .' (e.g., 202r/8, 227r/11)
- *lenger ṣal-* 'to weigh anchor' (e.g., 194v/10, 234r/12)
  deryāya ṣal- (ships) 'to sail' (e.g., 194v/9, 257r/2)

The word *çek-* is mostly to be found with *pişkeş* 'to bring presents' (e.g., 199r/3–4); *niᶜmet* or sorts of food 'to offer' (e.g., 211v/1); *ḳalem-i beyān* 'to draw the pen of explanation' (e.g., 225v/12); *kilk-i beyān* also 'to draw the pen of explanation' (e.g., 298v/2); *ḳalem-i ᶜafv* 'to draw the pen of forgiveness over . . .' (e.g., 286v/10–11).

The most intriguing peculiarity of Bostān's style is that he especially likes phraseological verbs with *göster-*. There is a total of 357 occurrences of verbs formed with *göster-*, out of which we could count 126 different verbs. This means that there is an average of about one such verb per folio. Thirteen of these verbs occur more than 5 times, thus covering more than 50% of all the verbs with *göster-*. The most common are verbs of movement and nonmovement, verbs that mean 'glow', 'shine', and others; verbs combined with abstract nouns; and those combined with words like *ṣūret*, *şekl*, and *ḥālet*, which may be met with in other texts as well. The subjects of these verbs are (quoted by

51. Prokosch, *Studien zur Grammatik*, 145ff.

decreasing number of occurrences) the sultan; the troops; high officials; time; waves, stars, swords, the sultan's grace, and so forth; and artists. These verbs are often part of izafet or *sec*^{c} constructions. Here are some examples: *müşārün ileyh paşa . . . semt-i ğaẓāya teveccüh ve* ^{c}*aẓīmet gösterdiler* 'the aforementioned pasha . . . turned to and set out on the path of fighting' (53v/13–54r/6); *ḥażret-i ṣāḥib-ḳirān-i se*^{c}*ādet-şi*^{c}*ār . . . on gün miḳdārı ol maḥal* (!) *ḳarar ve istirāḥat gösterdiler* 'His majesty, the lord of the conjunction of happiness, . . . stayed and rested there for ten days' (110v/6–111r/4); *leşker-i manṣūr mez̲kūr köpriden dakhı* ^{c}*ubūr eyleyüb şühüb-i rücūm gibi şeyāṭīn-i khuṣūma ḥücūm göstermişlerdi* 'The victorious troops crossed the aforementioned bridge and assaulted the devilish enemies as if they were meteor-like missiles' (188r/13–188v/4).

12. *Subordinate clauses.* Bostān very often (more than 90 times) uses subordinate clauses beginning with *ki* or *ammā ki*, some of which seem strange and rather burden the text.[52] These clauses mostly end with a verbal form that makes *ki* or *ammā ki* totally superfluous. I shall content myself with offering just two examples.

> 28v/13–29r/2
> *ammā ki maḥall-i meẓbūr sābıḳda maḳarr-i küffār ve ma*^{c}*had-i eşrār olmağın ṭarafeynüñ taṣādumından ḥavālīsinde olan memālik niçe günlük menẓil kharāb olub.*
>
> But as the aforementioned place earlier had been the home of the unbelievers and a gathering point of rebels, several days' journey of surrounding land had been devastated through the collisions of both sides.
>
> 25v/13–26r/5
> *ma*^{c}*a hāz̲ā ki be-ğāyet şitāb ile gidüb tüfeng u ṭopa ve sāyir ühübe* (!) *tevaḳḳuf ḳılmamışlardı ammā ki nabż-i ğayret-i islām ve* ^{c}*irḳ-i ḥamīyet-i īmān ḥareket ve żarabān édüb ṣavaşdan yüẓ döndermeyüb şolki ās̱ār-i şecā*^{c}*at ve merāsim-i celādetdür ẓuhūra getürdiler.*
>
> Although they had gone very hurriedly and not bothered about guns and cannons and other weapons, they instigated and made throbbing the pulsation of Islamic zeal and the veins of the heat of belief and did not turn their faces away from the battle and they showed the signs of bravery and the traces of courage.

We can conclude that Bostān's prose is as much influenced by Arabic and Persian as other contemporary works, and the Arabic vocabulary even seems to be a little more predominant than elsewhere. Vowels in non-first syllables

52. For other examples, see ibid., 174 and 178.

reflect the *Süleymānnāme*'s closeness to the spoken language of the middle of the sixteenth century. Although the *Süleymānnāme*, as a whole, is not too different in style from similar works of the same period, we can discern several of the author's distinctive characteristics. Bostān turns out to be a skilled writer, who handles well the stylistic devices of *inşā* prose (*sec*ᶜ, alliteration, parallelism, comparisons, and so on).[53] His tendency, however, to repeat whole passages with only small variations, wherever they fit into the context (just as he repeats his own poems and those of others),[54] is not necessarily a sign of a great literary gift. At the same time, the fluency of the *Süleymānnāme* is somewhat disrupted by Bostān's excessive use of subordinate clauses. These peculiarities make him a writer of second rank only, in comparison to such great masters of Ottoman prose as Muṣṭafā ᶜĀlī or Djelālzāde Muṣṭafā.

53. On the main principles of this art, see Tietze, "Muṣṭafā," 298–311; and Kappert, *Geschichte*, 36–40.

54. Römer, "Bostān," 242.

Language and Script in Ancient Egypt

Hans Goedicke

As much as it is a pleasure to congratulate Georg Krotkoff, it is also a problem to find an appropriate topic for a book honoring him. We have known each other for almost half a century. This brings a level of familiarity, but the disparity in our academic disciplines creates a few problems for communicating. Having grown up bilingual, Georg Krotkoff did not stop there, but language became the dominant theme of his intellectual life. However, for him, language was not to be treated with a dissecting, analytical attitude but primarily as communication. One could describe him as a polyglot in the traditional sense, rather than a linguist in the modern one. Although our first contacts were in the Institute of Egyptology in Vienna, ancient Egyptian was one of the languages that remained beyond his perimeter. It is thus only appropriate that some reflections about this language are presented on this occasion.

These days, when individual communication over distances in space or time becomes increasingly overshadowed by mechanical, extra-human technologies, it seems all the more necessary to reflect on the interaction of language and writing. Without the latter, communication between people would be limited to the immediate participants. It is also the single element that shaped what is fundamental to all human existence and generated the qualities that traditionally were considered the most profound human ones. Interest in writing is indeed nothing new, and there are reams of writings on writing. These works have, to dare a sweeping observation, two points in common: first, that "writing . . . (is) the use of graphic signs for the systematic description of spoken language," to quote the opening statement of a recent discourse on the topic by Joseph Naveh;[1] second, that there is a positive evolution from primitive "pictographs" to the system we use, the alphabet.[2]

Writing is certainly not an innate human form of expression in the same way that speaking is—that is, the production of sounds. If this notion needs any support, two arguments are readily available. First, *writing*, meaning the communicating outside of space and time with the help of graphic notations, has been in use for a little over 5,000 years. Compared with the biological history of the anthropoid, this span of time is minute. Second, it requires great effort, as we all know, to introduce a human being to writing—and not always with overwhelming success. If, as seems apparent, writing is a human invention of a fundamental nature, an important question arises: was writing invented recurrently, or is its ubiquitous use the result of the dissemination of a single invention?[3]

It is commonly known that the first comprehensive system for making meaningful notations belonged to the Sumerians in southern Mesopotamia. To attach a date to its appearance, ca. 3100 B.C., seems reasonable, although it

1. Joseph Naveh, *Early History of the Alphabet* (Jerusalem, 1987) 1.

2. The notion is expressed in a nutshell in Kurt Sethe, "Vom Bilde zum Buchstaben: Die Entstehungsgeschichte der Schrift," *Untersuchungen zur Geschichte und Altertumskunde Ägyptens* 12 (1939).

3. It was especially Ignace J. Gelb (*A Study of Writing* [Chicago, 1952], 190ff.), who stressed the interconnection between the various writing systems. The difficulty of linking the Meso-American writing with the otherwise closely intertwined efforts to write have spawned the notion of an indigenous invention. Chronologically, the emergence of writing in Central America is in good accord with the use of writing in other parts of the world. This writing appears full-fledged without any discernible preparatory steps, which seems surprising. Other systems that commence in an advanced stage are the result of either emulating or borrowing an already existing system. One of the obstacles concerning the Meso-American writing is the implicit notion that cultural contacts require firm and continuous links. However, when it comes to writing, a distinction should be made between a familiarity with the concept of writing and the technical know-how of its execution. The transfer of the former from one cultural area to another requires only one individual, who does not necessarily have to be trained in the execution of writing but is nevertheless familiar with its principles.

should not be taken with any excessive desire for precision. What we find at this date are small clay tablets onto which signs were scratched with a stylus. These "signs" represent simplified but nevertheless clearly recognizable pictures of objects. As a result they are frequently labeled pictographs, from which the notion of "picture writing" was born.[4] It is essential for the sake of clarity to analyze this conceptual hybrid. Man has been able to reproduce the optical images conceived around him in the Cro-Magnon caves.[5] Intriguing as some of these pictures are, they cannot be considered "writing." What separates these pictures from "writing" is obviously not the medium itself, because both depict objects of the physical world. It is, rather, a different aim underlying their making. While "pictures" are a rendering of impressions the physical world makes on the artist who fashions them, writing is principally an expressive notion. It is not motivated by capturing a vista, but rather aims at conveying something on the writer's mind that is outside of the immediacy of space and time. In other words, while pictures render impressions of and in the existential world, writing expresses thought and is thus the result of abstracting processes.

A picture, especially when motivated by eidetics,[6] can convey astounding aesthetic qualities, but it does not convey rational meaning. Writing, on the other hand, does not necessarily convey aesthetic qualities but does impart meaning, which is to say, it is the result of thinking. Aside from the technical merit, which plays a major role in the appearance of either product, the distinguishing feature of writing appears to be abstraction. However, this does not mean that pictures are devoid of any abstraction; on the contrary, early drawings—and this is not necessarily a chronological qualification—sometimes display a remarkable degree of abstraction. As a result, they convey meaning, which, however, due to the medium, remains general. For example, a depiction of a small group of people with gestures of greeting cannot indicate whether this action is in welcome or in farewell; nor can it distinguish the greeters from the greeted. The same ambiguity applies to the picture of a king: it conveys nothing about the person, such as age, name, qualification, or many other things. In short, pictures—and there are, of course, varying stages—can impart a more or less detailed impression but not specific communication. Indeed, pictures in one respect reflect the same mental process also responsible for the invention of writing because of their being influenced in differing degrees by abstraction, that is, the concentration on the typical at the expense of the general expression. It is

4. The term is commonly used without much effort to define the contradiction in it.

5. Most famously, of course, at Lascaux; see, e.g., M. Ruspoli, *The Cave of Lascaux: The Final Photographs* (New York, 1987).

6. E. R. Jaensch, *Die Eidetik und die typologische Wahrnehmungsmethode* (1933).

this very process that also constitutes the matrix of intellectual reasoning by abstracting the phenomenal as the prerequisite for any hermeneutics.

While, of course, "writing" did not spring forth in a fashion comparable to Athena's birth from Zeus' head and thus had forerunners for trying out the technical aspects, the only system that can be considered writing is the one that allows one to communicate fully and that is able to cope with such abstracts as names and similar specifications, individualizing the object of communication. The Promethean breakthrough can be assigned to the analysis and the abstraction of the flow of spoken communication into units, that is, words. Only the awareness of them as individual elements could provide the basis from which writing could evolve. The fact that *eye* and *fly* were idiomatic units made them conceptually isolated. The differentiation of semantic elements constituted an essential step but was not yet writing. Its creation is ultimately due to the realization that a "word," that is, an idiomatic unit, combines two aspects, namely a specific sound pattern and a "meaning." This dichotomy and its separation are not only the vertex of all inquiry into language, as de Saussure emphasized,[7] but also the matrix from which some human genius, whose identity we will never know, invented writing.

It is the realization that sound and meaning, the two aspects of a "word," can be separated that was in this case the proverbial "egg of Columbus." For example, *eye* as a sound-pattern not only indicates the organ for seeing but also the first person, the *ego*, or *fly* can be the phoneme for the insect or for the activity of suspension in the air. Based on this principle of identical or similar sound patterns, termed *homophony*, writing had its beginning. One could utilize the homophony of words to depict abstract ideas in writing in cases where one of the homophonous words represented a depictable object and the other represented a concept that did not lend itself to graphic representation. Consequently,  could be rendered phonetically as "I fly." However, the number of homophones in any language, even if applied liberally, is limited. This inspired as the next step the combination of word phonemes. As a demonstration, combining an  with (a runner), one could have indicated "i-ron." The same principle lies behind the game of charades, which used to be a favorite pastime. This form of notation has its obvious shortcomings. There are first of all not sufficient words that can be indicated graphically and that offer themselves for sound combinations based on the charade principle; in order to overcome this, short phonetic groups were adopted for filling in the gaps. Secondly, such a notation system on the basis of "word-signs" or "logograms" would have completely disregarded the other aspect innate in a word, namely the meaning, that is, its intellectual content. The two symbols  put together could pho-

7. Ferdinand de Saussure, *Course in General Linguistics* (New York, 1959) 14–15.

netically be read as "I run" or as "iron." Reflecting the double nature of language better than most of its modern counterparts, fledgling writing made use of a double system of notations, one indicating the sound pattern of a word, the other its meaning. In other words, early writing maintained a distinction between phonetic indicators and meaning indicators, or what de Saussure called "parole" and "langue," the latter being an addition to the former.

It is impossible to define the historical circumstances of the emergence of Egyptian writing beyond the impact of the Sumerian model. The very fact that it is an emulation rather than a direct acceptance has one major consequence. There is no need to envisage any specific physical contact between the Nile Valley and Mesopotamia to provide the basis for the unquestionable transfer of know-how.[8] One individual would ultimately suffice for it, without speculating as to details. The very fact that the earliest application of writing occurs in connection with the institution of kingship would make it likely that it attracted the bearer of authority in the land.

Because of the external impetus in its emergence,[9] writing went through a lengthy process before it became a medium for communication. The earliest writings preserved are names, which is the most abstract use of a word. The notion that *scorpion* as a king's name is to be taken literally in the sense that the person denoted this way was considered a "scorpion" would hardly have been flattering, especially in view of the negative reputation the scorpion had at all times in Egyptian lore.[10] The same applies to the famous Narmer, whose name takes on a curious note when rendered 'angry catfish'.[11] Again, the use of the catfish in writing cannot be explained on pictographic grounds but only as the result of the intellectual abstractions that form the basis of ancient Egyptian writing, namely as a phonetic indication. As a result, these names

8. The question of interrelationship between the hieroglyphic and the cuneiform systems is widely debated, with viewpoints frequently determined by emotional association. While a direct takeover due to ethnic movement (namely, migration) is highly unlikely, the possibility of an impetus from the Mesopotamian cultural orbit into the Nile Valley would seem the most satisfactory explanation. Once the impetus was received (see Wolfgang Helck, *Zeitschrift für Ägyptische Sprache und Altertumskunde* 80 [1955] 144–45), the further development followed different lines.

9. W. Schenkel (*Lexikon der Ägyptologie* [7 vols.; Wiesbaden, 1975–92] 5.726) is certainly to be followed when he denies a cultic origin of writing. However, he sees the origin of writing to be in the administrative needs of a central administration. Now, administrative needs unquestionably had a major impact on the formation of the skill, but I am not as convinced that it was the determining cause.

10. See my work in *LÄ* 5.98 9–90.

11. Wolfgang Helck, "Geschichte des Alten Ägypten," *Handbuch der Orientalistik* (1968) 22; Gérard Godron ("À propos du nom royal," *Annales du Service des Antiquités de l'Égypte* 49 [1949] 217ff.), rendering it 'aimé de $N^{c}r$'; cf. also Vladimir Vikentiev, *Journal of Egyptian Archaeology* 17 (1931) 67ff.

should be read as *Srq* and as *Nᶜr*[12] and understood as nominally used participles describing the bearer of the name as "the strangler" and "the fighter,"[13] both in relation to Horus, the "godhead."[14]

Although the principle of writing already prevailed in its earliest attestations in ancient Egypt, it was an extensive process before this tool became used for communication in the way familiar to the modern person. Names as the earliest form of "writing" are the outflow of a conceptual concern, namely the identification of personal dominion. In other words, the use of the early names is not part of a "communication" but is rather to be seen as a statement of personal association, that is, of possession. As indicators of property, the use of names appears to be a continuation of earlier efforts of this sort, namely the so-called "pottery marks."[15] Their specific quality consists in conveying to others the personal claim in the form of a statement.

The property indication continues to act as a force in the expansion of writing from annotating to a full communicative instrument. The identification of the proprietor as subject is followed almost instantly by the identification of the object of property, including place of origin, purpose of use, and so forth.[16] Out of this rudimentary form, the use of writing was developed as an administrative tool. One of its initial points of crystallization was the recording of immaterial property,[17] specifically in the form of titles or position in society—to some de-

12. Although it is customary in Egyptology to read the name **Nᶜr-mr* (see, e.g., W. B. Emery, *Archaic Egypt* [Baltimore, 1961] 43ff.), all other royal names of this period are monosyllabic. Only Winfried Barta (*Mitteilungen des Deutschen Archäologische Kultur* 24 [1969] 53) takes the name as *Nᶜr,* rendering it 'Horus der Wels', with the alternative 'Horus ist der Wels', which could be interpreted that the falcon is a fish. The sign read *mr* represents a dagger, and it seems more appropriate to consider it the king's own personal weapon. Especially in early representations, the king is shown wearing a dagger in his belt, which might be a continuation of the practice started by *Nᶜr.*

13. See my "Zum Königskonzept der Thinitenzeit," *Studien zur Altägyptische Kultur* 15 (1988) 123–41.

14. See my "Unity and Diversity in the Oldest Religion of Ancient Egypt," in *Unity and Diversity: Essays in the History, Literature, and Religion of the Ancient Near East* (ed. H. Goedicke; Baltimore, 1974) 201–17.

15. See the most recent study by Wolfgang Helck, "Thinitische Topfmarken," *Ägyptologische Abhandlungen* 50 (1990).

16. Peter Kaplony, "Die Inschriften der ägyptischen Frühzeit," *ÄA* 8 (1963) 49ff.

17. Titles are generally understood as social indicators, but the ranks they indicate are directly related to revenues and properties enjoyed as a result of it; see my "Titles for Titles," in *Grund und Boden in Altägypten, Untersuchungen zum Rechtsleben im Alten Ägypten* (2 vols.; ed. Schafik Allam; 1994) 2.227–34. It is indicative that the early tomb stelae not only provide the names and social positions of deceased persons but also their material status in various lists (cf. P. Kaplony, "Inschriften," 242ff.) These lists appear to serve a double purpose in being both retrospective as an indication of the material status achieved in this life and prospective as an expression of a hope of continuing it in the Hereafter.

gree an extension of the definition of the position of the monarch in the society by the formation of the royal titulary.

Although the Palermo Stone—which is most likely a copy dating to around 700 B.C.[18]—points to the existence of some form of annalistic records commencing as early as Dynasty One, it is impossible to say what form such records might have had.

Despite the fact that physical evidence is lacking, it would seem that by Dynasty Three (at the latest) the potentials of writing had been developed from a device for notations to a point that they could be used to convey statements. This does not mean in any way that the ancient Egyptians indulged in the fallacy of modern educators in writing as they spoke. They did, however, expand the medium of writing to a degree that it could convey a statement to someone outside the immediacy of contact with its originator. In the phenomenon concerning us here, this is not only a critical, but also an enormously creative step. The outcome of it is what is correctly labeled as **grammar**, a term used with great ease but remarkable inaccuracy.

As so often, etymology is a major help toward clarity. **Grammar** originates, of course, from the Greek, *grammatikḗ*, which actually had very little to do with linguistics and is basically to be recognized as "the art of writing." No doubt, any form of communication has its patterns, but what makes up conversation in the corridors or cafeterias might be difficult to reconcile with Fowler's English Grammar. The term **grammar** as a body of rules and principles has its sole raison d'être in the necessities of written communication. The lack of direct contact requires a coordination between sender/originator and recipient, that is not necessary for verbal communication. Beyond the mere "word," the recipient has an array of means available that the sender does not have. It is the realm of the "musical" aspect of communication, what might be called in Greek its *phýsis*, which in writing is reduced to a few diacritical marks, such as ! or underlining.

From the little remaining evidence on which we can base conclusions, we can determine that it was during the first two to three centuries of its use that writing evolved into a means of communication. We have no idea who is to be credited for it and can only guess that it happened as an outcome of the emerging profession of scribes.[19] In the forming of writing as a means of communication,

18. See Wolfgang Helck, in *LÄ* 4.652ff. If the available copy dates to the Twenty-Fifth Dynasty, the attempts to use it as a basis for the reconstruction of Egypt's early history (e.g., W. Barta, "Die Chronologie der 1. bis 5. Dynastie nach den Angaben des rekonstruierten Annalensteins," *Zeitschrift für Ägyptische Sprache und Altertumskunde* 108 [1981] 11–23) should be viewed with appropriate caution.

19. The formation of Demotic 2,500 years later provides a fascinating parallel. It is noteworthy that writing is a focal point of social distinction, as indicated in the carrying of writing equipment by noblemen, for example, Hesire[c].

two different approaches can be distinguished. Their difference has something to do with the disparity in usage. It stresses the two intertwined aspects of language, namely the semantic/conceptual and the phonetic/physical. In its use as written communication, the conceptual aspect dominates initially, which does not exclude the gradual incorporation of elements originally part of the spoken, that is, descriptive language. What we know as ancient Egyptian, in its earliest phases was an artificial vehicle for written communication and was not spoken (phonetically) in this form.[20] It is paramount that we keep this in mind. However, once an originally abstract standard was created for scribal use, it exerted an impact on verbal communication, just as the latter influenced the former.

That written Egyptian, the only kind available to us now, ought to be considered a **conceptual** language is best illustrated by the dominating role of the noun, that is, the conceptual element in language, to the point of forming a statement out of two nouns, that is, the nominal clause.[21] The **verb** at the same time lacks the *dynamic*, or descriptive aspect, permeating the Classical languages, Greek and Latin, as well as the modern ones. Nothing demonstrates the point better than the fact that the basic verbal expression in Egyptian, the *saḏm.f*, uses a possessive concept, resulting in an existential state specified by a possessive suffix. In other words, the *saḏm.f* does not indicate a dynamic act, as does 'he hears', but rather an acquired quality, 'his hearing'. The point is best illustrated by a look at Egyptian art. Neither the two- nor the three-dimensional rendering displays **actions** but rather, a condition or quality of the person depicted.

From its very beginning, Egyptian society was divided into a 'nobility' or 'patriciate' (*pᶜt*) and 'folk' or 'plebs' (*rḫyt*). This distinction, which in all likelihood had historical causes, was maintained even after new strata evolved in the society (they were the "burgers," the "priests," and the professional military, in approximately this time sequence). The intertwining of the two-tier

20. Kurt Sethe ("Das Verhältnis zwischen Demotisch und Koptisch und seine Lehren für die Geschichte der ägyptischen Sprache," *ZDMG* 79 [1925] 290–316) presented a step-by-step development of the Egyptian language. His presentation determined Gardiner's distinction of a series of "linguistic stages" in Egyptian (A. H. Gardiner, *Egyptian Grammar* [3d ed.; Oxford, 1957] §4) by equating scribal tradition and an imagined standard form of Egyptian but also shaped the view of Elmar Edel) (*Altägyptische Grammatik* [AnOr 34; Rome, 1955] §§ 6–14) in envisaging the Pyramid texts, as witness, "einer vergangenen Sprachphase . . . , die einmal als Vorläufer des Altägyptischen der 4.–6. Dyn. im lebendigen Gebrauch war." Bruno Hugo Stricker's evaluation was less compartmentalizing, emphasizing the standardizing effect of writing (*De indeeling der egyptische taalgeschiedenis* [1945]). A more complex differentiation is offered by Wolfgang Schenkel, in *LÄ* 5.1190–91, based on a variety of "Sprechhandlungen."

21. Kurt Sethe, "Der Nominalsatz im Ägyptischen und Koptischen," *Abhandlungen der philologisch-historischen Klasse der königlichen Sächsischen Gesellschaft der Wissenschaften, Leipzig* 33/3 (1916); Wolfgang Schenkel, *Einführung in die klassisch-ägyptische Sprache und Schrift* (Tübingen, 1987–88) 12ff.

stratification of Egyptian society was the fundamental sociological distinction permeating the entire ancient Egyptian society. The stolidity of the nobility as bearers of Egyptian social concepts was rendered in matching canonical terms, while the common folk were described in the artistic renderings. While no typological limits were imposed on them, the conceptual rendering of human representation was highly limited.[22]

The same limitation prevailed in the earliest stages of the Egyptian written language. This not only applies to the noun, but it is also indicative of the fact that in its conceptual approach, Egyptian grammar limits the verb to three possibilities. It is what de Buck[23] called the **actualis** and the **durative**, as well as the **retrospective**, meaning, the separation of act and actor by time.[24]

The central point is that ancient Egyptian, comparable to other ancient languages, is not the recording of a spoken idiom, but a creation by and for professional needs for written communication. This nature of written Egyptian has, of course, major consequences for approaching it. Modern linguistics are based on spoken forms of language and when applied to written ones—the only form available as far as ancient Egyptian is concerned—operate on the assumption that writing is a transcript of speech. The case of ancient Egyptian certainly does not conform to such a notion.

Realizing the fundamental difference between written and spoken language allows a number of conclusions to be drawn, which are applicable on a wider scale as well. While there can be no doubt of wide dialectal differences in the country,[25] geographically as well as socially, the existence of a communication standard was an outflow of the need for writing. It was ultimately an artificial formation, though it may have been influenced by personal or regional idioms. Language as we know it from the ancient Near East was a scribal product and had fundamentally limited linguistic substance. Differences may have been due

22. It finds its clearest expression in the development of a "canon" for the representation of the human form, specifically of those of an elevated social standing, while there is less rigidity as far as the lower ones, especially foreigners, are concerned; cf. Erik Iversen, *Canon and Proportions in Egyptian Art* (1975) 60ff.; idem, "The Canonical Tradition," in *The Legacy of Egypt*, (ed. J. R. Harris; 2d ed.; Oxford, 1971) 55ff.; Hermann Junker, "Die Feinde auf dem Sockel der Chasechem-Statuen," in *Ägytologische Studien* (ed. Otto Firchow; Grapow Festschrift; Deutsche Akademie der Wissenschaften zu Berlin, Institut für Orientforschung, Veröffentlichungen 29; (Berlin, 1955) 162ff.

23. Adriaan de Buck, *Grammaire élémentaire du moyen égyptien* (Leiden, 1952) §111.

24. It is indicative that it uses the element *n* for linking the two, which is also used for the "indirect genitive." In the Old Kingdom this construction occurs a few times in conjunction with the suffix pronoun.

25. Cf. W. F. Edgerton, "Early Egyptian Dialect Interrelationship," *BASOR* 122 (1951) 9–12; Rodolphe Kasser, "Dialectologie, textes et langages de l'Égypte Pharaonique," *BIFAO* 64/1 (1972) 107ff.

to geographic or temporal variations in scribal traditions but did not necessarily mirror linguistic developments. Needless to say, the written idiom did not remain unaffected by the simultaneously existing vernacular, just as the latter was influenced by the former.

It is the interaction between the two idioms that provides the fascination for the study of the language in ancient Egyptian texts. It was not necessarily an evolutionary process but one marked by social forces causing upheaval. At no point in the long history of ancient Egyptian writing is this more apparent than in the stage commonly labeled "Late Egyptian."[26] It is true that Late Egyptian is closer in its forms to the spoken language than to the Classical grammar. The love of "truth" of the ancient Egyptian heretic Akhenaten was, however, not responsible for it, as sometimes claimed.[27] Rather, it was the collapse of traditions due to social upheaval, as so clearly reflected in the recurrent claim, "I was a nobody, son of a nobody, who became somebody by accepting the word of the ruler."[28]

It is fascinating to observe how the freedom of the vernacular almost instantaneously brought forth its own grammatical concepts,[29] without which there would not have been any possibility of communication. The closer resemblance to the vernacular appears to have been largely a local and also a temporary phenomenon. After roughly a century of the crumbling of the traditional grammatical concepts for the sake of modernity, they fade out, giving way to an even more polarized dichotomy in communication: the spoken (phonetic) language had hardly any impact, while the written grammar became increasingly stolid. By emphasizing the conceptual structures, the texts lost the liveliness they had gained by a healthy balance with the life-force of descriptiveness. As a result, texts of the mid–first millennium B.C. are an impressive demonstration of academic learnedness, but unfortunately they were written in a dead language.

26. For its gradual emergence in the written idiom, cf. Burkhart Kroeber, *Die Neuägyptizismen vor der Amarnazeit* (Ph.D. diss., Tübingen, 1970) xiiiff.

27. For example, Frida Behnk (*Grammatik der Texte aus el Amarna* [Paris, 1930] §1) and John A. Wilson (*The Burden of Egypt* [Chicago, 1952] 207) make this claim.

28. Tomb of May = Maj Sandman, "Texts from the Time of Akhenaten," *Bibliotheca Aegyptiaca* 8 (1938) 61, 13ff.

29. Jaroslav Černý and Sarah Israelit Groll, *A Late Egyptian Grammar* (Rome, 1975) iii–vii.

Contributors

Asma Afsaruddin is Assistant Professor of Arabic Language and Literature at the University of Notre Dame and has previously taught at the Johns Hopkins and Harvard Universities. She works in Classical Arabic literature and Islamic studies and is one of the editors of this volume.

Roger Allen, Professor of Arabic at the University of Pennsylvania, has authored, translated, and edited a number of books in Modern Arabic literature. His publications include *The Arabic Novel* (1982, 1994) and *Modern Arabic Literature* (1987).

Yoël L. Arbeitman is associate director of the Institute of Semitic Studies (Princeton, N.J.) and researches Homer, philology of Jewish and Christian Scriptures, languages of Ancient Anatolia, and Indo-European linguistics. He edited *Fucus: A Semitic/Afrasian Gathering in Remembrance of Albert Ehrman* (1988).

Issa J. Boullata, Professor of Arabic Literature and Language at McGill University, is the author of *Trends and Issues in Contemporary Arab Thought* (1990) and the editor of *The Arabic Novel since 1950: Critical Essays, Interviews and Bibliography* (1992). He is former editor of *The Muslim World* and *Al-ʕArabiyya.*

Michael G. Carter is Senior Lecturer in Arabic at the University of Oslo. He previously taught at the University of Sydney, Australia, and New York University. His research interests include relations between grammar, law, philosophy, and theology in medieval Islam, on which he has published a number of articles.

Michael L. Chyet, formerly the Judaica and Middle East Specialist, Catalog Department, Main Library, University of California, Berkeley, has recently been appointed Senior Editor, Kurdish Service, The Voice of America, Washington, D.C. His areas of specialization are Kurdish language and linguistics and folklore.

Peter T. Daniels is an independent scholar who has translated and updated Gotthelf Bergsträsser's *Introduction to the Semitic Languages* (1983). With William Bright, he edited *The World's Writing Systems* (1996).

Werner Ende is Chair of Islamic Studies, Albert-Ludwigs Universität, Freiburg, Germany. He is the coeditor of *Die Welt des Islams* and is the author of *Arabische Nation und islamische Geschichte* (1977).

Hans Goedicke has taught at universities in Egypt, Europe, and America, including Göttingen, Brown, and the Johns Hopkins University, where he is now Professor Emeritus in the Department of Near Eastern Studies. Among his numerous publications are *Die privaten Rechtsinschriften aus dem Alten Reich* (1970) and *Perspectives on the Battle of Kadesh* (1985).

John A. C. Greppin, Professor of Linguistics at Cleveland State University, edits the *Annual of Armenian Linguistics* and is managing editor of *Raft: A Journal of Armenian Poetry and Criticism.*

Benjamin Hary, Associate Professor of Hebrew and Arabic and the Director of the Linguistics Program at Emory University, researches Judeo-Arabic dialectology and linguistics. He is the author of *Multiglossia in Judeo-Arabic* (1992) and the co-editor of the forthcoming *Bridging the Worlds of Islam and Judaism.*

Wolfhart Heinrichs, James Richard Jewett Professor of Arabic in the Department of Near Eastern Languages and Civilizations at Harvard University, works in the fields of Classical Arabic poetry and literary theory, Islamic legal theory, and Neo-Aramaic. He is the author of *The Hand of the Northwind* (1977) and the editor of *Studies in Neo-Aramaic* (1990). He is also one of the editors of the *Encyclopaedia of Islam.*

Robert D. Hoberman, Associate Professor of Judaic Studies and Linguistics at the State University of New York at Stony Brook, and author of *The Syntax and Semantics of Verb Morphology in Modern Aramaic* (1989), teaches Hebrew and Arabic.

Carleton T. Hodge, Professor Emeritus, Indiana University, engages in reconstructing proto bases common to Afroasiatic and Indo-European languages, using the consonant ablaut framework. Two of his books are *Hausa Basic Course* (1963, with Umaru) and *Serbocroatian Basic Course* (1965, 1969, with Janković).

Otto Jastrow, Professor of Oriental Philology at Erlangen–Nürnberg University, works mainly in the fields of Neo-Aramaic languages and Arabic dialectology. He is the author of *Der neuaramäische Dialekt von Hertevin* (1988), *Lehrbuch der Ṭuroyo-Sprache* (1992), and *Der neuaramäische Dialekt von Mlaḥsô* (1994).

Herrmann Jungraithmayr is Professor of African Linguistics at the University of Frankfurt am Main. He has published *Lexique mokilko* (1990) and *Lexique migama* (1992); a *Lexique mubi* is in preparation.

Alan S. Kaye, Professor of Linguistics, Arabic, and Hebrew and Director of the Laboratory of Phonetic Research at California State University, Fullerton, is the author of *Chadian and Sudanese Arabic in the Light of Comparative Arabic Dialectology* and *A Dictionary of Nigerian Arabic (English-Arabic and Arabic-English)* (1982/1986). With Judith Rosenhouse, he co-authored "Arabic Dialects and Maltese" in *The Semitic Languages* (ed. Robert Hetzron; London: Routledge, 1997 [forthcoming]).

Carolyn Killean is Associate Professor Emeritus of Arabic at the University of Chicago, where she developed *Electronic Al-Arabiyya,* a CD-ROM for computer-assisted instruction. She is the author of the entry for Classical Arabic in *Current Trends in Linguistics* (1963–76).

George Makdisi is Professor Emeritus in the Department of Oriental Studies at the University of Pennsylvania. His research interests include Islamic education, religion, and theology. He is the author of numerous publications, which include *The Rise of Colleges: Institutions of Learning in Islam and the West* (1981), *The Rise of Humanism in Classical Islam and the Christian West* (1990), and *Religion, Law, and Learning in Classical Islam* (1991).

Fedwa Malti-Douglas, is The Martha C. Kraft Professor of Humanities at Indiana University, where she is Chair of the Department of Near Eastern Languages and Cultures and Director of the Middle Eastern Studies Program. She is the author of numerous publications on Arab and Islamic studies, including: *Structures of Avarice* (1985), *Blindness and Autobiography* (1988), *Woman's Body, Woman's World* (1991), and *Men, Women, and God(s)* (1995).

Julie Scott Meisami is Lecturer in Persian at the University of Oxford and co-editor of *Edebiyât: The Journal of Middle Eastern Literatures*. Her books include *Medieval Persian Court Poetry* (1987) and an English verse translation of Nizami Ganjavi, *Haft Paykar* (1995); she is currently working on a study of medieval Persian historiography to the end of the twelfth century.

Edward Y. Odisho, Professor of Bilingual/Bicultural Education at Northeastern Illinois University and Adjunct Professor of Linguistics at Loyola University, Chicago, is the author of *The Sound System of Modern Assyrian* (1988).

Gary A. Rendsburg is Professor of Biblical and Semitic Studies in the Department of Near Eastern Studies at Cornell University. He is the author of *Diglossia in Ancient Hebrew* (1990) and *Linguistic Evidence for the Northern Origin of Selected Psalms* (1990).

Claudia Römer, Associate Professor at the Oriental Institute, Vienna University, works in Ottoman documents. Her book *Ösmanische Festungsbesatzungen in Ungarn zur Zeit Murads III* was published in 1995.

Karin Christina Ryding is Sultan Qaboos bin Said Professor of Arabic Language and Culture and Dean of Interdisciplinary Programs at Georgetown

University. She is the author of *Formal Spoken Arabic: Basic Course* (1990) and *Formal Spoken Arabic: FAST Course* (1993).

Yona Sabar, Professor of Hebrew and Aramaic at UCLA, has published several books and many articles on Neo-Aramaic, including *Targum De-Targum: An Old Neo-Aramaic Version of the Targum on Song of Songs* (1991). He has edited *The Folklore of the Kurdistani Jews* (1982).

Anton Schall is Professor Emeritus of Semitics and Islamic Studies at the University of Heidelberg. He has published extensively in comparative Semitics and philology; his works include *Studien über griechische Fremdwörter im Syrischen* (1960) and *Elementa Arabica: Einführung in die klassische arabische Sprache* (1988).

Hans-Rudolf Singer is Professor Emeritus of Arabic Studies at the University of Mainz and specializes in Arabic philology and dialectology. Among his published works are *Neuarabische Fragewörter: Ein Beitrag zur historischen und vergleichenden Grammatik der arabischen Dialekte* (1958) and *Grammatik der arabischen Mundart der Medina von Tunis.*

Barbara Freyer Stowasser is Professor of Arabic in the Department of Arabic and Director of the Center for Contemporary Arab Studies at Georgetown University. She is the author of *Women in the Qurʾān, Traditions, and Interpretation* (1994) and editor of *The Islamic Impulse* (1987).

Karl Stowasser (1925–1997) was Associate Professor Emeritus in the Department of History at the University of Maryland at College Park. He is the author of *Ein Muslim entdeckt Europa: Scheich Rifāʿa al-Ṭahṭāwī's Bericht über seinen Aufenthalt in Paris, 1826–1831* (1989) and, until his untimely death, was preparing a complete English translation of al-Maqrīzī's *Khiṭaṭ.*

Werner Vychichl is Professor Emeritus at the University of Freibourg in Switzerland. He specializes in the study of Ancient Egyptian and Coptic. His published works include *Dictionnaire étymologique de la langue copte* (1983); *La vocalisation de la langue Égyptienne* (1990).

Manfred Woidich is Professor at the University of Amsterdam and is the author of *Die ägyptisch-arabischen Dialekte* (1985) with Peter Behnstedt and has edited the Amsterdam Middle Eastern Studies (1990).

A. H. Mathias Zahniser, John Wesley Beeson Professor of Christian Mission at Asbury Theological Seminary, Wilmore, Kentucky, is interested in the application of discourse analysis to the Medinan *sūra*s of the Qurʾān. He is one of the editors of this volume.

Index of Authors

Abate, F. R. 385 n 1
Abbas 386 n 1
Abbott, N. 91 n 16, 93, 93 n 26
Abdala the Saracen 21
^{c}Abduh, M. 68, 103
Abelard, P. 17
al-Abnūdī, ^{c}Abd al-Raḥmān 204 n 20
Abū ^{c}Amr *see* al-Shaybānī, Abū ^{c}Amr
Abul-Fadl, F. 189 n 15
Abul Lughod, J. L. 192 n 25
Abū l-Ṭayyib al-Lughawi, ^{c}Abd al-Wāḥid b. ^{c}Alī 166 n 4, 177 n 8
Afsaruddin, A. viii, ix
Agius, D. A. 368, 368 n 21
Aḥīqār 241
Aḥmad, ^{c}Abd al-Ilāh 112 n 21
Ahmed, L. 94 n 28, 95 n 30, 99, 99 n 51, 100 n 52
Ākhūnd 62
Alavi, B. 70 n 28
Albright, W. F. 268, 268 n 4, 268 n 9, 269 n 12
Algeo, J. 385 n, 387 n 3, 396 n 32
^{c}Ālī, M. 418
^{c}Alī, ^{c}Abd al-Raḥīm M. 62, 62 n 3
Aliyo, K. 358 n 12
Allen, R. 107 n 3, 110 n 14, 111 n 16
Alvaro 24
Ambrose, A. A. 72 n 4
al-^{c}Āmilī, B. al-Dīn 67
al-^{c}Āmilī, Z. al-^{c}Ābidīn 68
al-Amīn, M. 66 n 16
Amīn, M. M. 175 n 1
Amīn, Q. 98, 98 nn 42–44, 100, 112
al-Amīn, S. M. 69
al-Amīnī, M. H. 69 n 22
Amram, H. L. 302, 303
Anderson, L. 369 n
al-Anṣārī, A. Z. 169 n 11
Anter, M. 292, 297
Anṭūn, F. 115
Apamea, P. von 239
Aqiva, Rabbi 270–71
al-^{c}Aqqād, ^{c}A. M. 116
al-A^{c}rābī, Abū Khiyara 168
Arberry, A. J. 397, 397 n 38
Aristotle 25, 172 n 14
Arjomand, S. A. 66 n 15
Arkoun, M. 28, 28 nn 1–2, 29 n 4, 30, 30 n 6, 32, 32 nn 13–14, 52 n 2, 53, 53 n 6
Arnaldez, R. 44 n 16
Arnold, W. 272 n 27
al-Aṣbahānī, al-Rāghib 52 n 3
al-Ash^{c}arī 98 n 45
Ashley, L. R. N. 321 n 12
^{c}Āshūr, N. 204 n 20
al-Assad, H. 395
Atatürk *see* Kemal Atatürk
Ateş, A. 406 n 22
Augustine 31 n 10, 32 n 14, 48, 48 n 34
Aurel, M. 242
Avicenna *see* Ibn Sīnā
Avishur, Y. 203 n 12
Avneri, U. 121, 121 nn 1–2
^{c}Awwād, ^{c}Abd al-Ḥusayn M. 65 n 12
^{c}Awwād, K. 63 n 4
^{c}Awwād, T. Y. 116
^{c}Ayyād, S. 108
Ayyūb, Dhū l-Nūn 116
al-Azharī 173, 181 n 18
Azmeh, A. 28 n 2

Babinger, F. 407 n 22
Badawi, El-Said 204, 204 n 19, 212 n 43, 213 nn 45–48, 215 n 53

Badran, M. 110 n 13
Baer, G. 191 n 24, 192 n 25
al-Baghdādī, al-Khaṭīb 52–53, 53 nn 7–8, 55 n 14, 55 n 19, 56 n 23
Bagley, F. R. C. 70 n 28
Bahlūl, B. 180 n 16
Bahrām 41, 41 n 7, 41 n 9, 42 n 9, 43–44, 44 n 18, 46, 48, 48 n 33, 49
Baḥr al-ᶜUlūm, M. M. 67
Bakaev, C. K. 286–87, 290, 292, 297
Bakhtin, M. M. 111, 111 n 17
Bar Asher, M. 216 n 58, 224 n 71
bar Nūn, I. 167
bar Serapion, M. 241, 245
Barta, W. 424 n 12, 425 n 18
al-Baṣrī, al-Aḥmar 168
Batatu, H. 64 n 10
Bates, H. E. 108, 108 n 7
Bauer, D. 73 n 8
Baumgartner, W. 269, 269 n 13
Baumstark, A. 241
Bausani, A. 49 n 36
al-Bayḍāwī, ᶜA. ibn ᶜUmar 54 n 11, 55 n 20, 56 n 21, 91 nn 18–19, 92, 92 nn 20–21, 93 n 24, 96, 96 n 34, 97 n 37, 97 n 40
Bazzi, M. J. 255, 255 n 2, 256, 256 n 3, 259 n 22, 261 nn 34–35, 262, 262 n 36, 262 n 38, 263 n 39
Beaussier 227 n 13, 228 n 16, 229 n 19, 229 n 29
Beekman, J. 73 n 8
Beeston, A. F. L. 33 n 15, 385 n, 393 n 16
Begzade, P. T. 302, 303 n 6, 306
Behnk, F. 428 n 27
Behnstedt, P. 186 n 4, 187 n 6, 187 n 8, 188 nn 9–12, 190 n 17, 192 n 27, 196 n 39, 209 n 29, 297, 297 n 21
Behrens-Abouseif, D. 175 n 2, 178 n 9
Beinin, J. 122 n 6, 126 n 15
Bell, R. 73 n 6
Benfey, T. 237
Bengston, H. 246
ben Sūsān, Y. 218 n 63, 221 n 66, 223
ben Yehiel, N. 270
Ben Yehuda, E. 270 n 20
Bergsträßer, G. 33 n 16, 167 n 7, 331 n 16
Bezzenberger, A. 366, 366 nn 14–15
Bickerton, D. 204 n 17
Bikoma, E. J. 255, 256, 256 n 4, 260 n 32, 261 n 34, 262
al-Bīrūnī 49 n 36
Bishai, W. B. 297, 297 n 20
Bitton, S. 120, 121 n 1, 122 n 5, 127 n 17
Blanc, H. 200 n 1, 209, 209 n 31, 212 n 42
Blau, J. 218 n 63, 223 n 68, 273 n 32
Blust, R. A. 156 n 1
Bohas, G. 29 n 3, 37 n 29
Boissier, A. 268, 268 n 10
Bolinger, D. 296 n 32
Bolozky, S. 223 n 69
Bostān, M. ibn Meḥmed 401 n 1, 402, 404–6, 409, 410–14, 414 n 47, 415–18
Bright, W. 376 n 11
Brockelmann, C. 31 n 7, 31 n 9, 180 n 15, 271 n 23, 355, 355 nn 1–3, 356, 356 nn 4–5
Browne, E. G. 397, 397 n 37, 397 nn 39–40
Brugman, J. 110 n 11
Bruijn, J. T. P. de 44 n 16, 45 n 20, 47 n 30
Bryan, M. A. 356 n 6
Buck, A. de 427, 427 n 23
Buhl, F. 388 n 6
Burckhardt, J. 26, 26 n 12
Burnett, H. 108
al-Bustānī, Saᶜīd 111 n 15
al-Bustānī, Salīm 111 n 15
al-Bustī, Abū ᵓl-Fatḥ 21

Cachia, P. 110 n 14
Callow, J. 73 n 8
Cannon, G. 385, 385 n 1, 393, 393 n 17, 394, 394 n 22, 395 n 26, 396 nn 28–29, 397, 397 nn 41–44, 398, 398 nn 45–49, 596
Caprona, P. C. de 72 n 4
Carter, M. G. 30 n 5, 34 nn 20–21, 36 n 27
Castro, G. de 24
Cella, J. 369 n
Černý, J. 428 n 29
Channing, M. 386 n 1
Chekhov, A. 112
Chelhod, J. 89 n 5, 89 nn 8–9, 90 n 10, 90 n 12
Chyet, M. L. 294, 294 n 15
Cicero 25
Civil, M. 270 n 19
Cobban, A. B. 16, 16 n 2
Cohen, D. 357 n 9
Colish, M. L. 32 n 14
Colless, B. E. 157, 157 n 9, 160 n 22
Cooke, M. 110 n 13
Corbin, H. 47 n 26
Corneille 24
Cornelius, F. 269, 269 n 12
Corré, A. A. 203 n 12
Czermak, W. 5, 5 n 4, 6

Dahan, J. 211
Dahlstedt, K.-H. 186 n 2
Daiber, H. 177 n 8
Dale, S. F. 38, 38 n 33
Dalman, G. H. 268 n 8
Daniels, P. T. 370–71, 380, 385 n, 394 n 22, 395 n 23, 396 n 32, 397 n 44
Dante 25
Darwich, M. *see* Darwīsh, M.
Darwīsh, M. 119–21, 121 nn 1–3, 122, 122 nn 4–5, 122 n 8, 123–24, 124 n 12, 125, 125 n 14, 126, 126 n 15, 127, 127 n 17, 128
Dashtī, ᶜAlī 70, 70 n 28
Davies, H. 200 n 1, 212 n 42, 214 n 50, 215 n 52
Deeters, G. 249 n 12
Delitzsch, F. 291
Destaing, E. 358 n 10
Dhuᵓayb, A. 171
Dickens, C. 111

Diem, W. 177 n 6
Diez, E. 175 n 2, 179 n 12
Dihkhudā, ᶜAlī Akbar 182 nn 21–22
Dihoki, H. E. A. M. (Abu Abdallah) 302–3
Dilçin, D. 406 n 22
Dimitrakos, D. 178, 178 n 11
Doerfer, G. 405, 405 nn 18–19, 406, 406 nn 20–22, 407 n 23, 408, 408 nn 24–27, 409, 409 nn 28–30, 410, 410 n 31, 410 n 33, 410 nn 35–36
Dolgopolsky, A. B. 176 nn 3–4
Dols, M. 38 n 30
Donaldson, D. M. 69 n 23
Doron, D. 218 n 63, 221 n 66
Dozy, R. P. A. 95 n 29
Dresden, S. 25
Dumas, A. 110
Dunkling, L. A. 319, 319 n 1, 320, 320 n 8, 321, 321 nn 10–12
al-Dūrī, ᶜAbd al-ᶜAzīz 7
Dzhalilov, D. 290–91
Dzhalilov, O. 290–91
Dzhangoev, A. A. 294

Eccel, A. C. 62 n 2
Edel, E. 426 n 20
Edessa, A. 243
Edgerton, W. F. 427 n 25
Edmonds, C. J. 294
Ehret, C. 338 n 8, 339 n 12
Ehrlich, B. 4, 4 n 2
Elamrani-Jalal, A. 29 n 3
Elliot, R. W. V. 162 nn 31–32
El Nouty, H. 122 n 9
Emery, W. B. 424 n 12
Ende, W. 64 n 10, 69 n 24
Endreß, G. 29 n 3
Epstein, Y. N. 271, 271 n 24, 271 n 26
Erasmus 32, 32 n 12
Erman 251 n 22
Errico, R. A. 259 n 22, 261 nn 34–35, 262 n 36, 263 n 39
E'vdal, E. 291, 294
Ewald, H. 241

Falkenstein, A. 269 n 16
al-Farābī 29, 35, 44 n 16, 181 n 18
al-Farahī, Ḥ. al-Dīn ᶜAbd al-Ḥamīd 72 n 2, 73 n 7, 74 n 11
Faraj, A. 107 n 2
al-Farazdaq 170
Faulmann, K. 2, 2 n 1, 3
al-Fayyūmī, S. ibn Yosēf 202
Ferdī (Kazasker of Anatolia) 401, 401 n 1
Ferdōsī 397
Ferguson, C. 191 n 23
Ferguson, M. W. 53 n 4
Ferguson, S. 111 n 18
Ferruolo, S. C. 16 n 3
Fineman, C. S. 369 n
al-Fīqī, M. K. 101 nn 54–56
al-Fīrūzābādī 180 n 17

Fischer, W. 177 n 7
Fleisch, H. 157 n 5
Fleming, I. 381
Flemming, B. 404 n 13
Flügel, G. 75 n 18
Fowler, W. C. 425
Fraenkel, S. 285 n 8, 286 n 11
Franklyn, J. 320, 320 n 5
Friedrich, J. 268 n 9
Frye, N. 53 n 5
Fuller, T. 319, 319 n 1

Gabrieli, F. 31 nn 7–8, 38 n 32
Gamal, A. S. 38 n 30
Gandz, S. 158 n 10
Gaᵓon, S. 216
Garbell, I. 284, 284 n 4, 303, 303 nn 6–7, 312 n 83, 312 n 85, 312 n 88, 313 n 96, 313 nn 92–94
Garcin, J.-C. 196 n 38
Gardiner, A. H. 426 n 20
Gelb, I. J. 269 n 16, 269 n 18, 420 n 3
Gibb, H. A. R. 73 n 6, 134 n 8
Gibbon, E. 135 n 12
Gil, M. 201 n 4
Gleichen, E. 380 n 17
Godron, G. 423 n 11
Goedicke, H. 423 n 10, 424 nn 13–14
Gogol, N. V. 112
Goitein, S. D. 38 n 33, 200 n 1, 203, 203 nn 13–14, 211 n 36
Gordimer, N. 108
Gordon, C. 365
Gottschalk, H. 6
Grabar, O. 179, 179 n 14
Gragg, F. A. 21 n 6
Gran, P. 70 n 27
Gray, L. H. 332 n 17
Greppin, J. A. C. 249 n 11, 250 n 15
Grimes, J. E. 73 n 7
Groll, S. I. 428 n 29
Großen, A. den 239
Grotzfeld, H. 210, 210 n 34
Grunebaum, G. E. von 134 n 8
Guillaume, J.-P. 29 n 3

Haarmann, U. 34 n 19
Haas, M. R. 380 n 18
al-Ḥabbūbī, M. S. 63, 63 n 6, 66
Ḥaddād, N. 115
al-Ḥaḍramī, ᶜAbd-Allāh 167
Hāfez 397
Hafez, S. *see* Ḥāfiẓ, Ṣ.
Ḥāfiẓ, Ṣ. 107 n 4, 110 n 14, 395
Hahn, R. F. 373 n 7
Haile, G. 389 n 8
al-Hakim, M. B. 395
al-Ḥakīm, T. 7, 107 n 2, 113, 116
Halkin, A. S. 202 n 8
al-Hamadhānī 133 n 8
Hanks, P. 319, 319 nn 2–3, 388 n 7, 389 nn 8–9, 391 n 13

Hanson, C. 107 n 5
Ḥaqqī, Y. 108, 112 n 21, 113
al-Ḥarīrī 133 n 8
Harris, J. R. 427 n 22
Hary, B. 199 n 1, 200 nn 2–3, 201 n 3, 202 n 11, 202 n 6, 202 n 8, 203 n 15, 204 nn 17–18, 206 n 23, 207 nn 24–25, 208 n 26, 209 n 27, 211 n 37, 212 n 40, 214 n 50, 218 nn 62–63, 220 n 65, 221 n 66, 224 n 70
ha-Sandlar, Y. 270
Haupt, P. 364, 364 n 2, 365 n 6
Hava, J. G. 339 n 14
Hawkins, J. D. 367, 367 n 19, 368
Hayes, J. 385 n, 386 n 2
Haykal, M. Ḥ. 115
Ḥazzan 211
Hegel, G. W. F. 109
Heine, P. 67 n 18
Helck, W. 423 n 8, 423 n 11, 424 n 15, 425 n 18
Heninger, S. G., Jr. 45 n 19, 47 n 27, 48 n 33, 49 n 36
Hesychius of Alexandria 178, 178 n 10
Hibbard, A. 73 n 5
Hill, R. J. 4, 4 n 2
al-Ḥillī, al-ᶜAllāma 67
Hinds, M. 212 n 43, 213 nn 45–48, 215 n 53
Hoberman, R. D. 256 n 4, 256 n 7, 271 n 23, 284
Hocke, H. H. 191, 191 n 22, 194 nn 34–35, 196 n 41
Hodge, C. T. 338 nn 5–7, 342 n 25
Hodges, F. 319, 319 nn 2–3, 388 n 7, 389 nn 8–9, 391 n 13
Hoffmann, G. 167 n 6
Hoffner, H. A. 272 n 28
Holma, H. 365, 365 n 7
Holman, C. H. 73 n 5
Horn, P. 284 n 3, 286 n 9
Hübner, B. 269 n 15
Hübschmann 247 n 1
Huffman, F. E. 380 n 18
Hunwick, J. 389 n 8
Ḥusayn, Ṭ. 7, 116
al-Ḥuṣrī, S. 64 n 9

Ibn al-ᶜAbbās, ᶜAbd Allāh 168
Ibn ᶜAbd al-Aᶜlā, ᶜAdnān 168
Ibn ᶜAbd Rabbihi 52 n 3
Ibn ᶜĀdiyāᵓ, al-Samawᵓal 201
Ibn Aḥmad, K. 166
Ibn ᶜĀᵓidh, A. M. ᶜAbd Allāh 166
Ibn al-ᶜAjjāj, R. 171
Ibn al-ᶜAlāᵓ, A. A. 167, 168 n 9
Ibn Anas, M. 58 n 32
Ibn al-Anbārī 34
Ibn al-Aᶜrābī 181 n 18
Ibn al-ᶜĀṣ, ᶜAmr 135 n 12
Ibn Bābashādh 32
Ibn Durayd 31, 173, 181 n 18, 183 n 24
Ibn Durustawayh 165
Ibn Ezra 305 n 20
Ibn Fāris 34, 180 n 17, 182 n 22, 183
Ibn Ḥabīb al-Ḍabbī, Y. 168
Ibn Ḥajar, A. 170
Ibn Ḥanbal, A. 96 n 32
Ibn Ḥawqal 24
Ibn Ḥayyān, J. 48, 156 n 3, 158 n 10
Ibn ᶜĪsā Rummānī, A. 157 n 6
Ibn Isḥāq, Ḥ. 95, 96 n 31, 167
Ibn al-Jawzī 21 n 7, 52, 52 n 3, 57, 57 n 25, 58 n 29, 58 n 31
Ibn Jinnī 29 n 4, 30, 34–35, 35 n 22, 36, 36 nn 23–26, 37, 37 nn 28–29, 156, 157 n 5
Ibn Kathīr, I. ibn ᶜUmar 90, 90 n 13, 91 n 16, 91 nn 18–19, 92, 92 n 21, 93 n 24, 97 nn 37–38, 98 n 41
Ibn Khaldūn 133 n 6, 166, 166 n 5, 168, 168 n 10, 169, 169 n 12, 174, 174 n 18
Ibn Kirkira, A. M. A. 168
Ibn Makkī, M. 68
Ibn Mālik, A. 91 n 15
Ibn Manẓūr, M. ibn Mukarram 87 n 1, 89 nn 6–8, 158 n 10, 166, 180 n 17
Ibn Masᶜūd 31, 31 n 9
Ibn Muḥammad, J. 53
Ibn al-Muqaffaᶜ 31, 31 n 7, 33 n 15, 111
Ibn Muṭarrif, Abū l-Wazīr ᶜU. 168
Ibn al-Nadīm 165, 165 n 1, 166, 173 n 15
Ibn Qutayba 52, 57 n 27
Ibn Saᶜd 91 nn 16–18, 92 nn 22–23, 93 n 24
Ibn Salama, al-Mufaḍḍal 173
Ibn Sīda 170 n 13, 171, 173
Ibn al-Sikkīt 157 n 6
Ibn Sīnā, al-Ḥusayn (Avicenna) 19, 38 n 30
Ibn al-Tawᵓam 56, 56 n 22
Ibn Yaḥyā, al-Faḍl 58
Ibn Zayd, N. 168 n 9
Ibrāhīm, L. ᶜA. 175 n 1
Idrīs, Y. 115, 115 n 24, 117 n 27, 205 n 21
Ingham, B. 193 n 31
al-ᶜIrāqī, S. Ā. Ḍ. 66
Irving, W. 386 n 1, 387 n 3, 388
Iṣfahānī, Abū l-Ḥasan 66
Ishōᶜ, ᶜAnān 167
Iṣlāḥī, A. A. 72 n 2, 73 n 8, 74 n 14, 76 nn 24–25, 85 n 37
Iversen, E. 427 n 22
Izolî, D. 287, 291

Jaba, A. 285–92, 294
al-Jābirī, M. S. 112 n 21
al-Jābirī, S. 113, 116
Jacob of Edessa 166
Jaensch, E. R. 421 n 6
al-Jāḥiẓ 31, 52, 54 n 12, 56, 56 n 22
Jansky, H. 4, 4 n 3
Jastrow, M. 268 n 6, 268 n 8, 285 n 7, 291
Jastrow, O. 8 n 11, 177 n 7, 193 n 30, 272 n 27, 276 n 3, 297 n 18
Jawāhirī 66
al-Jawharī, Abū Naṣr I. ibn Ḥammād 173, 181 n 18

Jazayery, M. A. 372 n 6
Jehlitschka, H. 379 nn 16–17
Johanson, L. 411, 411 nn 38–39
John of Salisbury 31, 31 n 10
Johnston, T. 176 n 5
Johnstone, T. M. 272 n 30
Jones, R. B. 380 n 18
Jones, W. 387 n 3, 395 n 26, 397, 397 n 44, 398
Jong, R. de 187 n 5
Josephus 241
Jubrān, J. K. 112, 112 n 19
Jungraithmayr, H. 346–47, 349, 358 n 12
Junker, H. 427 n 22
al-Jurayrī, A. S. A. ibn Taghlib 168
Justi, F. 285–92, 294
Justinian 178 n 10

Kafāʾī, ʿAbd al-Ḥusayn M. 63 n 3
Kāshif al-Ghiṭāʾ, Shaykh M. Ḥ. 66
Kaplony, P. 424 nn 16–17
Kappert, P. 404 n 13, 418 n 53
Karabacek, J. 401 n 1
al-Kāshī, J. 183 n 26
Kasser, R. 427 n 25
Katz, D. 381
Kaufman, T. 156 n 1, 192 n 28
Kaye, A. S. 148 n 3, 372 n 6, 376 n 11, 398 n 45
Keddie, N. R. 65 n 14
Kemal Atatürk 380 n 17
Kenan, A. 121, 127 n 17
al-Khafajī, A. 96, 96 n 35
Khalaf al-Aḥmar, K. 22, 22 n 10
Khalaf Allāh, M. A. 103, 103 n 62
Khalidi, T. 64 n 11
Khalīfa, M. 73 n 6
al-Khalīl, ibn Aḥmad 157 n 7, 158, 158 n 11, 159, 159 n 14, 160, 163, 165–67, 167 n 7, 169, 172–24, 181 n 18
al-Khalīlī, J. 63 n 5, 68 n 21, 70 nn 25–26
Khan, G. 209 n 28, 212 n 41, 376 n 11
Khān, S. A. 68
al-Khāqānī, ʿA. 68 n 21
Khawam, R. R. 31 n 7
Khiḍr, ʿA. 112 n 21
Khin, U. 380 n 18
al-Khunāʿī, Khuwaylid 181 n 19
al-Khunāʿī, M. b. Kh. 181, 181 n 19
al-Khurāsānī, M. K. 62–64, 66 n 15
Killean, C. 132 n 5
Kippel, E. 196 n 38
al-Kirmilī, A.-M. 63, 63 n 7, 64 n 8
al-Kisāʾī, ʿA. ibn Ḥamza 168, 169 n 11
al-Kisrāwī, Abū ʾl-Ḥasan ʿA. ibn Mahdī 166
Klingenheben, A. 345
Koch, J. 31 n 10
Kofler, H. 5
Kohut, A. 270 n 21
Kopesec, M. 73 n 8
Kouloughli, D. E. 29 n 3
Kraemer, J. L. 28, 28 n 1
Kraus, P. 156 n 3, 158 n 10
Krauss, S. 238, 240
Kristeller, P. O. 25–26, 26 n 11
Kroeber, B. 428 n 26
Krotkoff, B. 2–4
Krotkoff, G. viii–ix, 1–5, 5 n 4, 6, 6 nn 5–6, 7, 7 nn 8–10, 8, 8 n 11, 9, 9 n 12, 10–11, 11 nn 13–15, 39, 39 n 1, 46 n 25, 48 n 33, 71–72, 72 n 1, 158, 158 n 13, 256, 256 n 5, 257, 257 n 9, 258, 258 nn 13–14, 258 nn 18–20, 259 nn 23–24, 271 n 23, 273, 273 n 37, 283–85, 285 n 8, 287–89, 292, 301 n, 320, 320 n 4, 331, 331 n 15, 369 n, 379 n 17, 385 n, 389 n 8, 390, 398, 419
Kulan, Y. 276
Kunitzsch, P. 33, 33 n 16
Kurdoev, K. K. 285, 294
Kutscher, E. Y. 271 n 26, 284, 284 n 2

al-Laʿabī, ʿAbd al-Laṭīf 122
Labib, S. Y. 31 n 7
(Lal)la-Ḍawya 225
Lamb, D. 390, 390 nn 10–11
Lambert, W. 8
Lamsa, G. M. 262 n 38
Landersdorfer, S. 268–69, 269 n 11
Lane, E. W. 162 n 30, 107 n 2, 173, 339, 339 n 10, 339 n 13, 341 nn 17–18, 342 n 21, 365, 365 n 8
Lāshīn, M. Ṭ. 113
Lawrence, T. E. 398, 399 n 51
al-Layth 166, 173
Lazar of Parp 249
Lebedev, V. V. 200 n 1, 209, 209 n 30
Lemke, W.-D. 62 n 2
Lescot, R. 287, 290, 292
Leslau, W. 272 n 31, 337, 337 nn 1–3, 338 n 9, 340 n 15, 370 n 2, 385 n
Levy, J. 268 n 6, 268 n 8
Lewin, B. 181 n 20, 183 n 25
Lewis, M. B. 373 n 9
Lewis, B. 392 n 15, 395 n 23
Lidzbarski, M. 381
Lieberman, S. J. 269 n 16, 269 n 18
Lockman, Z. 122 n 6, 126 n 15
Loucel, H. 36 n 23
Löw, I. 251 n 22
Luizard, P.-J. 66 n 17
Lukas, J. 358 n 11
Lyall, C. J. 22, 22 n 8

MacKenzie, D. N. 182 n 23, 291, 375 n 10, 378
Maclean, A. J. 271 n 23, 286–88, 290–92, 314 n 100, 314 n 103
MacMichael, H. A. 195 n 38
al-Maḥallī, J. al-Dīn 55 n 20
Maḥfūẓ, N. 105, 106 n 1, 116
Makdisi, G. 15 n 1, 18, 31 n 11, 34, 34 n 18, 51 n 1, 52 n 2
Malkiel, Y. 157 n 8
Malti-Douglas, F. 51 n 1, 52 n 2, 53 nn 7–8, 55 n 14, 56 n 22, 58 n 28, 116 n 26

Māmaqānī, S. A.   66 n 15
al-Manfalūṭī   110, 112
al-Maqdisī, Ḍiyā' al-Dīn al-Khālidī   285–87, 288–92
Marçais, P.   225–26, 226 n 1
Marzolph, U.   52 n 2
Māsawayh, J.   167
Massignon, L.   158 n 10, 160 n 21
Massoud, R.   368, 368 n 21
al-Masʿūdī   38 n 31, 47 n 26
al-Mawdūdī, A. al-Aʿlā   98, 98 n 45, 99, 99 nn 46–50, 100
al-Māzinī, I.   116
McCarus, E. N.   373 n 8, 379 n 15
McIlwain, B.   369 n
Medvedev, P. N.   111, 111 n 17
Mehiri, A.   36 n 24
Meillet   366
Meinhof, C.   346
Meisami, J. S.   40 nn 2–4, 42 n 9, 43 n 15, 44 n 18, 48 n 33
Melchert, H. C.   367, 367 n 18
Melikian-Chirvani, A. S.   47 n 26
Mélikoff, I.   48 n 33
Melk'es   288
Mercier, M.   226
Mernissi, F.   90 n 11, 91 n 14, 91 n 16
Mervin, S.   67 n 18
Merx, A.   167 n 6
Meyerhof, M.   6
Middlemore, G.   26 n 12
Milroy, J.   196 n 40
Mingana, A.   255–56, 256 n 6, 259, 259 nn 21–23, 259 nn 26–27, 260 n 29, 261 nn 34–35, 262 n 36, 263 n 39, 264 n 41
Mir, M.   72 n 2, 72 n 4, 73 nn 6–8, 74 n 11, 75 n 14, 76 nn 24–25, 85 n 37
Mirandola, G. P. della   21, 21 n 6, 24
Miskawayh   28 n 2, 41 n 6, 42 nn 10, 12
Mommsen, T.   245
Monroe, J. T.   134 n 8
Moosa, M.   110 n 14
Morag, S.   302
Moravia, A.   108, 108 n 8
Morell, S.   270 n 22
Morison, S.   369
Morpurgo Davies, A.   367, 367 n 19, 368
Mubārak, ʿAlī   110, 113
Müller, A.   379 n 16
Müller, D. H.   81 n 31
Mughnīya, M. J.   68 nn 20–21
Muḥammad   33
Muḥsin, Shaykh   67 n 19, 70
Munīf, ʿAbd al-Raḥmān   113–14
Muruwwa, Ḥ.   70, 70 n 27
Muṣṭafā, D.   402, 410, 418
al-Mutanabbī   35
al-Muwayliḥī, M.   111, 113–14, 114 n 23, 115

Nadīm, ʿAbdallāh   110, 112
Naim, C. M.   370–71, 375, 376 n 11, 377
Naimy, N.   112 n 20

Nāʾīnī, M. Ḥ.   66
Nakash, Y.   66 n 17
Narekatsi (Gregory of Narek)   248, 248 n 3
al-Nāṣir, C.   45 n 18, 47 n 28
Naṣīr al-Dīn Ṭūsī   see al-Ṭūsī, N. al-Dīn
Nasr, S. H.   41 nn 7–8, 43 n 14, 44 n 16, 45 nn 21–23, 48 n 32, 49 nn 35–36, 67 n 18
al-Nassāj, S. Ḥ.   112 n 21
Naveh, J.   420, 420 n 1
Nawabi, Y. M.   182 n 23
Nazhdip, E. N.   373 n 7
Naẓmī, W. J. ʿU.   63 n 6
Nelan, B. W.   386 n 1
Neusner, J.   271 n 22
Neuwirth, A.   72 n 4, 73 n 8, 74 nn 9–13, 75, 75 n 19, 76 n 23, 79, 79 n 30, 82 n 35, 122, 122 n 7
Newby, G. D.   201 nn 4–5
Nicholson, R. A.   22, 22 n 9, 133 n 8, 397, 397 n 35
Nijland, C. J.   112 n 20
Nikator, S. I.   239
al-Nisāʾī, al-Ḥasan ibn al-Sabbāḥ   53
Niẓāmī   39–40, 40 n 3, 41, 41 n 9, 42 n 10, 43 n 15, 44 n 18, 45–46, 47 n 28, 48
Nöldeke, T.   88 n 3, 93, 93 n 25, 245, 254 n 1
Nuʿayma, M.   112

O'Connor, M.   369 n, 371, 385 n
Odisho, E.   322 n 14
Önler, Z.   406 n 22
Örnek, S. V.   288 n 13
O'Faolain, S.   108
O'Leary, De Lacy   214 n 51
Oraham, A. J.   271 n 23, 286, 290–92
Ornan, U.   373
O'Rourke, W.   108 n 6
Otto, B.   319 n
Owen, D. I.   269 n 14, 272 n 28
Owens, J.   156 n 4

Papadopoulo, A.   46 n 25, 47 n 28
Paper, H. H.   372 n 6
Parkinson, D.   200 n 1
Parunak, H. v. D.   73 n 8, 74 n 11, 81 n 31, 81 n 35
Payne-Smith, R.   180 n 15
Peck, R. A.   45 n 23, 46 n 24, 48 n 31, 48 n 34, 49 n 36
Peled, M.   121, 121 nn 1–2, 124 n 12, 125 n 14
Pellat, C.   31 n 7
Pennacchietti, F. A.   284, 284 n 5
Penzl, H.   371
Péres, H.   226, 226 n 4
Peters, E.   33 n 17
Pettinato, G.   272 n 29, 274 n 38
Phillott, C.   215 n 54
Pike, K. L.   372
Plöger, O.   270 n 19
Poe, E. A.   107
Poetto, M.   367, 367 n 17
Pokorny, J.   365, 365 n 11, 366

Poonawala, I. 385 n
Porter, K. 108
Powell, A. 215 n 54
Pretzl, O. 167 n 7
Pritchett, V. S. 108, 109 n 9, 112
Procházka-Eisl, G. M. 403 nn 11–12, 404 n 13, 411 n 41, 413 n 45
Prokosch, E. 415 n 49, 416 n 51, 417 n 52

al-Qabbānī, A. K. 107 n 2
al-Qadhdhāfī, M. 388, 391, 394
al-Qarāfī 6
al-Qāsim, S. 121 n 3
al-Qāsimī, M. J. 81 n 33
al-Qifṭī 135 n 12
Quilligan, M. 53 n 4

Rahman, T. 388 n 4, 395 n 27
al-Ramlī, L. 129–30, 132–33, 137, 140, 141 n 16
Rashdall, H. 16, 16 n 4
Rashi 305 n 15, 305 n 19, 305 n 21
al-Rashīd, H. 58
Raẓavī, M. T. M. 47 n 30
al-Rāzī, A. Ḥ. A. ibn Hamdān 158 n 10
al-Rāzī, A. ibn Muḥammad 160, 160 n. 23, 163
al-Rāzī, F. al-Dīn 19–20, 20 n 5, 81 n 32
Reitzenstein, R. 178 n 10
Reizammer, A. 269 n 15
Rendsburg, G. A. 267 n 2, 271 n 26, 272 n 31, 273 n 33
Reynolds, J. H. 380 n 17
Ribichini, S. 272 n 29
Ritter, H. 285 n 7
Rizzitano, U. 7
Robinson, N. 79 n 29
Römer, C. 4 n 3, 402 nn 3–4, 403 n 10, 415 n 50, 418 n 54
Roper, E. M. 359 n 14
Rosenthal, F. 240, 284 n 1
Rossi, E. 406–7 n 22
Rubenson, S. 389 n 8
Rugh, A. B. 103, 103 nn 60–61
al-Rumma, D. 170
al-Rummānī 30
Rushdie, S. 389 n 8
Ruspoli, M. 421 n 5
Russell, B. 38 n 32
Rypka, J. 47 n 28

Sabah, J. A. 394
al-Sabah, S. A. 395
Sabar, Y. 223 n 69, 256, 256 n 8, 258 nn 16–17, 284, 285 n 6, 302 n 2, 303 n 7, 304 nn 8–10, 304 nn 12–13, 305 nn 14–15, 306 n 22, 314 n 100
Sadān, Y. 52 n 2
Ṣadr, M. 70
al-Ṣāḥibī 34 n 21
Said, E. W. 387 n 3
Ṣāliḥ, al-Ṭayyib 113–14
Sampson, G. 370
Sanāʾī 45, 45 n 20, 47
Sandman, M. 428 n 28
Ṣannūʿ, Y. 110
Ṣarrūf, Y. 115
Sasson, J. M. 267 n 1
Saussure, F. de 422, 422 n 7
Savage-Smith, E. 47 n 27
Schenkel, W. 423 n 9, 426 nn 20–21
Schimmel, A. 389 n 8, 399, 399 n 52
Scholes, R. 109 n 10
Schwartz, M. 283 n
Schwyzer, E. 237, 241
Seibert, U. 353 n 3
Sells, M. 72 n 4
Sephiha 223
Sethe, K. 420 n 2, 426 nn 20–21
Sezgin, F. 181 n 19
al-Shabībī, M. R. 66
al-Shahīd al-Awwal 67
Shahid, I. 72 n 4
al-Shahīd al-Thānī 67–68
al-Shahrastānī, H. al-Dīn al-Ḥusaynī 63–64, 63 n 5, 66
Shakespeare, W. 36 n 26
Shamir, Y. 121
Sharaf al-Dīn, ʿAbd al-Ḥusayn 70
Sharāra, M. 64, 64 n 11, 65, 65 n 12, 65 n 13, 66–69, 69 n 23, 70, 70 n 27
al-Shaʿrāwī, M. M. 101, 101 n 53, 101 n 56, 102, 102 nn 57–59
al-Sharqī, ʿA. 65, 65 n 12, 66
al-Shārūnī, Y. 108
Sharvit, D. 211
al-Shaybānī, Abū ʿAmr 181 n 20
Shboul, A. 38 n 31
al-Shidyāq, A. F. 106, 113
Shīrāzī, M. H. 65, 65 n 14
Shklovsky, V. 109 n 10
Sībawayhi 34, 172, 172 n 14
Sidilio, Rabbi 211
Ṣidqī, N. 97 n 39
Singer, H.-R. 226 n 2
Singer, I. 123 n 11
Skjærvø, O. 182 n 23
Smith, M. B. 47 n 27
Smith, P. 285 n 7
Soden, W. von 285
Sokoloff, M. 271, 271 nn 25–26
Sophocles, Evangelinus Apostolides 178
Spitaler, A. 75 n 18
Steiner, F. 275 n 1
Steingass, F. 286 n 9
Steinschneider, M. 202 n 8
Stewart, D. 7
Stillman, N. A. 201 n 3, 202 n 9, 202 n 11
Stilo, D. 283
Stock, B. 32 n 14
Storch, A. 353 n 3
Stowasser, B. F. 96 n 36
Stowasser, K. viii, x
Stricker, B. H. 426 n 20

al-Sukkarī 181 n 20
al-Suyūṭī, J. al-Dīn 55 n 20, 166 nn 2–3, 168 n 9

al-Ṭabarī, A. J. M. Ibn Jarīr 91 n 16, 91 nn 18–19, 92 n 20, 93 n 24, 96, 96 nn 32–33, 97 n 37, 97 n 40
Taeschner, F. 45 n 18, 47 n 28, 380 n 17
al-Ṭahṭāwi, R. R. 113
Taimur, M. *see* Taymūr, Maḥmūd
Talay, Š. 276
Tarrāzī, F. D. 110, 110 n 12
al-Tawḥīdī 28, 28 n 2, 29 n 4
al-Tawwāb, R. ^{c}A. 157 n 6, 158, 158 nn 10–11, 158 n 13, 159 n 18, 160, 160 n 23
Taylor, F. W. 377 n 14
Taymūr, Maḥmūd 7, 7 n 7, 113, 116, 116 n 25
Taymūr, Muḥammad 113, 113 n. 22
Tedghi, J. 210 n 35, 217 n 60, 218 n 61
Telfan-Gebirges, A. 351
Testen, D. 369 n
al-Tha^{c}ālibī 52, 58, 59 n 34
Tha^{c}lab 181 n 18
al-Thaqafī, ^{c}Ī. 167
Thomason, S. G. 192 n 28
Thomsen, M.-L. 269 n 17
Thrall, W. F. 73 n 5
Thury, J. 401 n 1
Tietze, A. 412 n 42, 413 n 46, 415 n 50, 418 n 53
al-Ṭihrānī, Ā. B. 63 nn 5–6, 65 n 14
Tingey, R. 1
Tischler, J. 367 n 17, 367 n 20
Tolkien, J. R. R. 370
Tourneux, H. 357 n 8
Traina, R. A. 73 n 8
Treimer, K. 251 n 21
Trevoux, G. 158 n 10, 160 n 21
Trilling, L. 109
Trubetskoy, N. 3–4
Trudgill, P. 187 n 7, 190, 190 nn 18–21
Tsereteli, K. 176 n 3
Tsukerman, I. I. 294
Tucker, A. N. 356 n 6
al-Tūnsī, B. 204 n 20
al-Ṭūsī, N. al-Dīn 41 n 7, 42, 42 nn 10–12, 43, 43 n 13, 44, 44 n 17

^{c}Ubayd, Abū 181 n 18
^{c}Ubayda, Abū (Ma^{c}mar ibn al-Muthannā) 168
Uğur, A. 404
Ullendorff, E. 272 n 31
Ullmann, M. 339, 339 n 11, 339 n 13
^{c}Umar b. al-Khaṭṭāb 94, 392
Urdang, L. 385 n 1

Vajda, G. 158 n 10, 201 n 3, 202 n 8
Van Ess, J. 33 n 15
Velten, C. 377 n 13
Versteegh 204 n 17, 206 n 22
Vickers, N. J. 53 n 4
Vikentiev, V. 423 n 11
Vollers, K. 215 n 57
Vryonis, S. 55 n 16
Vycichl, W. 358 n 13

Wade, D. 47 n 29
Waetzoldt, H. 269 n 14
Wahby, T. 294
Wahrmund, A. 379 nn 16–17
Walde, A. 365, 365 n 10, 366, 366 n 13
Walters, S. D. 72 n 2, 73 n 8
Walton, R. A. 146, 146 n 1, 147, 151–52
Wannūs, S. 107 n 2
Watt, W. M. 7, 38, 38 n 32
Wazin, ^{c}A. 122 n 9
Wehr, H. 146, 159 n 18, 365, 365 n 8
Weinreich, U. 284
Welch, A. T. 388 n 5
Wensinck, A. J. 58 n 32
Weryho, J. W. 284 n 3, 286, 290
Wieland, R. 116 n 25
Wierzbicka, A. 163, 163 n 34
Willard, T. 158 n 10
Willmore, J. S. 215, 215 n 55
Wilson, J. A. 428 n 27
Windfuhr, G. L. 156 n 2, 163 n 33
Woidich, M. 186 n 4, 187 n 6, 187 n 8, 188 nn 9–12, 189 n 16, 190 n 17, 192 nn 26–27, 193 n 29, 196 n 39, 196 n 41, 209 n 29
Wolters, A. 273 n 33, 274
Wurzel, W. U. 186 n 2

Xella, P. 272 n 29

Yāqūt 165 n 1, 166 n 3, 168 n 9, 173, 173 n 16
al-Yāzijī, N. 106, 113
Yeghishé 249
Yegorova, R. P. 376 n 12
Yishay, H. 302–3
Yisraeli, Y. 268 n 3, 272 n 27
Yurdaydın, H. G. 401 nn 1–2, 402, 402 nn 4–7, 404, 404 n 16, 410 n 34, 411, 411 n 40

al-Zabīdī, M. 55 n 17, 180 n 17
Zahniser, A. H. M. viii–ix, 1, 71, 72 n 4, 79 n 30
Zajączkowski, A. 406 n 22
al-Zamakhsharī, M. 32, 91 n 16, 91 nn 18–19, 92 n 20, 93 n 24, 97 n 37, 97 n 40
Zaydān, J. 114–15
al-Zeebari, A. 386 n 2, 387 n 2
Zevit, Z. 273 n 35
Zimmern, H. 337 n 1
Zuhayr 20